TEACHING THE
LANGUAGE ARTS
Engaging Literacy Practices

MICHELANN PARR
Nipissing University

TERRY CAMPBELL
Nipissing University

BICENTENNIAL
BICENTENNIAL
1807
WILEY
2007
BICENTENNIAL
BICENTENNIAL

John Wiley & Sons Canada, Ltd.

Library and Archives Canada Cataloguing in Publication

Parr, Michelann
Teaching the language arts: engaging literacy practices/Michelann Parr, Terry Campbell.

Includes bibliographical references and index.
ISBN-13: 978-0-470-83775-7
ISBN-10: 0-470-83775-6

Language arts. 2. English language–Study and teaching.
I. Campbell, Terry, 1951–II. Title.

LB1576.P358 2006   428'.0071   C2006-902545-2

Production Credits
Acquisitions Editor: Michael Valerio
Editorial Manager: Karen Staudinger
Publishing Services Director: Karen Bryan
Developmental Editor: Gail Brown
Editorial Assistant/Permissions Coordinator: Sara Vanderwillik
Cover and interior design: Interrobang Graphic Design Inc.
Anniversary Logo Design: Richard Pacifico
Typesetting: Emerson Group
Printing and Binding: Tri-Graphic Printing Limited

Printed and bound in Canada
11 10 09 08 07 TRI 5 4 3 2 1

John Wiley & Sons Canada, Ltd.
6045 Freemont Blvd.
Mississauga, Ontario L5R 4J3
Visit our website at: www.wiley.ca

For Taralyn, Ashley, Jonathon (MP),
and Alex Maeve (TC)

About the Authors

Michelann Parr is Assistant Professor in the Faculty of Education at Nipissing University. She received a Hon. B.A., B.Ed., and M.Ed. from Nipissing University and is currently pursuing doctoral studies at McGill University. Her Ph.D. work focuses on the relationship between multi-sensory approaches to reading (i.e., text-to-speech software) and dialogue and collaborative sense-making in elementary classrooms. Pre-service curricular areas include language arts, literacy, drama, Kindergarten, outdoor and experiential education; she also teaches special education in the in-service department. She has elementary classroom experience in both English and French immersion from Kindergarten to Grade 6 and is also trained in Early Literacy Intervention. Workshops presented at local, national, and international levels include those prepared for the International Reading Association, Ontario Ministry of Education, and Language and Literacy Researchers of Canada.

Terry Campbell is Assistant Professor in the Faculty of Education at Nipissing University. She specializes in language arts, literacy, drama, and Kindergarten, and also teaches in-service courses on developmental reading. Dr. Campbell graduated from University of Toronto, where she received a Hon. B.A., M.A., and Ph.D. on "Good Talk about Great Literature: Addressing the Problem of Subjectivity in Moral Education." She also completed a B.Ed. at Nipissing University. She has taught in elementary classrooms from Kindergarten through to Grade 6, has practised as a trained Reading Recovery® teacher, is a professional storyteller, and regularly presents workshops for local school boards and at conferences such as the International Reading Association Convention and the World Congress on Reading.

Preface

Literacy is and must be a social undertaking, to be sought in pluralistic classrooms where persons come together in speech and action to create something in common among themselves.
—Maxine Greene

Wherever illiteracy is a problem, it's as fundamental a problem as getting enough to eat or a place to sleep.
—Northrop Frye

These are exciting and challenging times for teachers. We know that many years of hard work, planning, and preparation have led you to make the decision to teach language and literacy, and we invite you to continue your journey with us. This text is designed to help pre-service educators as they cross the threshold into the diverse world of today's classroom, as well as to assist in-service educators with a series of theoretically driven, practical strategies for teaching the language arts of reading, writing, listening, speaking, viewing, and representing.

GOALS OF THIS TEXT

The concept of literacy has grown beyond reading and writing to include listening, speaking, viewing, and representing. It is influenced by social and cultural practices, as highlighted in UNESCO's (2003, 2001) conceptualization of literacy as not only communication, but also as freedom. Recognizing and building on these conceptualizations, this text promotes the idea that literacy is a *recursive and lifelong process* that requires active engagement and reflection. Throughout the text, we encourage you to think of yourself and your students as lifelong learners of literacy. As pre-service educators and authors, we want to help you understand the importance and utility of literacy within the context of social and cultural practices in your everyday lives so that

you can in turn share this awareness with your students. One of our primary goals is to encourage you to investigate theories that provide students with multiple ways of knowing and multiple ways of demonstrating knowledge. You will find suggestions to help you as a teacher of literacy as you seek to understand your literate life and your own way of knowing and demonstrating knowledge. This will, in turn, lead you to an understanding of your own personal literacies—an understanding that is fundamental to teaching.

We believe that your personal stories lead directly to the social and political world of the classroom. We encourage you to reflect on your previous experiences and build upon your own background to enrich instruction. We believe that the best literacy teachers are also the best literacy learners—they are the teachers who learn by doing and have a wide repertoire of knowledge, skills, and values and are ready and waiting to teach. It is our sincere wish that this text will further inspire you in your journey as a successful, lifelong learner and teacher of literacy.

Let your mind start a journey through a strange new world. Leave all thoughts of the world you knew before. Let your soul take you where you long to be... Close your eyes, let your spirit soar, and you'll live as you've never lived before.
—Erich Fromm

FEATURES OF THIS TEXT

A variety of pedagogical features support the approach of this text and have been designed to support readers as they explore engaging language and literacy practices.

Guiding Questions and Key Terms

Each chapter opens with a set of questions to guide your learning and a list of key terms that you should understand by the end of the chapter. These are intended to introduce the key themes and questions that will be addressed throughout the chapter.

Looking Back, Looking Ahead

Each chapter begins with a summary of the previous chapter as well as a vision of where the next chapter intends to take you. This organization encourages you to reflect on what you have read as well as establish purposes for reading new material. This also enables you to see the connections and interrelationships among the language arts.

Cumulative Literacy Portfolio (Lit-Folio) Approach

Using a cumulative portfolio approach (described in Chapter 2), this text allows you to collect evidence of your development as a language and literacy teacher. The lit-folio is intended to provide concrete and performance-based evidence of yourself as both a literacy learner and a literacy teacher.

Literacy Notebook: Stop, Think, and Write

Literacy Notebook is designed for you to stop, think, and write about the content in question. This underscores our belief that reading text is not a passive process and that we need to take time to think, interrogate, and connect to the content we are reading. Many of the literacy notebook elements are excellent starting points for your lit-folio (for example, keeping a log of favourite children's literature).

Theory into Practice

Throughout the text, we have made every effort to connect theory with practice. Theory into Practice illustrates how chapter content can be incorporated in the classroom. In addition, Chapter 10 provides an alphabetical listing of strategies discussed in the text, and a detailed list of strategies—cross-referenced with literacy focus areas—is provided following the table of contents as an overview and for quick reference.

Teacher Talk

Teachers in the field are eager to share their thoughts and ideas with new teachers, and in Teacher Talk, teachers reflect on some of the strategies incorporated throughout the text. They speak to the technical aspects or subtleties of implementation as well as "lessons learned along the journey." Chapter 15 includes contributions from teachers in the field who offer their advice and tips for getting ready for September.

Student Teacher Practice

Student Teacher Practice features insights, realizations, and reflections from teacher candidates as they transition to the world of the classroom, putting into practice the ideas and concepts contained within the text.

Figures

To summarize or provide a concise reference to chapter content, figures are presented throughout the chapter. The figures include information that will be useful to you as a reader and as a teacher in the classroom with your students.

Glossary

In order to support the introduction of new terms, a running glossary has been incorporated into the margins of each chapter. Each new term is boldfaced in the text, defined in the margin, and then listed in a full glossary at the end of the text. This running glossary will enable you to access quickly new terms as they are encountered in the text, freeing you to focus on content and sense-making.

Resources to Support Your Learning

In keeping with a research and literature based approach to language and literacy, extensive resources to support your learning are provided at the end of each chapter. These include educational books and journals, children's literature, and websites.

ACKNOWLEDGEMENTS

A project of this size requires the participation of many people and we would like to acknowledge the contributions of family, friends, mentors, colleagues, and our publisher.

Thank you to the many colleagues who provided us with assistance and guidance. Even before writing began, colleagues willingly provided feedback and suggestions upon our proposal to write this text. Their thoughtful comments and feedback greatly helped us in writing this text.

Marguerite Campbell, *York University*
Mary Clare Courtland, *Lakehead University*
Janette Holmes, *York University*
Shelley Peterson, *Ontario Institute for Studies in Education of the University of Toronto*
Ruthanne Tobin, *University of Victoria*

We would especially like to thank those colleagues who reviewed chapter material. Their insights were invaluable and helped to shape the text.

Geraldine Balzer, *University of Windsor*
Annelies Browne, *University of Victoria*
Jan Buley, *Acadia University*
Marguerite Campbell, *York University*
Mary Clare Courtland, *Lakehead University*
Rachel Heydon, *University of Western Ontario*
Luigi Iannacci, *Trent University*
Larry Swartz, *Ontario Institute for Studies in Education of the University of Toronto*
Ruthanne Tobin, *University of Victoria*

Special thanks go to Marguerite Campbell, Mary Clare Courtland, and Ruthanne Tobin who contributed their time and energy to reviewing the different stages of this text's development

A huge thanks to all of those at John Wiley & Sons Canada, Ltd. who offered assistance, support, and encouragement throughout the process. A special thanks to Michael Valerio, our Acquisitions Editor who believed in and supported the project from the beginning; Gail Brown, our Developmental Editor who patiently sifted through a multitude of correspondences, and was a constant presence throughout the writing and publication process; and Joan Lewis-Milne, Marketing Manager.

A special thanks to all of the contributors to this text—from those who contributed children's writing samples to those who contributed to Teacher Talk and to Chapter 15. Without your efforts, our text would lack the practical and experienced voices of those who teach and learn in the field.

Thanks also goes to Nipissing University, particularly the research department and our Dean, Dr. Ron Common who provided us with the necessary resources for this project.

Over the years we have both been touched by the lives of many students—both elementary and post-secondary. Thank you for guiding us and showing us what works best.

Although not with us anymore, we would like to extend our sincerest gratitude to Dr. Elizabeth Thorn. She was a constant inspiration and mentor as we worked through this text. Her countless hours of language and literacy practice influenced us significantly and provided us with the necessary foundation to write this text.

And finally a heartfelt thank you goes to our family and friends for their tireless support and patience throughout the entire writing process. Thank you for accepting the hours that we dedicated to research, writing, and conceptualizing, and for recognizing our need to relax at the end of a long day. It's now time to celebrate!

Michelann
Michelann Parr

Terry
Terry Campbell
North Bay, Ontario, August 2006

Brief Table of Contents

Table of Contents

CHAPTER 11   Teaching and Learning Writing 373

CHAPTER 12   Real Writers Writing 409

LITERACY STRATEGY	LITERACY FOCUS
ABC Bookmaking, Chapter 10	comprehension, summarizing, vocabulary building, word play
Anticipation Guides, Chapter 10	activating prior knowledge; predicting; clarifying, confirming, and re-establishing predictions; generating questions
Author's Chair, Chapter 10	building literacy communities; language arts: listening, speaking, reading, writing; questioning
Book Talks, Chapter 10	language arts: speaking, representing; summarizing
Choral Reading, Chapter 10	comprehension; fluency, expression; language arts: listening, speaking, representing
Choral Speaking, Theory into Practice 7.2	language arts: listening, speaking, representing
Cloze Procedure, Chapter 10	comprehension; language arts: reading, writing; predicting; sense-making
Content Area Reading, Theory into Practice 9.12	activating prior knowledge, finding main ideas/details, generating questions, summarizing, vocabulary building
Continuum of Support: Reading Read Alouds, Theory into Practice 6.1, 9.1, 9.2 Think Alouds, Theory into Practice 6.3, 9.3, 9.4 Shared Reading, Theory into Practice 9.5, 9.6 Guided Reading, Theory into Practice 9.7, 9.8 Independent Reading, Chapter 9 Interactive Reading, Chapter 9	activating prior knowledge, comprehension, constructing knowledge, gradual release of responsibility, responsive support, scaffolding
Continuum of Support: Writing Modelled Writing, Theory into Practice 12.1 Shared Writing, Theory into Practice 12.2, 12.3 Interactive Writing, Theory into Practice 12.4 Guided Writing, Theory into Practice 12.5, 12.6 Independent Writing, Chapter 12	activating prior knowledge, comprehension, constructing knowledge, gradual release of responsibility, responsive support, scaffolding
Critical Inquiry and Critical Literacy Literacy Events, Theory into Practice 13.1 Written Conversations, Theory into Practice 13.2 Habits of Mind and Lived Experiences, Theory into Practice 13.3 Touchstone Texts, Theory into Practice 13.4 Drama, Theory into Practice 13.5 Poetry, Theory into Practice 13.6 Multi-Media, Theory into Practice 13.7	activating and connecting prior knowledge, asking questions, comprehension, critical inquiry, exploring and understanding multimedia, exploring perspective, social action
Directed Listening-Thinking Activity, Theory into Practice 4.1	asking questions, comprehension, critical inquiry, listening
Directed Reading and Thinking Activity, Chapter 10	asking questions, comprehension, critical inquiry, language arts: reading
Elkonin Boxes, Chapter 10	phonemic awareness, phonics, spelling, word study
Expository Text Strategies/Efferent Reading and Writing, Chapter 10	activating prior knowledge, finding main ideas/details, generating questions, summarizing, vocabulary building, writing
Five-Finger Book Test, Chapter 10	self-monitoring, gradual release of responsibility, language arts: reading, self-monitoring

LITERACY STRATEGY	LITERACY FOCUS
Found Poetry, Theory into Practice 7.1	language arts: reading, writing; poetry; word play
Goldilocks Strategy, Chapter 10	reading, self-monitoring
Grammar, Chapter 12 Using Drama, Theory into Practice 12.7	understanding grammar, syntax, parts of speech, sentence structure, punctuation in context
Graphic Organizers, Chapter 10	activating prior knowledge, setting goals, vocabulary building summarizing, finding main ideas/details, generating questions, reflecting on learning
Home-School Connections, Chapter 10 A Note to Parents, Theory into Practice 15.1 Weekly Newsletters, Theory into Practice 15.2	building literacy communities; language arts: listening, speaking, reading, writing, viewing, representing; motivation; vocabulary building
Instructional Conversations, Theory into Practice 4.1	building literacy communities; comprehension; constructing knowledge; language arts: listening, speaking
Integrated Units, Chapter 10	curricular areas; language arts: listening, speaking, reading, writing, viewing, representing; making connections
Journals, Chapter 10 Reader Response Journals, Theory into Practice 8.1, 8.2	constructing knowledge, generating questions, making connections, reflecting on learning, setting goals, writing
Keys to Comprehension, Chapter 10	connecting to prior knowledge, drawing conclusions, finding main ideas/details, inferring, predicting, self-monitoring, summarizing, synthesizing, visualizing
Listening to and Re-telling Tales Theory into Practice 5.2	comprehension; fluency; expression; language arts: listening, speaking, representing
Literacy Cafés, Chapter 10	building literacy communities; engagement; language arts: listening, speaking, reading, writing, viewing, representing; motivation
Literacy Centres, Theory into Practice 9.10	engagement, gradual release of responsibility, independence, word solving
Literary Conversations, Chapter 9	building literacy communities; comprehension; constructing knowledge; language arts: listening, speaking
Literature Circles, Chapter 5, Theory into Practice 9.11	building literacy communities; comprehension; constructing knowledge; language arts: listening, speaking
Lit-Folios, Theory into Practice 2.1	constructing knowledge; critical thinking; engagement; language arts: listening, speaking, reading, writing, viewing, representing; making connections; reflection
Multiple Intelligence Responses, Chapter 10	engagement, motivation, responsive instruction
Music and Literacy, Chapter 10	engagement, motivation, responsive instruction
Novel in a Day, Chapter 10	building literacy communities; language arts: listening, speaking, reading, writing, viewing, representing; making connections
Oratory or Public Speaking, Chapter 10	language arts: listening, speaking, reading, writing, viewing, representing
Poetic Surfing/Pre-Reading Strategies, Chapter 10	making connections, summarizing, vocabulary building
Poetry Gallery, Chapter 10	building literacy communities; comprehension; language arts: reading, writing, making connections; questioning
Praise-Question-Polish, Chapter 12	asking questions; comprehension; conferencing; critical inquiry; language arts: listening, speaking
Questioning-Answer Relationships, Chapter 10	asking questions, comprehension, critical inquiry, self-monitoring

LITERACY STRATEGY	LITERACY FOCUS
Questioning the Author, Chapter 10	comprehension, constructing knowledge, critical inquiry, establishing purposes for reading, exploring perspective generating, asking questions
R.A.F.T. Writing, Chapter 10	exploring perspective; language arts: writing; making; connections
Read Alouds, Theory into Practice 6.1, 9.1, 9.2	comprehension; establishing purposes for reading; language arts: reading, listening
Reader Response Journals, Theory into Practice 8.1, 8.2	building vocabulary, clarifying, comprehension, critical inquiry noticing language, predicting, questioning, visualizing
Readers' Theatre, Theory into Practice 5.1	comprehension; fluency; expression; language arts: listening, speaking, representing
Readers' Workshop, Chapter 9	comprehension; constructing knowledge; establishing purposes for reading; language arts: listening, speaking, reading, writing, viewing, representing; self-monitoring; setting goals
Reciprocal Teaching, Chapter 10	building literacy communities; constructing knowledge; gradual release of responsibility; language arts: listening, speaking
Running Records, Theory into Practice 9.9	assessment, comprehension, cueing systems, fluency, expression, self-monitoring
Sketch to Stretch, Theory into Practice 6.2	comprehension; language arts: reading, representing; visualizing
Survey-Question-Read Actively-Recite-Review (SQ3R), Chapter 10	comprehension, language arts: reading, questioning, reviewing, self-monitoring, skimming, summarizing
Storytelling, Theory into Practice 5.3	comprehension; fluency; expression; language arts: listening, speaking, representing
Subtext Strategy, Theory into Practice 9.4	comprehension; exploring perspective; language arts: listening, speaking, writing, viewing
Think Alouds, Theory into Practice 6.3, 9.3, 9.4	assessment; comprehension; explicit explanation of reading; language arts: listening, speaking; self-monitoring
USSR, Chapter 10	establishing purposes for reading, language arts: reading, setting goals
Visualization, Chapter 10	forming mental images, inferring, representing
Vocabulary Work, Chapter 10, 12	comprehension, phonemic awareness, phonics, vocabulary building, word play
Word Splashes, Chapter 10	comprehension, phonemic awareness, phonics, vocabulary building, word play
Word Walls, Chapter 10	comprehension, phonemic awareness, phonics, vocabulary building, word play
Writers' Workshop, Chapter 12	constructing knowledge; establishing purposes for writing; language arts: listening, speaking, reading, writing, viewing, representing; making connections; setting goals for writing
eXtremely Engaging Ways to Teach about Story Elements, Chapter 10	language arts: listening, speaking, reading, writing, viewing, representing; reader response, comprehension; constructing knowledge, vocabulary building, story structure
Yearn to Read, Chapter 10	comprehension, engagement, motivation
Zeroing in on Reading Strategies, Chapter 10	comprehension, cueing systems, self-monitoring

1

Understanding Ourselves as Literate Beings

Constructing Our Own Stories

> We are what we do,
> especially what we do to change
> what we are;
> Our identity resides in action and in struggle.
> —*Eduardo Galeano*

key terms

aesthetic purposes
efferent purposes
listening
literacy story
reading
representing
speaking
viewing
writing

questions to guide your learning

By the end of this chapter, you should understand the key terms and be able to answer the following questions:

- Who am I as a literacy learner?
- What memories do I have regarding language and literacy?
- What do I remember about listening, speaking, reading, writing, viewing, and representing?
- What is my literacy story?
- Why is it important to construct a literacy story?
- How will my literacy story shape me as a teacher?
- Why is it important for my students to be able to tell their literacy stories?

Looking Back, Looking Ahead

This chapter will engage you in the recall and construction of your own story as an independent literacy learner. It is our belief that uncovering our literate selves and our literate lives shapes who we are in the classroom and how we interact with our students. Our stories often help us to "understand what happened and why" (Meyer, 1996, p. 1). To write our stories, we must think about them, investigate them, rehearse them, and then reconstruct and write them in ways that enable us to understand their parts and patterns in ways we hadn't thought of before.

> *These stories become a kind of primary text in classes, enabling us to un-*
> *cover our unspoken assumptions; examine the contradictions between our*
> *pedagogies and our experiences; complicate our understandings of lit-*
> *eracy, learning, and teaching; integrate our examined experiences into our*
> *working conceptions of literacy and learning; develop intimacy and build*
> *community. They also provide us with a sense of our own authority to*
> *resist and revise the powerful culture of schools.*
>
> (Wilson & Ritchie, 1994, p. 85)

Many of us, both literacy educators and future literacy educators, arrive at this point in our literacy lives equipped with the strategies and tools common to literate beings. Often what we lack is an awareness of how we acquired them and the many influences, positive and negative, that have shaped who we are today. Teaching requires an awareness of who we are as literate beings and why we behave as we do. The intuitive ideas we have about literacy—about listening, speaking, reading, writing, viewing, and representing—underlie our literacy teaching, our planning, and our interactions with students. Recognizing these implicit assumptions is critical to understanding; it will help us decide which ideas we need to set aside, to reconsider, or to retain.

This chapter initiates the exploration of your literate life; the suggested notebook and lit-folio activities are designed to help you understand who you are as a literate being and the literate life you have lived. Throughout the book, we will provide many suggestions to help you to become more critically conscious as you explore your literacy life and how, when examined in light of the times in which we live, it will shape your teacher story. These prompts and suggestions are given in the Literacy Notebook: Stop, Think, and Write sections, which we invite you to complete. We recommend that you consider each box as an opportunity for holistic reflection. Respond to those questions that resonate with you; add and delete to suit your purposes. We have included a feature called Student Teacher Practice (written by B. Ed. students) to help you get started.

Your reflections and your stories will become a dynamic text, ever-evolving and continually influenced by the people and events in your past, the present in which you are immersed, and the future that you have yet to encounter. You will keep these stories as part of your dynamic text as long as they are useful to you.

Meyer (1996) argues that the stories we carry forward and the memories we retain are the ones we continue to learn from. Van Manen (2002) reminds us that "how and what we *see* depends on who and how we are in the world" (p. 23). That is why we will ask you to continue to explore and reconstruct your story as you read, interact with other literacy learners, engage in literacy practices, and learn to be a literacy teacher. Your story will form the foundation for your lived experiences as you continue your literacy journey.

> *Our lived experiences frame our stories. That living and framing include writing inside when it is lovely outside; they include not writing; they include losing ourselves in the events of our classrooms; and they include a long weekend away from our classrooms—in the garden, by the ocean, near a stream, or in the desert, or wherever it is that we let ourselves explore what we are creating—in our minds. Our frames are made of our relationships with ourselves and our students. Framing our stories means understanding who we are and being sensitive to and respectful of who we are. Framing also means being open to the voices in books, articles, and presentations. The frames for the stories that unfold in our classrooms provide us with insights into understanding and move us toward the goal of creating classrooms that uncover the hidden possibilities for our students.*
>
> (Meyer, 1996, p. 129)

As your identity and role in this teaching world change and evolve, so too will how and what you see. One will be continually informed by the other, ultimately leading you to a greater understanding of who you are as a learner and your way of being in the classroom, both as a literacy learner and a literacy teacher.

Stories to Learn From: Exploring Our Experiences

Making the transition from independent literacy learner to teacher of literacy requires that you first identify your key experiences with language, literacy, and literature. A critical examination of and reflection on these stories will be the foundation for your developing attitudes, understandings, and preconceptions about teaching, learning, and literacy. Once you are aware of the stories, you can take a critical stance and situate yourselves not only in the research on best practice, but also in who you want to become as literacy teachers. You will be able to retain the best of what you have experienced and develop alternative conceptualizations of language and literacy teaching and learning (Applegate & Applegate, 2004; Ellis & Bochner, 2000; Meyer, 1996; Palmer, 1998).

The journey toward self-understanding and transformation requires your full engagement as literacy learners. No longer can you be passive in your pursuit of knowledge. You must be active in becoming who you are so that you can in turn teach who you are. Teachers who are engaged and enthusiastic literacy learners themselves are more likely to plant and cultivate the seeds of literacy in their classrooms (Applegate & Applegate, 2004; International Reading Association, 2002; Parr & Campbell, in press). As literacy educators, when we are planning our programs, these questions guide our explorations and will likely guide yours in the classroom as well.

How do we help you, as independent literacy learners, experience education as something you do, not something done to you? How do we help you to become more active, more critical, more reflective, and thus more powerful as literacy teachers? How will you bring your experiences of engagement and participation in this course into your own classrooms? How do we help you to critically examine your own experiences, to dialogue about beliefs and assumptions, to reflect on the many ways in which you are literate and how you have become literate?

Engaging Literacy Learners: Our Goals for You

Goal 1: *To engage you in reading and writing for pleasure, in your own time and for your own purposes.*

Reading and writing for pleasure, in your own time and for your own purposes, is a reflection of your self-confidence and sense of self as readers, as writers, and as literacy learners. When literacy learners find reading and writing too difficult, they will often not reach the level of engagement that most effectively fosters learning (Adams, 1998). It becomes easier and safer to withdraw than to repeatedly experience failure (Stanovich, 1986). Those who struggle with or do not enjoy reading and writing spend less time reading than capable readers, and less time writing than capable writers.

> They read and write less than their higher performing peers, do not choose to read and write (even actively avoid doing so), are less meta-cognitively aware, less strategic, less persistent, less likely to connect learning to their own experience, less likely to generalize new learning, less likely to take control of their own learning, and more likely to construct and cling to simplistic interpretations. In other words, they adopt a relatively passive stance to learning: they lack a sense of agency in literacy learning.
>
> (Center on English Learning & Achievement, 2001, p. 2)

Goal 2: *To help you envision yourself as a listener, speaker, reader, writer, viewer, and representer.*

Students who do not envision themselves as readers and writers will likely lack the confidence to read independently and as a result, will withdraw from the tasks of reading and writing (Dymock, 1993). It is our goal to help you to envision yourself as a reader and a writer as well as a speaker, a listener, a viewer, and a representer (see Chapter 2 for a full discussion).

Goal 3: *To build an aesthetic enjoyment of language and to value the role of literacy in your life.*

Aesthetic enjoyment often reflects a readiness to relate to and focus one's attention on the experience of what is being heard, spoken, read, written, viewed, or represented. It is making connections and perceiving text through the senses, feelings, intuitions, images, and ideas from previous experiences and opportunities.

> The aesthetic reader pays attention to—savours—the qualities of the feelings, ideas, situations, scenes, personalities, and emotions that are called forth and participates in the tensions, conflicts, and resolutions of the images, ideas, and scenes as they unfold. The lived-through meaning is felt to correspond to the text. This meaning, shaped and experienced during the aesthetic transaction, constitutes the "literary work," the poem, story, or play. This "evocation," and not the text, is the object of the reader's "response" and "interpretation," both during and after the reading event.
>
> (Rosenblatt, 1994, p. 1373)

Listening to Learn

Despite the fact that **listening** is at the heart of learning, it has often been referred to as a lost art. It is often neglected in the classroom with little at-

Listening is at the heart of learning.

tention given to instructing students on how to improve their listening skills, regardless of whether they are listening for information (efferent purposes) or listening for pleasure (aesthetic purposes) (Rosenblatt, 1985). As listeners, we often find fault with speakers—they are not interesting, what they are talking about doesn't interest us, we don't like the sound of their voice, they are talking too fast. The list goes on. Effective listeners know that listening is an active process—not something done to us but something we do.

How do listeners actively make sense of oral texts? If we accept that listening is an active process, there are many things that we can do to counter the common faults we find in speakers when we find ourselves in primarily efferent listening situations, situations where we might consider ourselves to be passive. Figure 1.1 lists 10 strategies to help you identify your strengths and needs as an efferent listener.

Your ability to listen for aesthetic purposes will be critical in the classroom. It is therefore important that you identify your strengths and develop an action plan to improve those areas where you are in need. Listening is far more than providing what has often been referred to as "a listening ear." Effective listening strategies for conversations with friends, colleagues, family, and students are provided in Figure 1.2.

FIGURE 1.1 Top Ten Strategies for Listening to Lectures, Presentations, Discussions, and Conversations

1. Choose to find the story, topic, or subject useful and interesting.
2. Concentrate on the words and message, not on the speaker's looks, clothes, or delivery.
3. Suspend judgement when you hear something you're not sure you agree with. React slowly and thoughtfully. Try to make connections to something you already know or something the speaker has previously said.
4. Identify the "big ideas," those fundamental concepts to which everything else in the story, topic, or lecture is related.
5. Adjust your note-taking system to the speaker's pattern.
6. Stay attentive.
7. Aggressively tackle difficult material.
8. Don't get derailed by emotionally charged buzz words that trigger negative responses.
9. Get to know the speaker and listen to the clues used to convey a message.
10. Understand and use the differential between the speed of speaking and the speed of thinking.

Source: Adapted from Culbertson (2000/2001) and Saskatchewan Education (1997).

Awareness of strategies to improve your aesthetic and efferent listening will benefit you not only as a listener and meaning-maker this year, but you will benefit as you talk to students in your future classroom.

FIGURE 1.2 Listening for Aesthetic Purposes	
Effective listeners are interested and attentive	• They look at the speaker. They do not fidget or move unnecessarily. • They pay full attention to the speaker's message and respond in a way that paraphrases or builds on the speaker's message and extends the conversation as opposed to stopping it.
Effective listeners encourage talking and listen patiently	• They do not interrupt the speaker. They give them time to finish their idea and respond to the speaker's requests at appropriate times.
Effective listeners are aware of non-verbal messages	• Effective listeners can monitor both the words being spoken and non-verbal communication in terms of tone of voice, facial expression, energy level, posture, or changes in behavioural patterns.

STOP, THINK, AND WRITE

literacy
notebook
1.1

How Do I Listen? Let me Count the Ways

Choose one lecture or class this week and apply the top 10 strategies. Reflect on their effectiveness.

■ Which were natural? Which required effort? How have they changed the way you listen?

■ What did you find interesting about the subject?

■ List two or three words or messages the speaker was trying to get across. How did you react to these words or messages?

■ What were the big ideas the speaker was trying to get across?

■ How did you take notes? What supports did the speaker provide for you to take notes?

■ Was there anything you found challenging, difficult, or controversial? How did you deal with it?

■ What did the speaker use as supporting evidence?

■ What is one thing you learned about the speaker?

■ Were there any instances where you felt that your thoughts were not on the speaker or on the discussion? Why?

Student Teacher Practice/1.1

THE ART OF LISTENING TO SCIENCE

What did you find interesting about the subject?	• I was fascinated by the discussion of how science allows us to have an understanding of the world around us, and is a natural phenomenon, unlike technology.
List two or three words or messages the speaker was trying to get across.	• Don't be afraid to take risks. • Be willing to experiment.
How did you react to these words or messages?	• At first I was hesitant to take part in the subject discussion because of what I consider to be a lack of personal knowledge of the subject. The professor's encouraging, non-judgemental tone gave me the confidence to offer opinions and become involved in the conversation.
What were the big ideas the speaker was trying to get across?	• As teachers we need to motivate our students by giving them a problem to solve and a method of inquiry for solving it.
How did you take notes? What supports did the speaker provide?	• Handwritten notes were taken. • Handouts were provided. • An overhead projector was used to support the lesson.
Was there anything you found challenging, difficult, or controversial? How did you deal with it?	• The only thing I found difficult was the initial challenge to take risks and offer opinions. • I faced the challenge rather than ignoring it, and got involved in the conversation. Admittedly, it wasn't easy, at least not in this class.
What did the speaker use as supporting evidence?	• The speaker backed up his thoughts and ideas by using the class as an example. He conducted some fascinating experiments that completely captured our attention and left us eager to learn the scientific principles involved in the experiments.
What is one thing you learned about the speaker today?	• I learned that the speaker sometimes rides his bike to school, and encourages us to do the same. • I learned that the speaker is a dynamic individual who is skilled at capturing the attention of the class and is able to keep them focused on the task at hand.
Were there any instances where you felt that your thoughts were not on the speaker or on the discussion? Why?	• There were some instances where my mind stayed focused on an idea that had already been discussed and as a result I missed some of the ongoing lecture. • I was able to successfully avoid daydreaming in class. At times my mind wandered, but my thoughts were always on class-related matters.

Student Teacher Practice/1.1

THE ART OF LISTENING TO SCIENCE (continued)

REFLECTION

I found that being exposed to the top 10 strategies helped me stay focused and attentive in class. I don't mean to imply that I have a difficult time staying focused, but I must admit that there are times when my mind wanders off topic and I miss some of what is being said.

These strategies felt natural; I found the subject interesting, I stayed attentive, and I focused on the big ideas. The challenge now is to implement these strategies in other classes on a consistent basis.

Mike Poluk is a 2005-2006 graduate of Nipissing University's Bachelor of Education program.

STOP, THINK, AND WRITE

literacy
notebook
1.2

Recall what you consider to be a positive conversation you have had with a friend or a student recently. Visualize the situation in your mind.

- How did you demonstrate that you were interested and attentive to the speaker?
- How did you encourage the speaker to continue talking?
- How did you respond?
- What non-verbal messages were you aware of?

Contrast this positive conversation with one that did not end as you would have liked.

- What were the differences?
- How might your response or interest as a listener have influenced the conversation?
- What non-verbal messages might you have missed?
- What would you do differently next time?

Speaking

Speech is the oldest form of expressive communication. Many of us overlook the necessity to look at how we achieve "speaking in a listening way" (van Manen, 2002, p. 246). Most adults would choose **speaking** as a method of responding over writing, drawing, or representing. Just as with listening, though, it is set aside in many classrooms in favour of what is perceived to be a more critical task: the improvement of read-

Student Teacher Practice/1.2

TALKING ABOUT CONFIDENCE, FEAR, AND APPREHENSION

In terms of my speaking, I would say that I don't have the type of confidence in it that I would hope for. With my close friends, I never think about the things I'm going to say, I just say them. With my colleagues, that is, my fellow section mates, I suppose I do censor what I say according to the situation. I consider whether the bit of information that I'm about to share is interesting enough to bring up. I've always had a fear of seeming boring in the eyes of others, so before I speak, I like to know that what I will say is going to be received well. I constantly try out what I am going to say before I say it. This habit severely limits the conversations that I enter into. This is a habit that I remember having and perpetuating since I was young. With my parents, this is also the case—this kind of self-censorship that takes place in my mind before I speak. I've found myself trying to get away from this since it is a hindrance. I remember a few times when I was relaxed enough to speak my mind, and often times that works out well: I say something that I myself approve of. Yet other times, this is not the case. I look back on what I've said and feel unsatisfied with the conversation. This does not enter into my thought pattern as much when I am in the classroom. There, I feel that I already have the intellectual respect that I crave from the students, so I don't monitor myself as closely. Although, I do remember times when I wish I had not said certain things. I believe that everyone should have a handle on what comes out of their mouths, but I sometimes feel that I restrict myself in this sense.

Do I speak in a listening way? I don't know. I find myself not listening to what I say some of the time. I suppose I would rather speak for efferent purposes as opposed to aesthetic ones. I really don't like people who speak just to hear the sound of their voice. If I am going to take the time to say something, I want it to mean something, and I want people to take it as such. I definitely prefer to speak in smaller groups; in a large group of people, I often get lost in a strange competitive pattern in that I try to outwit the people I'm speaking with. Also, it is easy to hide in a large group; only small speech offerings are necessary to remain part of the group. In a smaller group, I can't hide behind any sort of jargon and am forced to make complete sense all the time. If given the choice, I would also choose to partake in small group presentations and discussions, for the same reasons. It is so easy to get lazy in a big group, so I like to keep myself engaged and working while in a smaller group. In a big group, when the focus shifts from one person to the next, 16 pairs of eyes come your way expecting something, and you are forced to deliver. In a small group you have many opportunities to contribute without feeling rushed when it is your turn.

I do think about the delivery in terms of volume, pitch, etc., but not as often as I monitor the content. I suppose I know that I have made a meaningful contribution when my audience gives me the clues I'm looking for. I can tell if someone truly understands or values what I've just said.

Scott Wood is a 2005-2006 graduate of Nipissing University's Bachelor of Education program.

STOP, THINK, AND WRITE

- How do you assess your own speaking skills with friends, colleagues, professional acquaintances such as parents and administrators, and with your students?

- In the previous section, we talked about assessing yourself as a listener. What about your practices as a speaker?

- Do you speak in a listening way?

- If given a choice, do you prefer speaking for aesthetic purposes or efferent purposes? Which one is more comfortable?

- Do you prefer to discuss in small groups as opposed to large groups?

- Do you prefer making presentations to small groups and facilitating small group discussions, rather than delivering speeches and lectures?

- Do you assess your own 'delivery' in terms of volume, pitch, timing, and animation?

- How do you know if you have improved?

ing and writing. Many of us recall classrooms where talk was not encouraged, where we were rewarded for silence, when silence meant learning. Earlier we said that "listening was at the heart of learning;" in fact, if we observed real teaching-learning situations, we might find that students spend just as much time listening as they do any other activity. If this is indeed the case, then it is even more critical that we examine our strengths as a speaker in both aesthetic and efferent situations and acknowledge our role as an oral language model in the classroom. For some children, you will be the consistent oral language model in their lives; it is not a role to take lightly.

Reading

Teachers who are engaged and enthusiastic readers are more likely to encourage and cultivate at least some kindred spirits in their classrooms. It is in the classrooms of such teachers that children are more apt to encounter teaching strategies that foster a love for reading and a high level of engagement in reading.

(Applegate & Applegate, 2004, p. 555)

Motivation and engagement are crucial in the development of ideal readers.

Engagement as a reader appears to be a critical factor in the development of ideal readers, regardless of whether we are discussing adults or children. Stanovich (1986) coined the term "The Matthew Effect" to describe the relationship between active engagement in reading and the developing reader; it is by actively engaging in reading that effective readers develop the characteristics that make them ideal readers. The more they read, the more they develop; therefore, those who are rich in reading get richer, and those who are poor in reading get poorer.

According to Rosenblatt (1978), there are two primary stances that influence the way a reader approaches a text. Readers who read with an efferent stance are primarily concerned with the information they can take away from the reading. Readers who assume an aesthetic stance are more concerned with becoming actively involved in the text and immersing themselves in the story, living vicariously through the characters.

Literacy teachers have a profound influence on the stance assumed by their readers. Teachers who have a primarily efferent stance toward reading, who view reading primarily as a means to information, are likely to pass this stance on to their students (Applegate & Applegate, 2004). While the efferent stance is highly effective for content area material, when used with literature it may reduce story and narrative to facts and chunks of information; often the real meaning is lost. "Readers may neutrally accept a text, actively embrace it, or vehemently resist it for one reason or another" (Sipe, 1999, p. 129). Texts that are externally imposed or reduced to a collection of facts and extensive analysis are more likely to be rejected by readers because they do not reflect their ideological, social, cultural, or interest needs (Bogdan, 1992; Sipe, 1999). For readers to actively embrace texts, they need to be internally motivated to read for a variety of purposes. Figure 1.3 presents an overview of sources of internal and external motivation and readers' purposes for engaging in reading.

Teachers' beliefs and habits with regard to reading have a significant effect on the motivation and engagement of students. Reading proficiency itself does not distinguish influential teachers from non-influential teachers. What is critically important is the teacher's ability to "involve students in meaning negotiation based on the text by encouraging interaction between the students, yourself as a teacher, and the classroom community of learners" (Ruddell, 2004, p. 994). If teachers do not experience this meaningful negotiation of text and interaction in their university community of learners, it is unlikely that they will be able to create this kind of transaction with their own students in a regular classroom (Applegate & Applegate, 2004). Spache (1976) drew a strong connection between the success or failure of a reading approach and teacher attitude, especially with regard to expectations of success and the degree of enthusiasm with which the method is taught. These factors were found to be far more significant than the quality of the program or the materials (Robinson, 2002). It is, therefore, important to explore your current reading habits, attitudes, and beliefs in order to understand the influences that have shaped your stance as a reader.

FIGURE 1.3 Internal and External Sources of Motivation for Reading

Internal Motivation	Purpose
Problem Resolution (Conflict Resolution)	Enables readers to see themselves as successfully solving problems or conflicts.
Prestige (Self-Esteem)	Enables readers to perceive themselves as significant persons, receiving attention and exerting control in their lives.
Aesthetic (Pleasure)	Enables readers to appreciate literature that ranges from an appreciation of beauty in nature to enjoyment of family or friend interaction and harmony.
Escape	Enables readers to leave the realities of daily existence and travel to far away places doing strange, unfamiliar, and exotic things.
Intellectual Curiosity (Information)	Enables readers to discover through text new concepts and new worlds.
Understanding Self (Self-Concept)	Enables readers to understand personal motivations through the motivations of story characters.
External Motivation	**Purpose**
Teacher Expectations (Content Learning, Work)	Enables readers to participate in what is considered an efferent instructional stance where they are expected to respond to explicit text-based questions and participate in discussions involving pre-determined responses.

Source: Adapted from Ruddell (2004).

literacy notebook 1.4

STOP, THINK, AND WRITE

Consider your engagement as a reader. Using the following questions as a guideline, write a one or two paragraph description of your stance, motivation, and experience as a reader.

- How often do you read? When do you read?
- What do you read? How do you make sense of what you read?
- Do you read primarily to gather information or do you read to immerse yourself in another world?
- What are your motivations for reading? (See Figure 1.3). Can you classify books you have read recently by internal or external motivation?
- What reading did you do this past summer?
- Do any titles or authors stand out?
- What did you read for aesthetic purposes? What did you read for efferent purposes?
- When you think of yourself as a reader, how much enjoyment do you associate with reading? Explain your reasons for feeling that way.

Source: Applegate & Applegate (2004).

Writing

When I was a kid, this is what I thought:
Writers are strange beings born with "the gift."
They never stew over spelling.
They never forget the rules of punctuation.
They never worry where or not to start a new paragraph.
They never have to rewrite in better cursive because of picky
*   fifth-grade teachers.*
They glide where I trudge.
They soar where I end up flat on my face.
For them writing is a piece of cake. Sitting alone in small attic rooms, they
*   need only to stare out the gable window, and inspiration is sure to hit.*
*   Then they just write it all down, as simple as that! No help is needed.*
                                        (Birdseye, 1993, pp. 179-180)

What is your image of the effective and independent writer? Is it similar to the one presented by Birdseye? Which of these statements apply to you? Did you find yourself nodding your head in agreement? Did you find yourself thinking differently? Are some destined to be exemplary writers where others are simply writing to get their ideas down and no art is involved?

Our needs as adults as we continue to explore, discover, and construct our own literacy are quite similar to those of children. We need invitations to read and to write for a variety of purposes, and the opportunity to see ourselves as authors. We need co-learners on our journey as writers and demonstrations of writing that we can emulate, discuss, depart from, and argue over. Each writing experience needs to be viewed as the doorway into subsequent writing experiences for a lifetime of writing, thinking, reading, and learning (Meyer, 1996, p. 107).

Each writing experience contributes to our development as effective and independent writers.

Despite invitations and optimal conditions, a blank sheet of paper will often be one of the scariest things there is for literacy learners. Why? Some are afraid to fail. Some are afraid that it won't be good enough, that it won't be long enough, that it won't be interesting, that the spelling, grammar, and conventions aren't perfect, that there are run on sentences or sentence fragments. Some will be concerned about awkward ideas, jumbled sequences, repetition. Yet others are afraid because somewhere in their experience there is a memory of not being good enough, of red marks on a returned paper, of not receiving the gold star that was awarded for excellent work.

Many of us can relate to these fears. Some of us have learned to overcome them. Some of us will tread carefully, taking risks only within supportive environments. Regardless of where we find ourselves, it is an awareness of who we are as writers that is critical to our emergence as literacy educators. This understanding is the first step in constructing and rewriting our stories.

Discomfort is part of the tension that writers feel. The discomfort and tension are part of being creative because creativity requires energy: tension and discomfort (as well as other emotional or cognitive states) put stress on our lives and we can learn to use that stress to push ourselves as writers. We live our lives, feel the tension, live the story as it unfolds, tell the story in order to relive and enhance it, and then eventually write the story. This can be a long, slow process, one that allows us to understand all the many facets of the story, the players involved, and the context in which it all takes place.

(Meyer, 1996, pp. 143-144)

literacy notebook 1.5

STOP, THINK, AND WRITE

Take a few minutes to jot down your strengths and needs as a writer.

- Do you like to write?
- What are the best conditions for you to write?
- Why do you write?
- What purpose does writing serve in your life? (See Figure 1.3, substituting *writing* for *reading*.)
- Who do you write for?
- Who do you write to?
- Are you creative/imaginative?
- Can you write with vivid detail engaging your audience fully in your text?
- Do you have exemplary spelling, grammar, and command of vocabulary?
- Is your handwriting and printing neat and conventional for modelling with students?

Student Teacher Practice/1.3

WRITING OUR WAY TO UNDERSTANDING

I love to write essays. I love watching the argument in my head develop into a clearly articulated document. I usually write for academic purposes, although I do try to write poetry periodically. I love and am comfortable writing factually, so I do not believe that my poems are very creative or good. I would like to someday improve my writing ability in this genre. A good friend of mine has told me that I write exactly the same way I speak. Usually my writing is done to fulfill course requirements. My spelling and grammar are above average. My handwriting and printing is absolutely atrocious though—it has always been that way.

– Laura Crawford

Over the years, I have realized my strength of writing as an effective communication tool. I have personally found that it is preferable to write and re-write until I have communicated my message effectively. My writing tends to be clear and coherent in comparison to speaking. Accordingly, I find myself writing things out in quiet surroundings when I am unsure how to express my feelings or message. Often writing things out allows me to critically think about what I want to communicate orally.

– Kyla Dillabaugh

Laura Crawford and Kyla Dillabaugh are 2005-2006 graduates of Nipissing University's Bachelor of Education program.

Viewing

It is often said that a picture is worth a thousand words, but is it really? Arguably, the picture is only worth a thousand words if we have the vocabulary to talk about it and the skills to observe, view, and interpret it. Without these foundations, a picture is worth very little. Viewing, like listening, is often overlooked in our language and literacy classrooms. We take for granted that viewing or watching is part of our experience and we neglect the strategies that enable us to make sense of visual information and then talk about it. Beyond simply understanding the message or looking at the visual text, we also need viewing skills that help us to understand the impact of media on shaping our selves and society, in both positive and negative ways.

How do you view and interpret visual information? What do you need to be aware of? How can the presentation and arrangement of visual texts alter attention, meaning, comprehension, and appreciation of a message? Viewing, like listening and reading, is an active process. Viewing enables us to acquire information from a range of visual media such as performance, television, movies, videos, diagrams, symbols, photographs, drawings, sculpture, and paintings.

Viewing is not unlike reading or listening from a comprehension, critical thinking, or critical literacy perspective. (See Chapters 8 and 9 for a discussion of comprehension from a reading perspective and Chapter 13 for a discussion of critical literacy). For the time being, what we need to know is that many of the strategies such as previewing, predicting, and making inferences that are effective in reading and listening can also be extended to viewing.

STOP, THINK, AND WRITE

Think about memorable advertisements on radio, television, in print.

- What is it about these visual texts that appeals to you and makes them stand out?
- How do you react to certain forms of media?
- What do you definitely like? Dislike?
- How do you deal with the bombardment of media images?
- How do you work with the visual images and graphics you encounter in textbooks? In books you read for pleasure?

literacy
notebook
1.6

Representing

How do you view the connection between being literate in terms of reading and writing, and being able to represent feelings, thoughts, and ideas in visual, non-verbal forms? Do you think of pictures as more primitive than encoded symbols? When we think of artistic development historically, there seems to be a progression from schematic drawings such as cave pictographs to the complex masterpieces of Emily Carr or Picasso. Similarly, children draw and make uncomplicated pictures and constructions at first, and later make the transition to the more sophisticated use of symbols. It is the latter phase we identify as the more literate. But does it follow that purely pictorial or three-dimensional constructions are less sophisticated than communication expressed in alphabetic symbols? When we think of what artists engage in as they create, we can see that this is not necessarily true. Artists, whether creating in the visual or performance arts, engage in highly complex problem-solving processes. Integral to the creative process is the ability to solve problems as they arise, and to anticipate problems before they arise by visualizing them and imagining possible solutions.

Representing enables us to communicate ideas in a variety of forms.

We can create meaning in and through many modes of communication, including the creative arts such as visually representing, through drawing or sculpture, or through performing music, drama, or movement. We can take what is known in one system and transpose it into another using new signs and symbols. The ability to take something verbal that has been read about (and talked and written about) and express it in a new form is a highly sophisticated process involving the deepening and broadening of concepts, thoughts, and feelings experienced when one is reading or writing. **Representing** enables us to communicate information and ideas through a variety of media such as video presentations, posters, diagrams, charts, multimedia performances, visual art, drama, mime, and models.

The benefits of representing verbal meanings in nonverbal forms are numerous. By using a variety of representing strategies, we can discover and refine ideas, create representations with increasing confidence and skill, and demonstrate understanding in a variety of ways. In addition to an increase in depth and breadth of comprehension, representing through visual and performance modes provides learners from diverse cultural and linguistic backgrounds with an alternative medium of expression, which we argue is in fact a means of rehearsal for writing. Students with strengths in the arts or technology are given the opportunity to flourish; creative problem-solving is encouraged for all.

STOP, THINK, AND WRITE

Set aside the language arts of writing and speaking for now.

- How else do you represent your learning?
- Do you draw, doodle, sketch?
- Do you like to create graphic representations to support your writing and speaking?
- Do you sing to learn?
- Do you play with words?
- Do you create poetry?
- Do you enjoy multimedia (such as photography, computer graphics)?
- What do you consider to be non-traditional forms of representing and extending your learning?
- What is the role of movement, drama, music, and visualization in your learning and acquisition of new information and concepts?

**literacy
notebook
1.7**

Constructing Our Stories

As you arrive at this point in the chapter, we anticipate that you have a heightened awareness of the many strengths and perhaps areas of need (we all have them!) that you have as a literacy learner. How can you best represent your story? Who would you like to share it with? What format or genre will best represent your literate self and your literate life? A story? A timeline? A collage? A scrapbook? A memory box? The formal presentation of your literacy story will be as unique as you are as a literacy learner. Take your time, enjoy the process—remember that the journey is the destination. Let us hear your voice and your journeys to other times and places. Student Teacher Practice 1.4 and 1.5 present two different perspectives on literacy stories. In Student Teacher Practice 1.4, Heather Crawford created a memory box of items that represented her literacy story. Each item was accompanied by a description of its signifance. In Student Teacher Practice 1.5, Jason Mills told his story through the voice

Student Teacher Practice/1.4

MY MEMORY BOX

A Watch: The summer before I went to Kindergarten, I was pressing my mom to buy me a watch. Then in September, I went to school for the first time to meet my Kindergarten teacher and she had a prize box. I was allowed to pick anything out of the box and I was so excited when I found a blue watch. Reflecting on this experience, I believe that my desire for a watch was a symbol of my eagerness to learn all that I could about the world and my first experience with school was a fulfillment of that desire.

Old Yeller: I did not have a television when I was a child, so I clearly remember the first movies I ever saw, which were *Black Beauty* and *Old Yeller*. I recall that I was already an avid reader at that point, and seeing these two movies piqued an interest in the books. So, when I went home, I searched for those books and read them. In this case, a visual representation of a written work inspired me to search out books and read them.

A Loonie: I remember my first formal speech at school in Grade 4 (on the subject of loons). I was so scared to stand up in front of my classmates. However, I survived and in Grade 8, I remember that I was much more confident when I stood up at the front of the classroom to do my speech. Oral presentations were never my strongest point, but these early experiences demonstrated my desire to consciously work on becoming more comfortable in front of other people. Public speaking is very much a work in progress but, with lots of reflection and practice, I improve every time that I present.

A Christmas Tree: I recall with fondness the times as a child that my family would gather around the piano at Christmas to sing carols. We would turn off all the lights except for those by the Christmas tree and light candles and sing all together. The piano was perhaps my greatest exposure as a child to expression through music. Although I did not appreciate it so much at the time, later on in my life I increasingly found music to be a channel for me to release intense emotion. Today, I often listen to classical music because I find that the music can express how I am feeling much more than I could express myself in words. Thus, the Christmas tree is a symbol of my experience with the literacy skill of listening.

A Flashlight: In my grade school years, before I was allowed to stay up as late as I wanted, I would hide under the covers and read a book with a flashlight or with the light from my alarm clock. My passion for reading was so strong that I could not or would not stop reading when my parents turned out the light. I felt compelled to continue until I had finished the chapter or the book. (Even today, I prefer to read a book as quickly as possible, so I won't start a book unless I can sleep in the next day).

Anne of Green Gables: *Anne of Green Gables* was my favourite book as a child and young adult. I felt that I related to Anne, who at first felt out of place in Avonlea but who worked her way into the hearts of everyone in Avonlea (or almost everyone). She was a girl who was searching for "kindred spirits" and I felt that, had I known her in real life, I would have been one of those special friends. Anne's penchant for finding trouble constantly made me laugh. Although I always tried to stay out of trouble, Anne's experiences showed me that trouble can lead to some interesting and exciting

Student Teacher Practice/1.4

MY MEMORY BOX (continued)

experiences! I included this book because it was the first of many Canadian classics that I read throughout my childhood and it inspired me to read past the first chapter of books instead of giving up on them at first glance.

Watson's Mill Story: In Grade 9 history, I wrote a story based on a legend in my local town. I worked hard to gather facts for the story and I remember carefully distinguishing between the parts of the story that had actually taken place and the parts that I had fictionalized to make my story flow. It was one of the few short stories that I had attempted to write and I was very proud of it. When I handed it in, my teacher said that I was a natural storyteller. That comment gave me confidence in my abilities as a writer, especially in story writing, which I had not tried before. I included this work because I remain proud of it. It was definitely one of my best written works in Grade 9.

Journal: In my Ontario Academic Credit (OAC) year, I took an English Literature course in which we were asked to write in various forms. That was a difficult point in my life and I found that the open-ended nature of this course allowed me to express my feelings about what was happening around me. By writing out my feelings on paper, I truly found a way to visualize and represent the emotions I felt. The things I wrote that year helped me to understand not only how I was unique, but also how my uniqueness was valuable. Through those writings I truly developed the ability to understand myself and to envision where I was going in my life.

My Quotes: After watching the movie *A Walk to Remember* I decided to begin a journal in which I would keep quotes that I found from various sources. In quotes, I found words of wisdom, humour, sadness, and joy. I found the wisdom of people who had a deep sense of self and who constantly reflected on the meaning of life. Now when I hear a quote, I pay attention and remember it so I can record it later. I also frequently describe people in terms of a saying I have heard in the past. Collecting poems and quotes is an ongoing process and I plan to use them when I am teaching—both for myself to make sense of the world and for my students to reflect upon their own experiences and dreams.

Toothbrush: This summer, I worked as a program director at a summer camp. It was often a challenge to deal with the problems that arose, but I had one special person beside me and we helped each other when it felt like everything was against us. Through this experience, I learned the value of truly listening to another person. I represent this experience with a toothbrush because I feel that the time that we truly listened to each other was when we brushed our teeth at night. This may seem strange, but as the two staff members who were responsible for managing the camp, these times late at night were often the only times when we could be truly honest with each other and say things from our hearts. There were no distractions at this time, and we were only focused on what the other person was saying. From this experience, I carried away a deeper understanding of the value of active listening, which I hope to consciously practise in the future.

Heather Crawford is a 2005-2006 graduate of Nipissing University's Bachelor of Education program.

Student Teacher Practice/1.5

THE BOY AND THE MASK

There once was a boy who lived on the island of storybooks. This was a wonderful place of writers and readers. The writers would write and the readers would read and every so often they'd switch. The writers would reach for a book to read and the readers would pick up a pen. How the boy loved storybooks. How the boy loved to read and write amazingly incredible, beautifully fantastic storybooks. How the boy loved creating worlds to play in and characters to play with. The boy had learned to bring to life castles and dragons, pirates and ships right from the page. The boy would often dress up in costumes and go racing on magic carpets, or swim to the bottom of the sea, or play chess with an alien on the moon.

One day the boy woke up and realized that he was bigger. His bed seemed a bit too short. He went to his costumes and tried on his pirate hat. His head had grown too big for his pirate hat! The boy's armour and space suit would not fit. His sword seemed less a sword and more a cardboard cut-out. The boy did not know what to do. He went for a walk to think about his problem. The boy walked, and walked, and walked all the way to the top of a very high hill. The boy looked up and out across the sea. The boy saw something out there in the sea that he'd never seen before, an island, away over there. The boy looked really hard and he was able to see tall shiny buildings all over that island with machines that raced about and with people all big and old, wearing strange costumes, and playing strange games. The boy wondered about what they were doing, and what was over there, and what he could read there.

The boy thought then what he must do. He made a disguise to be his strange costume with a made up mask to look like the others. The boy packed a bag with no room for a book and left on a boat without a backward look.

The boy landed and asked, "Where is this?" The reply came: this was the Island of Facts. The boy was excited. "This is what I've been missing," he thought, "I'll read lots of books here and get really smart." So the boy hopped in a car and went into the city, he went to school, and he got down to work. The boy learned lots of good things about the world and how real things worked.

The boy learned to read books about figures and facts. He learned to write research papers and experimental procedures. He learned to question and to ask, "what, when, where, how, and who?" Time went by. The boy had good teachers and bad ones, good friends and bad ones, but no one to talk to about the old stories that he knew. Soon he forgot about space ships and dragons, pirates and sea monsters. Soon he forgot all about the island of stories. Soon he forgot that he was wearing a disguise. Soon, the boy forgot what he looked like under his mask.

One day, after a long time had passed, the boy woke up to find a horrible feeling of nothing and oldness inside him. The boy thought, "Something big is missing inside," and, "What can it be?" The boy thought, "I don't understand, I know lots about how things work, and about facts and figures. I have scientific knowledge, a job, and money to boot. This feeling of empty inside just won't do."

Student Teacher Practice/1.5

THE BOY AND THE MASK (continued)

The boy went for a walk to think about how to solve his problem. The boy walked, and he walked, and he walked. The boy walked out of the city, away from the noise and down to the beach. The boy walked across the beach and down to the sea and found a strange group of people all dressed in costumes of a strange and various designs. The boy thought, "I'll ask one of them if they know were to find the answer to my problem of this emptiness inside."

The boy walked up to a girl in a funny dress, and asked, "What, when, where, how?" and "Who are you?". The girl turned to the boy and said in a slightly annoyed way, "You ask a lot of questions. Can't you see? We are sailors, and scholars, and pretenders, and thinkers, and writers and readers of books of all fashions." The girl looked the boy up and down, and said, "I like your costume, it's very realistic. You could do without the mask though, it's looking kind of tattered." The boy replied, "What mask? This is me!" The girl looked again for a second time and said, "No, that is a mask, an ugly old mask, hiding a person that is not from this island. Come sail with me and maybe you'll find that the world looks better out from behind that ugly old mask that you say is you."

The boy reached up to find that there was a mask there with a person behind it! The boy took off that ugly old mask that he'd learned to call me and left it in the sand, on the beach, on the Island of Facts. The boy went out exploring for a new way to be. The girl wrote him poems and stories galore, filling his emptiness with what he had been missing. She told stories of people and places, both real and imagined, beautiful ones, horrible ones, and lots of others. She had stories and poems of hope and pain, laughter and sadness. Her stories took him on trips under the sea, to the stars, and to other magical places.

The boy remembered, after awhile, some treasures he'd forgotten, an ability to imagine things that can't be measured and a sense of wonder. The boy also taught the girl in a very complementary way, to ask "Why, and how, and when, and where, and who?" He taught her a language to see the stars as gas and fire as well as dragons and gods and thunder. The girl and the boy sailed off, writing and reading, to who knows where. I guess we'll find out when they get there.

Jason Mills is a 2005-2006 graduate of Nipissing University's Bachelor of Education program.

of his main character as he journeys from the land of story to the land of content and back again.

Figure 1.4 lists additional prompts that will help you to think and reflect on your previous experiences, language practices, curriculum, teaching opportunities, literature, and values. This is not intended to be a question and answer exercise but instead these prompts may further stimulate your reflection in a way that does not confine or restrict. You might also want to reflect on your literacy notebook responses, since

FIGURE 1.4 Prompts to Construct our Literacy Stories

Language Practices with Family and Friends

- Recall your experiences, as a child and adolescent, of being spoken to, read to, listened to, written with, of actively viewing, and visually representing. What are your favourite memories? Which stories do you remember best from childhood? What is it that you remember about them?

- What were your first words? How did your speech and language progress from these first words to today? Do you like making presentations? Do you like speaking in public? What are your strengths as a speaker? What are your strengths as a listener (see Figure 1.1)?

- Before you were able to read on your own, do you remember pretending to read books? What were your favourites? Who did you read to?

- Can you recall your early writing attempts (such as scribbling, labelling drawings)? Where did you like to write? What did you like to write with? What did you like to write about? Do you still have samples of your work or pictures that would help you to recall this writing?

- Can you recall seeing family members making lists, receiving and sending mail or e-mail? Did you receive and send mail (such as birthday cards, thank-you notes, letters, e-mail) when you were younger? What are your preferred methods of communication today?

- Did you watch TV? If you did, what did you watch (for example, sitcoms, cartoons, news, movies)? Did you talk about the programs at home, at school, or with friends?

- Recall specific opportunities to talk, communicate, and discuss at home, at school, or with friends (for example, dinnertime or bedtime conversations).

- Did your parents belong to a book club? Did they borrow books from a library? Did they buy books? Did they read for pleasure? Did they maintain a personal library of books?

- Recall specific experiences of visually representing and dramatizing. What were your favourite "Let's pretend" games? What types of roles did you like to play? How were these influenced by your reading and writing? How did these games influence your reading and writing development?

Teaching and Learning in Elementary School

- Can you detail your first memories of reading and writing instruction? Do you remember the purposes for your reading and writing? Are your memories of reading and writing primarily positive, negative, or neutral and why? Do you recall any particular type of instruction you received? Can you describe any instructional materials that were used? Do you recall any specific content areas?

- Can you detail your first memories of listening and speaking instruction? Do you remember the purposes for your listening and speaking? Do you recall any particular type of instruction? Can you describe any instructional materials that were used? Do you recall any specific content areas?

- Can you detail your first memories of viewing and visually representing? Do you remember the purposes for your viewing and visually representing? Do you recall any particular type of instruction you received? Can you describe any instructional materials that were used? Do you recall any specific content areas?

- Can you recall reading and writing for pleasure? Can you recall pleasurably sharing books with your friends?

FIGURE 1.4 Prompts to Construct our Literacy Stories (continued)

- Can you recall the first book you chose to read? Can you recall how you worked with narrative (story) text and content-based texts in school?
- Can you recall your first writing assignment? Do you remember writing stories? Reports? Speeches?
- Can you recall your first oral presentation? What was the topic?
- Can you recall being taught how to listen, how to speak, how to view presentations, or how to visually present information?

Literature

- What is your all-time favourite children's book? Novel? Non-fiction work?
- When did you first visit a bookstore? What was it like?
- Did you have a library card? Did you use it then? In later school years?
- Have you ever read a book that has made a difference in your life?
- Have you ever read a book that you knew had been challenged or censored? How did you feel about reading it? Did you read a certain type of book (such as mysteries or biographies) at a particular age? Why do you think you made such choices?
- Do you recall feeling dissatisfied with any of the books you read in or out of school? Why?
- Have you ever seen a book you've read turned into a film? What were your reactions?
- What do you look for in a good book to read for pleasure?
- List some books, authors, or genres that you enjoy reading. Why those books, authors, or genres?

Awareness of Self

- What are you currently reading and writing? Do you read and write for pleasure? Are you a member of a book club? Do you own books? Do you maintain a personal library of books? Do you borrow books from a library?
- Have there been times in your life when you have viewed reading and writing as a means to resolve problems and conflicts, build a sense of interconnectedness and relationship to others, enhance self esteem, escape, fulfill intellectual curiosity, learn new information, or broaden your understanding of self?
- Have you ever read a book that was so evocative or provocative that you felt you just had to talk to someone about it?
- What do you currently like to listen to, talk about, view, visually represent? What purposes do these literacy practices serve?
- Were there any literacy experiences (books, people, places) that you wish you could have had?
- Do you feel comfortable modelling, reading, writing, listening, speaking, viewing, and visually representing for your students?
- What impact do *your* literacy experiences have on *your* developing sense of self as a literacy teacher and therefore the future literacy experiences of your students?

Source: Applegate & Applegate (2004), McLaughlin & Vogt (1996), Ruddell (2004), Vacca, Vacca, Begoray (2006).

they were intended to help you recall memories and experiences with regard to literacy, and it is likely that the initial seeds of your story were planted there. As you recall and construct your story, remember that just as the two examples provided were unique, so too will yours be.

Stories to Live By

Constructing and writing your literacy story is hard work; it will require energy, focus, and commitment. Your story will not be finished when you write "The End"; your literacy journey, once begun, will become a life-long process that will require continual exploration, discovery, and re-vision. Sharing the story of your ongoing literacy life with your students is equally as important as modelling exemplary teaching and learning practice. Your literacy story will become a model of literacy that you can retell and live by in the classroom, a story that is composed of stories experienced throughout a lifetime. Our lives are lived through texts that may be read, chanted, experienced, observed, or come to us, like the murmurings of our mothers, telling us what conventions demand. Whatever their form or medium, these stories have formed us all; they are what we must use to make new fictions, new narratives (Heilbrun, 1988).

Your use of stories and your growing awareness of students through self-awareness will be what makes you unique in your classroom. These understandings will also enable you to engage in authentic conversa-tions about language, literacy, and its many component arts, strategies, and skills. Recall the stories of Heather Crawford and Jason Mills. Imagine the variety of literature these teachers will have in their classrooms, the learning experiences they will plan, and the conversations they will have with their students! By understanding your own past literate life, you will be better situated to understand the literate lives of your students.

Taking Our Stories into the Classroom: From Knowledge of Self to Knowledge of Learners

To teach, not only must teachers know themselves but they must also know their learners—who they are as listeners, speakers, readers, writers, viewers, and representers. Some of this information will be gained from classroom assessments (discussed throughout the text) but other pieces of information can be provided directly by the learners, through such activ-ities as conferences, interviews, structured writing, and journaling.

Educators always have had a special biographic interest in the educational lives of individuals. Educators want to gain insights in the lives of particular students in order to understand them or help them. It is important to know where a child "is coming from" (for example the home background or what it is that the child brings to school) in order to understand more sensitively where a child "is" at present, and where he or she seems "to be going." And educators have a professional interest in (auto) biographies because from descriptions of lives of individuals they are able to learn about the nature of educational experiences and individual developments.

(van Manen, 1997, pp. 71-72)

All learners will be able to tell you about their experiences, especially when guided with questions such as those we have suggested for evoking your own literacy stories or activities such as question and answer, storytelling, or memory boxes. Throughout this chapter we have guided your journey in self-awareness; in a similar way, you will guide your students on a journey of self-awareness.

As teachers, it is important to realize when and how to enlist the support and input of parents. Some teachers choose to use open-ended prompts to stimulate discussions with parents (for example, "Tell me about your child's language and literacy development."); others choose a more structured format with specific questions (for example, "What are your child's strengths? What do they like to read? Talk about your child's favourite reading time. What were your child's first words?").

In her book *The Art of Teaching Reading*, Lucy McCormick Calkins (2001) describes the importance of understanding the traditions, rituals, landmarks, and tools of children's literate lives outside of school. Teacher Talk 1.1 is an excerpt from the book, which describes how to help children make a place for reading in their lives and co-author the rituals and tools of the classroom community. Sharing in the development and retelling of our students' stories values their experiences, permits them to make connections between home and school, recognizes parents as one of the primary educators of their children, and supports us as teachers in program planning and resource selection.

Moving On

The story of your literacy life that you have begun to tell will form the foundation for your future learning and perhaps a schema within which to organize future learning. Your story is not a static piece of work. It is a

Teacher Talk/1.1

LUCY McCORMICK CALKINS: MAKING A PLACE FOR READING AT SCHOOL AND AT HOME

In the independent reading workshop more than anywhere else, we help our children build richly literate lives. We begin the year by learning about their reading lives outside of school. Then we invite them to join us in fashioning even richer reading lives by working together within the classroom.

"Reading and writing will be at the heart of everything in our classroom this year," Kathy Collins, a teacher at P.S. 321 in Brooklyn, told her big-eyed first graders at the start of their first morning meeting to launch their independent reading workshop. "We need to make this a classroom where reading is so, so special," she continued. "I'm wondering if anyone has a book at home that is an absolute favourite?"

Hands shot up. "I do..." "I've got the best book..."

"Wait a minute. Do you think you'd be willing to bring your special book to our classroom tomorrow?" Kathy asked over the commotion."

The next morning, as the kids unpacked and rushed to show Kathy their choices, she began having mixed feelings about her idea. "They certainly didn't bring in Faith Ringgold's *Tar Beach*!" Kathy said, recalling the ambivalence she'd felt showcasing *The Little Mermaid* and *Titanic* and books that beeped and bopped.

These books may not have been Kathy's idea of great children's literature, but they did come into the room layered with life stories. Josh, holding up his cross-section book of automobiles and trains announced, "My dad reads it to me." That was all Josh planned to say. He was done. A flurry of hands popped up as the circle of children clamored onto knees and waved frantically, pleading, "Call-on-me, call-on-me!"

But Kathy's attention remained steadfastly fastened on Josh. With one hand, she quelled the appeals as if to say, "Wait, I'm listening to Josh. Listen with me." Looking into Josh's face, Kathy said, "You read with your dad? That is *so cool.*"

Josh nodded, "He reads to me, but last night, he was tired. We just laid on my bed and went through the pictures."

"Don't you just love it when someone reads with you?" Kathy asked. "And in bed! That's the best! I'm just like you Josh. I can't fall asleep without a story. I was like that as a kid and I'm like that as a grown-up. I need to read before I can sleep."

Soon the room was full of talk about bedtime stories and read-aloud times. "After my baby brother goes to sleep, my mom sometimes reads to me," Marissa said.

"You and Josh are alike in that way. You both have parents who read aloud to you. That is so neat."

"My grandma reads the Bible and then she puts a little piece of paper in it to save her place," Cheltzie said.

"Wait a minute!" Rohan blurted out. "My mom does the exact same thing. She folds up a Kleenex and uses it for a bookmark." From all corners of the room children compared notes on bookmarks.

Teacher Talk/1.1

LUCY McCORMICK CALKINS: MAKING A PLACE FOR READING AT SCHOOL AND AT HOME (continued)

"My grandma gave me one you can buy at the store. Wanna see it?" Emma said, and raced of to dig through her backpack, producing a laminated kitten-bookmark with pink silk tassel.

"You can use a Popsicle stick," Meon added.

"Wow," Kathy said. "Maybe we should all save Popsicle sticks. Then we could use them as bookmarks the way Meon suggested, or we can use Kleenex. Or if anyone has a birthday coming up, they can ask for a bookmark from the store, like Emma's. Because we're going to be doing tons of reading this year and you are right; readers need ways to mark our places in books." When we and our children work together to bring the tools, traditions, rituals, and landmarks of literacy into our classroom, we are deeply engaged in the project called Making a Place for reading in our schools and in our lives. The reading lessons are giant ones. Whether made from Kleenex or from a Popsicle stick, bookmarks have everything to do with making a commitment to stay with a book and to carry books back and forth between home and school, and this work is not at all inconsequential. Likewise, what could be more important work for readers to do than to talk together about the times and places for reading throughout their day? We help children develop identities as avid readers by inviting them to join us in building the habits and the places for reading.

Source: From Calkins (2001). Published by Allyn & Bacon © 2001 by Pearson Education. Reprinted by permissioin.

flexible and dynamic text that will help you to uncover your assumptions and implicit theories about language, literacy development, and learning. As you continue on your journeys to becoming teachers of literacy, you will find it necessary and practical to a) review and question your beliefs, attitudes, practices, values, and experiences within a framework of contemporary research and best practice; b) plan and implement learning experiences that will further your development as literacy learners and literacy teachers; c) examine and re-interpret the meaning of literacy in your lives and therefore that of your students.

Throughout this chapter, we have attempted to build your motivation for literacy learning in a way that activated your prior knowledge in order to bridge the gap between your present experience and future learning. We have emphasized that in understanding yourself, you will be better positioned to understand your students. Meyer (1996) reminds us that "when we take care of ourselves, let ourselves be learners, hopers, and dreamers, we are developing one of the most powerful teaching tools in our classrooms: ourselves" (p. 137). Literacy is an active process that requires a high level of engagement and understanding.

We are what we repeatedly do.
Excellence, then, is not an act, but a habit.

—Aristotle

LIT-FOLIO UPDATE

The process of lit-folios will be outlined in depth in Chapter 2. Understanding yourself as a literate being and your literacy life is a critical step in your formation as a literacy teacher. As a result of fully engaging with this chapter, you should have a good insight into the story of your literate life. As your initial entry for your lit-folio, begin to draft your literacy story. What best reflects you as a literacy learner? A story? A timeline? A collage? A scrapbook? A memory box?

Throughout the rest of the text, you will be asked to continually reconsider who you are as a literate being and who you are becoming as a literacy educator. Literacy Notebook boxes have been designed for this purpose as have portfolio suggestions outlined in the next chapter. These boxes are similar to guided learning logs or journals. They will be a record of the insights you have gained and will enable you to discern patterns in your thinking and in your literacy works-in-process.

As you continually look back on your Literacy Notebook entries, comment on the patterns you notice—patterns of thought, practice, change, and transformation.

Resources to Support Your Learning

Professional Resources

Graves, D.H. (1990). *Discover your own literacy*. Toronto, ON: Irwin.

Meyer, R.J. (1996). *Stories from the heart: Teachers and students researching their literacy lives*. Mahwah, NJ: Erlbaum.

Paterson, K. (2001). *The invisible child*. New York: Dutton.

Paterson, K. (1989). *The spying heart: More thoughts on reading and writing for children*. New York: Lodestar.

Powling, C. (1998). *Roald Dahl: a biography*. Minneapolis, MN: Carolrhoda Books

Children's Literature: Our Favourites

Grandfather's journey, Allen Say
❧ *Hey world, here I am!* Jean Little

Jeremiah learns to read, Jo Ellen Bogart
❧ *Little by Little*, Jean Little
Only Opal: The diary of a young girl, Barbara Cooney
Reading with Dad, Richard Jorgensen
Thank you, Mr. Falker, Patricia Polacco

Multimedia Connections

Finding Neverland, has some wonderful perspectives about writing and what it means to be a writer.

The Neverending Story and *The Pagemaster* both demonstrate the power of story and knowing literature.

the verbs.
cat ran up the tree.

ase pass the butter.

From Independent Literacy Learners to Lifelong Teachers of Literacy

key terms

conditions of literacy learning
constructivist learning theory
cueing systems
gradual release of responsibility
literacy works-in-process
presentation lit-folio
process lit-folio
ranges of instruction
socio-cultural learning theory
strategic supports
zones of proximal development

questions to guide your learning

By the end of this chapter, you should understand the key terms and be able to answer the following questions:

- What do lifelong literacy learners and literacy teachers have in common?
- What is the progression of development from independent literacy learner to lifelong literacy learner and teacher?
- How do literacy teachers use what they know about themselves as literacy learners?
- What do literacy teachers know about models of learning, curriculum, instruction, and assessment?
- What do literacy teachers know about literature?
- How do literacy teachers demonstrate what they know about literacy and teaching literacy?

Looking Back, Looking Ahead

This chapter introduces the essential characteristics of literacy teachers and guides students in an exploration of how these characteristics fit into a language arts curriculum. It provides an overview for the rest of the book and establishes key expectations for learning, applying, and making sense. It also introduces the *lit-folio*, a strategy that will allow you to reflect on your engagement in literacy practices and your personal development as a literacy teacher. Readings, discussions, cooperative and collaborative experiences, engagement in literacy practices, and application of theory to practice are interwoven into this journey of becoming literacy teachers.

What do literacy teachers have in common? What do they believe? What do they value? Who are literacy teachers? What do teachers know and understand about literacy and language learning? What do literacy teachers look and sound like? What do the classrooms of literacy teachers look and sound like?

Today you continue your journey into literacy—using what you know as a literacy learner to become a lifelong literacy learner and teacher, a journey that began at the time you were born and continues today. For some, the journey is exhilarating and exciting, for others it may seem overwhelming. Chapter 1 helped you to explore yourself as a literacy learner; in this chapter, we continue with a discussion of exemplary literacy teachers and a vision of who you would like to become. This look to the future is a critical step in the process; the journey of becoming a literacy teacher that will never be over, because we know that exemplary literacy teachers are first exemplary teachers. Figure 2.1 provides an overview of the beliefs that effective teachers share about teaching. It is important that we explore these commonalities, especially as they relate to our classroom practice.

Developing literacy teachers begin their journeys as independent literacy learners and with time, experience, and instruction will progress seamlessly to lifelong literacy teachers as described in Figure 2.2.

We know that teachers make a critical difference in the literacy journeys of their students and that every student has the right to an exemplary literacy teacher. Although exemplary literacy teachers are diverse, they share characteristics that you can examine, and behaviours that you can strive for in terms of language theory and practice. These characteristics include values, knowledge, and skills related to their own literacy and that of their students; these language and literacy processes will become their companions on the journey (International Reading Association, 2001; Routman, 1988; Ruddell, 2004, 2006; Tompkins, 2003; Wray & Medwell, 1999).

In Chapter 1, we led you to an understanding of who you are as independent literacy learners. Through an exploration of literacy teacher characteristics and behaviours, we will now help you to understand the various influences on your literacy development including curriculum, literature, teachers, and contexts. Quite likely, one of the most significant influences is the teachers you have encountered, regardless of their

FIGURE 2.1 Shared Beliefs of Effective Teachers

Teaching: Quality of Instruction	• makes material personally relevant
	• stresses basic communication: clear writing, comprehension of text, critical thinking
	• develops logical and strategy-oriented instruction:
	  (a) clearly states problems
	  (b) uses familiar concrete examples
	  (c) extends to more abstract examples
	  (d) analyzes abstract concepts involved
	  (e) applies concepts to new contexts
	• identifies issues that should be considered before conclusions are reached
	• engages students in the process of intellectual discovery

Excitement: Personal Characteristics	• shows energy, commitment, passion • is warm and caring • is flexible • has high expectations of self
Attitude: Attitude toward subject	• exhibits enthusiasm • creates intellectual excitement • considers alternative points of view
Caring: Understanding of Learner Potential	• is sensitive to individual needs, motivations, and aptitudes • understands where students are developmentally • places high demands on learners
Helping: Life Adjustment	• is concerned with students as persons • is attentive to academic problems and personal problems

Source: Excerpted from Ruddell (2006, p. 6). Reprinted by permission of Robert Ruddell and the International Reading Association.

FIGURE 2.2 A Seamless Progression from Literacy Learner to Literacy Teacher

Phase	Independent Literacy Learner	Emerging Literacy Teacher	Developing Literacy Teacher	Enacting Literacy Teacher	Lifelong Literacy Learner and Teacher
What You Might Say	• I can't teach language and literacy. • It's too hard, and I don't know enough.	• Maybe if I find out about language and literacy, it's possible that I'll be able to teach it.	• I'll do exactly what the experts say. • I'll follow the strategies and techniques outlined in the programs and research.	• I'll adapt the experts' work to my own contexts. • I will plan a responsive literacy environment that meets the needs of my literacy learners.	• I trust myself as a student-teacher-observer-evaluator. • I am a lifelong learner and expect to learn as much from my students as they learn from me.
Understanding of the Nature of Language and Literacy	• Independent and flexible use of six language arts to make sense of the world and transform students' lives	• Exploration of self as a literacy learner and deconstruction of personal preconceptions and assumptions	• Understanding of literacy practices and how previous experience shapes literacy teacher development • Learning about literacy by doing what the experts say	• Understanding the contextualized nature of language and literacy practices • Adapting expert practice to diverse students and multiple contexts	• Understanding literacy as a social act that has the potential to reciprocally and interdependently transform the realities of teachers and students
Language and Literacy Strategy Use	• Flexible and independent use of language and literacy strategies for meaningful and authentic purposes	• Developing awareness of contemporary language and literacy teaching/learning strategies	• Supported implementation of language and literacy teaching/learning strategies of experts	• Implementation and adaptation of language and literacy teaching/learning strategies of experts	• Skilful and responsive integration, implementation, and balance of a variety of language and literacy teaching/learning strategies

Source: Routman (1991, p. 27).

Teacher Talk/2.1

MICHELANN'S GRADE 1 CLASSROOM IN SEPTEMBER

As the bell rings, I take one last look around my classroom and am pleased with what I see. At the front of the room, there is a primary manuscript alphabet in the students' line of sight. Each letter card is big, bright, and bold and contains a strong image to represent the corresponding sound. My word wall is organized at the carpet where students have easy access to words and can review them while waiting for morning circle. I have placed each student's name under the letter it begins with. The class calendar is on an easel, waiting for students to dictate key sentences about today, the first day of school. *Chrysanthemum*, a picture book by Kevin Henkes, sits on the ledge of the easel. I plan to use this book to introduce a lesson on names and our unit on "All about Me." I know that this is a logical place to begin as most of the children will recognize their classmates' names from Kindergarten. In the centre of the carpet, there is a box surrounded by the students' name cards. The students will pick up their name cards as they enter and put them in the box—an easy way to take attendance.

My pocket chart is hung where the students can reach it; it contains a poem for shared reading and independent investigation during readers' and writers' workshop. My work board contains visual and word representations of each centre as well as a schedule for rotation. I walk from area to area, reading the room, making sure that labels on windows, doors, computers, etc. are in place and that each student's name is recorded on their clothes hook at the back of the classroom. Although not bare, there is lots of wall space for the students to make themselves visible in the classroom. The bulletin board has a big welcome sign in the middle, ready for the picture, name, and a paragraph of introduction for each student.

I glance at my desk. There is a checklist for concepts about print and a schedule for reading assessment. **Browsing boxes** that organize levelled books are colour-coded for easy access. Large file boxes are distributed around the room, each containing a folder for each student that will house their **literacy works-in-process.** On the corner of my desk is a novel I am currently reading and a book on the implementation of guided reading in primary classrooms. When I assign uninterrupted sustained silent reading (USSR) today, I will read as well. My daybook is open and lists a full day of activities for the students. We will read a story, engage in oral introductions, practise writing names on mini-white boards, and organize ourselves in various formations by our first names. I wait with quiet anticipation for the group of Grade 1 students about to appear in the classroom. I look forward to the magic of learning that is about to begin.

progression point—developing, enacting, or lifelong. Your ultimate goal as developing teachers is to strive for the very highest level on the progression, that of lifelong literacy learners and teachers. We begin with a discussion of how lifelong literacy learners and literacy teachers implement their knowledge of themselves, learning models, curriculum, instruction, assessment, and literature. We then return to learners and the implications for instruction.

STOP, THINK, AND WRITE

Reflect on your memories of exemplary literacy teachers in your elementary, secondary, and post-secondary education, of movies you have seen, and of articles in professional journals you have read. Before going any further, envision the "ideal literacy teacher."

■ What would this teacher look like?

■ Sound like?

■ What characteristics would this teacher possess?

You might consider using a metaphor to encapsulate your vision and aid in your description. For example, an ideal literacy teacher is a tree...

How Do Literacy Teachers Use What They Know about Themselves as Literacy Learners?

Literacy teachers believe that all children can learn and engage in literacy processes. They recognize that learners are diverse in terms of language, culture, multiple intelligences, and learning styles, and that we must be aware of and responsive to these differences. They recognize that some learners need more opportunities to use language in order to grow and develop and that more does not mean more of the same thing. It means different strategies, texts, opportunities, and experiences. "One simply takes the child from where he or she is to somewhere else" (Clay, 1985). Literacy teachers use their understanding of children and language development to help them teach language and literacy. They value the role of language in children's learning and recognize and appreciate the impact of learners' **discourses** or unique ways of being in the world (for example, personal, social, cultural, familial). They create a community of learners because they know that learning does not occur in isolation but instead involves collaboration and shared construction, talking and thinking, making meaning by responding, and active and interactive learning. They show that they care about their students' lives, motivations, interests, strengths, and needs; they teach with enthusiasm and excitement (Cambourne, 2000/2001; Clark, 1997; Tompkins, 2003; Wray &Medwell, 1999; Ruddell & Unrau, 2004).

Literacy teachers are more than competent in their own command of language and their ability to use language for a variety of purposes

discourse
Communication through language, which is largely influenced by our ways of being in the world.

(for example, to learn, grow, express thoughts and ideas, persuade). They share their "in the head" processes with their students by thinking aloud. They correctly apply the conventions of grammar, spelling, and punctuation. They recognize that they should know more than they teach—more in terms of strategy, more in terms of value, and more in terms of content.

What Do Literacy Teachers Know about Models of Learning?

Literacy teachers understand that a comprehensive and balanced approach to literacy instruction uses principles from two major learning theories: socio-cultural and constructivist. They relate assumptions about learners and learning to classroom practice in meaningful and authentic ways.

Literacy teachers must be aware of and respond to their learners' differences.

SOCIO-CULTURAL LEARNING THEORY

Students construct understandings and interpretations primarily through interaction with others. Learning is a social process that reflects the community and culture in which children learn and live (Gee, 1990; Heath, 1983; Vygotsky, 1978, 1986); language is used for social purposes, to learn, to communicate, and to share experiences with others. Children's social interactions with family, friends, teachers, and community enhance learning and provide students with meaningful and authentic purposes to use language and literacy. Figure 2.3 is a summary of assumptions about learners evident in socio-cultural learning theory and its implications for teachers' classroom practice.

CONSTRUCTIVIST LEARNING THEORY

Constructivists argue that learners make sense of their world by connecting what they already know or have previously experienced with what they are learning. Piaget's early work (1969) and other research (Anderson, 1994; Rumelhart, 1994) show that new learning often requires modification of learners' existing cognitive frameworks or **schemata**. Integration of new information and modification of existing

schema (*pl.* schemata) Organizing principles, such as rules, based on a learner's knowledge.

FIGURE 2.3 Socio-Cultural Perspectives

Assumptions about Learners	Role of Teachers
• Learning is a social process that requires interaction with peers, family, community, and teachers. • Social interaction between learners enhances meaning construction.	• Plan activities that incorporate opportunities for social interaction (for example, cooperative learning, literature circles) and discussion about learning.
• Children learn very little by performing tasks that they can already do independently. There is a significant difference between what learners can do on their own and what they can do with the support of an adult or more capable peer.	• Scaffold/support new learning experiences by relating new learning to previous experience. Model or demonstrate new procedures. • Ensure that tasks are not too easy nor too difficult but in the learner's **zone of proximal development** (or instructional range).
• Learning is highly contextualized and reflective of the community and culture in which children learn and live.	• Respond flexibly to the strengths and needs of individual learners and move along the continuum of support as necessary. • Provide activities that are inclusive and culturally diverse. • Help students make the link between home, school, community, and culture.

schemata are not passive processes; they require students to be active, to be attentive to how new information can be related to prior knowledge, and to actively organize and integrate information into schemata. Figure 2.4 presents a summary of constructivist assumptions about learners and the implications for classroom practice.

Teachers link learning theory to practice and work within learners' zones of proximal development by providing a continuum of support that helps students to make the critical links between familiar and strange, home and school, self and other. Figure 2.5 describes how teachers plan for a gradual release of responsibility from a high level of teacher support to a high level of student independence. Teachers who gradually release responsibility for learning to their students recognize and value constructivist approaches to learning as well as the learners' capability to make sense of their experiences and the world around them.

FIGURE 2.4 Constructivist Perspectives

Assumptions about Learners	Role of Teachers
• Learning is an active process that requires learners to actively organize and integrate new information into pre-existing schemata or cognitive frameworks.	• Help students to make connections between pre-existing schemata and new information. • Pose relevant problems that prompt student inquiry. • Structure learning experiences and literacy events around key concepts (for example, help students to understand the purposes of literacy in real life).
• Learning is highly individualized despite its contextualized nature. No two students will have exactly the same schemata or background experience.	• Value students' point of view. • Activate prior knowledge when necessary. • Help students to develop new schemata within which to organize new information by explicitly teaching organization structures (for example, narrative story structures). • Build background knowledge for those who may lack prior experience with what is being taught. • Assess students within the context of instruction.

FIGURE 2.5 Continuum of Support from Teacher Modelling to Student Independence

Level of Support	Role of Teachers
Modelled	Model and demonstrate in-the-head thinking, sense-making, and strategy use.
Shared	Share learning and literacy experiences and opportunities with learners to facilitate success and growth.
Interactive	Plan learning and literacy experiences that permit learners to contribute what they know and can already do independently, with the teacher filling in the gaps to facilitate success and growth, and build self-confidence.
Guided	Scaffold to bridge the gap and prepare students to undertake unfamiliar or novel tasks. Group students by similar strengths, needs, and experiences to provide intensive strategy instruction.
Independent	Independent learners engage in selection and negotiation of meaningful, relevant, and authentic learning and literacy experiences, texts, and strategies.

What Do Literacy Teachers Know about Curriculum, Instruction, and Assessment?

A comprehensive and balanced approach is not "one-size-fits-all" but is instead a responsive approach where each learner's diversity is valued and optimized. Understanding their students' diversity, teachers organize literacy instruction in a variety of ways including learning experiences that are formal/informal, planned/incidental, explicit/implicit, isolated/contextualized. It is important that these types of instruction be seen not as a dichotomy but as ranges of instruction. As well, we should not associate any one type of instruction with a higher level of success than any other. What is important and what is best is what helps students to experience success at any given time. Regardless of where we place ourselves in the range of instruction, our focus should be on meaningful, authentic, and real-life learning experiences as presented in Figure 2.6.

Understanding the need for social interaction, teachers use a range of grouping strategies including individual, partners, small group, and large group. They have a variety of strategies, for example, readers' workshop, writers' workshop, guided reading, and interactive writing. They know when and how to use each strategy and how to combine them in a comprehensive program that maximizes learning. They continually assess their students, recognizing that assessment informs instruction. Literacy instruction is linked to learners' previous experiences as well as to assessment. Literacy instruction, assessment, and previous learning are connected in relevant, meaningful, and authentic ways.

Literacy teachers know that certain conditions are necessary for optimum language learning; their classrooms must reflect these conditions (Cambourne, 2001). Although Cambourne makes specific reference to print and text, we feel that this is an effective model for literacy learning in the classroom and draws together a range of instructional methods to optimize language learning. Figure 2.7 presents Cambourne's theory and conditions of literacy learning as they relate to classroom practice.

Teachers integrate many opportunities for students to use the six language arts throughout the school day in all curricular areas. They link them to the content areas in meaningful and authentic ways. They provide frameworks for reading content (for example, expository text structures) and they link and extend language and content in real-life ways across the curriculum. See Figure 2.8 for further definitions of the six language arts and implications for practice.

FIGURE 2.6 Ranges of Instruction

Explicit	Implicit
Explicit instruction is direct teaching. Teachers present information and have students use the new learning in novel situations. Teachers present the new concept or strategy, involve students in guided practice, and then provide opportunities for independent practice, application, and assessment, and opportunities for review and reteaching when necessary. The teacher directs the learning.	Implicit instruction is associated with constructivist theories of learning: students actively gather information, look for patterns, and construct meaning. Teachers structure opportunities that allow students to discover and work through problems on their own, ultimately constructing their own meaning. Teachers are facilitators. Students are self-directed learners.
Sequential	**Just-in-Time**
Sequential instruction uses lessons previously sequenced by curriculum guidelines, research results, published programs (for example, spelling and handwriting programs). It assumes a hierarchy of skills and strategies that build on each other and increase in complexity.	Just-in-time instruction is responsive to the strengths and immediate needs of the students. Through systematic instruction and assessment, teachers have realized what learners need to know right now in order to succeed. Just-in-time instruction often takes the form of mini-lessons. Teachers group and regroup students on an as-needed basis for skill and strategy instruction.
Planned (Formal)	**Incidental (Informal)**
Planned instruction encompasses the multitude of learning experiences and opportunities that teachers plan to teach systematically over the course of an hour, a day, a term, or a year. Details are provided in daily lesson plans, unit plans, long range plans, and standardized curriculum guidelines.	Incidental instruction occurs in the many teachable moments that emerge over the course of an hour, a day, a term, or a year. These opportunities are often unpredictable, unplanned, and unforeseen. They capitalize on classroom or community events such as the first snowfall of the year or the emergence of a Monarch butterfly from its cocoon.
Isolated	**Contextualized**
Isolated instruction takes place when teachers teach isolated skills and strategies, for example, sight word instruction, phonemic awareness training. The learning experiences are designed to teach these concepts, for example, word sorts for the sound <a>, phonics worksheets.	Contextualized instruction takes place when skills and strategies are taught within the context of literature, classroom events, and authentic, meaningful, and engaging language activities. For example, teaching idioms and maxims might involve finding an idiom, defining it literally, dramatizing it, and illustrating it.

FIGURE 2.7 Conditions of Literacy Learning

Condition	What we think this condition means	Some possible classroom strategies that we can employ to implement this condition
Immersion	Providing multiple opportunities for student to experience (a) visual saturation of print and text and (b) aural saturation of sounds of written texts.	• Make functional use of wall print through regular "print walks"; sustained silent reading (SSR); teacher read alouds; shared reading (SR); taped books; choral reading (e.g., poems, songs) on wall print.
Demonstration	Doing lots of teaching modeling of the processes of reading, with special emphasis on making explicit the invisible processes that make reading possible. Collecting, displaying, and discussing models (examples) of different kinds of texts.	• Do teacher read alouds and SR accompanied by think alouds. • Use joint construction of texts accompanied by think alouds. • Focus on processes, knowledge, and understandings that make effective reading, spelling, and writing possible.
Engagement modelling	Continually communicating and modelling a set of reasons for becoming powerful, critical readers [literacy learners]. These reasons must be relevant to the pupils we teach.	• "Propangandize" the value of reading through constant messages, explicit reasons, personal stories, "nagging," posters, models, and demonstration of power and value of reading.
Expectations	Communicating, through language and behaviour, the message that every pupil is capable of learning to read, and that you expect every child to become a reader.	• Make explicit the processes, knowledge, and understanding that effective readers use. • Constantly remind students that they all learned to talk—a much harder task.
Responsibility	Encouraging pupils, and giving them opportunities, to make some, not all, decisions about what and how they learn. Making explicit the idea that good learners know how to make learning decisions.	• Devise activities that don't have simple right-wrong answers. • Insist that comments and judgments be justified wherever possible. • Set up support structures, processes that allow pupils to take responsibility for learning.

FIGURE 2.7 Conditions of Literacy Learning (continued)

Modelling	Modelling and demonstrating examples of "taking responsibility" or "ownership" of learning.	• Use language that invites open-ended responses and reflection (e.g., What else could you do when you're reading and you come to something you don't understand? Why would you do that?).
Approximation	Communicating through discourse, (i.e., language and behaviour) such messages as these: Having a go (i.e., making an attempt and not getting it perfect at first) is fundamental to learning. Mistakes are our friends in that they help us adjust and refine our knowledge, understandings, and skills so that next time we do better. Ultimately our approximations must become conventional (expectations).	• Share stories of how we learn to do things outside of school, e.g. skate. • Highlight the role that approximations and responses play. • Model and demonstrate good/bad miscues as approximations that help/hinder the reader. • Discuss spelling approximations as temporary spellings (not invented) and study similarities/differences to conventional spelling. • Model/demonstrate how effective readers deal with approximations.
Use	Providing multiple opportunities for learner-readers to apply their developing skills and understandings about reading and the reading process in authentic and meaningful ways.	• Use reading for a range of purposes, do lots of meaningful and authentic writing, and develop a pool of authentic reading/writing activities and tasks that can be constantly reused without boring the students (e.g., read and retell on different text types).
Response	Paying close attention to learners' approximations and recycling demonstrations and models that contain information; knowledge they've not yet got under control. Drawing explicit attention to salient features of demonstrations/models that will help learners modify approximations.	• Set up structures/processes that make it possible for learners to receive feedback (response) from multiple sources, e.g., other students as well as the teacher. • Constantly model how effective readers use various cues available to create/understand meaning.

Source: Excerpted from Cambourne (2000/2001, pp. 415-416). Reprinted by permission of Brian Cambourne and the International Reading Association.

FIGURE 2.8 The Six Language Arts

Listening, speaking, reading, writing, viewing, and representing fit into the domains of oral, written, and visual language and cover both receptive and expressive language. Receptive processes require students to take in language through their five senses whereas expressive forms of language require students to output or perform language in a variety of ways.

	Receptive	Expressive
Oral Language	**Listening** Making meaning and accessing information from speech or talk (for example, question and answer, oral discussion, audience participation).	**Speaking** Expressing information or narrative orally (for example, drama, storytelling, song, role-playing, debate, speech, improvisation, oral discussion).
Written Language	**Reading** Making meaning and accessing information from print (for example, environmental print, books, magazines, song lyrics, expository text structures).	**Writing** Expressing information or narrative in print (for example, script writing, quickwrite, journal, creative writing, transactional writing).
Visual Information	**Viewing** Making meaning and accessing information from sources other than print (for example, maps, pictures, videos, graphics, dance, art, drama).	**Representing** Expressing information or narrative in a form other than print (for example, art, craft, charts, drama, storytelling, models, song, dance, graphic symbols, multimedia, photography, technology).

Literacy teachers recognize that it is their role to support and scaffold, leaving the real work for the literacy learner. They do this by supporting learners' use of four cueing systems: semantic, grapho-phonemic, syntactic, and pragmatic (Goodman, 1968; Smith, 2004; Adams, 1998). Teachers recognize that not only must learners be effective readers, writers, listeners, speakers, viewers, and representers, they must also be able to describe what they are doing and why. They recognize that strategic learners solve the puzzles of language far more effectively than students who have been taught to memorize rules, forms, and words. Figure 2.9 presents an overview of the four cueing systems and strategic supports that teachers use when supporting students.

FIGURE 2.9 Cueing Systems and Strategic Supports

Cueing System	Strategic Supports Teachers Use
Semantic: Engages the schemata that individual literacy learners bring to the literacy event. These include background knowledge, life experiences, world awareness, conceptual understandings, beliefs, attitudes, and values.	Ask: Does that make sense? Scaffold new learning, activate prior knowledge, talk to students about the purposes and functions of literacy.
Grapho-phonemic: This system engages literacy learners' visual awareness of letter-sound relationships; in part, it is the act of perceiving letters, graphic marks, on a printed page.	Ask: Does that look right? What word would you expect to see? Point out letters during shared reading and help students to make the connection between what they see and what they hear.
Syntactic: Engages literacy learners' knowledge about how the language system works. It is primarily related to structure and grammar. Allows literacy learners to use their understanding of sentence patterns to construct meaning.	Ask: Can we say it that way? Does that sound right? Engage students in many opportunities to explore oral language. Scaffold tricky sentences and sentence patterns.
Pragmatic: This system engages a literacy learner's awareness of how language functions and is used in social/cultural situations.	Ask: What is the purpose and function of this literacy event? How should your use of language vary given the context? Talk to students about the purposes and functions of language; engage them in activities that help them to understand that how we say something, when we say it, and who we say it to, are often more important than what we say.

What Do Literacy Teachers Know about Literature?

Literacy teachers recognize that text selection should be negotiated with students and reflective of their needs and interests. They are aware of a range of genres (for example, fairy tales, science fiction), levels of difficulty (easy, instructional, hard), and formats (for example, picture books, magazines, e-texts, anthologies) and effectively match texts to the purposes of the language experience and the needs of the learner. Teachers have a wide variety of materials on hand. Their goal is to get students reading and then challenge them to go beyond their comfort zone to new and diverse texts.

What Do Literacy Teachers Understand about Literacy and Themselves as Literacy Learners?

They continue to learn about language and literacy after their formal education is completed. Not only do they engage in language and literacy practices, but they reflect on their understanding, relate them to the curriculum they are following and to their learners. They ask themselves the following questions:

- How does this relate to my development as a literacy teacher?
- How does this relate to my understanding of learners?
- How does this relate to curriculum, instruction, and assessment?

What Do Literacy Teachers Know about Learners?

Literacy teachers understand how theory informs their understanding of the unique needs of each student. They see their primary roles as helping children to: develop their ability to think; develop their confidence and abilities as readers, writers, listeners, speakers, viewers, and representers; and to nurture a reverence for language, a fascination with it, and an appreciation of how it works. Teachers do this by negotiating and implementing a literacy learner's Bill of Rights such as the one in Figure 2.10.

Our Image of the Lifelong Literacy Teacher

Based on our discussion of the characteristics of literacy teachers and the research conducted by Ruddell (2004, p. 994) 10 key insights emerge and hold implications for increasing our effectiveness as literacy teachers. Literacy teachers:

1. Develop clear purposes and instructional plans that facilitate successful development and resolution of instructional episodes.

FIGURE 2.10 A Literacy Learner's Bill of Rights

I am a literacy learner...

I need to understand the purposes of literacy so that I can fully appreciate it and enjoy it in my life.

I need opportunities to use language to express myself, to choose books I want to read and topics I want to write about, and to create or find my own voice.

I need to use language aesthetically to read literature, talk with others, and enrich my life and that of others.

I need to hear, speak, read, write, view, and represent language so that I can learn how language works and how I can use it to investigate concepts and issues in language and across the curriculum.

I need opportunities to collaboratively construct meaning through language and make connections between my experiences and my social world.

I need to work with continuous texts and a variety of genres in order to develop a wide range of strategies to enhance comprehension, share my ideas, and expand my knowledge about language.

I need to use language to solve problems, persuade, and take action.

I need to use language to evaluate learning experiences, question personal and social values, and think critically.

Source: Adapted from NCTE (1996); Pinnell & Fountas (1998).

STOP, THINK, AND WRITE

literacy
notebook
2.2

If you looked at your literacy story (conceptualized and constructed in Chapter 1) through the eyes of a developing literacy teacher, how would you answer the following questions:

- How much value did you place on strategy development? Independence? Choice? Engagement?

- What were your strengths and needs as a literacy learner?

- What models of learning were you exposed to? What did your teachers believe about literacy learning, learners, and literature?

- Knowing what you know now about ranges of instruction, conditions of literacy learning, and the six language arts, how would you plan for that learner in your classroom?

2. Emphasize activation and use of students' prior beliefs, knowledge, and experiences in the construction of meaning.

3. Incorporate higher-level thinking questions, questioning strategies, and sensitivity to students' responses in conducting instruction.

4. Orchestrate instruction using a problem-solving approach to encourage intellectual discovery by posting, exploring, and resolving problems.

5. Monitor students' thinking, use verbal feedback, and ask subsequent questions that encourage active thinking.

6. Understand the importance of text, task, source of authority, and socio-cultural meanings in negotiating and constructing meaning.

7. Involve students in meaning negotiation based on the text by encouraging interaction between the students, yourself as a teacher, and the classroom community of learners.

8. Share teacher authority in discussions to encourage student thinking, responsibility, interaction, and ownership of ideas in discussion.

9. Understand instructional stance, the role it plays in setting instruction purpose for students, and the importance of using internal reader motivation to enhance student interest and authentic meaning construction.

10. Develop sensitivity to individual student needs, motivation, and aptitudes but hold appropriate and high expectations for learning.

literacy notebook 2.3

STOP, THINK, AND WRITE

Let's consider some questions about Michelann and her classroom.

- What does Michelann have in common with lifelong learners and literacy teachers?
- What does she believe?
- What does she value?
- Is she a lifelong literacy teacher?
- What does she know and understand about literacy and language learning?
- What does she do that reflects a comprehensive and balanced approach to language and literacy?
- If you were working in Michelann's classroom, what would you discard?
- What would you add?
- What would you continue?

Your Lit-Folio: Evidence of the Seamless Progression from Independent Literacy Learner to Lifelong Literacy Learner and Teacher

WHAT IS A LIT-FOLIO?

A lit-folio is a portfolio that focuses on growth specifically in the area of language and literacy; it can also be considered as one component of a professional portfolio. A lit-folio is more than just a collection of "stuff": it is not simply a file of tasks, assignments, and projects, nor is it a scrapbook or memory box of memorabilia.

The primary purposes of a lit-folio include:

- To provide organized, goal-driven documentation of your growth as both a continuing literacy learner and a developing literacy teacher

- To address the following questions:

  - What do I know about myself?

  - What do I know about learners?

  - What do I know about curriculum, instruction, and assessment?

- To provide a multi-levelled, individualized record that fosters learner-to-self, learner-to-text, and learner-to-world connections (including learner-to-peer and learner-to-professor collaboration)

No two lit-folios are the same; each is a reflection of the literacy learner you are and the literacy teacher you have become. What will vary from lit-folio to lit-folio will be highly dependent on the learner, curriculum, or program expectations and the goals that are negotiated with learners.

Why is the creation of a lit-folio important in teacher development? We believe that in order to teach language and literacy, you must have first experienced language and literacy and reflected on personal learning. Our students also tell us that their lit-folios become impressive and supportive evidence during job interviews or also during conferences with parents.

THE LIT-FOLIO PROCESS

Although not exactly the same as the writing process described in Chapter 12, the lit-folio process is similar. The process lit-folio contains your *process* work, which is the evidence you will gather throughout your course or throughout your reading. The presentation lit-folio is the *product*, the final representation of who you are as a literacy learner and a literacy teacher.

Our vision of the lit-folio process is a multi-stage process similar to the writing process. It begins with rehearsal and planning and progresses to polishing and sharing as presented in Figure 2.11.

Process Lit-Folios: Literacy Works-in-Process

Consistent with McLaughlin and Vogt's (1996) approach to portfolios in teacher education, we emphasize both *process* and *product*. The items in your process lit-folio represent the *process* that you have undergone as a literacy learner and a developing literacy teacher. Your process lit-folio will always be much larger and more complete than your presentation lit-folio. It is an ongoing and systematic collection of unabridged literacy works and texts that represent your development as an independent literacy learner and a developing literacy teacher. For example, it might contain entire reflective journals, completed curriculum units, unique materials you have made, your notebook entries, and videos of your teaching. Figure 2.12 contains a comprehensive list of literacy works-in-process possibilities. Works-in-process may be stored on your computer and in notebooks. Your process lit-folio is the foundation of your presentation lit-folio and your ongoing reflection on personal and professional growth.

Presentation Lit-Folios: Professional Evidence

A presentation lit-folio provides an effective and easy-to-read portrait of your professional competence. A presentation lit-folio is selected and streamlined because other people usually do not have the time to review all the material in your works-in-process folder. In making a presentation lit-folio, you will find that less is more. For example, since you would be unlikely to take to an interview all your teacher-made learning materials, you might rely on photographs. Sample pages from a large project would replace an entire project. Figure 2.13 presents a formatted sample page from Michelle Petreman's presentation lit-folio during the 2005–2006 school year. As a student who participated in a laptop initiative at Nipissing University, Michelle has showcased not only her awareness of a variety of language and literacy strategies, but she has also highlighted her expertise with technology and organization. Michelle's lit-folio presented the full continuum of support (from modelled to independent) for both reading and writing, evidence of her ability to teach the other four language arts (listening, speaking, viewing, and representing), and her awareness of how to integrate language for learning across the curriculum.

FIGURE 2.11 The Lit-Folio Process

Process Lit-Folio	Key Characteristics
Rehearsal	*Brainstorming, Planning, Conceptualizing* Purpose: To demonstrate professional growth in literacy. Audience: Self, as a record of learning, and interview or hiring committees, as a record of professional growth. Goal Setting: Consider and deconstruct your own literacy story and determine personal goals to move you further along the continuum from literacy learner to literacy teacher.
Drafting	*Doing, Creating, Practising* Full engagement in literacy works: Tasks will be selected to either accomplish personal goals, course expectations, or practicum requirements.

Presentation Lit-Folio	Key Characteristics
Revision	*Designing and Formatting, Selecting, Assessing, and Evaluating* Designing and Formatting: Design an appropriate presentation format; one that reflects who you are as a literacy learner and teacher. Selecting: Who am I? Who am I as a reader-writer-listener-speaker-viewer-representer? Assessing and Evaluating: How does this document demonstrate your growth with regard to personal goals or course expectations?
Editing	*Conventions* Spelling, grammar, punctuation
Publishing, Sharing	*Interview, Conference*

Your presentation lit-folio is oriented toward product and the goals you have set for yourself. These goals may change and evolve over the course of a lifetime, and will enable you to plan a relevant curriculum for yourself (Hansen, 1992). Your presentation lit-folio is characterized by a selection of the items that represent your growth, level of achievement, individuality, and creativity as a literacy teacher. Items are chosen because they answer the questions: "Who am I?" "Who am I as a reader-writer-listener-speaker-viewer-representer?" "Who am I as a literacy teacher?" "How does this item show my growth?" (Hansen, 1992).

In the preface to your presentation lit-folio, outline your philosophy of literacy teaching. In the introduction, explain the importance of your lit-folio so that your audience understands the context of your work and who you are as a literacy teacher.

FIGURE 2.12 Literacy Works-in-Process

Literacy works-in-process should reflect a comprehensive and balanced literacy program. Growth demonstrated should be holistic and reflective of the six language arts across the curriculum. Works-in-process include:

- a table of contents or concept web outlining the artifacts in the lit-folio
- an "About the Author" page: "Who I am as a literacy learner," for your students; "Who I am as a literacy teacher," a statement of your philosophy
- drawings, pictures, photos, and descriptions of favourite people, places, memories, objects
- lists of words read and written on demand, spontaneously, or independently
- copies of letters, cards, or e-mails sent to friends, authors, or characters in books
- reading responses such as journal entries, notetaking, notes made outside the classroom, summary charts, anticipation guides, creative responses; literature circle assessments, videotapes of performances, readers' theatre, drama, visual arts, storytelling
- writing samples of the five stages of the writing process and of several genres (e.g., expressive, poetic, transactional)
- journal entries (e.g., free flow, quickwrite, "what I think", personal, social skills, reflections)
- literacy learner's notebook, which might include notes, observations, pictures, ideas, thoughts, questions, experiences, interests, sources to look for, books I have read, books I would like to read, interesting words encountered in reading, conversation, or other media, words or concepts that need to be remembered (e.g., glossary), memorable quotes or poems
- evidence of oral communication (listening and speaking) which might include talk and listening checklists, videotapes, audiotapes, or photographs of oral presentations, drama, storytelling, role play, debate, interview, tableau
- completed viewing guides for performances, movies, and videos
- anything the learner wants to include from home, community, or school that reflects your process as a literacy learner: listener, speaker, reader, writer, viewer, representer
- a rationale for each artifact may be required if you are combining the cumulative lit-folio with the presentation lit-folio

Teacher literacy works-in-process may also include the following:

- lesson plans, unit plans, long-range plans, individual education plans
- classroom schedules and timetables
- maps or pictures of classroom setup: centres, bulletin boards, student activities
- assessment ideas: checklists, rubrics

Source: Summarized and compiled from Booth (1996); Sullivan (1995); Wiggins & McTighe (1998).

FIGURE 2.13 Michelle's Comprehension Page

Comprehension Strategies

What is it?
Comprehension strategies are used to help students understand what they are reading, hearing, or viewing. These strategies aid in the process of teaching students to read like a writer and write like a reader.

Question, Answer, Relationship (QAR)
Example: Fanny's Dream

Right There (Answer in the text)	Think and Search (Answer must be sought out)
• How many children did Fanny and Hebert have? • What was Fanny waiting for?	• Compare Fanny's idea of a Prince to Hebert. • Why did Fanny want to go to the ball? • What happened when the fairy godmother finally came? • Compare Fanny's dream to her real life. (Venn diagram)
Author and you (Answer is not in the text; you need information the author has given you combined with what you already know in order to respond) • Why didn't Fanny want to go to the ball at the end of the story? • What took the fairy godmother so long to get to Fanny? • Was Fanny happy with the life she chose to live? Find evidence.	**On My Own (Answer not in text, do not need text to respond)** • What could cause someone to change their dreams? • What is your dream? • Would you marry for love or money? • Did you ever want to be a prince or princess?

Bloom's Taxonomy
Example: Applying Bloom's Taxonomy to Cinderella

Knowledge	Comprehension	Application
Who are the members of Cinderella's family?	What happened when the clock struck midnight?	Can you think of a time when you were treated unfairly?
Analysis	**Synthesis**	**Evaluation**
Compare the stepsisters with each other.	How else could the Prince have found the woman who fit the glass slipper?	Were the stepsisters showing Cinderella respect? Why or why not?

Retell, Relate, Reflect
Example: Video on modelled, shared, and interactive writing

Retail (Retell text using your own words)	Relate (Memories, connections, feelings related to the text)	Reflect (Wondering, sharing thoughts, asking questions)
• Writing about a theme (e.g. a critter hunt) • Examined the different critters they found and what they had done that morning. • Teachers that writing is a process and it needs to be planned. • Brainstorms with the class what they did. • Teacher used science books and literacy centres.	My associate had an entire writing unit based on *The Jolly Postman*. By Christmas, students finish their own book that gets published for their parents. Throughout the term, he would use modelled reading, shared reading, and guided reading to help the students create their finished product. I remember him telling me that guided writing is exhausting.	My next placement is a JK/SK class, so it would be most beneficial to use modelled and shared writing. The students may not yet be at the level to begin writing on their own.

In Student Teacher Practice 2.1, Neil McLeod discusses his lit-folio from process, product, course expectation, and reflective perspectives. The following questions can be used to guide your lit-folio reflection:

- How does this relate to my development as a literacy teacher?
  Consider both course expectations and standards for professional practice. Make a direct link between the artifacts and your personal and professional growth as a literacy learner and as a literacy teacher.

- How does this relate to my understanding of learners?
  Link and relate your own literacy development to that of your students. Make a direct link between the artifacts and the methods you use to motivate, engage, and support learners (e.g., learning styles, multiple intelligences, multiple ways of knowing, multiple levels of support, etc.)

- How does this relate to curriculum, instruction, and assessment?
  Consider relevant curriculum documents and language and literacy methods. Make a direct link between the artifacts and critical awareness of the curriculum and its implications (e.g., standardized curriculum, standardized testing, literacy initiatives, etc.) and exemplary methods of language instruction and assessment.

BENEFITS OF LIT-FOLIOS

Regardless of whether we are discussing the implementation of lit-folio assessment processes for elementary school children or B. Ed. students, lit-folios have a number of clear benefits (Booth, 1996; Bressler & Siegel, 2000, McLaughlin & Vogt, 1996; Sullivan, 1995). Lit-folio assessment provides a dynamic, fluid, ongoing, and collaborative perspective on learner performance (Booth, 1996; Graves & Sunstein, 1992).

literacy
notebook
2.4

STOP, THINK, AND WRITE

- What do you understand about lit-folios and the process of creating them both as an independent literacy learner and a developing literacy teacher?

- What might you include in your process lit-folio?

- What are the major differences between a process lit-folio and a presentation lit-folio?

- What do you still need to know to further your understanding of the lit-folio process?

Lit-folios:

* encourage students to engage in *student-centred and self-directed learning*: set goals, engage in self-assessment (continuous review of strengths, needs, effort, growth), and reflective thought

Student Teacher Practice/2.1

LIT-FOLIO REFLECTION

In creating this lit-folio, I fulfilled the following course expectations:
* Develop a personal philosophy of literacy education to guide classroom practice.
* Understand factors influencing language learning and how these apply to the classroom.
* Become familiar with curriculum documents related to language.

I believe that by working on and compiling this lit-folio, I have fulfilled a number of the course expectations. I say this, because it was only as I brought all of the components together that I began to fully understand what I was learning. Putting it together in this format helped me to organize the information in my mind much more so than just attending classes.

First, creating this lit-folio gave me the opportunity to think about and articulate my own philosophy of literacy (found on preceding pages). It was only after going through practicum experiences and then working on this lit-folio that my philosophy began to take shape. I believe that it is a sound philosophy and one that I can and will implement in my own classroom.

By doing reading and writing assessments (found near the end), I could see how developmental factors influence how we learn to read and what tasks we can assign to students of different ages to help them read better. For example, children in Kindergarten are just learning about the concepts of print (left to right, spaces between words, etc.), so it is important to emphasize these ideas when implementing guided reading or journal activities. Similarly, I see that junior level students need to focus on reading comprehension strategies, organizing their thoughts into writing, and using greater detail in their writing.

Also, working on my literature focus unit required me to become more familiar with the curriculum documents related to language. I chose to create units for Grade 2 and Grade 5. In order to choose appropriate activities for each unit, I needed to review the curriculum documents to see what was expected of those students. Though I have not committed all of the expectations to memory, I am more familiar with them than ever before.

I admit that at the beginning of and throughout this year, I was very intimidated by this lit-folio, even by the idea of implementing a literacy program of my own. However, after compiling this lit-folio and seeing everything I have learned in one place, I can now make the connections among all the elements in Balanced Literacy. I have a much greater understanding of what is required of a Primary/Junior literacy program, and I feel that I am on my way to creating a meaningful one for my own students in September.

Neil McLeod is a 2004–2005 graduate of Nipissing University's Bachelor of Education program.

- enable students to explore the *interconnections and interrelationships of learners, curriculum, instruction, and assessment.* Negotiating literacy learning goals helps students to situate their learning in not only a school context but a world and home context as well. Authentic lit-folios are reflective of world, community, and family literacy practices as well as school practices

- offer a great opportunity for *legitimate and meaningful literacy conversations* between parents, teachers, and learners; these conversations often extend beyond the technological or practical aspects into conversations regarding "what counts as literacy and what it means to grow as a literacy learner" (Bressler & Siegel, 2000, p. 153)

- offer a *meaningful and authentic means of performance-based assessment* that encourages students to demonstrate knowledge, skill, and values in ways that are reflective of multiple intelligences, learning styles, and multi-literacies

A collection of literacy works-in-process provide a cumulative record of each learner's interests, motivations, thoughts, feelings, backgrounds, strengths, and needs, which can be used to develop and assess programs (whole class, small group, individualized), participate in parent-teacher conferences (Hansen, 1992; Bressler & Siegel, 2000), and take part in school and division planning. Assessment of portfolios encompasses considering student growth over a period of time (measured both against goals and a standard where appropriate), each individual learner's process and not just product as described in reflections, and the final product. Rubrics, checklists, conferences, peer assessment, and self assessment are all valid methods of assessment; the key to lit-folio assessment is to connect assessment to instruction in an authentic and relevant way (Wiggins & McTighe, 1998).

Lit-folios are a performance-based method of assessment; they contain evidence and artifacts of growth related to both literacy process and product. Successful implementation of lit-folios requires systematic thought regarding their purpose, procedures, assessment, and implementation. Lit-folios have both a process aspect and a product aspect. Essentially, the process lit-folio contains a full representation of a literacy learner's works-in-process whereas a presentation lit-folio contains a selection of artifacts that reflects the learner's goals, expectations, and learning.

Theory into Practice 2.1 provides a complete description of the process of implementing lit-folios in the regular classroom.

LIT-FOLIOS IN THE REGULAR CLASSROOM

Before implementing lit-folios:

1. Establish a purpose/focus for the lit-folio.
    Ask: What are the learner, course, and program expectations?
    How will goals be negotiated with learners?
    Who is the audience for the lit-folio?
    How will lit-folio contents be used?
    What is the vision of the learner implicit in the lit-folio?
    What is the vision of the lit-folio for the purposes of this program, grade, or assignment?

2. Establish procedures for review: feedback, assessment, and evaluation.
    Ask: What do I expect to know about the learner in terms of knowledge, skill, and value?
    How do I expect to see growth throughout the lit-folio?
    How will students be involved in the review and sharing process?
    How will I share assessment and evaluation criteria with my learners prior to implementation?
    What will be assessed? How will the lit-folio be assessed? Who will assess the lit-folio?
    Who will provide feedback? How will feedback be provided? When will feedback be provided?
    How will the lit-folio be evaluated? Who will evaluate the lit-folio?

During the process:

3. Engage learners in comprehensive and balanced language and literacy works-in-process.
    Ask: What do learners need to understand about literacy works-in-process?
    How will literacy works-in-process or artifacts be collected?
    What are some artifact possibilities?
    How will works-in-process/artifacts be stored?
    How will works-in-process/artifacts be logged during the collection phase?

4. Negotiate goals and expectations for lit-folio, evidence selection, and final product construction.
    Ask: What do learners need to understand about presentation lit-folios?
    How will evidence of expectations and goals be selected?
    Who will select evidence?
    How will evidence be displayed?
    What decision criteria will be used for selecting and including evidence?
    How will learners and teachers justify choices for evidence selection?
    How will the lit-folio be organized?

After lit-folio implementation:

5. Implement pre-established criteria and process for review: feedback, assessment, and evaluation.
    Ask: How is this lit-folio reflective of the negotiated criteria?
    What do you know about the learner in terms of knowledge, skill, and value as a result of this lit-folio?
    What growth is evidenced throughout the lit-folio?

Source: Adapted from Campbell et al. (2001).

MANAGING LIT-FOLIOS IN THE CLASSROOM

Managing lit-folios in the classroom requires a high level of organization and communication with students, parents, and other teachers. Below, we list our hints and what we have learned about lit-folio assessment and instruction from both personal practice and research (Booth, 1996; Manning & Manning, 1994; Sullivan, 1995).

1. Be clear about the purpose and uses of the portfolio with your students and their parents. Involve parents by sending a letter that explains the process and invites them to participate. Engage parents in the development of a literacy learner profile.

2. Choose a container that works best for you and your students. Some teachers like loose-leaf notebooks, large pocketed folders, or plastic containers. Some store the materials in cardboard boxes, plastic crates, file cabinets, or cupboards. The important thing is that the portfolio containers are manageable for you and the children.

3. Establish a convenient place in the classroom to store the containers.

4. Establish criteria for selecting and evaluating work for the lit-folio. This will help students to build ownership in the process.

Ensure portfolio containers are manageable for you and your students.

5. Contents in the portfolio differ from level to level. Ensure that students add items into their working lit-folios on a regular basis. Without continual attention and focus, evidence selection for their presentation lit-folio will be limited.

6. Focus on collecting data on only one or two students each day (running records, oral language assessment, writing conferences, etc.).

7. Write anecdotal notes when you think you've observed an important event in a student's literacy development. These are often referred to as "literacy events" and document important realizations, attitudes, and skills.

8. Schedule time to review portfolio contents with students, individually or in small groups, and provide individualized feedback for growth.

9. Schedule time for lit-folio conversations with parents. Respond to their observations and concerns about their child's literacy development.

10. Exchange lit-folio tips with other teachers.

In conclusion, we believe that lit-folio development and assessment support a comprehensive and balanced approach to literacy; they provide opportunities for instruction and assessment that are meaningful, authentic, and real-life. Lit-folio assessment:

- requires performances that demonstrate students' meaning construction
- is collaborative, necessitating interactions and support from others
- nurtures students as inquirers
- demonstrates students' progress over time, valuing increasing knowledge and application of what is learned
- requires students to self-reflect and self-assess, promoting reflectivity about practice (McLaughlin & Vogt, 1996, p. 10)

In pre-service education, McLaughlin and Vogt (1996) state that "just learning about the philosophy inherent in an assessment practice is not sufficient" (p. 11). We believe, as do they, that in order to emerge as knowledgeable teachers able to develop lit-folios with students, teachers must first experience lit-folio development and assessment themselves.

Moving On

As we near the end of this chapter, review the enduring understandings (Wiggins & McTighe, 1998) that we have presented throughout this chapter. We began with a discussion of exemplary literacy teachers and the characteristics they share and finished with a description of how transformational literacy teachers can demonstrate their developing expertise and understanding of theory into practice. Keep your literacy notebook as a central focus during the rest of your reading assignments so that you demonstrate your growth through your lit-folio. It is only by being fully engaged and critical that we can hope to become more than great teachers who inspire.

The good teacher explains,
The superior teacher demonstrates,
The great teacher inspires,
The lifelong teacher changes the world!
Adapted from William Arthur Ward

LIT-FOLIO UPDATE

You now have a comprehensive understanding of what lit-folios are, how you can trace your own development as a literacy learner and a literacy teacher, and how you can implement them in a classroom. If you haven't already, establish some goals for your lit-folio, set up a log sheet to keep you on track. Collecting literacy works-in-process for your process lit-folio does not happen overnight. It requires thoughtful and critical attention throughout your course, your program, and your lifetime.

LIT-FOLIO TIP

As you think about collecting information for your process lit-folio, we suggest that you develop an organizational structure that works for you. For example, some of our students have maintained divided sections in a binder (or on their computer) where they can file:

- Children's literature
- Class notes, activities, and assignments
- Text notes
- Practicum ideas, notes, and/or lesson plans

Resources to Support Your Learning

Inspirational Books on Teaching

Layne, S.L. (2001). *Life's literacy lessons: Poems for teachers.* Newark, DE: International Reading Association.

McCourt, F. (2005). *Teacher man: A memoir.* New York, Scribner.

Palmer, P.J. (1998). *The courage to teach: Exploring the inner landscape of a teacher's life.* San Francisco, CA: Jossey-Bass.

Teacher Portfolios and Literacy Portfolios

Campbell, D.M. et al. (2001). *How to develop a professional portfolio: A manual for teachers* (2nd ed.). Boston, MA: Allyn & Bacon.

Manning, M. & Manning, G. (1994). Managing literacy portfolios. *Teaching Pre-K-8, 24*(7), 84-86.

Mitchell, J.P., Abernathy, T.V., & Gowans, L.P. (1998). Making sense of literacy portfolios: A four-step plan. *Journal of Adolescent and Adult Literacy, 41*(5), 384-387.

Children's Literature: Our Favourites

A fine, fine school, Sharon Creech
Dear Mr. Henshaw, Beverly Cleary
First day jitters, Julie Danneberg
Ish, Peter H. Reynolds
T is for teachers: A school alphabet, Steven Layne
Thank you, Mr. Falker, Patricia Polacco
The dot, Peter H. Reynolds
The three questions, Jon J. Muth
Rainbows, head lice, and pea-green tile: Poems in the voice of the classroom teacher, Brod Bagert

Multimedia Connections

Films that portray inspirational teachers:
Dangerous Minds
Dead Poets Society
Mona Lisa Smile
Mr. Holland's Opus
The Breakfast Club
The Miracle Worker
The Prime of Miss Jean Brodie
To Sir With Love

3

Literacy as a W.O.R.L.D. View

key terms

discourses

literacies

literacy

multiliteracies

multiple intelligences

orality

re-vision

W.O.R.L.D. view

word

questions to guide your learning

By the end of this chapter, you should understand the key terms and be able to answer the following questions:

- Is literacy a technical skill or a generalizable ability related to reading and writing print?

- Is literacy a static or dynamic concept? How is literacy influenced by its purpose or use?

- Is literacy defined the same by all? Is it a single concept or skill?

- Does literacy favour a particular view of the world?

- How can awareness of literacy ideologies and practices help us to assess, critique, and evaluate assumptions inherent in curricular and instructional materials and processes and traditional school contexts?

- How can you take a critical approach toward the development of literacy in your students and the use of curriculum materials and processes?

Looking Back, Looking Ahead

In Chapter 1, you explored your perspective as a literacy learner: a listener, speaker, reader, writer, viewer, and representer. In Chapter 2, you were introduced to the characteristics shared by literacy teachers and encouraged to set goals for your own personal development as a literacy learner and a literacy teacher. In this chapter, we ask you to think critically about what you currently believe about literacy and how those beliefs will shape your literacy practices.

Critically reviewing traditional and contemporary research will help you to make sense of the diverse meanings of literacy and of what counts as literacy. This will bring you closer to selecting literacy practices that will meet the needs of all students in a responsive and inclusive manner.

As an active and critical reader, we encourage you to challenge and problematize your own language and literacy beliefs and practices (Lankshear & Lawler, 1987), in an effort to address the critical questions:

> *Whose interests are emergent technologies and pedagogies serving? Are they helping all social groups and individuals? Who is being excluded and why? We also need to raise the question both of the extent to which multiplying technologies and literacies are preparing students and citizens for the present and future, and producing conditions for a more vibrant democratic society, or simply reproducing existing inequalities and inequity.*

> (Kellner, 2004, pp. 26-27)

We begin by problematizing the term "literacy" in a way that will enable you to reflect on your beliefs about literacy and the language arts curriculum, both as you have experienced it and as you will be expected to teach. These beliefs, experiences, and ideologies lead to positive and negative assumptions about learners and learning as well as about teaching practices. Without critical inquiry into your beliefs and assumptions about literacy, you may rely on the memory of your own literacy experi-

literacy notebook 3.1

STOP, THINK, AND WRITE

- What does literacy mean to you?
- What are the ideological, societal, and educational consequences of literacy?

ences and be less likely to develop alternative conceptualizations of language and literacy that will better serve you in today's classrooms (Boomer, 1993; Gardner & Boix-Mansilla, 1994; Gitlin, 1995; Palmer, 1998).

Problematizing Literacy

What does it mean to be truly literate in the twenty-first century? Does it mean we can read the details of a contest on the back of a cereal box and correctly fill in the entry form? Does it mean that we are graduates of high school or post-secondary education? Does literacy mean that we have a literate state of mind, a literate way of knowing, an ability to communicate effectively with others, or an ability to interact with the world around us? Is literacy the result of schooling, education, or learning? Is literacy a creative, imaginative, critical, dialogic process? What are the purposes, functions, and goals of literacy? What is it about literacy that makes it valued, highly sought after, and idealized?

> *Many people would no doubt regard such questions as pointless... After all, there is a pervasive folk wisdom about literacy. Surely we all know what it is and why it is so valuable and important. Conventional wisdom assumes the necessity and value of literacy for social and economic development, for advancing and maintaining democratic institutions, and for individual betterment.*

> (Lankshear & Lawler, 1987, p. 37)

Conventional wisdom attributes literacy to the individual, the teacher, and the school, instead of looking to social and cultural institutions, and the necessity to reconceptualize literacy and its corresponding practices in the home, school, and community. We often hear of a "literacy" crisis: not enough students are passing the literacy tests, remediation is needed, it is the school's responsibility; but what role do political and societal ideologies play? What conceptualizations of literacy drive our educational system? Are these conventional understandings in the best interests of learners and society? While the value of literacy

> *for achieving fulfilling productive, expanding, and participating lives of freedom in modern societies is undoubted and unquestioned... literacy does not seem to be well understood, popularly or academically... Whether seen as a concept; a skill, tool, or technique; or expected consequences from possession of the tool, discussions of literacy suffer from serious confusion.*

> (Graff, 1981, p. 1)

What is the root of this confusion? Surely we do not need to expend more time and energy investigating and researching answers to what appears to be so transparently necessary and good. Can we not assume that our educational institutions understand the nature of literacy and its vast implications for teaching and learning?

Schooling approaches that rely on conventional wisdom have long-perpetuated statistics regarding adult literacy in Canada that are alarming. According to the Canadian Education Association (2004), "two out of five Canadians would have difficulty reading this sentence, following the instructions on a prescription label, finding out information about how to vote, or filling out a permission form for their child's school trip" (p. 1). According to "Reading the Future: A Portrait of Literacy in Canada" (2003), about 22% of adult Canadians 16 years and over have serious difficulty dealing with printed materials and most likely identify themselves as people who have difficulties reading; another 24-26% can deal only with material that is simple and clearly laid out, and in which the tasks involved are not complex. They read, but not well. Not only do they not read well enough, but a recent study published by Statistics Canada (2004) suggests that reading proficiency may affect students' likelihood to graduate from high school and pursue postsecondary education (Statistics Canada, 2006). We must call into question how much of the problem rests with the literacy learner and how much with our current conceptualization of literacy and the way we measure "what counts as literacy" in today's society.

Consider the UNESCO (2003) conceptualization of literacy that is frequently cited in language and literacy curriculum documents across Canada:

> *Literacy is more than reading and writing—it is about how we communicate in society. It is about social practices and relationships, about knowledge, language and culture. Literacy... finds its place in our lives alongside other ways of communicating. Indeed, literacy itself takes many forms on paper, on the computer screen, on TV, on posters and signs. Those who use literacy take it for granted, but those who cannot use it are excluded from much communication in today's world. Indeed, it is the excluded who can best appreciate the notion of "literacy as freedom."*
>
> (UNESCO, 2003, p. 1)

Whose interests are served by this definition? What assumptions about literacy are implicit in this definition? Does it allude to the dynamic nature of literacy or is literacy viewed as a finite and concrete skill? Does this definition encompass non-traditional literacies or is it restricted predominantly to print literacies? Our world is filled with such diversity that we can no longer be satisfied with a conceptualization of literacy that perpetuates a focus on the printed word. We must look to theorists such as Eisner (1987) who define literacy as a search for meaning:

> We are condemned, it seems, to searching for a life of meaning. Trying to negotiate the environment in which we live, trying to determine who is friend and who is foe, trying to apply the social codes we learn through our social experience, these are the ubiquitous and defining characteristics of our nature. This process of creating meaning is largely a matter of learning to read. But here I am speaking of reading as a generic human process of decoding the expressive forms we create as social organisms. It is a process not limited solely to the written word. When we speak of reading, particularly in the context of schooling, we think of it as a process dealing with the words, sentences, and paragraphs found in books, articles, and stories. And it is true that reading these codes in these forms is a crucially important social act. But reading can also be thought of as any process that involves the decoding of any type of expressive form, whether it is constructed intentionally or not. Reading in this sense is so pervasive an aspect of our existence that we have become desensitized to the ways in which we read and the range of material to which it is applied.
>
> (Eisner, 1978, p. 14)

Literacy, in its broadest sense, is much more than reading individual words on a page. Much more than reading "in page-bound, official, standard forms of the national language" (New London Group, 2000, p. 9), literacy is about reading, making sense of, and transforming events, art, expression, life, self, essentially the world.

A W.O.R.L.D. View of Literacy

With such a diversity of opinion and belief about what counts as literacy, we suggest an approach that acknowledges the contributions of a variety of researchers and of perspectives. Our comprehensive and balanced view of literacy is one that draws from literacy research about Words, Orality, Re-vision (or transformation), Literacies, and Discourses (W.O.R.L.D.), each of which is defined in this chapter. The ideological perspective that we offer is one that embraces literacy beyond the classroom and recognizes the need to examine and revise social and educational practices that privilege one group of learners or one individual learner over others. At the core of our inquiry and re-vision is the development and critical analysis of values and practices that respect the right of each learner to be successful. Your classroom should be a place where all students are encouraged to listen, speak, read, write, view, represent, and revise their worlds—acts and practices that are grounded in social interaction, not in individual autonomy (Collins Block, 2003).

Literacy teachers with W.O.R.L.D. views of literacy recognize and value the following:

- Literacy always begins with the needs of the learner. Local and dominant (contextual) literacies and discourses need to be valued. It is our role to take students from where they are to somewhere else (Clay, 1985).
- The needs of literacy learners change over time; this requires flexible teaching.
- There is no one conceptualization of literacy that is globally accepted or universally useful. Regardless of which concept we use, literacy will always include reading the word (hearing, viewing, reading) and writing the word (speaking, visually representing, writing).
- Literacy can enable students to create and revise some aspects of their worlds, providing them with a literacy passport to access and navigate the W.O.R.L.D. independently and powerfully.
- Literacy develops most effectively within an environment of acceptance, risk-taking, co-operation, and respect.
- Literacy is multiple in terms of purpose and function. Some literacies are better suited to different domains and contexts.
- Literacy is multidisciplinary and cross-disciplinary and must be taught accordingly. Literacy permeates every aspect of education.
- There is no single or right way to teach literacy, although there are exemplary literacy practices.
- Literacy practices are most often shaped by social institutions and power relations beyond teachers' control. Some are more dominant, visible, influential, and demanding than others (for example, program and curriculum development, standardized testing, evaluation research).

(Armstrong, 1994; Bruner, 1986; Cambourne, 1988; 2000/2001; Collins & Blot, 2003; Egan, 2001; 1988; Freire, 1987; Gardner, 1991; 1987; 1995; Gee, 1990; Heath, 1983; Kellner, 2004; Lankshear & Knobel, 1998; Lankshear & Lawler, 1987; Leland et al., 2000; Lonsdale & McCurry, 2004; New London Group, 2000; Pérez, 2004; Richards & McKenna, 2003; Smith, 1988).

Framing our inquiry through a W.O.R.L.D. view allows you to investigate not only the meaning of literacy but also its implications for literacy learning that culminate in the individual's re-vision of self, world, and W.O.R.L.D. views. In order to do this, we must first understand what is meant by each individual letter in the acronym W.O.R.L.D.

W FOR WORD

Reading and writing the word are philosophical inheritances that we must contend with; they date back to the creation of the alphabet, the invention of the printing press, and now the impact of computers. Reading and writing the word are commonly accepted as literate behaviours in today's ideological, educational, societal, and global institutions. Understanding this dimension requires us to understand literacy as more than the traditional and historically embedded processes of reading and writing the word. Underlying standardized testing and many instances of contemporary curricula, we see the influences of this traditional conceptualization. Chapters 8 through 12 deal exclusively with reading and writing theories and practices.

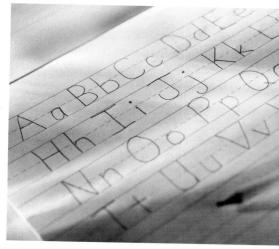

Literacy is more than reading and writing the word.

Although reading and writing the word is a core component of our W.O.R.L.D. view, we must also acknowledge that words need not always be written. "The word" in this reconceptualization requires us to understand how words work in a wide variety of contexts for a variety of purposes, the empowering nature of words, the ability of words to construct our realities, communicate with others, and transform the world. Consider Frederick's ability to read the world and transform his reading of the world into words and thoughts, ultimately contributing to a transformation of reality not just for himself but for his comrades as well (see Figure 3.1).

Paulo Freire (1987), like Frederick, recognizes the importance of reading words as an extension of reading his world, and uses words to paint a powerful image of the impact of reading his world on his emerging literacy.

Deciphering the world flowed naturally from my reading my particular world; it was not something superimposed on it. I learned to read and write on the ground of the backyard of my house, in the shade of the mango tress, with words from my world rather than from the wider world of my parents. The earth was my blackboard, the sticks my chalk…

The texts, the words, the letters of that context were incarnated in a series of things, objects, and signs. In perceiving these, I experienced myself, and the more I experienced myself, the more my perceptual capacity increased. (p. 32)

FIGURE 3.1 *Frederick* by Leo Lionni

Frederick is a field mouse. While all the other field mice were preparing for the winter, Frederick appeared to be daydreaming, not contributing to their day-to-day work. When asked why he doesn't work, Frederick insisted that he did work; he gathered "sun-rays for the cold, dark winter days."

Then they saw Frederick sitting and staring at the meadow and asked what he was doing this time, and he replied, "I gather colors. For winter is gray."

Another time when Frederick appeared to be asleep, they reproachfully asked him if he was dreaming. But Frederick replied that he was gathering words for the long winter days when they ran out of things to talk about.

During winter the food ran out, the little mice got cold, and they ran out of things to talk about, so they asked Frederick about his supplies.

As he shared his work, he effectively transformed their world. As he spoke about the sun the other mice began to feel the warmth. Was it because of Frederick's voice? Or was it magic?

He spoke about the bright, colourful flowers, like the blue periwinkles and the red poppies, and they could see the colours clearly and vividly in their minds.

Source: Summarized from Lionni (1967).

Literacy develops by reading the world and reading the word simultaneously, each one influencing the other in a positive way; reading and writing words enable learners to read and write their worlds; one cannot occur in isolation from the other. To this end, Freire (1987)

> [insists] that words used in organizing a literacy program come from what [he calls] the "word universe" of people who are learning, expressing their actually language, their anxieties, fears, demands, and dreams. Words should be laden with the meaning of the people's existential experience, and not of the teacher's experience. Surveying the word universe thus gives us the people's words, pregnant with the world, words from the people's reading of the world. We then give the words back to the people inserted in what [he calls] "codifications," pictures representing real situations. (p. 35)

Literacy is not reduced to words but instead words are used as reflections of reality. In this way, words become a symbol of value and power; they are not only reflections of the changing world but come to represent the transforming self as well. As a summary, we have provided an overview of how word theory can be transferred into classroom language practice in Figure 3.2.

FIGURE 3.2 Word Theory into Language Practice

Word Theory	Language Practice
How Words Work – Context and Purpose	• helping students understand the processes of reading and writing words (for example, genre, format, purpose, audience, context) • supporting students with a range of word-solving and grammar strategies (for example, word meanings, parts of speech)
Empowering Nature of Words	• making use of students' vocabulary as a starting point for language exploration • helping students to understand the purpose of language in their lives and the power gained through the use of words
Words as Communication	• providing legitimate and meaningful opportunities to use language for a variety of purposes in the classroom (for example, writing letters about social issues, asking questions, seeking information, interacting with others)
Words as Means to Shape and Transform Reality and World	• helping students to explore texts and stories, make connections, and reflect on their own realities • teaching critical literacy strategies such as questioning the author and question-answer relationships that allow students to question the authority and fallibility of texts (print, visual, oral, multimedia)

O FOR ORALITY

There is no doubt that navigating the W.O.R.L.D. requires an ability to read and write the word but necessary precursors to reading and writing the word are hearing and saying the word. Historically, researchers have had a tendency to separate literacy and orality, seeing them as distinct and discrete entities (Havelock, 1991). It is interesting, though, that a fully literate culture cannot exist without orality but the converse is not true. Primary oral cultures have prospered in the past and continue to exist today without the written word. Educators are increasingly recognizing the importance of orality in literacy. For this reason we devote two chapters (Chapter 4 and 5) to the nature of oral language and its relationship to literacy in the classroom.

For some,

the purely oral tradition or primary orality is not easy to conceive of accurately and meaningfully. Writing makes 'words' appear similar to things because we think of words as the visible marks signalling words to de-

Orality is important in the development of literacy.

> coders: we can see and touch such inscribed 'words' in texts and books. Written words are residue. Oral tradition has no such residue or deposit. When an often-told oral story is not actually being told, all that exists of it is the potential it creates in human beings to tell it.
>
> (Ong, 1982, p. 11)

That being said, we must acknowledge the importance of orality in the development of literacy. We cannot say with certainty that there is a direct causal relationship between orality and literacy but what we can say is that literacy will not develop in isolation from orality. We can use what we have learned about learning oral language to support us in effective language literacy instruction in the classroom. How do children best learn language?

> They learn by apprenticeship—hunting with experienced hunters, for example—by discipleship, which is a kind of apprenticeship, by listening, by repeating what they hear, by mastering proverbs and ways of combining and recombining them, by assimilating other formulary materials, by participation in a kind of corporate retrospection—not by study in the strict sense.
>
> (Ong, 1982, p. 9)

Egan (1988) draws from oral cultures for his rich description of what it means to understand the world and how we acquire literacy. He argues that literacy is mediated by tools inherited from oral cultures that are used to remember and transmit information from one generation to the next. These tools include narrative story structures, metaphors, jokes, and rhythm.

> They are cultural universals, observable in all human cultures—they seem to be cognitive tools that we cannot not use. They do not go away

with the development of literacy, even though they are all influenced in one way or another by literacy.

(Egan, 2001, p. 11)

These capacities or tools are, in fact, residue from oral cultures; while we do not have formal texts reliably and consistently passed from one generation to the next (as we do in literate cultures), we do have genres or formats within which to frame our talk. Feldman (1991) speaks about the nature of these oral inheritances and their resultant impact on literate development.

> *Though we may not have oral systems of text and interpretation in our culture, the appropriate genres having been handed over to writing, many oral cultures seem to have such oral genres in the absence of a system of writing. Moreover, some of those cultures seem to show the same general preoccupation with the nature of interpretation itself that is of concern to literary theorists. In those oral cultures that have them, artful genres are a privileged and valued form of life, one that is an occasion for reflection and for elegance and beauty that go beyond adaptive necessity.* (p. 62)

With regard to recording or "fixing" texts for interpretation, she argues that there are two universals of human culture at play that determine how something is to be remembered. First, is the human ability "to salivate over words or seek for elegant expression, and second, to want to interpret or make meanings of utterances, to strive to look behind the surface of what is said or merely seen to what is meant" (Feldman, 1991, p. 52). If this is truly the nature of the human condition, one could argue that it is as equally present in an oral culture as it is in a literate culture. Both of these represent the true essence of the continuous arts of listening, speaking, reading, writing, viewing, representing, and re-visioning. Figure 3.3 presents a summative overview of how our thoughts about orality can be transferred into classroom language practice.

R FOR RE-VISION

> *Re-vision involves both critically seeing the past and present and imagining a different future. It implies as well reconstructing education, using informed theory to guide novel pedagogical practices, and to fundamentally restructure educational institutions. Re-visioning education also involves another way of seeing and doing, grounded in historical practices of the past and present and looking toward a different and better future.*

(Kellner, 2004, p. 10)

Paulo Freire (1987) discusses the fact that the differentiation between reading the world and reading the word often serves to empower certain

FIGURE 3.3 Orality Theory into Language Practice

Orality Theory	Language Practice
Oral Language Is Learned through Apprenticeship	• providing opportunities to learn through modelling (for example, conversing, imitation, approximation, storytelling, drama, reading aloud, and thinking aloud)
Orality Is a Necessary Rehearsal for Literacy	• providing multiple opportunities for storytelling, information gathering, drama, public speaking, readers' theatre, choral speaking/reading, sharing, show and tell, literature circles
Oral Language Provides a Structure for Written Language	• structuring oral language practices for transfer into written language (for example, narrative stories, poems, arguments/debates, conversations/dialogues, speeches, metaphors, idioms, grammar, drama)

individuals (those who can become literate within the generally accepted standard or conceptualization), which consequently means that an inability to read the word leads to domination and oppression. He is not alone in this view, but is supported by many theorists (Foucault, 1988: Galeano, 1988; Pattanayak, 1991) who suggest that traditional approaches to education seek to perpetuate the divide between those who have and those who have not. Indeed the UNESCO definition cited earlier highlights this differentiation between those who have and those who have not.

Students who do not have the "cultural capital" (Bourdieu & Passeron, 1977), "funds of knowledge" (Moll, Amanta, Geff, & Gonzalez, 1992), or "ways with words" (Heath, 1983) are often oppressed and their voices silenced in the process of education and therefore the development of literacy. Galeano (1988) paints a dismal picture of domination and oppression where "illusions of wealth are sold to the poor, illusions of freedom to the oppressed, dreams of victory to the defeated and of power to the weak. One need not be literate to consume the inviting symbols presented by television, radio, and films in their effort to justify the unequal organization of the world" (p. 117). No longer is it enough to simply read and write words, but critical literacy calls for

individuals [to] be helped to develop the competencies to understand, critique, and transform the social and cultural conditions in which they live, gaining the ability to be creative and transformative subjects and not just objects of domination and manipulation. This requires developing abilities for critical thinking, reflection, and the capacity to engage in discourse, cultural creation, and political action and movements. Active and engaged subjects are produced in social interaction with others, as well as with tools and techniques, so social skills and individual capacities for communication, creativity, and action must be part of the multiple literacies that a radical reconstruction of education seeks and cultivates.

Crucially, developing multiple literacies and alternative pedagogies must become reflective and critical, aware of the educational, social, and political assumptions involved in the restructuring of education and society currently under way.

(Kellner, 2004, p. 26)

This dimension of re-vision is one of social action and empowerment of individuals through literacy. The power of individuals to re-vision, reconstruct, and transform their world and themselves is an essential characteristic of literacy. Without this power, we would live our lives in much the same way humans came to exist in Lois Lowry's *The Giver*, which is summarized in Figure 3.4.

What this community gained was sameness, an equality of sorts, but language was reduced to a technical skill that enabled them to communicate for functional purposes only. What they lost was the memory of what had come before, the ability to think critically, and the capacity to see beyond the present; essentially what they lost was literacy as an ability to read, write, and reconstruct their world. There was no need—the Giver remembered and provided memories and insights only when necessary, but it was a tremendous burden to be the only keeper of knowledge. In order to be literate in the twenty-first century, we need the same

---

FIGURE 3.4 *The Giver* by Lois Lowry

Jonas was selected to be the next Receiver of memory. Throughout his twelve years, he had shown all the qualities that a Receiver must have... 'Intelligence, Integrity, Courage, Wisdom, and the Capacity to See Beyond'. In Jonas' community, only the giver was privileged with memory of what had come before; it was the role of the Giver to share the memories of times past with the Receiver, "back and back and back". The Committee, the ones in power, had oppressed memory in an effort to eradicate war, fear, pain, and ultimately knowledge. Only the chosen ones, the Receivers who would become Givers, received the memories and the capacity to develop intelligence and wisdom, protecting the others from pain, suffering, and chaos. Each member of the community had an assignment. They were all very well trained—they understood the scientific facts and knew what they needed to know. They had no memory of the past, therefore they knew no different. In the end, Jonas recognized the power of memory and his capacity to see beyond the present, he recognized his ability to revise not only his world but that of his Community as well.

Source: Summarized from Lowry (1994).

attributes as the Giver: intelligence, integrity, courage, wisdom, and the capacity to see beyond. This is literacy, but as with the Giver, it does not come without cost nor does it come without benefit. Without our oral inheritance, without memory of what came before, we would be unable to read the world, make sense of it, and see beyond it to reconstruction and re-vision. It is interesting to note that re-vision falls in the centre of our W.O.R.L.D. view; indeed, re-vision is the centripetal force of our W.O.R.L.D. view of literacy. Theories about critical literacy and re-vision can be applied to classroom language practice as we have described in Figure 3.5.

L FOR LITERACIES

We consider literacies as multiple, flexible, and individualized; we include the theories of multiliteracies extended by the New London Group (2000) and multiple intelligences described by Howard Gardner (1987; 1999 a). These theories will "extend the idea and scope of literacy pedagogy to account for the context of our culturally and linguistically diverse and increasingly globalized societies; to account for the multifarious cultures that interrelate and the plurality of texts that circulate" (New London Group, 2000, p. 9).

The use of multiple literacies, multiple modalities, and multiple ways of knowing to teach literacy did not begin with the recent wave of research and contemporary pedagogy. Ivan Illich (1973) discussed problems with

FIGURE 3.5 Word Theory into Language Practice

Re-vision Theory	Language Practice
Communication	• negotiating texts, purposes, audiences, questions, problems, and solutions with students • using language for meaningful and authentic purposes
Critique	• adopting a questioning and interrogative stance (for example, questioning the author and text)
Empowerment	• providing students with choices about text, purpose, audience • allowing students to make limited and legitimate choices about language
Transformation	• encouraging intertextuality, making connections between texts and personal lives • learning from texts and others about what and how to be in the world

education that related to monomodal instruction with "one-size-fits-all" lesson plans, curricula, testing, and pedagogy that did not address challenging educational, social, cultural, political, or ecological problems. What is new, however, is the re-visioning of literacy that we are suggesting, as a W.O.R.L.D. view that incorporates multiple literacies in a way that respects the diversity of learners, classrooms, schools, and contexts, and recognizes that there is no one conceptualization of literacy, no one right way to teach literacy, and no best time or place to teach literacy.

This emergent theory of multiliteracies (New London Group, 2000) includes a description of modes of meaning that mediate the way we construct meaning with a variety of texts:

- linguistic meaning: of print texts, words, written texts

- audio meaning: of music, sound effects

- visual meaning: of images, page layouts, screen formats

- gestural meaning: of body language, sensuality

- spatial meaning: of environmental spaces, architectural spaces

- multimodal meaning: the most significant, as it relates to all other modes in dynamic ways (See Figure 3.6 for a description of how multiliteracy theory can be transformed into classroom practice.)

"In a profound sense, all meaning-making is multimodal" (New London Group, 2000, p. 29). Multimodal meaning-making is best achieved when all six strands of language are woven into a classroom program that is comprehensive and balanced. Rarely is any one language experience or language practice characterized by only one strand of language or one mode of meaning. Instead, meaning-making is best characterized by flexibile **hybridity** and **intertextuality** where students engage all senses and all modes of meaning when necessary. Hybridity involves the mechanisms of creativity and of culture-as-process where people create and innovate by hybridizing and making connections. Relevant and meaningful elements are woven together in unique ways that cut across traditional and conventional boundaries. Intertextuality refers to the complex relationships that emerge or are created between text and other modes of meanings, real or imaginary, print, media, or otherwise (New London Group, 2000).

While the theory of multiliteracies offers us significant food for thought and momentum for re-vision, the research appears to be oriented to and grounded in what we do with print text and how we represent texts, not to how we acquire literacy. We, therefore, turn to the

hybridity A characteristic of meaning-making that requires the producer and consumer of text to creatively merge, connect, and activate prior knowledge related to texts, culture, and personal experience.

intertextuality A characteristic of meaning-making that refers to the complex relationships that emerge or are created between text and other modes of meanings, real or imaginary, print, media, or otherwise (New London Group, 2000). When readers make these "text-to-text" connections they enhance their meaning-making processes.

Meaning	Language Practice
FIGURE 3.6 Multiliteracy Theory into Language Practice	
Linguistic	• helping students decipher the underlying message of a variety of print texts and words • understanding idioms, colloquial expressions
Audio	• use of music to express and enhance learning in language, and content areas • drama and dance: ways of learning, rehearsing, and understanding world views and culture
Visual	• making sense of visual representations of information: graphs, charts, concept webs, web pages, electronic texts • looking at how messages are reinforced with visual representations
Gestural	• helping students to understand body language through drama, role play, viewing, and representing • exploration of supporting words with gestures
Spatial	• exploring alternate spaces for learning: outdoors, home, community
Multimodal	• integrating the five literacies listed in meaningful, authentic, and real-life activities, for example, a multimedia recount of a field trip involves: • spatial: experiencing the field trip in an alternative learning space • visual: using photographs to help recall a previous experience and using a concept mapping software (for example, Kidspiration to brainstorm memories of the field trip) • gestural: analyzing the photographs for body positions, facial expressions that reveal students' feelings and reactions • linguistic: transforming the concept web into an outline to write a recount • auditory: recording the recount with sound effects to represent the entire experience

contributions of Gardner's theory of multiple intelligences to further conceptualize literacy. While Gardner's theory (Armstrong, 1994; Gardner, 1987; 1999 a) of multiple intelligences is not specifically a theory designed for literacy, it is significant as it presents an alternative view of how we come to understand who we are and what we can do. Gardner's goal is an understanding of the world that goes beyond fascination and curiosity. It is an understanding that positions us to reconsider and readjust our world view, thus making the world a better place, one student or one classroom at a time (Gardner, 1999 a). His theory of multiple intelligences (while continuously evolving) currently consists of eight intelligences:

1. Linguistic intelligence involves sensitivity to spoken and written language, the ability to learn languages, and the capacity to use language to accomplish certain goals. This intelligence includes the ability to use language to express oneself rhetorically or poetically as well as the use of language as a means to remember information.

2. Logical-mathematical intelligence is the capacity to analyze problems logically, carry out mathematical operations, and investigate issues scientifically. It entails the ability to detect patterns, reason deductively, and think logically. This intelligence is most often associated with scientific and mathematical thinking.

3. Musical intelligence involves skill in the performance, composition, and appreciation of musical patterns. It encompasses the capacity to recognize and compose musical pitches, tones, and rhythms.

4. Bodily-kinesthetic intelligence entails the potential of using one's whole body or parts of the body to solve problems (for example, expressing oneself through dance or physical movement). It is the ability to use mental abilities to coordinate bodily movements.

5. Spatial intelligence involves the potential to recognize and use the patterns of both wide space and confined space.

6. Interpersonal intelligence is concerned with the capacity to understand the intentions, motivations, and desires of other people. It allows people to work effectively with others.

7. Intrapersonal intelligence entails the capacity to understand oneself, to appreciate one's feelings, fears and motivations. It involves having an effective working model of oneself and the ability to use such information to regulate one's life.

8. Naturalist intelligence enables human beings to recognize, categorize, and draw upon certain features of the environment (Gardner, 1999a, pp. 41-43, 48; Smith, 2002, pp. 5, 8-9).

Ways that these intelligences are useful to language and across the curriculum are presented in Figure 3.7. In this figure, it is evident that language permeates every aspect of the curriculum, regardless of whether or not it is set as a focus.

To the New London Group's theory of multiliteracies, Gardner's multiple intelligences add the concepts of multiple ways of knowing, multiple access points for learning, and multiple ways of performing. Using the language of multiliteracies, we can hybridize and intertextualize these two theories into a workable understanding of literacies for learning where multimodal learning involves any two or more of modes of meanings or ways of knowing. Teaching with multiliteracies and multiple intelligences expands communication potential and provides access to ways of knowing other than linguistic for learners whose cultures are different than ours, who may have found in the past that traditional school settings did not serve their learning potential well.

What is emphasized in this *literacies* dimension of the W.O.R.L.D. view is the multiplicity of meanings and their complex interrelationships in response to the ever-changing diversity of learners, texts, and contexts. The types of connections we make are not simply within our own literacies, but require us to be social as well, which brings us to our final dimension, discourses.

STOP, THINK, AND WRITE

■ How do you make sense of your world?

■ How does this impact your literacy development?

■ How might this impact your development as a teacher?

FIGURE 3.7 Multiple Intelligence Theory into Language Practice

Intelligence	Language Practice
Linguistic	• Word and language play, puzzles and problem-solving, drama, storytelling, jokes, reading aloud (see Chapters 4-6) • Across the curriculum: written language work: story and report writing, journal writing, written reading responses, guided and independent reading (see Chapters 7-10, 13)
Logical-Mathematical	• Pattern and sequential stories, cause and effect, questioning strategies, word and sentence patterns • Across the curriculum: transactional writing, story problems, sequential and process writing

FIGURE 3.7 Multiple Intelligence Theory into Language Practice (continued)	
Intelligence	**Language Practice**
Musical	• Choral reading, soundscapes, participation stories, songs turned into stories (see Chapters 6, 12) • Across the curriculum: poetry and songs in content areas and language
Bodily-Kinesthetic	• Dramatic and hands-on approaches to language: magnetic letters, sandpaper letters, rehearsal for writing, oral communication, body language • Across the curriculum: drama, charades, puppetry, role playing, skill demonstration
Spatial	• Use of visual tools and graphic organizers for writing (for example, concept webs, storyboards, mindmapping), listening, planning oral presentations, note-taking, study skills, visualization and imagery as comprehension strategies for reading, visual games for word study • Across the curriculum: integration of tools and organizers in content areas, use of games to support content, integration of visual arts (diagramming, illustrating, model building)
Interpersonal	• Multiple opportunities for social interaction and good talk: cooperative learning, class meetings, social skills, group discussions, grand conversations, literature circles • Across the curriculum: setting and establishing goals with regard to learning, using literature to teach interpersonal skills, active listening, understanding point of view, critical literacy (see Chapter 11)
Intrapersonal	• Understanding of self as a learner: identifying strengths and needs as a literacy learner, personal and expressive journal writing, understanding of self and point of view through literature, media • Across the curriculum: goal setting, planning and accepting responsibility for learning, using feedback for growth, use of self-directed learning
Naturalist	• Recognition that observing and reading the world are natural precursors to reading print, selection of literature, viewing the natural environment as rehearsal for writing • Across the curriculum: understanding interdependence, research skills, classification, developing a questioning frame of mind

Source: Bellanca, Chapman, & Swartz (1997); Campbell, Campbell, & Dickinson (2004); Wilkens (1996).

D FOR DISCOURSES

The dimension of **discourses** extends literacies by arguing that

> *Language is a communicative act embedded in social interactions, and that in order to understand language we need not focus on language itself but on discourses: "ways of being in the world, or forms of life which integrate words, acts, values, beliefs, attitudes, social identities, as well as gestures, glances, body positions, and clothes."*
>
> (Gee, 1990, cited in Wilkinson, 1999, p. 142)

In other words, it is not enough to possess literacies and their interrelationships. In a sense, Gee's notion of discourses circumvents literacy and puts localized and contextualized communication and dialogue at the core of meaning making. Heath's (1983) study *"Ways with Words"* and even Moll et al.'s (1992) research on "funds of knowledge" clearly demonstrated that literacy practices develop in direct response to the context and community within which the child grows, learns, and develops. This research indicates that children who enter school environments where the assumptions, beliefs, and values regarding literacy are different than those at home experience dissonance and often default to the mainstream school culture, where they are often unsuccessful. These same children can clearly articulate that they do not believe that school will give them the foundational skills that they need to be successful in life. Teaching students as opposed to teaching curriculum requires us make our classrooms places where all students' experiences and values are considered relevant, valued, and important. We can do this by asking questions similar to the following:

- Is what is valued in the classroom congruent with what is valued in the students' homes and communities?

- Which students may be marginalized by what is happening at school?

- How can bridges be built between the literacies valued by students' homes and communities and those valued by the school?

- How can students learn to value the different kinds of discourses that are demanded of them, particularly those that count outside the classroom?

(Wilkinson, 1999, p. 10)

> *Discourse practices are always embedded in the particular world view of particular social groups; they are tied to a set of values and norms. In apprenticing to new social practices, a student becomes complicit with this set of values and norms, this world view.*
>
> (Gee, 1990, p. 67)

As with literacies, this dimension places great emphasis on diversity and the multiple discourses within which we live, work, and learn—literacies are extensions and expressions of discourses; one cannot exist without the other. As literate individuals, we must be alert to and capable of entering appropriately into a variety of discourses, whether educational, social, research, religious, political, or otherwise. Figure 3.8 asks you to consider the discourse of instant communication, adopted by many young people today. It is embedded in social interaction and communication, often with its own language and social identity. One only need look at the shortened and streamlined spelling and grammar of text messaging, user names, and accompanying photos to understand that instant communication is worthy of consideration in language and literacy.

As literate beings we must be able to enter into a variety of discourses.

Quite often a literacy conflict occurs when students cannot engage with the dominant discourse of mainstream, school-based literacy: "mainstream ways of using language in speech and print; mainstream ways of taking meaning, and of making sense of experience" (Gee, 1990, p. 67). Understanding is dialogic in nature; "without *one's own* questions one cannot creatively understand anything other or foreign" (Bahktin, 1986, p. 7). Dialogue requires first that we engage words and orality relevant to individual discourses. Without recognition of individual discourses, students are often denied access to learning, and consequently literacy. In order to alleviate what has been called a literacy crisis, literacy for the twenty-first century must acknowledge a broader W.O.R.L.D. view, one that is respectful of the discourses of diverse social groups, cultures, and contexts. No longer can we privilege a dominant social group with a dominant discourse—or word view—as opposed to recognizing the merit of their world view. Teachers who acknowledge the impact of students' unique discourses apply practices such as those listed in Figure 3.9.

Classrooms with W.O.R.L.D. Views

What have you learned from this cursory glance at theory and literacy discourse? What have you gained from our W.O.R.L.D. inheritance? What is it that you need to be aware of in order to move beyond the dominant discourse of the word and bring your emerging W.O.R.L.D. views into your classrooms?

First and foremost, we suggest that you continually revise your conceptualization of literacy and your beliefs about literacy. Literacy teachers with W.O.R.L.D. views:

FIGURE 3.8 The Discourse of Instant Communication

Will instant messaging and other forms of information technology affect language acquisition in terms of vocabulary and grammar? Will access to instant communication privilege one group of learners over another, creating situations of marginalization and inequity? How does instant communication enable students to build friendships and communication skills? Will cyber-communication and cyber-socialization emulate that of real life? Will cyber-bullies emerge?

These questions and many more are currently under investigation and bear mention here as we see a new discourse emerge in the lives of our students. Are opportunities for face-to-face interaction being reduced as a result of instant communication? What are the effects of this type of communication on oral conversation? Is this discourse of instant communication any different than passing notes, writing letters, or long hours spent on the telephone? Perhaps the greatest distinction is the number of conversations and the number of contacts students make on a daily basis, not simply with those friends they have seen at school, but with others around the world.

If we acknowledge that individual discourses are ways of being in the world and that they have a critical role to play in the literacy development of our learners, we should investigate ways to acknowledge and include what is now becoming the natural discourse of instant communication into our teaching practice. Do we study the language and communication usage of instant communication? Do we capitalize on the motivational aspect of computer mediated communication to get at writing, keyboarding skills, homework, teamwork, and problem-solving? Do we ensure that all students have access to this particular discourse by allowing some instant communication time in class? Or do we leave it alone, outside the walls of the school, hoping that our students will do the same?

FIGURE 3.9 Discourse Theory into Language Practice

Discourse Theory	Language Practice
Social, Cultural, Gender, Religious, Political Identities Are Valued	• using literature that is balanced and reflective of diversity • adopting a questioning and interrogative stance toward text and literacy that recognizes that some views are privileged and valued more than others
Discourses Are Contextualized and Localized	• understanding the school community within the larger societal, political, and cultural contexts • understanding students in view of their familial, cultural, gender, and social discourses • asking students and parents to provide information about personal and local contexts
Individual Discourses and Identities Are Valued	• providing students with choices, interesting and meaningful activities • planning multiple entry and exit levels

must first imagine a new instructional world before we can create it. It is this interplay between theory and practice that rightfully drives curriculum. In some ways, it is all art—a matter of seeing; in other ways it is all drama—living the life we want to live, being the people we want to be.
(Leland, Harste, & Helt, 2000, p. 114)

Your views and beliefs about literacy are often represented in what we call a literacy philosophy—a one page statement that outlines what you believe about language, literacy, and teaching and learning language and literacy. Carrie Anderson's philosophy (Student Teacher Practice 3.1) represents her developing thoughts and ideas about language and literacy. Whether you record your literacy philosophy on paper or discuss it with others, we contend that it is critical that you articulate it in a way that makes sense to you and might make sense to others who ask, "What do you believe about language and literacy? About teaching and learning literacy? About language learners? How might I see this enacted in your classroom?"

Second, we suggest that you take a critical and active stance toward curriculum, program, and instructional materials recognizing that there is no one right way to teach students to become literate. Figure 3.10 presents a checklist of essential and critical questions to guide you in the assessment, design, and practice of your long-range plans, instructional materials, classroom environments, and individual lesson plans. This will necessarily involve a consideration of diverse perspectives, including curriculum and policy expectations, culture, language, gender, program, and instructional materials.

Third, we suggest that you take the time to envision the setup and structure of your classroom and your program. Many schools talk of bal-

STOP, THINK, AND WRITE

Throughout this chapter, we have described a research-based view of literacy. It is important at this point that you begin to shape your own personal literacy philosophy.

- What is it that you believe about literacy?
- About students?
- About environments that foster literacy success?

Keep in mind that your philosophy is intended to be your belief statement, not necessarily how you would transfer it into practice.

Student Teacher Practice/3.1

CARRIE ANDERSON'S LITERACY PHILOSOPHY

Though I have, at least on an unconscious level, always been aware of the many facets of literacy, I have always placed the greatest emphasis on the written word. From childhood, even my pictures and sketches have been littered with words and letters. It was as though my illustrations could not speak for themselves.

Recently, I have been exposed to the many dimensions of literacy—oral, dramatic, written, and visual, among others – and have discovered that I lack a balanced approach to embracing these. I have always felt that a reader should be able to visualize the images that, to me, are ingrained in the text. While this creative pictorial imagination is useful to have, it is not realistic to expect that the written word be the sole basis upon which a student learns literacy. In fact, it is vital for readers to have the opportunity to scan illustrations for hints about what that tricky word looming on the page might mean. For others, the look on someone's face, the way his or her mouth forms a word, or the manner in which that person moves a hand may be the clues from which a listener gains insight into one of the possible interpretations of a story.

There are many diverse facets of literacy that I will have the pleasure of introducing to my students. To do this, though, I must continue on my journey as a literacy learner. I will continue to read, to learn from colleagues and students alike, and to develop professionally on a continuous basis. It is only by learning new literacy strategies that I can expose my students to them, which I intend to do in a classroom that fosters continual growth and development. My classroom will be one that surrounds students with words and drawings. They will be encouraged to trust and respect each other so they can comfortably participate in drama and small group activities that expand their abilities to communicate both verbally and non-verbally.

My classroom will be one that encourages literacy development across the curriculum, not just during several periods of language arts each week. I will encourage my students to make connections between subject areas, such as when I introduce mathematical word problems or social studies report writing.

I aspire to become a balanced teacher of literacy. At the same time, I hope that my students challenge me enough that my teaching practice remains dynamic and flexible, and that this balance is always far enough out of reach that I am continuously working to achieve it.

Carrie Anderson is a 2005-2006 graduate of Nipissing University's Bachelor of Education program.

anced and comprehensive literacy—words that you will hear us use throughout the text. What does this mean? What does it look like? What are the necessary components? How will time be allocated? What will the physical setup look like? How will you ensure that you plan for optimal instruction by addressing: multiple levels of support with a gradual release of responsibility, ranges of instruction, conditions of literacy learning, and strategic supports as outlined in Chapter 2? How will students access materials?

FIGURE 3.10 W.O.R.L.D. View Design

W.O.R.L.D. View	Essential Questions
W Word **(See Chapters 8 - 12)**	❑ Do I recognize students' strengths and needs to read the world simultaneously with reading the word? ❑ Do I provide a significant amount of experience with the world prior to reading the world? ❑ Have I made sufficient connections between the worlds of my students and the words in my classroom? ❑ Have I immersed my students in words relevant to their world views? ❑ Do I continually conceptualize and revise my own understanding and value of the word?
O Orality **(See Chapters 4 - 6)**	❑ Do I provide multiple purposes and functions of talk: to communicate, to explore, to learn? ❑ Are the conditions for oral language learning present in my classroom? ❑ Do I provide diverse opportunities for talk: drama, storytelling? ❑ Do I model, demonstrate, and explicitly teach students about effective talk strategies: narrative, persuasive, metaphor, humour? ❑ Do I constructively respond to student talk? Do I probe and prompt for higher level thinking? ❑ Do I use assessment of talk as opportunity for learning? ❑ Do I continually conceptualize and revise my own understanding and value of talk?
R Re-Vision **(integrated through-** **out Chapters 1, 3,** **13, 15)**	❑ Do students use literacy for meaningful and authentic purposes? ❑ Is literacy viewed as a natural extension and application of real life? ❑ Do I encourage students to review, rediscover, reconstruct, and re-vise their selves, their worlds, and their W.O.R.L.D. views? ❑ Do I accept students' rights to become critical, independent, and effective users of language and literacy? ❑ Do I scaffold their learning experiences in a way that helps them to revise their W.O.R.L.D. views? ❑ Do I continually see opportunities for my own re-vision of self, world, and W.O.R.L.D. views, and their complex interrelationships?
L Literacies **(integrated through-** **out Chapters 7, 10)**	❑ Do I plan an inclusive program that incorporates multiple ways of knowing, multiple modes of meaning, and multiple ways of performing? ❑ Do I model a range of ways of knowing, modes of meaning, and ways of performing? Do I incorporate exemplary practice? ❑ Do I respect students' rights to know and learn literacy differently? ❑ Are all students permitted access to successful learning?

FIGURE 3.10 W.O.R.L.D. View Design (continued)

L Literacies (integrated throughout Chapters 7, 10)	❑ Do I address adequately the diversity of learning needs in my classroom: cultural, linguistic, religious, technological? ❑ Do I acknowledge and make use of the changing information technologies influencing and impacting literacy (for example, computers, media, games)? ❑ Do I continually conceptualize and revise my own understanding and value of multiple literacies?
D Discourses (integrated throughout Chapter 14)	❑ Have I included time for students to engage in meaningful and relevant discourse for learning? ❑ Do I recognize the formal and informal, planned and incidental, local and dominant discourses that underlie education? ❑ Do I value and capitalize on local and student discourses? ❑ Do I continually conceptualize and revise my own understanding and value of multiple discourses?
W.O.R.L.D. (See Chapters 2, 3, 13, 15)	❑ Do I continually conceptualize and revise my own W.O.R.L.D. view? Am I active in this conceptualization and re-vision? ❑ Do I use my W.O.R.L.D. view to improve life in and out of the classroom? ❑ How do I share my W.O.R.L.D. view with my students? ❑ How can I share this W.O.R.L.D. view with others? ❑ What effect does my W.O.R.L.D. view have on my understanding of self, students, society, and global issues of literacy?

In some cases, you will be bound by your local board and provincial ministry policies in terms of designated programs and instructional materials. This is where your role as a literacy teacher with a W.O.R.L.D. view becomes critical. How can you extend your philosophy and your views into a mandated curriculum or program? How can you adapt program and instructional materials in a way that is responsive to your students' literacies and discourses? Figure 3.11 presents a sample allocation of time for language and literacy instruction; it is equally effective for primary and junior grades. It is important to note that this framework represents the time that should be spent formally teaching language over the course of the day. Depending on the setup of your classroom and program, you might distribute these activities throughout your day. For example, setting up your whole day might be done from a cross-curricular perspective, a read aloud might be done to introduce a social studies concept, oral language activities might take place during science, and closure might wrap up the whole day, as opposed to simply the language block. Envisioning your day like this will allow you to teach literacy in real life contexts and see the connections to language for learning across the curriculum. Figure 3.12 outlines a sample daily planning format for your language arts block. Note that you should try to incorporate as many levels of support into each day as possible.

It is important to envision the structure and setup of your classroom and your program.

Fourth, we remind you to be patient—with yourself, with your students, and with the world. Change is a process, not an event. It requires time, effort, and re-vision. Accepting literacy as our W.O.R.L.D. inheritance means that we allow literacy to empower us in much the same way as our students; we must recognize that we stand at the heart of *"some of the most crucial educational, cultural, and political issues of our time"* (Gee, 1990, p. 67). We can simply choose to close our doors and teach literacy from a conventional or traditional standpoint, or we can

> *accept the paradox of literacy as a form of interethnic communication which often involves conflicts of values and identities, and accept [our] role as one who socializes students into a world view that, given its power here and abroad, must be viewed critically, comparatively, and with a constant sense of the possibilities for change.*
>
> (Gee, 1990, p. 68)

FIGURE 3.11 Language Arts Time Allocation	
Literacy Practice	**Time**
Preparation for the Day Morning meeting, morning message, daily agenda	15 minutes
Oral Language Block: Time for Sharing A blend of drama, storytelling, literature circles, readers' theatre, sharing circle, news reports, current events	15 minutes
Workshop Block: Time for Teaching and Conferencing A blend of modelled, shared, interactive, guided reading and writing, word study, viewing and representing, reading/writing workshop	60 minutes
Read Aloud: Time to Just Enjoy	15 minutes
Independent Reading and/or Paired Reading	15 minutes
Closure: Time for Sharing, Reporting, and Reflecting	10 minutes

FIGURE 3.12 Daily Planning for Language Arts Instruction

Date:	Grade(s):

OVERALL OBJECTIVES:

PREASSESSMENT
a) Learners:
b) Learning Environment:
c) Resources:

TEACHING CONTENT AND STRATEGIES

Morning Entry Activities	Class Sharing or Closure Activities

Modelled Reading (Read Aloud/Think Aloud):

Shared Reading	Guided Listening/ Reading/Viewing	Modelled/Shared/ Interactive Writing	Literacy Centres and Independent Activities (Readers'/ Writers' Workshop)
Before:	Students:	Before:	Centres:
During:	Text Level:	During:	Routines:
After:	Strategy:	After:	Tracking and Assessment:
Mini-Lesson Focus:	Mini-Lesson Focus:	Mini-Lesson Focus:	

(Chapters 9 and 12 have detailed lesson plans for the continuum of reading and writing).

CONTINUAL ASSESSMENT:

Moving On

Throughout this chapter, we have asked you to explore traditional assumptions about literacy and re-examine what you understand literacy to be. It is only when we critically and habitually make conscious unexamined assumptions, definitions, and inadequacies that we can formulate appropriate responses in ways that make positive change possible (Boomer, 1993; Gardner & Boix-Mansilla, 1994; Harste, Leland, Schmidt, Vasquez, & Oceipka, 2004). As Galeano (1988) argues, "We are what we do, especially what we do to change what we are: our identity resides in action and in struggle" (p. 121). Literacy is what we do and what we use to change ourselves and reconstruct our worlds; it requires us to make conscious our beliefs and assumptions, change ourselves through action and struggle and find the "courage to teach" (Palmer, 1998), which sometimes requires us to be unconventional and non-traditional.

In this chapter, we presented literacy as a W.O.R.L.D. view where words, orality, re-vision, literacy, and discourses play an equally important role. We provided you with a checklist of questions that will enable you to quickly assess and critique an approach, a classroom, a school, or even a lesson. We pointed you in the direction of balanced and comprehensive literacy programs that would engage and extend the worlds of your students, as well as your own. This chapter provides a theoretical and conceptual framework for the remainder of the book; what is introduced here will be further clarified, described, problematized, and practised in the next chapters. Throughout the text, we will continue to take both a theoretical and a practical stance to provide you with a foundation to explore, critique, and further develop your own perspective and your own identity as a literacy teacher. Extending and re-visioning your literacy story (Clandinin, 1990) will permit you confident, convincing, and critical access into the discourse surrounding literacy in its many different forms, and therefore critical access to the world views of your students.

As we move on to oral language and creative expression, we ask you to keep a W.O.R.L.D. view insight as you

imagine a day...
... when [the world] swings open on silent hinges,
and a place you've never seen before welcomes you home.
Imagine... today.
—Sarah L. Thomson

LIT-FOLIO UPDATE

Consider what might count as evidence to include in your portfolio to show that you have *personally* grown in your understanding of literacy and the implications of your current conceptualization. How will this conceptualization translate into classroom practice?

LIT-FOLIO TIP

You should, at this point, be starting to think about who the primary audience will be for your lit-folio and the big picture that you want to present as a literacy teacher. As you begin to conceptualize your audience and purpose, put together a sample table of contents. Some of the strongest lit-folios that we have reviewed include:

- Introduction and Orientation to Lit-Folio, Table of Contents
- Philosophy
- Balanced Literacy
- Listening
- Speaking
- Reading (1-2 page(s) each for Modelled, Shared, Interactive, Guided, Independent, Assessment)
- Writing (1-2 page(s) each for Modelled, Shared, Interactive, Guided, Independent, Assessment)
- Viewing
- Representing
- Language for Learning across the Curriculum

Designing one to two pages per strategy or topic will allow you to organize and reorganize until you find the exact presentation that suits you as a literacy teacher.

Resources to Support Your Learning

Professional Resources

Bellanca, J. C. Chapman, & E. Swartz, (1997). *Multiple assessments for multiple intelligences* (3rd ed.). Arlington, Heights, IL: Allyn & Bacon.

Campbell, L. B. Campbell, & D. Dickinson, (2004). *Teaching and learning through multiple intelligences* (3rd ed.). Boston, MA: Pearson Education.

Egan, K. (1988). *Primary understanding: Education in early childhood.* New York: Routledge.

Richards, J.C., & M.C. McKenna, (2003). *Integrating multiple literacies in K-8 classrooms: Cases, commentaries, and practical applications.* Mahwah, NJ: Erlbaum.

Wilkens, D.K. (1995). *Multiple intelligence activities: Grades K-4.* Huntington Beach, CA: Teacher Created Materials.

Children's Literature: Our Favourites

Crow boy, Taro Yashima
Frederick, Leo Lionni
Only Opal: The diary of a young girl, Barbara Cooney
The Giver, Lois Lowry
Three pebbles and a stone, Eileen Spinelli

Websites

Canadian Education Association—Focus on Literacy: http://www.cea-ace.ca/foo.cfm

Canadian Language and Literacy Research Network: http://www.cllrnet.ca/

National Adult Literacy Database: http://www.nald.ca/

4

Literacy Learning as a Seamless Progression

> Before we enter into the life of language, we have already begun to organize our lived experiences perceptually and imaginatively.
> —Maxine Greene

key terms

Cambourne's model of literacy learning
concepts about print
four language systems
Halliday's functions of language
heuristic function of language
imaginative function of language
instrumental function of language
interactional function of language
orality
personal function of language
recursive learning
regulatory function of language
representative function of language
scaffolding

questions to guide your learning

By the end of this chapter, you should understand the key terms and be able to answer the following questions:

- Why is it important for me as a teacher to understand how oral language and literacy are connected?
- What are some of the key connections between oral language and literacy development?
- What are some strategies and approaches for enhancing oral language development?
- What are some of the purposes of oral communication in the real world? How do these purposes or functions relate to the purposes of literacy?

Looking Back, Looking Ahead

In Chapter 1, we explored our personal perspectives as literacy learners. In Chapter 2, we examined the characteristics of exemplary literacy teachers and invited you to set goals for your own personal development through an investigation of your own underlying beliefs and assumptions regarding language and literacy. This chapter discusses the progression of language development as well as the optimal conditions for literacy learning. It considers theoretical and practical approaches to language development and looks at some of the connections between language and literacy development, particularly with regard to creating conditions for learning. We will examine how these connections inform classroom practice. An understanding of how oral language learning is intimately related to literacy learning is necessary in order for teachers to implement language programs that skilfully include and build on oral language development strategies. This will in turn help students understand the purposes of literacy so they can fully appreciate and enjoy literacy in their lives; hear print texts read aloud so they can learn language structures; take in new information and ideas; become aware of and enjoy the sounds of language; and use this knowledge as a tool in becoming literate (Fountas & Pinnell, 1998, p. 3).

What is the relationship between activities that involve speaking and listening (oral language) on the one hand, and the activities of reading and writing (written language) on the other? How can knowing how oral language is acquired and how it develops help us, as teachers, know more about how to teach both oral language and literacy skills?

Before we begin a discussion of oral language development and its implications for practice, we will first outline the relationship between orality and literacy. Eric Havelock (1991) stated that orality and literacy "are sharpened and focused against each other… yet… interwoven in our own society… their relationship is one of mutual, creative tension" (p. 11). Havelock is speaking here about our historical conceptualizations of literacy and orality and how these conceptualizations have influenced society (see Chapter 3). This notion of "mutual, creative tension" can be applied to our ongoing endeavours and those of our students as we acquire and develop both oral language and literacy. This chapter investigates the interconnections between oral language and literacy development—an investigation that invites you to examine some of the theories of linguists as well as the literacy practices informed by those theories.

Teacher Talk/4.1

AMANDA BROWNLEE FINDS THE ORAL LANGUAGE-LITERACY LINK IN CAMEROON

During my time spent practice teaching in Cameroon, the magnitude and significance of a strong early literacy program became apparent to me, and how closely linked oral language is with literacy success.

After one day of observation, I was required to teach the students the following subjects: English, environmental education, health education, science, and arts and crafts. I noticed that this classroom was completely teacher directed and much of the learning was by rote. I hoped that I would be able to introduce the students to some other forms of learning during my time there. On my first day, I taught four lessons. This was quite an introduction to teaching abroad, as the students could barely understand me, and I could barely understand them. Although this was an English school, our accents differed greatly, and our pronunciation of words varied. To help the learners, I spoke very slowly and with distinct breaks between my words. After my first day of teaching, my associate informed me that the students seemed to be responding very well to my teaching.

In the area of language arts, my associate teacher asked me to teach a unit on writing a letter to a friend. When I collected the first drafts, I realized that the students had no concept of sentence structure, spelling conventions, or even a sense of phonemic awareness. It was on this third and fateful day of practice teaching that I discovered that most of my class could not read or write. This was a very hard realization for me. I felt terrible that I did not notice before the third day, but I have dealt with this, and have attributed it to a combination of things, such as culture differences, a different school setting and system, and the fact that I was suffering from a bad case of culture shock. What was I going to do? How do I assess the students based on this writing sample? How am I to teach this complex curriculum to a group of students who cannot read or write? Where do I start?

Needless to say, I had my work cut out for me...

Through this experience, the importance of a focus on literacy became clear to me. How can children learn when they cannot read or write? It should be the principal focus of a primary school teacher to ensure that all of their students can read and write. It seems that in Cameroon the goal of education is to learn to speak English, not to read or write it. This may be one reason that literacy is not a focus of school. Another factor which explains the lack of literacy in the schools in Lewoh is the simple fact that it is a small village in a remote part of Cameroon where reading and writing are not necessary. In the village there are no signs, newspapers, television, maps, or other sources of print on which to practise literacy skills. Although there is a library, the schools do not use it, and one must pay a fee to borrow a book or simply enter the building. I asked my associate teacher, the students, and several other Cameroonians about oral storytelling, and if it was a presence in their culture. It was not. This explains why the students seemed puzzled by the story that I read to them each day. They had no sense of story structure. They did not understand the concept of story because very few of them had ever been told stories. All of these realizations saddened me. I felt that my efforts were futile and my time was wasted.

Although I was feeling defeated about the situation of my students, I was motivated by the simple hope that, at least, I could plant a few seeds and that I could show my associate a few

Teacher Talk/4.1

AMANDA BROWNLEE FINDS THE ORAL LANGUAGE-LITERACY LINK IN CAMEROON (continued)

strategies that she could use in the future. I introduced my students to shared writing and reading sessions, choral reading, independent reading at the library, spelling bees, sentence building exercises, and even a short retelling exercise. I implemented a two-day lesson on the fable of King Lion and the Beetle. I had the class reread the story in many different ways (shared, choral, independent), I debugged some tricky words, we talked about the story through question and answer, we cut it up and put it back together, I gave a retelling, and I even dramatized the story with the help of one of the students. By the end of the two days spent on the story, two students were able to retell it in their own words. This is when the fact that the oral language-literacy link works both ways really hit me: the two students who were able to do this were the ones who were already literate! Although this was a shock, I realized that the others would still benefit, because these students modelled this skill to the rest of the class.

Amanda Brownlee is a 2005 graduate of Nipissing University, and was in Lewoh, Cameroon for her placement.

As educators, we rarely underestimate the power of language, in both its oral and written forms. In fact, many authors have written about the power of language and words. When asked to contribute her personal perspective on literacy to a collection of articles by well-known Canadian authors, Joy Kogawa (1990, p. 124) offered a poem entitled, "Where There's a Wall." The following lines taken from that poem beautifully express the power of language:

> **Where There's a Wall**
> *where there's a wall*
> *there are words*
> *to whisper by a loose brick*
> *wailing prayers to utter*
> *special codes to tap*
> *birds to carry messages*
> *taped to their feet*
> *there are letters to be written*
> *novels even*

Teachers and literacy educators must be able to articulate explicitly the assumptions they make about language development in the real world, in the classroom, and at home. Such assumptions are often commonly accepted beliefs and understandings that inform our awareness of language (Ontario Ministry of Education, 1991). In fact, these assumptions should provide you with an organizational framework for the remainder of the chapter:

- Language is a meaning-making tool. Children seek to understand the world around them by engaging in dialogue, making observations, and asking questions.

- Language learning is interactive and requires interaction with models of successful language in use. Children learn language through imitation, trial and error, repetition, and practice. They will use what they hear in conversations, in stories, in videos, in songs. They will use what they overhear when inadvertently eavesdropping on conversations. Children must therefore have high quality models of oral language in their lives: speakers who use language clearly and correctly, and show how language can be used effectively for many different purposes. Teachers must be aware of their contribution to oral language development and strive to use language that is not biased in terms of gender, culture, or ethnicity.

- Language is learned in use. It flourishes in an atmosphere of trust and respect. Children learn what they live. Children who are spoken to will speak, children who are listened to will listen. Children whose questions are answered keep asking questions. The best way to improve oral language is to provide meaningful opportunities for language use, both in the classroom and beyond.

- Language learning is an integrated process. Rarely will it develop in an environment that does not include all six of the language arts: listening, speaking, reading, writing, viewing, and visually representing are interrelated and overlapping processes. Early language learners demonstrate the ease and facility with which most children learn how to integrate all six language arts without explicit instruction.

- Children learn language according to general principles (see Figure 4.1) rather than according to specific rules. Infants and children learn oral language through modelling and interaction, not explicit rule instruction. How often does one hear a parent instructing their two-year-old, "Now dear, don't forget that your sentence needs to have a noun and a verb." And yet, if we listen in on early sentence formation, we do indeed hear young children creating sentences that include both nouns and verbs, often with an adjective or two thrown in for good measure.

- Language development is not a linear process but instead develops within given contexts and discourses, for different purposes. It is an expressive process, similar to writing, but it is not permanent. The oral word is often considered to be "winged"; once spoken, words are gone; they are spoken

FIGURE 4.1 General Principles of Language Acquisition

Although it is a highly complex process, we can identify some generally agreed principles of oral language acquisition:

- Children listen to and observe those around them using language in meaningful ways.
- Children imitate, invent, and try out language on their own.
- Specific tasks involved in the acquisition of language include:
  - acquisition of vocabulary
  - **metalinguistic awareness** (phonological, syntactic, semantic)
  - overcoming egocentrism (interactive)
  - learning to use language in different settings (pragmatics)
- Children learn language by inventing it, not simply by copying or imitating.
- Young children have the ability to abstract regularities in an environment where examples are not presented in any orderly sequence, rules are not explained or directly stated, and little or no attempt is made to emphasize patterns.

Source: Britton (1970, 1993); Halliday (1975); Tough (1977); Wells (1986).

STOP, THINK, AND WRITE

literacy
notebook
4.1

The assumption underlying this chapter is that oral language is logically and developmentally linked to literacy. Write some provisional definitions of "oral language" and "literacy" and list some ways in which you think they are related, both in terms of your definitions, and how you think each develops in children.

■ Do you see them as separate and distinct or as interconnected?

When you have completed this chapter, go back to these thoughts, to make any revisions you deem necessary and record your after-thoughts.

■ How does the assumption that language is learned "in use" influence the ways in which we approach the teaching of reading and writing?

in a given context, in a given tone, heard by individuals. Written words, on the other hand, have the possibility of permanence. They can be read over time, in different contexts, by different individuals.

How Does Language Develop?

There is no simple answer to this question; rather, there are various theories. We provide a brief overview of current theories while recognizing that this is a complex field of study that continues to attract new research. Please note that these approaches to language learning are closely connected to those models of learning presented in Chapter 2 as "socio-cultural" and "constructivist." Here they are applied to how language is learned.

According to the most widely accepted general theories of language learning, children are able to learn language because of their socio-biological nature. Chomsky (1975) argues that language acquisition is biologically inherent in the human species because we have at birth a "language-acquisition device" requiring interaction with speakers According to this behaviourist account, children seem to learn to speak "naturally" when they are exposed to speech. On the other hand, the cognitive or constructivist models place the learners' own efforts at the centre of language learning processes. Language learners' efforts include seeking patterns and using prior knowledge of language systems to assign meaning to new information (Vygotsky, 1978; Dyson, 1999).

Children learn language, as they learn other new things, by forming and testing hypotheses (Piaget, 1959), and experimenting with sound and word combinations. This learning often occurs in interactions with expert language users who support or "scaffold" children's efforts as they move from simpler to more complex usages (Bruner, 1983). **Scaffolding** is a metaphor used to describe the kind of temporary support and guidance provided for learners in order to acquire skills and understandings they are almost, but not quite, capable of managing on their own. Most parents and caregivers provide scaffolding to provide support for the language development of children. They demonstrate and model the successful speaking and listening levels of the expert language user while accepting the children's attempts at their appropriate levels of difficulty. At the same time, they motivate the children to attempt slightly more difficult language tasks (for example, developing more complete sentences from three-word phrases). In the classroom, teachers who provide effective scaffolding sequence their teaching activities so that they match the students' current levels and at the same time challenge and extend what the students are able to do. Since it is aimed at enabling students to perform independently, the support or scaffolding is withdrawn as the learners become increasingly capable.

Children learn language by experimenting with sound and words, often with support from expert users.

The psycholinguists make a case for "learning by doing": children make linguistic meanings by seeing, feeling, and doing. This approach has implications for classroom practice, since it argues that we learn by sharing and exploring our beliefs and ideas—by talking, debating, playing, and participating in conversations (Goodman, 1987; Smith, 1990, 2004; Harste, 1994).

Recent researchers have contributed to our knowledge of more specialized areas of language learning, such as vocabulary and grammar development. For example, Nagy and Scott (2000) show that learning new words is more complex than adding them to an existing list: "knowing a word is more like being able to use a tool" (p. 273). This supports our contention that one of the key features of language learning is that it is learned in use—in interaction with other language learners.

Regardless of which theory we espouse, the assumption common to all three—behaviourist, constructivist, psycholinguistic—is that the development of language follows a fairly orderly and predictable course. This sequence or continuum of development is dictated by the nature of language and by a set of basic learning strategies which allow young children to interact with expert speakers and to gradually use and understand language at increasingly complex levels. Although not all children follow identical sequences of language learning, we must accept on principle that as they emerge as language users, their receptive and expressive understandings become more complex with experience and practice. What is important is to understand that children develop their listening and speaking abilities gradually (over time), recursively (by repeating or returning to previous learning to build new learning), and in increasing complexity (building greater storehouses of speech patterns and abilities to do things with a greater number and variety of words).

What does this mean for us as we make decisions about how to teach so that our students develop their language capabilities to their full potential? It means that our role is to provide high levels of support or scaffolding for new learning, to lessen that support gradually as the learners become more proficient, and eventually to remove the temporary supports when learners are able to understand and perform independently. As we stated in Chapter 2, *teachers of literacy understand that effective language learning occurs within a continuum of support that proceeds from a high level of teacher support to independence.*

The following questions are significant in gaining an understanding of oral language from both a theoretical and practical perspective.

1. How does oral language (listening and speaking) develop?

2. How is language used in the real world? What functions does language serve?

Oral language development and how it moves into literacy development in a "seamless progression," and how the conditions that allow oral language learning can inform our literacy teaching practices, are considered first. We then take up the second question, emphasizing the need to continue to provide instruction in oral communication along with reading and writing instruction.

Although we acknowledge a developmental continuum for language development (Piaget, 1959), we do not view these stages as discrete, non-overlapping entities. Instead, we view language learning in terms of a more **recursive** process, which is closely aligned with constructivism, *whereby the learner repeatedly revisits previous learning and builds increasing complexity and sophistication on earlier foundations.* Early language use can be viewed as developing along a continuum, without necessarily accepting that this occurs in a non-varying, stage by stage progression. Understanding language learning in terms of recursive growth allows for individual variation, while recognizing that similar patterns emerge over time; therefore, learning, or progressing along the continuum, can be facilitated through guided support or scaffolding. Let us keep this in mind as we look into how oral language develops and how this development continues into literacy.

How Does Oral Language Develop?

What is of interest to educators is how learners typically move along a continuum from relatively simple speaking and listening behaviours to those of greater complexity, usually, though not necessarily, following a progression such as the one outlined below (Britton, 1970; Halliday, 1975; Tough, 1977, Collins Block, 2001):

- **Names for things ("holophrastic" speech; usually by age 2)**

  This stage is often referred to as holophrastic speech. Single words are used as sentences or whole phrases, since "holo" means whole, and "phrastic" refers to a phrase. For example, "baba" might be generally understood in the family to mean anything relating to a baby bottle. It might mean, "Mommy, I dropped my bottle" or "Daddy, I'm hungry. Please get me my bottle." What a single word means depends on the context.

  Typical vocabulary of a 2-year-old: 300-500 words

- **Combining words**

  At this stage, the appearance of word strings signals the early use of grammar and syntax. For example, young children often learn to direct their requests by joining names to individual words. "Dada baba" may mean, "Daddy, you are the one I want to listen to me. Please get me my bottle."

- **Early sentence formation ("telegraphic" speech; usually ages 2 to 5)**

  This stage is often referred to as telegraphic speech since it resembles a telegram; some words and word endings are omitted but words that are most critical to the meaning are included. For example, a child who says "Me go park" is clearly making the purpose of his/her speech known: she or he wants to go to the park.

  Typical vocabulary of a 4- to 5-year-old: 3,000-5,000 words

- **Language used for a variety of functions (usually by ages 6 to 7, with continuing development in later years, if instruction is provided)**

  By the time children are in Kindergarten, they can usually use oral language for a range of functions: to get things done, to regulate, to personalize, to find out why, to imagine, and to inform (Halliday, 1973, 1975; Collins Block, 2001); see Figure 4.7. How to "instruct" so that children continue to develop their oral language abilities is discussed in the section, How Is Oral Language Used in the Real World? and throughout the rest of this chapter.

Typical vocabulary of a 6-year-old: 10,000 to 15,000 words

(Estimates of vocabulary size are based on research by Loban, 1999, p. 98).

How does the relatively restricted language of early sentence formation become more complex and more conventional? We know that language is acquired in use, in real-life contexts, in interaction with proficient, responsive role models. Listening in to conversations between oral language learners and sophisticated language users (see Figure 4.2) demonstrates how this theory is transferred into everyday practice, without explicit attention being focused on teaching a more complex language structure.

Parents, particularly when their children first enter school in Kindergarten, often ask teachers "What can I do to help?" In Figure 4.3, we offer some suggestions, emphasizing modelling good listening and communication skills. The emphasis here is on how parents can help their children develop their communication (listening and speaking) skills regardless of the first language spoken in the home. The suggestions offer good advice to all language users with whom young children interact: parents, caregivers, teachers, and older peers whose language

FIGURE 4.2 Child-Parent Conversations

In her article, "Talking, Reading, and Writing," psychologist Marie Clay, founder of the Reading Recovery® program, give us a snapshot of the sort of parent-child interaction that is so fundamental to a child's language acquisition.

Mothers talking with preschoolers go straight for the message. They ignore how the child is making the message or how the child is transmitting the message. They respond to what the child says.

"I built a fence," says the child.

"You built a lovely fence," says the mother.

"Yeah, I built a fence," says the child.

That is how the limited language of the preschool child becomes the more complex language of the high school graduate. How does the school entrant learn more about talking, begin to use his own language in his early writing, and allow both these activities to interact with early reading? A complex network of language acquisition underwrites so much of a child's future education.

Source: Clay (2004, p. 13).

FIGURE 4.3 The Home-School Connection

Adults, parents, older peers, and teachers set a powerful example of good or poor communication. Communication skills are influenced by the examples children see and hear. Parents and teachers who listen to their children with interest, attention, and patience set a good example.

The greatest audience children can have is an adult who is important to them and interested in them. These are suggestions only. As always, adapt them to your local circumstances as a teacher with your classroom community.

Parent and Teacher Guidelines for Modelling Good Listening Skills
- *Be attentive*. Children can tell whether they have a parent's interest and attention by the way the parent replies or does not reply. Maintain eye contact.
- *Encourage talking*. Some children need prompts to start talking.
- *Listen as patiently as possible*. People think faster than they speak. Children often take longer than adults to find the right word.
- *Hear children out*. Avoid cutting children off before they have finished speaking. This models a listening skill that is often neglected.
- *Listen to nonverbal messages*. Be attentive to tone of voice, facial expressions, energy level, and posture. You can often tell more from the way a child says something than from what is said.

The following suggestions for parents are included in a Welcome to Kindergarten folder provided by a school board in Sudbury, Ontario.

Suggestions for Strengthening Listening Skills
- Listen and identify neighbourhood sounds.
- Identify voices on the telephone.
- Listen for the stove timer.
- Listen for weather reports, commercials, music on the television or radio.
- Listen to sounds of household appliances (blender, vacuum cleaner, washing machine).

Suggestions for Developing Children's Language
- Sing simple action songs with repeated patterns, for example *Row, Row, Row Your Boat*.
- Practise saying nursery rhymes, for example *Humpty Dumpty*.
- Play *I Spy*, encouraging your child to describe what he or she sees.
- Read traffic signs, street signs, and store signs.
- Talk about directions, for example "We turn left at the next corner and then travel on to School Street."
- Help your child recognize and name colours, shapes, labels, numbers, and letters.
- Encourage your child to recall and share his/her experience by talking in short phrases or sentences.

Source: Sudbury District Catholic School Board (2004).

use is more proficient than that of the child, and can therefore provide more sophisticated modelling and encouragement to use new vocabulary and try out more complex syntactic and semantic structures.

LANGUAGE SYSTEMS BECOME CUEING SYSTEMS

While learning language, which occurs in the context of everyday activities while interacting with other language users, children are at the same time taking in the principles and rules that govern that language, although they are not consciously aware of this. To become fluent language users, they must orchestrate the four language systems that govern how language works.

1. **Phonological system** determines all the possible sounds that can be combined to make meaning in that language. This is the basis for "sound-symbol" correspondences (which is why it is sometimes referred to as the *grapho-phonemic* system: "grapho" for written and "phoneme" for sound). These are the correspondences children must learn to be able to "crack the code" as part of becoming a reader and writer. Children need to know the phonological system to emerge into literacy, although this awareness may not be at the conscious level (Cazden, 1992).

2. **Semantic** refers to the meanings of individual words and how words can be combined to make meaning in a given context. To develop semantic awareness, children need many opportunities to develop vocabulary and features of language, such as poetic and story sense, through listening, speaking, reading, and writing activities. Listening to stories and talking about them are strong stimulants for pre-schoolers who are not yet reading and writing (See Chapter 6).

3. **Syntactic** refers to the set of rules governing the arrangement of words to form sentences. This refers to the grammar or structure of lan-

Phonics: Instruction that teaches children the relationships between the letters (graphemes) of written language and the individual sounds (phonemes) of spoken language.

Phonemes: The smallest part of spoken language that makes a difference in the meaning of words. English has about 44 phonemes. A few words, such as "a" or "oh" have only one phoneme. Most words have more than one phoneme. The word "if" has two phonemes (/i/f/); The word "check" has three phonemes (/ch/e/k/).

Phonemic Awareness: the ability to hear, identify, and manipulate individual sounds in spoken words.

Phonological Awareness: a broad term that includes phonemic awareness. In addition to phonemes, phonological awareness activities can involve work with rhymes, words, syllables, and onsets of rimes (where "st" is the onset of the rime "op" in stop).

Source: Ontario Ministry of Education (2003).

guage. This includes an ordering system for words, the endings that can be added to nouns and verbs, and where phrases can be placed in sentences. Clearly, opportunities for informal talk allow much of this knowledge to be acquired incidentally as language is learned. When teaching reading and writing, the more formal aspects of grammar require explicit instruction.

4. *Pragmatics* include the variable linguistic cues relating to cultural and social uses of a language. This is the system that must be attended to when using language for specific purposes for designated audiences. It involves understanding how discourse must be adapted to fit specific contexts; for example, when to use standard and non-standard (including dialects, everyday informal speech, and slang) forms of English.

You will recognize these systems from Chapter 2, Figure 2.9. We discussed the strategic supports used by effective teachers of literacy to prompt early readers and writers as they decode, make meaning, use awareness of the structures of language, and use reading and writing for specific purposes. But these cueing systems were already known—mostly at an unconscious level—to the beginning reader and writer.

We use these four systems whenever we talk and listen. When young children are learning to read and write, they must learn how to use these systems as cueing systems to engage in literate behaviours such as successfully decoding and encoding words, making meaning using print, recognizing and forming sentences, and varying how language is used to match specific purposes (for example, writing dialogue). Knowledge of the four systems must be built at the foundational level of oral language; this knowledge can then be used to "do things with words" at the literate level. This is why it is vital to continue to provide opportunities to develop oral language abilities along with reading and writing.

A Seamless Progression from Orality to Literacy

If we think first about the syntactic system, the structures of language children use as they talk, we can make connections to the structures they encounter and use when they begin to read and write. "In their early years children build a common syntactic base that serves all three activities (talking, reading, and writing), and this means that language use may be expanded as children read and as they write, as well as when they talk" (Clay, 2004, p. 1).

Language structures acquired while listening and speaking are likely to be transferred to reading and writing in the classroom. To illustrate, consider the impact of singing and reciting on talking, reading, and writing. We are not claiming here that the ability to sing songs and recite poems and rhymes necessarily results in the ability to read and write. Clearly the ability to sing and recite is not sufficient for the work of decoding and encoding that is necessary for reading and writing skills. What we do emphasize is that these activities create strong links to the ability to do many of the things required of readers and writers, such as being able to hear and manipulate sounds, attend to similarities and contrasts in words, and being able to attend to individual sounds. Children are more likely to become enthusiastically literate if playing with the sounds and with literal and metaphorical meanings is taken seriously in the early years.

There is strong evidence that reading development is closely connected with phonemic awareness (National Reading Panel, 2000; Adams, 1990; Juel, Griffith & Gough, 1986), which is part of our knowledge about the phonological system. Phonemic awareness includes the abilities to play with and manipulate sounds; match, compare, and contrast sounds; and the ability to listen for certain sounds, for alliteration or rhyming endings, for example. Songs, chants, poems, and nursery rhymes provide opportunities that encourage phonemic awareness. Many research studies have shown that pre-schoolers who have considerable informal experience of sharing rhymes, songs, alphabets, picture books, and daily routine talk with carers are already sensitized to language and literacy and likely to make an early start in reading (Bryant & Bradley, 1985; Goswami & Bryant, 1990). We know that English-speaking children's reading development is closely connected with their knowledge of rhyme (Whitehead, 1999, p. 23).

As we shall see in Chapters 8 through 12, learning to read and write is a complex process. Reading and writing require the abilities related to the semantics of language, to make meaning, the syntax of language, to determine appropriate structures, and the phonological (and visual) aspects of language to analyze sound-symbol relationships and use knowledge of letter and word patterns. Learners also need to call on the pragmatics of language use, since language can serve various functions in a variety of forms and contexts. We consider the pragmatic system in the section of this chapter titled How Is Oral Language Used in the Real World?

At the word knowledge level alone, part of the phonological system, readers and writers must develop the ability to decode words by analyzing letters (and letter clusters) and sound correspondences, and to encode words by hearing sounds and recording corresponding letters. They must also have a bank of known words as automatic reading and writing vocabularies (this overlaps with the semantic system), and they must be able to use knowledge of word patterns and analogies. When first learning these complex processes, we can see many benefits for experiences with rhymes, chants, and songs.

At the holistic level, exposure to familiar stories, themes, speech patterns, and vocabulary in nursery rhymes, songs, and poems prepares children for the semantic meaning-making and syntactic recognition required to understand those patterns and words when they encounter them later in print. Figure 4.4 discusses this critical link between orality and literacy.

Keeping in mind the crucial connections between strong oral language development and literacy learning, we turn now to the practices involved in setting up successful learning in listening, speaking, reading, and writing. First, we examine some of the similarities between the conditions that must be present when learning to listen and speak, and when learning to read and write.

FIGURE 4.4 Poetry and Oral Tradition

"Poetry is the first genre that most children hear" (Manning, 2003, p. 86); it is rooted in oral tradition (Cramer, 2001). Babies hear lullabies, toddlers listen to nursery rhymes and finger plays, emergent and early readers often have their first literacy experiences with Mother Goose rhymes, and poems by Dr. Seuss, Jack Prelutsky, and Dennis Lee. Children experience poems before they enter school, during school, and outside of the classroom (Hopkins, 1987); they "are natural poets, and poetry surrounds them as they chant jump-rope rhymes on the playground, clap out the rhythm of favourite poems, and dance in response to songs" (Tompkins, Bright, Pollard, & Winsor, 1999, p. 414). Chances are if they can sing it or recite it, they will soon be able to read it, and if they can read it, they will soon be able to write it. Poetry is fun and rhythmic; it engages and captivates students' interest; they just can't help chiming in with a familiar poem (Cornett & Smithrim, 2001; Heard, 1989).

"Poetry isn't just whimsical but contributes to increasing reading abilities. Lower primary teachers use nursery rhymes to develop phonic awareness and one-to-one correspondence, and poetry helps children of all ages develop vocabulary. Reading poetry aloud over and over creates fluency with expression" (Manning, 2003, p. 86). Awareness of rhyme, rhythm, and alliteration in addition to phonemic awareness are characteristics that often distinguish effective readers from readers at risk. The sad fact that some children enter school without the benefit of this rich background of language experiences makes it all the more imperative that we provide these opportunities throughout the school day.

Source: Parr and Campbell (in press).

CONDITIONS FOR LANGUAGE LEARNING

If oral language learning, in spite of its complexity, is natural, relatively painless, and almost universally successful, how might we apply its principles to the teaching and learning of literacy? Brian Cambourne (1988, 1995, 2000/2001) developed a research-based **model of literacy learning**, of how the teaching and learning of literacy can be made more effective and less painful by recreating the conditions that naturally facilitate oral language learning.

First of all, what are some of the principles involved? Two assumptions made by Cambourne (1988) reveal the thinking that enables effective teachers of literacy to draw on their knowledge of how children learn to speak to discover powerful clues as to how children might more efficiently—and less agonizingly for many—learn to read and write.

*The oral and written forms of language
are only superficially different. (p. 28)*

They are different in important ways, but not at the deep levels that affect how we learn them:

*The same neural processes are involved,
using the same neural machinery. (p. 29)*

Thus, if the conditions of learning are the same for learning oral and written language, then each should be able to be learned in much the same way.

*Learning to talk is a stunning
intellectual achievement. (p. 30)*

Once we identify the optimum conditions for oral language learning, we can determine whether they are applicable to the teaching and learning of literacy.

Let's review the conditions for the successful learning of oral language introduced in Chapter 2 and how they might then be applied to the teaching and learning of literacy. The key conditions (Cambourne, 1988, 1995) include:

- *Immersion* in resources and opportunities for practice (lots of talk, plenty of texts).

- *Demonstration* or expert modelling of the ability (talking or reading) to be acquired.

- *Expectations* on the part of those with whom the learner is bonded, that the learners will achieve or succeed (these expectations must be explicitly discussed).

- *Responsibility* for decision-making on the part of the learners about what, when, and how to learn.

- *Responses* consisting of relevant, timely, and appropriate feedback from knowledgeable others.

- *Employment* or *use* of the time and opportunity to practise what is being learned in functional, authentic ways.

- *Approximations* or the freedom to make mistakes as the desired model is approached.

- *Engagement* as the key condition throughout all of the above conditions.

Cambourne sees engagement in literacy learning as dependent on factors such as seeing oneself as a "potential doer," seeing the activity or skill as part of or as furthering one's own purposes, seeing the risks as "sufferable and livable-through," and being bonded with the person who is demonstrating (1988, pp. 50-55).

Cambourne's model reveals how intimately interrelated the processes of listening, speaking, reading, and writing are. The claim that oral language is the foundation of all literacy is verified when we consider everyday classroom practices and contexts where children are learning to read and write. Learning by demonstration requires a teacher who is talking and demonstrating while the learners are listening, and perhaps reading along. If we take each of Cambourne's conditions and picture it in practice, the learners and teachers must be engaged in at least three or four of the language arts—listening, speaking, reading, and writing—and will likely include viewing and representing along the way.

CONTINUUM OF LITERACY DEVELOPMENT: FROM ORALITY TO LITERACY

Children acquire written language with the same social constructivist process as with oral language. As was the case with language development, literacy also develops along a continuum. It is dependent upon a complex interplay of factors, including early language (lots of interactive conversations) and literacy experiences (being read to) at home, at day care, and at pre-school as well as the classroom practice of a teacher who knows how language and literacy develop together in young children. When the ideal home or pre-school foundations are missing before children enter Kindergarten, good first teaching is essential. Fortunately, there are successful early intervention programs in place in many schools, most of which include a home-school connection to ensure success (for example, Reading Recovery® developed by Marie Clay).

If the conditions for learning are present, and the children willingly engage along the way, most young children, most already amazingly proficient in oral language, emerge into essential understandings about the concepts of print (see Figure 4.5) and into the approximation stages of early readers and writers. With the necessary scaffolding provided by expert models, immersion in a world of print, and encouragement to take risks and give it a go, children begin to approximate reading and writing behaviours. They read the pictures, inventing a corresponding story using book language, then move on to patterned and predictable

FIGURE 4.5 Where to Begin: The Concepts about Print

Based on Marie Clay's early literacy assessment framework, these are the key concepts about print an emerging reader must understand in order to experience success learning how to read and write.

- How to handle a book; where the front (cover) of a book is, how to hold it, how to turn the pages.
- The print carries the message to be read, not the picture (although print and pictures are related in meaning-making).
- Directionality: print is read (and written) in English from left to right beginning in the top left corner, then back to the left from the end of each line ("the return sweep").
- One-to-one or word-by-word matching: the ability to point to each word in such a way that it matches the words being uttered.
- The concepts of "first and last": where a word, line, sentence, or entire text begins, and where it ends. Knowing about the spaces between words, in reading and writing, sometimes called "word boundaries," is normally established in Grade 1.
- The orientation of print concept: that upside down, or reversed, for example, is not conventional.
- The left page precedes the right when reading.
- Some familiarity with the basic uses of punctuation: the period to stop, the question mark to ask, etc.
- The concepts of, and the relation between, capital letters (upper case) and small (lower case) letters.
- The concept of a **letter**.
- The concept of a **word**.
- The concept of a **sentence**.

How do students learn concepts about print? Most children come to school with many concepts about print, primarily by being read to early and often by their caregivers. How print works is learned through direct and/or indirect demonstration or modelling by an expert reader. Some children require explicit, direct teaching of these concepts, while others seem to learn through more implicit and incidental "teaching." The primary classroom context for this teaching and learning is the read aloud (Chapter 6); and shared reading (Chapter 9) where the text is large enough for a small or large group to see the textual features being discussed and taught. Modelled and interactive writing (Chapter 12) also reinforce concepts about print. See in particular Theory into Practice 12.1.

Source: Clay (2000a).

books, recognizing more and more about words, letters, and punctuation. Once they establish one-to-one correspondence (saying one word for each word in print) and acquire decoding strategies, such as using initial consonants, making use of meaning or context cues and knowledge of grammatical structures, they can progress to texts of less predictability and greater complexity.

The full development of the ability to read and write is more complex (see Chapters 8 to 12), but successful initial steps into literacy require a strong oral language foundation, which includes listening to lots of stories, and talking about how print works during read alouds (Chapter 6), shared reading (Chapter 9), and modelled and interactive writing (Chapter 12), where the conventions of print can be explicitly demonstrated and discussed.

At the same time, these emerging readers progress from scribble writing that exhibits the same concepts about print required for success in reading: that print goes from left to right, from top left down the page with a return sweep at the end of each line, and so on. They begin to print their own names, understand that these are words, and learn that there is an association between the sounds we make and the letters we write. As emerging writers increase their repertoire of familiar words and letters, and establish the sound-symbol relationship, they have taken an essential step to cracking the code—a vital aspect of becoming literate.

In addition to concepts about print, the following principles and practices for leading young children—emergent readers and writers—into literacy are, recommended for effective pre-school and Kindergarten programs. These are research-based, and summarized by Lesley Morrow (2000):

1. Thematic instruction: to support a comprehensive approach to literacy instruction, themes create a context for broad-based learning

2. Using nursery rhymes

3. Developing oral language and vocabulary

4. Teaching phonological and phonemic awareness

5. Beginning print concepts ("Concepts about Print"): use big books, storybooks, and environmental print (bulletin boards, signs, labels around the classroom)

6. Alphabetic knowledge: activities to promote knowledge of letter names and sounds

7. Reading aloud

8. Beginning writing: set up a writing centre

9. Home involvement

The continuum of language development is reflected in the developing characteristics of emergent, early, transitional, and self-extending literacy learners. As discussed in oral language development, these are not necessarily discrete stages or phases but instead provide insight into how most learners develop as literacy learners and into the developing characteristics that provide information about how and what the students should be taught. It is generally assumed that emergent literacy learners require a higher level of teacher support than self-extending literacy learners as evidenced by the continuum of support described in Chapter 2 (modelled to independent). This is not to say that we begin with modelled instruction in Grade 1, aiming for independence in the higher grades; instead, we are suggesting that the level of support must be matched to individual learners, the environment, and the task at hand. The ultimate goal is a gradual release of teacher responsibility so that the children are able to have a go on their own and experience success.

Recognizing where an individual child is on this continuum at a given time is important. It allows teachers to set realistic goals, to scaffold and provide appropriate teaching at the optimum time, and to select and make available the learning resources required for success. See Figure 4.6 for an overview of the continuum in reading and writing. Further information and detail will be provided in Chapters 8, 9, 11, and 12 on reading and writing.

Note: Development is individual and highly complex; these phases represent a framework to help teachers to observe change and should not be viewed as a lock-step sequence that all children must go through at the same time.

How Is Oral Language Used in the Real World? What Functions Does It Serve?

It is our contention that oral language is the foundation of literacy learning, and that facility in using oral language must continue to develop along with abilities in reading and writing. Beyond Kindergarten, the importance of continuing to provide instruction in oral language seems to fade. We argue that, on the contrary, it is more important than ever. We need only think about how varied the purposes of oral language are in the

FIGURE 4.6 Literacy Learning as a Seamless Progression from Emergence to Independence, from Orality to Literacy

Phase	Emergent	Early	Transitional	Self-Extending	Independent
Approximate Grade Level	Pre-school – early Grade 1	Kindergarten – Grade 1	Kindergarten – Grade 2	Grades 1–3	Grades 4–6
Developing Reading Characteristics	Attends to picture, has awareness of environmental print, and forms oral stories using "book language." Attends to some features of print; begins to link own oral language to print. Constructs, tests, and perfects hypotheses about written language.	Has less reliance on pictures: increasing awareness of and attention to print. Has increasing control of reading strategies. Knows high-frequency words. Has some fluency. Monitors and cross-checks; self-corrects when reading.	Has full control of early reading strategies. Uses multiple sources of information and cues when reading, Has large core of frequently used words. Notices, but does not need pictures. Reads fluently; reads longer, more complex texts.	Uses all sources of information flexibly. Solves problems independently. Reads wide range of texts. Reads for meaning; reads longer, more complex texts and a variety of genres.	Uses all sources flexibly and independently. Solve problems using a wide range of strategies. Reads wide range of texts and genres for multiple purposes. Reads increasingly longer, more sophisticated texts.

Suggested Strategies

Emergent to Early: explicit and incidental teaching of the "concepts about print" through Read Alouds, shared reading, modelling, and interactive writing, making and breaking words using magnetic letters

Emergent to Early: patterned, predictable books with strong picture-text connection; nursery rhymes, cumulative tales, circular stories (see resource list the end of this chapter)

Early to Independent: guided reading to ensure continued growth, levelled books of increasing length, difficulty, and range in genres

FIGURE 4.6 Literacy Learning as a Seamless Progression from Emergence to Independence, from Orality to Literacy (continued)

Phase	Emergent	Early	Transitional	Self-Extending	Independent
Approximate Grade Level	Pre-school – early Grade 1	Kindergarten – Grade 1	Kindergarten – Grade 2	Grades 1–3	Grades 4–6
Developing Writing Characteristics	Drawing as writing, scribble writing	Letter-like units, non-phonetic letter strings, copying from environmental print	Invented, phonetic spelling	Conventional spelling	Conventional spelling/risk-taking based on knowledge of spelling patterns, meanings, and derivations.

Suggested Strategies

Emergent to Early: phonemic and phonetic awareness activities and games (rhyming, picture-sound-symbol association), word games

Early to Independent: word and spelling games, modelled, shared, interactive, and guided writing, independent writing in writers' workshop setting

Emergent to Independent: teacher think alouds (see Chapter 6); opportunities for writing for real purposes (lists, recipes, thank you notes, letters, invitations)

Source: Adapted from Fountas & Pinnell (1996).

real world, and how these purposes are related to the purposes of reading and writing, to see how vital it is that we provide many varied opportunities for listening and speaking activities, as well as explicit instruction in how to improve oral communication skills.

The categories, purposes, and functions of oral language in the real world and in the classroom reflect the purposes and functions of all forms of language and therefore help us forge the link and ease the tension between orality and literacy. Understanding how language works and the functions that it serves is not only essential for teachers, but critical for students as well. What are the primary purposes of language?

The First Steps Oral Language Developmental Continuum (1994) identifies three strands of talk:

- **Language of social interaction**: language used to converse, discuss, brainstorm, cooperate

- **Language and literacy**: language used to tell news, tell stories, describe events, give instructions
- **Language and thinking**: language used to clarify thoughts, analyse information, form conclusions, solve problems.

These are useful as broad categories. They illustrate how intimately connected are the oral and literate uses of language. The work of Michael Halliday—a linguist who looked closely at how language is used for distinct purposes—is useful for teachers as they plan practical ways to enhance and extend their students' use of language for a wide variety of purposes.

PURPOSES AND FUNCTIONS OF LANGUAGE

Halliday (1973, 1975, 1993) suggests that language learning is not a unified achievement—that children don't just learn language—they learn *languages,* seven different variations of the same one, to be exact. Each "language" serves a distinct function which children combine and blend for different purposes. Figure 4.7 provides a detailed outline of Halliday's functions of language with examples from Primary and Junior students.

Based on Halliday's seven functions, there are many opportunities we can provide in the classroom to extend the range and power of oral language. One of the richest sources of the variety of language use is children's books. For example, Byrd Baylor's *Everybody Needs a Rock* provides illustrations of the regulatory function ("I'm giving my own ten rules for finding a rock...."). This and many other examples of children's books can be used to model the wide range of possibilities language opens up for us. It is suggested that you keep notes and plan direct teaching events to record your own ideas and suggestions.

Once the link is made between the functions of oral language and examples of those functions in literature, it becomes clearer how these same functions apply in the literary world, as parallel purposes of the decontextualized language of print. One of the difficulties children encounter when emerging from totally oral, pre-literate language into understanding how language is used in print, is the fact that when a poster has only "Stop that!" printed on it, there is no context to help the reader (listener) figure out who is speaking to whom or why, and what the word "that" refers to. The print by itself is decontextualized. The wealth of detail in picture books provide a context rich with clues. In *No, David!* by

FIGURE 4.7 Halliday's Seven Functions of Language

Function	Primary Language in Action	Junior Language in Action
Instrumental: language used to get things done	Gimme!	Can I borrow your cell phone?
Regulatory: language used to tell how	Stop that!	Before I act, I have to think fast.
Heuristic: language used to find things out	What's that?	I don't understand. Can you explain?
Interactional: language used for social relationships	How are you feeling?	I found math class really hard today. How about you?
Personal: language of feelings	I'm scared.	I'm not sure. I'd like to go but it makes me nervous.
Imaginative: language of the imagination	Knock, knock, who's there?	When I grow up, I think I'd like to...
Representative: language used to talk about the world	It's snowing.	The ice is as hard as diamonds. It sparkles in the sun too!

Source: Adapted from Halliday (1973).

David Shannon, each page contains the words "No, David!" and is accompanied by an illustration of behaviour David's mother wants him to stop doing, for example, hitting a ball with a bat inside the house.

Just as we can speak and listen in order to get things done, to tell how, to find things out, to interact socially, to express feelings, to represent what we imagine, and to talk about the world, we can also demonstrate these uses of language outside of their real-world contexts by writing and reading to accomplish them. The language itself shifts when it "goes to print" but the various purposes found in written texts are similar to those used in oral language.

Children who have control over a wide range of functions in their oral language abilities and are aware of the power it affords them, are more likely to be motivated to extend those powers through control over the printed word. They are also more likely to be aware of the purposes of reading and writing.

STOP, THINK, AND WRITE

- Which of these functions are most commonly heard in the classroom?
- How can you encourage the development of those functions that may have been neglected?

LISTENING: THE NEGLECTED ART

We hear with our ears, but we listen with our minds.
Gorman & Gorman; quoted in Opitz, Ford, & Zbaracki (2005)

The International Listening Association (1996) defines listening as the process of receiving, constructing meaning from, and responding to spoken or nonverbal messages. It is far more than the perceptual act of hearing. Listening is not passive. It is an active process that requires effort to extract and reconstruct meaning. Effective listeners do not just hear an oral text; they live it and are able to reflect on its meaning, integrating new meaning into their existing knowledge base. Listening and speaking are reciprocal acts. Speaking requires that we have a message to share or something important to say. Listening means that we are willing to consider and incorporate someone else's ideas and thoughts into our personal schema. Being listened to means that we are being taken seriously, that our feelings, ideas, and words are valued, and that what we have to say matters. We know that we learn from and about our culture primarily through listening.

We know that listening is often a neglected art in our families, our schools, our communities, and our cultures, perhaps because we assume that listening will develop naturally and does not require conscious effort. We disagree with this view. What follows is a discussion of effective listening behaviour and how it can be enhanced and developed in the classroom. Effective or active listening involves making sense of what we hear as well as what we observe. Effective listening requires that we not only hear what someone says but also how they say it; we not only pay attention to what we are listening to but also how we are listening. Current research on listening comprehension suggests that there is a strong link between listening and reading comprehension. In order to make sense and comprehend print text, learners must first be able to comprehend oral texts (Opitz, Ford, & Zbaracki, 2005). Listening is part and parcel of the reading experience: "What does it mean to listen while you read? First, it means to attend to the voice of the text—to tune in, with one's mental ear, to the way the sentences sound." (Bomer, 2006, p. 525).

Here is what Donald Graves (1990) has to say:

> *Listening is the heart of learning for both children and teacher. Unless we listen we have no window on the world. We can see, touch, and feel, but the world of words is lost to us. But if we are to live the life of words in our teaching and in our writing, we need to hear the words of children and adults, both when they speak and when they write. (p. 83)*

What does it mean to listen not only with our ears, but our minds as well? What does effective listening behaviour look like? What distinguishes effective listeners from ineffective or poor listeners? Some of the characteristics we identify may appear to be surface level behaviour in that they are directly observable; however, surface behaviours such as looking at the speaker, making eye contact, and sitting still are habit-forming. They are indicators of listening etiquette. Go back to the listening assessment and suggestions for listening in Chapter 1 (Literacy Notebook 1.1). These will benefit you as a listener and meaning-maker, and influence your interactions with your students. It is also likely that awareness of yourself as an effective or ineffective listener will be reflected in your skill as a speaker. *Why does the teaching of listening skills and abilities seem to be neglected?*

Listening can be difficult to assess and difficult to teach. How can we tell if someone is "really" listening? Listening is not just a matter of adopting an appropriate behavioural or physical stance; it is an "inside-the-head" activity. Focusing on the outward behaviours of "good listeners" does not guarantee true listening development. Here we are thinking of those classroom wall charts telling children what "good listeners do," for example, keep your eyes on the speaker, your lips together, hands folded, etc. In addition, teachers may feel they don't have time. Our response to this is to point out that listening need not be taught as a separate "subject" all on its own—weave it in!

STOP, THINK, AND WRITE

As you read the suggestions below, which merely scratch the surface of the whole topic of listening, jot down some of your own ideas on how children can be taught to be really good listeners.

literacy notebook **4.3**

The following are suggestions to promote listening skills:

- Be conscious of opportunities for explicit teacher modelling.
- Set clear expectations and purposes for listening.
- Forge the link between orality and literacy (Figure 4.8).
- Use directed listening-thinking activities (Theory into Practice 4.1).
- Read aloud to the children every day.
- Don't repeat yourself or student responses (this makes students dependent upon repetition, and devalues their contributions).
- Set the stage (provide the context, the content, and a warm-up).
- Scaffold: make sure that students have the prerequisite knowledge for what they are listening to.
- Give feedback and have students assess their own growth as listeners.
- Keep listening activities brief; use a multi-sensory approach when appropriate (for example, model, demonstrate, provide visuals, engage students in acting).

FIGURE 4.8 From Theory to Classroom Practice: Progressing along the Language Continuum

The **Language Experience Approach**, (shared writing) which uses speaking, listening, reading, and writing to reinforce one another, is particularly effective with emergent and/or struggling readers and writers, including ESL or ELL students. The learners say what they think, you as the teacher write what they say, and they read back what you wrote. This can be incorporated into individual, small group or large group dictated stories or accounts, written on chart paper and read repeatedly. On subsequent days, the story can be used to emphasize vocabulary; for example, students can underline new words, circle known words, or add new words such as adjectives. The chart story can be used to teach concepts and skills such as story structure and identifying the main idea. On another day the students can be assigned independent work such as preparing word cards with new or "almost known" words.

Source: Adapted from Collins Block (2001).

Other listening and speaking activities include:

- **Add-a-sentence** stories are built by starting with the teacher, and then having each child around the circle add a sentence. This can also be used to develop an account of a special event, school trip, or science experiment.
- **That reminds me of** is a fast-paced game that engages students in recalling favourite memories or stories. The teacher begins with a quick story and students jump in with their memories, beginning with the line, "That reminds me of…"
- **Meanwhile, back at the ranch** is similar to "that reminds me of," but instead of telling reminders the children can completely switch the direction of the story beginning with "Meanwhile back at the…"

FIGURE 4.8 From Theory to Classroom Practice: Progressing along the Language Continuum (continued)

- **Fortunately... Unfortunately** is a game that requires students to think of the flip side of situations, for example, "Fortunately, I found a $100 bill. Unfortunately, it's counterfeit."
- **Yes I can** is a fast-paced game during which a leader asks a question such as, "Joanna, can you brush your hair?" and Joanna responds, "Yes I can brush my hair," mimes the action, then addresses another student with a new question.
- **Place names** is played by chaining place names or other related words and focuses on the sounds in words. Each addition has to begin with the same sound as the ending of the previous word; for example, "Toronto – Owen Sound – Dartmouth," and so on. Besides reinforcing phonemic awareness, it can be used to emphasize specialized vocabulary or word categories.
- **Barrier games** build listening skills, concept knowledge, and understanding of the language of instruction. Two students sit on either side of a screen. Each student takes turns giving instructions to the other to perform certain tasks; they take turns being speaker and listener. Instructions must be clearly given and carefully followed since they cannot see one another. Materials such as crayons, magnetic letters, shapes, and coloured tokens can be used.
- Engage students in **participation stories** where they listen for specific words or sounds and add in sounds or phrases to make the text more interesting. They may also join in on sequential and recurring refrains or patterns; this is often referred to as chiming in or shared reading, for example, children love chiming in on the chorus "terrible, horrible, no good, very bad day" as they listen to Judith Viorst's, *Alexander and the Terrible, Horrible, No Good, Very Bad Day*.
- Daily **read alouds**, occasionally using Directed Listening-Thinking Activity (DLTA) (see Theory into Practice 4.1) and emphasizing a variety of sounds, rhymes, word types, new vocabulary, and grammatical structures.
- Through **teacher modelling,** personal experiences are shared through "show-and-tell": using a favourite photo, talking about who you are, where you came from, and what you like.
- After a read aloud, involve students in a **cooperative retelling** staying close to the plot of the original at first, and then adding twists to create a new story.
- In the **story maker game** students draw one card from each of four piles: plot, setting, characters, and dialogue. In small groups, they begin telling a story based on their cards.
- It's not what you say, but how you say it! games encourage students to hear and listen beyond words to nonverbal cues, emotion, tone, etc. **Minimal scripts** (four-line conversations) work well, as do nursery rhymes. The object of the game is to use only voice and nonverbal communication to change the meaning of the text, for example, Humpty Dumpty could be recited using a very agitated tone or a very sad tone.
- **Instructional conversations:** Use explicit teacher modelling to teach speaking and listening skills.
- **Readers' theatre:** Another motivating classroom strategy that reinforces the reciprocity between oral language and print. There is no need to memorize lines as learners always have the script before them; however, they must listen to one another very attentively in order to know when it's their turn to read. (See Chapter 5 for a more detailed explanation.)

For more detailed step-by-step instructions refer to: Booth & Swartz (1996); Collins Block (2001), Swartz (2002), Temple & Gillet (1996); Trehearne (2000).

Theory Into Practice/4.1

DIRECTED LISTENING-THINKING ACTIVITY

A directed listening-thinking activity enables students to learn how to set purposes for listening, and to listen attentively, actively, and critically. It is effective, in both narrative and content area listening, in helping students to use their own thinking abilities and prior knowledge as they listen. The teacher's role is to engage students in critical thought before, during, and after listening, and to encourage creative, divergent thinking, the use of logic, and a heightened curiosity and interest in the text. The steps outlined below are appropriate for a narrative text, but can be adapted for content area text.

Before:
Choose a story with a clear plot and distinct episodes. Plan your stops just before important events. Two to four stops are recommended.

During:
At each stop, elicit summaries of what happened so far, and "wonder statements" about meanings "between and beyond the lines," and about what might happen next. Ask children to explain or justify their wonder statements based on information provided so far. Avoid "Right" or "Wrong;" use terms such as "possible" or "likely." After listening to a section, review wonder statements, invite students to revise wonder statements, then continue.

After:
Review the wonder statements and revisions, focusing on the statements and the inferential reasoning processes involved, not who made which predictions, or which were "true" or the "best." Invite feedback from the learners themselves on how this exercise focused their listening: "Did you listen in a different way because of your predictions and wonder statements?"

Source: Temple & Gillet (1996).

- Be an excellent model of real listening, "with your mind." Listen to your students and respond in ways that model active, critical listening.

High level listening comprehension ability is critical for reading comprehension (Opitz, Ford, & Zbaracki, 2005).

Moving On

Throughout this chapter, we discussed the progression of oral language development and how it is best learned in use, with effective role models, in a variety of contexts, and for multiple purposes. We emphasized the interconnectedness between oral language development and the development of literacy, and discussed the relationships between listening and reading, speaking and writing. In Chapter 5, we extend this theory into practice, as we present strategies to engage students in meaningful and authentic talk for literacy and language across the curriculum. We will also ask you to reflect on the roles of teacher talk and student talk in teaching and learning.

Clearly, we cannot return to the landscapes of those prereflective days.
We can only become present to them by reflecting on them.
—Maxine Greene

LIT-FOLIO UPDATE

Consider what you might include in your portfolio as evidence that you have increased your oral language abilities. What speaking, talking, discussing activities have you participated in, and how have your contributions developed in depth and breadth? How have you developed as an oral communicator with your students? How have you grown as a listener, with your colleagues and with your students? Review Chapter 1, Figure 1.1 to help you further develop your listening skills. How will these help you to become a better listening teacher? How can you plan ahead, so that even when you are a busy teacher with 1,001 things to do, you will make time to listen to your students?

LIT-FOLIO TIP

Refer back to Figure 4.3 and develop a plan for modelling good listening with your students.

Resources to Support Your Learning

Professional Resources

Booth, D., & Swartz, L. (2004). *Literacy techniques for building successful readers and writers.* Markham, ON: Pembroke Publishers.

Cambourne, B. (2000/2001). Conditions for literacy learning: Turning learning theory into classroom instruction: A minicase study. *The Reading Teacher,* 54 (4), 414-417.

Clay, M. (2000a). *Concepts about print: What have children learned about the way we print language?* Portsmouth, NH: Heinemann.

Swartz, L. (2002). *The new dramathemes.* Markham, ON: Pembroke Publishers.

Trehearne, M. (2000). *The Kindergarten teacher's resource book.* Scarborough, ON: Nelson.

Websites

Early Years of Schooling:
http://www.sofweb.vic.edu.au/eys/lit/litpp.htm

International Listening Association:
http://www.listen.org

International Reading Association:
http://www.reading.org/

National Association for the Education of Young Children (NAEYC), Learning to Read and Write link:
http://www.naeyc.org/about/positions/PSREAD0.asp

ReadWriteThink (for lesson plans):
http://www.readwritethink.org/

Children's Literature for Emergent Learners

Nursery Rhymes

My very first Mother Goose, Iona Opie
Sing a song of Mother Goose, Barbara Reid

Rhyming Picture Books

Dr. Seuss's ABC, Dr. Seuss
Each peach, pear, plum, Janet and Allan Ahlberg
We're going on a bear hunt, Michael Rosen

Pattern Books

Brown bear, brown bear, what do you see? Bill Martin, Jr.
Have you seen my cat? Eric Carle
Mrs. Wishy Washy, Joy Crowley
Puffins climb, penguins rhyme, Bruce McMillan

Repetitive, Rhythmic Books

Howdi do, Woody Guthrie
How do dinosaurs say good night? Jane Yolen
Miss Mary Mack, Mary Ann Hoberman
Teeny tiny woman, retold by Jane O'Connor

Cumulative Stories

Ten big babies, Robert Priest
The napping house, Audrey and Don Wood

Traditional Folk and Fairy Tales

Goldilocks and the three bears, retold by Jan Brett
Little Red Riding Hood, retold by James Marshall

Something from nothing, retold by Pheobe Gilman
The three little pigs, retold by Paul Galdone

Circular Tales

Beware beware, Susan Hill
Dog and cat, Paul Fehlner
The tale of Peter Rabbit, Beatrix Potter

To Increase Listening and Speaking Skills

Big Sarah's little boots, Paulette Bourgeois
Bread and jam for Frances, Russell Hoban
Chicka, chicka boom boom, Bill Martin, Jr.
Everybody needs a rock, Byrd Baylor
Heckedy Peg, Audrey and Don Wood
Journey, Patricia MacLachlan
Joyful noise: Poems for two voices, Paul Fleischman
No David! David Shannon
Ramona Quimby, age 8, Beverly Cleary
Rosie's walk, Pat Hutchins
Sarah and the people of sand river, W.D. Valgardsen
Stella, queen of the snow, Marie-Louise Gay
The tale of Desperaux, Kate DiCamillo
The true story of the three little pigs, Jon Scieszka
Tikki Tikki Tembo, Arlene Mosel
Wemberly worried, Kevin Henkes
Willy and Hugh, Anthony Browne

5

The Oral Tradition
Literacy through Talk

> It matters very little what one knows if one cannot express and communicate what one knows.
> —Northrop Frye

key terms

good talk

grand conversations

literature circles

readers' theatre

real discussions

storytelling

questions to guide your learning

By the end of this chapter, you should understand the key terms and be able to answer the following questions:

- What is the role of talk in learning across the curriculum?
- How does classroom talk contribute to overall literacy learning?
- How can you promote peer talk that is fair and productive for everyone?
- What are some strategies for promoting the kind of talk that enhances literacy development by deepening comprehension of story, as well as improving reading fluency and writing skills?
- What are some methods for both student and teacher assessment?

Looking Back, Looking Ahead

Talk and discussion are vital in language development. In this chapter, we suggest a range of strategies that engage learners in real talk for real purposes. Oral language development strategies will be introduced here and will be an ongoing theme in the rest of the book.

In Chapter 4, we investigated the interconnections between oral language development and literacy development. The fact that oral language is learned *in use*, in a variety of real-life contexts, and under identifiable learning conditions, influences the teaching and learning of literacy. We have already explored these conditions through Cambourne's model and looked at its implications for choosing effective teaching strategies (see Figure 2.7 and the section on conditions for language learning in Chapter 4). We continue the theme of the intimate, interdependent links between oral language development and the processes involved in becoming literate, by looking at how literacy develops through *talk*.

ABOUT TALK

We use "talk" as an umbrella term that covers the wide range of activities involved in listening, speaking, conversing, discussing, and engaging in dialogue, from the informal clamour on the playground to the formal, structured dialogues of a literature circle discussion. The main emphasis in this chapter, and throughout the book, is that talk is a vital medium through which learning of all kinds occurs. In many cases, it is talk that makes learning possible.

Just as you explored and made explicit your own assumptions about language and literacy in Chapters 3 and 4, in Chapter 5 you will uncover your presuppositions about the role of talk in literacy teaching and learning. Talking is a daily activity—we use it as a primary medium in our teaching—and yet, talk itself often remains unexamined by teachers engaged in daily classroom practice, as expressed in this quotation from Donald Rubin (1990):

Talk is like the sea…. A traditional homily tells us that fish would be the least likely creatures to ever become aware of water. For those of us who teach, talk surrounds us and it also constitutes our primary mode of action. It is our medium, our atmosphere, and also our substance. And it is therefore invisible to us much of the time. Because talk is invisible to us, we rarely treat it as a matter of deliberate concern for teaching and learning. Of course, students do learn about talk in the classrooms, but the lessons they learn may not be ones we would choose to teach if we thought about it. Sometimes students learn more about silence than about talk, for example, and more about hearing than about listening. (p. 5)

In this chapter, we invite you to consider the roles of teacher talk and student talk in teaching and learning as an antidote to poisonous consequences such as silence, as Rubin suggests. We will explore opportunities for the development of language and literacy through talking and listening activities, including some specific classroom strategies. These strategies are linked in important ways to research findings that support the importance of talk in the classroom. We will encourage you to explore ways in which you can become more articulate about your perceptions of the role of oral language in learning, how those perceptions influence how you teach, and how you can become a more effective oral communicator. The strategies will encourage your students to value talk in their own learning, to become metacognitively aware of the key roles talking and listening play in their learning, and how to nurture their own growth as oral communicators, and by extension, their growth as readers, writers, and learners across the curriculum. Figure 5.1 outlines the many benefits of talk, not only in language learning but across the curriculum.

FIGURE 5.1 Consequences of Oracy

From 1988 to 1993 the UK Department of Education conducted a National Oracy Project, which identified talk from the earliest years with the use of language as a means of learning. Oracy was assumed to be not a subject "but a condition of learning in all subjects" (Barnes, 1993, p. 28). The five-year study found that children who value talk in their learning:

- are more likely to explore beyond facts, into situations, causes and consequences
- know more about the language in which knowledge is expressed
- have a greater repertoire of learning strategies
- have greater insight into the relationships among bits of information
- have greater understanding of the possibility of multiple solutions to problems and questions
- have a greater understanding of why they are working within a particular area of knowledge

Source: Barnes (1993, pp. 28-29).

The Importance of Talk in the Classroom

Once again, our assumption is that there are inseparable links between literacy and oral language. In the classroom context, we are assuming that:

1. Literacy is interwoven into the cultural and social contexts in which and through which it is acquired and practised.

2. Classroom talk, especially in the form of real discussions, is a primary component of the literacy process.

literacy notebook
5.1

STOP, THINK, AND WRITE

Talk, especially the sort of unstructured talk typical of play, is encouraged in the early primary years—Junior and Senior Kindergarten—and in primary classrooms where learning centres are part of the classroom set-up. It has often been observed that as students move through the grades and divisions, classroom talk among peers occurs less and less frequently—even the structured, teacher-sanctioned sort of talk that characterizes literary discussion groups.

■ Why do you think this is so?

■ Have you ever hesitated to use a peer talk strategy in your classroom? Why?

■ Have you felt constrained by circumstances? Comment on the nature and the reasons for these constraints.

Note: The criteria for real discussions and what constitutes good talk in the classroom is presented later in the chapter.

WHY SHOULD TALK BE EXPLICITLY TAUGHT?

There are powerful social, emotional, and moral reasons for ensuring that our students develop their oral language abilities.

Many students have endured traumatic experiences beyond their years and beyond their abilities to express in language. Their defence is often silence. Without a supportive classroom community, without your personal care, encouragement, and instruction, they may never believe that what they have to say is worth listening to.

There are enormous challenges involved in creating physically and emotionally safe environments for all your students in all of their diversity. This is one of the moral dimensions of your job as teachers. Since much of the school day involves talk in the broad sense defined above, you need to ensure that talking and listening activities are conducted fairly and honestly, with care and respect for one another, in a collaborative spirit that does not allow language or behaviour that harms or silences some students. Just as your students learn how to become more proficient readers and writers through your instruction and guidance, they can learn how to conduct and participate in fair discussions —good talk (Ayim, 1997; Campbell, 2005)—through modelling and guided practice. There are many opportunities to foster moral growth, social confidence, and emotional security.

As students and teachers we spend more of our time listening than we do reading, writing, and speaking together (Werner, 1975). The ability to speak well—to communicate clearly and effectively—is valued in social and school life, and in personal and professional life.

> *Talk is the medium by which we convey and receive most of our information.*

In classrooms where peer discussion is awarded time and encouragement, oral language abilities improve because, rather than demanding little more than brief right or wrong answers to teacher-posed questions, students become aware of a variety of viewpoints, and learn to value the multiplicity of perspectives generated through the extended conversations around questions students themselves formulate and explore together.

> *Those who have well-developed oral abilities are likely to have significantly higher reading and writing achievement.*
>
> (Ruddell & Ruddell, 1994; Cazden, 1988; Chall, 2000; Collins Block, 2001)

Oral proficiency includes a well-developed vocabulary, which increases the number of words students can recognize and decode. Students who speak effectively are more readily able to recognize the **graphemes** in print that correspond to the **phonemes** that are spoken (Adams, 1990; Juel, 1991). These students are also able to talk to their friends about new words they encounter in print, and are less self-conscious about asking friends about words they don't know. In the course of further conversations, they are more likely to use the new word; this immediate transfer guarantees that this new learning will become part of their reading, writing, speaking, and listening vocabulary (Collins Block, 2001). Being able to talk about what they have read or written or learned about through talking in turn strengthens **metacognition** and comprehension.

The opportunity to pronounce and use new words in a low-risk environment fosters a rapid buildup of oral vocabulary (Block & Mangieri, 2005; Templeton & Morris, 1999). As the research of Nagy and Scott (2000) indicates, "knowing a word means being able to do things with

grapheme The smallest part of a word that represents a phoneme (a single sound). For example, a/pp/le, p/l/ay.

phoneme The smallest unit of sound in a word. For example, a single letter (c/a/t) or several letters (ph/o/t/o/g/r/a/ph)

metacognition The process of thinking about one's own thought processes and so being able to be responsible for one's own learning.

it: To recognize it in connected speech or in print, to access its meaning, to pronounce it—and to be able to do theses things within a fraction of a second" (p. 273). This rapid acquisition of oral vocabulary and its transfer into reading and writing vocabularies is crucial to both native speakers and second-language English students; however, a non-threatening environment is particularly beneficial for English as a Second Language (ESL) learners. Correct pronunciation is also the key for emergent writers who are learning how to say a word slowly, and hear and record all the sounds as accurately as possible—a crucial step for early problem solving as writers. Figure 5.2 provides an overview of the specific strategies learned in oral situations that are directly generalizable to print. Chapter 9 continues this discussion in greater depth.

> *Talking is the first language art children use to express their own original ideas and to further their own purposes.*

In Chapter 4, you became familiar with the range of purposes for which talk is used—purposes that most young children demonstrate before they enter school. Once children are in school, they must add the language of learning, such as teacher talk (Newman, 1991) and exploratory talk (Barnes, 1993) to their repertoire—language that grows out of functions such as Halliday's (1975) heuristic and representative models. When young children become familiar with the language of learning, they learn that they can *learn through talk*. Since you want your students to value how they can learn through talk, you must provide opportunities to use language for expressing more than their immediate needs, feelings, and observations.

This is a good time to revisit the First Steps: Oral Language Developmental Continuum (1994); see Chapter 4, which describes three strands of talk and language:

- **Language of social interaction:** language used to converse, discuss, brainstorm, cooperate

- **Language and literacy:** language used to tell news, tell stories, describe events, give instructions

- **Language and thinking:** language used to clarify thoughts, analyze information, form conclusions, solve problems

"Language and literacy" and "language and thinking" are the components of "language for learning." Language and thinking refers to metacognitive awareness of how talk is used that leads to the active valuing of talk as a medium for learning.

When students are members of a peer discussion group, learning occurs directly through explicit teaching (how to conduct a discussion session, for example) and indirectly through participation in the talking and listening activities that constitute group discussions. This is the main theme of the rest of this chapter. Peer discussions, such as "literature circles" (Daniels, 2002) and

> *The social context of the classroom provides students with opportunities to participate in the construction of meaning and to observe how group processes work.*

FIGURE 5.2 Problem Solving through Talk

The following strategies have been identified by many researchers as those developing readers and writers need to become capable problem-solvers when dealing with text. Some researchers refer to these strategies as metacognitive processes, describing how proficient readers think about their own thinking as they read (Keene, 2002). Allington (2001, 2006) refers to the development of "thoughtful literacy" through effective comprehension instruction that focuses on the *thinking* students need to engage in while reading. All strategies are co-dependent with talking and listening skills. Each of these strategies is directly applicable to talk. Each can be taught through modelling and other forms of direct and indirect instruction; each can be learned, practised, and brought to metacognitive awareness through talk:

- activating prior knowledge or **schema** before, during, and after reading
- determining important ideas and themes
- visualizing or creating other sensory imagery before, during, and after reading
- asking questions of oneself, the author, and the texts (Beck & McKeown, 2002)
- making inferences: using prior knowledge and textual information to interpret and make critical judgments
- synthesizing: combining information from different sources to create summarized restatements of central ideas
- applying fix-up strategies: using strategies such as think alouds to re-think and repair comprehension using semantic, syntactic, or graphophonic cues (for example, Did that make sense? Does that sound right? Does that look right?)

Source: Adapted from Keene (2002, pp. 80-105).

In addition, Almasi et al. (2005) provide an overview of recent research supporting the effectiveness of directly teaching these strategies in order to stimulate active thinking and improve comprehension. *Direct teaching* includes teacher modelling through think alouds (see Theory into Practice 6.3), and guided practice with opportunities for students to talk about the strategies. Think alouds are particularly important to use in context, in order to show how the flexible problem solving is used, and how talking our way through the problems helps us to understand when we are reading.

Peer discussion is a valuable classroom strategy.

"grand conversations" (Peterson & Eeds, 1990), show constructivist learners at work. Discussing books that are worth talking about allows students to become part of the "active conversation that is reading, the conversation between the reader and the text, between text and community, and among readers" (Straw & Bogdan, 1993, p. 4).

To provide a rationale for the claim that discussion is a valuable classroom strategy, we will consider first the importance of setting genuine purposes and authentic contexts for these activities, and then look at the major benefits of discussion as reported in the research.

WHAT IS A "REAL DISCUSSION"? WHY MUST TALK OCCUR IN AUTHENTIC CONTEXTS?

Courtney Cazden (1988) identified the "most common pattern of classroom discourse at all grade levels" as involving the following three-part sequence:

1. Teacher **initiation (I)**: The teacher initiates the sequence by asking a question, or calling on a student to share.

2. Student **response (R)**: The nominated child responds by answering the question, or by telling a narrative, etc.

3. Teacher **evaluation (E)**: The teacher comments on the response before calling on next child or "moving on."

Her research supports her contention that "all analyses of teacher-led classroom discourse find examples of this pattern, and anyone hearing it recognizes it as classroom talk and not just informal conversation" (p. 30-31). Figure 5.3 is an example of the contrast between a genuine conversation and artificial classroom talk.

FIGURE 5.3 Classroom Conversations

CONVERSATION (real discussion)	CLASSROOM TALK ("recitation")
What time is it, Sarah?	What time is it, Sarah?
Half-past two.	Half-past two.
Thanks.	Right.

Cazden calls these teacher-led lessons, following the I-R-E pattern, "recitations" in contrast to conversations or **real discussions**; the teacher controls topic initiation and development, determines what is relevant, and decides who gets a turn to talk (and when). Aside from the critical question of teacher control, we notice that recitation is not like a real discussion; the final statement by the teacher, which is an evaluation, effectively chokes off further talk. In real discussion, the social convention of saying "Thanks" might stop a conversation, but not necessarily. In a real social context, one would not respond "Right" when told the time.

Cazden refers to the teacher control evidenced in the recitation example as imposing an "assymetry of speaking rights" in the classroom.

> *Teachers have the right to speak at any time and to any person; they can fill any silence or interrupt any speaker; they can speak to a student anywhere in the room and in any volume or tone of voice. And no one has any right to object. But not all teachers assume such rights or live by such rules all the time. (Cazden, 1988, p. 54)*

Teachers can choose whether and how to exercise these powers. Effective teachers structure the conditions for classroom discussions so that they have a real purpose (for example, to explore ideas that are of concern to the students) and that they are conducted without the direct intervention of the teacher; this happens when the teacher takes the role of *evaluator*, for example. How can teachers shape the conditions for discussions so that they have real purposes and so that they can proceed without the constraints of too much teacher influence?

Three conditions are necessary for real discussion:

1. **Timing:** The discussion takes place after an event in which the whole class or a small group of students have participated. This may be going on a class trip, watching a film, listening to a news event, or reading an evocative story.

2. **Topic:** The students identify the question or problem they want to discuss, rather than being given recall or comprehension questions composed by the teacher.

3. **Know how:** The students know how to participate in a discussion that is a fair, honest, and caring collaboration. Everyone in the group contributes equally. No one is afraid of being silenced.

When these three conditions are met, the students are ready for a real discussion or what we call good talk (Campbell, 2005).

These conditions correspond to Cambourne's conditions of learning. Each of the three conditions echoes at least one of the conditions he identified: a topic worth discussing relates to *immersion* and *engagement*; the choice of discussion questions relates to *responsibility* and *use*; and that the discussion be conducted fairly, relates to *demonstration* (since this will have to be taught), *response, responsibility,* and *engagement*.

With this model, the students construct their own learning collaboratively. This is an obvious, intuitive benefit of engaging in discussions. What support do we have from research studies on student discussion and its benefits?

What Does Research Tell Us about Discussion?

Effective planning enables students to gain deeper literary understandings, to improve communication skills, to enhance aesthetic enjoyment, and to increase cognitive skills.

DEEPER LITERARY UNDERSTANDING

Research supports our intuition that discussing literary texts that have been listened to or read fosters deeper understanding (Palinscar, 1987; Eeds & Wells, 1989; Whitmore, 1997). From Kindergarten (Morrow & Smith, 1990) to middle school (Alvermann, 1996) to secondary school (Townsend & Pace, 2005), this is an observable result of engagement in group discussions where meaning is constructed and texts are interpreted by the students themselves. Research on groups that meet over time to discuss their reading shows that interpretations are modified as a result of interactions within the group (Gambrell, 1996). In many instances, students achieve insights based on their interactions with other group members (Freedman, 1993; Whitmore, 1997). Figure 5.4 reports a classroom conversation that illustrates this process.

These modifications of initial responses or changes of opinion would not occur in a debate format, where each person or team must defend a stated point of view. In a debate, the point is to continue to argue for one's assigned point of view, and to rebut what the other team says. As James Moffett (1968) put it, "taking a position is not difficult and hardly needs to be taught…. What takes learning is the sense of alternative possibilities and the reasons for choosing one over another" (p. 97). This requires a willingness to be influenced; the debater wants to persuade others while remaining unchanged. In a collaborative discussion, the goal is to encourage perspectives and interpretations to evolve as the result of openness to the thoughts and ideas expressed by other group members.

IMPROVED COMMUNICATION SKILLS

Studies have documented increases in student-student interaction, recognition and acknowledgement of the previous speaker, requesting verification, and the ability to consider a position different from their own (Almasi et al., 2001; Goatley & Raphael, 1992) as a result of participating in discussion groups. Students do seem to need coaching about how to solve conflicts with regard to group process issues (Almasi & Gambrell, 1997); however, once they are coached on how to solve such problems themselves and then allowed the freedom to problem-solve on their own, their proficiency as a group noticeably improves (Almasi et al., 2001).

ENHANCED AESTHETIC ENJOYMENT

Participation in discussions may produce emotional and cultural benefits such as greater enjoyment of reading. The scope or range of reading has been shown to increase when students discuss ideas in the texts they have read (Morrow & Weinstein, 1986); students who talk about

---

FIGURE 5.4 Literary Understandings

A group of students in a Grade 3-4 class, discussing the illustrated book *Rose Blanche* by Roberto Innocenti, which is set in World War II, wondered why Rose Blanche was pictured waving a Nazi flag.

Colin: I think one of the reasons that she was waving that is because a lot of the people didn't know that the Nazis were so mean to the Ger, um to all those people.

Travis: Yeah.

Aaron: Yeah.

Trevor: *WOW! I never thought of that!*

Caryl: You hadn't thought of that before?

Trevor: No, I think it might be right.

Caryl: Why do you think so, Trevor? Why does that make sense to you now?

Trevor: I just didn't know. I just didn't know about that. I thought everybody in the world knew that Nazis were mean.

Source: Whitmore (1997, pp. 107-108).

what they have read are more likely to engage in reading, and to respond aesthetically to their reading (Many & Wiseman, 1992). Student engagement in reading, in the sense of intrinsic motivation to read and enjoyment in reading for its own sake, increases when there is opportunity for "social discourse among students in a learning community that enables them to see perspectives and to construct knowledge socially from text" (Guthrie & Wigfield, 2000, p. 143).

INCREASED COGNITIVE SKILLS

Discussion promotes higher-level thinking and problem solving. Almasi's (1995) study seemed to show that student-led discussion groups, as opposed to teacher-led, engaged students in higher level thinking and wider participation. Other studies (O'Flahavan et al., 1992; McGee, 1992) indicate that without strategic input from the teacher, little progress is made by literary discussion groups. Since some of the studies yield conflicting conclusions, and since the role of the teacher in peer discussion groups is so important, it will be considered in some detail later on. Another factor is the size of the group—small groups work better (Townsend & Pace, 2005; Almasi, 1995; Morrow & Smith, 1990).

If students are to receive maximum benefit from participating in group discussions, the teacher must arrange the safe and practical conditions that make it possible for them to engage in productive discussions conducted within appropriate moral parameters such as fairness, collaboration, and care. The conversation must be allowed to flow with a minimum of teacher intervention and interference.

The Role of the Teacher: Balancing Good Pedagogy and Student Independence

> *The problem with the use of class discussion as pedagogy is that the teacher tends to control it, almost with a set of vice grips.*
>
> — Lauren Freedman

Classroom discussion groups provide the forum for the recursive growth of literacy involving reading, listening and responding, re-reading, and revisiting responses. These discussion groups are pedagogically arranged; they may be more or less formally organized with or without assigned roles. However, we are using the dynamics of the informal conversation—resembling Cazden's real discussion—as the model for the unscripted, unpredictable, and creative responses and exchanges that take place when such groups are functioning at their finest (Campbell, 2005). The talking and listening interactions resemble a real-life conversation, where the teacher or authority figure, if present at all, is there *to participate and not to evaluate performance*. The assertion that the teacher's presence as evaluator has a detrimental effect on discussion groups has both theoretical and empirical support (Cazden, 1988; Freedman, 1993). This does not mean, however, that discussion groups should be allowed to function on an "anything goes" basis. Teachers know that this is a recipe for disaster. The question then becomes one of *balancing teacher control with student freedom*. Figure 5.5 provides some insight into the relationship between teacher belief and practice.

FIGURE 5.5 Belief vs. Practice

Research on teacher talk (Alvermann, O'Brien, & Dillon, 1990) indicates a discrepancy between teacher belief and practice: teachers believe in discussion as a forum for open exchange and yet they set the questions, use student answers to evaluate recall of facts, and insist on students raising their hands (being acknowledged by the teacher, thus really addressing the teacher, not their peers) and/or writing down their discussion points prior to the discussion (Freedman, 1993).

STOP, THINK, AND WRITE

- How can you set up a classroom discussion group so that the talk stays on track, everyone participates without fear of being wrong, no one dominates the discussion, and where the students feel autonomous and become fully engaged in a conversation of real interest to them?

- If you should not overtly evaluate students' performance, how can you assess their participation to provide feedback for improvement?

literacy
notebook
5.2

WHAT DO RESEARCH REPORTS CONCLUDE ABOUT HOW STUDENT DISCUSSION IS INFLUENCED BY LEADERSHIP?

Some studies have focused on group discussions where a teacher or researcher acts as a group leader; others have looked at student-led groups (Evans, 1997); and at least one has explicitly compared teacher-led versus student-led discussion (Almasi, 1995). Looking across these studies, we can conclude that the type of leadership affects how group members interact and the levels of thinking that are achieved. It appears

meta-talk A form of metacognition whereby students talk about their own talk processes and articulate how they learn through talking.

that discussions are most dynamic and the students most engaged *when the teacher serves as a guide or coach.* As guide, the teacher helps students achieve autonomy and authority in expressing their interpretations of the text and articulating their opinions during **meta-talk**—conversations about taking turns, staying on topic, and resolving conflicts.

One study (Almasi, O'Flahavan & Arya, 2001) compared two discussion groups over time, one more significantly proficient than the other, and contrasted the role of the teacher in each group. They found that the teacher of the more proficient group adopted a hands-off role with regard to initiating and managing topics and other group process issues. She "modeled strategies for managing topics in the beginning and gradually released this responsibility to the students" (p. 114).

> *Ms. Evans relinquished her responsibility as group process monitor after week two, and her students assumed the role throughout the rest of the study. In contrast, the teacher of the less proficient group continued to initiate group process meta-talk throughout the investigation, and the amount her students initiated declined. (p.117)*

The key, according to the conclusions drawn in this study, is "to teach students how to recognize and resolve their own interaction dilemmas" (p. 117). The goal should be to create enough structure so that the students develop autonomy: they must have control over group processes and feel that they have the authority to express opinions and interpretations.

A note of caution is needed here, however. Research studies also suggest that if teachers take too much of a hands-off approach, and remove themselves completely from the discussion process, students' interpretive responses do not develop (O'Flahavan et al., 1992). A study of a Grade 1 class (McGee, 1992) revealed that while it is vital to allow exploration of stories on their own, it is equally important that the teacher structure and centre the discussion for the students, for example, through a specific focus question. Taking this one step further with older students, teachers can teach them how to formulate their own focus questions, and encourage them to pose questions that are likely to stimulate good discussion.

Teachers whose students become proficient discussants do not turn the classroom over to the students, but effectively share power with them by supporting their choices, ideas, and personal connections, while being available as a guide when needed. Teachers can make suggestions, which the students can accept or reject.

Discussions are more dynamic and students become more engaged when the teacher serves as a guide or coach.

Figure 5.6 is a transcript of a discussion where a suggestion is made by the teacher to stimulate higher-level thinking about the moral question raised by an event in Mark Twain's *The Adventures of Huckleberry Finn*.

There is no perfect method for finding a balance between teacher control and student freedom. How this should best be handled will vary from group to group, teacher to teacher, according to the individuals involved, their background, and their sophistication in conducting group discussions. Factors such as developmental level, gender, ethnic, racial and cultural diversity, the size of the group, as well as a number of situational details can play a role in how students can learn how to successfully engage in good talk. How to communicate across these

---

FIGURE 5.6 Talking about Moral Thinking

This Grade 7 class had been reading that part of the novel, *The Adventures of Huckleberry Finn*, where Huck is faced with the dilemma of whether or not to turn in Jim, a runaway black slave, during pre-civil war times when the punishment for Jim would have been severe. The discussion is about Huck's struggle between "doing wrong" and helping Jim, who was well-known and liked by Huck, or "doing right" and turning him in. In this discussion, the teacher acts as a participant in exploratory talk (Barnes, 1993) where ideas are not yet fully formed. Rather than direct the conversation, the teacher (T) adds to the discussion, offering a new idea for them to explore—the idea of "two consciences."

S1: They're saying wrong and right are the same thing.

S2: Well, it sort of is.

S3: Well, if you don't get in trouble, or get caught lying.

T: What is the struggle here that Huck is having? Is it fair to say that Huck has two consciences?

S2: Yeah—one from how he was raised.

T: What society has taught him.

S4: The other side being fair.

T: Loyalty.

S5: Friendship.

S3: But, Huck believes in the rules.

T: He just doesn't follow them all the time or even most of the time.

S2: Could Huck get in big trouble, I mean hanged if he got caught helping Jim?

S1: It's sort of like the Nazis killing Christians when they helped the Jews.

Source: Freedman (1993, p. 232).

differences can itself best be addressed through further dialogue. Lisa Delpit (1990) expresses the difficulty this way:

> One of the most difficult tasks we face as human beings is communicating meaning across our individual differences, a task confounded immeasurably when we attempt to communicate across social lines, racial lines, cultural lines, or lines of unequal power (p. 263).

Figure 5.7 outlines some concerns about gender balance.

FIGURE 5.7 Gender Balance in Classroom Talk

There has been considerable research on the issue of male dominance in discussions, especially in the classroom.

Some of the findings are startling. French and French (1984) describe a primary classroom where, out of 66 turns at interactions, 50 were from *"boys who numbered less than half the class."* Spender (1982) documented situations where teachers consciously strove to *"balance the amount of time and attention they gave to the girls and boys"* and subsequently felt that they gave too much attention to the girls, unfairly discriminating against the boys. But an analysis of videotapes showed that even then, *"over two-thirds of their time was spent with the boys who comprised less than half the class"* (Ayim, 1997, p. 38).

In another study, three gifted adolescent students, two girls and a boy, in the beginning were all perceived as outspoken, but after just six months, one of the girls was effectively silenced (Alvermann 1996). Evans (1997) details how boys in a discussion group challenged any girl who tried to position herself in a role of authority. Two of the girls who were leaders in the beginning became silent after just three sessions as a result of intense pressure from the boys in the group.

Jane Miller (1990) notes that "language is learned within actual conversations and it is a rare conversation which is not internally unsettled by the inequality of its participants. Age, size, gender, class, authority: these are not the context of conversation, they are its organizing principles" (p. 127). When arranging for learning through talk, all of these issues must be on the table, for teachers and students alike. We must keep in mind that talking about talk is part of the process: teacher guidance and evaluation, and student self-assessment must take into account the conditions of the discussion format, or its "organizing principles" as Jane Miller puts it. It is now time to look at some of the classroom strategies used to arrange learning so that real discussions can take place; that is, discussions that are truly collaborative, where the teacher may be a participant, but is not in full control of topic initiation and development, and may not decide what is relevant or who gets a turn to talk (and when).

Good Talk about Good Books: Literature Circles and Grand Conversations

> *Participants in dialogue experience in a dramatic way what it means to construct meaning. For the most part, our individually constructed meaning happens unnoticed. But in a group we can take note of the shifts in thinking that occur as the interpretation of the text evolves. Group members also learn about the feelings and experiences of others as they interact. Members seek to know ideas on other people's terms as they collaborate in the construction of meaning*
>
> (Peterson & Eeds, 1990, p. 21).

The key elements of literary discussion groups, regardless of what they are called, or the details by which they are organized involve:

- reading, thinking, listening, and talking about literature

- collaborating with others to reflect on, interpret, analyze, and criticize literature

- developing and sharing aesthetic responses to literature

- extending understandings through talk

- using the students' own questions to deepen understanding, not teacher-made, comprehension check questions.

Briefly, literature circles (Daniels, 2002) gather to discuss self-selected literature, with each student adopting a specific role in the group following specific guidelines, and keeping written records, including self-assessment checklists. This model is described in depth in Chapter 9.

In grand conversations (Peterson & Eeds, 1990), the focus is on aesthetic appreciation of literature and on awareness that the process of interpreting stories takes place over time by listening to one another's viewpoints. After an individual reader's initial unconsidered, unexamined response is stated, the readers then consciously deliberate over and re-shape their meanings through their conversations with co-readers. Interpretations evolve, critical dispositions gradually develop, approximations are accepted, and peers and teachers provide modelling and feedback. Grand conversations are more open-ended, and less structured than literature circles, particularly in terms of the roles of the group members. There are only two rules: participants must (1) listen and respect one another's opinions, and (2) follow the spontaneity of a conversation; that is, there must be no agendas; everyone must be "open to respond to whatever emerges in the encounter" (Peterson & Eeds, 1990,

p. 22). Grand conversations are similar to literary conversations discussed in Chapter 9, which refer to student-directed discussions addressing specific aspects of a piece of literature, specific story elements, or particular themes or genres of literature. The focus of a literary conversation is a literary element, in other words, while the focus of a grand conversation is the interpretation of a story.

A powerful way to increase the enjoyment and comprehension of a shared story or poem, and to further develop oral language skills, reading fluency, and collaborative skills, is **readers' theatre**. Readers' theatre, as shown in Theory into Practice 5.1, is a way to share a story or an episode from a novel with the rest of the class. To do this, the teacher needs to teach the class how to select an appropriate scene, and when and how to use narrative and dialogue based on the original. Throughout this process, reading, writing, listening, and speaking, operate reciprocally.

literacy notebook 5.3

STOP, THINK, AND WRITE

What are some meaningful response projects that students can create that will extend their aesthetic appreciation, deepen their understanding, and build their collaborative skills as a group? (Remember that, although creating a diorama is a fun and creative thing to do, it does not necessarily relate in a significant way to the story or novel.)

Storytelling

Storytelling is an ancient art. Before the invention of alphabets, storytellers were the keepers of the history and culture of the tribe or community. While now it may seem that storytelling is used only for entertainment, it remains a valuable activity in our everyday lives for sharing news, passing on gossip, or telling jokes. For students emerging into literacy, developing their literacy, or well on their way to becoming independently literate, what is the role of storytelling?

Under the term storytelling, we can list everyday anecdotal storytelling, the telling of family stories, sometimes passed down over generations, chanting nursery rhymes, telling folktales and fairy tales "by heart," and the polished, performance-style telling of epic tales by master storytellers. Why are stories so important for students as they journey into literacy? The stories themselves are vital as a cultural way into literacy, and

Theory Into Practice/5.1

READERS' THEATRE

In readers' theatre, a group of readers prepare and perform a script, usually with one or two narrators and several characters, using their voices to convey the meaning of the tale. The many benefits include collaborative group work, literary appreciation, building confidence in oral language ability, reading fluency, and increased vocabulary through repetition. In our experience, the entire process of preparing and performing a readers' theatre production is highly motivating, especially for reluctant readers.

Before:

1. Assign one director: you or a trained assistant interested in providing a meaningful oral language experience for students.

2. Arrange students: divide the students into manageable groups to match the number of characters and narrators in the script.

3. Choose an appropriate story: the story could be a published one that you have adapted or one written by the students; it should be instructional or easy reading level, be of reasonable length, and have interesting characters.

4. Provide stools, chairs, benches or other props for the performers to practise and perform with (in readers' theatre, there is little or no dramatic movement).

5. Put copies of script in black folders.

6. Read the script over with the students.

7. Assign parts: the students may have some input here, but you will likely make the final decisions.

During (includes practising and performing):

1. Help the students practise their parts: the focus is on developing fluency and interpreting the characters' words using intonation, pitch, and volume.

2. Set up a performance area as per the needs of the script.

3. Distribute minimal props and costumes if appropriate, but they are usually used sparingly if at all.

4. While the group practises, prepare the audience for its role as listener.

5. During the performance, have the audience play the role of active listeners and constructive critics in order to make helpful suggestions.

After:

Evaluate collaboratively the reading as a performance, with a view to making improvements. Have the group assess its own work—both the rehearsal and the performance.

Source: Worthy & Prater (2002, pp. 294-297).

it is through the fundamentally human activities of receiving and telling stories, that we build a foundation for our understanding of written stories and our ability to understand and appreciate story in all its forms, whether spoken, as dramatic movement, as song, or as written word.

WHY USE STORYTELLING IN THE CLASSROOM?

Storytelling is an essential component of a comprehensive and balanced approach to teaching literacy. Its major benefits are literary awareness, integration of the six language arts, social, emotional, and moral growth, and cross-cultural and intercultural understanding.

Literary Benefits

There are vital reciprocal connections between the listening and speaking activities that constitute storytelling, and the other essential language arts of reading, writing, viewing, and visually representing, as shown in Figure 5.8.

Social, Emotional, and Moral Benefits

There are powerful immediate benefits of engaging in talk in a risk-free environment, and there are long-term benefits to students' social, emotional, and moral well-being as they develop the ability to speak well and confidently, and to listen attentively and critically. Storytelling provides an opportunity to explore characters and situations that may be similar to some of our students' harsh realities, but are safe to talk about and explore because "it's just a story" (Bettelheim, 1976).

Storytelling is an essential component of teaching literacy.

For teachers the rewards of storytelling are well worth the initial risks. The degree of direct interaction with your listeners made possible when telling a story by heart, using only voice and gesture, is magical; there is nothing to compare with the joy of watching a story brought to life in the eyes and faces of enchanted story listeners. Storytelling invites participation; the story is created by the teller's voice and the listeners' imagination. Storyteller and author, Tololwa Mollel described the difference for her between the freedom of a told story and the bonds of a written one: "Yes…there's a difference, it slips off your tongue differently—reading the written word and telling a story—it gets so attached to the page that you can't lick it off."

By encouraging students to tell their own stories and to learn how to tell their favourite stories, you honour each student's unique voice.

Teacher Talk/5.1

ROSEMARY SIDORKO'S THOUGHTS ON STORYTELLING

Before entering the education program, I had thought of drama and storytelling as being just a small and separate part of a language program. I have learned that so much of language can be taught through storytelling. Reading comprehension can be learned when the student retells a story. Summarizing, sequencing, and making connections can be developed while retelling. Vocabulary and grammar structures can be learned by listening to and telling stories. Understanding different genres, point of view, and story sense can all be developed through telling stories.

In the past, I had thought about drama as being about the performance, as when my children would learn their parts for the Christmas pantomime. Now I understand drama for primary school students to be about teaching students to express themselves, to communicate, to enhance comprehension, and foster oral language development. Drama can be a way to engage students who may be having difficulty with the written language; a way to express themselves through their bodies or their voices.

I believe that as children communicate more and more via computers (e-mail, instant messenger) and that as television programs, video, and computer games become their primary entertainment choices, they are losing the art of conversation and storytelling. As busy families find less and less time to talk to one another directly and as grandparents often live separately, we are not passing on traditional stories and family legends. When I was a child (beware whatever follows that clause) my mother did not read books to us; rather, she told us stories in Polish—Hansel and Gretel, Little Red Riding Hood, the Seven Billy Goats. We also heard stories about the war and our Polish aunts and uncles whom we would never meet. I have read lots of books to my own children and also told stories at the public library and for the Literacy Association.

In my teaching practice, I would love to have lots of drama, poetry, and storytelling throughout the day and across the curriculum; even something as simple as a mime reflection after recess to calm the children and to get them focused on learning. I would love to tell stories without a book or other props. I want to look into the eyes of the children and know how they are experiencing the richness of the language. I would like them to learn about the structure of language through the spoken word. I will encourage the students to tell their stories and help them by providing the scaffolding they need. For example, when Kindergarten children bring in an item for show and tell, they can learn to answer the questions with what, how, when, where. With all the wonderful resources available it shouldn't be difficult to incorporate drama activities into the classroom so that the children with different learning styles and different intelligences can demonstrate what they know.

Finally, as demonstrated in our class, drama and storytelling are a great way to team build. Students are engaged and motivated to become active participants in their learning.

Rosemary Sidorko is a 2004 graduate of Nipissing University's Faculty of Education Program.

FIGURE 5.8 Storytelling and the Development of Reading, Writing, and Visual Strategies

Storytelling enhances the following strategies:

- visualizing, forming sensory images summarizing and retelling strategies
- sequencing events
- making connections to other stories, own lives
- understanding genres
- developing story sense and story structure
- understanding point of view, and the perspectives of diverse characters and cultures
- enriching vocabulary, and the semantic and syntactic structures in book language
- monitoring comprehension (when retelling "in your own words," for example)
- contributing to increased oral language skills; for example, public speaking, general communication, social skills
- contributing to the development of writing skills through all of the above, as well as organizational awareness (for example, the beginning-middle-end pattern of traditional stories) and audience and voice awareness

Promoting Understanding across Differences

Listening to stories from a variety of cultures and learning to tell our own stories and those of other times and places deepen our knowledge and appreciation of our profound similarities; we are more alike than different. At the same time, telling of tales of diverse origins helps us to recognize and appreciate the many differences in cultural practices.

STORYTELLING ACTIVITIES FOR THE CLASSROOM

The activities we describe are "tried and true." We have used these with elementary school children and with pre-service teachers. The bonus exists implicitly in their intimate links to literacy growth. We have included anecdotal storytelling (Figure 5.9), learning how to tell a tale by heart (Theory into Practice 5.2), and traditional storytelling techniques (Theory into Practice 5.3). Finally, at the end of the chapter we have included our favourite teacher resources and children's literature for storytelling.

Notes on Assessment

Finding appropriate assessment tools for storytelling and the other spoken arts that often overlap with drama is difficult. The goal is to have

FIGURE 5.9 Anecdotal Storytelling

The purpose of these activities is to demonstrate that we are all storytellers. Some are best used by partners, others in small or large groups.

Liar's Contest: Everyone sits in a circle as the leader chants this counting-off rhyme:

> *As I sat beneath the apple tree,*
> *All the apples fell on me*
> *Apple pudding, apple pie,*
> *Did you ever tell a lie?*
> *Yes you did, you know you did,*
> *You broke your mother's teapot lid!*

The last person counted is "it" and must tell a story about something that happened to him or her. It may be true or false. The others in the group vote on the story afterwards. If they think the story is true, they raise their fingers in a 'V'; if they think it is false, fingers are crossed. The teller must then say if the story is true or false. The goal is to fool the listeners by making a true story seem implausible and a false story seem plausible.

The teacher should model first, and stress that even when telling a simple anecdotal story, the tale must be shaped with a beginning, middle, and end, embellished with as many details as possible, and include dialogue between characters, as with any good story.

Benefits: The development of story sense and extending oral language use to imagine and to persuade (Halliday's instrumental and imaginative language functions).

Stupid Things I've Done Stories: Tell anecdotes about "The day I did something so stupid." Again, the teacher should model this first, stressing that the story should be shaped and embellished.

Connections and Extensions: Compare classroom stories with well-known folktales about "noodleheads and numbskulls" for example, or "Jack" stories (see resources list). This is a particularly good warm-up for composing written versions of the story.

Object Stories: Pass a treasure chest or magic bag around the story circle. Each person tells a short tale that an object calls to mind. The story may begin "This stone reminds me of the time..."

FAMILY STORIES OR STORY ACTIVITIES TO BE PREPARED WITH FAMILY MEMBERS

Name Stories: Tell the students to ask their parents why they were given their names. Each child then tells a story about how or why he or she was given his or her name.

Heroes and Heroines Stories: Ask the students to make up hero/heroine tales about themselves for the next day. The next day, group those with stories together, and those without tales together. Those without tales create their stories in class. Combine mixed groups when everyone has a tale to tell.

Eldest, Middle, Youngest, and Only Child Stories: Begin by telling the *Three Billy Goats Gruff*. In a large group, discuss the advantages and disadvantages of each of the three goats. Also discuss the "what-if" situation of a single, "only child" goat. (You may also bring in an '"only child" story, for example, *Rapunzel* or *Jack and the Beanstalk*, for comparison.) Arrange the students in small groups to share their own stories about the advantages and disadvantages of their position in their families.

Theory Into Practice/5.2

LISTENING TO AND RETELLING TALES

This strategy is a critical step in preparing students to tell a traditional story by heart. We encourage you to learn a favourite story–folktales and fables are good to start with–and tell it to your class without using a script or notes (see Theory into Practice 5.3). Prepare a story that you like and then set up a listening and retelling activity as described below.

Before:

Select a story with a clear structure (this is why folktales are best) and strong possibilities for visualizing characters and scenes. Have the students make predictions based on the title and the story's place of origin. For example, "I am going to tell you the story, *The Name of the Tree* a Bantu tale from Africa. What do you think it might be about? What do the title and place lead you to wonder about?"

Tell the students that they should visualize and focus on sensory images as they listen. If you have not yet taught and practised this as a comprehension strategy (see Chapter 10, Visualization) then do so before this exercise. Tell them you will be asking about their mental pictures after the story.

During:

Listen and visualize.

After:

Ask your listeners to engage in one or more of the following:

- Visualize and form sensory imagery: describe a scene that stands out, one you were able to visualize, and imagine scenes, smells, tastes, feelings, and sounds.
- Compare to other folk tales. Ask the students to discuss differences and similarities; display on a chart or use a Venn diagram (see the section on expository text strategies in Chapter 10).
- Tell and write your own versions.
- Create **tableaux** of three scenes, freezing each one for 10 seconds.
- Retell the story to a partner from the point of view of a minor character or an object.

the students assess and improve their oral language skills, as individuals and as group members. Assessment need not be a formal, separate practice when you listen to a story for the specific purpose of assessing recall, sequencing, and comprehension; you can assess speaking skills as well depending on your desired focus, such as vocabulary use, grammar, fluency, or pronunciation. Many assessment checklists are available for teacher, self, and group assessment of storytelling, drama, and literature circle activities (for example, Swartz, 2002; Daniels, 2002; and Booth, 1996).

STORYTELLING THE TRADITIONAL WAY

WHERE TO BEGIN: SHORT FABLES

Before:

Make a collection of short fables (such as those in Arnold Lobel's *Fables*), and folktales. Organize students in pairs who work well together, and who will help each other to read the story they choose. Assure them that they will not be required to perform a story for the entire class unless they want to.

During:

Each person is given a one-page fable or folktale and reads it several times, at least once out loud to a partner. Work in pairs, as in Figure 5.10. The pairs may be working on the same story to tell in tandem or each may be learning separate stories. The partners practise telling the story to each other *using their own words* and visual images. The pairs should not memorize the text. When they memorize, they just say words. When they make the story their own, they tell a living story.

   Variation: Pairs may choose one story to tell in tandem, called a "two-hander," with the tellers alternating as the story suggests (alternating characters or scenes).

EXPANDING STORYTELLING CIRCLES

When a pair knows its story well enough to tell it without the text or prompts, that pair joins another to form storytelling circles of four, then eight. When the pair has told the story at least three or four times, it is ready to tell it to the whole class, and eventually to other classes.

After:

When you and the students have participated in story circles several times, you may be ready for a public performance for another class or for parents. The storytelling session usually ends with the following verse:

> *Three apples fell from heaven*
> *One for the teller,*
> *One for the listener,*
> *And one for the one who heard.*

SELF-ASSESSMENT THROUGH META-TALK

We now focus on students' growth in oral communication abilities through self-assessment within the context of literacy learning through talk. We emphasize self-assessment through meta-talk—talk about talk.

   We recognize how important it is that your students realize the value of talk in their learning. Students develop their speaking and listening skills in contexts such as literature circles and storytelling. This development is more likely if *they talk about these activities* with their groups. In addition to becoming aware of how they are doing both as individuals and as a group, meta-talk should include plans for improvement and progress toward good talk that is fair, honest, caring, and collaborative. Literature circles and grand conversations about great literature provide rich contexts for this kind of progress. While the students are engaging in real discussions about issues that matter to them, they are co-constructing the kind of **recursive** development of literacy so essential to achieving full *literary literacy* as Deanne Bogdan (1992) calls it. Taking time for self-assessment through meta-talk becomes part of this learning—learning that has cognitive, social, emotional, and moral dimensions. Without the social structure of the discussion group scaffolded by an effective teacher, these improvements would not be possible. But can teachers assess progress toward good talk that enhances literacy development?

recursive learning A learning strategy that focuses on repeating or returning to previous learning in order to build new learning.

We have developed Figure 5.11 based partly on Cambourne's conditions of literacy learning and partly on Bogdan et al.'s (2000) method for combining literary experiences or "direct participating responses," with literary criticism to gradually construct an integrated "literary literacy." We have added the vital ingredient of talk about literary experiences and meta-talk about the discussion groups in order to enhance literacy. The

---

FIGURE 5.10 Terry Campbell's Ten Steps for Storytellers

1. Choose a story you really like. Plan to read at least 10 stories, until the right story chooses you.
2. Read it silently several times, picturing the story in your mind as you read.
3. Read the story out loud to your partner.
4. Visualize all the details of the story and discuss this with your partner.
5. Create a storyboard, using at least three cartoon boxes, to show the main events of the story with pictures and captions. (You will be using this to help you learn to tell the story.)
6. Tell the story to your partner using your storyboard. Don't worry about using the exact words from the book.
7. Tell the story again, without the storyboard. Remember to visualize as you tell.
8. Re-read the story from the book to check for missing parts, or special words you want to remember.
9. PRACTISE! PRACTISE! PRACTISE!
10. Trust the story and yourself. Tell it to your story circle.

Note: The goal is to be able to tell a tale in the ancient way. The idea is to make the whole story your own, rather than memorizing the words.

STOP, THINK, AND WRITE

■ How do you assess your own communication with friends, colleagues, parents, administrators, and students?

■ In Chapter 4, we discussed listener self assessment. What about your practices as a speaker?

■ Do you monitor your delivery in terms of volume, pitch, timing, and animation? How do you know if you have improved?

■ Do you ensure your own literacy development by talking about what you are reading, including novels and professional texts?

■ Have you kept your reading up to date so that you are articulate, using recent vocabulary about contemporary practices?

■ Have you tried to learn something new in the spoken arts, such as storytelling, or reciting poetry by heart?

■ Try storytelling yourself before you try teaching it to your students. Your performance does not have to be professional. If you choose a story you feel enthusiastic about, your students will be enthralled!

literacy notebook
5.4

key learning, which can be assessed by both teachers and students, is the growing ability to clearly articulate and to refine a point of view. Points of view include the expression of literary interpretations of the text and meta-talk about group processes and the value of talk in learning about multiple points of view.

Figure 5.11 is a simplified guide to a complex process. The crucial role of great literature in these processes is discussed in Chapter 6.

Figure 5.12 is a student self-assessment checklist that has been modified to include meta-talk. Most of the questions require self-monitoring of speaking and listening behaviours, while some refer explicitly to the quality of the talk as an individual and as a group. This self-assessment is easily adaptable for students in early primary grades by using "yes" or "no" responses or happy/sad symbols for the categories of good speaker, good listener, and sharing of ideas and by limiting each category to two to three criteria, phrased in language suitable for the grade level. Where self-assessment is carried out with a teacher, it can be used in its present form in a conference. The items in the checklist can be modified to fit the grade level and the discussion format. Such an extensive self-assessment would be used occasionally—not after every discussion.

FIGURE 5.11 A Three-Phase Process toward Progress in "Good Talk"

	Reading and Talking	Meta-talk
Demonstration and Engagement	Engaging with texts; early talk sessions include asking questions and sharing initial responses.	Teacher, peers, or sample dialogue from texts overtly model "good talk" in literary discussions.
Immersion and Identification	Strong engagement with texts and with other group members. Revisions and reconstructions of initial responses begin.	Group members participate in and talk about processes and dynamics, including how talking and listening allow seeing others' points of view.
Return Engagement	Re-reading, talking about reading and responses; revising, reading, and talking about related readings. Critical awareness, listening to alternative perspectives, and ongoing formulations and refinements of moral and literary points of view.	Continuing rounds of talk about how conversations are meeting criteria of "good talk" and the role of talking and listening in learning how to better articulate one's own point of view; include the impact of listening to other perspectives.

Source: Campbell (2005, pp. 223-4).

Moving On

In this chapter, we have explored many of the ways literacy develops *through talk* and emphasized the central role of discussion as a powerful means of building classroom community, improving literacy skills, and increasing literary awareness. Special attention was given to what research has to tell us about the role of the teacher in discussion groups. Moving from theory into practice, specific "tried and true" strategies were suggested: literature circles, grand conversations, readers' theatre, and a variety of storytelling activities. We concluded with some ideas for assessing talk in the context of these classroom activities and stressed the importance of student self-assessment to encourage growth in oral language as well as increasing awareness through meta-talk of the value of talk in learning. The goal for teachers and students is to fully appreciate the crucial role talking and listening plays in our social learning-teaching environments, both inside and beyond the classroom walls. One

FIGURE 5.12 Self-Assessment of Collaborative Group Discussions (Recommended for Grades 3–6)

I talked with the group about how I can improve as a: A. Speaker B. Listener C. Ideas Collaborator	Never	Often	Comments
A. As a speaker			
1. I spoke so everyone could hear me.			
2. I made eye contact with the group members.			
3. I contributed my fair share to the discussion.			
(a) more than I should have			
(b) less than I should have			
4. I feel group members listened to me.			
B. As a listener			
5. I listened to each speaker.			
6. I did not interrupt the speaker.			
7. I thought about the speaker's ideas.			
8. I made comments or asked questions.			
C. As a collaborator			
9. I was prepared for the discussion (I read the text, had questions ready, and brought all needed materials).			
10. I expressed my ideas clearly and backed them up with reasons and evidence from the text.			
11. I think I spoke so that everyone could understand me.			
12. I extended other students' ideas.			
13. When I disagreed, I made sure I understood the other point of view, and backed up my view with reasons.			
14. After listening to others, I thought again about my own view, and changed or refined it, or found better reasons to support it.			
15. I helped keep the discussion on topic.			
16. I helped keep the discussion fair for everyone.			
17. I participated in the "group talk" after the discussion.			
18. I talked with the group about how we can improve our discussions.			

Source: Adapted from Collins Block (2001, p. 175).

clear and powerful way of communicating across the walls of difference is through the ability to speak articulately and listen attentively.

In Chapter 6, we will explore the importance of story and of high quality children's literature in literacy development and learning. We will discuss how essential it is that teachers are aware of the characteristics of high quality children's literature and the impact that it has in the classroom and beyond.

> *It matters very little what one knows if one cannot express and communicate what one knows.*
> —Northrop Frye

LIT-FOLIO UPDATE

Do you treat talk as *"a matter of deliberate concern for teaching and learning"* (Rubin, 1990)?

Consider what might count as evidence to include in your portfolio that you personally have shown growth in your awareness of the role of talk in your own learning, and in the learning processes of your students. Have you learned a poem and recited it to your students? Have you told an anecdotal story or a favourite folktale? What plans do your have to encourage the full development of your students' voices, in the fullest sense of "voice," that is, speaking with authenticity and authority?

LIT-FOLIO TIP

The next time you are involved in a group discussion, complete the self-assessment form in Figure 5.14 and then comment on the possible uses of this self-assessment for your students in the classroom.

While on placement, learn a poem or a story by heart and recite or tell it to your students during read aloud time. Record their oral responses.

Resources to Support Your Learning

Teacher Resources for Storytelling

* Barton B., & Booth, D. (1990). *Stories in the classroom.* Markham, ON: Pembroke Publishers.
* Barton, B. (1992). *Stories to tell.* Markham, ON: Pembroke Publishers.
* Barton, B. (1986). *Tell me another: Storytelling and reading aloud at home, at school, and in the community.* Portsmouth, NH: Heinemann.
* Booth, D. W., & Lundy, C. J. (1985). *Improvisation: Learning through drama.* Toronto, ON: Harcourt Brace Jovanovich.
* Booth, D. (1996). *Literacy techniques.* Markham, ON: Pembroke Publishers.
* Booth, D. (2005). *Story drama.* Markham, ON: Pembroke Publishers.
* Booth, D. (2000). *Story works: How teachers can use shared stories in the new curriculum.* Markham, ON: Pembroke Publishers.
  Cornett, C. E., & Smithrim, K. L. (2001). *The arts as meaning makers: Integrating literature and the arts throughout the curriculum.* Canadian Edition. Toronto, ON: Prentice-Hall.
  Daniels, H. (2002). *Literature circles: Voice and choice in book clubs and reading groups.* Markham, ON: Pembroke Publishers.
  Peterson, R., & Eeds, M. (1990). *Grand conversations: Literature groups in action.* Richmond Hill, ON: Scholastic.
  Rog, L.J. (2001). *Early literacy instruction in Kindergarten.* Newark, DE: International Reading Association.
* Swartz, Larry. (2002). *The new dramathemes.* Markham, ON: Pembroke Publishers.
* Trehearne, M. (2000). *The Kindergarten teacher's resource book.* Scarborough, ON: Nelson.
  Wells, G. (1986). *The meaning makers.* Portsmouth, NH: Heinemann.
* Worthy, J. (2005). *Readers" Theatre for building fluency.* Toronto ON: Scholastic.

Children's Literature

Literature Focus Unit Comparing Cinderella Versions

Bubba the cowboy prince, Helen Ketteman (fractured Cinderella story)
Fanny's dream, Caralyn Bruehner
Mufaro's beautiful daughters: An African tale, John Steptoe
The Egyptian Cinderella, Shirley Climo
The Irish Cinderlad, Shirley Climo
The rough-face girl, Rafe Martin
The Korean Cinderella, Shirley Climo
Yeh-Shen: a Cinderella story from China, retold by Ai-Ling Louie

Folktales for Telling

Knots on a counting rope, Bill Martin, Jr.
Something from nothing, Phoebe Gilman
The bone talker, Shelley A. Leedahl
The name of the tree, Celia Barker Lottridge
The trial of the stone, Richardo Keens Douglas
The wolf of Gubbio, Michael Bedard

Traditional Literature Anthologies for Storytelling and Drama

* *Canadian fairy tales,* Eva Martin
  English fairy tales, collected by Joseph Jacobs
  Fables, Arnold Lobel
  Favorite folktales from around the world, Jane Yolen, ed.
  Once upon a time, Alan Garner
* *Out of the everywhere: New tales for Canada,* Jan Andrews, ed.
  The magic orange tree, Diane Wolkstein, ed.
  The wonder child and other Jewish fairy tales, Howard Swartz, et al.
  World folktales, Atelia Clarkson, ed.

For Early Primary Learners (suitable for read alouds, storytelling, and discussion)

Chester's Way, Kevin Henkes
Chrysanthemum, Kevin Henkes
Goldilocks and the three bears, Jan Brett
How the robin got its red breast: A legend of the Sechelt people, Charlie Craig
Just one more story, Dugald Steer
Little Red Riding Hood, James Marshall
Lon Po Po: A Red-Riding Hood story from China, Ed Young
Officer Buckle and Gloria, Peggy Rathman
Rapunzel, Rumplestiltskin, Hansel and Gretel, Paul O. Zelinsky
Seven blind mice, Ed Young
The gingerbread boy, Paul Galdone
The mitten, Jan Brett
The napping house, Audrey Wood
The three billy goats gruff, Robert Bender
The three little pigs, Paul Galdone

There was an old lady who swallowed a fly, Simms Taback
This little pig stayed home, Donna Guthrie
Wemberly worried, Kevin Henkes
Wemberly's weekend, Kevin Henkes
Who's in rabbit's house? (African Masai tale),
    Verna Aardema

Books for Read Alouds and Storytelling

Something from nothing, Phoebe Gilman
Talk, talk: an Ashanti legend, retold by
    Deborah M. Newton Chocolate
The crane wife, retold by Sumiko Yagawa, translated by
    Katherine Paterson
The legend of the bluebonnet, Tomie dePaola
The legend of the lady slipper: An Ojibwe tale, retold by
    Lise Lunge-Larson, Margi Preus
✤ *The name of the tree*, Celia Barker Lottridge
✤ *The trial of the stone*, Richardo Keens Douglas
The wolf of Gubbio, Michael Bedard

Developing Primary Problem Books for Literature Circles Discussion

A chair for my mother, Vera B. Williams
Ira sleeps over, Bernard Waber
Smoky night, Eve Bunting
The ghost-eye tree, Bill Martin, Jr.
The hundred dresses, Eleanor Estes

Junior Level Books for Literature Circles

Knots on a counting rope, Bill Martin, Jr.
Monster Mama, Liz Rosenberg
Rose Blanche, Roberto Innocenti
Sarah and the people of Sand River, W. D. Valgardson
Smoky night (also *The wall*, *Fly away home*), Eve Bunting
The bone talker, Shelley A. Leedahl
The divorced kids club and other stories, W. D. Valgardson
The table where rich people sit, Byrd Baylor

Problem Novels for Literature Circles

Are you there, God? It's me, Margaret, Judy Blume
Journey, Patricia MacLachlan

Keri, Jan Andrews
✤ *Lesia's Dream*, Laura Langston
✤ *Naomi's road*, Joy Kogawa
✤ *Owls in the family*, Farley Mowat
Sadako and the thousand paper cranes, Eleanor Coerr
✤ *Shadow in Hawthorn Bay*, Janet Lunn
✤ *Underground to Canada*, Barbara Smucker

Websites

Resources

School Talk: Between the Ideal and the Real World of
    Teaching, an online journal from NCTE:
    http://www.ncte.org/collections/earlyliteracy
The Children's Literature Web Guide (for stories, author
    links, and readers' theatre scripts):
    http://www.acs.ucalgary.ca/~dkbrown
Read Write Think, International Reading Association
    (for high quality lesson plans):
    http://www.readwritethink.org

The Early Years of Schooling

An excellent website from Australia with links to literacy,
    parent participation, and reading:
    http://www.sofweb.vic.edu.au/eys/lit/litpp.htm
Primary English Teachers Association (PETA): Another
    first-rate site from an outstanding association in
    Australia: http://www.peta.edu.au/
NCTE: National Council of Teachers of English, Early
    Literacy Link: http://www.ncte.org/
UNICEF: www.unicef.ca/eng/unicef/story/main.html
✤ Storytellers of Canada/Conteurs du Canada:
    www.sc-cc.com
✤ Storytellers School of Toronto:
    www.storytellingtoronto.org

Website for Conducting Readers' Theatre

Readingonline (International Reading Association):
    http://www.readingonline.org/electronic/carrick/

Starting with Story
Literacy through Literature

All that people have ever thought, done, or dreamed
lies waiting to be discovered in books.
Literature begins with Mother Goose. It includes Sendak
as well as Shakespeare, Milne as much as Milton, and
Carroll before Camus. Children's literature is a part of the
mainstream of all literature, whose source is life itself.
—Charlotte S. Huck

key terms

genre
read aloud
reader response activities
story sense
think aloud

questions to guide your learning

By the end of this chapter, you should understand the key
terms and be able to answer the following questions:

- In what ways is it important for children to develop a
  sense of story? How does this play a role in their literacy
  development?

- How does experience with high quality children's literature
  contribute to literacy and language development?

- Why is it vital that you know how to select quality children's
  books? What are some of the criteria you can use?

- What are some reasons you can offer to those who
  challenge your choices?

- Why is it essential to present a variety of genres, and to
  include many from diverse cultures?

- What purposes does the teacher read aloud serve?

Looking Back, Looking Ahead

In Chapter 5, we emphasized the importance of talk and discussion in language development, and we suggested a range of strategies to engage learners in authentic talk for learning. The language development strategies introduced there will be referred to often in this chapter, which focuses on the key role of literature in literacy development. Oral language, story, literature, and literacy are closely interwoven. Oral language is the initial vehicle of the story and the best children's literature can often be traced to traditional beginnings in oral cultures. The emergence and growth of literacy is nurtured through story—in both its spoken and written forms. Good stories inspire good talk. Reading and sharing stories play an important part in the continuous development of both oral language and literacy.

This chapter underscores the importance of story and of children's literature in literacy development and learning. We will discuss how essential it is for teachers to know the characteristics of children's literature and the impact that good literature has in the classroom and beyond. Literature will be explored for its teaching and learning value for language-based abilities, for social aptitude, and for the development of emotional well-being and moral awareness.

As a child I was immersed in story—living the literature of everyday life—without really being consciously aware of the powerful role narrative was playing in my life. Story made my world come alive, sparking my imagination and creating a sense of wonder and enjoyment. Even the most mundane, everyday story that a relative or neighbor told was often sprinkled with adventure and intrigue.
—Richard T. Vacca

Why *Story?*

Stories are how we explain, how we teach, how we entertain ourselves, and how we often do all three at once.
—Robert Fulford

Why are stories so important in literacy learning? Would it not be possible for a child to become literate through non-fictional print—environmental print, everyday transactions such as letters, lists, and messages, the world of newspapers, magazines, informational texts, the instructions

STOP, THINK, AND WRITE

Think back to your childhood.

- How important were stories when you were growing up?
- Were stories told in your family and by your friends and neighbours?
- Do you remember stories being read to you? At home? At school?
- Make particular note of any differences between your home and school experiences with stories, both in oral form and in books.
- Do you believe these experiences played a role in your learning to read, and learning to love reading?
- What stories and books do you remember most vividly?
- What made them memorable?

Examine your beliefs

- Do you believe all children, regardless of their background, can learn to read and can learn to love reading?
- Do you believe that good literature is the best vehicle for teaching children how to read and write?

Challenge

- What can you do to enrich the story life of children who enter school without the experience of listening to stories being told and read to them?

for video games? Technically, there is no reason why the sole use of such materials would not allow the successful acquisition of literacy. Certainly they should not be neglected; understanding how non-fictional print works is a crucial aspect of full literacy, since this is a major part of real-life reading and writing. But what would children be missing if they were not immersed in story as part of their journey toward literacy?

Let's look first at some of the research on the role of narrative and story sense in linguistic and literacy development, and in social and emotional development. Evidence is available in educational and psychological theory and research about why story matters. Bruno Bettelheim (1976) and Howard Gardner (1991) explain the role of story in healthy mental and emotional development. Lev Vygotsky (1962, 1978) supports its role in social and cognitive development. Literary theorists such as

Northrop Frye (1963) and Robert Fulford (1999) have shown how it is through narrative that we learn to give form and meaning to our lives.

When Gordon Wells (1986) conducted his 15-year longitudinal research into language development, he found evidence of the central role of story sense in children's extending control over language and long-range literacy success. Wells observed that young children learned language through a collaborative meaning-making process, a collaboration that occurred naturally in conversations between parent and child while they were engaged in activities of mutual interest. By contrast, in most learning situations at school, the teacher did most of the talking and asked the kinds of questions that actually limited children's participation in conversation. But Wells's most important finding was that listening to stories read aloud at home was the best predictor of school achievement.

> Of three frequently occurring activities [looking and talking about a picture book, listening to stories, and drawing and writing] that had been considered as possibly helpful preparation for the acquisition of literacy, only one was significantly associated with later test scores...That activity was listening to stories. (p. 151)

Wells found that even when children came to school as competent oral language users, if their preschool experiences did not include lots of stories listened to and talked about, they did not do well in terms of literacy and long-term school achievement. Why are frequent experiences with listening to stories and talking about them so crucial? Wells suggests three main reasons.

First of all, when children listen to stories long before they can read themselves, they begin to gain experience with "the sustained meaning-building organization of written language and its characteristic rhythms and structures" (p. 151). When they come to read books on their own, the language will be familiar. Those children who are familiar only with context-bound language are not as able to make sense of the de-contextualized language of books.

Second, children can extend the range of their experiences through story. In this way, they develop a richer mental model of the world, as well as an expanded vocabulary.

Third, stories provide a perfect starting point for collaborative talk between parents and children. Through strong interactive conversations about a story, parents can help children explore their own world in light of what happens in the story, and to use their own experience to understand the characters and events in the story. These conversations are vital.

Such talk and the stories that give rise to it also provide a validation for the child's own inner storying—that internal mode of meaning making which is probably as deeply rooted in human nature as is language itself.

(Wells, 1986, p. 152)

More recently, other researchers have reached similar conclusions regarding the fundamental role of literature and story sense in the development of literacy. For example, a study of a Grade 2 literature-based reading-writing program revealed that over the school year the students "demonstrated high levels of engagement with books, developed skill in word identification, fluency, and comprehension; and grew in written comprehension abilities" (Gambrell, Morrow, & Pennington, 2000, p. 6).

In their article "Literature for literacy: What research says about the benefits of using trade books in the classroom," Lee Galda and Bernice Cullinan (2003) cite wide-ranging support for the following links between literature in the form of quality trade books—books intended for general readership, not just for school reading—and literacy development.

Parents can help children explore their world through story.

READING ACHIEVEMENT

In the pre-school years, being read to has been shown to promote a positive association with books (Holdaway, 1979), familiarity with the concepts and conventions of print (Clay, 1979), an understanding of the differences between oral and written language (Smith, 1978/1979), and familiarity with the language of narrative. "Children who spend time interacting with adults around books develop understandings about the functions and the processes of reading that help them develop literacy skills when they enter the traditional classroom" (Galda & Cullinan, 2003, p. 641).

Many studies highlight the positive effects of reading stories and books aloud to children throughout the school years. In a study of students with a low socio-economic status, a group of 4-year-olds were read to daily one-on-one. After 10 weeks, they were asking better and more frequent questions, giving more interpretative responses to the stories, and responding more often to print and story structure (Morrow, 1988).

Studies conducted in the higher grades show that students continue to enjoy being read to well into secondary school, that this is an important factor in their positive attitude toward books and an interest in reading, and that this results in their reading more often. Other studies show a strong link between frequent reading and stronger reading ability: "those who read most read best" (Galda & Cullinan, 2003, p. 643).

Reading and listening to literature builds the essential background knowledge required for comprehending stories encountered later. This prior knowledge includes awareness of narrative **schema** and of life experience in general, since every story contributes to the students' storehouse of knowledge of people and the world.

schema (*pl.* **schemata**) Organizing principle, such as a rule, script, or concept based on a learner's prior knowledge.

ORAL LANGUAGE DEVELOPMENT

Being read to from good literature positively affects children's general language development. Galda and Cullinan (2003) cite studies that show a positive relationship between experiences with literature and

- vocabulary development
- use of increasingly sophisticated syntactic and semantic schemata
- increase in students' "linguistic data pool," using previous encounters with stories to make sense of subsequent language encounters.

WRITING

Some studies have shown evidence of a link between reading literature and becoming a capable writer, with a variety of reasons for this link.

- There are similarities between the acts of comprehending and composing (Goodman & Goodman, 1983).
- Doing one affects the ability to do the other (Smith, 1983).
- Contact with literature provides young writers with exposure to "a variety of lexical and syntactical choices as well as to a variety of narrative patterns that they then may call on in their own production of written text" (Chomsky, 1972, cited in Galda & Cullinan, 2003, p. 643).
- The narrative schemata found in children's books, especially those using folktale schemata, "serve as 'rhetorical models' for beginning writers" (Galda & Cullinan, 2003, p. 643).
- "Children exposed to quality literature reflected that quality in their own narrative writing" (Dressel, 1990; Lancia, 1997 cited in Galda & Cullinan, 2003, p. 643).

CLASSROOM COMMUNITY

Classrooms rich in story contribute to the formation of socially collaborative communities in which learning thrives. Having a classroom full of good books is not just an aesthetic frill; there is strong research support for the connections between positive social experiences with literature and good models, and literacy learning (Galda & Cullinan, 2003, p. 643). One study in particular is worth mentioning. In their "Book Club" project, McMahon and Raphael (1997) developed a classroom model involving the sharing of reading and writing, including small group discussions in book clubs using children's literature. "Book clubs extended the social nature of the classroom by providing opportunities for students to interact in a structured manner" as well as opportunities for "demonstrations of fluent reading behaviours" and "for linking the language arts" (Galda & Cullinan, 2003, p. 644). This is further evidence to support our theory that good books stimulate good talk, and that this promotes further growth in literacy.

A classroom community that is rich in story promotes further growth in literacy.

The best of children's literature keeps us all grounded in that powerful touchstone to our own humanity—*story*. We humans are storytelling animals. The drive to story is basic in all people, and exists in all cultures. Stories shape our lives and our culture—we cannot seem to live without them (Booth & Barton, 2000).

Why High-Quality Children's Literature?

A literature program should help students understand the formal elements of literature and lead them to prefer the best that our literature has to offer. Children need to hear and read fine literature and to appreciate authors who not only have something to say but also say it extremely well. Educators must be able to identify the best books in literature and share these books with children.

—Jack Zipes et al., *Norton Anthology of Children's Literature*

Why is it important that you use high-quality children's literature, the best that our literature has to offer? Why should you be knowledgeable about children's literature, and especially about what makes certain books outstanding?

First of all, literature is part of our cultural inheritance as members of our own communities and of the world community. When we study children's books and determine what makes some excellent and others inferior, we are using criteria that apply to all literature for any age. Children's literature has a distinctive status, since it is primarily based on the body of stories we have inherited from unknown authors through our various oral traditions. These include folktales, fables, myths, legends, and folk rhymes from around the world. These stories form the basic structure upon which all literature is constructed; they tell of journeys into danger and safe return, of struggles where good deeds are rewarded, and of finding lasting values and one's true identity. As Northrop Frye (1963) put it, quoting a line from the Robert Graves poem *To Juan at the Winter Solstice*, "there is one story and one story only." This story is "of the loss and regaining of identity"—of leaving home and returning—and is, according to Frye, "the framework of all literature" (pp. 19-21). We can see how stories such as Beatrix Potter's *The Tale of Peter Rabbit*, Maurice Sendak's *Where the Wild Things Are*, and C.S. Lewis's *The Chronicles of Narnia*, have the same circular plot as Homer's *The Odyssey*. Peter Rabbit, Max, and the four Pevensie children leave home, take risks, encounter dangers, get lost, and then find their way home again—just like Odysseus.

Second, children's literature is worthy of our respect and critical scrutiny because it is widely understood to be crucial to children's literacy and to their learning in the broadest sense. Good books provide children with knowledge about the world and their place in that world alongside other human beings who are both alike and different from them. Good books "inform the intellect" (Frye, 1963) with factual knowledge and problem-solving strategies; they cultivate the imagination with what-ifs, and foster an appreciation of the power of language.

These two reasons identify literature as uniquely suited, indeed indispensable to a child's developing literary background. This background is essential to becoming literate in the fullest sense, where being literate includes the ability to understand and appreciate all forms of text from newspapers to poems. Children need to recognize and become familiar with the structures of traditional literature as these will be found in most of the books they will encounter, and will become the foundation for their own writing. These traditional and formal text structures will be further explored in Chapters 9 and 10.

Interwoven with the role of literature in the reading and writing dimensions of literacy is its role in providing the linguistic structures for oral language growth. As discussed in Chapter 5, this has important social repercussions. However, knowledge of literary language provides more than a means of communicating well; it allows learners to participate with confidence and enjoyment in discussions with peers and adults about particular stories and about literature in general. This allows learners to become part of the "literacy club" (Smith, 1988). A large part of the aesthetic pleasure and the pure entertainment value of many stories is due to this background knowledge and the ability to express this knowledge through re-telling and comparing. Imagine how difficult it would be for a child to enjoy and talk about Jon Scieszka's spoof, *The True Story of the Three Little Pigs!* without knowing the original folktale. A wide background in traditional literature provides children with what Jane Yolen (1981) terms "a landscape of allusion."

> *As the child hears more stories and tales that are linked in both obvious and subtle ways, that landscape is broadened and deepened, and becomes more fully populated with memorable characters. These are the same folk that the child will meet again and again… Stories lean on stories, art on art. This familiarity with the treasure-house of ancient story is necessary for a true appreciation of today's literature. (p. 15)*

Terry's Favourite Books as a Child

My favourite story growing up was *The Tale of Peter Rabbit*, by Beatrix Potter. It was the first book I took out of the public library when I was five years old. It has the wonderful language and gorgeous water colours of course, but I think what really attracted me was the size; its smallness made it seem like a treasure, which it is. Now my favourite children's books include *The Secret Garden*, by Frances Hodgson Burnett and the C.S. Lewis's Narnia series. I realize now that all of these books are connected by the magic garden theme, and by the fact that they are most beautiful when read aloud.

A Few of Michelann's Favourites

The books that stood out in my childhood were *And to Think that I Saw it on Mulberry Street*, by Dr. Seuss and *Are You My Mother?* by P. D. Eastman. As a tween, I was an avid mystery reader and loved the Nancy Drew, Trixie Belden, the Bobbsey Twins Series, and *Harriet the Spy*. Later in my teen years, I immersed myself in case studies of students with emotional and social differences. The ones that have stuck with me over the years and the ones I continually return to are *P.S. Your Not Listening* by Eleanor Craig and *Lovey* by Mary MacKracken. As an adult, I cannot part with *Frederick* by Leo Lionni, the tale of a fieldmouse who realizes the transformational power of language, and *The Giver, Gathering Blue*, and *Messenger*, all by Lois Lowry, which talk of world views and the work we, as human beings, do in this world. Literature, both children's and adults', is a central force in my world; it gives me a sense of permanence, the chance to escape every once in a while, and the opportunity for immense growth and learning.

Qualities of First-Rate Children's Literature

What are the qualities of a first-rate children's book? We have identified the following: appeal, good story, vivid language, richness, true-to-life story, not too moralistic, and integrity. These qualities are common to our childhood (and adulthood) favourites as well as to those works that have been critically acknowledged as "greats."

Appeal

Children's books with appeal are books that are delightful, entertaining, and enlightening for children. They engage children on an emotional and intellectual level because they portray characters with whom they can identify and situations that are familiar enough for them to understand. Even when the main character is an animal—for example Peter Rabbit—children can relate to the story essentials of disobedience, getting lost, and returning to safety. Children can even identify with an adult central character such as Cinderella (in all of her many versions from various cultures), a struggling underdog character type, whose personal qualities may include being caring, resourceful, brave, and honest.

Good Story

First-rate children's literature must have drama that unfolds through a clear, clean plot structure. For younger children, this means a linear plot, sequenced with a definite beginning, middle, and end. Stories with subplots and flashbacks can be introduced with older children, but should be well-structured so that readers or listeners are able to follow. A good story should focus on a limited number of characters, a distinct problem, and a clearly delineated setting. There should be a real problem or conflict, with rising dramatic action, and a solution, along with a strong forward momentum allowing children to become caught up in the action.

Vivid Language

Language must make the story come alive. It should not be overly complex for the young reader or listener, but yet it should offer some challenges—

STOP, THINK, AND WRITE

Without background knowledge of folklore, imagine a young reader trying to understand and take pleasure in reading the poem "Picture Puzzle Piece" by Shel Silverstein, which makes reference to Snow White and her stepmother, a magic bean, a woman who lived in a shoe, an evil genie inside a bottle, and a witch of the West.

Discuss the following questions with a partner before writing down your thoughts.

■ Most of the allusions in the Silverstein poem refer to literature that would be familiar to those steeped in Western culture. Does making sure that your students are familiar with these staples of the English language mean that we value this body of literature over those from diverse cultures?

■ How can we ensure balance has been achieved in our book selection and teaching procedures?

such as descriptive or technical vocabulary. In *Miss Rumphius,* for example, Barbara Cooney describes a conservatory where "the warm moist air wrapped itself around her, and the sweet smell of jasmine filled her nose." If there are illustrations, the language and pictures should enhance one another. In *Miss Rumphius* there is a clear illustration of a conservatory. If there are no illustrations, there must be sufficient description for the reader to visualize the setting and characters. Dialogue should add to characterization and move the plot along. Finally, because children's stories are often read aloud, the language should be poetic, vivid, and powerful; it should flow with an easy rhythm and be pleasing to the ear.

Richness

First-rate literature offers many layers and the possibility of multiple interpretations, stimulating conversation, and the possibility of nurturing literary awareness. One of the reasons for this is that literary forms such as novels written for young adults provide richly detailed representations of many types of characters, in a wide variety of social, historical, cultural, and moral settings. Usually the main characters are depicted embroiled in conflicts and dilemmas that are complicated and engaging, and, therefore, are worth discussing. In the case of simpler stories, such as those told in picture books, high-quality books offer an original way of looking at an old situation; it stretches the reader's mind by offering a new perspective and invites transformation.

True-to-Life Story

Strong literature addresses truths about life, regardless of possible controversy. For example, *The Tenth Good Thing about Barney*, a picture book by Judith Viorst, and *Bridge to Terabithia*, a novel by Katherine Paterson, tell two very different stories about children coming to terms with death. The first book, (which is suitable for Primary children in Grades 1 to 3), is about a young boy dealing with the death of his pet cat. The second book (suitable for late Junior to Intermediate children in Grades 6-8), involves adolescents in the much more complicated situation of facing the death of a friend.

Sometimes a serious topic is given humorous treatment; for example, Beverly Cleary's *Ramona and Her Father* and Barbara Robinson's *The Best Christmas Pageant Ever* address issues of unemployment, class division, and poverty with humour and sensitivity. In books such as these, topics of real significance are tackled using believable characters, leading the readers to their own valuable insights. David Booth (2000) wrote: "With young adolescents it is often thought that the stories must necessarily be fast-paced and tinged with gore to capture this seemingly complacent audience. Adolescents may appear worldly on the outside, but deep down they want to learn about life's complexities" (p. 43).

Not Too Moralistic

While great literature has the potential to transform the reader morally, and many stories offer lessons through their themes, this should not be an obvious explicit purpose. As Temple et al. (2002) express it: "If a book seems too obviously contrived to teach a lesson, children (and critics) will not tolerate it" (p. 7). The only overt purpose of literature should be to tell a story that will delight, entertain, move, or enlighten the reader.

Integrity

All of the story elements, including plot, character, setting, problem, theme, illustrations, and language must come together to create a whole, a complete work that says something that matters in an arresting and original way. One of the dimensions of this quality of integrity is the authenticity of the author's voice—the ineffable presence of the writer's personality.

WHO DECIDES?

The above list of qualities may sound as though we are saying that it is the text alone that determines whether a book becomes "great." Our theory of reading—that reading is a transactional and constructive conversation among reader, author, and other readers—means that we do not limit our critical analysis to the qualities of the text alone. Although a successful author must meet the criteria, it is not the author alone who creates a great piece of literature. Nor is it the award jury or the critic. Ultimately, it is the readers who decide, and in the case of children's literature these readers include children, parents, teachers, and librarians, as well as the critics and award juries.

We define "great literature"—including literature designated as children's literature—partly following Northrop Frye (1988), as a collection of literary works that "refuse to go away" (p. 139). This is literature that "insists on its own value" and persists as worth discussing, but that is not part of a sacred canon. This is literature that is also great in a broad sense, and that reflects a wide range of cultural perspectives. Thus, although there may be a core group of books considered great, and this can be attributed in part to their intrinsic value, the list fluctuates over time, as determined by readers.

Truly great literature refuses to go away because readers want to return to it. Greatness, or literary merit, is conferred on texts over time by readers through various means including the reading experience itself, which includes talking and listening with other readers. This requires literature that readers want to continue to be fully engaged with because it delights them, or because they are deeply disturbed by it and are thereby motivated to talk and write about it. This requires literature that inspires the intellect and moves the heart. This requires literature that has the potential to transform, transport, or even "transfigure"[1] the reader. If literature has this power to transform, it can influence for good; however, and this is a significant "however," we must then acknowledge that it can also influence for ill, and we have to be able to come to terms with this. We must now face the thorny issue of censorship.

Censorship and Teacher Censorship through Selection

I believe that good questions are more important than answers, and the best children's books ask questions and make the readers ask questions. And every new question is going to disturb someone's universe.
—Madeleine L'Engle

---

[1]Bogdan (1992), *Re-educating the Imagination*. More than transformation, transfiguration represents a "genuine shift in consciousness" (quoting de Lauretis, 1987, 10) as expressive as "poetry" in the sense that it is "expressive of something fundamental to the human condition" (p. 267).

We presented the L'Engle quotation to a group of teachers and asked them to comment on her words in light of the "current climate of censorship and self-censorship regarding some children's books." Teacher Talk 6.1 contains the response from Carrie McKay, one of those teachers.

Teacher Talk/6.1

CARRIE McKAY EXPRESSES HER POINT OF VIEW ON THE CENSORSHIP QUESTION

This is definitely a discussion topic open to much debate. The only literature I remember from elementary and high school are the works of high quality, which contained something memorable. Whether it be the lesson taught, the battles fought, or the controversy, I can honestly say the only works I even have inklings of are currently not taught (or taught very safely) as a result of censorship or political correctness. Interestingly enough we as teachers are criticized for not teaching critical literacy skills or for not teaching the kids to think. It's awfully hard to teach them to be critical readers when all the topics worthy of their interest have been taken out of the classroom.

I have taught *Shiloh* and *Charlotte's Web* to Junior students and we talked about death and survival of the fittest, etc. I have taught *The Outsiders* to grades 6, 7, and 8 and we talk about gangs and smoking. I have taught Shakespeare to grades 6, 7, and 8 and we talked about the "dirt" in his life and the naughtiness in his plays (even though I am obviously teaching an age-appropriate version). I have taught *Catcher in the Rye* and *Animal Farm* to Grade 8s and the students were interested and they read the books. When I teach with books without any controversy or real-life in them, the kids don't read and they don't write.

I always let my principal know what I am teaching and how we will handle the topics and ask them to direct any concerns to me. Not once have I not been supported. Having said that, I am careful to teach to my audience appropriately—so yes, I self-censor. But, I would prefer to self-censor and still use great works of children's literature than be censored and not introduce the children to these works at all. My usual response to a parent telling me that Shakespeare is too raunchy for their child or that *Charlotte's Web* is too sad is to ask them if they only let their children watch G movies. Then I ask them which types of movies they are allowed to watch, most of which are far more graphic and controversial than any of the books we are reading. And, I always invite the parents to read the books with their children and to discuss any issues or concerns as they arise if they are worried that I will not be doing it satisfactorily. Not once has it ever gone beyond this point. Having said that, I always have a backup book and unit ready for a student just in case a parent does continue with their complaint.

My only warning to new teachers is to make sure your principal will support you beforehand. My Grade 7/8 class presented *A Midsummer Night's Dream*. We had boys dressed as girls and girls dressed as boys. Not once was there an issue about cross-dressing or sexual overtones among the kids. They could have cared less that one of the lead male love-interests was a girl or that some of the fairies were boys with wings and flowers in their hair until we presented it to the parents. A few of the dads had heart failure at first but as the play unfolded to cheering parents, everyone recovered from their issues.

Carrie McKay is an Ottawa-area elementary school teacher.

McKay makes several well-argued points, and justifies them from a strong knowledge base about literature and about her students, an openness about what she is teaching and how, and a willingness to remain flexible. But what can teachers do when a student, group of students, or parents find a work of literature so offensive that they insist on its removal from the classroom or school library?

Here we are thinking of extreme cases such as one that occurred in Toronto, where parents and students objected to the inclusion of *Lord of the Flies* in the curriculum because of its use of a deeply insulting word referring to persons of colour. Setting aside the issues surrounding the principle of non-censorship, we believe that sensitivity to both students and their parents is essential, as McKay suggested. Facing similar objections is the new edition of the banned *Little Black Sambo*, which, it has been argued, featured a stereotypical colonial portrayal of persons of colour. Should books that are challenged be removed entirely so that they can offend no one? Or should they be retained and, with knowledgeable teacher guidance, be used to address issues of "critical literacy"?

What can teachers do when well-meaning, protective parents want to shield their children from any book containing anything unpleasant, sad, or violent? As McKay pointed out, this would rule out children's classics such as *Charlotte's Web*. Without "unpleasant" and even "violent" conflicts, what would become of stories about King Arthur, or Snow White, or stories such as *The Lion, the Witch and the Wardrobe*?

From her perspective as a well-known children's author, Katherine Paterson has this to say about the censorship of one of her books:

> *Though no one has ever told me why* Bridge to Terabithia *is on the Banned Books List of the American Booksellers Association, I must conclude that it is the scene in which the articulate Mr. Aarons seeks to comfort his grieving son. "Hell, ain't it?" he says. I tried to comfort my son when his best friend died, and it* was *hell, though I think fire is the wrong image. Hell is not burning but utter coldness. It is the desolation, the outer darkness, the separation from the one who loves us.*

> *Nobody has ever told me that she was uplifted or refreshed by reading* Bridge to Terabithia. *People tell me how angry they were or how much they wept. But you see, my job is not to expand vocabularies or teach proper, reverent speech, or even, in the most obvious sense, to uplift. My job is to tell a story—a story about real people who live in the world as it is. I dare to believe that such stories, even when they are painful, have a power to illumine the reader in a way that a nice tale with exemplary characters does not. But then, I know that the only raw material I have for the stories I tell lies deep within myself, and somehow when I go in-*

side I find there a troubled child reaching up for comfort and under-standing (1989, p. 137).

We do not have the absolute answers, since teachers must make collaborative decisions based on an empathetic response to local contexts. Our own experience, and that of many of our colleagues, suggests that the following conditions help us to make the best decisions:

- knowledge of a wide range of children's literature (as teachers we are obliged to read the books and to read about them)

- knowledge of our students, parents, and administration

- knowledge of the issues and the ability to articulate our own point of view

- sensitivity to and respect for our students as individuals and as members of distinct cultural communities with their points of view

One suggestion is that we stay informed about the topic of censorship—which books are being challenged, and why. The American Library Association (www.ala.org) keeps lists of "most frequently challenged books" along with databases with analysis of challenging institutions and the types of reasons given. It is sobering to see how many children's books headline the "100 Most Frequently Challenged Books." Among the top 10, only two are not children's book.

1. *Scary Stories* (Series), Alvin Schwartz
2. *Daddy's Roommate*, Michael Willhoite
3. *I Know Why the Caged Bird Sings*, Maya Angelou
4. *The Chocolate War*, Robert Cormier
5. *The Adventures of Huckleberry Finn*, Mark Twain
6. *Of Mice and Men*, John Steinbeck
7. *Harry Potter* (Series), J.K. Rowling
8. *Forever*, Judy Blume
9. *Bridge to Terabithia*, Katherine Paterson
10. *Alice* (Series), Phyllis Reynolds Naylor

As one well-known children's author said:

[I]t's not just the books under fire now that worry me. It is the books that will never be written. The books that will never be read. And all due to the fear of censorship. As always, young readers will be the real losers.
— Judy Blume

Culturally Diverse Literature

Since the question of censorship often arises in the context of members of minority groups, including those with distinct cultural and religious beliefs, an important preventative measure is the inclusion of a wide range of literature representing diverse cultural origins.

We are fortunate to have an excellent selection of Canadian quality children's books representing our multiplicity of cultural and historical perspectives. Figure 6.1 contains a small sample of these books.

Reading and listening to a wide variety of traditional and contemporary tales from around the world and from the cultural worlds within our own and our neighbouring communities is a powerful way to open doors to new perspectives, to build cultural awareness and multiethnic understanding. In addition to this plurality of points of view, we find

---

FIGURE 6.1 Multicultural Literature

Andrews, Jan, *The Very Last First Time* (about an Inuit girl)

Edmunds, Yvette, *Yuit* (Traditional Inuit)

Eyvindson, Peter, *Red Parka Mary* (contemporary Aboriginal)

Garrigue, Sheila, *The Eternal Spring of Mr. Ito* (Japanese Canadian internment in WWII)

Gilman, Phoebe, *Something from Nothing* (Jewish folktale)

Gilmore, Rachna, *Roses for Gita* and *A Gift for Gita* (South Asian)

Keens-Douglas, Ricardo, *The Nutmeg Princess* (Caribbean tale)

Kogawa, Joy, *Naomi's Road* (Japanese Canadian internment in WWII)

Lottridge, Celia, *The Name of the Tree* (African Bantu tale)

McGugan, Jim, *Josepha* (immigrants in Canada, 1900)

Mollel, Tolowa, *The Orphan Boy* (African Maasi legend)

Oberman, Sheldon, *The Always Prayer Shawl* (Jewish traditions)

Smucker, Barbara, *Underground to Canada* (slavery)

Spalding, Andrea, *Finder's Keepers* (Aboriginal Canadian)

Truss, Jan, *A Very Small Rebellion* (Aboriginal Canadian)

Wallace, Ian, *Chin Chiang and the Dragon's Dance* (Chinese Canadian)

Waterton, Betty, *A Salmon for Simon* (Aboriginal Canadian)

Wiseman, Eva, *A Place Not Home* (refugee child from Hungary)

Wolf, Gita, *Mala: A Woman's Folktale* (Indian folktale)

Yee, Paul, *Ghost Train* (Chinese Canadian)

Yee, Paul, *Roses Sing on New Snow* (Chinese Canadian)

Selections by Aboriginal Canadians

Bouchard, David, *The Elders Are Watching*

Bourdeau Waboose, Jan, *Morning on the Lake*

Campbell, Maria (Ed.), *Achimoona*

McLellan, Joe, *The Birth of Nanabosho*

Paul-Dene, Simon, *I Am the Eagle Free* (Sky Song)

Plain, Ferguson, *Amikoonse* (Little Beaver)

For more suggestions, visit the Canadian Children's Book Centre website (http://www.bookcentre.ca/).

STOP, THINK, AND WRITE

- Can you remember books that were potentially controversial as you were growing up?
- What criteria will you use for literature and media choices in your classroom?
- Will you take a safe approach?
- How will you explain your choices to students, parents, colleagues, and administrators?

within these ancient tales and traditions many instances of common human concerns and values found anywhere, anytime:

> *One of the common behaviours of children from many cultures is to join hands in a circle and dance around in joyful movement. The circle is a universal symbol of friendship and celebration of life. It's been said that a child who reads holds the world in his or her hands, so we can enhance and extend the circle of friendship with print and pictures that celebrate the human experience…*
>
> (Livingston & Kurkjian, 2005, p. 696)

Literature Selection and Genres

When choosing literature for the classroom there are a number of factors to consider. These include criteria for quality literature, variety in terms of cultural diversity, the inclusion of works by Canadian authors and illustrators, and a balance of classic and contemporary texts. In addition, we want students to become aware of the many different genres. We want them to be proficient readers and writers of many genres of fiction, poetry, and non-fiction. Exposure to a wide range of genres helps children learn to appreciate the language and forms of discourse that authors use. This in turn influences what students choose to write and the quality of that writing. Providing a wide variety of literary genres, including informational texts on topics that interest students or are relevant to the curriculum, is essential for motivating them to read and write. Students themselves, particularly those in the junior and upper grades, often complain about lack of choice when it comes to classroom reading materials and writing topics. To put it plainly, *choice is motivating*. This conventional wisdom is supported by research (Sweet, Guthrie & Ng, 1998; Baumann et al., cited in Guthrie & Wigfield, 2000). We will return to this topic when we consider teaching writing (Chapters 11 and 12). The Genres Chart is a guide to choosing a range of literature for your language program, in particular for daily read alouds and for independent reading.

GENRES CHART

Fiction	Examples
Traditional Literature	• Nursery rhymes (*Sing a Song of Mother Goose*, Barbara Reid), folk and fairy tales, fables, legends, and myths
Historical Fiction	• *Ticket to Curlew*, Lottridge (1992)
Contemporary Realistic Fiction	• *Shiloh*, Phyllis R. Naylor (1991)
Science Fiction	• *Beckoning Lights*, Monica Hughes
Fantasy	• *Dragon Rider*, Cornelia Funke (2000)
Humour	• *The Adventures of Captain Underpants*, Dav Pilkey (2003)
Animal Stories	• *The Tale of Despereaux*, Kate Di Camillo (2003)
Mystery	• *Cam Jansen* (series), David Alder
Poetry	• *Seasons*, Warabé Aska (1990)
Non-Fiction	**Examples**
Informational	• How-to books (crafts, hobbies), nature books, history and culture, how-things-work and activity books
Biography	• *Who Was Albert Einstein?* Jess M. Brailler (2002)

Reading Aloud

Reading to children is the single most important activity for building the knowledge required for eventual success in learning to read.
—J. Hoffman, N.L. Roser, and Jennifer Battle

The vital role of reading aloud in the classroom program cannot be emphasized strongly enough. Research supports its key links to literacy, the love of reading, the development of story sense and story structure, and language development from the pre-schooler to the secondary student. Since it is such a powerful teaching tool, it deserves the well-informed attention of teachers when they choose literature and when planning presentation and follow-up procedures.

Reading aloud to students plays a key role in their love of reading and their development of story sense and story structure.

An engaging **read aloud** requires careful thought about what to read as well as the rehearsal and creative design. Not every child is going to love every story. However, we increase the likelihood of their emotional and intellectual engagement if we bring the stories of all children from their many cultures and backgrounds into our classroom, and if we include genres and topics that reflect a wide range of interests and backgrounds. In order to choose appropriate books, that is, to choose that "just right" book at the right time, you must have read widely, be able to evaluate according to criteria such as those listed above, and have the confidence to follow your own instincts about a particular book. One foolproof method for determining whether a text is suitable for reading aloud is to actually read it out loud, and read it with the listener in mind. If the language flows rhythmically and lends itself to the creation of dramatic moments, then it will most likely work. A quality literature program includes meticulous planning of all stages of a read aloud, including:

- providing the scaffolding required so that learners can tap into their experiences and concepts to comprehend the text

- modelling fluent reading and use of problem-solving strategies

- stimulating increasingly higher level responses

- designing questions and prompts to augment story sense and explicitly teach story structure

While the emphasis is often on modelling good reading strategies when conducting a read aloud session (see Theory into Practice 6.3 where we provide a detailed description of modelling using think alouds), we should remind ourselves that there are many times during the busy school day when all activity pauses for no other purpose than the enjoyment of a good story. Teachers relish the chance to enter into the world of a story through the medium of a well-illustrated picture book, or an image-evoking or thought-provoking novel. This is purely aesthetic reading and listening. At this point, we should also remind ourselves that the primary linguistic mode for the student during a read aloud is listening. Thus, when you are planning a read aloud for purposes beyond the aesthetic, you should remember that you can use the opportunity to reinforce excellent listening (and speaking) skills and strategies, in addition to reading and writing.

literacy
notebook
6.4

STOP, THINK, AND WRITE

■ How would you define "story"?

■ What shapes a series of apparently unrelated events into a *real story*?

Children develop what is called story sense over time. They acquire the set of concepts and expectations of how stories are structured through many repeated direct experiences with stories. This sense of story structure involves being aware of how events are shaped into the recognizable form of "who did what to whom and for what reason" (Temple, 1996, p. 49). Thus, the key literary elements of a story include:

Characters: the "who" in the story

Plot: the "what happens," typically with a beginning, middle, and end sequence

Setting: the "where and when" of the story; its place, time, and mood

Theme: the "why" or the unifying truth in the story; what is this story really about?

■ What experiences help to develop and deepen children's growing sense of story?

The following have been identified by researchers and educators. Since they focus on the emerging learner, add your own suggestions for extending and expanding the sense of story in older children who are fluent readers and writers.

1. Listening to stories, and hearing the same stories repeatedly.

2. Talking about the stories.

3. Talking about the structure of the story through teacher-led questions and prompts.

4. Comparing the structures of similar stories, especially predictable stories.

5. Retelling familiar stories.

6. Using these structures in their own storytelling and early writing.

Add to this list.

■ What experiences might help to deepen and broaden story sense in more mature readers and writers?

■ Investigate some teaching strategies for each of the story elements listed above, for example, the use of different forms of **story mapping** or **webbing** to demonstrate plot structure (see Graphic Organizers in Chapter 10).

Theory Into Practice/6.1

READ ALOUDS

Read alouds are an essential component of a literacy program. Being read to fosters a love of reading; promotes story, informational, and print awareness; stimulates language development; and motivates independent reading and writing. They allow teachers to introduce a variety of genres and forms of text (for example, the use of captions, or graphs and charts). They provide opportunities for teacher modelling of key reading strategies, such as making connections to life experiences, making comparisons to other books, and problem-solving unfamiliar words. Here is a general procedure for any read aloud, whether fiction or non-fiction.

NOTE: A single read aloud would not include all of these suggestions.

Before:
Plan
- Choose books that will interest the children and are relevant to your classroom context (students' lives, curriculum, and classroom events).
- Plan questions to ask during the read aloud and plan your script for a think aloud (verbalizing your thinking processes to model a reading strategy).
- Plan opportunities to respond and extend student comprehension.
- Rehearse out loud: practise volume, pitch, timing, and inflection.

Introduce the book
- Activate prior knowledge (background experiences in life and with texts).
- Talk about the author and illustrator.
- Encourage predictions or "wonder statements" about the story.
- Discuss unfamiliar or special vocabulary and concepts.
- Introduce unusual text features and formats (for example, tables, glossary).
- Invite questions.
- Set purposes for listening (refer to their questions).

During:
- Read with expression, enthusiasm, and appropriate intonation and pacing.
- Make connections to and draw comparisons with other texts or experiences.
- Make inferences and predictions.
- "Stop and think" to model incidentally how to use reading strategies to monitor one's own understanding (for example, visualizing, using context).
- Think aloud (see Theory Into Practice 6.3) to model explicitly how to formulate questions, solve problems, and confirm answers as one reads.

Note: Not every text is suitable for a think aloud. If these interruptions take away from the aesthetic flow of the story, read the story once, and go back on another day to use the text for modelling.

After:
Help students extend learning and comprehension by encouraging them in some of the following ways:

READ ALOUDS (continued)

- Connect to their own background knowledge and experiences in life and with the story.
- Apply their learning by retelling or mapping the story.
- Reinforce comprehension by making comparisons and inferences.
- Discuss story elements such as character, plot, and setting.
- Discuss questions posed before, during, or after the reading.
- Expand on one another's ideas.
- Discuss responses: "text-to-self; text-to-text; text-to-world" connections (Keene & Zimmerman, 1997, p. 55).
- Respond by retelling in a new form, for example, role-play, retelling in comic strip form, picture sequence, tableau, or **sketch to stretch** (see Theory into Practice 6.2).
- Record responses in a journal.

Beyond:

- Use the text or parts of it for readers' theatre (see Theory into Practice 5.1).
- Make the book available at a literacy centre with an appropriate activity, for example, an author, illustrator or genre study.
- Make the book available at a play or work station with an appropriate imaginative or curricular activity, for example, a post-office or construction site or a math, science, music, or visual arts station.

Source: Adapted from Ontario Ministry of Education (2003).

Not all read alouds are used for teaching purposes, nor do they require follow-up activities. However, there should be opportunities for talking about the story. There should be time to retell the puzzling beginning or the wonderful ending, to talk about favourite lines and passages, or to discuss unanswered questions.

Sketch to Stretch

Engaging in activities such as sketch to stretch serves many purposes. According to Louise Rosenblatt's transactional theory of reading, reading is experienced as a form of intense personal activity during which the reader "draws on past experience of life and language to elicit meaning from the printed words" (Rosenblatt, 1978, p. 26). She stated that "a text, once it leaves its author's hands, is simply paper and ink until a reader evokes from it a literary work—sometimes, even, a literary work of art" (1978, p. ix). In this approach, the spotlight is on the reader's involvement in the two-way, transactional relationship with the text. It emphasizes the role of the individual reader's responses to texts in making sense and interpreting meanings.

This does not imply an "anything goes" approach—that whatever the reader feels or thinks in response to a text is acceptable as long it is heartfelt. On the contrary, strategies designed to provide students with opportunities to respond in a variety of ways to the literature they are reading encourage higher level thinking, particularly since self-assessment, peer interaction, and teacher evaluation are built into each activity.

Theory Into Practice/6.2

SKETCH TO STRETCH

Sketch to stretch encourages students to go beyond a literal understanding of what they have experienced in a read aloud. This strategy helps them create meaning in and through many modes of communication, including language strands such as speaking, visually representing, art, music, drama, or movement. Taking what is known in one system and transposing it into another using new signs, symbols, and forms is called "transmediation."

1. Explain that sketch to stretch is an artistic interpretation of what a story means to an individual. Explain that it is not about artistic talent, for example, making a realistic drawing, but about representing in pictorial or symbolic form how you personally connect to or make meaning from the story. When students are first introduced to this, you may need to brainstorm some possibilities with them as a group.

2. Divide students into small groups of 4 to 5.

3. Read a story or a selection, pausing at the end or at an appropriate stopping point.

4. Allow students time to think and draw.

5. When sketches are complete, each person shows their sketch to the group and invites comments and interpretations. The artist gets the last word.

6. When everyone has shared, each group can identify one sketch for the large group to share. This can be shown on the overhead projector or scanned into a computer.

7. Discuss the variety of interpretations, and the fact that there is no one correct reading or sketch.

8. Discuss how communicating in pictorial or symbolic form opens a story for many ways of interpreting.

9. Encourage students to use this strategy independently to monitor their own comprehension both during and after reading.

10. Extend the use of sketch to stretch as a response to non-fiction, and as a technique to use when writing.

Source: Adapted from Harste et al. (1988, pp. 353-357).

Thinking Aloud

Theory Into Practice/6.3

THINK ALOUDS

Effective think alouds consider and explain what independent literacy learners do before, during, and after they read, listen to, or view texts. Tip: Make sure that you establish with students in advance how to distinguish between the two voices sharing information: your voice that is reading and the "voice in your head" that is sharing what it thinks the text is about and how you are making sense of the text.

Before Reading:

1. Choose a reading selection that causes you to think. You might choose a selection that uses primarily one type of thinking or one that requires a range of different thinking strategies (for example, connecting, predicting, self-monitoring, forming sensory images, inferring, drawing conclusions, evaluating). Find points in the text that best exemplify the use of the comprehension strategy (strategies) you have identified. We suggest marking these spots with yellow post-its and loosely scripting what it is you would like to share with your students.

   Note: When first introducing the think aloud process to students or when using the think aloud strategy primarily for comprehension instruction, we suggest focusing on one or two strategies only.

   Ask: What information do I want my students to focus on? How will I explain my in-the-head thinking to the students?

2. Tell the students that today you will be modelling how to think aloud to make sense of text. Depending on your purpose for using the think aloud, you might alert them to the strategy (strategies) you will be demonstrating.

   Ask: What do the students already know or believe about thinking aloud or the strategy that might influence how they engage with the story or the think aloud? How will I activate this background knowledge?

During Reading:

3. Think aloud to demonstrate your strategy (strategies). Ensure that you are modelling your in-the-head thinking. In some cases, especially as the students are working their way toward independence, you can stop and ask the students to share their in-the-head thinking.

   Ask: How am I helping students to understand this strategy in context?

After Reading:

4. Ask students to recall the strategy (strategies) you were modelling.

   Ask: Can students explain the strategy and how you used it to make sense of the text?

5. Ask students to recall instances where you stopped to use the strategy (strategies).

   Ask: Can students explain why you stopped at this point in the text?

6. Debrief the strategy and clues that can help us to identify when we are using this strategy (strategies) and why.

   Ask: Can students recall words or phrases characteristic of your selected strategy (strategies)?

THINK ALOUDS (continued)

Making Connections
This reminds me of...
I remember something like this happened when...
I read another book where the character...
This is like in our school when...
Our country doesn't have that holiday, but we have...

Predict and Anticipate
I wonder if...
I wonder who...
I think I know what is coming next...
He will be in trouble if...
I think we will learn how...

Summarize and Draw Conclusions
The most important thing I've learned so far is...
It didn't say why she did that, but I bet...
I know he must be feeling...
So far in our story...
So far I have learned that...

Question and Monitor Comprehension
I wonder what it means when...
I don't understand...

It didn't make sense when...
I'm going to re-read that because it didn't make sense that...

Imagine, Infer, and Visualize
Even though it isn't in the picture, I can see the...
Mmmm, I can almost taste the...
That sent chills down my spine when it said...
For a minute I thought I could smell...
I could hear the...
I can imagine what it is like to...
I can picture the...

Evaluate, and Form Opinions
My favourite part in this chapter was...
I really liked how the author...
What I don't like about this part is...
it was really interesting to learn that...
I am going to try this out when I...
I wish I could...
If I were her, I would...

Source: Adapted from Cunningham & Allington (1994, pp. 78-79).

Toward Independence

7. Once students are accustomed to the think aloud process, they will be ready to assume more independence and try it themselves.

    Ask: What indicators tell me that they are ready to try it on their own?

8. To make the transition to independence, teachers may choose to read and think aloud the first quarter or third of a text that the students are about to read independently. In this way, they are introduced to the selection, tricky words, and type of writing. After your introduction and think aloud, students work in small groups, reading the remainder of the selection, and sharing the "voices in their head."

    Ask: Can students effectively apply a designated comprehension strategy? Can students independently and effectively apply a range of comprehension strategies in order to make sense of the text?

For further information, see: Block & Israel (2004, pp. 154-167); Cunningham & Allington (2003, 2006); Wilhelm (2001).

Teacher Talk/6.2

NICOLE THINKS ALOUD WITH A LANGSTON HUGHES POEM

Poem: Dream Variation   **Author:** Langston Hughes
Reading Strategy: Visualizing [Nicole's thinking aloud is noted in square brackets.]

To fling my arms wide in some place of the sun,
To whirl and to dance, till the white day is done.

[I'm picturing a hot summer day, in a wide open field, a young girl with bare feet and a summer dress twirling around and around with her arms outstretched.]

Then rest at cool evening beneath a tall tree

[I'm picturing a large apple tree and the young girl is sitting underneath it. The sound of insects and the breeze blowing calmly.]

While night comes on gently, dark like me—

[I am thinking of the young girl and am adding more detail to the image of her in my mind. I'm also thinking about the words "white day" and how they contrast with the words "night" and "dark."]

That is my dream!

[I think about how children's lives are so filled with dreams. This young girl seems to be free spirited and probably has many dreams.]

To fling my arms wide in the face of the sun. Dance! Whirl! Whirl!

[I once again see the image of the young girl twirling in the field, but this time I see her as a slave and she is imagining herself as a young girl who is set free.]

'Til the quick day is done. Rest at pale evening...

[The young girl is exhausted at the end of each day, from working, and because of this she is pale and needs her rest. This poem includes several words that relate to colour—white, dark, and pale. I wonder if the poet is trying to make a point about colour.]

A tall, slim tree... Night coming tenderly black like me.

[There is another colour word—black. I think the poet has some kind of hidden meaning here but I'm not sure what it is. The poem seems to portray freedom. Maybe the title "Dream Variation" helps make this point. Is this poem about slavery and the only way to be free is in a dream? I think that I might want to look up some information about the author and the date that this poem was published. That might help me to understand it better.]

As Nicole emerged as a literacy teacher, she became more aware of the strategies that she used as a literate being, making it easier for her to share her in-the-head thinking with her students. Thinking aloud is an effective method for teaching about comprehension and thinking. When asked by Block and Israel (2004), second through sixth graders said that teachers could do the following things to help them comprehend: a) describe what they did to understand what happened in books, b) show how they figured out the meanings of words from context, and c) explain what they did in their heads to comprehend.

Nicole Lajoie is a 2004-2005 graduate of Nipissing University's Bachelor of Education program.

Reader Response Activities

Here is a list of our favourite reader response activities—favourites because they are "tried and true." These are used by many teachers, supported by evidence from research as effective strategies to deepen comprehension, and shown to enhance students' engagement and enjoyment.

1. *Literature Circles* (see Chapter 9)
   What: An effective way for small groups of students to read books they have chosen and talk about their responses to their readings, and about what they are learning about reading and writing.
   Variations: Grand conversations, book clubs
   When: During and after reading
   Why: Talking together deepens and broadens understanding, motivates further reading, encourages new perspectives, and promotes community in the classroom.
   Language Arts Focus: Speaking and listening
   Suggested Titles:
   Where the Wild Things Are, Maurice Sendak (Early Primary)
   The Rough Face Girl, Rafe Martin & David Shannon (Primary)
   ✦ *Hana's Suitcase: A True Story*, Karen Levine (Junior)

2. *Reader Response Journals* (see Theory into Practice 8.2)
   What: Written records of student responses to readings including immediate feelings and reactions, connections to one's life, other texts and media, and reflections expressing opinions and critical analyzes. The focus is on the development of the reader's interpretation and personal meaning-making, not on a single correct interpretation as dictated by a teacher or critic.
   Variations: Double Entry Journal—readers choose quotations they find important and meaningful, record the quotation and page number in one column, and then record their thoughts and feelings in the right hand column.
   Dialogue Journal—two people reading the same book interact by means of the journal, responding first to the text, to their correspondent. Readers can converse with a peer, a teacher, or a family or community member.
   When: During and after reading
   Why: Writing journal entries as they read novels for literature groups results in greater engagement in reading. By connecting reading and writing experiences through reader response journals, you

are enabling students to deepen their understanding of the texts they they are reading. Reader response journals enable students to make personal connections as well as strategy connections as they read.

Language Arts Focus: Reading and writing
Suggested Titles:
* *Omar on Ice*, Maryann Kovalski (Primary; grades 1-3)
Sarah, Plain and Tall, Patricia MacLachlan (Late Primary; grades 3-4)
Dear Mr. Henshaw, Beverley Cleary (Junior; grades 4-6)

3. *Sketch to Stretch (see Theory into Practice 6.2)*
What: A pictorial representation—sometimes with accompanying captions—of a reader's understanding of a text.
Variation: Quick Draw—students illustrate their interpretation of a read aloud (shared, or read independently) with an impromptu drawing done quickly, maximum 10 minutes. Although usually recommended for early primary learners who are not yet independent writers, this can be used at any level to encourage the expression of immediate reactions through non-linguistic means.
When: Immediately after reading.
Why: Using non-verbal means to express an interpretation of a text encourages making connections (between verbal thoughts and difficult-to-express feelings, for example) and allows learners who are less facile with verbal systems to express themselves in a potentially sophisticated visual form.
Language Arts Focus: Reading, representing, viewing, listening, and speaking (sketches are discussed after they have been drawn)
Suggested Titles:
Olivia, Ian Falconer (Primary)
* *The Very Last First Time*, Jan Andrews (Primary or Junior)

4. *Story Drama (see Chapter 7)*
What: Story drama is an improvised role-play based on a story. It involves a dramatization or re-enactment of a story that goes beyond a literal retelling of the plot.
When: After reading or listening to a story, and having time to discuss it, the children decide how they can dramatize it, using teacher prompts and structures to help them.
Variations: Dramatic role-play in literacy centres (see Teacher Talk 7.1 for an example of a Kindergarten application).

Tableaux—students re-create a story in small groups, using a series of silent depictions of selected scenes "frozen in time."

Why: Story drama is a powerful way to link drama and reading: the relationship resides in the meanings—meanings that are found well below the surface and beyond single, "correct" interpretations.

Language Arts Focus: Representing, viewing, speaking, listening, reading

Suggested Titles:

Who's in Rabbit's House?, Verna Aardema (Primary)

★ *The Name of the Tree*, Cecilia Barker Lottridge (Primary or Junior)

★ *A Promise to the Sun*, Tololwa M. Mollel (Primary or Junior)

5. *Poetry as Reader Response (see Chapter 7)*

What: Writing an original or a found poem (Theory into Practice 7.1) inspired by a story. In a found poem, readers collect words and phrases from the text and arrange them in poetic form.

Variations: An "I Am" poem, where each line begins with the words "I am" (or "I say," "I wonder," etc.) followed by descriptions that fit the character chosen from the text. A "Where I'm From" poem, where each line follows the title line with truths about a character's relationship to the setting of a story. Rewrite a poetic response as a song, adding a melody and instrumentation or recorded music.

Why: Writing poetry is similar to writing in a different language because of its rhythm and beat, creative word and line placement on the page, the occasional use of rhyme, and the opportunity to go beyond language conventions such as sentence structure and punctuation. It can be a potent medium for the expression of feelings and the representation of a "different way of knowing" (see Multiple Ways of Knowing in Chapter 7).

Language Arts Focus: Reading, writing, listening, speaking, viewing, representing

Suggested Titles:

Owl Moon, Jane Yolen (Primary or Junior)

The Whale's Song, Dyan Sheldon (Primary or Junior)

★ *Boy of the Deeps*, Ian Wallace

There is no better means of motivating students to engage in this kind of high-level talking and listening than to provide them with something worth listening to and worth talking about—they deserve nothing but the best stories told well; they deserve nothing but the best children's literature.

STOP, THINK, AND WRITE

Think back to a children's picture book you have read or listened to recently during a read aloud (in your Language Arts class). If you are drawing a blank, then read *Miss Rumphius* by Barbara Cooney, and complete this assignment using that wonderful book. Apply what you know about story structure, and use the sketch-to-stretch activity (Theory into Practice 6.2) as though you were conducting a read aloud lesson for a group of students.

You might use this story to explicitly teach circular plot structure by having the students draw a circular picture in the form of a clock, with 12 main events, in picture or symbol form, placed around the clock face in the positions of the numbers.

OR

Have the students sketch one important thing that had particular meaning for them, or "three important things," just like Miss Rumphius. Once you know what you want to teach about story structure, and how you plan to have your students express their understanding, include key questions and prompts designed to increase their sense of story. Remember to include opportunities to share their interpretations with one another.

literacy notebook 6.5

Moving On

In this chapter, we explored the crucial role of story in meaning-making and the value of high quality children's literature in literacy development and learning. Discussing issues such as reading achievement and censorship, we highlighted the importance of teachers' awareness of the characteristics of high quality children's literature and the impact that good literature has in the classroom and beyond. We explored the teaching and learning potential of literature in a range of domains, from language-based abilities and achievements to building a classroom community, emphasizing the central place of the daily teacher read aloud from superb children's literature as a key classroom event.

A sense of story is a condition; an appreciation of outstanding literature is the means; they are, in a sense, pre-conditions of full-fledged literacy, since they develop initially through listening and talking about stories—through "reading for" and "reading with" expert readers. But we also want our students to be able to enter these worlds independently; they must learn to read for themselves—this is "reading by" the children themselves. Chapter 8 introduces reading as a puzzle to be solved by readers in a variety of contexts for a variety of purposes. The sense of story and concepts about print that young learners have developed through listening to good literature now will be applied in their own reading as meaning makers, word solvers, concept builders, and architects (see Figure 8.4).

Chapter 7 builds on many of the literature response concepts developed in this chapter, and goes on to demonstrate further the value and importance of creative expression in learning generally. It enriches students' responses and written communication, helps them to make connections between texts, their own lives, and other persons, and promotes self-understanding through self-exploration, reflection, and expression.

> *Every day, every child everywhere has the right*
> *to hear a good story.*
> —Elizabeth Thorn

LIT-FOLIO UPDATE

Consider what might count as evidence that you have shown growth in your knowledge of high quality children's literature. What websites, libraries, and children's bookstores have you consulted or visited? How have you developed your ability to evaluate children's books and your confidence in articulating your reasons for your choices? Have you started a list of books of different genres and cultural traditions, suitable for different grades and ages? Have you developed your read aloud strategies by rehearsing your performance techniques, planning think alouds, and designing creative response activities? Finally, revisit your beliefs about the role of children's literature in promoting literacy (Literacy Notebook 6.1) and make revisions if your thinking has changed.

LIT-FOLIO TIP

If you have not started one already, begin to keep an organized Children's Literature list, with annotations that will be useful to you as a teacher; for example, suggested levels (Primary or Junior), possible uses when teaching reading and writing strategies, and developing listening and speaking skills. Think about including reader response activities for each book, ensuring that you include a range of modes of expression, including visual and oral as well as written responses.

Resources to Support Your Learning

Professional Resources

✤ Booth, D. W. (2002). *Story drama*. Markham, ON: Pembroke Publishers.

✤ Frye, N. (1963). *The educated imagination*. Toronto, ON: CBC Publications

Raphael, T., Pardo, L.S., & Highfield, K. (2002). *Book club: A literature based curriculum*. Lawrence, MA: Small Planet Communication.

Vasquez, V. (2003). *Getting beyond "I like the book": creating space for critical literacy in K-6 classrooms*. Newark, DE: International Reading Association.

Wells, G. (1986). *The meaning makers*. Portsmouth, NH: Heinemann.

Journals

✤ *Canadian Children's Literature* (University of Guelph)
The Reading Teacher (International Reading Association)
Language Arts
The Horn Book Magazine (http://www.hbook.com)

Children's Literature: Our Favourites

The following are two superb resources for the "best" in children's literature. We refer you to these, and to the websites listed for further information regarding high-quality children's literature.

Huck, C., Hepler, S., Hickman, J., & Kiefer, B.Z. (2004). *Children's literature in the elementary school*. (8th ed.) Dubuque: IA: McGraw-Hill.

Zipes, J., Paul, L., Vallone, L., Hunt, P., & Avery,G., Eds. (2005). *Norton anthology of children's literature*. New York: Norton & Co.

Literature of Outstanding and Enduring Quality

✤ *Alligator pie*, Dennis Lee
✤ *Anne of Green Gables*, Lucy Maud Montgomery
A wrinkle in time (trilogy) Madeleine L'Engle
Alice in Wonderland: Through the Looking Glass, Lewis Carol
Bridge to Terabithia, Katherine Paterson
Charlotte's web, E.B. White
Madeline, Ludwig Bemelmans
The black cauldron (Book 2 in the Prydain Chronicles), Lloyd Alexander
The borrowers, Mary Norton
The cat in the hat, Dr. Suess
The dark is rising, Susan Cooper

The giver, Lois Lowry
The hobbit, J.R.R. Tolkien
The lion, the witch, and the wardrobe, (Book 2 in the Narnia chronicles) C.S. Lewis
The secret garden, Frances Hodgson Burnett
The snowy day, Ezra Jack Keats
The tale of Peter Rabbit, Beatrix Potter
The velveteen rabbit, Margery Williams
The wind in the willows, Kenneth Grahame
The wonderful wizard of Oz, L. Frank Baum
Tuck everlasting, Natalie Babbit
Where the wild things are, Maurice Sendak
Winnie the Pooh, A.A. Milne

Primary Level Picture Books for Read Alouds to Develop Story Sense

✤ *Love you forever* (also *Paper Bag Princess*), Robert Munsch
✤ *Out on the ice in the middle of the bay*, Peter Cumming
✤ *Up in the tree*, Margaret Atwood
Alexander and the terrible, horrible, no good, very bad day, Judith Viorst
Anansi and the moss-covered rock, retold by Eric A. Kimmel
Heckedy Peg, Audrey Wood
Joseph had a little overcoat, Simms Taback
No, David! (also *David gets in trouble, David goes to school*) (trilogy), David Shannon
Once upon a golden apple, Jean Little
Stellaluna, Janell Cannon
Strega Nona, Tomie dePaola
Tiger soup: an Anansi story from Jamaica, retold and illustrated by Frances Temple
Tikki, Tikki, Tembo, Arlene Mosel

Junior Level Short Stories and Picture Books Recommended for the Development of Story Sense

✤ *Boy's own*, Tim Wynne-Jones (ed.)
✤ *Caribou song*, Tomson Highway
✤ *Chin Chiang and the dragon's dance*, Ian Wallace
✤ *Ghost train*, Paul Yee
✤ *Last leaf, first snowflake to fall*, Leo Yerxa
✤ *The bone talker*, Shelley A. Leedahl
✤ *The hockey sweater*, Roch Carrier
✤ *The very last first time*, Jan Andrews
Cold feet, Cynthia DeFelice
Crow boy, Taro Yashima
Knots on a counting rope, Bill Martin Jr.
Miss Rumphius (also *Only Opal*), Barbara Cooney
Owl moon, Jane Yolen

Snow White in New York, Fiona French
Thank you, Mr. Falker, Patricia Polacco
The true story of the three little pigs, Jon Scieszka
The polar express, Chris Van Allsburg

Primary Novels for Developing Readers

Fantastic Mr. Fox (also *Charlie and the chocolate factory, James and the giant peach, Matilda, The Witches, The BFG, The Twits*) Roald Dahl
⚘ *Jacob Two-Two meets the hooded fang* (also *Jacob Two-Two and the dinosaur, Jacob Two-Two's first spy case*), Mordecai Richler
Ramona Quimby, Age 8, Beverly Cleary
Sarah, plain and tall, Patricia MacLachlan
Stone fox, John Reynolds Gardiner
The whipping boy, Sid Fleischman

Canadian Novels for Independent Readers

⚘ *A time to choose*, Martha Attema
⚘ *Looking at the moon*, Kit Pearson
⚘ *Shadow in Hawthorn Bay*, Janet Lunn
⚘ *Tales from Gold Mountain*, Paul Yee
⚘ *The belonging place* (also *One to Grow On*), Jean Little
⚘ *Ticket to Curlew*, Celia Barker
⚘ *You can pick me up in Peggy's Cove*, Brian Doyle

Other Favourites

A series of unfortunate events, Lemony Snicket
Bunnicula, Deborah & James Howe
Cam Jansen, David A. Alder
Chocolate fever, Robert Kimmel Smith
Dear Mr. Henshaw (also *Strider*), Beverly Clearly

Dragonwings, Laurence Yep
Harry Potter (series), J. K. Rowling
Hatchet (also *Brian's winter*), Gary Paulsen
Holes, Louis Sachar
Julie of the wolves, George, J. Craighead
Shiloh, Phyllis Reynolds Naylor
Tales of a fourth grade nothing, Judy Blume
The best Christmas pageant ever, Barbara Robinson
The Indian in the cupboard, Lynne Reid Banks
The phantom tollbooth, Norton Juster
The sheep pig (also *The Fox Busters*), Dick King-Smith
The witch of Blackbird Pond, Elizabeth George Speare
The wizard of Earthsea, Ursula K. Le Guin
This can't be happening at MacDonald Hall, Gordon Korman
Wringer (also *Maniac Magee*), Jerry Spinella

Websites

⚘ The Canadian Children's Book Centre: http://www.bookcentre.ca/
⚘ The Children's Literature Web Guide (for stories, author links, Readers' Theatre scripts): http://www.acs.ucagary.ca/~dkbrown
American Library Association: http://www.ala.org
The 100 Most Frequently Challenged Books: http://www.ala.org/ala/oif/bannedbooksweek/bbwlinks/100mostfrequently.htm
National Centre for Research in Children's Literature (UK): http://www.ncrcl.ac.uk
UNICEF: http://www.unicef.ca/eng/unicef/story/main.html

Literacy through Creative Expression

> The purpose of art is not the release of a momentary ejection of adrenaline but rather the gradual, lifelong construction of a state of wonder and serenity.
> —*Glenn Gould*

key terms

- choral speaking
- drama
- found poetry
- literacy-enriched play centre
- multiple ways of knowing
- role-playing
- story drama
- storytelling
- tableaux

questions to guide your learning

By the end of this chapter, you should understand the key terms and be able to answer the following questions:

- Why are the arts in education important?
- What are the connections among play, the arts, and literacy development?
- How can creative expression enhance literacy learning?
- Why is it vital that you as a teacher engage in and demonstrate arts such as drama, storytelling, and poetry, both for and with your students?

Looking Back, Looking Ahead

In Chapter 6, we explored the crucial role of story in meaning-making and the value of high quality children's literature in literacy development and learning. We discovered the teaching and learning potential of literature in a range of domains, from language-based abilities and achievement to classroom community building. We emphasized the central role of the skilfully conducted daily teacher read aloud as a key classroom event.

This chapter expands on the development of literacy and literary traditions through story and literature to include the artistic media of visual art, drama, storytelling, poetry, music, and movement. One of our goals is to demonstrate how these creative endeavours can be effectively integrated into a comprehensive literacy program. This chapter demonstrates the value and importance of creative expression in learning: it enriches reader response, both oral and written, helps us to make connections between texts and our own lives and with others, and promotes self-understanding through self-exploration, reflection, and expression.

The specific forms of artistic expression in this chapter—visual art, drama, storytelling, poetry, music, and movement—have been chosen because of their central role in the elementary curriculum. They are uniquely suited for truly integrated learning; curricular areas traditionally treated separately can support, enhance, and harmonize with one another to generate new forms of learning that can be experienced at higher levels of intensity. In this chapter, we invite you to critically examine the role of the arts in your classroom, particularly in your language program. Do you consider the arts to be a frill or an add-on to the real curriculum? Do you think the arts require specialized, expert teacher knowledge? Do you participate in any form of creative expression—visual art, drama, dance, or music—regardless of whether you are good at it? What is the role of enjoyment in relation to engaging in creative activities—for you and for your students?

Although each of the artistic modes has its own unique characteristics and should be appreciated for its own sake, we emphasize an integrated approach, one that is more practical and achievable. We offer a variety of suggestions for infusing the curriculum with the arts and for their use in integrated learning. We end the chapter with three integrated literature-based units presented in a ready-to-go workshop format, one focusing on drama, another on storytelling, and a third on the theme of space.

STOP, THINK, AND WRITE

literacy notebook 7.1

- How important is the opportunity to express yourself through a creative medium? (Be specific; for example, gardening, playing the guitar, moving to music, writing poetry.)

- How would you feel if you were unable to continue this activity for any reason?

- Have you ever used one form of literary or creative activity to motivate or stimulate another? For example, do you sing to help you to think about the topic you are writing about?

- Has a book or film ever inspired you to write a poem or a song?

- Do you listen to music while you paint?

Examine Your Beliefs

- Do you feel the arts should be central in the classroom program? Why? Why not?

- Do you believe that every student's literacy profile should include the dimension of being able to interpret and communicate through non-verbal media?

- Do you think that there are particular benefits for students who have been labelled "at risk" or who have been identified as having learning difficulties in a classroom based on a multiple ways of knowing approach—that is, when there are many opportunities for creative expression?

Challenge

- What can you do to provide enriched opportunities for creative expression for your students?

How Is Creative Expression Important to Literacy?

Only through art can we get outside of ourselves and know another's view of the universe which is not the same as ours and see landscapes which would otherwise have remained unknown to us like the land-scapes of the moon. Thanks to art, instead of seeing a single world, our own, we see it multiply until we have before us as many worlds as there are original artists.

—Marcel Proust

Children engage in literate behaviours as they play.

There has always been a strong association between the arts and play. While this may have contributed to an undervaluing of the arts, and especially to the view that the arts are a frill in the school curriculum, we would be foolish to underestimate the implications of this connection with regard to learning. If, as John Dewey stated, learning occurs in and through experience, and if, as Lev Vygotsky taught, learning is socially constructed, then what better context for learning can we provide for children than play? Whether playing in role or with story, playing with colour, line, and shape, or with sounds, or playing with words or with movement, all are forms of play that are natural, inherently enjoyable, and connect intimately with literacy development.

Play promotes the kind of learning that connects children to one another, connects prior knowledge to new experiences, and promotes the construction of deeper understandings. This process involves intimate links to the learning of literate behaviours in very young children, and to the further development of literacy in children as they mature. When Kindergarten children engage in socio-dramatic play—pretending to be a police officer writing a speeding ticket, a principal writing a letter to a parent, or a teacher writing instructions on the board—written language often becomes part of the play activity. Older children involved in dramatic play and storytelling use the continuous and interdependent skills and problem-solving in reading, writing, speaking, listening, viewing, and representing. Play does more than lead to literacy—children engage in literate behaviours as they play. The fact that language is used in the context of play places language learning in a unique position, different from many of its other more school-like tasks.

When children are playing, they feel freer to take risks and therefore display greater confidence in their performance. As Bruner (1983, pp. 60-61) states "To play implies a reduction in the seriousness of the consequences of errors and of setbacks... Play is an activity that is without frustrating consequences... It is, in consequence, a superb medium for exploration." Play is also *the* medium for exploration in the arts.

Play is a superb medium for those children who are just becoming literate or developing new areas of literacy (for example, media, technological, visual, and critical literacies). Play through the arts is also an ideal medium for those children who are second-language learners and for learners with difficulties or exceptionalities in speech and language, because they benefit from the richly varied visual and contextual clues that are part of play. Facial expression, body language, gestures, as well as the sets, costumes, and props used in play, all contribute to greater ease in expressing and understanding linguistic meanings, learning new vocabulary, and developing confidence in oral language use.

Play opens up the emotional, social, moral, and intellectual aspects of our being. Learning through play is joyful learning. Becoming literate should not be the arduous, unpleasant task it becomes for many children. As Elliot Eisner reminds us, there are deep connections between the experience of play, the development of the imagination, and the ability to read.

> *The early forms of play of the young are precisely aimed at exploration, the seeking of possibility, and culminate in the discovery of patterns that hold meaning. Such behavior, formed in the context of play, provides the ground for meaning. Through play, imagination is exercised and combinatorial forms of exploration occur. New relationships are sought and new patterns established. These patterns, first discovered through play, eventually become formed into the codes necessary for games. Games…possess the codes that establish conventions for social forms of interaction. The acquisition of these codes or rules provides a form of learning that children use as a basis for learning the codes in reading… The ability to exercise imagination in reading is not, in my view, a marginal characteristic of the process; it is a necessary condition for its occurrence.*

> (Eisner, 1978, pp. 16-17)

Clearly, it is vital that we provide many opportunities for the kind of play that allows this exercise of imagination so essential in reading, and by extension, in writing. Most Kindergarten programs are play-based. They usually have activity centres or learning centres, defined by Lori Jamison Rog (2001) as "purposefully planned classroom areas where children can work with hands-on materials to guide their own learning" (p. 34). Because they provide the structure for learning through organized play, learning centres present opportunities for exploration, discovery, and creation of new learning, as well as practice and reinforcement of previously learned concepts. Centres allow students to work and play together, to problem-solve collaboratively and independently, and to manage their own time and take responsibility for resources. Viewed in this way, learning centres have a legitimate place in all classrooms well beyond Kindergarten. They are part of any well-designed elementary classroom, particularly in the primary grades. They are incorporated less frequently in the junior grades and beyond, but where they are found, one can observe excited, motivated learners engaged in enjoyable, productive learning.

Creative expression through play is a powerful scaffold for literacy-building. It allows integration of various artistic domains, and can easily be tied into content areas of the curriculum (see, for example, Debbie Diller's (2005) "Newspaper Work Station," pp. 80-82). Although Diller calls the literacy centres designed for Grades 3-6 work stations, they involve purposeful play, which should be at the heart of classroom practice for all learners at various points along the continuum of literacy development as meaning makers. As Eisner points out, play helps us to make connections, and it is through making connections that we are able to make meanings.

> *The ability to go beyond the information given, to piece together what is discrete and separate, requires both an inclination and an ability to treat materials or ideas flexibly, to be able and willing to play with the stimuli one confronts so they can be patterned. The early forms of play of the young are precisely aimed at exploration, the seeking of possibility, and* culminate in the discovery of patterns that hold meaning.
>
> (Eisner, 1978, p. 16; emphasis added)

Multiple Ways of Knowing

> *If children are to achieve common outcomes after two or three years in school it will be necessary to recognize that they enter school having learned different things in different ways in different cultures and communities. I assume that what one already knows is important in determining what one will come to know and, if teachers believe that, they would search for what each new entrant to school, or any slow-to-get-started learner, already knows about how one can learn.*
>
> (Clay, 1998, p. 1)

Not everyone learns in the same way; there are various individual paths to literacy. All too often, when children have difficulty in learning how to read and write, it is assumed that they have a learning disability and require specialized teaching. Sometimes this is true, but it is not the whole story. Sometimes not enough attention is paid to what children "already know about how one can learn." Observing attentively, we might find that a particular child learns in ways that are not considered typical. This requires acknowledging that there can be multiple ways of knowing

Teacher Talk/7.1

GRETCHEN OWOCKI TALKS ABOUT A LITERACY-ENRICHED PLAY CENTRE

Here is an example of a play centre described by Gretchen Owocki (2001) as a literacy-enriched play centre. It is designed as a play area based on a classroom experience; in this case, a trip to an art gallery. The centre is equipped for role play and the use of familiar reading and writing materials.

BUILDING BACKGROUND KNOWLEDGE

- Invite an artist, an art gallery director, or a museum docent to do a show and tell followed by a question-and-answer period. Some questions may be prepared ahead of time through a whole-group shared writing (see Chapter 12).

- Tour an art gallery, studio, museum, or framing shop. Prepare the students carefully by providing specific things to look for, do, and ask.

- Share books on art and artists (for example, *The Art Lesson,* Tomi dePaola; *It Looked Like Spilt Milk,* Charles G. Shaw; *The Magic Paintbrush,* Robin Muller).

DESIGNING PROPS AND MATERIALS

To create a gallery in the classroom, rope off a corner, so there is space to hang children's art, a shelf for sculptures, a stand for visitors to buy tickets and pick up brochures (produced by the children or from a real gallery), an easel, and tables for sculpting and framing.

MATERIALS TO PROVIDE

- paper of different sizes, colours, and textures; crayons, pastels, pens, paints, pencils, clay
- glue, tape, cardboard, mat boards (many frame-makers will donate seconds), bristol board for framing
- materials such as blank playing cards, high gloss paper, and permanent markers for making tickets, gallery maps, and brochures
- cash register and money
- index cards for art labels (name of artist, title of the work, brief description)

EXPLORING ROLES AND PERSPECTIVES

Before, during, and after play, explore the following with the children:

- Who works in an art gallery or frame shop? Who arranges the displays? What materials do they use? Generate other questions with the students: Who cleans the gallery? Who writes the brochures and advertisements?

- How are you using the art gallery to practise and explore what you learned about art (painting and sculpting techniques, for example) at other times of the day?

NOTE: Many children are impressed with how much time professional artists need to complete a painting or sculpture. Provide a classroom space where art can be worked on over a period of time. Build in routines for discussing progress and whether a work is finished.

Source: Adapted from Owocki (2001, pp. 164-167).

literacy notebook 7.2

STOP, THINK, AND WRITE

Based on the above description of a play centre, design a similar role play centre for Kindergarten or early primary students that involves creative expression and built-in literacy learning.

Use the same sequence to:

■ Build background knowledge
■ Design props and materials
■ Explore roles and perspectives

Tracking Progress

It is vitally important that play-learning centres are designed with procedures for tracking and documenting children's play and the learning time spent in the centre. Observe and record regularly: these records provide information for your teaching. Detailed and accurate documentation informs and enhances instruction and can be used to communicate with families. Some parents (and educators) question the importance of play; your profiles of individual students' play time literacies help you to articulate "the functions, the features, the formats, and the genres of written language that their children are exploring as they play" (Owocki, 2001, p. 164).

With this in mind, design an observational tracking record for documenting a child's literacy behaviours, including concepts about print (Figure 4.5).

Extending the Idea

■ How might you adapt this idea of a learning centre with opportunities for creative expression for older children in a junior level classroom?

Suggested resource: Diller (2005)

(Leland, Harste & Helt, 2000) and different conceptions of what counts as "literacy" conceptions that go beyond equating literacy with written language. Leland and her colleagues saw the need to redefine literacy when they looked at how old definitions make "severely labelled" students vulnerable.

We saw sign systems (art, music, drama, language, movement, math, and so forth) as representing the various ways humans have developed to mean. We assumed that each sign system made a unique contribution to a person's overall meaning potential and that any instance of literacy was in fact a multimodal event...

Since literacy events are multimodal, we need to look beyond the evidence of written expression. Encouraging our students to use oral language, art, and drama together allows them access to the discourse community and provides them with the tools to be literate in the 21st Century.

(Leland, Harste, & Helt, 2000, pp. 106 & 114)

This conception of literacy implies that students may demonstrate and develop their literacy in a different way, or may be "smart in a different way" (Gardner, 1993, 1999).

Howard Gardner famously identified seven intelligences (adding one more in 1999) recognizing that although we all have capacities in all eight domains, we usually have strengths in some more than others. Schools may have traditionally taught mainly to our verbal and logical intelligences, and seem to have neglected the visual, musical, interpersonal, intrapersonal, and kinesthetic intelligences and "naturalist intelligence which enables human beings to recognize, categorize and draw upon certain features of the environment" (Gardner, 1999, pp. 41-43; see also Figure 3.6). Individuals who do not exhibit strength in the verbal and logical domains often appear less successful in school settings. Gardner's theory of multiple intelligences offers strong support for providing more opportunities in the arts, so that students with greater strengths in those domains can make use of those intelligences to bolster the less dominant areas.

Expression through artistic media allows ways of communicating that might not otherwise be possible. In some ways, each of the arts is a distinct language in itself. A picture is not just *worth* a thousand words, it expresses ideas, feelings, and realities that *cannot be conveyed in words*. Painting, sculpture, dance, and song exhibit their meaning from another perspective. For some students, if given the opportunity, it is through the medium of colour and shape, or through sound and movement that they are able to solve problems and show how they are "smart."

Because the arts are hands-on, experiential, and problem focused, students in arts-based classes develop creative problem-solving and higher-order thinking skills that are essential 'smarts'; life the 21st century demands citizens who have diverse approaches—people who will readily use intuition, as well as analysis, synthesis, and evaluation to make judgments with moral ramifications.

(Cornett & Smithrim, 2001, p. 4)

Research supports this claim. Shirley Brice Heath's (2004) studies of middle-childhood and adolescent learners at risk who "participated intensely in high-demand, high-quality productions or performances in the arts" showed that they benefited from acceleration in "later language development of forms central to academic language and literacy." She found a significant relationship between time spent in "arts learning environments" (studios, theatres, and galleries) and the development of "fluent talk" about their artistic endeavours as well as engagement in "multiple forms of literacies—from art books to…video libraries" (p. 338). Although her research initially examined the links between the arts and oral and written language acquisition, she went on to find evidence of links between *enjoyment* in the arts to other forms of learning as well.

> *It appears artists see learning as ways of solving problems that may arise, and because much of the work of art involves casting the self forward and needing to anticipate variables or circumstances that may affect that performance, anticipatory problem seeing and problem solving have high appeal. (p. 340)*

While it is important is to see the potential for literacy learning for those who have strengths in the creative domains and weakness in others, the arts are an important and powerful means of teaching and learning for all of us. The arts are an integral part of everyday life; we see art in

literacy
notebook
7.3

STOP, THINK, AND WRITE

A dramatic revolution in cognitive understanding began in the 1970's.
Research now substantiates what some teachers and parents already knew intuitively—that the arts are critical to learning.

—E. Murfee

1. **Imagine yourself** in a staff room with several teachers who express skepticism about your plans to make the arts a central part of your program. They advise you to stay focused on the "basics"—literacy and numeracy—and save art for Friday afternoons. In your notebook write a detailed account of how and why you plan to integrate the arts (visual art, drama, storytelling, poetry, music, and movement) and infuse them throughout the program.

2. **Comment** on the role of aesthetic enjoyment in learning as experienced through engaging with the arts. How is learning more effective and memorable when it is joyful?

3. **List** some ways you can help your students to see the connections between the art they are viewing and creating in school, and the role of the arts in the "real world."

our environment on signs and billboards and in television advertisements; we listen to music; we hang art on the walls of our homes and offices; we read beautifully illustrated books; we attend theatre or dance productions; some of us dance, sing, act, make pottery, or tell stories every day. If art is so prevalent in our everyday lives, why do we have to justify and fight for its inclusion in the daily classroom program?

The Magic of Poetry

> *Poetry is the record of the best and happiest moments*
> *of the happiest and best minds.*
> —Percy Bysshe Shelley

> *And I must borrow every changing shape to find expression.*
> —T. S. Eliot

In our quest to recognize that students display multiple ways of knowing and to provide various ways and means for demonstrating different ways of being smart, poetry is particularly powerful. It is as much like a distinct language as music. From Mother Goose to T. S. Eliot, poets allow us, as Proust states, to "see landscapes which would otherwise have remained unknown to us like the landscapes of the moon." Poetic language employing compelling metaphors, such as Proust's use of "landscape," opens new vistas—new ways of seeing and feeling familiar terrain.

The "motive for metaphor," as Frye (1963) calls it, is a powerful drive to connect "the human mind with what goes on outside it, because the only genuine joy you can have is in those rare moments when you feel that although we may know in part, we are also a part of what we know" (p. 11). One motivation for reading and writing poetry, then, is the joy found in the act of expressing our most profound feelings and ideas. They cannot easily be expressed in words, which is why we reach for metaphors. How does Carl Sandburg express his experience of fog? He says that it "comes on little cat feet." How does Emily Dickinson see the setting sun?

> *Blazing in Gold and quenching in Purple*
> *Leaping like Leopards to the Sky...*
> *And the Juggler of Day is gone.*

And the rising sun?

> *I'll tell you how the sun rose—*
> *A Ribbon at a time—*

Sharing the beauty of such poetic expression with our students and inspiring them to write poems and verse is like introducing them to an intoxicating form of music. It brings language to life, and is more like play than many other forms of school writing. Because there are fewer rules, poetry is less likely to be full of errors; it allows greater freedom to take risks.

> Poetry can build immediate success with students and allow them to focus on the fun and joy of writing unencumbered by grammar and punctuation. It encourages language and word play, connects reading and writing, demonstrates the importance of word choice and word order, and frees students to write creatively (Routman, 2003). To this, Harrison and Holderith (2003) add that poetry helps students to learn and apply important content in fun and interesting ways.
>
> (Parr & Campbell, in press)

READING AND WRITING POETRY

Poetry is an art form to be appreciated for its own sake. To write one poem, you have to read and listen to many poems.

> Poetry is earprint. It longs to be said aloud. It plays with language and with the sounds and rhythms of language. Very young children know about poetry. They clap along, sing along, and join in with rhymes that are hundreds of years old. We can bring poetry to the ears of our children in many ways. It is the constant ear training that will bring children to see the need for poetry.
>
> (Booth & Moore, 2003, p. 72)

Teaching poetry begins with reading poems aloud. You must choose and rehearse them carefully so that the words leap off the page and into the hearts and minds of the listeners. One of our goals should be to introduce our students to all kinds of poetry, from free verse to the more structured forms, such as Haiku and rhyming narrative.

If we find that our students are unfamiliar with traditional nursery rhymes, this is a good place to begin. These ancient poem-stories tune the ear and demonstrate the amazing economy of poetic writing. Along with nursery rhymes, playground rhymes are an accessible way into poetry. The collections of Iona and Peter Opie, such as *I Saw Esau: The Schoolchild's Pocket Book,* are valuable sources of chants, riddles, and rhymes passed down through the generations. Using the humour of playground rhymes can entice the most reluctant poet.

Teacher, teacher, we don't care,
We can see your underwear.
Is it black or is it white?
Oh my gosh...
It's dynamite!
(Booth, 1993, pp. 47-49)

We feel that budding poets should begin their more serious or formal study of poetry reading and poetry writing by first playing with free verse, unbound by the constraints of rhyme schemes, metre, and syllable counting—they can all be taught later. Most children are probably familiar with rhyme—perhaps too familiar. Many children (and adults) think that all poetry must or should rhyme. This can result in artificial and stilted poetry, where the lines are written within an imposed rhyme scheme.

> **TEACHING TIP:** *Have children write their own playground rhymes and parodies of nursery rhymes, and collect them in a classroom anthology. It will become favourite reading during self-selected independent reading time. This genre is particularly appealing to Junior-level students.*

The teacher is also the model for writing poetry. Those who are hesitant need only try it; mastery is not essential (Parr & Campbell, in press). As with all teaching, it is our passion and enthusiasm that matter most.

In addition to valuing and understanding poetry as a distinct form of creative expression, poetry carries strong connections to the worlds of music, movement and dance, visual art, drama, and storytelling. It is to those connections we now turn.

STOP, THINK, AND WRITE

We believe that to teach anything successfully, the teacher should try the activity first whenever possible. This is particularly true in the case of poetry reading and writing.

First of all, answer the following honestly:

- Do you like reading poems?
- Have you ever written a poem?

Second of all, read some poems. Lots of them. Read different kinds. Read haikus, sonnets, narrative and lyric poems, free verse, shape and sound poems. Read long and short poems, funny and sad poems. Try writing a found poem (see Theory into Practice 7.1).

Finally, compose an original poem, copy it into your notebook, and share it with your students. The magic will begin!

literacy
notebook
7.4

Teacher Talk/7.2

DAVID BOOTH, AUTHOR AND TEACHER, SPEAKS ABOUT THE SOURCE OF HIS LOVE OF POETRY

At my mother's knee.... Those chestnuts of elocution: "The Boy Who Was Half-Past Three," "Little Orphan Annie," and we begged her to recite them again and again... I took all of the poetry books out of the Sarnia Public Library children's section—I'm not sure why. I think it was the words—so many that I had never seen, special and from long ago, used so well and so strangely. Did "kind" rhyme with "wind" after all?

Teaching my first classes of children, and meeting Bill Moore, my English consultant, who came to my classroom filling it with poems...

Assemblies to run every other Friday. Oh, the work! Choral speaking with 42 boys—and never having time to be afraid of their not liking the poems or their not wanting to read them aloud in front of their peers. Thousands of lines dramatized, chanted, interpreted, sung...

Using nursery rhymes for my first class in teacher education, as a professor, and realizing how much power was hidden inside them...

Forty years of poems. So many more I want to share. Find me a class. I'll just read one or two.

Source: From Booth, D., & Moore, B. (2003). Poems *please! Sharing poetry with children*. Markham, ON: Pembroke Publishers, pp. 7-8. Reprinted by permission.

WHAT WILL I TEACH?

I live in fear
  that I
  will teach the poem
  and they
  will lose the poet
  and the song
  and the self
  within the poem

I live in fear
  that I
  who love the poem
  and the children
  will lose the poem
  and the children
  when I teach the
  poem

But I will teach the poem
  Live with the fear
  Love the children
  Sing the song
  Find the self
  And know the poet
  is beside me
  Just as afraid
  But full of hope.

—David Booth

Source: Booth & Moore (2003, p. 136). Reprinted by permission.

POETIC FORMS: POETRY AND THE MAGIC OF TRANSFORMING

A translation is no translation... unless it will give you the music of a poem along with the words of it.
—J.M. Synge

Synge expresses one of the challenges of poetry, but also points to its tremendous potential for creativity, which often involves "transforming" or "transmediating" (Harste, 1988) from one medium to another, much like translating from one language to another. We use "transforming" to emphasize the creative process of shaping or "forming" from one form or shape into a completely different structure. But as Synge tells us, something of the original feel or "music" must be carried through.

Poetry is an excellent medium for identifying and trying out these transformations. By its very nature it is uniquely suited to illustrate how transforming from one medium to another is possible. The ability to transform, like magic, from one mode of expression to another is a sign of real understanding; this is most challenging when going from verbal to non-verbal or vice versa. Poetry is a bridge in this respect, because it goes beyond mere words to evoke images and feelings, sometimes using the shape of a poem on the page to express its meaning, such as the following poem by bpNichol. It is imprinted in the concrete of a laneway on the University of Toronto campus. Or the shape or concrete poem on the following page, which is formed into the shape of its subject matter.

A LAKE
A LANE
A LINE
ALONE

We can once again turn to children's literature to support our efforts to teach and learn about how poetry and visual images can be harmonized, and to encourage students to make transformations from one medium to another. The powerful connections between the paintings of the Group of Seven and Canadian poems are shown in David Booth's *Images of Nature: Canadian Poets and the Group of Seven*. Warabé Aska's *Seasons* combines his illustrations with poems chosen by Alberto Manguel.

We find links between poetry and music in rhythm and beat, lyrics, and classical favourites such as Vivaldi's *Four Seasons*; many poems about the seasons and weather fit the mood and tempo of each of these concertos. Playing music while reading poems aloud enhances the mean-

> **TEACHING TIP:** *With a wide selection of paintings collected from calendars, magazines and art books, and a collection of poetry books with poems of all kinds, students themselves can find poems and pictures that enhance one another. These can be used to create personal albums, or a whole class project book. The poems and paintings can also be used to inspire poetry and story writing during writers' workshop (see Chapter 12), or art work in any medium during visual art time. Use Booth's* Images of Nature *and Aska's* Seasons *as models.*

The rhythms and beats in music help to enhance the meaning of poetry.

Raindrop

A
drop
of rain is
like a sudden
knock at the door.
Unexpected, yet often
welcomed with a smile. It
can brighten your day or ruin
your plans. It can make you laugh
or make you sad. Whether the raindrop
is moving fast or slow, or is big or small,
it always gets everyone's attention. A rain-
drop contains many secrets. It is a bubble of
anticipation and surprise. It cleanses the earth,
it feeds the flowers, and fills the holes. The
raindrop is never silent. It bangs on the
roof, spatters on the window, or
splashes into a puddle.
A raindrop.
—Anonymous

ings of a poem. Similarly, listening to music can stimulate poetic writing. And, like music, poems can be performed—a fact quite evident to all of us through rap music. Song lyrics can be a highly motivating way to

Woke up, it was a Chelsea morning
And the first thing that I knew
There was milk and toast and honey
And a bowl of oranges, too
And the sun poured in like butterscotch
And stuck to all my senses

Oh, won't you stay
We'll put on the day
And we'll talk in present tenses.

—Joni Mitchell, lyrics from the song "Chelsea Morning," from the album, *Clouds*

My paddle's keen and bright,
Flashing with silver.
Follow the wild goose flight,
Dip, dip, and swing.

Dip, dip, and swing her back,
Flashing with silver.
Swift as the wild goose flies,
Dip, dip, and swing.

—A Traditional Round

introduce poetry to Junior-level and older students. The following examples might be used to introduce sense imagery and similes ("*the sun poured in like butterscotch*") to emphasize using the sounds of words to evoke images ("*dip, dip, and swing*").

PERFORMING POETRY: CONNECTIONS BETWEEN POETRY AND DRAMA

In their book, *Story Works*, David Booth and Bob Barton (2000) describe how they used **role-playing** to help a group of six-year-olds "wander inside a complex story poem" (p. 87). Reading a poem aloud in role, in the voice of the character telling the story in poetic form, can create the mood and atmosphere needed to explore the meanings embedded in the poem. The next step is to involve the students in dramatic readings of poems. This can be done in a variety of ways:

- Shared reading (see Chapter 9)

- Choral reading or speaking: Similar to shared reading, in that it involves reading as a whole group, but uses more dramatic effects, such as alternating between individual voices and group voices, and varying effects such as pitch, volume, and tempo. (See Theory into Practice 7.2 and Chapter 10.)

- Readers' theatre (see Chapter 5): Many narrative poems lend themselves to this format.

- Drama: Dramatize a poem through interpretative improvisation. Several students can role play a poem's characters or objects in words or by miming their actions, while other students may interview them about their feelings and points of view.

- Narration and mime: While the teacher or a student reads a poem out loud, students mime the actions. Students can interpret the words through their movements individually, in pairs, or in small groups.

- Dance drama: Individual students or groups can interpret a poem through patterns of dance movements that reflect the rhythms and feelings expressed in a poem. The dance moves can be accompanied by music, sound effects, an added chant composed by the students, and costumes and props.

Many of these dramatic activities can be used with either poems or stories as inspiration. The possibilities for integrating other art forms are virtually endless.

Theory Into Practice/7.1

FOUND POETRY

Found poetry is a natural link to reading since its foundation is in text. Students choose direct quotes, random phrases, or words from a variety of genres, texts, and formats to create an original poem. They manipulate these phrases and words, and piece them together in a novel way that creates a strong and powerful image. Found poetry often provides a scaffold to poetry writing that allows students to explore literary devices and vocabulary, in a non-threatening way. It also actively engages problem-solving and critical thinking as students must review their text source with a specific purpose and message in mind. They need not rhyme or impose a particular structure.

Before:
- After a read aloud, model by thinking aloud and recording on the board, chart paper, or overhead how to choose words and phrases from the author's text, and how to rearrange them into poetic form. Demonstrate repetition, word placement on the page, and how to find rhythmic sections. The poem does not have to be finished by the whole group; show them enough so they get the idea.
- Choose a variety of well-written picture books or stories from an anthology; include some non-fiction, too, as long as the writing is exceptionally good.
- Organize students in small groups (4-5) and provide a range of texts (at least 3-4) to choose from.

During:
- Students read the texts, first individually, and then together. They can decide which text will be their source for the found poems by taking turns reading aloud the best selections each has chosen. Once consensus is reached, the text should be read aloud in its entirety. While one student is reading, the others are noting words and phrases they like the sound of.
- One student becomes the scribe or recorder, while the group members contribute their favourite "deliciously poetic" lines from the text they have read together. Another student might re-read what has been written so far, as others search for themes, adjust the sequencing, identify lines for effective repetition, and finally reach a consensus on the final form.

After:
- Read found poems with the large group. Publish a final copy, revised and edited by the group. The entire process may take 3 to 4 days to complete if a 1 to 2 hour literacy block is used. Here is a found poem composed with Grade 4 students using Dyan Sheldon's book, *The Whale's Song*:

<table>
<tr>
<td>

Whales
most wondrous creatures
Whales
as big as the hills
as peaceful as the moon
Whales
as large as the mountains
bluer than the sky

</td>
<td>

Whales
moved as if they were dancing
their voices like the wind
Whales
enormous in the ocean
their singing filled up the night
Whales
most wondrous creatures

</td>
</tr>
</table>

A Note on Performance Presentations

Booth and Moore (2003) give the following advice that we have used when preparing public presentations by children.

> There may be times when children wish to take a particular activity out of the classroom environment to share it with a wider audience. When children are placed in performance situations, the point of view of the audience becomes the major consideration rather than the development of the children's own feelings and relationships. This type of sharing should occur only when the children are prepared and ready, and when the exploration and learning have been wholly satisfactory. (p. 101)

In the final sections of this chapter, we look specifically at how to integrate successfully drama and storytelling across the curriculum, using story as the focal point. We will continue with a brief discussion of the nature of story drama, drama, and storytelling followed by three classroom-ready workshops using drama, storytelling and the arts integrated with content areas of the curriculum. As we discuss each of these, we suggest that you focus on drama and storytelling as processes of learning rather than products and performances.

Story Drama: One Way to Integrate Literature and Language Study, Drama, and Storytelling

I believe that every child I meet understands deep, basic matters worthy of exploration but they may as yet have no language for them. One of the languages they may develop is through dramatic work.
—Dorothy Heathcote

A primary reason for integrating the arts with other aspects of the curriculum is purely practical and can be stated in a refrain echoed by teachers everywhere: "There is just too much to cover and not enough time!" Another main reason emphasizes the needs of the learners: Integration promotes meaning-making. It provides the conditions that allow students to use what they already know to explore, learn, and connect previous learning in new ways. In a fragmented, itemized curriculum, integration permits big-picture thinking and strategic problem-solving. Figure 7.1 is a detailed list of the links between reading and writing, oral and visual connections, drama and storytelling.

Storytelling and drama are two rich interrelated sources of possibilities for full integration. Although the classroom workshops (Figure 7.3,

Theory Into Practice/7.2

CHORAL SPEAKING

The simplest way to begin work in **choral speaking** with a classroom is to choose a short, rhythmic poem, and follow the "reading to, reading with, and reading by" sequence:

- **Reading to:** teacher reads aloud.
- **Reading with:** students join in where and when they can.
- **Reading by:** students read without the teacher.

A nursery rhyme is a good place to begin, or a poem such as "Flying-Man" as described by Larry Swartz (2002):

Flying-Man, Flying Man   Over the mountains
Up in the sky,   And over the sea.
Where are you going   Flying-Man, Flying-Man
Flying so high?   Can you take me?

Swartz had his class chant this rhyme together, and then experimented with:

- saying it softly, then loudly
- using call and response*
- repeating it as a round
- clapping it out
- singing (to the tune of "On top of Old Smokey" or "Twinkle, Twinkle Little Star")
- giving single words or lines to individual students, having them say it as dramatically as possible, and then adding a movement, followed by freezing into a position (Swartz, 2002, pp. 20-21)

Source: *There are specific poems that have been composed for choral speaking, for example, Paul Fleischman's poems in *Joyful Noise: Poems for Two Voices;* and *I Am a Phoenix: Poems for Two Voices.*

Figure 7.4, and Figure 7.5) provided below seem to separate them into two distinct categories, we wish to stress their interdependence by briefly describing the concept of **story drama**:

> Story drama—which I'll define for the moment as improvised role play based on story—surrounds my teaching, and allows children to at once become the co-constructors of a story, the story itself, and the characters living within the story: as the poet David McCord says, they are "the singer, the song, and the sung."
>
> (Booth, 1994, p. 7)

Story drama is a powerful way to link drama and reading: the relationship resides in the *meanings*—meanings that are found well below the surface and beyond single, "correct" interpretations.

Students can dramatize or enact a story in a variety of ways, but to count as *drama*, they must go well beyond a literal retelling of the plot.

FIGURE 7.1 Curriculum Connections

Reading Comprehension Strategies	Writing Skills	Oral/Visual Connections
• Retelling, relating, reflecting • Visualizing • Summarizing, sequencing • Predicting, speculating • Interpreting • Making connections (to other stories, own lives) • Understanding genres (traditional literature: folktales, fairy tales, fables) • Development of story sense (how the elements in a story function) • Development of vocabulary, especially "book language" • Development of knowledge of language structures • Monitoring comprehension (for example, when retelling in your own words)	• Development of story sense • Organizational awareness • Audience and voice awareness • Imagination; creativity • Adding detail • Descriptive language • Opportunity to use book language (vocabulary and language structures) • Opportunity to explore a variety of genres in writing	• Excellent preparation for public speaking skill development • Listening skill development • Oral language development (communication and social skills)

After reading or listening to a story, and having time to discuss it, the children can then begin the process of deciding how they can effectively dramatize it. Give them a structure to help them make the following choices:

• Who are the characters? Who is playing whom and how? Should we add other characters not in the original? Should some students role play as witnesses to the events or interview the main characters?

• What is the setting? Should we change where or when the story takes place? Do we need costumes or props?

• Who will do what? Why? (Encourage students to discuss deeper meanings, as well as the themes and issues the story presents.)

• What will we say? How will we say it? (Depending on the purpose of the activity, the students can write the dialogue as a script and include stage directions.)

We have found that this process unfolds best when small groups of students discuss the story and its transformation into drama while sitting in a circle and guided by the teacher. But to transform a story from the listening or reading mode into speaking, moving action, we need to first understand the concept of "drama" itself? Should this concept be explicitly taught along with the doing of drama in the classroom? To help you answer these questions, we will present our view of what drama is and what storytelling is, and then consider some of the conditions that need to be present in the classroom for these arts to flourish.

FIGURE 7.2 Tableaux

Tableaux are a good way to begin teaching story drama, since they are performed in small groups using just the participants' bodies and positions in relation to one another. No speaking lines are included.

A tableau is a frozen action shot or picture created by a group of individuals performing, in statue-like form. It is the essence of a significant moment in the action of a story.

Procedure
Groups do not talk in the final presentation, but work cooperatively using body language. All members of the group combine to create a scene, freeze for a few moments (approximately 10 seconds), then flow seamlessly into the next scene. Two to three scenes from a story may be presented in sequence.

Tips
Teach this in the gym, directing small groups to make shapes as a group, then freeze—a line, now FREEZE, a circle, now FREEZE, etc.

Next have them display specific scenes from a well known tale, such as *Little Red Riding Hood* (one person is Little Red Riding Hood, one the Grandma, one the wolf, one the woodcutter).

Think of the arrangement of the group members and how it will look visually, as for a photograph; individuals can be facing in different directions, their bodies aligned on different levels, etc.

Teach the students to use a pre-arranged signal, such as foot-stomp to signal the transition to the next scene.

Extension
After 2 to 3 scenes are presented, each person may speak one word or short phrase best expressing his/her feelings at this moment in the story.

NOTE: For practical and beautifully constructed integrated units using drama as the vehicle, see *The New Dramathemes*, by Larry Swartz. The activities have all been put into practice successfully by real teachers and real students in real classrooms. They are themed by topics such as humour, mystery, and community; they include all of the language arts and they focus on social-emotional skills by developing communication, collaboration, and problem-solving.

FIGURE 7.3 Classroom Drama Workshop

Using *A Promise to the Sun: An African Tale* by Tololwa M. Mollel.

A holistic drama approach allows students to explore story and content in oral, interpersonal, and low-risk ways; students get so involved in the fun and action of drama that there is less focus on the story/content, although that is what is truly driving the drama. Drama becomes an integral part of the reading response and transactional writing processes; students learn in authentic, natural, and meaningful contexts where drama serves as a scaffold to the independent expression of their learning in other formats.

Before the Drama

- Set a purpose for listening: See if you can figure out the water cycle while I am reading; try to determine what must happen before rain will come to earth.
- Read aloud *A Promise to the Sun*.
- Discuss personification and character development. Who are the characters? What do we know about them? How do we know this?
- Warm up using appropriate and relevant activities.
  Voice: Chant "Earth has no rain, Earth has no food, Earth asks for rain."
  Movement: Use hands and simple movements to create a rainstorm.
  Teamwork/Groupwork: In small groups, choose one character. Create **tableaux** to represent the character's perspective at the beginning, middle, and end of the story.

During the Drama

Divide into groups. Assign each group a task. In a regular classroom, every student has the opportunity to explore all tasks using a rotation system. Exploring all tasks will prepare them to engage in all of the post-drama activities.

Story Drama

- Task 1: Design and present a soliloquy on the sun's behalf expressing his feelings about not having his promise fulfilled.
- Task 2: Design and present a soliloquy on the bat's behalf expressing its feelings about not having the promise to the sun fulfilled.
- Task 3: Stage a debate between the bat and the birds about the reasons why they should or should not keep a promise.

Content Related Drama

- Task 1: Using the content and props provided, dramatize the water cycle making sure to present key information in a way that is accurate, relevant, and meaningful.
- Task 2: Present dramatically the information provided on the individual birds and the bat. Make sure to give details explaining why the bat is not a bird.
- Task 3: Using information provided in the story and on task cards, describe a drought. Speculate on the influences of drought on human beings.

FIGURE 7.3 Classroom Drama Workshop (continued)

After the Drama

All students participate in guided reflection on the drama process. Students choose one multi-level activity:

Story Related Activities

- Pretend you are the trees who salute the hero who brought rain to your forest. Create a thank-you card to the bat outlining what you are thankful for.
- Write a journal entry about the bat's journey to find rain and his feelings along the journey.
- Write a letter from the sun to the bat. Exchange letters with a friend and write the bat's response.
- Write an apology letter from the birds to the sun and the bat outlining why they didn't fulfill their promise.

Content Related Activities

- Keeping the personification that was present in the story, create a cartoon strip that demonstrates the water cycle.
- With global warming comes the possible depletion of the world's water resources. Draw a series of pictures (supported by single sentences) outlining the potential effects of this loss of water.
- Choose one bird or the bat. Develop an information concept web including: appearance, food, habitat, adaptive behaviour, reproduction.

Connecting to Other Areas of the Curriculum

Visual Arts: Introduce students to watercolours. Invite them to paint a picture of a drought or the argument between the bat and the birds. Have them look at other watercolours and investigate adding fine detail. Show students different ways to experiment with watercolour technique, for example, drawing with black ink, photocopying on a very faint setting, and then painting over the lines.

NOTE: This story unit can be used to introduce social studies units on topics such as community and interdependence; science units on the water cycle, eco-systems, animal groups; visual arts units on mixed media and illustration; music and movement units on rhythm; literature-social studies units on folktales of the different regions of Africa; or social skills or character education to discuss what is meant by a promise.

Other Literature Resources for Story Drama

Bringing the Rain to Kapiti Plain; The Name of the Tree, Celia Barker Lottridge

Rainbow Crow, Nancy vanLaan

Something from Nothing, Phoebe Gilman

Keepers of the Earth, Caduto & Bruchac

The Wolf of Gubbio, Michael Bedard

The Trial of the Stone, Richardo Keens Douglas

Dear Children of the Earth; Children of the Earth... Remember, Schim Schimmel

FIGURE 7.4 Classroom Storytelling Workshop

Using *The Name of Tree*, retold by Celia Barker Lottridge.

This workshop engages the learners in a literature-based unit integrating the six language arts with drama, storytelling, poetry, music, movement, and visual art. The storytelling and story listening with selected follow-up activities can be completed in an afternoon. If all the activities are to be included, the workshop can take place over a one-week period, requiring about two hours per day. The story is appropriate for Kindergarten to secondary levels. The workshop is suitable for Grades 3-6.

First of all, in the days leading up to the storytelling day (when students listen to a tale told in the traditional way without a text, pictures, or props), we engage in these warm-up activities to demonstrate to students that we are all storytellers. If students are unfamiliar with visualization (see Chapter 10) or drama strategies such as tableaux, these can be taught prior to this workshop, or the suggested activities can be adapted for your classroom.

Small Group/Partner Warm-Ups

- Favourite Place Stories: Arranged in partners or in small circles of 4 to 5, students introduce themselves by describing their favourite place, including as much detail as possible so that the listeners can imagine themselves in that place.
- Stupid Things I've Done: Teacher should model first.
- Object Stories: Pass a treasure chest or magic bag around the story circle. Each person tells a short tale the object calls to mind (for example, "This stone reminds me of the time...")
- Name Stories: Each person tells story about their name; how or why they were given that name or nickname. (This can be assigned ahead of time.)

The workshop then continues with the teacher or guest storyteller modelling storytelling by telling *The Name of the Tree*.

Before the Storytelling Begins

- Set the scene; set a purpose for listening.
- Engage in a brief visualization exercise: "In your mind's eye, picture a tree, imagine the look, smell, and feel of its leaves, bark, and fruit."
- Ask for predictions or wonder statements based on the title and place of origin of the tale: "This is a Bantu tale from Africa, *The Name of the Tree*. What do you think and wonder about its plot, characters, and setting?" Record the answers and explain that you will return to them later.
- Instruct the students to listen for the importance of *remembering* in this story.
- If the students have not listened to a story told in the traditional way, without books, or props or pictures, say, "Visualize as you listen. I will be asking you to tell us what you saw after the story."

During Storytelling

- Join in on the repeated refrain, "Ungali, Ungali, the name of the tree is Ungali," possibly using a drum or rhythm sticks.

After Storytelling: Choose any Combination of the Following

- Visualize: Ask students to describe their most vivid scenes (share with a partner first). Ask for volunteers to describe how they pictured the tree. Encourage detailed descriptions with prompts:

FIGURE 7.4 Classroom Storytelling Workshop (continued)

"Tell about the colours of the leaves, the smell of the fruit, the texture of the bark of the tree." Discuss the variety of interpretations that are possible. After they have described their own scenes, show them the picture book.

- Re-visit: Return to the wonder statements recorded before the story was told. Discuss whether they discovered answers while listening, and ask what they are still wondering about.

- Compare this story with similar stories; for example, other African morality tales such as *The Man Who Knew Too Much* by Julius Lester, *The Magic Tree* by Obinkaram Echewa, or life experiences. This can be done in the whole group, and recorded on a T-chart, with two titles recorded at the top, under the top line of the T, and comparisons and contrasts recorded on either side.

- Re-tell: With a partner, take turns re-telling this story from the point of view of one of the animals or an object in the story such as a tree in the jungle, or the rabbit-hole that three animals fell into.

- Story Drama: In small groups, re-enact a main event in the story, for example:
  - Show the animals' trek across the "great flat plain" up to the point where they reach the tree and look up. Each animal in the group should say one line to help identify which animal they are portraying (e.g., the giraffe might say, "Even with my long, neck I cannot reach the wondrous fruit.")
  - Other possibilities can be listed on the board or chart paper, such as the elephant getting her foot stuck, pulling it out, and then admitting that she forgot the name of the tree, or the encounter between the lion and the tortoise. This list should be started by the teacher, with added suggestions from the students. The first role play should be modelled with teacher guidance, with appropriate lines, body movements, and a time frame, before allowing small groups to rehearse their event.

- Alternative to story drama: Perform a series of tableaux representing three scenes from the beginning, middle, and end of the story. Since tableaux do not include speaking, percussion instruments can be used to signal scene changes or to accompany the entire performance.

- Sketch to Stretch (see Theory into Practice 6.2): Choose a symbol or picture to represent what this story means to you, and share it in small groups.

- Choral Speaking: Practise the chant from the story as a whole group. Discuss the purpose of the chant in the story. In small groups, choose one of the animals from the story, and have students create their own chant for their animal group "so that you will never forget." Provide materials for visuals, props, costumes, musical instruments, if desired. Add movement, moving as the animals would. This can be stylized, and should be performed with the beat of the chant. Add simple rhythm instruments. Perform the chants for the class.

- Visual Arts: Provide a variety of materials for the students to choose from, for example, paper of different colours, textures, and sizes, paints, crayons, pencil crayons, Plasticine, and glue. Invite the students to paint, draw, or construct a multi-media collage or sculpture of their version of the tree. For inspiration include picture books by Ian Wallace and other illustrators working in a variety of media such as painting (*The Cremation of Sam McGee*, Ted Harrison), Plasticine art (*Two by Two*, Barbara Reid), pencil and ink (*Jumanji* Chris Van Allsburg), coloured pencil and crayon (*Out on the Ice in the Middle of the Bay*, Alice Priestly), collage (*Something from Nothing*, Phoebe Gilman), mixed media (*The Orphan Boy*, Paul Morin), and sculpture (*The Mud Family*, Paul Morin).

FIGURE 7.5 Classroom Content Workshop: Learning to Love Content

Using a variety of fiction and non-fiction, this cross-curricular science-art unit on the theme of "Space" demonstrates our multiple ways of knowing approach to literacy and its integration with studies in the content areas. It involves aesthetic reading, the pure enjoyment of reading—for example, reading a poem—and efferent reading for real world purposes. In efferent reading, attention is focused on information that is to be extracted or retained from the text following the reading event. Every text can be read from both an efferent and an aesthetic stance that is a reflection of the reader's orientation, intention, or purpose for reading. This unit presents various non-traditional methods (for example, drama, storytelling, poetry, visual arts) for presenting content material that has been learned. This approach enhances student engagement, reduces the possibility of regurgitation and plagiarism, and strengthens the connection between what students know and what they need to learn.

Before

Use an **anticipation guide** to find out what children know and don't know, and to stimulate the desire to find out more on a topic.

Fact or Fib?

Distribute stars with a fact or fib statement about stars, constellations, etc. Have children decide which statements are facts and which are fibs. For example:

1. The Northern Lights, or aurora borealis, were once thought to be dead souls trying to tell the living that summer will return. (Fact: Saami people of Arctic Europe)
2. "Sun dogs" appear in the Arctic when sunlight passes through ice crystals in the air; they appear as a halo around the sun, or as two bright spots, or "sun dogs" on opposite sides of the sun. (Fact)
3. When you see the Northern Lights, if you whistle, they will jump closer and make a crackling sound. (Fib)
4. The North Star cannot be seen at the North Pole. (Fib)

See Love & Drake (2000) to compose additional facts and fibs, or invite students to compose their own.

Discuss or brainstorm with students the types of activities that extend culminating projects beyond the traditional written factual report. Examples include:

Poetry as Research Project

- Choral reading: "Twas the Night" in *Science Verse*, by Jon Scieska
- Poetic surfing: Make an acrostic using the word "constellation" and facts from the NASA website
- "Discovery circles" instead of literature circles: Find web-based information using guided Internet searches; for example, acrostic poetry, Stellar phenomena, Tessellation, astronomy, Rega
- Concrete poem (shape of star or constellation), found poems from literature, websites, etc.

Hypothetical Writing—Language of the Stars

- Write a plausible explanation for the following:
  - Why are celebrities in music, film, and sports called stars?
  - Why are stars given as awards or rewards?

FIGURE 7.5 Classroom Content Workshop: Learning to Love Content (continued)

- What is the origin of the expressions "starry-eyed" and having "stars in your eyes"?
- What does it mean to be "star-struck"?
- After composing your own "fact" or hypothetical explanation for the origins of these expressions, research the true fact.

A Musical Space—Challenge: Produce a model for your students

- In the spirit of "Twas the Night" and "Twinkle-less, Twinkle-less," write a parody to the tune of "Jingle Bells." Theme: What you know about space.
- Record in the K of your K-W-L (Plus) chart (see Chapter 10)

During: Using Websites to Gather Information

Provide a variety of non-fiction materials, including bookmarked websites

Before

- Focused Internet searches; poetic surfing; how to ask a really good question; vocabulary preparation; K-W-L Plus; choose from a variety of expository text structures to record information (see Chapter 10)

During

- Navigate using graphics, symbols, key words; how to skim; judge when to skim, when to slow down; select worthwhile text; take notes (using K-W-L); read ahead; revisit initial questions; monitor comprehension through mini-summaries; stay focused

After

- Decide if reading goals have been achieved; check whether questions have been answered; evaluate your own understanding; summarize major ideas in K-W-L chart or graphic organizer; seek additional information from other sources

During: Using the Arts to Gather Information

Provide alternative ways to gather information and prepare a presentation, using one of the arts as outlined below. The following ideas can be set up as work stations. The students can rotate through them over a few days, or they may concentrate on one station to explore their area in greater depth.

Idea 1: Starry, Starry Night
(http://www.princetonol.com/groups/iad/lessons/elem/elem67.html)

- Show a reproduction of van Gogh's *Starry Night* to the class and invite the students to discuss it. Ask about the lines van Gogh uses in the sky to show movement. Discuss foreground and background and what objects are in them.
- Give students crayons; neon colours are even better. Instruct them to press hard as they draw stars and moon like *Starry Night* and to repeat shapes around them so that it looks as though the stars are radiating. Add swirls to the picture.
- Paint over the crayoned sky with black paint (crayon resist) and let dry. During the next lesson, discuss silhouettes. Using black 6"x18" paper, have students draw a base line in chalk and attach

FIGURE 7.5 Classroom Content Workshop: Learning to Love Content (continued)

mountains, houses, a skyline of any type and then cut around the outside edges being careful not to cut off the baseline.

- Cover the side that has the chalk showing with glue, then turn it over and place at the bottom of your crayon resist painting. Voila! A beautiful starry night.
- While the students work, play the song "Vincent" by Don McLean for inspiration.

Idea 2: Cometrivia! (Drama and Movement)

- Materials: an assortment of rings, nerf balls or smooshie balls, ribbons, etc. to emulate tails, comets, sun, etc.
- Instructions: Students use props to teach information on cards prepared by the teacher. Cards must be read aloud as part of the presentation. Group must work as a whole to present information.
  - Comets get their name from the Greek word "kometes," which means "long hair," a reference to their long tails.
  - Some comets make repeated trips to the sun.
  - Jets of gas and dust form long tails that we can see from Earth. These tails can sometimes be millions of miles long.
  - Comets orbit the sun, but have such a big orbit it takes some comets millions of years to orbit.
  - Comets come into our solar system periodically.
  - When Earth passes through the tail of a comet, we see meteor showers.

Idea 3: Planetextravenganza!

- Materials: Information cards on each of the planets, prepared by the teacher or the students.
- Instructions: Students first read the cards and decide on the key information to present to the class. Students work in small groups to determine how to present the information. They may choose a dramatic piece, a poem, illustrations, a panel discussion, a debate (on whether Pluto is really a planet, for example).

Students may find the following site useful when preparing information cards on the planets: http://www.solarviews.com/eng/

After: Representing Learning through Non-Traditional Responses

- With a partner, interview a Star.
- Write a newspaper report using the 5 Ws + H; write a poem.
- Read other constellation stories and myths from around the world ("How Fisher went to Skyland: The Origin of the Big Dipper," in *Keepers of the Earth*—see Resources).
- View videos that relate to legends and origins of constellations (*The Bear* by Raymond Briggs).
- Write or tell a story about your own version of the origin of a constellation (hypothetical or plausible explanation).
- Create a graphic text (*Magic School Bus*).
- Write a song, develop a webquest, PowerPoint, or Kidpix presentation about space.
- Participate in a virtual field trip to space.
- Develop a list of other creative responses.

The link between drama and reading goes beyond retelling the plot; students should uncover meanings.

WHAT IS DRAMA?

Drama

…is something that happens when all the participants in and witness to a make-believe situation find themselves believing in that situation, because somehow the situation has come to represent things that are important to everyone. The learning in drama is like a voice saying: 'This is what life is like; this is how people are; this is the way that human encounters work.'

(Booth, 1985, pp. ix-x)

Drama is about participation and problem-solving; it is a process that *may* end in performance. Performance is a product of drama, but we would like you to value the process of participation in drama activities. As Dorothy Heathcote expressed it:

Educational drama can be defined as having two aspects and aims. One of these we can define as 'creative work,' the other as 'coping work'…A broad definition of educational drama is 'role-taking' either to understand a social situation more thoroughly or to experience imaginatively via identification in social situations… Dramatic activity is the direct result of the ability to role play—to want to know how it feels to be in someone else's shoes.

(Heathcote, 1984, p. 49)

WHAT IS STORYTELLING?

Storytelling is a "distinctive art form" and an important way to revive a "lost dimension of human experience" that draws on cross-cultural performances and practices (Livo & Reitz, 1986 in Piazza, 1999, p.162). Storytelling provides students with opportunities to identify important details and dialogue, understand and recall stories and story elements, and practise oral language skills such as vocal expression and exaggeration. Storytelling provides students with opportunities to share their stories orally and experiment with a literary tradition (Piazza, 1999).

In order to instil a sense of what storytelling is, and what its powers might be, consider the following quote:

School life is full of all sorts of contexts for story-making. The children live inside a story culture of gossip in the cloakroom, retellings of television shows, games and songs at recess, anecdotes about what happened

STOP, THINK, AND WRITE

Discuss the importance of teacher modelling in the development of concepts such as drama and storytelling. Write several comments about how you can model role-playing a character from a poem or story in order to teach what it means to dramatize and how you can model storytelling by telling an anecdote from your everyday life.

■ How can you impart a sense of the value of drama and storytelling in real life, and in the life of your classroom community?
■ What conditions should be present in your classroom so that drama and storytelling can flourish?

Teaching Tip

Ask your students to imagine what their lives would be like without stories.

literacy
notebook
7.5

on the weekend when they saw their teacher eating in a restaurant. We know that children have heard hundreds of stories before they come to school, family stories that are told over and over again... As teachers, we can tap into these home tales and home truths, and use them to connect with other stories from other families in other times and worlds. We can also share our own personal stories form our own lives, participating in the storying process. We must value the family stories, the recess rhymes, the urban rumours, the tall tales; they are gold spun into story and they add to our wealth as storyers.

(Booth & Barton, 2000, p. 29)

CONDITIONS FOR DRAMA AND STORYTELLING

What should a classroom ready for drama look and sound like? What skills and attitudes must either be present or built for effective drama and storytelling to take place? Revisit Cambourne's conditions for literacy learning and the conditions we have previously discussed as being essential for any type of learning to take place (see Chapters 2 and 4). The following is a brief list of the conditions that we found critical to the success of drama and storytelling in the classroom:

• safe environment/effective management

• trust/risk-taking

• focus/concentration

- cooperation/teamwork
- movement
- imagination/divergent thinking/creativity
- problem-solving
- use of voice
- opportunities for guided/independent practice
- language experience
- fun!

What about Assessment?

Many teachers are concerned about the fact that drama, storytelling, and the other arts can be difficult to assess. We feel that with clearly described expectations for each activity, and careful observation of the processes (not just an evaluation of the final product or performance), assessment is possible and many aspects of student participation can be assessed. The items in Figures 7.6 and 7.7 include criteria for the process, such as collaborative skills, and for performance, such as use of voice and movement. Through careful observation of a student's participation, related literacy skills and abilities can also be evaluated. The ability to successfully retell and re-enact a story, for example, is a powerful indicator that story structure is becoming internalized. Similarly, using story language and speech and mannerisms to portray a character are indicators of higher level comprehension. As with all meaningful assessment, its ultimate purpose is to inform future teaching and provide feedback to students that will encourage further growth. The checklists in Figure 7.6 and Figure 7.7 are designed with those principles in mind. They are worded in child-friendly language so that they can be used for self-assessment.

Moving On

In this chapter, we invited you to examine critically the role of the arts in your classroom, particularly in your language program. Reconsider our initial questions. Do you consider the arts to be a frill or an add-on to the real curriculum? Do you think the arts require specialized, expert knowledge on the part of the teacher? Do you participate in any form of creative expression—visual art, drama, dance—regardless of whether you are good at it?

Do you plan to try any of these activities? What is the role of enjoyment in relation to engaging in creative activities—for you and for your students?

We hope you feel it is a practical, achievable goal to integrate and infuse the arts into your program. The benefits for your students and for you are immeasurable. As former elementary school teachers, we have learned that teaching and learning the arts in all of its forms, in

FIGURE 7.6 Self-Assessment Checklists

Choral Speaking	Tableaux	Problem-Solving	Group Participation
I use my voice appropriately to convey mood and intent.	I focus my attention on the task.	I demonstrate the ability to:	I focus attention on the task right away.
I know what my role is in the group.	I contribute ideas when planning with my group.	• communicate • question	I follow instructions.
I contribute ideas to the choral presentation.	I offer suggestions to help my group revise and shape ideas for presentation.	• argue • persuade • negotiate	I contribute ideas when planning. I take turns during discussions.
I am supportive of others.	I accept different points of view.	• brainstorm • thypothesize • take risks	I accept different points of view and build on the ideas of others.
I have an appropriate sense of audience.	I collaborate in a variety of situations.	• collaborate • reflect	I collaborate in a variety of group situations.
I follow directions and accept advice.	I enjoy this form of dramatic presentation.		I enjoy working with others.
I experiment with pitch, pause, and pace to make the reading more effective.			I make positive suggestions to complete tasks.
I investigate possibilities of using voice, sound, and movement.			
I understand the importance of revising and rehearsing.			

Source: Adapted from Booth & Lundy (1985) and Swartz (2002).

FIGURE 7.7 Journal Questions

Joining In	Storytelling	Role-Playing	Improvisation
Did you feel most comfortable working with a partner, a small group, or the whole class?	Were there times you told a story by yourself? In partners? In small groups? As a whole class? Which did you prefer?	How is role-playing different from acting?	What skills are you developing as you improvise in drama?
Write down three things that you learned about yourself from joining in.	Was it easier to tell a story in the first person (I), or in the third person (he, she)?	Why do actors spend time in their training learning to role play?	Do you agree with the statement "Improvising is more listening than speaking."?
How do you think this type of activity will help your future work in drama?	Is it necessary to memorize a story in order to tell it? Is this the same process as learning lines from a script?	What roles do you find yourself playing in real life?	How important is your belief in the imaginary situation when you are improvising?
What skills does a person have to have to take part in drama?	Is a storyteller an actor?	How much of yourself did you find in the roles you played?	Is a prepared improvisation truly an improvisation?
What skills do you think you will have to develop to work effectively with others?	Why is storytelling one of the oldest forms of theatre?	Do you prefer to be involved in the role-playing or to watch others role play?	Why is improvisation essential in the training of professional actors?

Source: Adapted from Booth & Lundy (1985) and Swartz (2002).

many contexts, with many different children, connected us most deeply with our children and gave us more joy than we can express.

Chapter 8 introduces reading as a puzzle that readers must solve in a variety of contexts, for a variety of purposes. By listening to good stories, young children will develop a sense of story and concepts about print that they will be able to apply to their own meaning-making, word-solving, concept-building, and architectural processes.

The growth of the imagination demands windows—
windows through which we
can look out at the world and windows through
which we look into ourselves.
—Katherine Paterson

LIT-FOLIO UPDATE

Consider what might count as evidence that you now have a greater understanding of how creative expression, in its many forms, plays a valuable role in literacy development. Comment on whether you feel confident about teaching the arts. What can you do to develop greater assurance and expertise in the arts? Return to the questions in Literacy Notebook 7.1 and 7.3. Revise your answers with any of the following readers in mind: your principal, your colleagues, or a curious parent.

Resources to Support Your Learning

Drama, Storytelling, Poetry, and Play

✤ Booth, D. W. (2005). *Story drama*. Markham, ON: Pembroke Publishers.

✤ Booth, D., & Barton, B. (2000). *Story works*. Markham, ON: Pembroke Publishers.

✤ Booth, D. W., & Lundy, C. J. (1985). *Improvisation: Learning through drama*. Toronto ON: Harcourt Brace Jovanovich.

✤ Booth, D., & Moore, B. (2003). *Poems please! Sharing poetry with children*. Markham, ON: Pembroke Publishers.

✤ Cecil, N. L. (1994). *For the love of language: Poetry for every learner*. Winnipeg, MB: Peguis.

✤ Cornett, C. E., & Smithrim, K. L. (2001). The *arts as meaning makers: Integrating literature and the arts throughout the curriculum*, Canadian Edition. Toronto, ON: Pearson Education Canada.

Glover, M. K. (1999). *A garden of poets: Poetry writing in the elementary classroom*. Urbana, IL: National Council of Teachers of English.

Graves, D. (1992). *Explore poetry*. Portsmouth, NH: Heinemann.

Harrison, D. L., & Holderith, K. (2003). *Using the power of poetry to teach Language Arts, Social Studies, Math, and more: Engaging poetry lessons, model poems, and writing activities that help students learn important content*. New York: Scholastic.

Heard, G. (1989). *For the good of the earth and sun: Teaching poetry*. Portsmouth, NH: Heinemann.

Owocki, G. (2001). *Make way for literacy! Teaching the way young children learn*. Portsmouth, NH: Heinemann.

Piazza, C. L. (1999). *Multiple Forms of Literacy: Teaching Literacy and the Arts*. Upper Saddle River, NJ: Merrill, Prentice-Hall.

Piazza, C. L. (1999). *Multiple Forms of Literacy: Teaching Literacy and the Arts*. Upper Saddle River, NJ: Merrill, Prentice-Hall.

Routman, R. (2001). Everyone succeeds with poetry writing. *Instructor*, 111(1): 26-31.

✤ Swartz, L. (2002). *The new dramathemes*. (3rd ed.). Markham, ON: Pembroke Publishers.

Journals

Bookbird: A Journal of International Children's Literature, International Board on Books for Young People (IBBY), website: http://www.ibby.org

Poetry Anthologies

✤ Booth, D. W, (1989). '*Til all the stars have fallen*. Toronto, ON: Kids Can Press.

✤ Booth, D. W. (1993). *Dr. Knickerbocker and other rhymes: A Canadian collection*. Toronto, ON: Kids Can Press.

✤ Dakos, K. (1990). *If you're not here, please raise your hand*. New York: Four Winds.

Little, J. (1986). *Hey world, here I am!* New York: Harper & Row.

✤ Warabé, A. (1990). *Seasons*. Toronto, ON: Doubleday.

On the Space Theme

✤ Caduto, M.J. & Bruchac, J. (1989). *Keepers of the earth: Native stories and environmental activities for children*. Saskatoon, SK: Fifth House Publishers.

Carle, E. (1986). *Papa, please get the moon for me*. New York: Scholastic.

Carle, E. (1992). *Draw me a star*. New York: Scholastic.

Hinz, J. (2001). *Dot to dot in the sky: Stories in the stars*. Vancouver, BC: Whitecap.

✤ Love, A. & Drake, J. (2000), *Kids book of the far North*. Toronto, ON: Kids Can Press.

Morgan, J. (2002). *Born with a bang: The universe tells our cosmic story, Book One*. Nevada City, CA: Dawn Publications.

Scieszka, J., & Smith, L. (2004). *Science verse*. New York: Scholastic.

Van Allsburg, C. (2002). *Zathura: A space adventure*. New York: Houghton Mifflin.

Children's Literature: Our Favourites

- *Something from nothing*, Phoebe Gilman
- *The name of the tree*, Celia Barker Lottridge

The rough-face girl, Rafe Martin

- *A promise to the sun: An African story*, Tololwa Mollel

Resources for Found Poetry

Cloudy, with a chance of meatballs, Judi Barrett (use in conjunction with weather reports)

Northern lights: The soccer trails, Michael Kusugak

Owl moon, Jane Yolen

Smoky nights, Eve Bunting

Stella, queen of the snow, Marie-Louise Gay

Stellaluna, Janell Cannon

The polar express, Chris Van Allsburg

The very last first time, Jan Andrews

Tales of African Origin

- *The orphan boy*, Tololwa Mollel

Anansi does the impossible: An Ashanti tale, Verna Aardema

Anansi and the lizard, Pat Cummings

Mother crocodile, Rosa Guy

Travelling to Tondo, Verna Aardema

Why the sky is far away, Mary-Joan Gerson

The cow-tail switch, Harold Courlander, George Herzog

Websites

- Learning through the Arts – teaching ideas integrating drama, music, movement, and visual arts: http:// www.ltta.ca

Carol Hurst's website: http://www. carolhurst.com

Creativity Workshop for Educators: http://www.creativityworkshop.com/educators.html

http://www.readwritethink.org

UNICEF: www.unicef.ca/eng/unicef/story/main.html

- Storytellers of Canada/Conteurs du Canada: http://www.sc-cc.com

Technology School of the Future, Australia; resources for Teachers of English: http://www.tsof.edu.au/resources/english/

National Storytelling Network: http://www.storynet.org/Directory/

NASA: http://www.nasa.gov/audience/foreducators/k-4/features/index.html

Lesson Planet: http://www.lessonplanet.com/search/Science/Space/Stars

Multimedia Connections

Roch Carrier [video recording] / [produced by] TVOntario for Council of Ministers of Education, Canada.

Story telling [video recording] / [produced/directed by] Rick Seabrooke. (From the series Aboriginal Voices, The Canadian Collection).

The bear [animated video recording] / [produced by] Walt Disney Video.

The Sweater, a childhood recollection [animated video recording] / by Roch Carrier; a National Film Board of Canada production. (Based on the book, *The Hockey Sweater* by Roch Carrier).

The truth about stories [sound recording]: a native narrative / Thomas King.

Reading the Word

Solving the Puzzle

When a child can talk, 'tis time he [*sic*] should learn to read. And when he reads, put into his hands some very pleasant book suited to his capacity, wherein the entertainment he finds may draw him on, and reward his pains in reading.

—*Evelyn Waugh*

key terms

architect
attention
automaticity
comprehension
concept builder
expository texts
expressive texts
fix-up strategies
fluency
instructional level
meaning-maker
meta-cognitive awareness
poetic texts
schema (*pl.* schemata)
word-solver

questions to guide your learning

By the end of this chapter, you should understand the key terms and be able to answer the following questions:

- What do reading teachers know, understand, and do?
- What does "reading as a transactional process" mean? What are the implications of this description for teaching reading?
- What are the four roles of the reader? What are their implications for teaching reading?
- How do readers negotiate the four roles and how do they affect readers' comprehension?
- How might reader response journals support your reading program?
- How can you apply the continuum of support to comprehension instruction?

Looking Back, Looking Ahead

In Chapter 7, we discovered story and its importance in our lives. As we argued in earlier chapters, story is central to an understanding of self, others, and the world. Traditional cultures passed story from one generation to the next through oral tradition. Today,

> *what we know as a culture and who we are as a people is written into text. Without access to the world of text, one's knowledge is limited to what can be communicated orally, illustrated in pictures, or shared by demonstration. Without access to the world of text, one is thrown back in time to an era where books belonged only to the elite and learning was restricted to what was known locally.*
> (Burke, 1985, cited in Anderson-Inman & Horney, 1998, p. 15)

This chapter introduces reading as a puzzle to be solved by readers and teachers in a variety of contexts for a variety of purposes. Readers and teachers will know that they have solved the puzzle when the text makes sense. We understand reading as a transaction among the reader, the author, the text, the teacher, and the reading community. Because of these complex connections, no two puzzles will be the same; there will be as many reading puzzles to be solved as there are readers in the world. Despite this diversity, however, there are some pieces of the puzzle that you can look at and learn from as you teach readers how to coordinate the roles of meaning-maker, word-solver, concept builder, and architect. We will pay particular attention to comprehension and response as indicators that readers have solved the reading puzzle.

Our lives are laden with reading; we read our environment, we read numbers, we read people, we read words. Each of these tasks requires time, effort, and a range of energies including cognitive, emotional, and social within a variety of contexts. Some scholars (Gough, 1985; Samuels, 1994a/b) claim that the acts of reading our environment, numbers, and people require significantly different processes than the task of reading words. Freire (1987), on the other hand, tells us that the task of reading

literacy notebook 8.1

STOP, THINK, AND WRITE

- How do you conceptualize reading?
- What do independent readers do?
- How do you envision teaching reading in your classroom?

our world (our environment) is a necessary precursor to reading words (Eisner, 2002; Gee, 2001). For example, reading the weather, reading emotions, and reading words require similar skills.

> *Reading is a cognitive act, but there is nothing about reading that does not occur in other cognitive acts that do not involve reading. We perceive, recognize, interpret, comprehend, appreciate, and remember information that is not in text form as well as information that is in text form.*
>
> (Sadoski & Paivio, 2004, p. 1329)

Reading, in this conceptualization, is far more than simple perception; it is an active process that enables us to simultaneously perceive, understand, interact within, and transform our world. Reading the word, however, may require specific strategies to "crack the code" of print texts. This chapter focuses on those strategies unique to reading the printed word. As we proceed, you will see an overlap between reading the word and reading the world—this is intentional. One informs the other and the two cannot realistically be separated.

CONCEPTUALIZING READING: THE SEARCH FOR MEANING

As a research focus, reading does not belong to any one field. It has been a source of interest and often a source of debate (Chall, 1987; Vacca et al., 2003; Ruddell & Unrau, 2004; Snow, Burns, & Griffin, 1998) for many scholars, including psychologists, psycholinguists, and socio-culturalists. Each has a unique conceptualization of reading behaviours and the best way to teach reading. Figure 8.1 presents the contributions of the main disciplines that have undertaken reading research and their implications for teaching, learning, and instruction. This table makes it easy to see the principles and premises underlying the debate about what counts as reading. The debate stems predominantly from the

> *inherent ambiguity of where meaning resides. Does it reside in the text? In the author's mind as he/she sets pen to paper? In the mind of each reader as he/she builds a model of meaning unique to his/her experience and reading? In the interaction between reader and text?*
>
> (Pearson & Stephens, 1994a, p. 32)

It is likely that many of you experienced some of this debate as you were taught to read. Some of you will recall skill and practice programs whereby the more you practiced, the more it was assumed you learned; phonics, decoding, and word recognition were often the focus, especially in the early years. Some of you will have memories of indepen-

FIGURE 8.1 Cross-Disciplinary Understandings of Reading

Cross-Disciplinary Understandings of Reading

Behaviourist (Adams, 1990; Snow, Burns, & Griffin, 1998)

Reading is considered a bottom-up process that emphasizes the written or printed text. Reading is viewed as being driven by a process that is driven by text, and proceeds from part to whole. Reading is composed of highly developed sequences of subskills that enable readers to "crack the code" and include phonological awareness, phonemic awareness, phonics, word recognition, and decoding skills. Little consideration is given to the effect of the reader's world knowledge, contextual information, or other higher-order processing strategies. A lack of comprehension is due to a breakdown in word-level subskills; therefore readers require explicit instruction, drill, and practice in word-level behaviours that include:

- identifying letter features
- linking these features to recognize letters
- combining letters to recognize spelling patterns
- linking spelling patterns to recognize words
- proceeding sequentially from letters to words to sentence, paragraph, and text-level processing

Cognitive Psychology (Anderson, 1994; Rumelhart, 1994)

Reading is considered a top-down process that emphasizes what the reader brings to the text. Reading is viewed as being driven by meaning, and proceeds from whole to part. Readers identify letters and words only to confirm their assumptions and comprehension of the text. Reading is a constructive process that is a result of connections made by readers between unfamiliar or novel texts and prior knowledge or existing schema. Cognitive psychologists acknowledge that:

- Readers comprehend a selection even though they do not recognize each word.
- Readers use meaning and grammatical cues to identify unrecognized words.
- Reading for meaning is the primary objective of reading, rather than mastery of letters, letter/sound relationships, and words.
- Reading requires the use of meaning activities rather than the mastery of a series of word-recognition skills.
- The primary focus of instruction should be the reading of sentences, paragraphs, and whole selections.
- The most important aspect about reading is the amount and kind of information gained through reading.

Psycholinguistics (Gee, 1990; Heath, 1983)

The field of psycholinguistics adds to the research on top-down processes. Reading is a constructive process that focuses on making meaning and is only incidentally visual; it is largely a matter of making informed predictions. Readers make use of three cueing systems (syntactic, semantic, and grapho-phonemic) to make sense of text. When reading, readers often choose the least effective cueing system resulting in what is called a miscue. With psycholinguistics, the focus shifts from a breakdown in the reading process approach (remedial, skills-based) to a strength and value approach. For example, What was the reader doing at the time of the miscue? Because reading is a constructive process, text should be matched to reader interest and level, and readers' approximations and efforts

FIGURE 8.1 Cross-Disciplinary Understandings of Reading (continued)

must be valued. Psycholinguists do not ask what they need to teach, but instead ask, "What can I do to support this student as a reader?"

Socio-Cultural Theories (Gee, 1990; Heath, 1983)

Reading is again considered a top-down and constructive process that is always embedded in and inseparable from its multiple contexts (instructional, non-instructional, home and community, cultural, social, political). Because literacy and reading events and contexts are reciprocally influenced, reading is inherently a social and cultural construction. Socio-cultural theorists suggest that:

- We accommodate the learner's use of language and dialect in reading instruction.
- Language must serve a function for students.
- Students must learn how to use language appropriately in educational settings.
- We rethink the competitive atmosphere of classrooms and of school labels.
- We make changes within schools so that children learn from and with each other.

Interactive Models of Reading

Interactive reading models recognize the interaction of bottom-up and top-down processes simultaneously throughout the reading process. They often come under criticism for being eclectic approaches without a real focus. Interactive theorists believe that:

- Reading is at once a perceptual and a cognitive process.
- Skilled readers must be able to make use of sensory, syntactic, semantic, and pragmatic information to accomplish the task of reading.
- Sensory, syntactic, semantic, and pragmatic sources of information appear to interact in many complex ways during the process of reading.
- The diverse backgrounds and contexts of readers must be accounted for in text selection and in the teaching of reading.

Additional Sources: Alexander & Fox (2004); Pearson & Stephens (1994b); Vacca et al. (2003).

dent reading where texts were levelled and you progressed one level at a time, reading texts and responding to comprehension questions. Some of you will recall whole language approaches where you started with the whole text, broke it into component parts for analysis, and then returned to the whole text. Some of you will remember response-based programs where the focus of reading was your interaction with the text and the experiences that you brought to the text. Some of you will recall small groups organized by reading ability—you might have been in the red group or you might have been a blue bird; you progressed with your group; each group had texts and activities that were unique. Others will recall basal reader programs, where all students in the classroom read the same text, engaged in the same activities, and progressed along a predetermined path

literacy notebook 8.2

STOP, THINK, AND WRITE

Review your conceptualization of reading from Literacy Notebook 8.1.

- Would you classify your conceptualization of reading as bottom-up, top-down, or interactive?
- What stands out as key learning in this component or as an area that you have identified for learning?

Envision excellent reading teachers as yet another role that lifelong literacy teachers assume.

- What are their characteristics?
- What do they understand about learners?
- What do they practise in the classroom?

Now that you have recorded your ideas, continue with your reading. Figure 8.2 describes excellent reading teachers as envisioned by the International Reading Association.

- Which of these characteristics is part of who you are today?
- Which qualities are you most comfortable with?
- Which do you need to explore in further depth?

FIGURE 8.2 Excellent Reading Teachers: A Position Statement of the International Reading Association

Every child deserves excellent reading teachers because teachers make a difference in children's reading achievement and motivation to read. This position statement provides a research-based description of the distinguishing qualities of excellent classroom reading teachers. Excellent reading teachers share several critical qualities of knowledge and practice:

1. They understand reading and writing development, and believe all children can learn to read and write.
2. They continually assess children's individual progress and relate reading instruction to children's previous experiences.
3. They know a variety of ways to teach reading, when to use each method, and how to combine the methods into an effective instructional program.
4. They offer a variety of materials and texts for children to read.
5. They use flexible grouping strategies to tailor instruction to individual students.
6. They are good reading "coaches" (that is, they provide help strategically).

In addition, excellent reading teachers share many of the characteristics of good teachers in general. They have strong content and pedagogical knowledge, manage classrooms so that there is a high rate of engagement, use strong motivation strategies that encourage independent learning, have high expectations for children's achievement, and help children who are having difficulty.

Source: International Reading Association (2000).

toward becoming a reader. Each of these approaches has contributed to our understanding of reading—seen as parts of a whole, they represent a comprehensive reading program. In this chapter, we present the individual components of a comprehensive reading program from theoretical, pedagogical, and practical perspectives. Our intent is to have you understand the complexity of the reading process and the many roles simultaneously negotiated by the reader.

Students require individually tailored and responsive instruction, as no two readers have the same needs.

Individual Readers, Multiple Puzzles

Comprehensive and inclusive reading programs are responsive to and reflective of contemporary research, the needs of the student, the curriculum, and the context. Literacy teachers understand how to provide balanced and responsive reading instruction; they understand that the *only* right way to teach reading is to teach the student, and the *only* right way to teach the student is to teach flexibly, diversely, and responsively, not categorically, analytically, or sequentially (Clay, 1994; Stanovich, 1986; Treiman, 2001; Weaver, 1998).

> *Terms such as the reader are somewhat misleading, though convenient, fictions. There is no such thing as a generic reader or a generic literary work; there are in reality only the potential millions of individual readers of individual literary works… The reading of any work of literature is, of necessity, an individual and unique occurrence involving the mind and emotions of some particular reader.*
>
> (Rosenblatt, 1938/1983 in Rosenblatt, 1994, p. 1363)

No two students will have the same profile of reading behaviours (Aaron, Joshi, & Williams, 1999; Carbo, 1987; Stanovich, Siegel, & Gottardo, 1997); students will therefore require individually tailored and responsive instruction in order to solve their puzzles.

> *The question is not, How do I teach reading and writing? Rather, it is, How do I teach my students to read and write? The addition of the words my students here emphasizes that children bring with them particular experiences in using language, interacting with print, perceiving school, and acting in the world that are shaped by their particular cultural communities, and these experiences may be different from their teachers' experiences. These differences can have a major impact on how teachers perceive children and teach them.*
>
> (Lazar, 2004, pp. 132)

Reading as a Transactional Process among Reader, Text, Author, and Reading Community

Throughout this book, we not only present literacy as an individual construct but we also argue that it is a social construct. "To be literate involves not only learning from others but also learning to be literate with others" (Tierney & Readence, 2005, p. 387). If we accept this statement as true, then we must strive for ways to ensure that all students have access to this community of learners regardless of their reading level. Reviews and compilations of research leave no doubt about the impact of phonemic awareness training and phonics instruction on reading fluency (Adams,1990; Snow, Burns, & Griffin, 1998; National Reading Panel, 2000), but what they do not suggest are ways to alleviate the stress that learners feel when they simply can't decode or recognize words fluently and automatically. As, educators, we must find ways to help readers to access their cognitively appropriate, meaningful, and authentic discourse communities both inside and outside the classroom, regardless of their word recognition or decoding ability. Without access to print, they will not have access to these communities of learners and will therefore experience difficulty *learning to be literate with others*.

Regardless of the theory we choose to adopt, what remains of critical importance are the underlying beliefs we have about ourselves, our students, teaching, learning, reading, and what these beliefs impose. It is not enough to know what good readers can do (Beers, 2003). The most effective teachers understand reading from a holistic and inclusive view; they believe that all students, given appropriate support, can be successful readers. They listen to their students every day and individualize instruction in response to students' strengths and needs; they intervene at appropriate times to ensure that physical, cognitive, social, cultural, and affective differences are celebrated (Collins Block, 2003).

Children require access to texts in order to access discourse in the social context of schools. Without this access to context, we are prohibiting them from making the decision to engage or not engage, and therefore prohibiting them access to their socially and cognitively appropriate discourse communities and literacy practices that develop in direct response to the context and community within which the child grows, learns, and develops (Heath, 1983). Students who have not read the Harry Potter books cannot be part of classroom discussions, play in the school yard, or chit-chat in the hallway; they cannot access the critical discourse communities that will facilitate growth and learning. They are as excluded from the "literacy club" (Smith, 1988) as non-readers would be. You need to consider how your teaching may support or detract from student learning and access to discourse communities. The choices that you make, instructional and otherwise, may in fact prevent students from engaging in the reading events that provide the greatest opportunity for growth in reading.

> *Unless there are opportunities for subconscious acquisition through exposure to models as well as use of the discourse in meaningful social contexts, these students are unlikely to become proficient performers within the discourse; they will inadvertently reveal themselves as "outsiders." They may know about the discourse, but may not be able to demonstrate the same proficiency in using it as other students. One of the reasons for this is that any discourse is a complex way of saying-doing-thinking-feeling-valuing.*
>
> (Gee, 1990, p. xv)

You need to recognize the complexity of the environment and students' dominant world views as they are shaped by cultural, social, school, and political contexts, and the critical role that each of these play in the task of reading and the overriding school goal of literacy. Such awareness acknowledges that reading, as an extension of

> *language is a communicative act embedded in social interactions, and that in order to understand language we need not focus on language itself but on discourses: "ways of being in the world, or forms of life which integrate words, acts, values, beliefs, attitudes, social identities, as well as gestures, glances, body positions, and clothes."*
>
> (Gee, 1990, cited in Wilkinson, 1999, p. 142)

In other words, it is not enough to possess and acquire reading strategies and their interrelationships; in a sense, Gee's notion of discourses puts localized and contextualized communication and dialogue at the core of meaning-making. "Discourse practices are always embedded in the particular world view of particular social groups; they are tied to a set of values and norms. In apprenticing to new social practices, a student becomes complicit with this set of values and norms, this world view" (Gee, 1990, p. 67). Acknowledging the importance of context in the reading process respects the diversity and the multiple discourses within which we live, work, and learn. Comprehension, which is at the heart of reading, is an extension and expression of discourses; one cannot exist without the other. It is for this reason that we refer to reading as being a transactional process—an exchange of meaning among the reader, the text, the author, and the reading community.

Solving the Reading Puzzle: A Matter of Developing Strategies and Making Connections

Reading is a puzzle, and just like a puzzle where each piece successfully inserted brings us closer to the whole, so too does each piece of the reading puzzle bring us closer to the core meaning of each student's puzzle, which is ultimately reading.

> *In the reading situation, as in any effective communication situation, the message or text provides but one of the critical sources of information. The rest must come from the reader's own prior knowledge. Further, in the reading situation as in any other language situation, the learnability of a pattern depends critically on the prior knowledge and higher-order relationships that it evokes. In both fluent reading and its acquisition, the reader's knowledge must be aroused interactively and in parallel. Neither understanding nor learning can proceed hierarchically from the bottom-up. Phonological awareness, letter recognition facility, familiarity with spelling patterns, spelling-sound relations, and individual words must be developed in concert with real reading and real writing and with deliberate reflection on the forms, functions, and meanings of texts.*
>
> (Adams, 1990, p. 422)

When complete, the whole is much greater than the sum of its parts—meaning is far more than the independent subskills of word recognition and previous experience. Meaning is at the heart of reading from the very beginning. It is not some distant goal that we work toward—it is the primary purpose for reading. Word recognition should not be taught in isolation, reserving comprehension for a later time when students are independent solvers of their own puzzles. Figure 8.3 demonstrates some of the strategies readers use as they make multiple attempts to solve the reading puzzle in their progression from emergent to fluent readers.

The ultimate solution to the reading puzzle is the development of critical thinking, critical consciousness, and critical literacy through comprehension that can only occur as a result of the reader's quest to construct meaning and transact with the text and the author. It should not be confused or misused as simply retrieving information from the text. Comprehension, critical thinking, critical consciousness, and critical literacy are viewed as processes, rather than products, of learning to read (Palincsar, 2003) (see Chapter 13 for more details).

FIGURE 8.3 Menu of Reading Strategies

Emergent Readers	Early Readers	Transitional Readers	Fluent Readers
• I think about what I know about stories and texts. • I ask myself, "Does what I'm reading make sense?" • I use my finger to follow the words on the page. • I look at the pictures to help me figure out the story and words. • I use patterns to help me figure out new words (for example, repetition, predictable texts). • I look at the first letter and the last letter. • I look for the little words I know. • When I don't know a word, I look for little words I know in big words.	• I think about what I know about stories and texts. • I ask myself, "Does what I'm reading make sense? Does that sound right? Does that look right?" • I self-correct when it doesn't make sense, look right, or sound right. • I use my awareness of letter-sounds and spelling to figure out new words. • I can make my reading sound like talking (fluency). • When I don't know a word, I skip it, read on, and then re-read.	• I think about what I know about how texts are organized (for example, stories, poetry, **expository**). • I stop to think aloud or use **thinkmarks** to help me make sense of text. • I re-read to clarify the meaning of something I'm not sure of. • I use graphic organizers (for example, **story maps, KWL,** comparative frameworks, before and after charts) to organize information. • I retell chapters in writing.	• I preview the text and make predictions (for example, anticipation guides). • I use text features to aid my comprehension. • I research texts, take notes, and make data charts to organize information. • I use writing to deepen my understanding of stories, factual texts, and poetry. • I independently select appropriate **graphic organizers** to help me make sense of text.

The Role of the Reader

As readers strive to comprehend, make sense of text, and solve the reading puzzle, they coordinate four complex roles. In fact, in order to comprehend, they must coordinate these roles flexibly, fluently, and automatically, drawing on each at appropriate times in a variety of contexts for a variety of purposes. Figure 8.4 presents a description of the four roles of the reader: word-solver, concept builder, meaning-maker, and architect.

We now explore the four roles of the reader, trace the shape of each role, its research base, and its link to comprehension instruction. Our assumption is always that the goal of any form of instruction is independence; the aim is to teach students to self-monitor and self-regulate

FIGURE 8.4 The Four Roles of the Reader

The Reader as Word-Solver	The Reader as Concept Builder	The Reader as Meaning-Maker	The Reader as Architect
• Draws on a repertoire of known words. • Continually develops a reading vocabulary that allows access into a variety of texts. • Uses word-solving strategies. • Recognizes and uses visual information to aid comprehension. • Demonstrates continual awareness of personal reading strategies and processes.	• Selects texts and reading for a variety of purposes. • Knows and uses the structures and features of a variety of text forms to aid comprehension. • Uses language conventions (for example, punctuation) and text features to aid in comprehension. • Adjusts reading strategies and reading rate to match the text form and the purpose of reading. • Recognizes the author's voice in a text. • Thinks meta-cognitively to make meaning. • Demonstrates a continual awareness of one's own reading strategies and processes.	• Establishes a purpose for reading. • Recognizes that reading always involves a search for meaning. • Knows and applies a variety of comprehension strategies. • Self-monitors while reading, recognizing when comprehension breaks down, and taking steps to restore it and taking steps to restore it. • Sustains comprehension and maintains interest over extended periods of time. • Demonstrates a continual awareness of one's own reading strategies and processes. • Responds to texts in a variety of ways.	• Recognizes reading as a transaction among reader, author, and reading community. • Builds on and revises ideas, information, and perspectives in texts. • Engages in critical thinking, critical consciousness, critical literacy/inquiry. • Recognizes points of view, omissions, and multiple perspectives. • Demonstrates a continual awareness of own reading strategies and processes. • Responds to texts in a variety of ways.

Source: Adapted from Freebody & Luke (1990); Ontario Ministry of Education (2004). We have built on both sets of research, adjusting the roles of the readers to fit our vision of reading.

their own processes strategically as literacy learners. Guided practice, meaningful and authentic use, and mindful instruction will enable you to gradually transfer responsibility for learning to the students (see Figure 2.5).

THE READER AS WORD-SOLVER

> ...*it is the ownership of words that gives one confidence.*
> —Courtney B. Cazden

Word-solving abilities develop in the context of multiple and varied experiences in listening, speaking, reading, writing, viewing, and representing contexts. Word-solving is a process that involves phonemic awareness (sounds in spoken words), phonics (letter-sound relationships), and spelling (the orthography of words). (See Figure 8.5 for a summary of word-solving terms and definitions.) Students master these concepts as they build their banks of known words. As teachers draw students' attention to words in literature and words in their environment, they are broadening learners' vocabulary, building a repertoire of words that they will recognize in print, and helping them to understand the power of words. We suggest helping students to recognize high frequency words automatically and fluently, as they comprise close to 50% of the words they will encounter in reading. See Teacher Talk 8.1 where we present a balanced and multimodal approach to word study. Further word solving and vocabulary building activities are discussed in Chapter 10 under the headings Word Walls and Vocabulary Work.

Students develop word-solving abilities as they build and broaden their vocabulary.

Literacy learners' ability to solve words in reading and writing is closely linked to their vocabulary (receptive and expressive) (Durkin, 2004). We cannot overstate the importance of oral language work within the context of authentic literature and responsive classroom instruction. With guidance, support, and explicit instruction, the word-solving strategies learned in oral language will transfer to reading and writing. It is likely that the three expressive modes of language will develop concurrently, each reinforcing the other. As students emerge into word-solving, Bryan Cambourne's (2000/2001) condition of approximation—rewarding students for partially correct attempts—becomes critical.

FIGURE 8.5 Understanding Word-Solving Terms and Definitions

Phonological Awareness: the ability to focus on and manipulate *phonemes, syllables*, and words. Phonemic awareness is one component of phonological awareness. The focus of instruction in phonological awareness is teaching learners to segment sentences into words and words into syllables, and to blend syllables to make new words.

Phoneme: the smallest part of spoken language that makes the meaning of one word different from another. Phonemes may be represented by one letter or a combination of letters. The English language has approximately 44 phonemes (for example, *cat* has 3 phonemes -/c/, /a/, /t/).

Syllable: the smallest part of a word that includes a vowel (for example, *cat* has 1 syllable)

Phonemic Awareness: the ability to focus on and manipulate individual sounds or phonemes in spoken words. It is the basic understanding that spoken language is composed of a series of sounds. The focus of instruction in phonemic awareness is teaching learners to hear, identify, say, and manipulate phonemes in syllables and words. Initially this begins with individual letters and sounds so that students learn how to string individual sounds together to make words or to break words into component sounds. It involves work with *sound matching, sound isolation, sound blending, sound segmentation*, and *sound substitution*. It may also involve work with *rhymes, onsets*, and *rimes*. Phonemic awareness provides the foundation for word-solving and breaking the code (Yopp, 1992).

Sound Matching: matching words to correspondent sounds (for example, *cat* is the word that starts with the sound /c/).

Sound Isolation: isolating individual sounds in words (for example, isolating sounds at the beginning, middle, or end of a word (for example, /t/ is the end sound of *cat*).

Sound Blending: blending two or three sounds to form a word (for example, /c/,/a/,/t/ makes the word *cat*).

Sound Segmentation: segmenting or breaking a word apart into its beginning, middle, and end sounds (for example, *cat* can be broken down into three sounds /c/, /a/, /t/).

Sound Substitution: isolating one sound and substituting a different sound to make a new word (for example, changing *cat* to *hat* requires substituting the beginning sound /c/ with /h/).

Rhyme: when words have the same or similar endings, they are said to rhyme (for example, *fat cat hat*).

Onset: the consonant or consonants that occur before a vowel in a syllable (for example, *c* in *cat*).

Rime: the part of a syllable that contains the vowel and all that follows the vowel (for example, *at* in *cat*). Rimes are smaller than syllables but larger than phonemes.

Phonics: the ability to connect the words, syllables, and sounds they hear, say, identify, and manipulate to the corresponding words, syllables, and letters that they see on a printed page. The focus of instruction in phonics is teaching learners to understand the relationship between sounds or *phonemes* in oral language (also referred to as letter-sound relationships) and letters or *graphemes* in written language. It involves helping learners to apply their understanding of how oral language works to reading and writing words.

> ### FIGURE 8.5 Understanding Word-Solving Terms and Definitions (continued)
>
> **Grapheme:** the smallest part of written language that represents a phoneme in the spelling or orthography of a word. Like phonemes, graphemes may be represented by just one letter or a combination of letters (for example, *igh*).
>
> **Graphophonic Cues:** the visual cues in a text that help readers decode the text using their knowledge of letter-sound relationships, letter patterns, word families, sight words, etc. When readers ask the question, *Does that look right?* they are using the graphophonic cueing system.
>
> **Orthography:** the spelling of words. Initially this involves an understanding of phonics, but as students become more competent word-solvers, it will also require an understanding of how words work (root words, prefixes, suffixes, etc.).
>
> **Root Words:** the word that is left when prefixes and suffixes are removed (for example, *history* of *prehistoric*).
>
> **Prefixes:** a syllable added to the beginning of a word that changes its meaning (for example, *pre* in *prehistoric* means *prior to the history of humans*).
>
> **Suffixes:** a syllable added to the end of a word that changes its meaning (for example, *ic* in *prehistoric* means *of history*).
>
> Source: Durkin (2004); Ontario Ministry of Education (2003); Tompkins (2003).

Children will learn to read and write in the same way they learned to listen and speak. Nowhere in reading and writing is approximation more important than in word-solving as students stretch out words, make and break words, search for familiar words in bigger words, and try out language as a real reader.

MAKING SENSE OF THE RESEARCH ON WORD-SOLVING

Without a doubt, the task of reading requires the perception, recognition, and analysis of words on a printed page. Some students can do this independently and automatically. Many researchers (Gough, 1985; Just & Carpenter, 1980; Rumelhart, 1994 a/b); Samuels, suggest that reader attention is focused on the physical features of words that allow connections to be made to prior knowledge of the alphabet, letters, and sounds. On the other hand, a great deal of research (Adams, 1990; Chall, 1989; National Reading Panel, 2000; Samuels, 1994b; Snow, Burns, & Griffin, 1998; Stanovich, 1986) has demonstrated that word recognition and decoding are the most frequent inhibitors of comprehension. "It is quite possible for accurate decoding to be so slow and capacity-demanding that

Teacher Talk/8.1

MICHELANN'S FAVOURITE APPROACH TO EARLY WORD-SOLVING

Despite the fact that this is a whole class approach for the early primary grades, I think you'll find as I describe it that there is something in it for everyone because it is derived from the students' own oral language. Most school boards are encouraging teachers to incorporate sound or word work of some sort into their programs—some boards have bought into *Jolly Phonics,* others *Animated-Literacy*™. What I describe here is a generic approach that can be used in the classroom on a weekly basis: I use the same routine, the same activities, the same sequence every week. It may seem monotonous, but I assure you, after the first couple of weeks, once your students have settled into the process, it works like a charm. In using the same approach each week, what I am doing is freeing up my students to learn concepts instead of routines. I aim for about 30 minutes of letter-sound work each day (over the course of the whole day!). As you'll see, it's a multiple intelligence, multi-level, multiple learning style approach that blends explicit instruction with student-centred approaches.

BEFORE INSTRUCTION

In choosing which letters and/or sound patterns to target, I always observe and assess my students. I try to figure out the letters and sounds they already have a good grasp of and I set these up for review and consolidation at the beginning. From there, I read their journals, listen to their oral language, read through the texts they are reading, and listen in while they are reading aloud. I do a survey of the class and select the letter or sound that requires intensive study or instruction this week (based on the students' work).

DURING INSTRUCTION

On **Mondays**, I sit with my students and together we brainstorm as many words as we can think of that have that particular letter or sound in it. I don't worry about differentiating whether it is at the beginning, middle, or end of words—we listen to the sound, we decide as a group whether it fits the pattern, and then we look at the way it is written. Sometimes, as with "f" and "ph," we enter into a grand discussion that the "f" sound is sometimes made by "ph" and then we look at words like telephone and elephant, substituting "f" for "ph" to which they all respond, "That doesn't look right!" As each word is written, a picture cue is added. I'm not an artist but inevitably my pictures lead to giggles and that is what makes them memorable—not only memorable but then many of the children want to prove that they can draw a better elephant than me. "Perfect," I'll think, "they'll relate that sound to that word now." As a group, we usually choose the word that we like best or that we use most often and that becomes our key word for the sound. For example, you'll often hear me say, "Remember it is the "ph" of elephant." I then ask the students (each takes a turn) to come up and underline the targeted sound in one word on the chart, reinforcing the sound with the visual representation. In preparation for Tuesday, I take all the words they have given me and make a class visual dictionary page (see example below)—the key word is slightly larger than the others. Tomorrow they will have a chance to colour it and underline the targeted sound on their own page (this is a great transition or bellwork activity).

Teacher Talk/8.1

MICHELANN'S FAVOURITE APPROACH TO EARLY WORD-SOLVING (continued)

On **Tuesdays**, I introduce a poem, short text, song, or joke and engage the students in a shared reading experience. The text selected reflects not only the theme that we are studying but also contains the sound that we are studying that week. While studying the "ph" sound for example, we might use Dennis Lee's poem, "Willoughby Wallaby Woo" (*Alligator Pie*). We use the text throughout the week during transitions and reading the room activities with the goal that students should be able to read the text independently by Friday. Each student is then given their visual dictionary page and they are asked to choose their favourite words and draw a picture that uses as many of these words as possible in a meaningful way. I circulate as they are drawing and write their sentences with them (for example, *Philip and the elephant were talking on the telephone*). As the children become more comfortable with letters and sounds, many of them find a challenge in using alliteration to write tongue twisters. We do our best to ensure correct spelling of sight words since their pictures will go into our class book, which goes home with a different student each night as part of our "I Can Read" program. Parents are asked to sign-in, indicating that they have read the book with their child. In preparation for Wednesday, I review their sentences and the words they have used, and create mini-books for each student that reinforce the sight words I have targeted for the week, the key word they have selected, and words I know that they can read independently. The books are multi-level for the groups I have identified; some have pictures and some do not. I choose two or three sentences (depending on the level of students) and I create sentence strips that the students will cut apart, scramble, and then put back in order. Also for Wednesday, I choose pictures for the students to sort by letters or sounds we have previously studied, making sure that this week's sound is well-represented. The word is printed on the back of the picture. Students know that they must look at the picture, say the word, listen to the sound, decide what the word is, and then double check by turning the card over. Sometimes we'll vary this centre with a game of "Go Fish" or "Memory."

On **Wednesdays**, I rotate my students through centres for an hour (15 minutes per centre is more than enough), because a volunteer is coming to help supervise. At the first centre, the computer centre, students use KidPix to find and stamp as many words or pictures as they can that have the targeted sound. At the second centre they work with me. I use a guided reading approach and scaffold the words in their individual books. The first thing they do when they open these little "Keep Books" is highlight in yellow all the words they can read without even thinking. My favourite part is when they bring their books and proudly show me that it is almost all yellow! These books will go into the reading folders that they take home every night. At the third centre, the students sort the words they find in the box by sounds they hear and say. They record their findings in a Venn Diagram, demonstrating that some words will fit in more than one area. At the fourth centre, the volunteer is working with students as they unscramble the sentences I have made for them, glue them in their books, and illustrate them.

Teacher Talk/8.1

MICHELANN'S FAVOURITE APPROACH TO EARLY WORD-SOLVING (continued)

On **Thursdays**, they are ready to try some writing with these words. During writers' workshop, I ask them to include the words and sounds that we are studying. Although this is an independent activity, I circulate and engage in **interactive writing** as necessary. During this block of time, I usually sit with the students and try some writing of my own, modelling the process, showing them that I can write a joke, a poem, a recipe, a silly sentence, or anything else I want with the words we are studying (these words are from both their sound and theme work).

On **Fridays**, we reread our Shared Reading text. I give each of them a copy and they begin to busily highlight every word, sound, letter, sentence, phrase, that they can read independently, which should be almost the whole text. They can request support from either me or a neighbour. Students divide into small groups and go off to find a way to present the text orally. Remember, it's not always what you say but how you say it!

EVERYDAY

We play a quick game of *Wheel of Fortune*—this is where I usually hide my morning message full of the letter or sound that we are studying this week within the context of our theme. Sometimes this is quite a challenge! Students can ask for letters, sounds, words, and as they get to know my writing pattern or recognize the structure of sentences, they even ask for entire sentences!

To manage transitions and line ups at their clothing and snack area, I usually ask for a word with our highlighted sound as the key to unlocking the gates. Some students rise to the challenge of presenting me with a tongue twister. Some students take a little more time to figure it out than others. I love to watch them sneak a peek at the chart or lean in so close to the student in front of them that they are almost going to fall over. In the end, even if it means probing or dramatizing on my part, they all find a word.

To get the attention of the children during the day, I will often recite the shared reading text, helping students engage in oral rehearsal and a sort of repeated reading, as many of them will gather to look at the posted copy of the text so they can join in.

AFTER INSTRUCTION

On **Fridays**, we celebrate our sound of the week. We hang the brainstorming poster up with the others as our record of learning. Each student chooses their favourite piece of work and reads us a sentence from it and then each small group presents its interpretation of the shared reading text. All in all, it's good fun and sound learning practice!

it strains available cognitive resources and causes comprehension breakdowns" (Stanovich, 2000, p. 373).

Students who experience maximum benefit from independent reading, read with at least 95% accuracy in decoding and word recognition. This is considered to be their instructional level. Less than 95% accuracy will interfere with readers' ability to comprehend and interact with text

STOP, THINK, AND WRITE

Use the terms in Figure 8.5 to review the word-solving approach described in Teacher Talk 8.1.

- Can you find specific examples of each?
- If not, what might you add to this approach?
- What word-solving principles are followed?
- Are any missing?
- What incidental are they learning?
- How does this approach differ from others you might have seen in schools (for example, *Jolly Phonics, Animated-Literacy*™)?

(Adams, 1990; Clay, 1993). Quite often texts that can be read with 95% accuracy are those previously read in class during read alouds, read on multiple occasions during shared reading, or those that contain familiar content that may be below curriculum or grade appropriate expectations in reading (for example, high interest/low vocabulary books, graphic novels, comic books).

Contrary to the views of top-down researchers (Goodman, 1968; Smith, 2004), Just and Carpenter (1980) argue that good readers rarely skip over words and rarely need to rely on context, because their decoding and word recognition skills are so fluent and automatic. **Attention** operates on a continuum and determines the amount of information and the type of information that can be extracted from text. In the case of good readers, because little direct attention is required to actually decode and recognize words, more attention can be directed elsewhere. When attention is focused on individual letters and words, there is less energy and attention for comprehension and response. Some readers are more alert to certain features of text, certain text structures, and certain types of information. Other readers can effectively and efficiently select and attend to key pieces of information (main ideas and details) that both support and sustain attention and therefore comprehension.

"**Fluency** allows the mind to concentrate on comprehension" (Hirsch, 2003, p. 12). It is synonymous with flow and often speed. We prefer to discuss fluency in terms of a reader's ease with phrasing, expression, and intonation. A reader's ability to "make it sound like talking" often reflects the reader's fluency. There is a general, though not perfect, correlation between how quickly you can comprehend a text and how well you comprehend it. "A person who reads fast has automated many of the underlying processes involved in reading, and can, therefore, devote conscious attention to textual meaning rather than to the processes themselves" (Hirsch, 2003, p. 12). They can simultaneously negotiate and continuously check the cueing systems: Does it make sense? Does it sound right? Does it look right?

Automaticity is the ability to perform a task with little attention. Behaviours that have become automatized can be performed simultaneously with other tasks (for example, decoding, activating prior knowledge, and comprehension). Think about your drive to school this morning. What were you doing? Chances are you were listening to the radio, drinking a coffee, carrying on a conversation with your passenger, mechanically braking and shifting gears, paying attention to road signs and other vehicles—all the while driving the car. You did all this without even thinking about it. It is this type of automaticity that we want for our students. It is the ability to coordinate the complex strategies of reading (for example, word-solving, comprehension, activating prior knowledge, self-monitoring) on the run, without even realizing it.

In reading practice, fluency and automaticity are often taught through repeated readings, levelled texts, shared reading, buddy reading, readers' theatre, guided reading, choral reading, and peer/teacher mediated readings. Chapter 9 explores these methods in greater detail. Fluency and automaticity in terms of graphophonemic information, decoding, and word recognition are essential, but even more critical is the reader's meta-cognitive awareness: an awareness of what it is that good readers do and how they often transfer this awareness into writing. Figure 8.6 presents an overview of the meta-cognitive awareness required in word-solving. Readers and writers need to understand that good readers and writers do not always read and write with 100% accuracy, but good readers and writers know when they make errors and can apply fix-up strategies. (Figure 8.9 describes our conceptualization of the comprehension monitoring process.) Good readers and writers are flexible; they have a repertoire of strategies for solving unknown words when they are reading and writing.

As readers become more independent, they will need more than word recognition, decoding, and phonemic awareness to unlock the code of print. They will need word-solving abilities that extend to awareness of how words work: their origins, prefixes, suffixes, root words, etc. and how the meanings of words vary in specific contexts and usage. Independent word-solvers support their word-solving with tools that include dictionaries, thesauruses, and other reference materials. They will require contextualized and responsive instruction in the efficient use of these tools. (Chapters 10 and 11 will revisit word-solving and the connection between reading and writing.)

FIGURE 8.6 Meta-Cognitive Awareness in Word-Solving

Known Words

When Reading
There are some words I know on sight.

Some words I figure out from known words (into = in + to).

When Writing
There are some words I can write accurately, quickly.

Some words I construct from known words (in + to = into).

Analogies

When Reading
I know another word like this one, for example, I know "hat" because I know "cat."

When Writing
I can write "hat" because I can write "cat" and all I have to do is change the first letter.

Word Analysis

When Reading
Letter sounds

Letter clusters sounds

I know lots of examples of words beginning and ending with common letters and letter combinations.

When Writing
I can write "cat" because I can say it slowly and I know which letters to record to match the sounds. I know "cat" begins with a "c" because it starts the same way as my name "Cathy."

Word Patterns

When Reading
I know about word endings and prefixes and how they affect meaning.

I know about vowels in the middle of words and how they work when they appear at the end of a word.

When Writing
I can construct words from my knowledge of word parts, how words work, and what they mean.

Monitoring

When Reading
I know how to monitor my reading by checking:

Does it look right?

Does it sound right?

Does it make sense?

When Writing
I know how to monitor my writing by checking:

Does it look right? Does it sound right?

Does it make sense?

Does my writing express the meaning I intended?

THE LINK TO COMPREHENSION

Attention, fluency, and automaticity, and the use of cueing systems are critical because they free the reader to do the real work of reading, which is comprehension, meaning-making, and ultimately reconstruction of thoughts, ideas, or self. Although we often talk of reading comprehension, it is important to remember that often a student's ability to comprehend in reading bears a direct relationship to their ability to comprehend in listening as well (Hirsch, 2003; Kintsch, 2004). Think alouds, modelled reading, storytelling, drama, and read alouds are just a few of the activities that will support readers, writers, listeners, speakers, viewers, and representers as they learn to make sense of the many texts around them.

In conclusion, we offer the following principles for effective word-solving instruction:

- It is evidence-based, developmentally appropriate, and responsive to the strengths and needs of the students. (For example, Kindergarten students will likely need support in phonemic awareness activities whereas Grade 6 students are ready to discuss word origins.)

- It is planned and purposeful, not simply incidental to the reading process.

- It is part of a comprehensive and balanced literacy program. It is integrated with comprehension, listening, speaking, reading, writing, viewing, and representing activities and should not be viewed as a series of isolated activities (Pinnell & Fountas, 1998; Yopp & Yopp, 2000; Tompkins, 2003).

THE READER AS CONCEPT BUILDER

Good readers build many concepts during the reading process including concepts about print, forms, functions, authors, genres, expository text structures, even personal concepts such as what makes a good book (Cambourne, 2002). As they learn to read, they use existing concepts to build connections to new information. "It is these connections to the text, to the world, to background information, and to experiences (schema) that make readers feel like the characters, connect to the story, or remember similar experiences" (Ketch, 2005, p. 8).

Concepts about print are one of the initial text structures that literacy learners acquire. They learn that, in English, we read from left to right, top to bottom, front to back, and that words contain meaning (Clay, 1993). These are observable behaviours learned through demonstration and modelling, as discussed in Chapter 4. Some readers will require explicit and direct teaching of concepts about print in order to achieve independence.

As students move along the continuum toward independence, concepts about print will make way for concepts about text and the way texts are organized. Concepts about text include awareness of the functions of language and print, forms of text, genres, authors, and expository text structures. Readers encounter a variety of forms and genres including poetic texts, such as stories, poems, fairy tales; anthologies; expressive texts, such as letters, journals, diaries; and transactional texts such as dictionaries, glossaries, indexes, tables of contents, figures, charts, tables, recipes, directions, how-to manuals. These genres are found in print texts but they are becoming more frequent as multimedia texts, oral, and visual texts. Each form, genre, even author has its own rules or corresponding concepts that both readers and writers have to learn. Figures 8.7 and 8.8 provide a detailed outline of forms, functions, and concepts about text and genre that provide readers with clues to comprehension and how to use the underlying structure of text to expose its meaning.

In Chapter 6, we discussed the importance of narrative texts and literacy learners' awareness of story structure in order to make sense of text. Awareness of story structures will facilitate comprehension and allow students to apply what they understand about story to unfamiliar texts as they encounter them. For example, readers who understand the structure of narrative story can integrate previously learned information on character development to unfamiliar texts without focusing explicit attention on the concept about character.

In contrast to narrative texts, expository texts are written to inform or to clarify details on a topic that is somewhat unfamiliar. In the same way that we teach structures about story, we teach structures about expository texts (for example, comparison, sequence, description). Generally speaking, readers have "much less world knowledge about the ideas in expository text" than in narrative texts (Graesser, McNamara, & Louwerse, 2003, p. 86). In Chapter 9, we discuss content area materials—texts for efferent purposes. In Chapter 10, we discuss explicit strategy instruction in language and across the curriculum; expository text structures are described as well.

MAKING SENSE OF THE RESEARCH ON CONCEPT BUILDING

We have chosen to use the word "concept" in accord with Marie Clay's *Concepts about Print* (2000), which we feel are the first concepts developed by readers. We draw from the research base on schemata and reading that indicates that pre-existing schemata provide readers with a framework within which to organize, remember, and learn new ideas from a text. Readers' schemata provide conceptual scaffolding within which to activate prior knowledge, establish purposes for reading, in-

FIGURE 8.7 Forms and Functions of Print

	Expressive	Poetic	Transactional
Purpose of the Text Creator	To inform To explain To reflect To interpret	To entertain To tell a story To share language as an art form	To instruct To direct To guide To remind To report To inform To persuade To express a point of view
Purpose of the Text Consumer	To reflect To seek information	To enjoy To explore language	To seek information To understand another point of view
Text Type or Format Text creators select types or formats depending on their purpose and the anticipated consumer of their text. It is important to note that any of these types or formats can be drafted, rehearsed, or performed in oral and/or written contexts.	Advertisements Advice columns Ask-the-expert Autobiographies Brochures Comic strips Computer presentations Crossword puzzles Diagrams Dialogue Diary entries Directions Drama Editorials Fables Fairy tales Tongue twisters	Folk tales Friendly letters Games Guides Headlines Interviews Invitations Jokes Learning logs Legends Maps Menus Music videos Myths News stories Newspaper articles Performances Personal Anecdotes	Photo captions Photo essays Poetry Postcards Posters/slogans Rebus stories Recipes Reviews Riddles Scrapbooks Speeches Storytelling Surveys Television commercials Thank you notes Time capsules Timelines

tegrate text information, free up some of the reader's attention for comprehension or word-solving, and reconstruct or revise existing schemata to incorporate new information (Anderson, 1994).

Actually, what you are doing as you read this chapter is building a concept for reading. What is reading? What do good readers do? What is the research about reading? What is effective and responsive practice in reading instruction? With this concept in mind, you will be able to integrate new information as you encounter it, establish purposes for further reading or further practice, and reconstruct your schemata as you incorporate new information.

FIGURE 8.8 Concepts about Genre

Expressive

Favourite author studies are a good way to teach the concept of different writing modes and genres. For example, Byrd Baylor's books (*Everybody Needs a Rock*, *The Table Where Rich People Sit*) are written in the first person, making them ideal demonstrations of the concept of expressive writing. The style is easy for young writers to imitate: the purpose is to express one's personal thoughts and feelings.

Poetic

Use authors such as Chris Van Allsburg (*The Wretched Stone; The Mysteries of Harris Burdick*); and Bill Martin Jr. (*Brown Bear, Bear, Knots on a Counting Rope*). "Poetic" refers to a wide assortment, from rhyming text to fictional stories, which can be further broken down into traditional literature, fantasy, mystery, etc. Many examples should be demonstrated repeatedly.

Expository

Text series, such as the Eyewitness books, children's nature magazines, and instructional texts (for example, how to play string games), create a clear category or mode.

STOP, THINK, AND WRITE

- Who is your favourite author?
- What you have learned about this author's style, form, purpose for writing that motivates you to read his/her text?

Recall that reading is a transaction among the reader, the text, and the author.

- How is this evident in your reading?

Compare reading your favourite author with reading your language arts textbook.

- How do they differ?

literacy
notebook
8.4

THE LINK TO COMPREHENSION

Concepts about text allow students to recognize the pattern or formula that often exists in text, freeing up the reader for the real work of reading, which is comprehension. This brings new meaning to the phrase, "read like a writer and write like a reader" because to understand and use these concepts, we must indeed understand what it means to be a writer and what it means to be a reader. "When readers comprehend text, they mentally build meaning representations at multiple levels" (Graesser, McNamara, & Louwerse, 2003, p. 87). Each level has its own characteristics, which must be explored as readers engage in the transaction with text. Readers need to recognize the diversity of writing styles and genres used by authors, and how these factors influence and shape comprehension. Understanding that authors write multiple texts at multiple times in multiple contexts will facilitate reader comprehension, activate prior knowledge, and build purposes for reading. It will also allow readers to look at text from a more critical standpoint, and to ask: Why did the author write this text? When was it written? Where was it written? What was happening in the world at the time it was written? Answering these questions will help readers to understand the author's point of view and perspective at the time the text was written.

"What is being suggested is that the comprehension difficulties experienced by some students may be caused by the fact that the concepts and knowledge stored in the schemata cannot be rapidly and automatically accessed" (Samuels, 1994a, p. 1142). Comprehension difficulties stem predominantly from the organization and structure of the text; whether the text addresses a single concept or tries to explain several at once; the clarity and coherence of the explanation; whether the text is appropriate for the students and the purpose of the lesson; whether the information is accurate and consistent; whether referents are ambiguous, distant, or indirect; whether the reader lacks the requisite background for the concept; whether events are relevant to the text. To overcome these textual limitations, teachers can change how they teach for comprehension by thinking about the connections between real life experience and comprehending a text, and the connections between reading and composing or writing one's own text. Mini-lessons, think alouds, read alouds, and graphic organizers are just a few of the activities that will support readers, writers, listeners, speakers, viewers, and representers as they learn to make sense of the many texts they encounter.

Theory into Practice 8.1 and 8.2 describe how readers and writers might use information about concepts about text as they respond to text in reader response journals. Teacher Talk 8.2 shows how Janet McIntosh uses reader response journals to engage Junior-level students in deepening their understanding of text.

In conclusion, we offer you the following principles for effective concept-building instruction:

- It should be research-based, developmentally appropriate, and responsive to students' strengths and needs (for example, Kindergarten students are capable of building concepts about story, poetry, or nonfiction written at their level whereas Grade 6 students are ready to look at historical fiction and more complex forms of poetry).

- It should be planned and purposeful, not simply incidental to the reading process.

- It should be part of a comprehensive and balanced literacy program. It should be integrated with comprehension, listening, speaking, reading, writing, viewing, and representing activities and should not be viewed as a series of isolated activities where students retrieve information about characters, setting, etc. (Palincsar, 2003).

THE READER AS MEANING-MAKER

To construct meaning from text, readers have to be helped to understand the relationship between what they are reading, why they are reading, and how they should do the reading. They look beyond what is explicitly stated in the text to what the author is implying; they pose questions from literal, figurative, and inferential perspectives. They make use of cues provided by the author or illustrator (for example, comparisons, headings, graphs, labels, pictures). Durkin (2004) argues that successful comprehension has taken place if the reader has realized the purpose established for the reading. She compares comprehension to a journey in much the same way we have discussed literacy as a journey:

> *Little comprehension is likely to result if an individual wanders aimlessly through a piece of text. Instead adequate comprehension is the product of a journey guided by a pre-specified destination.*

> *Like travelers, successful readers sometimes slow down or even stop, perhaps to think about something of interest. Like travelers, too, they may encounter problems that need to be remedied before their reading proceeds. Throughout all this, the destination—that is, the purpose of the reading—is not forgotten.*

(Durkin, 2004, p. 295)

PRIMARY LEVEL READER RESPONSE JOURNAL

Dear readers:

Your reader response journal is a place where you can talk about books you are reading and how you feel about them. I will write back and ask you questions about your reading. Tell me about the things you like and dislike, and the things that you find confusing, unusual, or funny. Talk about what you think something means and make predictions about what might happen later. Doing this will help you get the most from your book.

Some suggestions to get you thinking:

Words: Find some interesting words. Do you know what the words mean? Can you draw them? How do they make you feel? Why did the author use these words?
How can you use words like these in your writing?

Connections: Talk about how the book reminded you of your life or school, other times and places, stories in the news, or other books or stories.
How can you help readers make connections to your writing?

Pictures: Draw something you liked about the story. It might be a picture of the setting, a character, an exciting part, a surprise, or a prediction. You do not need to copy a picture from the book but instead imagine the author's words.
How can you paint pictures with your words?

Questions: Think about the questions you have. What confused you? What questions would you like to ask the author?
What questions do you have about your own writing?

Passages: Choose parts of the story that you want to remember. What was good? What made you laugh? What was interesting? What was scary? What was good writing?
Why do you want to remember this writing?

You might find these sentence starters helpful:

I began to think...	I love the way...	I can't believe...
I wonder why...	I noticed...	I think...
I observed...	I wonder...	If I were...
I'm not sure...	I felt sad when...	I like the way the author...
I wish that...	This made me think of...	I was surprised...
It seems like...	I'm not sure...	This story teaches...
I began to think of...		

Thanks for sharing.

Source: Adapted from Daniels (2002).

JUNIOR LEVEL READER RESPONSE JOURNAL

Dear readers:

Your reader response journal is a place where you can talk about images, feelings, thoughts, reactions, interpretations, reactions, or anything else you would like to preserve or remember as a reader. Your comments may also be in response to the author's process as a writer as well as your process as a reader. Some of what you will collect as a reader will also help you as a writer. Keep track of interesting words, phrases, and ways of doing things that you might like to try. There are no right or wrong answers so take risks and be truthful, thoughtful, and thorough. Let me hear your voice. I will write back and ask you questions about your reading.

Remember your response journal is not a place to simply summarize what you've read. Sometimes a summary will be necessary to get your point across. But I am more interested in the things you like and dislike, and the things that you find confusing, unusual, or funny. Talk about what you think something means and make predictions about what might happen later. Doing this will help you get the MOST from your book.

Some suggestions to get you thinking:

- *Quote or point out details:* Quote a part of the book that you think is an example of good writing. What did you like about the quote? Write down striking words, images, phrases, or details. Speculate about them. Why did the author choose them? What do they add to the story? Why did you notice them? Divide your notebook page in half and copy words from the text onto the left side; write your responses on the right. On a first reading you might put use post-it notes to mark passages that intrigue you; on the second reading, choose the most interesting ideas, then write about them. *What makes you feel this is good writing? Why do you want to save it? How can you use these ideas?*

- *Experiences or memories/connections:* How does this book make you think or feel? Does the book remind you of anything or anyone? Do you see any similarities between this text (concepts, events) and other texts (concepts, events)? Does it bring to mind other related issues? *What kinds of ideas does this book give you for writing?*

- *Reactions:* Do you love/hate/can't stop reading this book? What makes you feel that way? What do you wish had happened? What do you wish the author had included or done more of? Try agreeing with the writer. Write down the supporting ideas. Try arguing with the writer. On what points, or about what issues, do you disagree? Think of your journal as a place to carry on a dialogue with the writer or with the text in which you actually speak with the writer. Ask questions; have the writer respond. What happens when you imagine yourself in their shoes? *What reactions do you have to your own writing, the writing of your peers, the world around you?*

- *Questions:* What confuses you? What don't you understand? What perplexes you about a particular passage? Try beginning, "I wonder why..." or "I'm having trouble understanding how...' or "It perplexes me that..." or "I was surprised when ..." Why did the author do something a particular way? What would you have done if you were the author? *What questions do you have about your own writing?*

JUNIOR LEVEL READER RESPONSE JOURNAL (continued)

- *Images:* How did the author paint pictures with words? How did the author help you to envision what was happening in the story? *What types of things do you do to help your readers visualize your writing and imagine your ideas?*

- *Evaluations:* How does this book compare to others you have read? What makes it an effective or ineffective piece of writing? Describe the author's point of view. How does the author's attitude shape the way the writer presents the material? *How is your writing going?*

Sometimes the story elements are important to our understanding of the text. If you need to talk about story elements, remember that you need to do more than summarize. Relate your personal experiences that connect with the plot, characters, or setting. These sentence starters might help:

Plot: This part of the story is very ironic because...
                 This part is humorous/sad/scary because...
                 I don't understand this part because...
                 I think this is symbolic in this novel because....
                 I think the point the author was trying to make in this part is that...
                 This situation reminds me of a similar situation my own life. It happened when...
                 This section makes me think about_____ because...
                 This section is particularly effective because...
                 This part is realistic/unrealistic because...
                 This scene reminds me of a similar scene in _____ (title of work) because...

Characters: _____ (name of character) reminds me of myself because...
                 _____ reminds me of somebody I know because...
                 If I were _____ at this point, I would...
                 The character I most admire/dislike is _____ because...
                 If the story were told from _____'s point of view, it would be different because...
                 A different way _____ could have handled the problem of would be to...
                 I could really "relate" to this part/character because....
                 I think the relationship between _____ and _____ is interesting because...

Setting: I think this setting is important because...
                 I could really picture the setting when the author wrote... _____

Thanks for sharing.

Source: Adapted from:
http://www.sdcoe.k12.ca.us/score/actbank/tjouguide.htm
http://www.readwritethink.org/lessons/lesson_view.asp?id=55
http://www.carman.k12.mi.us/Highschweb/hsstaff/sbobalik/readerwriterlog.htm
Retrieved August 15, 2005.

Teacher Talk/8.2

JANET MCINTOSH TALKS ABOUT READER RESPONSE JOURNALS

Writing reader response journals during the act of reading provides ideal opportunities for students to deepen and expand their understanding of literature. I've had junior level students write journal entries as they read novels for literature groups and I've observed that engagement in reading is the result. One classroom approach is to have students read an assigned portion of the text, and then pause, reflect, and write half page responses at regular intervals as they read. Writing *while* reading is a key component of response journals. Initially, this can cause students some difficulty as they may feel that they are interrupting their reading to write. With time and practice, many realize that it's easier to record their ideas when they are fresh in their minds. I've observed that pausing in the act of reading seems to spur them on to want to read more—as they move away from the text to write, they seem to be drawn back to it and want to return to their reading so they can gather more information.

Focusing on students' initial reactions to their reading is an ideal starting point for encounters with literature. Response to text often begins on an emotional level as they share personal experiences that they link to events or issues in the book they are reading. Reflective writing draws them into the text in a natural way. Some students benefit from response prompts, but many of my own students, when given the opportunity to journal, actively relate the text to prior knowledge and seem to better comprehend what they have read; in turn, they demonstrate greater confidence in their reading as they become more involved in the text. Students record initial reactions to their reading, prior to any small group, whole class, or teacher discussion; teacher-created questions are not the focus. The reader's experience of the text is emphasized and valued through use of the response journal. When students realize that they have a role in determining meaning, they become more actively immersed in reading. Independent reading and writing occur and, with practice, students gain confidence in their skills. Too often reluctant readers lack the motivation to read on their own. Some have had the experience of being told by teachers what the book means and believe that their teachers hold the correct interpretation of the text.

When Junior students are first exposed to reader response journals, they sometimes need to be encouraged to provide support for their ideas with text details when writing entries. Direct references are not required but textual interpretations seem to be strengthened when student writers refer to particular aspects of the novel they are reading. I've noted that providing in-class time for reading and journal writing is essential. When students see that I allot class time for journaling, then they become aware that it's a valued activity. They are happy to complete two tasks at the same time—the reading of a novel and producing a written response journal. Incorporating reading and writing experiences through use of reader response journals helps Junior-level students deepen their understanding of the text they are reading; effective meaning-making is a positive outcome of implementing this strategy.

Janet McIntosh is a professor in the Bachelor of Education program at Nipissing University. Her PhD research focused on the implementation of reader response journals with secondary students.

STOP, THINK, AND WRITE

Using texts that you are currently reading, apply the strategy of reader response journals to both children's literature you encounter in the classroom and on placement, as well as to your own personal reading.

■ What are your dominant strategies?

■ How do you make sense of text?

Try this over a period of time, expanding and experimenting with new strategies as you read diverse texts.

literacy notebook 8.5

One way that readers construct meaning from text is by asking questions.

How do readers monitor their comprehension? What do they do when it doesn't make sense? How do they restore comprehension? Comprehension monitoring requires that readers continually ask themselves the question "Does it make sense?" and engaging what we have referred to as the semantic cueing system (see Figure 2.9). When the answer is "no," they have to stop and explore alternative strategies, often referred to as "fix-up strategies." Figure 8.9 provides a description of the process and some fix-up strategies that are useful when readers find it difficult to comprehend and make sense of text (see also Figure 9.2).

As indicated in Figure 8.9, comprehension is a continual process that requires the reader's attention throughout the reading process. Teachers can facilitate and enhance the comprehension and sense-making process before, during, and after reading (see Figure 8.10 for a description of teacher scaffolded reading experiences). Teachers use a range of strategies to support and scaffold comprehension, ranging from think alouds to re-teaching strategies, always working toward reader independence and self-monitoring.

Meaning-making is a continuous process; it does not happen at the end of a text but occurs throughout the text. We have discussed scaffolding as a valuable teaching technique that allows teachers to bridge the gap between what students can do on their own and what they can do with the help of an adult or peer (Vygotsky, 1978). As students become more independent in their use of particular strategies, teachers should plan activities that gradually release the responsibility for comprehension to readers. Figure 8.11 describes levels of support in comprehension instruction in a reading classroom.

In conclusion, we offer the following principles for effective meaning-making strategy instruction:

FIGURE 8.9 A Process for Comprehension Monitoring

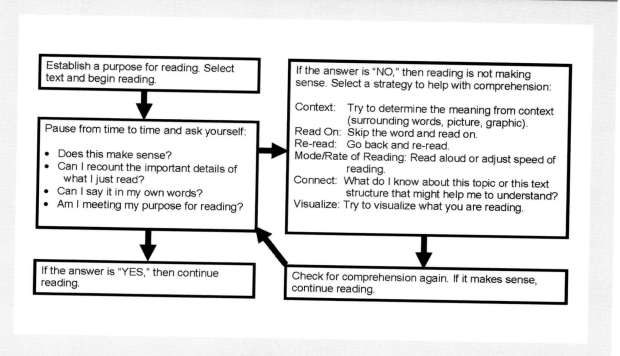

Source: Ontario Ministry of Education (2003); Wilhelm (2001).

- Strategies should be research based, developmentally appropriate, and responsive to what learners are telling you or showing you that they need in order to make sense of texts. It is a continuous and dynamic process and must be taught flexibly and comprehensively through a balance of modelling, thinking aloud, and opportunities for guided practice.

- Instruction should be planned and purposeful, not simply incidental to the reading process. Teachers learn what and how they need to teach from their students.

- Instruction is part of a comprehensive and balanced literacy program. It forms the foundation for comprehension and re-visioning, listening, speaking, reading, writing, viewing, and representing activities.

FIGURE 8.10 Teacher Scaffolded Reading Experiences

Before Reading	During Reading	After Reading
Relate reading to students' lives	Read aloud	Question students (Questioning the Author)
Activate and build on prior knowledge	Oral reading by students	Direct discussions
Motivate students	Comprehension monitoring by students	Structure application, response, and extension activities that involve writing, storytelling, drama, visual arts, poetry, etc.
Picture walks	Checking in or conferencing with students	
Pre-teach vocabulary	Reciprocal teaching	Help students to build connections—design for learning
Pre-teach text structures	Interactive reading	
Pre-teach concepts	Guided reading	Re-teach vocabulary, text structures, concepts, or strategies when necessary
Question, predict, set direction, and establish purpose for reading	Independent silent reading	
Explicit instruction of strategies that might be useful		
Suggest strategies that might be useful		

Source: Adapted from Clark & Graves (2004), p. 576.

The Reader as Architect

As Chapter 13 deals primarily with the role of listener, speaker, reader, writer, viewer, representer, and participant as architect in a multi-genre world, we will simply introduce the role here, leaving theory and instructional strategies and research for that chapter.

In Chapter 3, we discussed re-vision at the centre of reading the W.O.R.L.D., where re-vision is the ability to critically see the past and the present and imagine a different future (Kellner, 2004). At the heart of revision is the ability to comprehend the world and view it through a lens tinted by world views, texts, conversations, and experiences. Whether we are discussing reading words or reading worlds, the architectural role of the reader involves the ability to see past and present texts and then use these texts to envision a different future (Kellner, 2004). On a simplistic

FIGURE 8.11 Levels of Support in Comprehension Instruction

from	Level of Support	Comprehension Instruction
teacher	**Modelled**	Think alouds that demonstrate how the teacher is making sense of the text, the comprehension strategies being used, the self-monitoring processes being used to monitor words, text structures, and comprehension (see Theory into Practice 6.3, and Figure 8.9).
support	**Shared**	Moment-to-moment scaffolding (Clark & Graves, 2004) Teachers prompt, probe, and elaborate on student responses throughout reading and comprehension instruction. Teachers and students read through a text together and the teacher engages students' thought, comprehension, and sense making through careful questioning (see Theory into Practice 6.1).
to	**Interactive**	Reciprocal teaching allows teachers and students to work together to construct comprehension. It focuses on the development of four comprehension strategies: questioning, summarizing, clarifying, and predicting. Teachers pre-teach the four comprehension strategies and evaluate each student's progress with individualized instruction during reading. Teachers and students interact throughout the text with the teacher modelling and guiding, and the students filling in the bits of the comprehension strategies that they have mastered. Reciprocal teaching allows teachers to provide intensive instruction to those students who require it. As students become more comfortable with the strategies, they will assume the teacher's role, with the teacher modelling and prompting only as necessary.
student	**Guided**	Interrogating the author and text (see Chapter 13) Students focus on understanding, interpreting, and elaborating the author's meaning as they read the text. Questioning the author occurs throughout a text as readers progress through texts.
independence	**Independent**	Teachers incorporate mini-lesson approach where students sign in for mini-lessons or teachers post signs of those students participating that day (see Chapter 12). Independent learners engage in selection and negotiation of meaningful, relevant, and authentic learning and literacy experiences, texts, and strategies.

level, it might be the ability to crawl inside the role of characters and envision the world as they see it. On more complex levels, it means to be able to interpret critically a range of texts in a way that will transform the world and make it a better place. This is very much the role of an architect. We typically associate architects with structures and buildings, but most definitions include the primary roles of planning, creating, and designing schemata or plans. This is what we ask our readers to do: ask questions, plan their reading, design a plan for comprehension, and then create or design a new image or a new reality that will change their future. Readers, regardless of age, have the ability to envision the world as a different place and use texts for a variety of purposes. In Chapter 13, we will discuss grade appropriate strategies that help students to change the world one day and one situation at a time.

Moving On

In this chapter, we have discussed comprehension as the ability of the reader to engage in a transactional relationship with the text, the author, and the reading community and make text-to-text, text-to-self, and text-to-world connections (Keene & Zimmerman, 1997). In response to print texts, readers answer the question: Does this make sense to me? And if not, why? At higher levels, comprehension enables students to reconstruct, transform, and revise their world. It is the ability to interact with texts and ideas, integrating them into their own present and past schema in a way that enables them to imagine a different future. Comprehension in its broadest sense results in "some change in the way the mind views the world as a result of reading a text, that is, some sort of trace of the text read, including indirect effects cognitive as well as affective ones" (Kintsch, 2004, p. 1271).

As we have described, strategies to enhance comprehension are best learned within the contexts of literature, classroom, community, discussion, and active engagement (Alvermann & Eakle, 2003). In Chapter 9, we discuss specific strategies and methods that keep both the reader and comprehension at the centre of reading instruction, taking into account the diversity of learners, the need for multi-level engagement, the importance of literature, and the influence of context.

The primary purpose of reading in school is
to extend the experiences of boys and girls,
to stimulate their thinking powers, and to elevate their tastes.

*The ultimate end of instruction in reading is
to enable the reader to participate intelligently
in the thought life of the world
and appreciatively in its recreational activities.*
—William S. Gray

LIT-FOLIO UPDATE

If you haven't already done so, you should start your reader response journal now. This will record your developing awareness of not only literature, but strategies for reading and meaning-making as well. Take some time to review the strategies that you use as a reader. What have you learned about the reading process? What have you learned about how readers make sense of text? Comment on whether you feel confident with your own strategies as a reader. What can you do to improve or develop greater awareness of your own strategies so that you can in turn share these with your students?

LIT-FOLIO TIP

Our B.Ed. students kept a reader response journal for both self-selected literature and literature read in class. They began by simply responding as readers without paying attention to any particular strategy. As their awareness in reading and writing developed, however, they returned to their journals, analyzed their own dominant strategies, and began to experiment with those strategies they identified as areas of need. Using a balance of children's literature and their own selection of published literature allowed them to explore strategies from both a teacher perspective and a student perspective.

When preparing their reader response page for their lit-folios, many students made two entries as evidence: one that demonstrated their response to children's literature and a second that was evidence of their own personal reading.

Resources to Support Your Learning

Professional Resources

Ontario Early Reading Strategy. (2003). *A guide to effective instruction in reading, Kindergarten to Grade Three.*

Pinnell, G.S., & Fountas, I.C. (1998). *Word matters: Teaching phonics and spelling in the reading/writing classroom.* Portsmouth, NH: Heinemann.

Scott, R. (1993). *Spelling: Sharing the secrets.* Toronto, ON: Gage Educational Publishing Co.

Toronto District School Board. (2000). *Teaching children to read and write: A literacy guide.*

Weaver, C. (1996). *Teaching grammar in context.* Portsmouth, NH: Boynton/Cook.

Weaver, C. (2002). *Reading process and practice.* Portsmouth, NH: Heinemann.

Children's Literature: Our Favourites

Images of Reading and the Reader

Jeremiah learns to read, Jo Ellen Bogart
Reading with dad, Richard Jorgensen
Thank you, Mr. Falker, Patricia Polacco
Wednesday surprise, Eve Bunting
Wolf! Becky Bloom

Word Play and Word-Solving

❧ *I went to the zoo*, Rita Golden Gelman
❧ *There were monkeys in my kitchen*, Sheree Fitch

Websites

Ontario's Education Foundations Program eWorkshop with training modules: http://www.eworkshop.on.ca

Reading Practices

9

> The only right way to teach reading is to teach the student, and the only right way to teach the student is to teach flexibly, diversely, and responsively, not categorically, analytically, or sequentially.
> —Michelann Parr and Terry Campbell

key terms

efferent reading
guided reading
independent reading
interactive reading
literacy centres
literary conversatons
literature circles
modelled reading
read alouds
readers' workshop
running records
shared reading
subtext strategy
think alouds

questions to guide your learning

By the end of this chapter, you should understand the key terms and be able to answer the following questions:

- What does the continuum of support look like in reading?
- What are the essential features of shared reading?
- How does interactive reading differ from shared reading and guided reading?
- What are the essential features and goals of guided reading? How do I manage guided reading with literacy centres?
- What strategies and skills are assessed by running records?
- What is the goal of independent reading and how can independent reading be supported in the classroom?
- How can I facilitate classroom talk about great literature?
- How can I implement literature circles in the classroom?
- How do I manage readers' workshop and assess reading?

Looking Back, Looking Ahead

In Chapter 8, we introduced reading as a puzzle to be solved by readers and teachers in a variety of contexts for a variety of purposes. As we begin this chapter, we remind you of the complexity of reading, the individuality of each reader, and the nature of communication in the reading process.

In Chapter 9, we take a close look at the methods and strategies that literacy teachers use to help their students solve the puzzle and make sense of words, texts, and the world. As you read this chapter, remember that the reading strategies are equally effective for story and content texts; they are useful not only in language instruction but also as students are engaged in language for learning across the curriculum. Our discussion proceeds from modelled reading to independent reading; reading assessment is considered at each level. As well, we discuss efferent reading and special considerations to facilitate content area reading with students.

Chapter 10 describes our favourite strategies, acknowledging that because no two students, teachers, or classrooms are the same, you need a variety of strategies. As you come to understand yourself, your students, and the multiple contexts of your classroom, you will be better able to decide which strategy will work under which circumstances, and to plan multiple spaces, places, and times for reading, writing, and language for learning across the curriculum.

Recognizing that all students vary in personality, learning style, and reading behaviour, literacy teachers understand that there is no single method, theory, or set of learning materials that can successfully teach all children to read. A wide range of reading approaches and methods that will support all students in the classroom, regardless of grade level, personality, ability, or learning style, must be included in your repertoire. In this chapter, we present a range of strategies that will make reading interesting, fun, interactive, and engaging in both language instruction and language for learning across the curriculum. The strategies we describe reflect a continuum of support from modelled to independent. Figure 9.1 presents our conceptualization of how the continuum of support, introduced in Chapter 2 (Figure 2.5), can be applied in reading to support student growth and facilitate independence.

When we discussed literacy development in Chapter 4, we discussed the emerging characteristics of literacy learners and strategies to support learners as they progress from emergence to independence, from orality to literacy (see Figure 4.6). These strategies are not inextricably linked to an individual phase but instead run consistently across all

FIGURE 9.1 Applying the Continuum of Support to Reading

from	Level of Support	Reading Practices
teacher	**Modelled**	• Reading aloud, modelling, demonstrating, and thinking aloud to share their **in-the-head thinking**, sense-making, and strategy use. • Select texts that are often above what students can read independently, typically those that are at their **difficulty level**. Texts should be appropriate to the students' interest, cognitive level, and instructional theme (where appropriate). Only the teacher has a copy of the book.
support	**Shared**	• Share reading experiences and opportunities with students. Invite them to join in on repetitive or predictable words or phrases when they are ready. • Select texts that are at the students' **instructional level**. Texts should be motivating, engaging, and contain predictable patterns or rhythms that they will enjoy. shared reading is distinguished from other forms of reading by the presence of big books or enlarged texts accessible to all students in the reading group.
to	**Interactive**	• Share reading experiences and opportunities with students, interacting in ways that permit them to contribute what they know and can do independently. Students often read independently as much as they can, with the teacher filling in the gaps to ensure a successful reading experience. • Select texts that are at the students' instructional level. Texts should be motivating and engaging, and contain predictable patterns or rhythms that students will enjoy. A single text is shared between the teacher and usually a single reader.
student	**Guided**	• Scaffold in order to bridge the gap, activate prior knowledge, and prepare students to read unfamiliar texts. Students are grouped by similar strengths, needs, and experiences in order to provide intensive strategy instruction. Students read texts at their instructional level on their own, with the teacher listening in for appropriate strategy use and problem solving. • Select texts that are at the students' instructional level, challenging with just the right amount of reading work. Each student has a copy of the text.
independence	**Independent**	• Select methods and practices that foster learner independence. Make available a wide variety of texts for students that are at their instructional level. • Students select and read diverse texts, sometimes joining a literature circle or literary conversation.

phases, with teachers selecting strategies and levels of support in response to the students and the contexts of their classrooms. In the same way that strategies are selected responsively and flexibly, so too are the levels of support. Modelled, shared, interactive, guided, and independent reading are equally effective at all grade levels in all curriculum areas; the choice depends on the purposes, tasks, and contexts that support literacy learning.

The remainder of this chapter focuses on the levels of support and literacy strategies that enable literacy learning and language for learning across the curriculum. We will revisit concepts and strategies already introduced, not only to underscore their importance in a comprehensive literacy program, but also to link these strategies specifically to reading and the continuum of support that we are describing.

Modelled Reading

Modelled reading is composed of reading aloud and thinking aloud. Its primary goal is to model and demonstrate effective reading strategies.

READ ALOUDS

> *By reading to children, you introduce them to new authors, new illustrators, new forms of text. You make them more aware of the wonderful opportunities to experience adventure, humour, family life, and you help them to participate vicariously in all kinds of life events. You help them to know what it is like to be a sports star, or what it is like to go into space... You help them to imagine worlds they would never dream about. You help them to know what you can learn from books and to discover that there is a whole world of information at their fingertips. In other words, you give them purposes for life-long reading.*
>
> (Hornsby, 2000, p. 28)

Although the primary purpose of a **read aloud** is to demonstrate that reading is a source of pleasure and information, there are many other benefits that, although they may seem incidental, are of critical importance.

> *As we read aloud with children, we help them experience all the strategies of effective reading. We do the print-work, the phrasing, and the punctuating for children, deciding who is talking to whom and what their intonation will be, so that children's minds are more able to anticipate, infer, connect, question, and monitor for sense.*
>
> (Calkins, 2001, p. 59)

Read alouds were introduced in Chapter 6, but we cannot overstate their importance in the development of readers as well as literacy learners. Reading aloud is part of the first level in our continuum of support from modelled to independent. When you read aloud, you have the opportunity to model intonation, expression, pronunciation, and your own comprehension strategies for both story and content texts.

STOP, THINK, AND WRITE

literacy notebook 9.1

Your challenge in this chapter is to observe, implement, and reflect on as many strategies as possible. We encourage you to participate in all five levels of the continuum and gather evidence (for example, lesson plans, student work samples, and reflections on process) for your lit-folio.

At this point, you will likely also be engaged in practicum placements that require you to connect theory and practice. Select a range of strategies that are responsive to the needs of the students you are teaching. Try the strategies and reflect on what you notice about student engagement in literacy, student strategy use, and your own personal effectiveness.

- Which levels of support are you most comfortable with?
- Which do you need to work on?
- Which strategies do you find particularly useful?
- Which have you tried, changed, or adapted for a group of students?
- What strategies have you seen in place in a classroom that are not listed in this chapter and that you will add to your own repertoire of strategies?
- Which do you understand well?
- Which require more time, energy, and instruction to develop?

This will likely be a longer notebook entry, one that extends throughout many weeks as you try out new strategies and techniques. Organize your response using a retell, relate, reflect format:

- Retell the strategies you have used.
- Relate them to your course expectations, the goals you have set as a literacy learner, and the goals you have set as an emergent literacy teacher.
- Reflect on how these strategies enhance your awareness of literacy and how students develop literacy both in and outside a classroom.

Read alouds do not need to be restricted to story and fiction books. Reading aloud non-fiction will allow your students to learn and talk about real things in a highly supported environment (Taberski, 2001). Pairing up fiction and non-fiction texts for reading aloud is an excellent strategy that will enable your students to connect information gained through story texts and information gained through content texts. Thinking aloud about the similarities and differences will also allow you to alert your students to the unique strategies and skills required for reading informational texts. In Chapter 10, the strategy Teaching with Twin Texts explains how you can pair non-fiction and fiction texts in your literacy program.

Keeping in mind that there are times when you will simply read aloud for the pure enjoyment of sharing a great text with students, you also need to be aware of the fact that using literature for learning requires careful attention and planning (see Theory into Practice 9.1). In Theory into Practice 9.2, we show how *Stella, Queen of the Snow* by Marie-Louise Gay can be extended to a variety of balanced literacy activities that address the six language strands and incorporate language for learning across the curriculum. At the primary level, it will be your responsibility to select judiciously the activities to be completed before, during, and after reading. At the junior level, such concept webs are often used as a menu of response activities so that students have some choice about which activities to complete (for example, two from each strand).

Theory Into Practice/9.1

GETTING READY FOR READ ALOUDS

	Teacher's Role	Learner's Role	Strategies
Before Reading	**Plan:** • Plan questions to ask during the read aloud. Do not over plan; too many questions will interrupt the reading and pull students away from the text. • Plan opportunities to extend student comprehension. • Rehearse out loud: practise appropriate volume, pitch, timing, and inflection.	• Suggest texts to the teacher for the read aloud. • Participate in the selection of books or alternative texts where appropriate.	• Selecting • Skimming • Previewing • Anticipating

GETTING READY FOR READ ALOUDS (continued)

	Teacher's Role	Learner's Role	Strategies
Before Reading	**Introduce the text:** • Activate prior knowledge and set purposes for listening. • Introduce the author, illustrator, genre, unusual text features, and formats. When reading content area material, introduce an expository text structure that will enable students to mentally gather information as you read.	• Engage in conversation about the story. • Raise questions. • Build expectations; make predictions. • Notice illustrations and/or visual information in the text.	• Connecting • Questioning • Predicting
During Reading	• Read with expression, enthusiasm, and appropriate intonation and pace. • Make connections to and draw comparisons with other texts or experiences. • Make inferences and predictions.	• Listen actively, participating in discussions, making connections, drawing comparisons, making inferences, and revisiting predictions when requested. • Visualize the author's words.	• Connecting • Comparing • Inferring • Predicting • Revising predictions • Visualizing
After Reading	• Reinforce comprehension by helping students to make comparisons and inferences. • Discuss story elements such as character, plot, and setting. • Discuss questions posed before, during, and after the reading.	• Talk about the story, making text-to-self, text-to-world, and text-to-text connections. • Check predictions. • Respond by retelling in a new form; for example, role play, comic strip, or reader response journals.	• Connecting • Revising predictions • Retelling • Analyzing • Interpreting • Responding
Beyond Reading	• Plan activities that extend student comprehension, appreciation, and response to text.	• Participate fully in activities planned by the teacher.	• Connecting • Revising predictions • Retelling • Analyzing • Interpreting • Responding

EXTENDING READ ALOUDS WITH *STELLA, QUEEN OF THE SNOW*

Stella, Queen of the Snow by Marie-Louise Gay recounts a day in the life of Stella and Sam as they explore winter activities.

Reading:

- Make connections to personal experience by making predictions about the story by viewing the pictures and revising predictions after hearing the story read aloud.
- Read aloud a modified version of the story as readers' theatre.
- Separate words into parts and use patterns to determine the meanings of new words; focus on compound words (for example, snowbank, snowmen).
- Use awareness of punctuation (for example, quotation marks, question marks, exclamation marks) to read with expression and fluency.

Viewing:

- Before the first reading, have students view the illustrations and make predictions about the story. Record these on a chart for verification later.
- Notice details in the illustrations (for example, how the illustrator shows movement, birds flying south, footprints).
- Look closely at the illustrations in order to determine how the characters might be feeling: make use of a subtext strategy to step inside the characters' heads.

Speaking:

- Use appropriate vocabulary and oral language structures to discuss winter.
- Create winter dialogues, questions, and answers using the story as a model demonstrating awareness of conversational conventions and turn-taking.
- Retell the story of Stella and recount similar personal experiences.
- Participate in readers' theatre constructed of Sam and Stella's dialogue.

Writing:

- Identify winter nouns from the story (for example, snowman, snowbank, snowball, snowsuit).
- Brainstorm adjectives that describe winter.
- Participate in a shared writing experience about a winter field trip.
- Produce a short piece of writing that describes how to do a winter activity (for example, making a snow angel, a snow person, or a snowball).
- Extend their spoken winter dialogues, questions, and answers into writing.
- Use question marks appropriately in their questions and answers about winter.

Representation:

- Brainstorm what you would do if you were king or queen for the day and dramatize these activities.
- Extend the dramatization by creating images using KidPix or Storybook Weaver and adding text, voice, or music.
- Plan a dress-up day where students dress as kings or queens and read/represent their queen or king of the day stories.

Listening:

- Listen to a story read aloud.
- Participate in discussion connecting personal experiences to story.
- Apply the rules of participating in a conversation.
- Recognize the conventions of a question and answer conversation.

Theory Into Practice/9.2

EXTENDING READ ALOUDS WITH *STELLA, QUEEN OF THE SNOW* (continued)

Language across the Curriculum:

- Science: snow experiments, seasons, weather
- Physical and Health Education: snow activities and snow/ice safety, making snow angels, snowpeople, snowshoeing, catching snowflakes, follow the leader's footprints attempting to leave only one trail in the snow, frozen tag
- Visual Arts: watercolour illustrations using the illustrations as a model, snow sculptures
- Mathematics: creating six-point snowflakes using paper folding and cutting, using winter nouns to create patterns

Source: Based on Ontario Curriculum: Language, Grade 2

REVISITING THINK ALOUDS

Reading aloud will provide you with the time and opportunity to model reading strategies and your own in-the-head thinking as you read (see Theory into Practice 9.3 for a detailed description). The goal of **think alouds** is to demystify the comprehension process by making your in-the-head thinking explicit and visible to students so that they have a framework for thinking and a common language for talking about books. Think alouds require careful planning and conceptualization. Figure 9.2 provides prompts that you can use to support students as they think aloud. They are often used on second and subsequent readings (the exception is that making predictions is used only at the first reading). When planning a think aloud, consider the following questions:

- What should my students be able to understand about the strategy being modelled?

- Where could I stop to think aloud? Which two or three spots would best illustrate my point?

- How will I differentiate between reading aloud and thinking aloud?

EXTENDING THINK ALOUDS TO UNDERSTAND CHARACTER

As students make sense of text, they are often required to consider the multiple perspectives of characters. There are times when what a character is saying or doing in the story needs to be explored in more depth beyond what appears on the surface. A character's words and actions

Theory Into Practice/9.3

GETTING READY FOR THINK ALOUDS

	Teacher's Role	Learner's Role	Strategies
Before Reading	**Plan:** • Choose a reading selection, a strategy to model, and plan what you will say.		
	Introduce the book: • Talk about the type of text and explain to learners why you have selected it. • Read the text through once for pleasure and enjoyment. • Tell students that you will be modelling a think aloud strategy.	• Engage in conversation about the story. • Raise questions. • Build expectations, make predictions. • Discuss what they know about a given comprehension strategy.	• Connecting • Questioning • Predicting
During Reading	• Read with expression, enthusiasm, and appropriate intonation and pacing. • Demonstrate phrased and fluent reading. • Stop and think periodically to model incidentally how to use reading strategies to monitor one's own understanding. • Think aloud where appropriate and where planned.	• Listen actively and participate in discussions. • When prompted, learners orally share their in-the-head thinking or record their responses on a Post-it note (see Theory into Practice 9.4).	• Connecting • Comparing • Inferring • Predicting • Revising predictions • Visualizing
After Reading	• Debrief the strategy and clues that can help identify when this strategy is being used and why.	• Recall cue words that supported strategy use. • Recall a time when they used a particular strategy.	• Connecting • Analyzing • Interpreting • Responding
Beyond Reading	• Teachers plan activities that allow students to think aloud independently and with their peers (see Theory into practice 9.4).	• Use stop and think marks to keep track of passages where they thought aloud and analyze strategy use in a reader response journal (see Figure 9.2 for prompts for using fix-up strategies).	• Connecting • Analyzing • Interpreting • Responding

FIGURE 9.2 Think Aloud Prompts to Support the Use of Fix-up Strategies

Strategy	Sample Prompts
Use Fix-Up Strategies to Address Confusion and Repair Comprehension	Fix-up strategies are used when you can't grasp something or wish to check your understanding. All readers apply fix-up strategies at different points in their reading. They solve their problems by: • rereading • reading ahead to see if that will clear things up • reviewing and synthesizing previous ideas from the text and relating these chunks of concepts to the confusing ideas • replacing a word or words they don't know with one(s) that they know and think would make sense in this context; looking up a word in the dictionary • changing their ideas or visualization of the story to match new information. You may find that how you have visualized the story or what you thought about the text has changed and you need to make a self-correction, radically re-conceiving your ideas • asking someone for help ***Prompts*** Maybe I'd better... Something I could do is... Since I don't understand this word, a good strategy would be to... First I saw, but now I see... What I thought this was about no longer makes sense because... I need to revise my thinking by... Maybe I need to consider...

Source: Adapted from Wilhelm (2001).

do not always reveal their inner intentions, motives, or feelings. The sub-text strategy (see Theory into Practice 9.4) as described by Clyde (2003) provides students with the opportunity to "walk around inside a story—supplying characters' thoughts that are normally only implied by characters and their situations" (p. 150). This strategy allows students to make personal connections, relate to characters, and offer alternative perspectives based on their own experiences. Figure 9.3 provides an example of using the subtext strategy with *Stella, Queen of the Snow*. The subtext strategy is a natural extension of think alouds but directly focuses on the thoughts, feelings, and emotions of characters. Readers move beyond observation of a character to becoming the character, as

SUBTEXT STRATEGY: USING DRAMA, THINK ALOUDS, AND WRITING TO DISCOVER THE INNER WORLD OF A CHARACTER

Effective applications of the subtext strategy help students to understand characters in more depth and consider thoughts, feelings, and personalities beyond the surface level. Students can enter a character's mind and explore the character's perspective fully while making connections, inferences, and conclusions.

Before Reading:

1. Choose a reading selection that lends itself to exploring characters' thoughts, feelings, emotions, personalities, intentions, and motives. In order to teach the strategy to students, we suggest you find points in the text that best exemplify the use of the subtext strategy (the natural points in the text where characters' inner thoughts can be made explicit).

   Ask: How can I model sharing a character's inner thoughts and feelings? How will I differentiate between the character's dialogue and the hidden subtext?

2. Tell the students that today you will be modelling how to think aloud characters' thoughts to help them better understand the character and their perspective. Using a comic strip featuring speech and thought bubbles, demonstrate how subtext is often represented and how it is possible that what the character is thinking and saying are two different things. Explain that the illustrations often give clues about what the character is really thinking and feeling.

   Ask: What do the students already know or believe about this character or this character's experience? How will I activate this background knowledge? How will I help them to understand the character's perspective?

During Reading:

3. Think aloud (make the character's subtext visible) to demonstrate the subtext strategy. Ensure that you are modelling the character's in the head thinking. In some cases, especially as the students are working toward independence, you can stop and ask the students to share their in-the-head thinking (this can be done through drama, talk, or writing).

   Ask: How am I helping students to understand this character in a deeper way?

After Reading:

4. Ask students to recall instances where you stopped to use the strategy and vocalize subtext.

   Ask: What do students understand about the character's perspective, thoughts, attitudes, feelings, motives, intentions?

5. Provide opportunities for students to reread the story, using drama, think alouds, and writing as strategies to become the character and vocalize the subtext, recognizing that each student's vocalization will be affected by their thoughts, feelings, and experiences.

   Ask: Do students assume the role and perspective of a character? How can I help them to step outside their own world and experiences and into the story world and the experiences of the characters?

SUBTEXT STRATEGY: USING DRAMA, THINK ALOUDS, AND WRITING TO DISCOVER THE INNER WORLD OF A CHARACTER (continued)

6. Debrief the strategy and clues that can help to identify when they are using this strategy and why.

   Ask: Do students tap into all relevant resources and combine interpretations of illustrations, text, and experience to construct deeper understandings of text and of character?

Toward Independence:

7. Once students are accustomed to the subtext strategy, they will be ready to assume more independence and try it themselves.

   Ask: What are the indicators that demonstrate they are ready to try it on their own?

8. After the introduction and think aloud, students can be invited to read the remainder of the selection and share the voices in the characters' heads.

   Ask: Can students effectively apply the subtext strategy to make sense of the text, understand characters, and understand themselves?

Extending Reading: Supporting Independent Use of the Subtext Strategy

9. Once you have modelled the strategy, provided opportunities for guided practice, and noted that students are accustomed to the process, it is time to have them vocalize the subtext on their own. You can initiate this process by choosing a piece of literature with characters whose visible text differs from their in-the-head thinking or whose visible text does not clearly indicate how the character is really feeling.

   Ask: How might this character's visible text and words differ from their in-the-head thinking?

10. Prior to reading the story, do a picture walk using the illustrations to make predictions and get a sense of the character prior to reading. Remind students of the comic strip example that demonstrated speech and thought bubbles. Explain that while reading, you will be stopping and asking them to become that character and record their internal thoughts on a Post-it note.

    Ask: Are students becoming the character? Are they reacting in the role of the character?

Repeat Steps 5 and 6.

11. Once students have explored the character's inner thoughts and feelings, collate all the Post-it notes into a large group open-minded portrait that will support students as they explore the perspectives, thoughts, feelings, attitudes, and behaviour of the character. The last step might involve the students writing their own interpretation of the character's inner script from the beginning to the end of the book.

    Ask: Are students able to empathize with the character? Can they identify the character's thoughts, feelings, emotions, personalities, intentions, and motives?

Source: Adapted from Clyde (2003, p. 150-160).

FIGURE 9.3 Discovering Subtext with Stella

Sam had never seen snow.
This was his first snowstorm.

"Do snowmen eat *green* snowsuits?" asked Sam.
"No," said Stella. "They only eat pink ones."
"Are you sure?" asked Sam.
"Let's go skating on the pond," said Stella.

"Do snow angels fly?" asked Sam.
"Do snow angels sing?"
"Of course," said Stella. "Can't you hear them?"
"Yes!" whispered Sam.

Stella, Queen of the Snow by Marie-Louise Gay is an excellent book to use with the subtext strategy. Throughout the story, Stella and Sam engage in a question-and-answer dialogue about winter and snow. Sam's questions indicate his curiosity about the season but the pictures suggest that Sam might be feeling something a little beyond curiosity, perhaps apprehension and nervousness. Students can explore Sam's inner thoughts and dialogue and compare them to his visible dialogue, questions, behaviour, and body language. We have used Stella to demonstrate the process outlined in Theory into Practice 9.4.

Step 1: Select a text and mark think aloud spots.

Step 2: Do a picture walk and remind students of the comic strip example. The following might be used as an example for Stella.

Step 3: Model subtext think alouds and inner monologues.

Think alouds organized into a whole class open-mind portrait.

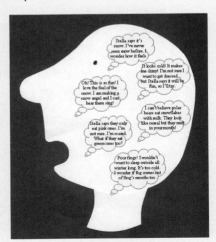

Sam's inner monologue from beginning to end.

Stella says when I look out the window I see snow. It looks cold. She says it's fun to play in, but I'm not sure. I have lots of questions. I wonder if she will be able to answer them all. I asked about a snowman. I'm a little nervous. She told me that they only eat pink snowsuits. I'm not sure I believe her. I mean, after all, how can a man made of snow really eat a snowsuit and what would it taste like anyway? I think of lots of other things that would taste better. We spent a lot of time outside in the snow today. I think I'm starting to feel a little better. I'm glad I made a snowman and listened for the frogs. What I liked most of all was making snow angels and listening to them sing. I think I'm going to like winter a lot!

they explore the personality, intentions, and motives of a character through drama, think alouds, and writing. This strategy enables students to make personal connections to text, further develop inferring skills, empathize with characters, and understand multiple perspectives.

> *If children are invited to examine the lives of others, trying them on for fit, looking around inside the story world, feeling the feelings of characters with life experiences different from their own, it's just possible that they might become kinder, more compassionate adults, able to empathize with and appreciate the perspectives of others whose lives at first glance seem incomprehensible. Imagine what a difference that could make.*
>
> (Clyde, 2003, p. 159)

EVALUATION AND ASSESSMENT OF READ ALOUDS AND THINK ALOUDS

Think alouds are one method that will help you to determine your students' strategy use and growth through conferencing, writing, and recording. As students show their in-the-head thinking, they are sharing strategies that they use and exploring the effectiveness of given strategies. They should also be encouraged to reflect on other strategies that might have been useful. As you assess student growth and awareness of reading strategies, use the prompts in Figure 6.3 and 9.2 to support your students as they think aloud.

STOP, THINK, AND WRITE

Choose a book that you have read recently.

literacy notebook 9.2

- Do you feel that the character's outward behaviour, actions, and personality are consistent with how they are feeling on the inside?

Select a passage that lends itself to exploring the character's innermost thoughts, feelings, emotions, personalities, intentions, and motives. Articulate what you feel the character might be thinking in their head.

- How does that differ from the character's outward dialogue or behaviour?

- How is your subtext influenced by your own thoughts, feelings, and experiences?

- How does this strategy help you to understand the character's perspective?

- How might this strategy help your students understand others' perspectives and explore attitudes and perspectives different than their own?

- How might this strategy be useful in social skills, moral development, empathy training, and character education?

Shared Reading

INTRODUCTION TO SHARED READING

Shared reading means exactly that: reading that is shared between an adult or an expert reader and a child or a developing reader. Shared reading experiences allow readers to integrate their story sense and extend their control over language (Wells, 1986). Researchers have learned a great deal by observing parents and children as they collaboratively negotiate text. We can all remember instances where we just couldn't help but join in on familiar rhymes or repetitive patterns as they were being read. *Alexander and the Terrible, Horrible, No Good, Very Bad Day* by Judith Viorst still engages adult readers in the chanting of the familiar phrase. The shared reading model was originally envisioned by Holdaway (1979). It builds on research that indicates that storybook reading is a critically important factor in young children's reading development (Wells, 1986). It extends the key features of reading aloud to a single child to small or large group contexts in ways that allow children to interact with both adults and texts in meaningful, authentic, and success-building ways.

Although often carried out with big books for emergent and early readers, shared reading is equally effective with transitional and self-extending readers as they are being introduced to new concepts and/or strategies. In addition to big books, teachers in the Junior grades may opt to use overheads, charts, or other technologies (for example, visual presentation systems) that allow the text to be enlarged so that all students can access it. shared reading often makes way for choral reading (described in Chapter 10) and readers' theatre.

Shared reading can take place with either a small group or the whole class. You will be able to work with students in fun and interactive ways, while modelling integrated use of the cueing systems and strategies applied to unfamiliar texts. In addition, shared reading provides opportunities for students to:

- activate prior knowledge, make predictions and connections, and set purposes prior to reading

- share a reading experience with the teacher (operating in the students' zone of proximal development)

- emulate the behaviour of real readers as they join in when comfortable and ready

- enrich concept and vocabulary development within the context of read alouds and shared reading

- engage in successful reading, which is possible when the text chosen is at an appropriate level and the reader has been provided with sufficient modelling, support, and scaffolding

- develop a sense of themselves as readers and the meta-cognitive strategies that will enable them to become lifelong readers

- have access to a body of known texts that they can use for independent reading

- have access to resources that can be used for writing and word study

- have the support and safety of a community of learners who share similar strategies and interests

- read and think about literature and extend these understandings through talk

- use prior knowledge to expand their knowledge and understanding through reading

ESSENTIAL ELEMENTS OF SHARED READING

Shared reading begins with a read aloud and extends into multiple readings, where you draw students' attention to key features of the text and alert them to tricky or unusual features that might interfere with independent reading. As a shared reading session unfolds, you will gradually release responsibility for reading to your students. At the beginning, your voice will be strong and clear, modelling and demonstrating the work of expert readers, with the ultimate goal being student independence. The essential elements of shared reading include:

1. Multiple readings (often referred to as repeated readings) of the text occurs over several days with increasing levels of discussion and engagement (for example, making connections, asking questions, drawing conclusions). The concept of multiple and repeated readings is particularly useful for students who require additional time and practice reading.

2. Each reading of the text serves a different purpose:
   - The first reading is often for enjoyment and the pleasure of being read to. During this reading, you will model reading and think aloud the strategies that students need to make sense of the text. You will guide students by pointing to each word as you read—this encourages students to attend to the print as the carrier of the story or text's message, and reinforces concepts about print.

- The second reading builds and extends comprehension, engaging students in active discussion of the meaning of the text and their personal connections.

- The third reading might focus attention on unusual text features or interesting language and vocabulary. During this reading, you will offer support to students as they apply reading strategies that enable them to access the text as independently as possible.

- The fourth reading might focus on word play and word solving with the increasingly familiar vocabulary from the story.

- Subsequent readings might involve students in exploring the effect of intonation, expression, volume, pitch, and speed on the reading of the story.

3. Students are encouraged to join in and chime in when they feel comfortable, thus apprenticing them into the reading community in a low-risk environment that fosters student success.

The primary goals of shared reading are to:

- build a positive reading community and to develop a low-risk environment where students are willing to take risks and "have a go"

- appreciate language and extend students' sense of text: story and content

- demonstrate thinking about reading strategies (for example, what makes sense, what sounds right, what looks right)

- develop and extend awareness of concepts about print, functions of print, language patterns, and basic text concepts (for example, title, author, characters)

- make the connection between oral language and print

- encourage fluency and expression

- identify words in a given text, both familiar and those figured out from context (this requires an already known reading vocabulary) (Taberski, 1998)

SELECTING TEXTS FOR SHARED READING

Books for shared reading in the primary grades should have:

- immediate interest for students

- strong storyline with accessible structure

- predictable language
- rhythm, rhyme, and repetition
- large, clear print
- one or two lines of print per page
- conventional placement of print
- complete sentence or idea per page
- strong, supportive illustrations
- appropriate vocabulary

With shared reading in the junior grades, the content of the text increases in complexity; many of the processes (before, during, after, and beyond) remain the same. Higher level shared reading uses an expanded repertoire of texts (for example, poetry, song lyrics, expository text) to model fluent oral reading and appropriate problem solving. Texts are generally not available in big book format, and will often be copied to charts, overheads, or other technologies that support the enlargement of text. In Theory into Practice 9.5, we outline the strategies addressed during shared reading as well as the teacher's and learner's role before, during, and after. Theory into Practice 9.6 presents a sample shared reading lesson. It is important to note that the planning process for shared reading in the early grades is the same as the planning process for shared reading in later grades.

EVALUATION AND ASSESSMENT IN SHARED READING

Shared reading enables you to observe students as they:

- develop sense of selves as readers
- gain awareness and use of symbols and conventions as they construct meaning from texts read or viewed
- interpret familiar letters and conventions
- make connections between background knowledge and new information
- recognize and use prediction strategies to develop meaning in text

Evaluation and assessment of students engaged in shared reading takes place as you conference with students (individually or in small groups), listen to them read a portion of the text, or listen to them retell the story. You can also evaluate students' awareness of sight words, letter-sound relationships, and sentence structure. When they make errors,

GETTING READY FOR SHARED READING

	Teacher's Role	Learner's Role	Strategies
Before Reading	• Choose an appropriate book, passage, or text with specific reading strategies/skills in mind. • Enlarge text for small group or whole class viewing. • Anticipate and plan areas where students can join in. • Introduce text and lead discussion/predictions based on the cover, title, and author. • Plan questions for the first reading.	• Engage in conversation about the story. • Raise questions. • Build expectations and make predictions.	• Connecting • Questioning • Predicting
During First Reading	• Read the entire book. • Read with expression, enthusiasm, and appropriate intonation and pacing.	• Notice illustrations, unusual features, and information in the text.	• Connecting • Comparing • Inferring • Predicting • Checking, confirming, and revising predictions
During Second, Third Reading	• Re-read the text and students join in reading. • Re-read the text and students participate in choral reading while focusing on specific strategy/skill, for example, punctuation and text features.	• Check predictions. • Talk about the story, making text-to-self, text-to-world, and text-to-text connections. • Revisit illustrations, punctuation, and special features of the text that enable students to read the text independently with fluency and expression.	• Connecting • Reading with fluency and expression
After Reading	• Add new words to the **word wall.** • Prepare **mini-books** of the story **(keep books)** so that students can re-read with partners.	• Sequence the events of the story. • Listen to a taped reading of the story and follow along in their individual book. • Respond in written, dramatic, or visual form.	• Connecting • Revising predictions • Retelling • Analyzing • Interpreting • Responding

A PLAN FOR JUNIOR LEVEL SHARED READING

Purpose:

The text provides students with the opportunity to apply and reinforce their knowledge of future tense, understanding of contractions, and the differences between genres of text (for example, narrative vs. poetry). The lesson encourages students to make personal connections to the text and understand how sometimes we all have a bad day. It also provides the opportunity for students to create their own "Today" poems and explore a variation of "I Can't" or free verse poetry.

Grade 6 Outcomes from Alberta Learning–English Language Arts:

General Outcome 2: Comprehend and respond personally and critically to oral, print, and other media texts

Use Strategies and Cues
* Use comprehension strategies: identify, and explain in own words, the relationship of the main ideas and supporting details

Respond to Texts
* Experience various texts: oral, print, and other media texts from a variety of cultural traditions and genres, such as autobiographies, travelogues, comics, short films, myths, legends, and dramatic performances
* Express ideas and develop understanding: engage in exploratory communication to share personal responses and develop own interpretations
* Construct meaning from texts: observe and discuss aspects of human nature revealed in oral, print, and other media texts, and relate them to those encountered in the community

Understand Forms, Elements, and Techniques
* Understand forms and genres: identify key characteristics of a variety of forms or genres of texts

Create Original Text
* Generate ideas: choose life themes from reading, listening, and viewing activities, and in own experiences and create oral, print, and other media texts

Text: "Today" in *Hey World, Here I Am!* by Jean Little

This poem recounts one of those days where nothing goes right. The author has trouble with peers, class contributions, volunteering, goal setting, achieving, and adjusting. She finally states that all that is needed is a rest.

Day 1:

Before Reading:
* Explain that today you will be working with a poem about a bad day.
* Read the title.
* Encourage students to make predictions about what they expect to hear in a poem about a bad day.
* Write predictions on a chart.

A PLAN FOR JUNIOR LEVEL SHARED READING (continued)

During Reading:
- Read the poem aloud.
- Ask students to check predictions on the chart.

After Reading:
- Review the predictions. Which were correct? Which were incorrect?
- Ask them to make connections between the poem and their own experiences. Which of these statements would apply to them? What might their bad day sound or look like?
- Word solving: Which words are new? Which words do they need to discuss and explore? Highlight these words and assign them to small groups of students to find the definitions.

Day 2:

Before Reading:
Ask students to present their research on words from Day 1. Discuss students' interpretations of the poem. What might have happened before the poet wrote this poem? What might have happened after the poem was written?

During Reading:
Read the poem aloud, asking students to record unfamiliar words on Post-it notes. Model the strategy of *reading on*, demonstrating that it is okay not to understand a word. Encourage students to join in the reading when comfortable.

Distribute copies of the poem and assign partners. Provide time for students to practise the poem aloud. Have them experiment with tone, voice, expression, and volume and how each of these can be used to evoke a range of emotions. Remind them that it is not always what they say, but how they say it that expresses meaning.

After Reading:
Ask for volunteers to share their interpretation of the poem.

Day 3:

Before Reading:
Ask students to recall the different interpretations of the poem from Day 2.
Tell them that today they will be writing their own version of "Today."

During Reading:
Read the poem together as a group once or twice, choosing one or two emotions explored yesterday (for example, frustrated, angry, nervous).

After Reading:
Ensure that each student has a copy of the poem.
Provide enough time to draft their own versions of "Today."

the students have opportunities to correct and apply **fix-up strategies** to their reading. You can use a variety of recording and assessment plans (for example, journals, anecdotal notes, checklists) for activities and strategies that were used by students. To inform your own practice, reflect on the effectiveness of your teaching approach and the text you chose by answering the following questions:

- What skills and strategies did the students learn and apply? What opportunities for additional practice do they need?

- How did the instructional strategies support student acquisition of selected skills and strategies?

- Was the text selection appropriate for the purpose of the lesson?

fix-up strategies
Alternate reading comprehension monitoring strategies to be used when the purpose for reading a particular text is not being met or when the text is not making sense to the reader.

Interactive Reading

We will not spend much time on interactive reading as it blends the best of Reading Aloud, shared reading, guided reading, and independent reading in ways that are responsive to students' strengths and needs and sets them up for success. interactive reading operates within a child's zone of proximal development. What students can accomplish with an adult or a more capable peer is significantly different from what they can do on their own. Anyone who has read with a child as they emerge into reading will recall pausing at words they know that the child can contribute or the child spontaneously chiming in on repetitive patterns. In this way, students build their sense of self as reader as they share the reading experience with a more capable reader.

In interactive reading, students contribute what they know to the reading process while parents, teachers, caregivers, or volunteers fill in any gaps. Interactive reading often occurs spontaneously during readers' workshop as students participate as members of the reading community. In formal classroom instruction, you will initiate interactive reading in the same way as in read alouds and shared reading. The goals, assessment, and instructional strategies from read alouds and shared reading can be extended to interactive reading as well; the major difference is that interactive reading is often informal and occurs at just the right time for student learning to be extended.

As readers gain increasing confidence (often as a result of multiple readings), increasing levels of responsibility are released to the reader

In interactive reading, children contribute what they know to the reading process while others such as parents, fill in the gaps.

and the reading is shared back and forth in a way that maintains the rhythm, fluency, and meaning of the text. Envision the students who are gaining confidence in their sense of self as reader; they have learned how texts work, they are beginning to internalize some of the structures and patterns of language, and they are willing to apply this awareness to an interactive reading event.

Texts that become interactive reading texts are often those that are particularly relevant or meaningful to students, or those that contain a repetitive pattern that supports students as they read independently. They are the ones that students want to read over and over, until it appears that they have memorized the text. This familiarity with text gives you a great opportunity to reinforce one-to-one word recognition, concepts about print, conventions, and expression. Students will have a great number of words that they recognize independently or sentences that they can recall from memory, but every once in a while they will encounter text that they are not sure of. This is when your role as a more capable reader is critical. You simply fill in the text, and keep on reading! Figure 9.4 contains Michelann's recollections of interactive reading with her children.

FIGURE 9.4 Interactive Reading Experiences

Kathy Stinson's books, *Big or Little* and *Red Is Best*, are ones that I remember reading with my own children, as they were experimenting with independence as both children and readers. I remember countless nights when my children chose these books, much to my dismay as they no longer held my interest. I remember inviting my parents to read interactively with my children, and I also remember my immense pride at hearing these little readers "do their stuff."

The power of interactive reading remains fresh in my mind, and the importance of books and stories in my children's literacy development was immense. Sitting in a big chair, side by side, the book in my children's grasp, we would read these books over and over, night after night. In *Big or Little*, the little boy explores all the things that he can do that remind him that sometimes he is big, and sometimes he is little. In *Red Is Best*, the little girl expresses her own thoughts about the colour red and attempts to convince her mother why red is best and why she should be able to wear red, even if it is not entirely appropriate for the season. Throughout the readings of both of these stories, as my children gained confidence, I would often fill in the trickier words or the ones that they could not figure out from the context or picture clues. The independence of the characters inspired my children to be independent as readers, and the images in both books were strong enough to support them as they had a go and tried out reading on their own. This was the primary goal of interactive reading with my children: I wanted them to focus on all the things that they could do as readers; I was aware of the need to celebrate their success and reward their approximations. This is what I share with parents who ask, "How do I read with my child? How do I support them as they read? How do I help them move beyond what appears to be memorization?"

Guided Reading

INTRODUCTION TO GUIDED READING

Guided reading is a small group approach to reading instruction based on the principles of reading recovery designed by Marie Clay (1993). Guided reading will enable you to support students as they develop the skills and strategies that will help them to become independent and flexible readers and writers. Guided reading provides opportunities for students to:

- enjoy reading and read for meaning, which is possible when the readers understand the story and are able to use problem-solving strategies successfully to meet challenges encountered in reading

- engage in successful reading, which is possible when the text chosen is at an appropriate level, and the reader has been provided with sufficient support and scaffolding

- use independently flexible problem-solving strategies in order to figure out words they don't know, deal with a tricky sentence structure, understand concepts they have not previously met in print, and negotiate meaning with text

- develop a sense of themselves as readers and the meta-cognitive strategies that will enable them to become lifelong readers

- work in a homogeneous group of learners who share similar reading levels and interests

- activate prior knowledge, make predictions and connections, and set purposes prior to reading

- read and think about literature, and extend these understandings through talk

- use prior knowledge to expand their knowledge and understanding as they read

Students are ready for guided reading when they can independently:

- demonstrate the basic concepts about print

- demonstrate an understanding and interest in story (for example, what's happening, what it's about)

- identify most words in a given text (This requires a bank of words—a reading vocabulary already known.)

- string words together orally with fluent language

If readers do not consistently demonstrate these behaviours, they are un-likely to experience success in guided reading and should instead continue to receive support through small group shared reading and interactive read-ing in addition to participating in whole class shared reading. And don't de-spair, even the best of teachers have introduced guided reading too early or have realized that the texts or strategies that they have selected for their stu-dents are too difficult or inappropriate. When this happens, cut your losses and accept the error. Tell the students that it is your mistake, finish the book as a read aloud, and try again tomorrow!

ESSENTIAL ELEMENTS OF GUIDED READING

In guided reading, the teacher works with a small group of students who require support with similar reading strategies.

In guided reading, you work with small groups of students often with similar reading levels, or students who require support with similar reading strategies, supporting them as they progress toward independence and increasingly challenging texts. Groupings for guided reading are flexi-ble and purposeful, and always keep the student at the centre of instruction. Students are grouped by similar strengths and needs, but they move among the groups flexibly, as they are ready. Because students are grouped by both reading level and strategy use, the stage is set for suc-cess and students are able to read independently with a minimum of support and frustration. Theory into Practice 9.7 details strategies, roles, and tasks that both teachers and students undertake before, during, and after guided reading. See Theory into Practice 9.8 for a sample junior guided reading lesson plan based on a biography of Terry Fox.

The purpose of guided reading is to enable children to use and develop strategies "on the run." They are enjoying the story because they can understand it; it is accessible to them through their own strategies sup-ported by the teacher's introduction. They focus primarily on con-structing meaning while using problem-solving strategies to figure out words they don't know, deal with tricky sentence structure, and under-stand concepts or ideas they have not previously met in print. The idea is for children to take on novel texts, read them at once with a mini-mum of support, and read many of them again and again for inde-pendence and fluency.

(Fountas & Pinnell, 1996, p. 2)

GETTING READY FOR GUIDED READING

	Teacher's Role	Learner's Role	Strategies
Before Reading	• Explain why the group has been called together. • Introduce the text, perhaps using a **picture walk** or **book walk**. • Scaffold tricky words or structures, leaving some reading work, questions, and challenges for the reader. • Activate readers' background knowledge and set purposes for reading. • Introduce and model a targeted strategy (for example, "I'm going to re-read that to make sure it makes sense").	• Engage in conversation about the story. • Raise questions. • Build expectations and make predictions. • Notice illustrations and/or information in the text.	• Connecting • Questioning • Predicting
During Reading	• Read 1 to 2. • Observe, listen, interact, confirm, or suggest strategies to assist with problem-solving. • Guide and support students as they independently apply strategies. • Prompt rather than tell. • Sampe teacher prompts include: "How are you going to figure that out?"; "What do you notice that will help you?"; "Look for a little word"; "What in the picture starts with the letter you see?"	• Independently read the whole text, or a unified part (softly or silently). • Use and practise targeted strategy. • Use the three main questions to self-correct: *Did that make sense?* *Did that sound right?* *Does that look right?* • Request help with problem-solving when needed.	• Reading with fluency and expression • Problem-solving • Monitoring comprehension • Self-monitoring • Applying fix-up strategies
After Reading	• Invite personal responses, encouraging reflective, inferential, and critical-level responses.	• Talk about the story, making text-to-self, text-to-world, and text-to-text connections.	• Checking, confirming, and revising predictions

GETTING READY FOR GUIDED READING (continued)

	Teacher's Role	Learner's Role	Strategies
After Reading	• Select one or two teaching points, focusing on strategies. • Engage children in word work and story extensions (drama, writing, art, more reading).	• Check predictions. • Revisit the text at points of problem-solving as guided by the teacher. • May re-read the story to a partner, or independently. • Sometimes engage in extension activities.	• Connecting • Analyzing • Interpreting • Responding

Source: Adapted from Fountas & Pinnell (1996), Taberski (2000).

A JUNIOR GUIDED READING LESSON PLAN

Text: *Terry Fox: A Story of Hope* **Author:** Maxine Trottier

Genre: Biography **Source:** Scholastic Canada

Lesson Objective/Reading Strategy:

Interpret information conveyed in illustrations, photographs, diagrams, graphs, maps, captions, letters, etc.

Time Frame:

This is the third lesson in a week-long plan for guided reading.

1. Instructional Expectations

Grade 4 Language curriculum expectations (the Manitoba Curriculum) addressed/modelled in this lesson are:

Comprehension Strategies
Confirm or reject inferences, predictions, or conclusions based on textual information; check and confirm understanding by rereading.

Textual Cues
Use textual cues such as headings and sub-headings, story elements, and key ideas in exposition to construct and confirm meaning.

Ask Questions
Ask general and specific questions on topics using predetermined categories.

Create and Follow a Plan
Select and use a plan for gathering information.

A JUNIOR GUIDED READING LESSON PLAN (continued)

Access Information
Use a variety of tools (including indexes, maps, atlases, charts, glossaries, typographical features, card or electronic catalogues, and dictionaries) to access information and ideas; use visual and auditory cues to identify important information.

2. Pre-Assessment
Learners:

- Reading level: early Grade 4 (instructional)
- On Day 1, this group of six learners read the text and were asked to extend what they know about character maps or biography maps as a note-taking strategy. On Day 2, they continued to read, taking notes as they read.
- This group requires guidance and support to explore fully the photographs, captions, and letters interspersed throughout the story in order to add detail to their biography maps (similar to character maps) and comment on his life based on the evidence in the story (they were not asked to survey the photos, letters, and articles yet).

Learning Environment:

- Seated at a round table, within sight of the Word Wall, beside the classroom library.
- Teacher is seated at the back, with a clear view of the entire class at their centres or work stations.
- The whole class is working on a famous Canadians theme and participating in the same literacy centres using text at their own reading level.

Resources:

- Seven copies of *Terry Fox: A Story of Hope*
- Partially complete biography maps for note taking
- Tracking/observation record (teacher)

3. Teaching Content and Strategies
Before Reading:
Introducing the Text
Ask: How will I activate students' prior knowledge? How will I prepare students for the lesson objective? How will I introduce the story?

Activating Prior Knowledge
Review what students already know about Terry Fox's life:
Ask: What do students remember about Terry Fox's life from their reading over the past couple of days?
Ask students to summarize, paraphrase, and discuss their biography webs.

Establishing New Learning
Ask: What is the targeted reading strategy or lesson objective? How will I introduce the strategy?

A JUNIOR GUIDED READING LESSON PLAN (continued)

How will I encourage students to practise the strategy prior to reading independently?

Ask questions

Ask: What questions do we still have or need more information to answer?

Have students develop questions they still have about Terry Fox's life (appearance, behaviour, family) and suggest that perhaps the answers to these questions can be found in the visual information on each page.

Access information

Ask: In our reading, there is often additional information that we set aside while we are reading the story. Where might we find this information? What more can we learn about Terry's life by consulting the photographs, letters, and captions on each page?

Think back to when you first read Terry Fox's story. On each page, there was other information that was not always referred to in the story. Where is that information?

Provide an example to illustrate how to access visual information

Ask: What visual information might students have ignored or set aside? Which pieces of evidence will require more support than others?

Let's take a look at some of the photographs on page 3 that have many people in them. How can we figure out which one was Terry? Teach students how to read photographs from left to right as well as clockwise.

Locate Information

Ask: Can students locate additional information independently?

Encourage students to further develop their biography webs by consulting the visual information on each page.

During Reading (Consolidation and Application):

Consolidation

Focus on students' application of strategies

Ask: Do students understand the text? Are they applying strategies appropriately?

Ask students to discuss strategies that they used while locating information and interpreting visual information and to evaluate their effectiveness.

Application

During: Each student reads the selection at an individual pace.

Teacher scaffolds word-solving and strategy use as required or requested.

After the silent reading, the story is discussed: personal responses (thoughts and feelings) are elicited. Which events or words prompted you to feel that way?

Ask: Was there a time when reading the story when you had to use visual information to determine information that was not written in the story?

Possible visual information questions: What do you think is more important in this story, the story or the surrounding visual information? What might have happened if the story was presented only with text? Only with photographs? Only through articles?

Theory Into Practice/9.8

A JUNIOR GUIDED READING LESSON PLAN (continued)

Beyond Reading:

Teachers provide opportunities for follow-up discussion and/or activities:
What activities will engage students in reflecting on the text? On their use of strategies?

a) Using their biography web as a foundation, write about Terry Fox's life.

b) Create a table of contents for *Terry Fox: A Story of Hope*, by labelling phases of his life.

c) Create a list of words that represent Terry Fox's life.

d) Track Terry Fox's life on a map as he travelled across Canada. Be sure to include dates.

e) Use Terry Fox's biography as a model for writing biographies. Encourage students to use visual evidence that is available, with captions where relevant that further explain the evidence.

Assessment

Teacher observes and records the strategies used, level of student engagement, rate of reading, and makes a Running Record of one or two students.

Source: Planning format adapted from Ontario Ministry of Education (2003); Nipissing University (2005).

The following are the essential elements of guided reading instruction (Fountas & Pinnell, 1996; Taberski, 2000).

1. The teacher works with small groups of learners (no more than four or five).

2. Students are grouped according to two criteria:

   • They are similar in their development of a reading process and are able to read at the same level; or

   • They are similar in their need for specific strategy instruction (for example, expository text structures, a genre lesson, a specific reading strategy lesson).

3. The teacher introduces the text and assists learners' reading in ways that help to develop independent reading strategies. The teacher supports and scaffolds but leaves the reading work for the learner.

4. Each learner reads the whole text on their own (all students whisper read simultaneously; this type of reading needs to be distinguished from choral reading and round robin style reading where each student takes a turn reading around the circle).

5. The goal is for learners to read independently and quietly.

6. The emphasis is on reading increasingly challenging books and on the independent application of strategies.

7. Learners are grouped and regrouped in a dynamic process based on ongoing monitoring, observation, and assessment.

SELECTING TEXTS FOR GUIDED READING

When selecting texts for guided reading, Taberski (2000) suggests the following criteria:

- It must be worth reading. It possesses the qualities of excellent children's literature: it has appeal, it is a good story, it uses vivid language, it is rich, it is true to life, not too moralistic, and has integrity.

- Everyone in the group can read it with the required rate of accuracy (between 90–95%).

- It supports your demonstration of the strategy you want your students to acquire.

EVALUATION AND ASSESSMENT IN GUIDED READING

You will know that you are using guided reading successfully when you see your students develop self-extending reading systems that allow them to become flexible and proficient problem solvers and readers. The level of student learning in guided reading is assessed through observation before, during, and after reading, and through formal running records. Theory into Practice 9.9 presents an overview of conducting, scoring, and interpreting running records. Assessment of guided reading provides significant information for subsequent planning and instruction; it concentrates mainly on the readers' acquisition and application of problem-solving using the four basic **cueing systems**. There are also the four basic prompting systems used to support students in their problem-solving as they read. For those of you who have not had experience conducting and scoring running records, e-Workshop, which is Ontario's Education Foundations program sponsored by TVOntario, offers an excellent training program and e-learning module at http://www.eworkshop.on.ca.

cueing systems The four systems (semantic, grapho-phonemic, syntactic, and pragmatic) that are part of every language and are used by teachers to support students' different methods of developing literacy.

Managing Guided Reading with Literacy Centres

Conducting guided reading sessions requires your full attention. It is, therefore, important for you to plan activities and learning experiences

THE ART OF RUNNING RECORDS

Running records are a systematic method of assessing a student's ability to read accurately for meaning developed by Marie Clay as part of *Reading Recovery*. When conducting running records, begin by introducing the text, scaffold where necessary, and listen while students read the text aloud. As each student reads, record the strategies that the student is using independently, the types of prompts used to support the reading, and the student's ability to make sense of an unfamiliar text. Many publishers sell running record kits and scoring sheets. You do not have to rely on published materials; any text can be used in a running record conference. Copy and enlarge a selection or create your own recording sheet in advance.

Types of Data Collected Through Running Records

- Instructional reading level
- Ability to read for meaning
- Integration of cueing and self-monitoring systems: meaning, structural, and visual cues
- Knowledge of print conventions

Administration Procedures

- Set the scene: explain the purpose of running records
- Introduce the book
- The running record
- Complete the comprehension section
- Score the reading record
- Analyze the student's reading behaviours and strategies

Follow-Up

- Plan your teaching (Identify what students need to learn next; determine the grouping method and instructional techniques that will be most effective
- Document change over time (Plot the assessment text level on the student book graph; place the running record in his or her literacy file)

Recording Conventions

Accurate reading is usually marked with a checkmark above the text contained within the story or text. We recommend leaving accurate reading alone as it is quite time-consuming and distracting to mark each word:

Auntie

Self-corrections are marked by writing the word the student reads above the word that is contained within the story or text. If they self-correct, a horizontal line is added and SC is recorded above the line:

Immediately after the error	Multiple attempts then self-correction	Error is corrected during a re-read
Aunt SC	All Aunt SC	Aunt SC R
Auntie	Auntie	Auntie

Theory Into Practice/9.9

THE ART OF RUNNING RECORDS (continued)

Problem Solving is marked by showing the strategies the student was using. When students stretch out or sound out words using individual letter sounds (decoding), it is coded using lower case letters with dashes in between, again recorded above the line as it is the student's response:

<u>st-e-p (child's response)</u>
stairs (text)

When students spell out words using letter names, it is coded using upper case letters with dashes in between, again recorded above the line, as it is the student's response:

<u>I-L-L (child's response)</u>
I'll (text)

Errors

Substitution is marked by writing the word the student reads above the word that is contained within the story or text:

<u>Aunt (child's response)</u>
Auntie (text)

Insertions are marked with editor's insertion marks, recording the word that was added above the insertion mark:

✓　　✓　　big　　✓
"What　　a　　^　　mess!"

Omissions are marked by drawing a line above the word that is contained within the text and then drawing a dash above that line to indicate that the word was missed:

–
Auntie

Repetition is marked by writing the letter R next to the word/phrase the student repeats. Note the differences in recording phrases that are repeated. The word/phrase is recorded as accurate reading:

✓ R

An **Appeal** is coded above the line, similar to a self-correction; the student's response is always coded above the line. It is simply recorded as "A." An appeal is usually turned back to the child, with the suggestion "Try it!" An incorrect response or no attempt after an appeal to "try it," and a reasonable wait time is followed by a "T" for Teacher Told. The "T" is recorded under the line to indicate that the student was told the text. It is the teacher's response:

<u>Church</u>　A　<u>R</u>　(child's response)
chair　–　T　(text or teacher)

A long wait can be coded by a line longer than that used for omissions.

Theory Into Practice/9.9

THE ART OF RUNNING RECORDS (continued)

Try That Agains are coded with TTA and are teacher prompted. It is assumed that something went wrong from the onset and if given another chance the student is likely to self-correct. A TTA is scored as one error unless additional
errors are made on the re-reread. TTAs are only used when the student's reading or your coding are so mixed up that it cannot be continued.

	"I found the steeple"	
Trial 1	"I'll fix your stairs	
‾	"I found the church."	
And	I'll fix your chairs.	TTA
Trial 2	"I'll fix your stairs."	100% accurate
	and "I'll fix your chairs."	

Recording TTAs can be tricky. It is often best to record the second reading on top of the first reading as you will often not have time to re-write the text. Alternatively, you could use a different coloured pen.

for the rest of the class that are meaningful and relevant. Literacy centres (or work stations) support the guided reading process and provide independent practice of literacy strategies previously taught. When rules, routines, and organization of literacy centres are well planned and consistent, student learning is facilitated and you are freed to work intensively with small groups of students. You must ensure that the quality of learning and instruction at literacy centres is equal to that which takes place with the teacher (Ford & Opitz, 2002). Prior to the implementation of literacy centres, consider the following four principles:

1. *Ensure that literacy centres provide practice for previously introduced strategies and content.*

   Students are far more likely to engage independently in Literacy Centre work if it provides the opportunity for independent practice of a previously introduced strategy or content area. You can introduce Literacy Centre activities in guided reading lessons, mini-lessons, and whole group instruction. Many teachers use a combination of permanent literacy centres and temporary literacy centres. Permanent centres are in place all year long. For example, computer centre, word-solving centre, poetry centre, read-the-room centre, and journaling centre are likely to be permanent centres in most primary classrooms; what might change is the theme or content of each centre. Temporary centres serve a specific purpose and are often dismantled once the task is complete, for example, following instructions to make a gingerbread house.

2. *Facilitate independent use of literacy centres through the use of task cards and a student designate.*

Many teachers ensure that all task cards follow a similar format and are at the instructional level of the majority of students. Task cards should include a list of materials as well as a set of procedures. For younger students, a pictorial list and set of procedures works well. Students who are taught how to use task cards through mini-lessons and shared reading are far less likely to require support at centres. We also find it particularly useful to designate one student who can interrupt you during guided reading sessions; all other students in the classroom ask questions of the designate, except under unusual or extenuating circumstances (for example, danger or blood!).

3. *Have a designated routine for transition time.*

Some teachers choose to have all students complete all activities by using a rotation system with a timer. Others allow groups of students to move freely from activity to activity until all activities are complete. Yet other teachers post a task board that requires students to verify the centres that have been assigned to their group for the day. Regardless of the system you choose to use, the key is to be consistent in the management of time and transitions and to ensure that your students are fully trained in the system that you have selected.

4. *Have a formal accountability structure in place.*

A learning centre approach fosters student independence and requires students to keep track of their activities, belongings, and learning. Options for tracking include task boards, individual student files for independent storage and retrieval of materials, learning logs, and tracking sheets. As with transitions and routines, the key is consistency. If students are aware of your expectations for accountability, they are far more likely to meet your criteria for success.

Theory into Practice 9.10 contains information for literacy centres. Note that this should be supplemented with visual information for earlier grades. (some centres adapted from Ford & Opitz, 2002).

PERMANENT LITERACY CENTRES, GRADE BY GRADE

Senior Kindergarten: Oral

Winter Play Dough
1. Roll the dough
2. Cut out your favourite shapes.
3. Tell a story using your shapes.

Grade 1/2: Listening Post/Centre

Can you hear what I hear?
1. As a group, listen to the story on tape and follow along.
2. As a group, listen to the story on tape and read along.
3. As a group, turn off the tape and read together.
4. Turn to a partner and read the story.
5. As a group, listen to the story on tape again.
6. Turn to a partner, and talk about your reading.
7. Be ready to share your story with the class.

Grade 3: Word Solving

Going on a Word Hunt
Materials: paper, pencils, markers, crayons
On your own, find three words in the classroom that:
1. Have more than six letters
2. End in 'ing' where the final letter was doubled before adding 'ing'
3. Mean the same as 'said'
4. Have the same sound pattern as 'make'
5. Are math, science, or technology words
6. Start with 'st'
7. Have the same spelling pattern as 'read'
8. Are contractions
9. Rhyme with 'bat'
With a partner, discuss the words you have found. Which ones are the same? Which ones are different? Write some silly sentences using as many words as possible from your word hunt.
On your own, choose one sentence, and draw a picture to go with it.

Grade 4: Readers' Theatre

To Read or Not to Read...Aloud!
Materials: readers' theatre scripts, props required to present script
1. Leader reads the story out loud.
2. Everyone reads the story together.
3. Partners read the story together.
4. Everyone is assigned a part.

5. Each person: practise your part on your own.
6. Everyone: practise your parts together.
7. Decide together whether you would like to make or use props and check with the teacher.
8. Sign up for a time, and present as a group to the class.

Grade 5: Procedural Writing

Reading How-do!
Materials: a selection of recipes, game directions, science investigation, art projects, paper, pencil
On your own
1. Read the recipes, game directions, activity instructions, and task cards provided at the centre.
2. What do you notice about the directions?
3. Choose an activity that you would like to teach to someone else.
4. Choose a format (e.g., recipe, game, directions).
5. Assume that the person you will be teaching has never done your activity before. Write out your directions step by step so that they can read your directions and do the activity independently.
6. With a partner, swap your instructions. Can your partner follow them easily? Are there any missing steps?
7. On your own, revise, edit, and write a polished copy.

Grade 6: Poetry Writing

Positively...Poetry: Read, Respond, and Write
Materials: a selection of literature, paper, pencils, "Fog"
1. As a group, or with a partner, choose one of the books at the reading centre.
2. Read it quietly.
3. Discuss how it made you feel, using emotion words from the word wall, and using the thesaurus at the centre.
4. As a group, make a list of these emotion words on the paper provided.
5. As a group, read the poem "Fog" by Carl Sandburg. This is a "free verse" poem.
6. With a partner or on your own, write a response to the story in the form of free verse poetry. Use your "response journal," and then edit and publish the poem.
7. On your own, choose a book and create a found poem using words from your story. Found poems are created by gathering words and phrases from other sources, such as stories, songs, and websites.

STOP, THINK, AND WRITE

Using the task cards provided as models, choose a grade level, curriculum expectations, a strategy focus, and develop a task card for a temporary or permanent literacy centre. Ensure that your task card contains a detailed list or pictorial representation of materials as well as a step-by-step description of the task.

Independent Reading

Independent reading builds on the knowledge, skills, and strategies introduced during modelled, shared, interactive, and guided reading. This is your students' opportunity to demonstrate independent engagement with text and strategies on a variety of levels; this is their opportunity to explore fully the four roles of the reader that you have been building through explicit instruction during read alouds, shared reading, and guided reading. When teachers plan for independent reading, they plan opportunities for students to engage in a combination of readers' workshop (independent response activities), literature circles, and literary conversatons.

Readers' Workshop

Readers' workshop creates a literary environment for students to read independently, explore texts, and discuss texts with peers. Students are provided with the time they need to engage fully and respond to text on a variety of levels (Atwell, 1989). During readers' workshop, students acquire and practise reading strategies to construct, extend, and revise meaning as they read a variety of texts for purposes that they choose and control. Literature circles, mini-lessons, grand conversations, journals, and conferences with you and other students enable readers to explore, construct, and revise their understandings, make inferences, and respond personally and critically to texts as they integrate reading and writing skills in meaningful ways.

In a readers' workshop, students have the freedom and the choice to select texts that they find personally relevant and meaningful. In order to run an effective readers' workshop, you will need to ensure that students have access to a range of texts in a variety of formats; you will also need to ensure that you have scheduled time for independent reading, discussion, reading work, journaling, response activities, literature circles, and grand conversations.

Readers' workshop offers the following benefits to students:

- Students select and read books at their instructional level; mini-lessons target strategy use and sense-making that students independently apply to texts of their choice.

- Independent and individualized selection of texts improves motivation by allowing students to select texts that suit their purpose, reflect their interests, and match their reading level.

- Menus of response allow students to reflect on reading, collaborate with peers, and select responses that suit the nature of the text and the reader.

- Response to texts in a variety of formats respects the individuality of each learner in terms of learning style and multiple intelligence.

- Some forms of response (i.e., literature circles, literary conversatons, and Individual Reading Conferences) support good talk about great literature.

- Responses provide a time for readers to reflect on reading and to collaborate with others in order to construct, extend, and revise meaning.

ESSENTIAL ELEMENTS OF READERS' WORKSHOPS

The essential elements of readers' workshops (Atwell, 1989) are:

1. *Literary Warm-Up (5 minutes)*
   Literary warm-ups can involve book talks generated by students and/or teachers. They might also contain highlights of previous workshops, quick presentations, or responses prepared by students that serve to motivate or interest other students.

2. *Mini-Lesson (5 – 10 minutes)*
   Mini-lessons are short, teacher-initiated, whole-group instructional sessions for constructing, extending, and revising meaning. Topics for mini-lessons are generally derived from the teacher's assessment and observation of what students need to know today to make them better readers tomorrow. Teachers select strategies that will prepare students to read unfamiliar texts successfully and independently or support them in their continued development as readers. Many mini-lessons are procedural in nature (responding to *how-to* issues), but flexibility is an important aspect as well. There are times when teachers conduct mini-lessons for small groups of learners. Topics for mini-lessons include:

   - components of readers' workshop and what readers need to be successful

- students' reading interests and how to select appropriate books
- rules for readers' workshop and management of time, space, and behaviour
- self-monitoring, self-assessment, and goal setting in reading
- reader response journals and different ways students may respond (see Theory into Practice 8.1 and 8.2)
- non-traditional response options that can be used to respond to text (for example, learning style, multiple intelligence, creative expression)
- story elements of setting, characterization, plot, theme, conflict, mood, and how students may explore them
- author's use of words, dialogue, imagery
- genre, author, theme studies
- introduce, model, or extend before-, during-, and after-reading strategies
- explore the causes of slow reading and instruct students in fix-up strategies that they can practise as they read
- demonstrate how to adjust reading rates according to reading purposes
- examine reading rates and appropriateness of each related to reading purpose
- include students in planning and implementing reading portfolios

3. *Self-Selected Reading and Response (remainder of the workshop)*
During self-selected reading (SSR), students may be involved in one or more activities. The choices depend on the needs of the students, goals established during mini-lessons, and the desire of the reader to re-spond in written, oral, or creative form to a text. Students complete most readings silently, but paired or group reading is a possibility. During this time students read, respond to reading, or update personal reading records. The teacher should communicate the importance of reading by setting an example: The teacher should spend part of each SSR time reading for pleasure or another purpose. During the rest of the period, teachers circulate, support, and conference with readers.

4. *Individual reading conferences should be held with each student as regularly as possible.*
The student and teacher listen to one another or they read, react, rein-force strategies, ask questions, and evaluate progress toward old goals and

set new ones. The teacher should establish rapport, share, listen, comment, encourage, and guide during these conferences. Conferences may include more formal assessments, such as informal reading inventories, running records, reader retellings, or think alouds.

ASSESSMENT IN READERS' WORKSHOP

Assessment within readers' workshop can take a variety of formal and informal shapes, but each should reflect the individual goals set by the learners and the teachers and curricular expectations. Through conferencing, observation, and response analysis, reader behaviours can be assessed. Teachers should look for student growth in both holistic behaviours such as reading fluency, self-monitoring, application of fix-up strategies, risk-taking, engagement of readers, recognition of good writing and what authors do, and more specific strategies such as making use of prior knowledge, predicting, critiquing, establishing criteria for selecting, and purposeful selection of books.

Since reader engagement is an essential characteristic of readers' workshop, part of the responsibility for assessment should be shared with the readers, especially as they evaluate their growth as readers and their progress toward goals. Teachers share the assessment process with students as they conference and examine reading responses. Additional forms of assessment include:

- goal setting through learning contracts (regular revisiting and reflection on progress)

- maintaining a list of *Books read* with initial reactions, jot notes, or comments

- maintaining a list of *Books I want to read* with comments

- workshop wheels of reading where students keep track of different genres or forms of literature they are reading (might simply be a frequency count or recording of title) to demonstrate willingness to take risks and try new forms

- mini-lesson products and reflections

- literacy works-in-process that includes projects completed before, during, and after reading (see Chapter 10, Extremely Engaging Projects)

- maintenance of reading portfolios: have students choose and polish their favourite response for their portfolio, with reflection and let parents and students make a list of observed growth indicators

- assess student preparedness, motivation, and commitment with periodic checks or student developed plans (Do they have a self-selected text, required journal entries, and up-to-date lists of *Books read* and *Books I want to read*?)

When you conference with students about reading, you should:

1. Listen to familiar reading first that they have selected, prompting appropriately and judiciously.

2. Talk about the story idea or topic; have a real conversation (try not to interrogate the reader). Think about whether your questioning style is *interview, comprehension check,* or *dialogue.* Teachers have a variety of questions at a variety of levels available for discussion (see Figure 9.5 for sentence starters designed to prompt higher-order thinking, consistent with **Bloom's taxonomy**).

Bloom's taxonomy (cognitive domain) A hierarchical classification of educational objectives, progressing from knowledge and memory to comprehension, application, analysis, synthesis, and evaluation. (Bloom et al., 1956)

3. In some cases, you will also use a reading conference to formally assess students using running records. When this happens, you should begin with a familiar text and then introduce a new text. The student then reads aloud as you listen, observe, and record, taking a running record with notes on "how it sounded." (See Theory into Practice 9.9, which details the art of taking and using running records for reading assessment and instruction.)

4. At the end of the conference, you should:
   - Give specific praise at the *cutting edge* of the reader's learning (for example a strategy tried for the first time, a noticeable improvement in fluency, a skill recently mastered).
   - Teach the *almost known* (choose one teaching point, based on an observation of the reader trying something, but not quite "getting it").
   - Assign further reading that is at the student's instructional level and is of interest to the reader (fiction or non-fiction). Try to make this a collaborative decision.

Literature Circles

One has only to look at the proliferation of adult book circles to appreciate the need to discuss what we read. When we, and the children, talk to others about our reading experiences, we can reveal our perceptions of the book, clarify concepts we found confusing, develop new perceptions based on those of our fellow readers, and take part in a shared, enjoyable experience that extends our personal and intellectual lives.

FIGURE 9.5 Conferencing à la Bloom (1956)

Knowledge	Comprehension	Analysis
• What is…? • How is…? • Which one…? • Where is…? • When did ____ happen? • Who was…? • When did…? • Do you recall…? • Who were the main…? • List three…	• How will you state or interpret in your own words…? • How would you rephrase the meaning…? • What facts or ideas show…? • What is the main idea of…? • Which statements support…? • Can you explain what is happening…? • Can you explain what is meant…? • What can you say about…? • Which is the best answer…?	• How would you use…? • What examples can you find to…? • How would you organize ____ to show…? • How would you apply what you learned to develop…? • What other way would you plan to…? • Can you make use of the facts to…? • What questions would you ask in an interview with…?
Application	**Synthesis**	**Evaluation**
• How is ____ related to…? • Why do you think…? • What is the theme… motive… assumption…? • What inference can you make? • How would you classify or categorize…? • What evidence can you find…? • What is the relationship between…? • What is the function of…?	• How would you improve…? • What would happen if…? • Can you propose an alternative…? • Can you invent…? • How could you change/ modify the plot (plan)…? • What way would you design…? • Suppose you could ____, what would you do…? • Can you predict the outcome if…? • Can you think of an original way for the…?	• Do you agree with the actions… • How would you prove/ disprove…? • Can you assess the value or importance of…? • Would it be better if…? Explain. • Why did the character(s) choose…? • How would you evaluate…? • What choice would you have made…? • How would you prioritize or justify…? • Why was it better that…? • How would you compare the ideas… people…?

Literature circles allow children to engage in this type of book talk. As they discuss aspects of their reading—their predictions, perceptions, and responses—they understand what they have read at a much deeper level, and can relate their reading to their personal lives and to the prior knowledge they already have.

(Booth, 1998, p. 52)

Literature circles fit into the balanced literacy program as an effective way for students to read self-chosen literature and talk about what they are learning about reading and writing. Literature circles are small discussion groups where students accept responsibility for book selection, independent reading, meaning-making, and group discussion of books. Literature circles are easily incorporated into a balanced and comprehensive language program and encourage students to make connections between their personal experience and ideas from books. In addition, literature circles provide opportunities for students to:

- read and think about literature, and extend these understandings through talk
- develop and share aesthetic responses to literature
- work together and learn effective co-operative and productive group skills (for example, listening skills)
- be accountable in the reading process
- support each other in the reading process
- participate fully in heterogeneous classrooms despite their learning style or reading level
- develop strategic approaches to comprehension
- develop their own questions to deepen understanding as opposed to relying on comprehension check questions, often designed by teachers
- develop meta-cognitive strategies that will enable them to become lifelong readers
- activate prior knowledge, make predictions, and set purposes prior to reading
- reread, remark, analyze, apply, evaluate, and synthesize what they have read
- use critical thinking skills as they apply to the reading process
- experience different cognitive approaches and multi-sensory approaches, and use **multiple intelligences** in the construction of meaning

multiple intelligences
Howard Gardner's (1987, 1999) psychological and educational theory asserting eight forms of knowing, learning, and performing: linguistic, logical-mathematical, musical, bodily-kinesthetic, spatial, interpersonal, intrapersonal, and naturalist.

In Theory into Practice 9.11, we have provided a summary of activities and roles that are occupied by the teacher and students before, during, and after literature circles are implemented in the classroom.

ESSENTIAL ELEMENTS OF LITERATURE CIRCLES

Daniels (2002, p. 18) identifies 11 essential elements of literature circles:

1. Students choose their own reading materials from a group that the teacher has previously selected (or students have suggested).

2. Small temporary groups are formed, based on book choice.

3. Groups read different books.

4. Groups meet on a regular schedule to discuss their reading (groups of five or six are best).

5. Students use written or drawn notes to guide both their reading and discussion.

6. Discussion topics come from the students.

7. Since the goal is to have open, natural conversations about books, personal connections, digressions, and open-ended questions are welcome.

8. The teacher serves as a facilitator, not a group member or instructor.

9. Evaluation is by teacher observation and student self-evaluation.

10. A spirit of playfulness and fun pervades the room.

11. When books are finished, readers share with their classmates, and then new groups form around new reading choices.

DAY-BY-DAY TRAINING USING SHORT STORIES, PICTURE BOOKS, POETRY, AND LITERATURE CIRCLES

Many teachers use role sheets to begin literature circles. Role sheets manage the transition from familiar, high teacher support, whole-class activities to more student controlled small group work. The role sheets bridge the gap between previous experience, knowledge, and the skills required to make literature circles work. They provide a structure or framework to temporarily guide the set-up of literature circles. Figure 9.6 contains a detailed description of individual roles that can be used in the preparation of role sheets. Role sheets are used only until students are

Theory Into Practice/9.11

GETTING READY FOR LITERATURE CIRCLES

	Teacher's Role	Learner's Role	Strategies
Before Reading	• Introduce books through a series of *book talks* where the title, author, and brief overview of the story are presented.	• Choose a book and form literature circles. • Set a schedule for reading and responding. • Make predictions about the book.	• Connecting • Questioning • Predicting
During Reading	**Practise:** • Provide opportunities for students to practise a variety of approaches and tasks in a non-threatening environment. • Monitor learning and intervene with mini-lessons or conferences when needed. **Explore:** • Teach a lesson on an element of story structure, author, genre, or reading strategy. • Encourage readers to go beyond simple retelling and apply higher-order thinking skills (for example, analyze, critique, compare, assess, evaluate).	**Practise:** • Read independently or with a partner. • Listen to a tape or a text reader if the book is too difficult. • Prepare for discussion by taking notes, recording favourite quotations and questions as they read (see individual roles). **Respond:** • Talk together about the book, beginning with questions such as "What did you think?" • Share reactions and ask questions to clarify and make connections. • Record in student reading logs or lists.	• Connecting • Comparing • Inferring • Predicting • Checking, confirming, and revising predictions
After Reading	**Debrief and Refine:** • Discuss effective procedures. • Provide ongoing training through mini-lessons, coaching, or modelling. • Focus on what went well to help children become independent thinkers who take ownership and pride in their learning.	**Apply:** • Meet to evaluate the Literature Circle, the book, and participation. • Have students share book and projects with class.	• Connecting • Revising predictions • Retelling • Analyzing • Interpreting • Responding • Discussing • Reacting

Source: Booth (1998); Daniels (2002).

FIGURE 9.6 Roles Fulfilled in Literature Circles

These six roles are considered to be appropriate for all students, regardless of whether they are reading narrative or content area texts. Teachers present these roles to students and often teach them individually through the use of role sheets (see Daniels, 2002 for examples or the many websites that have grade level role sheets and role sheets specifically designed for content or efferent reading).

Connector

Your job is to find connections between the book and you, and between the book and the wider world. This means connecting the reading to your own past experiences, to happenings at school or in the community, to stories in the news, to similar events at other times and places, to other people, or to problems that you are reminded of. You may also see connections between this book and other writings on the same topic or by the same author.

Connecting is what skilful readers most often do—connect what they read to their own lives, their feelings, their experiences, the day's headlines, other books, and authors.

Questioner/Question Asker

Your job is to write down a few questions that you have about this part of the book. What were you wondering about while you were reading? Did you have questions about what was happening? What a word meant? What a character did? What was going to happen next? Why the author used a certain style? Or what the whole thing meant? Try to notice what you are wondering while you read, and jot down some of those questions either along the way or after you're finished.

Questioners are always wondering and analyzing: Where is this text going? Why do these characters act as they do? How did the author evoke this feeling? Is this a plausible outcome? Sometimes questioners seek to clarify or understand; at other moments, they may challenge or critique.

Literacy Luminary/Passage Master/Passage Picker

Your job is to locate a few special sections or quotations in the text for your group to talk over. The idea is to help people go back to some especially interesting, powerful, funny, puzzling, or important sections of the reading and think about them more carefully. As you decide which passages or paragraphs are worth going back to, make a note why you picked each one. Then jot down some plans for how they should be shared. You can read passages aloud yourself, ask someone else to read them, or have others read them silently and then discuss.

Literary Luminary/Passage Masters return to memorable, special, important sections of the text, to savour, re-read, analyze, or share them aloud.

Illustrator/Artful Artist

Good readers make pictures in their minds as they read. This is a chance to share some of your own images and visions. Draw some kind of picture related to the reading you have just done. It can be a sketch, cartoon, diagram, flowchart, or stick-figure scene. You can draw a picture of something that happened in your book, or something that the reading reminded you of, or a picture that conveys any idea or feeling you got from the reading. Any kind of drawing or graphic is OK—you can even label things with words if that helps.

Illustrators remind us that skilful reading requires visualizing, and often invites a graphic, non-linguistic response to the text.

FIGURE 9.6 Roles Fulfilled in Literature Circles (continued)

Summarizer

Your job is to prepare a brief summary of the reading. The other members of your group will be counting on you to give a quick (one or two minute) statement that conveys the key points, main highlights, and essence of the reading assignment.

This is not a formal research report. The idea is to find some information or material that helps your group understand the book better. Investigate something that really interests you—something that struck you as puzzling or curious while you were reading.

Vocabulary Enricher/Word Wizard

The words a writer chooses are an important ingredient of the author's craft. Your job is to be on the lookout for a few words that have special meaning in today's reading selection. If you find words that are puzzling or unfamiliar, mark them while you are reading, and then later jot down their definition, either from a dictionary or some other source (for example a teacher, peer, or the Internet). You may also encounter words that stand out in the reading—words that are repeated a lot, used in an unusual way, or are key to the meaning of the text. Mark these special words with a Post-it note, and be ready to point them out to the group. When your circle meets, help members find and discuss the words that seem most important in this text.

Source: Daniels (2002).

familiar with how literature circles work and the roles that good readers fulfill. For further information on literature circles or prepared role sheets, consult *Voice and Choice* by Harvey Daniels (2002). He presents three different sets of role sheets: one primary set, one junior, and one for content materials. As you review the roles assumed by readers in literature circles, note that these roles are an extension of the roles of the reader that we introduced in Chapter 7.

DAY-BY-DAY TRAINING USING SHORT STORIES, NOVEL SETS, AND READER RESPONSE JOURNALS

This training can take up to two weeks. Reader response journals can be used with students who have previously written reader response journals or participated in literary conversatons, book clubs, cooperative learning, or collaborative learning. They add another level of student independence and provide students with increased flexibility as a reader and freedom to explore diverse roles simultaneously. They are also a natural extension of literature circles using role sheets and provide an alternative method of recording responses in preparation for literature circles.

Day 1	Days 2-5	Days 6-10
• Teachers explain how literature circles work and why they are important in the reading process. • Teachers provide live or videotaped demonstrations of literature circles. • Students read a good story and discuss it, using the role selected for the day. Students are then asked to complete the role sheet independently.	• Students learn one role per day using short stories, picture books, or poetry. • Groups of four students in the same role meet to discuss. • The whole class meets to debrief and clarify the day's target role.	• Students put the roles together while reading a short text. • Groups of four students in different roles meet to discuss; roles rotate daily. • The whole class meets daily to debrief and share. • Once students have mastered the first four roles, the second group should be introduced.
		Source: Daniels (2002).

Day 1	Day 2	Day 3	Day 4	Days 5, 6, 7 (meet every other day)
• Teachers explain how literature circles work and why they are important. • Teachers should provide live or videotaped demonstrations of literature circles. • Discuss reader response journals and model a reader response.	• Select book and form groups. • Groups make reading schedule. • Read the first chapter or about 25 pages. • Experiment with a variety of reader responses.	• Meet to discuss first reading. • Discuss and list key social skills. • Copy skills to journal.	• View classmates in video. • Revise social skills list. • Meet to discuss next reading or the second chapter.	• Conduct daily mini-lesson. • Groups read and discuss remainder of book, in thirds. • Conduct daily debriefing of management issues.
				Source: Daniels (2002).

Literary Conversations

Literary conversations are discussions held by the entire class. They are similar to literature circles because both are student directed; what makes them different from literature circles is their focus. literary conversatons are similar to instructional conversations in that they allow your students to explore literary understandings with indirect and informal support from you. Literary conversations may address one specific piece of literature, specific story elements, or particular themes or genres. When you use literary conversatons in the classroom, you allow for dialogue among students that is student directed; your students will have the opportunity to critique, debate, and extend each other's ideas. These conversations can be used to develop a reciprocal and recursive relationship between community building, talk, and understanding of literature. For example, the themes of literature discussed during literary conversatons are purposeful in that they facilitate literature knowledge and skills acquisition, while reinforcing the beliefs of community in the classroom.

Ideal literary conversatons have the following characteristics:

- All ideas are valued and everyone has a right to speak and be listened to.
- When an individual speaks, everyone else looks and listens attentively to the speaker
- Everyone is focused on the speaker and the idea being discussed.
- Speakers have the opportunity to discuss one idea in depth before moving on to the next.
- Speakers use evidence from the book to support their ideas and the points that they are making.
- Listeners ask questions that further their understanding of key concepts, themes, content, strategies, and genres.

EVALUATION AND ASSESSMENT OF LITERATURE CIRCLES AND LITERARY CONVERSATIONS

As you assess the effectiveness of literature circles and literary conversatons with your students, you should consider the following factors: level of discussion that occurs in literature circles and literary conversatons, your students' growth as readers and writers, how well your students follow the established rules, and participants' social behaviour. The best way to assess the quality of a discussion is to either sit in on the discussion or videotape/audiotape individual literature circles over the course of a book or literary conversatons with multiple texts. These tapes can then be used with groups to talk about the type of discussion, the overriding themes, the ability of the group to remain on task, the positive and negative elements of the discussion. Such tapes can also be used to help your students identify their own participation in and contributions to a literature circle or a literary conversation. Individual students and groups can self assess using checklists or rubrics you have designed or negotiated with students. Figure 9.7 contains a sample checklist for self and group assessment in literature circles and literary conversatons.

When assessing the effectiveness of literature circles and literary conversatons, look for a wide range of reader behaviour including understanding of literature, student interaction, critical thinking, and understanding literary content. Figure 9.8 contains a list of the types of questions you might ask yourself when assessing literature circles and literary conversatons as well as responses you might hear from your students.

FIGURE 9.7 Self and Group Assessment for Literature Circles and Literary Conversations

	Student:	Student:	Student:
Helped set the schedule.			
Completed reading on time. Fulfilled role responsibilities.			
Read thoughtfully.			
Brought the book to discussions.			
Participated in discussions.			
Made valuable contributions.			
Listened to other group members and commented positively.			
Helped share the book with the class.			
Other comments:			

Source: Tompkins (1999).

Reading from an Efferent Stance: Special Considerations

Efferent reading has real-world purposes such as reading the label on a bottle of poison to find the antidote. In efferent reading, attention is focused on information that is to be extracted or retained from the text

FIGURE 9.8 Teacher Assessment for Literature Circles and Literary Conversatons

What the teacher might look for or ask:	What the students might say:
Understanding of Literature Discussion: Do the students know what types of things to talk about? Is there trouble beginning a discussion or picking up a new topic?	What do we talk about?
Do the students articulate what confuses them?	I didn't understand why the character chose to return home.
Do the students theorize about confusing sections of the text?	I wonder if it means that she was sorry for what she had done.
Do the students give evidence from the text for their opinions and evaluations?	It says right here in the book that she was afraid.
What type of evidence do they give? Is it based on their own experiences or the text or something else?	I would never do that if it happened to me.
Can the students talk about who else might like the book?	My little sister would like this book better than I did.
Do the students try to understand the book from others' perspectives, such as the author or main character?	I think the author was making a point about how tough life was back then. I don't like that the main character joined a gang, but I guess he felt he had to.
Student Interaction: Do the students respond to each other's ideas? What are their responses like? Do they agree or disagree with each other's ideas?	I agree that she was selfish, but I think she had reasons for being a brat. It wasn't her fault.
Are the students willing to disagree? How do they go about disagreeing if they do?	I don't think that's right. I think she had a good reason for being mean to her little sister.
Are the students willing to share tentative ideas, things they haven't thought through completely?	I've been wondering if that wasn't because things were different then... well not different completely but... do you know what I mean?
Do the students ask questions of others? What types of questions do they ask?	Did you like the book, Ryan? What do you think the character should have done?
How does student participation change in different groups?	
Critical Thinking: Are the students willing to reconsider ideas in light of new evidence? What do students do when presented with conflicting evidence?	That's a good point... I forgot that she had made the promise to her friend.

FIGURE 9.8 Teacher Assessment for Literature Circles and Literary Conversations (continued)

What the teacher might look for or ask:	What the students might say:
Do the students actively theorize about the world or are they dependent on others to tell them the right answers?	Well, it might be that... as opposed to, I don't know. What do you think?
Are the students willing or hesitant to disagree with sources of authority?	I don't care if the book says... as opposed to, Well, the book says so... so it must be true.
Do the students see others as sources of expertise on which to draw?	Let's ask Drew. He knows a lot about baseball.
When the students give reasons for their opinions, are those reasons internal or are they external, depending on outside authorities, including their parents, peers, their friends, the book, or other adults?	Internal: That doesn't fit my experience... External: My teacher last year says it means this...
Do the students identify complexity in answers or do they just determine ideas as right or wrong?	I wonder if she was mean because of all the times people let her down, as opposed to, she was mean and that's all that matters.
Do the students look for multiple explanations or does one suffice?	He joined the army for excitement... or maybe he felt he had to join the army to help his sister... or maybe he wanted to get out of his terrible home situation.
Literary Content Knowledge: What content knowledge do students use? Do they use terms such as character, setting, tone, theme, foreshadowing? Do they talk about terms without having a name for them?	I really liked the way the author used those words to paint a picture in my mind of the sound. (onomatopoeia)
Do students notice the sound and feel of language? Do they attend to devices such as metaphor and simile and how they help them enjoy a book?	The comparison to...

Source: Excerpted and adapted from Day et al. (2002, pp. 166-168).

following the reading event. Any text can be read from either an efferent or an aesthetic stance that is a reflection of the reader's orientation, intention, or purpose for reading. We know that students who have previously and contextually developed frameworks, organizational structures, schemata, or awareness of expository structures (see Chapter 10) are more likely to learn and remember content quickly and to incorporate automatically new knowledge gained from print to construct and write new texts. Traditional and non-traditional methods (for example, drama, storytelling, poetry, visual arts, storybook writing, and games) can be used to support the acquisition, construction, and representation of content material and enhance student engagement, reduce the possibility of plagiarism, and strengthen the connection between what students know and what they need to learn. Just as students need to talk and collaboratively make sense of literature, so too do they need the same approach with content area reading.

> *We need to gather non-fiction materials that are discussable, that have some kind of narrative structure, some conflict or danger, some opposition of values, some kind of ethical or political dimension, some debate or dispute, some ideas that reasonable people can disagree about.*
> (Daniels, 2002, p. 201)

Essentially, if you want your students to talk, critique, discuss, write, and get excited about content, you must give them something to talk about and a reason for loving content! Reading in the content areas is most frequently linked to researching and writing, ultimately culminating in research projects. Research projects are effective ways of engaging students in reading and writing for real life purposes. While researching, your students are engaged in reading for very specific purposes (for example, gathering data), summarizing and recording information, sequencing and organizing ideas, and using language to inform and share a message with others.

When reading and writing in the content areas, you will follow many of the same procedures for reading before, during, and after as you do with aesthetic reading. The purpose of research and efferent reading is to increase students' ability to access information, ask questions, organize ideas, and share information with others. While we are not suggesting that every content area can be read the same way with the same strategies, what we do suggest is that the content areas share some general features and structures that can in turn be shared with students.

As you incorporate content texts into your reading program, you will make use of the continuum of support from modelled to independent

STOP, THINK, AND WRITE

Think back to your previous readings on oral discussion and good talk about great literature.

■ How will you fit literature circles and literary conversatons into your comprehensive literacy program?

■ What function will they serve?

■ What considerations will you keep in mind?

literacy notebook
9.4

reading that we have outlined in this chapter. Chapter 10 also provides additional information on explicit instruction, expository text structures, graphic organizers, and ways that language for learning can be incorporated across the curriculum. As you approach content area reading, you will have to give great consideration to the types of texts you select, the interests of your students, the context of the classroom, and the background experiences of your students. Theory into Practice 9.12 contains a detailed description of the teacher's and learners' role before, during, and after content area reading.

EVALUATION AND ASSESSMENT OF CONTENT AREA READING

Content area reading requires you to observe students' ability to:

• access and use a variety of reference materials for information

• gather and organize information

• paraphrase and summarize information in their own words

• use language to share ideas and convey messages to others

• organize main ideas and supporting details in a logical fashion

• choose an effective reporting format and project for sharing information in a variety of ways

Effective assessment in the content areas is linked to curriculum and teacher expectations. Both checklists and **rubrics** are useful in supporting student learning and helping students to make sense of the content areas. In Teacher Talk 9.1, Mike Parr talks about making the connection between content area reading and real life. Two examples of non-traditional projects and rubrics and checklists are provided with enough information to stimulate your thinking and get you started.

rubric A scale used to score performance according to a set of criteria or descriptors for each level of achievement (usually 3-4 levels) from least to most proficient.

Theory Into Practice/9.12

GETTING READY FOR CONTENT AREA READING

	Teacher's Role	Learner's Role	Strategies
Before Reading	• Introduce topics and content areas by activating prior knowledge and encouraging students to explore myths and misconceptions about given topics (for example, anticipation guides). • Consider individual students' needs and interests as topics and content areas are selected. • Brainstorm sources of information and data available in the school and community (for example, information books). • Select high-quality content area literature that students will enjoy and learn from.	• Choose appropriate reading and data gathering strategies for specific reading situations (see Efferent Reading in this chapter). • Establish a purpose for reading; select audience; and explore potential form of writing, reporting, and representing learning. • Form non-fiction literature circles (discovery circles) with four to six members on a given topic (if group work).	• Activating prior knowledge • Connecting • Predicting • Planning • Selecting appropriate literature • Questioning • Previewing • Scanning
During Reading	**Practise:** • Provide opportunities for students to practise a variety of approaches and tasks in a non-threatening environment. • Monitor learning and intervene in the form of mini-lessons or conferences when needed. **Explore:** • Teach a lesson to help students interpret information conveyed in tables of contents, indexes, glossaries, sidebars, and headings.	**Practise:** • Gather information using a variety of reference materials and sources. • Read independently or with a partner. • Use a listening centre or a text reader if the book is too difficult. • Take notes and record information and questions as they read. • Sources and page numbers should be noted by students to assist in the development of a bibliography at appropriate grade levels.	• Connecting • Comparing • Inferring • Predicting • Revising predictions • Visualizing • Scanning • Outlining • Note taking • Reading ahead • Sequencing • Determining main ideas • Locating specific facts and details • Paraphrasing

GETTING READY FOR CONTENT AREA READING (continued)

	Teacher's Role	Learner's Role	Strategies
During Reading	• Teach a lesson on a fiction reading strategy (expository text structures). • Teach a lesson to help students interpret information conveyed in illustrations, pictures, diagrams, graphs, and maps. • Encourage readers to go beyond simple retelling and quoting in order to apply higher-order thinking skills (for example, analyze, critique, compare, assess, evaluate); this will reduce the likelihood of plagiarism.	• Use expository text structures, graphic organizers, subheadings, initial questions, and frameworks to organize information (question and answer, KWL, problem and solution, cause and effect, sequence, and comparison). **Respond:** • Discuss the content area, beginning with questions such as "What did you think?" • Share reactions and ask questions to clarify and make connections.	• Rereading • Skimming • Summarizing • Interpreting information conveyed in visual representations • Detecting opinions and biases
After Reading	**Refine:** • Provide ongoing strategy instruction and modelling to improve content area reading through a range of teaching strategies and approaches (for example, mini-lessons, coaching). • Provide multiple opportunities for students to explore content area reading and writing that allow them to internalize content.	**Apply:** • Decide if reading goals have been achieved. • Check whether questions have been answered. • Evaluate own understanding. • Summarize major ideas in a KWL chart or graphic organizer. • Seek additional information from other sources. • Have students share projects with the class.	• Connecting • Revising predictions • Retelling • Analyzing • Interpreting • Responding • Organizing • Writing • Representing • Organizing • Writing • Representing • Retelling
Beyond Reading		**Plan:** • Students consider potential audiences and how they will share what has been learned. • Audiences may include other research groups, the class, or younger students. **Create a project:** • For example, ABC books.	

Teacher Talk/9.1

MIKE PARR TALKS ABOUT MAKING THE CONNECTION BETWEEN CONTENT AREA READING AND REAL LIFE

To fully engage students in learning, you need to provide your students with a purpose for completing the tasks associated with inquiry. Setting the stage for learning allows students to further refine their purpose and helps them to be self-directed, self-motivated problem solvers. In science, for example, setting the stage for high levels of engagement typically requires that you first draw on your students' previous knowledge and then present a series of facts or a body of knowledge, most appropriately accompanied by teacher/student generated questions for inquiry. Brainstorming, initial investigation, and exploration at this early stage can be provided through a variety of teacher directed activities (for example, direct teaching, videos, facts and figures, class discussions). These can be followed by group discussions that allow students to identify central issues and themes that relate to the curriculum, but just as importantly, to draw clear links to the meaning and relevance of their own lives as well.

Identifying several central issues worthy of further exploration and investigation without rigidly defining how to achieve the objectives of the unit gives students a sense of ownership over the direction their learning will take. Once the expectation for what is to be explored and learned is set, appropriate tasks or samples of types of appropriate learning activities should be explored. The teacher's role is to ensure that all students come to see that they have an active part in determining exactly what their learning activities, and their role in constructing these activities, will be.

In further defining purpose, it is important for most students to see that the extension of their own learning goes beyond themselves and has wider benefit and application. Without such a purpose and application, students who have acquired knowledge and developed skill often resent demonstrating this awareness for the sake of assessment (simply handing a project in for marking and then throwing it away).

Linking students' work to the community (school and beyond) adds to the development of purpose. If there is opportunity for application outside of assessment, students see that they are not just learning for themselves but that their learning and efforts can be of benefit to others as well. The book and ecology game assignments below serve a purpose to the wider community; both are designed to share a message with others. All students have something to teach others; we have to tap into this potential and capitalize on each student's natural desire to share something good about themselves. This sharing goes beyond merely presenting knowledge gained to classmates at the end of a unit through a series of class presentations.

Teachers should challenge students to be creative, collectively where needed, and to demonstrate that they are able to produce a product that is worthwhile and has purpose. Sharing activities and products that reflect student learning can be done in the class, with other classes throughout the school, in other classes throughout the board, and even in the wider community. When students share their work and see the learning and excitement that their work can generate, they see purpose! Such opportunities allow even reluctant learners to stand back and reflect with

Teacher Talk/9.1

MIKE PARR TALKS ABOUT MAKING THE CONNECTION BETWEEN CONTENT AREA READING AND REAL LIFE (continued)

pride on the fact that they have shared something of themselves that is good and benefits others. It's difficult to find greater purpose than that. Added to this is the fact that all this learning and sharing also leads into and facilitates your summative assessment.

Example: Book

Students write and publish a book that will deliver an environmental message. It will involve the identification of an ecological issue such as global warming, pollution, or species extinction. This is a very student-directed project and accordingly the topics are endless. The objective is for students to take whatever ecological issue interests them, write a description of the problem, and deliver their message in a way that will educate and interest readers. Ideally, the book will motivate readers to want to learn more and become involved in finding solutions to the issue.

Points to consider:

- Students may work alone or with a partner; select a topic and do a story map.
- Books must have a cover, illustrations, an About the Author page, and a list of resources where the reader may find more information.
- The audience may be primary, junior, or intermediate students or even adult readers.
- If the book is of high quality and the student would like to donate it to the school library, it will be catalogued and shelved in the right section for use by other students. (This is a great way for the student to earn bonus marks!)

Example: Ecology Game

Students construct a game board that teaches about ecological or environmental issues. The game board could be similar to other games such as Monopoly, or Trivial Pursuit. At each turn, players have question or issue cards that test their knowledge. Points are won or lost on chance cards that describe things we do that are good or bad for the environment. Students will be required to research issues and solutions to problems using the class textbook and outside resources.

Points to consider:

- Students may work alone or with a partner.
- Points are awarded for neatness and construction of the game board and cards.
- Complete and detailed instructions on how to play the game must be included.
- The game should teach its players about ecology as they play.
- The game should keep players interested and motivated to want to learn more about ecology and not just accumulate more chips, money, or points.
- The more informed the students become on ecology, the better your game challenges will be!

Mike Parr is an assistant professor in the Faculty of Education at Nipissing University.

literacy
notebook
9.5

STOP, THINK, AND WRITE

Discuss your preferences for content area reading and writing.

- What are your dominant reading strategies?
- What are your favourite reporting strategies?
- What else might you add to our list of projects?

Moving On

Throughout this chapter we have encouraged you to see meaningful and interdependent links between literacy assessment and instruction, where one informs the other. In order to teach the students in your class to read, you will need to use a range of grouping strategies including individual, partners, small group, and large group activities, multiple levels of support, and a variety of organizational strategies (for example, readers' workshop, guided reading). The following list represents our 10 favourite strategies for linking reading instruction and assessment in authentic and meaningful ways.

1. Running records
2. Readers' theatre, choral reading
3. Cloze passages (see Chapter 10)
4. Retell, relate, reflect
5. Literature circles, literary conversatons, instructional conversations
6. Reading conferences
7. Checklists, inventories, and assessments for students and parents
8. Reader response journals
9. Guided comprehension activities
10. Student portfolios or lit-folios

In Chapter 10, we present more specific literacy strategies that are useful throughout the six strands of language and with any grade level. We include a comprehensive plan for strategy instruction with ideas for adaptations for the diversity of learners.

Reading instruction...
More than a list of activities or description of strategies,
It's about how all the parts of our teaching can work together.
It's about helping children see connections and make new ones.
—Sharon Taberski

LIT-FOLIO UPDATE

At this point in your reading, your lit-folio should contain evidence of your developing awareness of the continuum of instruction as well as specific strategies that support learners in their acquisition of literacy. We suggest setting aside a summary page for modelled, shared, guided, and independent reading where you record your understanding, your questions, and your practical application of these approaches throughout your practicum experiences.

LIT-FOLIO TIP:

Our students pass on this bit of advice:
Make sure to gather artifacts for each reading strategy as you are introduced to them in class or as you apply them on practicum. Having a variety of artifacts or pieces of evidence will provide you with the opportunity to select the very best pieces. Each component of your lit-folio should have a healthy blend of theory, practice, and tips that you want to remember in the future (for example, management or assessment tips).

Resources to Support Your Learning

Professional Resources

Atwell, N. (1987). *In the middle: Writing, reading, and learning with adolescents.* Portsmouth, NH: Boynton/Cook.

Booth, D. (1998). *Guiding the reading process: Techniques and strategies for successful instruction in K-8 classrooms.* Markham, ON: Pembroke Publishers.

Booth, D. (2001). *Reading and writing in the middle years.* Markham, ON: Pembroke Publishers.

Calkins, L.M. (2001). *The art of teaching reading.* New York: Longman (Addison-Wesley).

Clay, M. (2000). *Running records for classroom teachers.* Portsmouth: Heinemann.

Daniels, H. (2002). *Literature circles: Voice and choice in book clubs and reading groups.* Portland, ME: Stenhouse Publishers.

Fountas, I.C., & Pinnell, G.S. (1996). *Guided reading: Good first teaching for all children.* Portsmouth, NH: Heinemann.

Fountas, I.C., & Pinnell, G.S. (2001). *Guiding readers and writer: Grades 3-6.* Portsmouth, NH: Heinemann.

Ontario Early Reading Strategy. (2003). *A guide to effective instruction in reading, Kindergarten to Grade Three.* Toronto, ON: Queen's Printer for Ontario.

Taberski, S. (2000). *On solid ground: Strategies for teaching reading K-3.* Portsmouth, NH: Heinemann.

Toronto District School Board. (2000). *Teaching children to read and write: A literacy guide.*

Websites

Ontario's Education Foundations program sponsored by TVOntario: http://www.eworkshop.on.ca. This website includes literacy training modules for guided reading, independent reading, running records, and shared reading.

Multimedia Connections

Fountas, I.C., & Pinnell, G.S. (2001). *Classroom management: Managing the day; Planning for effective teaching*, NH: Heinemann.

Fountas, I.C., & Pinnell, G.S. (2001). *Guided reading: Essential elements; The skillful teacher.* Porstmouth, NH: Heinemann.

❧ Metropolitan Toronto School Board.(1997). *Guided reading: Key features (Grades 6-8).* North York, ON.

Children's Literature: Our Favourites

Picture Books for Reading Aloud

Jolly Pocket Postman, Janet Ahlberg
The Canadian children's treasury, Key Porter Books

Novels for Reading Aloud

Charlie and the chocolate factory, Roald Dahl
Sarah plain and tall, Patricia MacLachlan
❧ *Jacob Two-Two meets the hooded fang*, Mordecai Richler

Abel's island, William Steig
Charlotte's web, E.B. White

Shared Reading

Bringing the rain to Kapiti Plain, Verna Aardema
Goodnight moon, Margaret Wise Brown
❧ *Something from nothing*, Phoebe Gilman
The wheels on the bus, adapted by Maryann Kovalski
❧ *Alligator pie*, Dennis Lee
❧ *The ice cream store*, Dennis Lee
❧ *Hey World, here I am!* Jean Little

Interactive Reading

You read to me: I'll read to you, Mary Ann Hoberman
❧ *Big or little*, Kathy Stinson
❧ *Red is best*, Kathy Stinson

Independent Reading and Literature Circles (Junior Level)

❧ *Naomi's road*, Joy Kogawa
❧ *Lesia's dream*, Laura Langston
❧ *Hana's suitcase*, Karen Levine
❧ *Ticket to Curlew*, Celia Barker Lottridge
❧ *Shadow in Hawthorn Bay*, Janet Lunn
❧ *Owls in the family*, Farley Mowat
❧ *Underground to Canada*, Barbara Smucker

10

L is for Literacy

Strategies and Techniques
from A to Z

> There is not a single method or single combination of methods that can successfully teach all children to read. Therefore teachers must have a strong knowledge of multiple methods for children in their care so they can create the appropriate balance of methods needed for the children they teach.
> —*International Reading Association*

key term

strategy instruction

questions to guide your learning

By the end of this chapter, you should understand the key terms and be able to answer the following questions

- How do I select strategies appropriate for my students' needs and the context of my classroom? How do I teach effective strategy use by applying the continuum of support?

- How do I gradually release responsibility for strategy use to my students?

- What are some effective strategies that support students as they make real-world connections between reading and writing?

- How do I manage the quantity of information and the number of literacy strategies?

Looking Back, Looking Ahead

In Chapter 9, we discussed the continuum of support and the reading approaches that should be used to organize instruction in a comprehensive literacy program. We suggested a seamless integration of the six language arts in order to support students as they make the transition into literacy.

In this chapter, we present a variety of literacy strategies that are equally applicable in listening, speaking, reading, writing, viewing, and representing. We have placed this chapter strategically between the chapters on reading and writing as we feel that its many strategies should be the central focus of a comprehensive literacy program. It is critical that you view the relationship between reading and writing as reciprocal and transactional, mediated by the connections you make, the types of real-world connections you encourage your students to make, and the types of strategies you select for your classrooms.

This chapter is not intended to be read from start to finish. Rather, it should be browsed, skimmed, and mentally catalogued. It will be an invaluable resource as you engage in long-term program planning, midrange unit planning, and daily lesson planning regardless of grade level. You will note that we have not indicated which strategies should be used as aesthetic experiences and which should be used for efferent purposes. This reflects our conviction that strategy use permeates the boundaries of curriculum and that one of the best ways to plan for effective and comprehensive literacy instruction is to look for opportunities to teach language and literacy across the curriculum.

Teaching for Effective Strategy Use

Strategy instruction involves explicit instruction and teaching in strategy choice, use, and reflection (Wilhelm, 2001). It is most effective when it is taught in a structured environment; the goal of explicit strategy instruction is student independence. In explicit strategy instruction, the strategies are explained, demonstrated, and practised within a structured supportive environment. It proceeds along the continuum of support from modelled to independent strategy use (see Figure 10.1), beginning with a high level of teacher support and gradually releasing responsibility to the students as they gain independence.

Teachers select strategies for instruction based on their observations of learners in addition to curriculum demands. When teachers are demonstrating strategy choice, use, and reflection, they think aloud their thoughts and strategies. Explicit strategy instruction begins with establishing a purpose for learning and activating the prior knowledge of the students. This is followed by a clear introduction of the strategy and an explanation of what to do. Teachers then model the process and provide multiple opportunities for guided and independent practice.

BEFORE STRATEGY INSTRUCTION

- Introduce your chosen strategy within the context of your lesson, theme, or content area.
  Ask: What strategy do I want the students to use? Why did I select this strategy?

FIGURE 10.1 Applying the Continuum of Support to Strategy Use

from	Level of Support	Reading Practices
teacher	**Modelled**	• Teachers model, demonstrate, and think aloud to demonstrate sense-making and strategy use until the students are ready to share the application of strategies.
support	**Shared**	• Teachers and students apply the strategy together; the teacher models and demonstrates while students apply the same strategy (see Theory into Practice 9.4).
to	**Interactive**	• Teachers share the application of strategies with learners, interacting in a way that permits learners to contribute what they know and can do independently, while the teacher fills in the missing steps. • Teachers model and demonstrate the strategy while students observe and call out instructions. • Teachers provide a balance of examples and non-examples to prompt student awareness of effective strategy use.
student	**Guided**	• Teachers scaffold to bridge the gap, activate prior knowledge, and prepare students to apply the strategy independently. • Task cards with step-by-step instructions support independent application of strategies. Learning experiences and opportunities are designed to guide and facilitate student practice.
independence	**Independent**	• Students effectively and appropriately choose from a variety of strategies that allow them to make sense of a variety of texts for a variety of purposes.

- Explain the purpose of the strategy.
  Ask: Why are we using this strategy?

- Explain the steps of using the strategy and provide examples of when the strategy would be useful.
  Ask: How and when should we use the strategy?

DURING STRATEGY INSTRUCTION

- Demonstrate the strategy by modelling the graphic organizer or the strategy itself. Combine demonstrating and modelling with a think aloud making sure to explicitly state how the strategy can be applied in reading or writing contexts.
  Ask: How can we model effective use of the strategy?

- Review the steps while using the strategy with the students and ensure consolidation of learning.
  Ask: Do the students understand the purposes of the strategy and how and when to use it?

- Provide students with many opportunities for guided practice as they gain independence. Intervene and support when necessary.
  Ask: What types of opportunities for guided and independent practice can I provide for students? How are students gaining independence in their use of the strategy?

AFTER STRATEGY INSTRUCTION

- Encourage students to reflect on information gathered through the use of the strategy and the process they followed. How did the strategy help them to understand the text as well as themselves as readers and writers? Assess students in their mastery of the strategy and re-teach through mini-lessons as required.

  Ask: What information did the students acquire? How effectively did they follow the process? What do I need to revisit and re-teach?

  Note: For students who require additional practice with individual strategies, consider whether the strategy can be broken down into smaller, more manageable chunks with multiple opportunities for success.

References: Tierney & Readence (2005); Wilhelm (2001)

literacy
notebook
10.1

STOP, THINK, AND WRITE

Your challenge in this chapter is to observe, try, and reflect on as many strategies as possible. At this point, you will likely be engaged in practicum placements that require you to apply theory to practice. Select a range of strategies that are responsive to the needs of the students you are teaching. Try the strategies and reflect on what you notice about student engagement in literacy, student strategy use, and your own personal effectiveness.

- Which levels of support are you most comfortable with?

- Which do you need to work on?

- Which strategies do you find particularly useful?

- Which have you tried, changed, or adapted for a given group of students?

- Which strategies have you observed in classrooms that are not listed in this chapter?

Consider adding these strategies to your personal repertoire.

- What evidence can you provide to demonstrate your learning with regard to strategy instruction (lesson plans, journal entries, learning logs, class notes, and student work samples)?

ABC Bookmaking

Making books using the alphabet as an organizer or framework can build content area vocabulary as well as improve motivation and engagement. Students use what they know about the alphabet and how alphabet books work to organize a content area or unit of study in a fun and interesting way. As they explore each letter of the alphabet and each word they have selected, they will need to discover meanings and create appropriate contexts for each word, using words, definitions, and pictures.

BEFORE WRITING

- Provide alphabet books that represent a range of reading levels (for example, *M is for Maple: A Canadian alphabet*, Mike Ulmer, *ABC of Canada*, Kim Bellefontaine and Per-Henrik Gürth).

- Read and review an alphabet book with the group. Brainstorm essential characteristics and qualities of good alphabet books. Have students identify the differences between alphabet books written for younger audiences and older audiences. For example, ABC books for younger readers are often designed to help them learn the alphabet, whereas ABC books for older readers often use the alphabet as a way to present new information.

- Students work in small groups to evaluate an alphabet book, using the criteria brainstormed.

- Students establish purpose and audience for their ABC book: Are they writing for younger students, same age students, parents, etc.?

- Students decide what style of writing to use: Should they write in paragraph or poetry style? Should they include a range of visual representations such as graphs, lists, and charts, or should they simply use pictures?

- Students choose the format of their book: Do they want a computer generated book or do they want a book that is done by hand?

- Students use an alphabet planning sheet or a storyboard to brainstorm, select, and organize information in preparation for writing. They should record the words they are going to use as well as resources that will be useful. Students may also include sources for illustrations or preliminary drawings for their alphabet books.

DURING WRITING

- Once students finish planning, they should begin writing their definitions for each word, reviewing the alphabet books on display to explore how other authors write and organize definitions.

- Teachers select small groups of students for mini-lessons including note taking while reading, finding resources, paraphrasing, definition writing, revision, and editing.

- Students then write their alphabet books, including charts, lists, and illustrations where appropriate. They will follow the writing process (outlined in Chapter 12) from start to finish.

AFTER WRITING

- Students share their books with their designated audience or peers, in either small groups or with the whole class.

- Books could be put on display in the library or at a book fair for parents.

For further information, see: the ReadWriteThink website (http://www.readwritethink.org) and the International Reading Association website (http://www.reading.org/resources/tools/lessons), both of which provide lesson plans.

Anticipation Guides

Anticipation guides help students to explore what they already know and understand about given concepts. They are particularly effective in content area reading and help students to build a framework for new learning and connect new knowledge to existing knowledge. The teacher's role is to engage students in active and critical thought before, during, and after reading.

BEFORE READING

- Identify major concepts or topics.
  Ask: What information do I want my students to focus on?

- Consider the previous knowledge and experiences of your students.
  Ask: What do the students already know or believe about this concept that might influence how they will read the selection?

- Depending on the age level, create 5 to 10 statements that will require students to challenge or modify what they already know or understand about the concept.
  Ask : Did I create statements that require investigation and discussion?

- The anticipation guide can use a true/false, before/after, agree/disagree, or open-ended response format. It can be distributed to students individually, posted on an overhead, as part of a computer presentation, or written on chart paper. Once each student has had the opportunity to reflect on the statements, engage the group in discussion, statement by statement. As each statement is read, they must justify their thoughts, opinions, and responses, drawing on previous knowledge and experience.
  Ask: Did I select a format that will facilitate investigation and discussion with my group of learners?

DURING READING

- Engage students in reading. As they read, they should be focused on collecting new information that either supports or refutes the statements introduced.
  Ask: How will they collect and record new information?

AFTER READING

- Return to the original anticipation guide and read it through statement by statement, engaging students in discussion. If they have changed their mind, they must provide new information from the text that justifies their new thoughts, opinions, and responses. Encourage students to compare their initial responses to the intended meaning of the author.
  Ask: Can students locate text selections that support their decisions?

For further information, see: Vacca, R.T., Vacca, J.L., & Begoray, D.L. (2005). *Content area reading: Literacy and learning across the curriculum.* Toronto, ON: Pearson Education.

Example: Anticipation Guide for Chapter 3

Beliefs and Assumptions about Literacy

Directions:

1. Before reading the chapter, read each statement and mark "A" for agree or "D" for disagree.

2. As you read, write down page numbers or references that either support or refute your initial response.

3. After reading and discussion, re-read each statement and mark an "A" for agree or "D" for disagree. Is there a difference between your initial thoughts and your responses after reading and discussion?

Author's Chair

Author's chair is often used in conjunction with the writing process. It usually occurs at the culmination of the writing process and is associated with the polishing, publishing, and sharing stages. Teachers often allocate a special time and place in writers' workshop when writers read their writing to their peers. Peers, at this point, have the opportunity to respond and provide positive feedback. The primary purposes are to extend students' sense of self as writers and to emphasize that students' ideas and experiences are worthy of sharing with others.

Authors face the class and read their writing aloud, showing any illustrations or graphics. Peers give positive comments about favourite events, characters, or interesting and impressive uses of language. If students are reading a draft, peers provide feedback regarding the clarity and effectiveness of the writing, language structures, and use of vocabulary, with suggestions for improvement.

Sample Questions:	Before	During (Reference)	After
Literacy is a technological skill related to print; it is a generalizable ability that involves the interrelated skills of reading and writing print.	____	_____	____
Literacy represents the same one thing for everyone; it is a single concept or skill.	____	_____	____

Author's chair can be used for written work across the curriculum, with a variety of forms and genres of writing shared. Particularly useful is a "math author's chair" that allows students time to share their thinking, problem solving, and reasoning. Teachers can also choose an "author of the week" and display individual writer's work.

For further information, see: Saskatoon Public Schools (http://olc.spsd.sk.ca/DE/PD/instr/strats/author/).

Book Talks

Book talks are intended to entice students to read books recommended by teachers, parents, librarians, and peers. They can be teacher developed or student generated. Book talks are like quick advertisements or brief commercials for a book (Fountas & Pinnell, 2001). Tell why you chose it and what you liked about it. Make sure you provide just enough information to hook your audience, but not enough to give the story away. Book talks should take only one to two minutes. Good book talks involve:

- talking about the title and the author of the book
- showing the cover and some of the illustrations or reading an exciting or interesting passage (if it is a longer text)
- talking about the book or briefly summarizing it without giving away the ending
- providing insight into the plot or a character in the book
- dressing, talking, and/or acting like one of the characters
- connecting the book to the students' lives, other texts, authors, or issues in the world
- posing and answering questions about the theme, or characters
- sharing your personal response, reaction, or connection to a text

BEFORE A BOOK TALK

- Read the book and prepare the book talk.
- Write down pages and references that are relevant to your book talk.
- Practise the book talk and any selected passages (if you intend to read one).

DURING A BOOK TALK

- Look at your audience.
- Speak so that everyone can hear.
- Avoid "reading" your book talk.

AFTER A BOOK TALK

- Answer questions without giving too much away.
- Make the book available for others to read.
- Discuss the book with others once it has been read.

For examples of book talks, visit: Nancy Keane's Book Talks—Quick and Simple (http://nancykeane.com/booktalks/).

Choral Reading

Choral reading allows readers to collaboratively participate in an interpretive reading of text, often poetry or songs. Students may read individual lines or stanzas alone, in pairs, or in unison. The focus is on how the text is read in addition to what is being read. Choral reading, sometimes called "unison reading," provides opportunities for repeated oral readings of texts from a variety of perspectives, using tone, volume, movement, and gesture. It is well suited to rhymes, poetry, and song lyrics. As a culminating activity, the texts can be 'performed' for others' enjoyment. Learning comes from the process of figuring out how to read the text rather than the performance itself. Choral reading is a fun way to practise reading and reduces the risk that is often associated with reading aloud by providing a supportive network of students and repeated practice.

BEFORE CHORAL READING

- Teachers select texts that are relatively short and simple, within the students' instructional level.

- Texts with catchy titles, exciting rhythms, or silly content will often engage students in imaginative and creative work. Poems by Shel Silverstein, Dennis Lee, and David Booth are fun and work well for choral reading

- Texts selected should come alive when read aloud—teachers should look for texts that have words with interesting sounds (onomatopoeia), contrast or content that bears interpretation, moods that can be altered depending on tone, volume, speed, etc., or dialogue that can be interpreted and personalized.

- Teachers ensure that there is a copy of the text for each student or that the text is large enough for all students to read in unison.

DURING CHORAL READING

- Each reader has the opportunity to read through the selection. Teachers might choose to do this through a shared reading approach. Readers can buddy up and practise the text in a variety of ways: echo read, read every second line, or one could read while the other follows along. This is the opportunity for repeated readings in order to build confidence and ensure successful reading.

- Once students can read the text independently, they can play with how to say it, and find ways to read the text that will reinforce the meaning that they have constructed. Exploring interpretation using choral reading can involve the following voice and communication elements:

  - Alternate slow/fast, loud/soft, low/high, happy/sad lines, calm/angry stanzas, or slow/fast paragraphs.

  - Change your body language: shake hands, show no interest in the conversation, stare at each reader, make no eye contact, sit back to back, or read as though talking on a telephone.

  - Find a rhythm that works and sing or rap the lines. Shout the lines across the room.

  - Echo your partner's lines.

  - Emphasize key words and phrases by reading them in a louder or softer voice.

  - Pause for a specified number of silent "beats" before you join in and continue reading.

  - Clap or make a certain sound at the end of certain lines, stanzas, or paragraphs.

AFTER CHORAL READING

- Small groups of readers can be encouraged to share their interpretation of a particular passage.

- Point out that how things are read reflects our interpretation of a text and shapes how our audience will interpret the text.

Cloze Procedure

A cloze procedure is a technique in which words are deleted from a passage and students are required to insert the missing words as they read in order to complete and construct meaning from the text. Cloze passages can be used to assess students' vocabulary, knowledge, and comprehension of literary, content, or theme related information. The cloze procedure allows students to predict words that make sense, therefore demonstrating their understanding of the three main cueing systems.

To prepare cloze passages, follow these steps:

1. Select or write a self-contained text at the students' instructional level. Do not alter the first and last sentences and leave all punctuation intact.

2. Carefully select the words for deletion. To assess students' knowledge of the topic or their abilities to use semantic cues, delete content words that carry meaning, such as nouns, main verbs, adjectives and adverbs. To assess students' use of syntactic cues, delete some conjunctions, prepositions and auxiliary words.

3. When preparing the final draft of the passage, ensure that all blanks are of equal length to avoid including visual clues about the length of omitted words. Tell students to read the entire passage before they begin to fill in the blanks. Encourage the students to fill in all blanks if possible.

4. Although there should be no time limit for this exercise, record the time the students spend on the task.

5. Tell students to reread the passage once they have filled in the blanks.

Variations:

• Provide the first letter of each missing word.

• Provide students with choices for each blank (for example, choose A or B).

• Provide a bank of words students can use to make sense of the text.

Directed Reading-Thinking Activity

A directed reading-thinking activity enables students to learn how to set purposes for reading, and read attentively, actively, and critically. It is effective in both narrative and content areas. It helps students to engage thinking abilities, activate prior knowledge, and become aware of comprehension strategies. These might include predicting, evaluating, confirming, clarifying, and revising. The teacher's role is to engage students in critical thought before, during, and after reading, and to encourage creative, divergent thinking, the use of logic, and heightened curiosity and interest in the text.

BEFORE READING

• Encourage students to skim the text and make predictions based on the title, subheadings, organization, illustrations/pictures, captions, sidebars. Encourage them to make wonder statements.

• Ask students to explain how they reached these conclusions.
Ask: What information did they make use of?

• Explain to students that they will be reading the text independently but will be stopping periodically to discuss their predictions and wonder statements, summarize the content, and make new predictions and wonder statements.

DURING READING

• Stop. Elicit a summary of what has happened so far or what they have learned. Have students revisit their predictions and wonder statements. Ask them to read between and beyond the lines and make further predictions or wonder statements about what might happen next. Avoid terms such as "right" or "wrong"; use terms such as "possible" or "likely" instead. Ask students to provide evidence from the text to support their predictions, wonder statements, and summaries.
Ask: Can students provide supportive evidence from the text to revise or confirm predictions and wonder statements? Can they effectively summarize the events of the story or the content?

• Continue reading, stopping periodically, until students have finished reading the text.

AFTER READING

* Review the predictions, wonder statements, and revisions, focusing on the statements and the inferential reasoning processes involved, not who made which predictions, or which were "true" or the "best." Invite feedback from the learners on how this exercise focused their reading: "Did you read in a different way because of your predictions and wonder statements?"

For further information, see Temple, C. & Gillet, J. (1996). *Language and literacy: A lively approach*. New York: HarperCollins.

Elkonin Boxes

Elkonin Boxes are an effective word-solving strategy for emergent to early writers (K–2). Initially, the focus is on *hearing and recording sounds*. "Sound boxes" are used to record sounds using this sequence:

1. Make a few picture cards for simple words with just two or three sounds, such as cat, dog, and jump. Under the picture, draw boxes with a square for each sound, and have some counters ready, one for each sound (not for each letter):

c–a–t

2. Say the word "cat" slowly, and have the child say it slowly.

3. Model how to slowly push the counter into the box as the sound is pronounced.

4. Have the child move the counters as you say the word. Change roles until the child is able to both say the word and move the counters with each sound.

5. Teach the child how to record the sounds in the boxes, using prompts such as, "What do you hear at the beginning?" "What sound is next?" Have the child record the corresponding letters and record the unknown ones for them.

Examples:

The goal is to show the child how to write "cat" by saying "c-a-t" slowly, and hearing and recording each sound in each box.

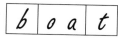

The word "boat" is written with the single sound "oa" in one box.

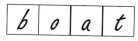

6. Once the child has mastered hearing and recording sounds and spelling patterns are being taught, individual letters can be recorded in the boxes.

Expository Text Strategies

Content area reading often requires a special way of looking at, previewing, and reading text. Strategies used for content area reading depend on the reader's purpose as well as the complexity of the material. Ensure that a wide variety of content area texts are available (videos, newspapers, magazines, encyclopedias, CDs, websites, etc.). Note that the process used to apply expository text strategies can also be applied to graphic organizers.

BEFORE READING EXPOSITORY TEXT

- Select a text that matches students' reading level and suits their purpose. Apply strategies for book selection: Is the text at their instructional level? Does it provide enough information? Preview the table of contexts, glossary, and index to ensure that the information they are seeking is in the text.

- Preview the material, paying particular attention to headings, graphics, pictures, and charts.

- Choose an appropriate method to read the text, depending on students' purpose. If they are looking for information, they should skim and scan. If they are learning information, they should read more in depth and study the material.

DURING READING EXPOSITORY TEXT

- Read the material, highlighting, annotating, and taking notes when necessary (using Post-it notes).

- Determine the expository text structure used by the author and take notes using the selected structure as a framework. Expository text structures help students to understand the layout of the text as well as the way that information is communicated by authors. The dominant expository text structures are comparison, cause and effect, problem and solution, sequence, and description. Give students graphic organizers or concept webs to support their note taking as they read and to enable them to extract information in a meaningful and useful way. This often reduces the likelihood of direct copying and subsequent plagiarism, especially if the intent of information gathering is to produce a report or presentation.

EXPOSITORY TEXT STRUCTURES:

Comparison Using Venn Diagrams

The author explains how two or more things are alike and/or how they are different.

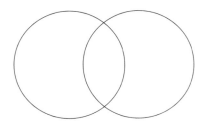

Signal words: different, in contrast, alike, same as, on the other hand

Problem and Solution

The author states a problem and lists one or more solutions. A variation of this pattern is the question and answer format: author poses a question and then answers it.
Signal words: dilemma is, puzzle is, solved, question… answer

Sequence

The author lists items or events in numerical or chronological order.
Signal words: first, second, third, next, then, finally, after

Cause and Effect

The author lists one or more causes and the resulting effect or effects.

	Effect 1:
Cause:	Effect 2:
	Effect 3:

Signal words: if… then, as a result, therefore, because

Description

The author describes a topic by listing characteristics, features, and examples.

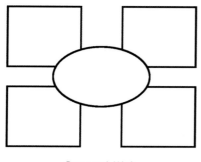

Concept Web

Signal words: for example, characteristics are

AFTER READING EXPOSITORY TEXT

- Students should identify a purpose for writing and a target audience.

- Use the information gathered to create a report using a selected expository text structure.

- Encourage students to explore a full range of reporting strategies including computer presentations (for example, PowerPoint), writing stories with messages, representing learning through ABC books, poems, songs, drama, news reports, and interviews.

Five-Finger Book Test

This is a quick strategy that helps students decide if the book is too hard, too easy, or just right. As students read, they place a finger on each puzzle word they encounter on a page. Five fingers down means the book is too hard. No fingers down means the book is too easy. More than five fingers per page means that the processing of words is likely to interfere with the comprehension of text. (See the five-finger test on the following page.)

For further information on the five-finger test, see: The Kentucky Virtual Library (http://www.kyvl.org/html/kids/p4_use/FiveFingerTest.html)

Goldilocks Strategy

Do you remember the fairy tale *Goldilocks and the Three Bears* and Goldilocks' search for the porridge, chair, and bed that were "just right"? Selecting a book that is not too hard nor too easy can sometimes feel the same way for your students, especially when they do not have a strategy. When your students are reading a book, suggest that they ask themselves the following questions to help them find books that are just right.

Too Easy Books

As the students read, they should ask themselves the questions below and if they answer "yes" to most of them, then the book is probably too easy. Tell the students that they can still have fun reading the book, but suggest that next time they choose one that is a little more challenging.

1. Have I read this book many times before?

2. Do I understand the story well without much effort?

3. Do I know and understand almost every word?

4. Can I read it smoothly and fluently without much practise or effort?

Too Hard Books

As the students read, they should ask themselves the questions below and if they answer "yes" to most of them, then the book is probably too hard. Tell them not to forget about the book, but to try it again later and that as they gain experience in choosing "just right" books, they may find that when they pick up the book again it is "just right."

1. Are there more than a few words on a page that I don't recognize or know what they mean? (Remind them about the five-finger book test.)

IS THE INFORMATION RIGHT FOR YOU?

The five-finger test will show you whether a book is a good one for your project.

Choose a book or a webpage that you would like to read. Begin to read. It is best to read aloud or whisper read so that you can hear the places where you have trouble. If you find a word you don't recognize, hold up a thumb.

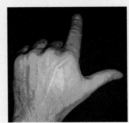

Thumbs Up!

If you still have only one thumb raised at the end of the page, this book will probably be easy for you to understand and easy for you to read.

Keep reading. If you find a second word that you don't understand, hold up your thumb and first finger.

Two fingers make an "L" to signify learning. You might have to stretch your mind a bit, but the book is probably a good resource. It will help you to grow as a reader.

If you find a third word you don't understand, hold up the next finger, too.

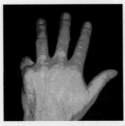

This book might be hard to read, or you'll have to ask for help. You might want to find a reading partner or see if you can find the book on tape or CD so that you can read and listen at the same time.

If you find a fourth word, hold up the next finger in line, as shown.

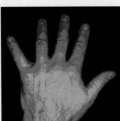

Warning! This book will probably be too much of a struggle to help you in your current project.

If there's a fifth word, open your hand fully. This is a warning for you to stop for now. It is probably too difficult to read independently right now.

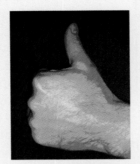

You can always read the book later after you've learned a little more about your subject or later in the year when you have learned other reading strategies. If you need help finding an appropriate book, ask your teacher or a librarian.

2. Am I confused about what is happening in most of the book?

3. When I read, am I struggling and does it sound choppy?

4. Is everyone busy and unable to help me if I hit a tough spot?

Just Right Books

As the students read, they should ask themselves the questions below and if they answer "yes" to most of them, then the book is probably "just right." Tell them that these are the books that will help them make the most progress in their reading and that they should read, enjoy, and learn from the experience!

1. Is this book new to me?

2. Do I understand most of the book?

3. Are there a few words per page that I don't recognize or know the meaning of instantly? (Remind them about the five-finger book test.)

4. When I read, are some places smooth and some places choppy?

5. Can someone help me with the book if I hit a tricky spot?

For further information, see: Ohlhausen, M.M. & Jepsen, M. (1992). Lessons from Goldilocks: "Somebody's been choosing my books but I can make my own choices now!" *New Advocate*, 5, 31-46.

Tompkins, G.E. (2004). *50 literacy strategies*, 2nd ed. New York: Merrill Prentice-Hall.

Graphic Organizers

Graphic organizers are visual tools that allow students to represent information and help them to create pictures, patterns, and relationships. They help students to organize, sort, classify, and represent information in a variety of ways. They are often referred to as "maps" as they en-

Examples

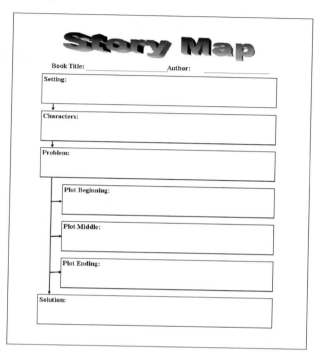

Story Map

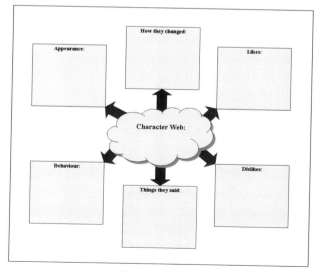

Character Web

USES OF GRAPHIC ORGANIZERS			
	Before	**During**	**After**
Reading	• Make predictions. • Make connections. • Activate prior knowledge. • Structure presentation of new content.	• Gather, record, and organize key information. • Check predictions.	• Analyze text features, characters, and story elements. • Summarize, represent, and elaborate on information. • Identify relationships between prior knowledge and new content.
Writing	• Rehearse and plan. • Organize ideas for writing.	• Gather and record information in a way that reduces direct copying.	• Support text with a visual representation

Source: McTighe (1992).

able teachers and students to 'map out' their ideas and establish relationships in a visual manner. Some are used as advance organizers, whereas others are used to organize or represent learning (for example, concept maps and webs). Story maps, character webs, and concept of definition webs (McLaughlin & Allen, 2002) are but a few of the graphic organizers we can use each day before, during, and after reading and writing. For further information on implementing graphic organizers, see Expository Text Strategies.

For further information, see: McTighe, J. (1992) Graphic organizers: Collaborative links to better thinking. In N. Davidson & T. Worsham (eds.), *Enhancing thinking through cooperative learning.* (pp. 182-197) New York: Teachers College Press.

Home-School Connections

Teachers recognize that parents want to support their children's literacy development, but sometimes need guidance and support to do so. Many schools start off the year with a Meet the Parent or Curriculum Night when teachers introduce their program, get to know the parents, and outline expectations for the year. We recommend sending home a literacy newsletter that highlights the curriculum expectations for each term and specific suggestions for parents. In addition to the term newsletter, many teachers find it useful to send home a weekly or bi-weekly newsletter telling parents what the theme of the week is, the poems or texts the students will be studying, special activities, and perhaps spelling words. A sample literacy newsletter is provided on the following page.

Integrated Units

Planning integrated or interdisciplinary units requires that you look at curricular expectations and connect them in meaningful, authentic, and efficient ways. Planning integrated units allows you to make links between subjects and to dissolve the boundaries that often exist between areas of study. Look for the logical and natural areas of integration and develop units accordingly. With integrated units, students are encouraged to think critically and transfer knowledge between the school and the community as well as between the literacy

HOW CAN I SUPPORT MY CHILD'S LITERACY DEVELOPMENT?

As a parent, there are many meaningful, positive, and authentic experiences that you can provide for your child that will support their reading development. We have highlighted those that we feel are most important to your child's development this year.

Read to and with your child every day

We recommend that you choose a consistent time and space, therefore creating what we call literacy traditions and rituals that will be memorable in your child's life. As you read to your child, you should recognize the importance of your modelling and demonstration. Read with enthusiasm and excitement, sharing the pleasure and joy of reading with your child. As your child emerges into reading, let him/her do some of the work, interacting and filling in gaps when necessary. This will set your child up for success and build a sense of self as reader. Take the time to read a variety of texts to and with your child (newspaper, books, poems, or websites) and talk to your child about the importance and purpose of literacy in your life and theirs. Make sure your child sees you reading at different times and for a variety of purposes. Talk to your child about what you are reading and how you are making sense of the text. Share your love of reading and nurture that same love in your child.

Create a language-rich environment

Your home environment should be language-rich. For younger children, you might have poems or rhymes posted to help them make the connection between oral language and spoken language. Provide access to a variety of print and books by joining the public library, participating in a book-sharing program, or borrowing books from the school library. Encourage your child to see the print in their environment (stop signs, labels on food, etc.) and help to make sense of all this print. Teach your child how to read it and what it means.

Talk to your child

Talk to your child about what is happening at school, with friends, in books, and in TV programs. Engage your child in language play before, during, and after reading. Play language games (for example, Simon Says) and sing songs that support oral language development (for example, "Old MacDonald," "Down by the Bay"). As your child develops oral language, provide names for items and engage your child in meaningful and authentic conversations. Help your child to recount experiences and describe ideas and events that are important to him/her. Engage your child in talk about books: have your child predict and talk about these predictions; have your child connect his/her experiences to the experiences of characters in books.

Encourage your child's literacy development

Provide many opportunities for your child to read, write, draw, and paint with a variety of materials (for example, markers, chalk, paint, pencil). Accept their early attempts at writing (drawing, scribbling, letter-like symbols) and encourage your child to share his/her stories with you. Encourage your child to participate in activities that involve reading and writing (for example, making grocery lists or following a recipe).

These are but a few of the supports that you can provide your child as he/she grows into literacy. Throughout the year, we will send home poems, songs, stories, strategies, etc. that we have been learning at school. We encourage you to talk to your child about his/her learning and continue to be fully involved in your child's literacy development.

Thank you for your cooperation and support.

classroom and other subjects. Integrated units often incorporate a constructivist approach where key learning and essential understandings are emphasized. The following approach to integrated unit planning is summarized from Wiggins and McTighe (1998).

Stage 1: Identify Desired Results

In this stage, goals and target understandings are identified using the following key questions.

Key Questions:

1. What expectations does the unit address?

2. What are the "big ideas"? What "enduring" understandings are desired?

3. What questions will foster further inquiry, understanding, and transfer of learning?

4. What key knowledge and skills will students acquire as a result of this unit?

Stage 2: Determine Acceptable Evidence

A backward design orientation suggests that we think about a unit or course in terms of the anticipated assessment evidence needed to document and validate that the desired learning has been achieved, not simply as content to be covered or as a series of learning activities.

Key Questions:

1. Through what authentic performance task(s) will students demonstrate achievement of the desired results?

2. Through what other evidence (quizzes, academic prompts, observations, homework, journals) will students demonstrate achievement of the desired results?

3. How will students reflect upon and self-assess their learning?

Stage 3: Plan Learning Experiences and Instruction

With identified results (enduring understandings) and appropriate evidence of understanding in mind, it is now time to plan learning activities. What questions will serve to "uncover" the big ideas you want students to come to understand? What

Effective Assessment	Informal Checks for Understanding	Assessment Tools
• Should include multiple sources of evidence • Should address many facets of understanding: explanation, interpretation, application, perspective, empathy, self-knowledge • Should address Bloom's taxonomy • Should address Gardner's Multiple Intelligences	• Hand signals (thumbs up, thumbs down) • Index card or one-minute summaries/questions • Question box/board • Analogy prompt • Web/concept map • One-minute essay • Misconception check	• Formal observations • Informal observations • Written products • Oral products • Visual products • Student exhibits • Student models • Student demonstrations • Reflective journals • Rubrics • Checklists • Quizzes and tests • Performance criteria: content, process, quality, result

enabling knowledge and skills will students need in order to perform effectively and demonstrate the desired results? What will you need to teach and coach, and how can you teach it most effectively in light of the performance goals? In planning the learning activities, consider the WHERE elements. Note that choices about teaching methods, sequence of lessons, and resource materials are made after you have identified the desired results and assessment instruments.

Key Question: Use of the Acronym WHERE
What sequence of learning experiences and instruction will enable students to achieve the desired results?

W *How will you ensure that all students know where they have come from (assess prior knowledge and interests), where they are headed in the unit, and why they are headed there? How will you orient them toward the purpose of work, key assignments, performance tasks, and the criteria by which they will be evaluated?*

- Directly state the desired results and/or culminating performance task requirements at the beginning of a unit.
- Present course/unit outline, requirements, schedule at the beginning of a unit.
- Have students participate in a mini-seminar to explore the overarching understandings and essential questions as they begin the unit.
- Have students complete an initial journal entry in which they react to the overarching understandings and essential questions.
- Ask students to complete a listen-think-pair-share.
- Videotape students at the beginning of the unit, each giving a "headline" or 25-word summary of their expectations about the unit.

- Hold a town meeting in which students explore together their expectations for the unit and how they need to operate during it.
- Use a three-minute pause at key points in an initial mini-lecture.
- Have students create a visual organizer to assess their initial knowledge and understandings.
- Use KWL charts (individual and/or group).
- Ask students to help create preliminary evaluation criteria and provide scoring rubrics in advance.
- Show models/exemplars.

H *How will you hook and hold the student through engaging and thought-provoking experiences (issues, oddities, problems, challenges) that point toward big ideas, essential questions, and performance tasks? How will you address different learning styles, interests, and abilities?*

- Engage students in a relevant "upfront" simulation or scenario activity.
- Use "weird facts," "strange ideas," mysteries, provocative entry questions, problems, issues, emotional connections, personal anecdotes/stories, etc. to interest and intrigue students.
- Employ media to provide interesting examples of key ideas and overarching concepts.
- Ask students to engage in performance tasks involving key facets of understanding to explore the unit's big ideas and questions.
- Use role playing and related activities to engage student interest in the overarching understandings and essential questions.
- Incorporate student interests, personal goals, and experiences into the design of both initial and ongoing activities.
- Use engaging daily "warm-ups"/anticipatory sets (guides, word splashes).

E *What events will help students experience and explore the big ideas and questions in the unit? What instruction is needed to equip them with needed skills and knowledge for their final performance(s)?*

- Stress hands-on, experiential, and cooperative learning activities.

- Use research-based reading and writing frameworks, including the writing as process model, SQ3R, reciprocal teaching, and before-during-after activities.

- Use simulations and related activities to stress multi-sensory and multiple intelligence learning.

- Integrate a true coaching model, based upon effective athletic coaching strategies (modelling, shaping/rehearsal, and internalization).

- Introduce new concepts through concept attainment activities.

- Encourage students to create visual representations of key ideas.

- Incorporate problem-based learning and decision-making into units.

- Engage students in seminar experiences using interpretive questions.

- Employ a variety of question types (application, analysis, synthesis, interpretive, evaluative) with accompanying follow-up probes.

- Teach students to employ and create mnemonic devices.

- Design activities to reinforce the six facets of Bloom's taxonomy and higher level thinking skills and processes.

- Use guided imagery, visualization, and investigation to engage students in real-world issues and applications for learning to the world beyond the classroom.

R *How will you cause students to reflect and re-think and to dig deeper into the core ideas? How will you guide them in rehearsing, revising, and refining their work based on feedback and self-assessment?*

- Use a variety of metacognitive tools including reflective journals, think logs, critiques (individual/peer), and peer responses.

- Model and encourage student use of think aloud strategies.

- Model and emphasize students' use of productive habits of mind, including self-regulation and critical and creative thinking.

- Encourage students to: shift perspective, reconsider key assumptions, revise based on feedback, confront alternative versions, make the strange familiar, make the familiar strange, play "Devil's Advocate," re-examine the argument/evidence/view, review the apparent truth/error, conduct research, consider new information, rethink the naïve idea, argue, confront surprises and anomalies, see the problems and weaknesses.

- Allow for ongoing interviews and dialogues with all students.

- Emphasize that editing is an ongoing process of revision.

E *How will students exhibit their understanding through final performances and products? How will you guide them in self-evaluation to identify their growing skills, knowledge, and understanding throughout the unit, the strengths/needs in their work, and set future goals?*

- Ensure that all students know and follow evaluation guidelines, which are articulated in scoring tools, analytical guides, and rubrics.

- Incorporate ongoing self-reflection and assessment activities.

- At key points in the unit, build in time for presentations, small and full-group reflections, and related evaluation activities.

- For projects and performance tasks, build in exhibition time.

- Use idea starters such as: What do you really understand about…? What questions/uncertainties do you have about…? What was most effective in…? What was least effective in…? How could you improve…? What would you do differently next time? What are you most proud of? What are you most disappointed in? How difficult was…for you? What are your strengths in…? What are your needs in…? How does your preferred learning style influence…? What grade/score did you deserve? Why? What goals do you have for the future? What follow-up work is needed? What issues remain?

For further information, see: McTighe, J. (2002). *Understanding by design: Teaching and assessing for understanding*. Pitt Meadows, BC: TW Branun & Associates.

Wiggins, G. & McTighe, J. (1998). *Understanding by design*. Alexandria, VA: Association for Supervision and Curriculum Development.

Journals

> *A journal is like a good friend who is never too busy to listen.*
> —Saskatoon Public Schools

Journal writing is based on the idea that we write our way to understanding and learning, as opposed to writing about learning or writing after learning. Journal entries should be written purposefully by both students and teachers and should demonstrate students' developing understanding of literacy, learning, and content. Journal writing serves many purposes, depending on the format selected by teachers and students. Sample purposes include:

- providing students with the opportunity to reflect on their world and expand their awareness of what is happening in their lives

- making students more thoughtful about literature and language/learning processes

- raising student engagement in language and literacy by encouraging students to explore writing as a way of understanding self

- encouraging students to reflect on their literacy and learning processes and make it visible both to others and self

- promoting self-evaluation of the six language arts, motivation, and engagement in literacy and learning

Journal entries should be thoughtful and conversational, with a focus on meaning and understanding. Introduce journal formats through mini-lessons, displayed descriptions and examples, and a personal list for each student's reference. Encourage students to select and label their format. Journals are draft writing and should be used for assessment, not evaluation.

A SAMPLE OF JOURNAL FORMATS

Art journals provide a place for students to plan, to gather resource and research materials, do preliminary drawings, and experiment with media; they are often recorded in sketch books where students can explore and document their personal creative processes in much the same way they record the writing process (from rehearsal to sharing).

Math journals provide a space for students to explain their thinking about mathematical ideas and then to re-examine their thoughts by reviewing their writing. Writing in math enhances students' understanding of math as they articulate thought processes in math problem-solving, math problems, and concept development. Pairing math journals with a retell, relate, reflect formula is highly effective (for example, Retell what you did; Relate this to the strategies that you have been taught; Reflect on how you might use this concept again or how you might use it in real life).

Science journals are a way to incorporate personal ideas with observation and inference. Students can express their opinions with experiments as they are conducted in class. Students can be encouraged to record questions about process or outcomes of explorations. Science journals often include drawings, diagrams, data charts, and graphs.

Dialogue journals are conversations about literature and learning between two individuals (student to student, student to teacher, student to adult). With this variation of the reader response journal, students receive responses to what they have written that may extend their thinking or have them rethink their interpretations.

Double entry journals are often done using a T-chart format. On the left hand side, list student selected references from the text or a wonder statements that arise while reading. On the right hand side, students reflect on their wonder statements or their selected passages, making text-to-text, text-to-self, or text-to-world connections.

Multiple entry journals provide students with the opportunity to track their thinking or their progress over time by making multiple entries on the same subject, same book, or even the same prediction. These can take the form of before, during, and after reading, writing, drama, and storytelling.

Learning logs provide students with an opportunity to reflect on what they are learning, how they have learned it, how they apply knowledge, and what they still need to learn. They represent a balanced integration of content, process, strategy use, and personal feelings. Teachers may guide learning logs or they might be more open ended in terms of a KWL (tell me what you have learned). Your literacy notebook is a great example of a learning log. Many teachers provide five minutes at the end of each class or day to allow students to reflect on what they have learned. Sample questions for learning logs include a) What did I do in class today? b) What did I learn? c) What did I find interesting? e) What questions do I have about what I learned? f) What was the point of today's lesson? and g) What connections did I make to previous ideas of lessons?

Personal journals provide students with the opportunity to write freely for themselves and express their thoughts and ideas with regard to school activities. These entries are not read (unless requested by the writer) nor are they evaluated, and students should be cautioned not to confuse this type of journal with a personal diary.

QuickWrite journals are designed to have students respond quickly to selected literature or an experience. They are often short, frequent bursts of writing that allow students to react quickly without excessive planning and thought. The focus is on exploring ideas freely without worrying about spelling, grammar, punctuation, judgement, or evaluation. Younger students can be encouraged to use a combination of quick writing and quick drawing.

In *quotation journals*, students begin with a quotation that they find particularly interesting or thought provoking and they write their interpretation, connections, thoughts, and ideas about the quotation. At times, teachers will designate quotes for students to use for their reflection.

Reader response journals are student responses to what they have read, during and after reading. They record student feelings, responses, and reactions to a variety of texts; students are also asked to reflect on how these responses would be useful to them as a writer. This interaction between reader and text extends the reading experience and encourages students to make text-to-text, text-to-self, and text-to-world connections. Reader response journals allow students to ask questions about a text, form opinions, make and value judgements, and think critically for a variety of purposes. Theory into Practice 8.1 and 8.2 provide detailed descriptions of reader response journals.

Retell, Relate, Reflect (3R) journals encourage students to summarize and recall learning experiences or readings they have encountered. This journal format goes beyond simple recall to asking students to relate what they have read to their own experiences or another book they have read, and then reflect on what might happen or how this might be personally beneficial. Swartz & Bone's *Retelling, Relating, Reflecting* provides a detailed description of how we might use this type of journaling with students and the types of sentence starters we might use to support students in retelling, relating, and reflecting.

For further information, see: Saskatoon Public Schools (http://www.saskschools.ca/curr_content/techclass/instr/strats/journal/index.html)

Senn, J.A. (1992). *325 creative prompts for personal journals*. New York: Scholastic.

Schwartz, S. & Bone, M. (1995). *Retelling, relating, reflecting: Beyond the 3Rs*. Toronto, ON: Irwin.

Keys to Comprehension in Reading and Writing

Key	What Readers and Writers Do
Connect	Use relevant prior knowledge before, during, and after reading to enhance understanding of what they are reading and writing.
Determine Main Ideas	Identify key ideas or themes as they read and write, and distinguish between important and unimportant information.
Evaluate	Use prior knowledge, reactions, and information to judge and compare the text to others they have read and written and assess their effectiveness.
Infer	Use prior knowledge and information to make predictions, seek answers to questions, draw conclusions, and create interpretations that deepen understanding of the text.
Predict	Generate questions before, during, and after reading and writing, revisit questions, and clarify meaning while reading.
Question	Generate questions before, during, and after reading and writing to clarify meaning and focus attention on what is important.
React	Become emotionally involved with what they read and write and describe what makes them love, hate, or can't stop reading or writing.
Self-monitor, Cross-check, Self-correct	Are aware of when they understand and when they don't. If they have trouble understanding specific words, phrases, or longer passages, they use a wide range of problem-solving or fix-up strategies including skipping ahead, re-reading, asking questions, using a dictionary, and reading aloud, and apply these skills to writing.
Summarize	Track main ideas, retell details in their own words, and focus on what is important.
Synthesize	Track thinking as it evolves during reading and writing, to get the overall meaning.
Visualize	Create a wide range of visual, auditory, and other sensory images as they read and use this information to writing.

For further information, see: Keene, E.O. & Zimmerman, S. (1997). *Mosaic of thought: Teaching comprehension in a reader's workshop.* Portsmouth, NH: Heinemann.

Zimmerman, S. & Hutchins, C. (2001). *Seven keys to comprehension: How to help your kids read and get it!* New York: Three Rivers Press.

Literacy Cafés

Literacy café, a term from the organization Literacy Alberta, refers to the permanent time or space in the school set aside for student and adult readers to celebrate and share their written work, what they are reading, favourite book reviews, and book talks. As extension activities, they may also have the opportunity to engage in literature circles, grand conversations, literary conversations, and book clubs. Participants may come dressed as their favourite characters or arrange a space to reflect the setting of the story. Discussion may be followed with video viewing, presentations from guest authors, round robin writing, read arounds, creative and dramatic presentations, and art galleries. Literacy cafés provide opportunities for readers and writers to share what they are reading and writing with others in an informal but structured setting.

Literacy cafés provide opportunities for students to develop "networks for literary support." A phrase coined by David Booth (2001), networks for literary support refers to the networks that we, as mature literate persons, cultivate. Examples are membership in book clubs, taking courses, and meeting with colleagues to discuss literacy education. Booth encourages teachers to model these forms of literacy by talking about them with students and engaging them in real life networks that extend beyond the walls of the classroom to include real-world readers and writers.

Literacy cafés are a little like Chapters bookstores on a Saturday night or public libraries during sponsored events. If you've ever spent time in a Chapters on a Saturday evening or attended a library book club, you'll know what we mean. There are readers everywhere—in front of warm fires, relaxing with hot, steaming lattés, snuggled up with good books, and engaged in deep and passionate conversation with other readers. What binds these people together is the desire to get lost in a good story, spread the word, and celebrate the passion of books!

Bookstores are sanctuaries. Places to lose yourself, escape the harsh demands of daily life, find new ways to dream and new sources of inspiration. I love all booksellers; anybody who helps spread the word is doing noble work. But my favourite bookstores are the small eccentric independents run by passionate and usually slightly mad book lovers. These are some of the best.
—Jeremy Mercer

For further information, visit the Literacy Alberta website (http://literacyalberta.ca/)

More Cloze Procedures

Cloze passages can be modified to reinforce knowledge of parts of speech. Students are asked to list random words under each part of speech (any noun, any adjective, any verb). They copy these words in the correct place in sentence, paragraph, or poetic frames. This requires that students know the parts of speech to be substituted into the frame. When complete, the syntax will be fine, but the semantics can be hilarious! This is an excellent partner activity: one asks the questions and the other provides the answers. Try the example on the next page with a partner.

For an added challenge, you can add the rhyming scheme into the frame as well.

(Adapted from *'Twas the Night Before Christmas* by C. Clement Moore)

'Twas the night before _____ (NOUN that names a special holiday)

When all through the _____ (NOUN that names a place)   <u>Rhyme 1</u>

Not a _____(NOUN that names an creature) was _____

VERB that ends in 'ing')

Not even a _____ .(NOUN that names a creature)   <u>Rhyme 1</u>

Multiple Intelligence Responses in Reading and Writing

Designing response activities with multiple intelligences in mind allows full expression of individual understandings of diverse learners, and allows opportunities to strengthen less dominant areas. (See Figure 3.7, Chapter 12, and eXtremely Engaging Ways to Teach Story Elements later in this chapter.)

A sample multiple intelligence response plan for *Lesia's Dream* by Laura Langston is provided on the next page.

Music and Literacy

The impact of singing on reading and writing has long been recognized and has been used extensively and effectively by primary teachers, particularly during the Kindergarten years. Songs and poems foster an increased awareness of rhyme, rhythm, and alliteration in addition to phonemic awareness—characteristics that often distinguish effective readers from readers at risk.

The music–literacy link can be extended throughout junior, intermediate, and senior years by reading aloud the lyrics to popular songs. Music can be used for choral reading, shared reading, readers' theatre, or incorporated into drama and storytelling activities. Students can also be asked to create musical scores or soundscapes to accompany read arounds, read alouds, dramatic performances, and readers' theatre.

For further information, see: Cornett, C.E. & Smithrim, K.L. (2001). *The arts as meaning makers: Integrating literature and the arts through the curriculum.* Canadian Edition. Toronto, ON: Prentice Hall.

Novel in a Day

Novel in a day is a whole class strategy that fosters teamwork and group building. The whole class works together to collect evidence, reconstruct a story, and make sense of text.

BEFORE READING

- Choose a book with a surprise, a mystery, or an interesting plot, which no one in the class has read.

- Consider the reading level of the students and choose a book that is within students' instructional range.

- Divide the book into equal sections. The number of sections will depend on the size of your class. You will need enough sections for each group of three or four students and for yourself. You may give yourself a longer section if you need to keep the other sections equal.

Intelligence	Language Practice for *Lesia's Dream*
Linguistic	Write a series of letters that might have been sent back and forth between Lesia, her mother, and her father while they were imprisoned.
Logical-Mathematical	Keep track of the sequence of events from the beginning of the book until the end (for example, before they left the Ukraine until Lesia's marriage in Canada).
Musical	Research the traditional music of the Ukraine and its transfer into Canada. Choose a passage of text and create a musical score or soundscape to accompany its reading.
Bodily-Kinesthetic	Create a series of tableaux that represent Lesia's working of the land. What type of strength and skill would she have needed?
Spatial	Create a character sociogram that describes the relationships between Lesia and other characters in the book.
Interpersonal	Engage students in literature circles, grand conversations, or literary conversations about the story.
Intrapersonal	Become Lesia and write a journal from Lesia's perspective as she settles in Canada. How does her life differ from yours? How does hearing about her life help you to understand yourself?
Naturalist	Use R.A.F.T. writing discussed later in this chapter to write a set of directions from the land to Lesia, telling her how to clear and maintain it.

• Scaffold words (through the set-up activity described below).

• Set up the activity. Set the opening scene of the novel to pique students' interest. Ask the students to be detectives, to collect evidence, and try to figure out what happened. They will need to make predictions, ask questions, and draw conclusions based on the scene structured before them. They may ask questions about the scene to deepen their awareness and draw them closer to what really happened. Students who have figured out the book are encouraged not to divulge its true nature (they will now become witnesses to the "crime"). They will be asked to write in role (as a detective) the opening paragraph of the novel. This paragraph should describe what they think happened leading to the scene of the "crime" (helps to set a purpose for reading).

• Once students have composed their preliminary report, notify them that one witness (or more if other students recognize the book) was found by one of the detectives. They have five minutes to ask as many questions as they can that will help them to draw further conclusions.

• Students will then be organized into groups of three or four and will compose a group report (opening paragraph) that represents a group consensus but will also contain something of each individual's quick write. Groups are then asked to read their reports aloud.

• Once reports have been shared, read the first chapter. Students reflect on how closely their paragraph resembled the true story and why.

• A variation is to ask students to create dramatic presentations of each section that will need to be sequenced in order to retell the story.

DURING READING

- Divide the class into heterogeneous groups (the number of which is determined by the number of sections). Remind them that there are many different ways to read a text (for example, listening or taking turns). Ask each group to nominate a recorder. After telling the class they will read a novel in an hour, distribute Post-it notes and random sections of the book to the group leaders.

- Do not tell them which section they have or how many chapters or pages are in the book.

- Each group reads its section by taking turns reading aloud a page at a time.

- Whenever a question pops in their head about the story, they ask the recorder to write it on a Post-it note.

- When a group has finished reading, it should construct a summary, which all members of the group should be able to retell or read.

- A variation of the question and summary approach is to use a recording sheet similar to the following:

Novel: **Name:**

This section begins with:

The main events include:

The problem in this section is:

The chapter ends with:

I think that this chapter is at the (beginning/middle/ending) of the book.

AFTER READING

- When everyone is finished, gather together and choose a group that had a middle section of the book to read a question on its Post-it notes. Someone in the room should be able to answer it. The group that answers the question then gets to ask its first question. And so on. If a question cannot be answered, write it on the board or on a chart.

- When all of the questions have been asked, the students should be asked to sequence themselves in a logical and sequential fashion. Try to let them figure it out based on the first chapter and the responses to the questions they recorded and answered.

- Ask each group, in order, to retell the main events of its section or read its summary.

- Then read aloud the end of the book and see which questions were answered; some will probably remain unanswered.

EXTENDING THE READING

- Depending on the novel selected, novel in a day can be paired with multiple intelligence response activities and/or cross-curricular activities that engage students in different ways with the text.

- The novel could be compared and contrasted to a similar video or a contemporary and familiar movie.

For further information, see: Teachers.Net – Four Blocks Chatboard (http://teachers.net/) and Turning Points – Transforming Middle Schools (http://www.turningputs.org/).

Novel in a Day: *Abel's Island* by William Steig
Opening Scene

Set up a picnic with as many clues from the opening scene as possible: a bottle of champagne, a book of poetry, an umbrella, a croquet mallet and ball, etc. Ask students to be detectives, collect evidence, and try to figure out what happened. They will need to make predictions, ask questions, and draw conclusions based on the scene structured before them. Students may ask questions about the scene to deepen their awareness and draw them closer to what really happened. Students will be asked to write in role (as detectives) the opening paragraph to the novel. This paragraph should describe what they think happened leading to the scene of the "crime."

Extension Activities for *Abel's Island*

• Watch the video of *Abel's Island*. Compare what you know of the novel to the movie.

• Watch the film *Castaway* and compare *Abel's Island*. Offer an intact copy of the book for U.S.S.R. (discussed later in this chapter).

• Sculpt a model of Abel as Abel did of his family.

• Draw a picture of Abel's island.

• Name your own island. Draw a map of your island. Use a key and show locations of major features with grid lines.

• Design your own survival kit. Use magazines and catalogues to cut out pictures of items you would include in the kit.

• Write a paragraph or essay entitled "How to Survive on an Island."

Oratory or Public Speaking

Oratory or public speaking is the art or practice of making a speech before an audience. Its purpose is to develop confidence in speaking formally in front of an audience and communicate effectively to other individuals. Speakers choose a purpose for their speech and a message. Speeches can describe, inform, persuade, entertain, or share information. Oratory or public speaking experiences provide meaningful, real life opportunities to blend all six language arts.

PLANNING THE SPEECH

1. Engage students in brainstorming reasons for writing speeches, topics, and the process.

2. Energize students by engaging them in table talks (impromptu talk and discussion on random topics) and quick writes.

3. Discuss topic considerations with students:

   a) Selection of topic – Sources of speech topics include direct experience, knowledge gained through participation and indirect experience, and knowledge gained from outside sources such as television and reading.

   b) Types of topic – Students can choose between informative, persuasive, or entertaining topics.

4. Discuss audience with students.

5. Help students to understand the relationship between their personality and how the audience will receive their speech.

6. Discuss the influence of context (for example, time and place).

WRITING THE SPEECH

1. Help students to write their speech using the following guidelines:

   a) Informative speeches
   Ask: Do the main ideas of the speech answer the questions of who, what, when, where, why, and how?

   b) Persuasive speeches
   Ask: Do the main ideas of the speech reflect the principal reasons for the desired belief or action?

   c) Entertaining speeches
   Ask: Will the main ideas of the speech amuse the audience?

2. Enable students to select supporting and relevant information for the speech. Use graphic organizers and expository text structures to support planning.

3. Introduce the three main parts of the speech:

   a) Introduction

     Ask: Does the opening tell the audience about the intent of the speech and the value the topic has for the audience?

   b) Body

     Ask: Is there a flow to the speech? Is there a repetitive statement that draws the audience in?

   c) Conclusion

     Ask: Is the conclusion of the speech reflective of the original purpose? Does it summarize the information, the persuasive message, or the entertainment?

DELIVERING THE SPEECH

1. Help students to plan an outline and set out the main ideas of their speech on cue cards.

2. Practise, practise, practise! Students should feel at ease in front of the audience and should have strategies to support themselves if they lose their place. Pitch, volume, and speed all require attention.

Poetic Surfing and Other Pre-Reading Strategies for the Content Areas

POETIC SURFING AND FOCUSED INTERNET SEARCHES

Give students a key word and a brief list of appropriate Internet sites, and tell them to gather preliminary information on the topic and arrange in the form of an acrostic poem using the word.

For example, using the word "constellation," find information from the NASA site and record a word or phrase for each letter in the word. This can be posted or used as an introduction to a research project.

KWL PLUS

KWL Plus charts are graphic organizers that provide students with the opportunity to explore what they know about a given topic, establish questions for inquiry, and then summarize learning after the inquiry is complete. Students also connect new learning to existing knowledge and reflect on what they still want to know or learn.

For further information, see: Banaszewski, T. (1999). "Poetic surfing: How I used a focused Internet search to keep students on the crest of a wave." *Learning and Reading with Technology*, 26(4), 20-21

Tompkins, G.E. (2004). *50 literacy strategies*, 2nd Ed. New York: Merrill Prentice-Hall.

As a pre-reading strategy, design a KWL Plus for the specific topic under investigation by providing categories for the "L" column "L" (learned) entries; for example, information on whales can be categorized under A – abilities, D – description, F – food, and L – location. This information can then be organized as a concept map using those categories as the four headings.

A space can also be provided at the bottom of the KWL for a record of Internet sites and other information sources used, along with the dates.

K What I Know	W What I Want to Know	L What I Learned	Plus What I Still Want to Know

Abilities	Description	Food	Location

Other pre-reading strategies referenced and described throughout this text include advance organizers, anticipation guides, concept webs, expository text structures, and graphic organizers.

For further information, see: Ogle, D.H. (1986). K-W-L: A teaching model that develops active reading of expository text, *The Reading Teacher*, 39, 564-570.

Poetry Gallery

A poetry gallery showcases 10 to 15 poems that are age appropriate, relevant, and engaging for students. Poems are enlarged or copied onto poster board and displayed around the classroom at students' eye level. Students will be asked to read and make sense of poems using a variety of reading comprehension strategies.

BEFORE READING

- Teachers use the think-aloud strategy to model how a poem can be read using reading comprehension strategies that the class has been working on (making connections, predicting, questioning, inferring—see Keys to Comprehension). If a specific strategy is being studied, teachers should suggest that students use that strategy. This can also be a culminating activity where students select strategies that are appropriate for particular poems.

- Teachers explain the purpose of the poetry gallery walk and outline the rules and routines that will be in place for the duration of the activity (silent reading, no more than four students at each poem at any given time.

- Teachers provide each student with 5 to 10 post-it notes to record their sense-making, connections, predictions, and questions, for a designated number of poems.

DURING READING

- Students wander around the gallery, looking at

and reading a variety of poems (15 to 20 minutes). This is a silent and reflective activity and can be enhanced by quiet background music that reflects the theme(s) of the poems.

- As students read poems, they record any connections, questions, predictions, inferences, reflections, or reactions on their Post-it notes and stick them on the poem. (Note: these reflections can be specific to the designated strategy or to one selected by the student.)

AFTER READING

- Students return to their seats and are assigned a partner. Each pair reads a poem and its Post-it notes.

- While reading, students consider and discuss the following questions:

  - What kinds of questions and connections did readers make?

  - How did the Post-its inform your reading of the poem?

  - What did reading the notes with the poem teach you about reading and writing?

- After five minutes of paired discussion, pairs write a one-page reflection on the poem.

- These reflections are attached to the poems and left up for about a week.

For further information, see: Turning Points – Transforming Middle Schools (http://www.turningpts.org/pdf/Poetry_Gallery.doc)

Question-Answer Relationships (QAR)

QAR is a reading and literacy strategy that helps students to realize that there is a relationship between the question asked and the answer found. QAR, developed by Raphael (1986), is "designed to demystify the questioning process, providing teachers and students with a common vocabulary to discuss different types of questions and sources of information for answering these questions…" (Anthony & Raphael, 1989, p. 319). It teaches students that answering different kinds of questions requires different reading behaviours, different sense-making strategies, and different thought processes. Some questions require students to find an answer in the text, explain something that they have read in their own words, elaborate and make connections, or evaluate their own thinking and sense-making about a given topic. Confronted with questions, students must be able to read a question and determine where they are likely to find the answer, whether they are using books, videos, media presentations, or websites. Below are four categories of questions that students must become aware of during strategy use and practice.

Right There

The answer is in the text, and if we pointed at it, we'd say "It's right there!" Often, the answer will be in a single sentence, and the words used to create the question are often also in that same place. "Right There" questions often elicit a one-word or short response and require one right answer.
Signal Words: who is, where is, list, when is, how many, when did, name, what kind of

Think and Search

The answer is in the text, but you might have to look in several different sentences or several different places to find it. It is broken up or scattered, or requires a grasp of multiple ideas across paragraphs or pages. "Think and Search" questions require students to understand how the information or ideas in the text relate to one another and to search through the entire passage to find the information they need.
Signal Words: summarize, what caused, contrast, retell, how did, explain, find two examples, why, compare

Author and You

The answer is not in the text, so you need information that the author has given you, combined with what you already know in order to respond to this type of question. "Author and You" questions require that students read the text material to understand what the question is asking.

On My Own

The answer is not in the text, and in fact you don't even have to have read the text to be able to answer it. "On My Own" questions can be answered with information from the students' background knowledge.

For further information, see: Anthony, H.M. & Raphael, T.E. (1989). Using questioning strategies to promote students' active comprehension of content area material. In D. Lapp, J. Flood, & N. Farnan (eds.), *Content area reading and learning: Instructional strategies.* Englewood Cliffs, NJ: Prentice Hall.
Beck, I. L. & McKeown, M. G. (2002). Questioning the author: Making sense of social studies. *Educational Leadership*, 60 (3), 44–47.
Raphael, T.E. (1984). Teaching learners about sources of information for answering comprehension questions. *Journal of Reading*, 27, 303-311.
Raphael, T.E. (1986). Teaching question-answer relationships. *The Reading Teacher*, 39, 516-520.

Questioning the Author (QtA)

Questioning the author (McKeown, Beck, & Worthy, 1993) is a text-based strategy to help students build deeper-level understandings of text as they consider ideas in depth with a writer's and reviser's eye. It can be used with both narrative and expository (content areas) texts. QtA requires students to think about what the author is saying in addition to what the text states. Through QtA, students can explore deeper meanings to make the text more understandable and to construct personal meanings.

EXAMPLES OF QAR ACROSS THE CURRICULUM				
Curricular Area	Right There	Think and Search	Author and You	On My Own
Mathematics	What is the name for a triangle with three congruent sides?	Explain the relationship between a square and a rectangle.	Can you draw a shape that has at least three lines of symmetry?	What shape of container would you recommend a company use to package candy?
Science	What is a mammal?	Compare and contrast solution and suspension.	Based on the author's information about energy sources, which would you use in your ideal home?	Identify three constellations that you have observed in the winter sky.
Social Studies	What was the Underground Railroad?	Describe the roles of community helpers.	Relate what you have read about life in pioneer times to your life today.	Identify somewhere in the world you would like to travel and explain why.

BEFORE READING

- Consider the previous knowledge and experiences of your students.

  Ask: What do the students already know or believe about the text content that they can bring to the reading situation?

- Explain that sometimes texts are difficult to understand because authors leave out important details, imply, or assume that the reader has previous knowledge or experience.

  Ask: Who wrote this text? What does the author think the reader will already know? What does the author expect that the reader will be able to do with the text? What could the author have done to make the text more understandable than it is?

- Select an appropriate text for modelling and demonstration. For example, a narrative text that has some story elements provided but others implied. Here the goal is to enable students to "read between the lines" of the text to discover and explore the author's real intent. You might choose an expository text that provides some of the important information but assumes reader experience of other details; in this case, the students' role is to identify what information is missing, implied, or assumed.

  Ask: Did I select a text that gives me something to model and discuss with students?

DURING READING

- Use an authentic text to model using questions to determine what the author really means. As you read, use a think-aloud strategy to model and articulate questions that you might ask the author to deepen and clarify understanding. Make sure that you share your in-the-head thinking and responses as you model.

Ask: What is the author trying to tell us? What is meant by that? Why is the author telling us that? Does the author say it clearly? How could the author have said things more clearly? What would you say instead?

- Engage students in discussion (partner, small group, whole class) using the above questions. Ask them to contribute information and responses that can be discussed, challenged, or refuted later by peers and teachers. Questioning strategies such as those in Figure 9.5 and Figure 13.1 would help students to further engage in QtA.

  Ask: What is the author trying to tell us? What is meant by that? Why is the author telling us that? Does the author say it clearly? How could the author have said things more clearly? What would you say instead?

AFTER READING

- Encourage students to generalize this strategy to other texts (oral, print, visual, multimedia).

  Ask: Do students independently question and query the fallibility of texts and the author or do they simply accept text as truth?

For further information, see: McKeown, M.G., Beck, I.L., & Worthy, M.J. (1993). Grappling with text ideas: Questioning the author. *The Reading Teacher*, 46, 560-566.

McLaughlin, M. & Allen, M.B. (2002). *Guided comprehension: A teaching model for Grades 3-8*. Newark, DE: International Reading Association.

R.A.F.T. Writing

The R.A.F.T. strategy (Santa, 1988) provides a nontraditional approach to enhance understanding of content material or informational text. Writing in role requires that students process information, adopt alternative perspectives, make connections, organize information, elaborate on details, and draw conclusions. R.A.F.T. writing en-

courages creative thinking and motivates students to reflect on their learning and understanding in unusual and fun ways. R.A.F.T. is an acronym for:

Role of the writer	Who are you as a writer?
Audience for the writer	For whom are you writing?
Format of the writing	What form will it take?
Topic to be addressed	What are you writing about?

When engaged in R.A.F.T. writing, students adopt a specific role from a real life, literature, or content-oriented context and write from that perspective (for example, a fictional character, an animal, an expert in a content area). R.A.F.T. writing assumes a viewpoint or perspective different than the student's, an audience other than peers or teacher, and a form different than those typically used (reports, essays). The chart on the following page demonstrates how R.A.F.T. writing is useful across the curriculum.

For further information, see: Instructional Strategies Online, Saskatoon Public Schools (http://olc.spsd.sk.ca/DE/PD/instr/strats/raft/index.html) and Santa, C. (1988). *Content reading including study systems*. Dubuque, IA: Kendall/Hunt.

Reciprocal Teaching

Reciprocal teaching (Palincsar & Brown, 1984) is a technique that actively engages students and teachers in dialogue about texts (whether print, multimedia, or electronic). Teachers initiate the comprehension strategies through modelling, demonstration, and thinking aloud, gradually releasing responsibility for the dialogue to students. Reciprocal teaching is a shared experience where teachers and students work together until students are ready to apply strategies indepen-

EXAMPLES OF R.A.F.T. WRITING ACROSS THE CURRICULUM				
Curricular Area	Role	Audience	Format	Topic
Language and Literature	*Salmon for Simon*	Simon	Thank you note	Freedom and life
Physical and Health Education	Lungs	People	Advice column	How to take care of us
Visual Arts	Clay	Potter	Advice	How to mould and shape me

dently. It is particularly useful with students who struggle with comprehension. When students are ready to "become the teacher," the teacher's role becomes that of a guide who prompts for higher levels of thinking and participation. The reciprocal teaching dialogue involves the four key strategies of summarizing, questioning, clarifying, and predicting.

Summarizing provides the opportunity to review, identify, and integrate the most important information in the text. Text can be summarized across sentences, across segments, and across the text as a whole. Students ask:

- What does the author want me to remember or learn from this passage?
- What is the most important information in this passage?
- What kind of "teacher" question can I ask about the main idea?
- In my own words, this is about ...
- The main point was...
- The author wanted me to remember...

Questioning reinforces the summarizing strategy and requires that students generate their own questions. To do this, they have to find information that would generate a question, pose the question, and then answer it. Questioning can be used flexibly with QAR and Bloom's taxonomy to engage students in questioning at a multitude of levels. Students ask:

- One question I had about what I read was....
- What was I thinking about as I was reading?
- What question(s) can I ask about what I have read?
- I'm curious about...

Clarifying is particularly useful with students who struggle with comprehension. When students are asked to clarify, they must attend to reasons why they do not understand the text (tricky vocabulary, difficulty concepts). They are taught to summarize, ask questions, and apply fix-up strategies that allow them to restore meaning. Students ask:

- One of the words I wasn't sure about was...
- What other words do I know that I can use in place of...?
- What words or ideas need clarifying?
- This is confusing to me. I need to _____ (strategy) to try to figure out this word.

Predicting occurs when students think about what will happen next. To make predictions, students must activate prior knowledge and establish a purpose for reading (to confirm, clarify, reformulate, or reject predictions) and what the author will discuss next in the text. To do this successfully, students must activate the relevant background knowledge that they already possess. Expository text structures are useful as students make predictions and learn that comprehension is facilitated by paying attention to headings, signal words, and questions embedded in the text. Students ask:

- I can look at the title and all the visual clues on the page. What do I think we will be reading about?

- Thinking about what I have read and discussed, what do I think might happen next?

- I wonder...

- I predict...

For further information, see: Palincsar, A. S. & Brown, A. (1984). Reciprocal teaching of comprehension-fostering and comprehension monitoring activities. *Cognition and Instruction*, 1(2), 117-175.

North Centre Regional Education Laboratory (http://www.ncrel.org/sdrs/areas/issues/students/atrisk/at6lk38.htm)

Newton Public Schools (http://www.newton.k12.ks.us/Dist/curr/bp/lit/reciprocal_teaching.htm)

SQ3R: Survey-Question-Read Actively-Recite-Review

SQ3R is a five-step study plan that helps students construct meaning while reading. It is particularly effective for content area material and can be extended as a study system for student-generated notes, textbooks, websites, visual information, and other forms of print text, especially when students are searching for pieces of information to support knowledge construction, sense-making, and research. It involves the five ordered steps of survey, question, read actively, recite, and review.

SURVEY

Skim or scan the text before reading it. Establish purposes for reading. Apply the KWL strategy if appropriate.

- Think about the title and the topic. Predict what will be included in the text.

- Determine the structure or organization of the text.

- Read the introduction. What are the main ideas? What are the relationships between the main ideas?

- Read the questions or summary at the end of the chapter. These will help to identify the important parts of the chapter.

- Read the main headings and subheadings. These are the author's main ideas.

- Look at the visual information (charts, pictures, graphics). How do they support the main ideas?

QUESTION

As you survey the text, write down any questions that you have. Finding the answers to some of these questions establishes your purpose for reading. In addition to your own questions, review the questions posed by the author throughout the text or at the end of the text. These will guide your reading and help you to identify main ideas and details. A double-entry journal is useful to record the questions and answers.

- Reword the author's question in a way that makes sense to you, as a reader.

- Turn titles, headings, and visual aids into questions.

- Write down any questions that come to mind during the survey stage.

- Apply the QAR strategy and consider where you will find the answers.

READ ACTIVELY

Read to answer your questions, both in your mind and in writing. Your survey and question stages have already helped you to identify the main ideas. During this stage, you read selectively and actively, sorting the main ideas from extra information that is not as important. Remember some answers are "right there," some will require you to "think and search," some require the "author and you" to construct the response, and some questions must be answered "on your own."

- Make sure to rephrase the answers to questions in your own words. It is not necessary to write in full sentences. Point form, graphics, charts, and pictures are acceptable.

- Sometimes you don't have to read the whole text. Instead you can move quickly, read fragments of text, sort ideas, and quickly evaluate them. If the content does not relate to your specific question, give it a glance, quickly familiarize yourself with the content, and then move on.

RECITE

After you have answered all of your questions, it is helpful to read and retell the questions and answers. To do this, you should:

- Recite each question out loud, one at a time.

- Quickly review the answer that you have written down and then verbally summarize the information.

- Try responding to the question, retelling your answer without looking at your written response or the text.

- Go back and read actively for any questions that are still unanswered or require further clarification.

REVIEW

Depending on your purpose for reading (to study, write an essay, write a speech, engage in a group discussion, you will need to go back and review your notes and your questions and answers.

- When you are studying, it is a good idea to review the material within 24 hours of first reading it, asking yourself questions and clarifying your understanding. If you are still unsure, then you need to go back to the "questioning" and "reading actively" stages.

- When you are writing an essay or a speech, review your notes, familiarize yourself with the content, and then write off the top of your head. You can add references later. Writing this way reduces the likelihood of copying as rarely do we write or restate another person's exact words off the top of our heads.

- When you are engaging in a group discussion about the content, it is a good idea to review the material a few times before the discussion. This will help you to confirm and clarify your understanding, sometimes returning you to the "questioning" and "reading actively" stages.

For further information, see: Robinson, F.P. (1961). *Effective study* (rev. ed.). New York: Harper & Row.

Teaching with Twin Texts or Text Sets

Twin texts (Camp, 2000) or text sets are groups of interrelated titles usually connected by a topic or a theme. They generally include both narrative and expository texts. In many cases, expository texts (or non-fiction) answer questions the students have with regard to detail and content, whereas the structure of a narrative (or fiction book) might be more accessible and interesting. Teaching with twin texts enables your students to balance reading for pleasure with reading for content as they become familiar with a variety of topics and vocabulary, activate prior knowledge, scaffold more complex content materials, draw comparisons, learn how to reference, and make connections between different genres of texts (for example, print, visual, oral, multimedia, performance). Here is a sample print text set for an "O Canada" theme.

O CANADA TEXT SET

Fiction or Narrative

ABC of Canada, Kim Bellefontaine, Per-Henrik Gürth
Bud the spud, Stompin' Tom Connors
By the sea: An alphabet book, Ann Blades
Canada 1, 2, 3, Kim Bellefontaine, Per-Henrik Gürth
A Canadian children's treasury, Janet Lunn (ed.)
Canadian hauntings, Michael Norman, Beth Scott
Canadian poems for Canadian kids, Jen Hamilton (Ed.)
Digging Canadian dinosaurs, Rebecca Grambo
The elders are watching, David Bouchard
Goodbye to Griffith Street, Marilynn Reynolds
Heartland: A prairie sample, Jo Bannatyne-Cugnet
The hockey sweater, Roch Carrier
If you're not from the prairie, David Bouchard
My Leafs sweater, Mike Leonetti
O Canada: Our national anthem, Scholastic
Our song: The story of O Canada, Peter Kuitenbrouwer
A prairie alphabet, Jo Bannatyne-Cugnet
A salmon for Simon, Betty Waterton
The story of Canada, Janet Lunn, Christopher Moore
Tales the elders told, Basil Johnston
Waiting for the whales, Sherry McFarlane

Non-Fiction or Expository

A is for Algonquin: An Ontario alphabet, Louvenia Gorman
Canadian explorers, Maxine Trottier
Eh? to Zed, Kevin Major
The great B.C. alphabet book, Nicola Morgan
An island alphabet, Erica Rutherford
The kids book of Canadian exploration, Ann-Maureen Owens, Jane Yealland
The kids book of Canadian history, Carlotta Hacker

The kids book of great Canadians, Elizabeth MacLeod
The kids book of the far north, Ann Love, Jane Drake, Jocelyne Bouchard
M is for maple: A Canadian alphabet, Mike Ulmer
A mountain alphabet, Margriett Ruurs
A Northern alphabet, Ted Harrison
Seaside alphabet book, Donna Grassby
Snow and ice, Nicole Mortillaro
Terry Fox: A story of hope, Maxine Trottier
The wildlife ABC: A nature alphabet, Jan Thornhill

When teaching using twin texts, you can select from a broad range of literacy strategies. The following are some examples.

KWL

1. Read or view a narrative text to activate prior knowledge and support students in making connections to new content (for example, an aboriginal story about how the loon got its necklace, *The Loon's Necklace*, retold by William Toye). Engage students in a KWL, helping them to record information that they gained through the narrative text and questions they still have.

2. Read or view an expository text on the same topic (for example, a fact book about loons in Canada). After reading, invite students to record their learning in the "L" column of the KWL chart.

EXPOSITORY TEXT STRUCTURES

1. Ensure that students have prior knowledge of the text structures modelled throughout the expository text (for example, comparison, cause and effect, sequence, description, problem and solution, question and answer).

2. Read or view both texts. Engage students in an analysis of the texts using one of the expository text structures. For example, they might read or view a narrative text, generate four or five questions, and then search for the answers

in the expository text. Or they might compare the information gathered from the expository text to the information gained from the narrative text. This will help them to understand the importance of consulting multiple sources.

DRAMA, STORYTELLING, AND CREATIVE EXPRESSION

1. Follow up either of the previous approaches, by providing additional opportunities for students to encounter texts in the classroom.

2. Encourage students to create a drama, tell a story, or write a poem that combines narrative texts that tell a story with those that provide content.

For further information, see: Camp, D. (2000). It takes two: Teaching with twin texts of fact and fiction. *The Reading Teacher*, 53(5), 400-408.

U.S.S.R.

Uninterrupted Sustained Silent Reading (U.S.S.R.) is an important component of Readers Workshop. This is a designated period of time where all students and the teacher read in class, usually for pleasure. They select texts that are motivating, engaging, and interesting. With younger students, teachers often begin with shorter periods of time, gradually increasing to a 20 to 25 minute period per day in the upper grades. Most teachers use a consistent block of time each day, building U.S.S.R. into their daily schedule and routine. Teachers should spend most of their time reading their own texts, modelling that they, too, are lifelong readers. Many teachers set aside one or two blocks of U.S.S.R. each week to conference individually with students or talk about what they are reading. You will often find what is called D.E.A.R. (Drop Everything and Read) in place in schools as well. This is similar to U.S.S.R., although in many schools it is school-wide and everyone who is in the school must drop every-

thing and read. D.E.A.R. may be slightly less predictable than U.S.S.R.; many teachers use D.E.A.R. to manage transitions, control unpredictable situations, or simply for the pure pleasure of dropping everything and spending time reading.

BEFORE U.S.S.R.

- Discuss the rules and procedures for U.S.S.R. with students before beginning. Students can be asked to brainstorm rules and routines for U.S.S.R.

- Explain to students that they will be reading self-selected reading material and should bring a book, magazine, game manual, or something they really want to read each day.

DURING U.S.S.R.

- Set a time limit. Start small, gradually increasing as students become accustomed to the process.

  - Everyone reads.

  - There are to be no interruptions during U.S.S.R.

  - No one will be asked to "report" what they read.

- Give a warning when there is one or two minutes left to let students know that they have time to finish that sentence or page. Keep in mind that those students who do not stop reading when the timer goes are likely not breaking the rules but are so engaged in their reading they don't want to stop. Give them the benefit of the doubt, and encourage them to finish up.

AFTER U.S.S.R.

- Once U.S.S.R. is firmly established and valued in the classroom, teachers might ask students to share what they are reading in literary conversations, literature circles, book clubs, literacy cafés, or grand conversations.

- Beginning sharing and discussion too early can

reduce the likelihood that students view U.S.S.R. as a time to read for pleasure and enjoyment.

For further information, see: Tierney, R.J. & Readence, J.E. (2005). *Reading strategies and practices: A compendium*, 6th ed. Boston, MA: Pearson.

Visualization (Forming Mental Images)

When we read good books, we can picture in our mind's eye what the characters look and sound like, and how they are acting. Visualization is closely related to inferring. When we visualize, we are inferring mental images based on the information the author has given us; instead of describing with words, we are visualizing images. The author's words and our own background knowledge help us to create pictures and movies in our minds. Visualizing enables students to experience situations first hand, take on the role of characters, allow their imaginations to take them places they have never been before, and respond with their senses to the mental images that they have formed.

Many students spontaneously visualize as they are reading, forming images of objects, events, situations, and settings in ways that they feel that they are part of the story or text, able to imagine various solutions to problems, and what might happen next. Teachers can support students as they learn to visualize by reading aloud texts that are not full of images or reading aloud the words of a text before showing them the pictures, then having them compare the images in their mind to the pictures in the text. Remind students that they can paint pictures or make movies in their minds and then describe them orally or recreate them visually or artistically. Visualization involves all senses. Teachers can connect reading visualization with poetry writing where students can be asked to describe an object, sensation, or feeling using information from the five senses.

Teaching the strategy of visualization can be done with think alouds as well as the subtext strategy. Poems work particularly well as they are often full of rich imagery and descriptive phrases.

BEFORE STUDENT VISUALIZATION

- Ensure that you have done sufficient thinking aloud, modelling, and demonstration of the visualization strategy, telling students what you see in your mind's eye as you are reading.

- Ask them what it means to visualize. Revisit and reinforce the strategy that you have previously taught.

DURING STUDENT VISUALIZATION

- Tell students that today, you will be trying something a little different.

- Ask the students to close their eyes as you read the poem aloud and to make pictures and movies in their minds as you read.

AFTER STUDENT VISUALIZATION

- Ask students to describe what they saw in their mind's eye.

- Ask students questions to determine their ability to visualize and apply the strategy.

- Provide materials for students so they can reproduce what they saw in their mind's eye using both words and pictures.

For further information, see: Tierney, R.J. & Readence, J.E. (2005). *Reading strategies and practices: A compendium*, 6th ed. Boston, MA: Pearson.

Zimmerman, S. & Hutchins, C. (2001). *Seven keys to comprehension: How to help your kids read and get it!* New York: Three Rivers Press.

Vocabulary Work

Vocabulary work helps students explore words, word meanings, and effective use of words. Depending on the strategy selected, students have opportunities to organize information related to a specific word, play with words and word meaning, use the words in oral language situations and conversations, and develop working definitions of words in both written and oral form.

Definition Maps

Students are asked to develop and create working definitions for words that are contextually appropriate. Students are asked to describe the word, what it is like, provide an example, and provide a comparison. As an extension, they should try to use the word in a sentence. Graphic organizers can be used to organize information to build definitions of words and concepts of definition.

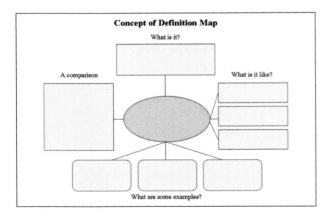

Vocabulary Storms

Vocabulary storms are similar to brainstorming and concept of definition maps. Through brainstorming, students and teachers respond to the following:

What is the word?
What does the word mean?
Write a synonym or provide an example.
Use it in a sentence.
Draw a picture or a diagram of the word.
Name three people who would use this word.
Using it as a root word, how many other words can you form?

Definition Challenge
(Adapted from Balderdash™)

Players develop plausible definitions for words and then attempt to persuade their peers that their definition is the real definition. Teachers can create a classroom version of the game by developing lists of thematic, literature-based, or content oriented words that can be used in the game. Each list should have five words. The words are written and numbered on the front of a card with the real definitions on the back. In each round, a player is chosen to lead. The "leader" selects a card and rolls the die; the number rolled will be the word selected. If a six is rolled, the leader can select any of the five words. The leader reads the word aloud to the rest of the students. Each student develops a plausible definition of the word, in an effort to bluff the other players. As the students create their definitions, the leader copies the real definition and collates it with the players' definitions. The leader then reads aloud all definitions. Each student chooses the definition they think is correct. After each player has guessed, the leader reveals the true definition. Students win two points for guessing correctly, one point for each vote they received.

Dictionary Barrier Game

Teachers create thematic, literature-based, or content oriented dictionaries (with real definitions). One student sits behind a screen with the dictionary, picks a word at random, and reads the definition and perhaps its part of speech. The opponent must guess the word. If correct, 10 points are awarded. If wrong, the first letter of the word is given and the second definition read. A correct answer at this point is worth five points. Play proceeds in this fashion until all letters and definitions have been provided, ultimately resulting in a score of zero if the word is not guessed.

Picture This!
(Adapted from Pictionary™)

A great word guessing game that taps into the visual representation of words. Students choose a word from a list of five (they do this by rolling the die). Teachers can create a classroom version of the game by developing lists of thematic, literature-based, or content oriented words that the students can then use as part of the game. Students have up to one minute to sketch a drawing of the word for their classmates. If the word is guessed within the one minute period, the team is awarded a point. If the word is not guessed, then the other team can guess the word and if right, gain a point.

Word Categories
(Adapted from Scattergories™)

Students are asked to think of and develop a list of words in various categories. This is a great activity to find out the words students know about a given theme before teaching and after teaching. Depending on the complexity desired, teachers can ask students to brainstorm only words that begin with a given letter or they can ask students to brainstorm words that use letters from a specific phrase or word. If trying to assess content area vocabulary, it is preferable to leave the task more open-ended.

BEFORE TEACHING
- Provide students with a global theme. Explain that they will have a given period of time to list as many words as they can think of that relate to that theme. This can be done individually, with a partner, or in small groups.

- When time is up, ask one individual or group to read their list of words. Students or groups of students must listen attentively and cross off any duplicate words. The next group is asked to read the words left on their list, and so on.

Each group is awarded a point for each word that no other group has.

AFTER TEACHING
- Provide students with 25 to 30 words from the unit. Individually, with a partner, or in small groups, ask students to review the meaning of the words and sort them into four or five categories (these can be teacher provided, student developed, or any combination thereof). There may be words that students are unable to categorize. These should be marked and set aside for further inquiry.

- A reporter from each group reads the categories and words to the rest of the class, justifying, analyzing, and debating placement as required. The key is that all students must be able to justify their sorting and categorization of words (this requires that they understand the words and how to use them appropriately).

- Provide time for students to revisit words not sorted or categorized.

Category Framework

Sort a list of content-oriented words into four categories using a structured framework. Highlight the words you are unsure of; you will be able to revisit these words and categorize them later. Keep in mind that some words may fit in more than one category. The key is that you must be able to justify your sorting and categorization.

Variation

To check students' global awareness of familiar vocabulary, a truer game of Scattergories™ might

Vocabulary	Geographical Feature	People or Places
	Wildlife	Weather

be used. In this game, teachers select a category and a letter of the alphabet. For example, colours that begin with "p." Students then brainstorm as many colours as they can think of that begin with "p." They are encouraged to be creative and to think of as many original colours as possible (for example, pig pink, periwinkle blue, poppy red).

Word Splashes

"Splash" refers to random arrangements of key words around a curriculum topic. Word splashes are natural extensions of predicting, brainstorming, making connections, and activating prior knowledge.

Variation 1: Teacher-Generated Word Splash

Word splashes, generated by teachers, act as scaffolding for a text or concept that may or may not be accessible to all students or might have unfamiliar content. Students examine the words posted randomly and are asked to construct meaning from seemingly unrelated words.

Topic: Word Solving

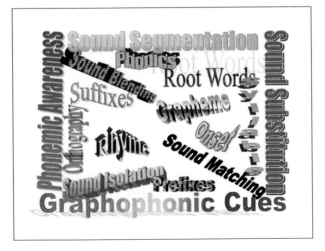

Variation 2: Engaging Word Splash

Students are asked to use as many words as possible to create a plausible story or scenario. This is usually limited to five minutes. Students can then share their writing with a partner or small group. Once the sharing has taken place, students may then be asked to find and underline the splash words in a text, make connections, and explore word meanings.

Variation 3: The Organized Word Splash

Teachers ask students to order sequentially or categorize the words that they generated in a word splash. Students do this in an appropriate written format (for example, graphic organizer).

Category: Phonemic awareness

Variation 4: The Directed Word Splash

Students are encouraged to use the words to answer a question asked by the teacher. For example, *How would these terms be applicable in a comprehensive word study program?*

Variation 5: Student-Generated Word Splash

Students are asked to brainstorm as many words as they can on a given topic. All words are valued, but students must explain the connection they are making when they add a word. Students then present their word splashes to the large group. The student reviews these words with the class, asking individual students to use the word in a sentence, either in written or oral form. Teachers can also explore the meaning of words and the association a word has with the given topic or concept. Word splashes can serve as anticipation guides as students explore and discover whether their associations and connections with the words need to be clarified, revised, or set aside.

For further information, see: Turning Points – Transforming Middle Schools (http://www.turningpts.org/pdf/Word_splash2.doc)

Word Walls

A word wall is not simply a display of words, but a systematically organized collection of words that are useful tools for students as they read, write, and emerge into full literacy. The primary purposes of word walls (Wagstaff, 1999) are to:

- support the teaching of important general principles about words and how they work
- promote independence on the part of young students as they work with words in writing and reading
- provide a visual map to help children remember connections between words and the characteristics that will help them form categories
- develop a growing core of words that become part of a reading and writing vocabulary

The following are some general guidelines for creating and using word walls:

- Make words accessible by putting them where every student can see them. They should be written in large black letters, with a variety of background colours used to distinguish easily confused words.
- Be selective about the words that go on the word wall. Try to include words that children use most commonly in their reading and writing. Words should be added gradually—five words per week.
- Provide enough practice so that words are read and spelled automatically, and ensure that when the words on the word wall are used in children's daily writing that they are always spelled correctly.
- Use the word wall daily to practise words incorporating a variety of review and multi-sensory activities such as chanting, snapping, cheering, clapping, tracing, word guessing games, as well as writing.

SELECTED WORD WALL ACTIVITIES

I Spy...

The teacher or student thinks of a word on the word wall and provides five clues that increasingly support students as they guess the word.

It's one of the words on the word wall.

It has four letters.

It begins with the same letter pattern as...

It rhymes with pen.

It begins the sentence "_____ will the bell ring?"

Word Wall Bingo

The teacher distributes bingo grids to students and asks each one to choose a word. Students write the words wherever they choose on each other's, card, setting aside one free space. Once cards are filled, play Bingo. Play for one line, two lines, four corners, Xs, etc. Once students have become accustomed to their own cards, have them swap with a peer.

Rhyme with the Word Wall

Teachers choose words from the word wall and ask students to spell words that rhyme. For example, for the rhyming word "be," students should be able to spell, "me," "see," "tree," "three."

Word Sorts

Teachers provide students with a variety of sorting rules (for example, number of letters, number of syllables, blends, onsets, rimes). Students choose a sorting rule and organize and classify words according to the rule.

For further information, see:

Cunningham, P.M. (1995) *Phonics they use*. New York: HarperCollins.

Fountas, I.C. & Pinnell, G.S. (1998). *Word matters*. Portsmouth, NH: Heinemann.

Wagstaff, J.M. (1999). *Teaching reading and writing with word walls*. New York: Scholastic.

EXtremely Engaging Ways to Teach Story Elements and Respond to Text

Traditional approaches to teaching story elements focus on students' understanding of narrative elements through literal examination of the text, often asking questions such as *What is the setting? Who are the characters? What is the problem? What is the solution?* Response-based approaches focus on student engagement and construction of meaning through interaction with texts, other readers, and classroom contexts. Students respond to texts by reflecting on their own emotions, attitudes, beliefs, interests, and personal experience, and then relating these to the text. Strategies for aesthetic reading include visualizing, predicting, engaging, empathizing, elaborating, noticing opposites, monitoring, connecting to life, evaluating, and analyzing. Students are encouraged to make individual and unique connections to the text, which reflect their literary experiences, their metacognitive awareness, and their links to story concepts.

BEFORE READING

Set a purpose for reading using anticipation guides, questionnaires, book boxes, book bits, contrast charts, semantic maps, KWL charts, preview-predict-confirm charts.

DURING READING

Interrogate and/or discuss the text through the use of: literature circles, literature maps, character maps, character webs, character perspective charts, journals, feelings charts, contrast charts.

DURING AND AFTER READING

Sustain great talk about great literature through: literature circles/instructional conversations, interviews, reading conferences/workshops, think alouds, read arounds, book talks, whole class meetings, panel discussions, debates, and co-operative group jigsaws.

AFTER READING

Respond, explore, and extend through the use of: lists, timelines, jot notes, questions, graphs, diagrams, family trees paragraphs, predictions, reports, maps, letters, webs, reactions, articles, charts, diaries, plot lines, posters, sketches, critiques, documentaries, illustrations, journal entries, dialogue journals, buddy journals, double-entry journals, writing in role, newspaper reports, story sequels, creative writing, advertisements.

Responding through the Arts

Visual Arts: story illustrations, water colour paintings, papier mâché, drawings, collage, 3-D models, dioramas, murals, photography

Music: song lyrics, medleys, singing, listening to music, selecting music to accompany reading

Dance: improvisational dance, creative movement, choreography

Drama: mime, tableaux, improvisation, role play, scripted stories, readers' theatre, choral reading

Multimedia: animation, special effects, film production

Culmination/Sharing of Novel/Literature Study

Novel exhibition or museum display, readers' circle, book talks, literary conversations

For further information, see:

Cornett, C.E. & Smithrim, K.L. (2001). *The arts as meaning makers: Integrating literature and the arts through the curriculum.* Toronto, ON: Prentice Hall.

Luongo Orlando, K. (2001) *A project approach to language learning.* Markham, ON: Pembroke Publishers.

Yopp, R.H. & Yopp, H.K. (2001). *Literature-based reading activities.* Needham Heights, MA: Allyn & Bacon.

Yearn to Read

Yearning to read refers to the motivation and self-confidence that readers develop that keeps them going and instils in them a desire to "get lost in a book." What teachers do to motivate readers represents a balance of internal and external sources of motivation. Although external motivators often spur readers on (for example, incentive programs with goal setting and rewards), it is important to note that external sources of motivation will not always predominate. Most of us can list external sources of motivation easily—grades, tangible rewards, and "because the teacher said so", but the internal sources of motivation remain a little more elusive. How can we arouse natural curiosity in our readers and instil in them a desire to learn more? How can we empower them and build that sense of "I can do it!" How can we help them to become aesthetically involved and enjoy literary texts for the pure love of reading? And lastly, how can you challenge and dare them to become more active and responsible readers?

Motivation and engagement are not conditions that simply appear in a classroom. They require careful consideration and thought on the part of the teacher.

Classroom contexts can promote engaged reading. Teachers create contexts for engagement when they provide prominent knowledge goals, real-world connections to reading, meaningful choices about what, when, and how to read, and interesting texts that are familiar, vivid, important, and relevant. Teachers can further engagement by teaching reading strategies. A coherent classroom fuses these qualities.

(Guthrie, 2001, retrieved December 29, 2005, from http://www.readingonline.org/)

When teachers structure the classroom context before, during, and after reading, they increase the likelihood that students will become internally motivated and actively engaged, ultimately yearning to read!

BEFORE READING

- Activate students' prior knowledge, connecting texts to students' real-world experiences.
- Scaffold tricky vocabulary to build in success points and the sense of self as reader.
- Establish specific and explicit purposes for reading.

- Set goals for reading.
- Ensure that there is a wide variety of texts that reflect students' interests, reading levels, dominant intelligences, learning styles.
- Provide students with authentic and legitimate choices.
- Teach about book selection and how to judge if books are too hard, too easy, or just right.

DURING READING

- Provide students with strategies that allow them to monitor their comprehension and keep track of their purposes for reading. This chapter provides a range of comprehension strategies that will engage students in active sense-making instead of passive reception of text and information.
- Provide just enough support to ensure that students are successful and do not experience unnecessary frustration.
- Praise and reward effective reading behaviour and effort.

AFTER READING

- Link assessment and instruction in meaningful, authentic, and relevant ways.
- Provide students with opportunities to assess their own comprehension of text.

- Provide students with opportunities to collaborate and engage in talk about great literature.
- Plan activities that allow students to extend, explore, and elaborate on ideas from the text in a variety of traditional, creative, and non-traditional ways.

For further information, see: Guthrie, J.T. (2001). Contexts for engagement and motivation in reading. *Reading Online*, 4(8).

Zeroing in on Reading Strategies

Not only do teachers need to zero in on reading strategies to teach students, but students need to have full access to the reading strategies available to them when they encounter tricky words. They need to be able to apply these strategies independently, flexibly, appropriately, and quickly in ways that will not interfere with comprehension or sense-making.

Post these strategies in the classroom for quick reference or glue them to the front of their reader response journal. Another fun way to remind students of the strategies is to accompany the strategies with music or rhythm and use these texts for shared and choral reading.

Moving On

In this chapter, we have presented many strategies and techniques that lifelong literacy teachers use as part of a comprehensive literacy program. We opened the chapter with a statement that not all techniques and strategies will work with all students and that the key to effective strategy use is flexibility. We underscored the importance of using a consistent procedure for strategy instruction that moves along the continuum of support from teacher modelling to student independence. Pay particular attention to those strategies that underscore the importance of students' motivation to read. How do the strategies and techniques in this chapter encourage students in their quest to "yearn to read"? How can we take what we know about "yearning to read" and transfer it into "yearning to write"?

In the next chapter, we continue our journey through literacy, exploring the strong connections between reading and writing and how one rarely occurs without the other. Also, we examine the theoretical development of writers as they learn to write, write to learn, write to understand, and write to re-vision and transform their own realities.

I hear and I forget. I see and I remember. I do and I understand
—Confucius

LIT-FOLIO UPDATE

As you conclude this chapter, your lit-folio should have concrete evidence of your application of a variety of strategies. In some cases, you will have personally tried these strategies (QAR, SQ3R), and in other cases, you will have used the strategies or techniques with students. Lesson plans, pictures, work samples, reflections, and unit overviews, are all considered appropriate evidence of awareness, knowledge, skill, and value gained as a result of this chapter. Use a reflective journal entry to summarize your experience with these strategies and techniques. How do they support student development? How do they motivate students to "yearn to read" and thus "yearn to write"?

LIT-FOLIO TIP

Many of our students found that it was useful to keep track of strategies that they had used as well as their own tips for success. When they returned to discuss their strategy use, they were able to problem-solve and troubleshoot. As well, they were able to talk about some of the intricacies of strategy instruction in conversation with colleagues, parents, during a job interview.

Resources to Support Your Learning

Professional Resources

Journals: *The Reading Teacher*, International Reading Association; *Language Arts*, National Council of Teachers of English

❀ Cornett, C.E. & Smithrim, K.L. (2001). *The arts as meaning makers: Integrating literature and the arts through the curriculum.* Toronto, ON: Prentice Hall.

❀ Harvey, S. (1998) *Non-fiction matters: Reading, writing and research in Grades 3-8.* Markham, ON: Pembroke Publishers.

❀ Harvey, S., & Goudvis, A. (2000). *Strategies that work: Teaching comprehension to enhance understanding.* Markham, ON: Pembroke, Publishers.

Keene, E.O., & Zimmerman, S. (1997). *Mosaic of thought: Teaching comprehension in a reader's workshop.* Portsmouth, NH: Heinemann.

McLaughlin, M. (2003). *Guided comprehension in the primary grades.* Newark, DE: International Reading Association.

McLaughlin, M., & Allen, M.B. (2002). *Guided comprehension in action: Lessons for Grades 3-8.* Newark, DE: International Reading Association.

❀ Schwartz, S. & Bone, M. (1995). *Retelling, relating, reflecting: Beyond the 3 Rs.* Portsmouth, NH: Heinemann.

Tierney, R.J. & Readence, J.E. (2005). *Reading strategies and practices: A compendium,* 6th ed. Boston: Pearson.

Vacca, R.T., Vacca, J.L., & Begoray, D.L. (2005). *Content area reading: Literacy and learning across the curriculum.* Toronto, ON: Pearson.

Weaver, C. (1996). *Teaching grammar in context.* Portsmouth, NH: Boynton/Cook.

Zimmerman, S. & Hutchins, C. (2001) *Seven keys to comprehension: How to help your kids read and get it!* New York, NY: Three Rivers Press.

Websites

International Reading Association Lesson Plan website: http://www.readwritethink.org

Saskatoon Public Schools – Instructional Strategies Online: http://olc.spsd.sk.ca/

Ontario's Learning Foundations: E-Workshop for Teachers: http://www.eworkshop.on.ca/

11
Teaching and Learning Writing

> Children want to write. They want to write the first day they attend school. This is no accident. Before they went to school they marked up walls, pavements, newspapers with crayons, chalk, pens, or pencils, anything that makes a mark. The child's marks say, "I am."
>
> *—Donald Graves*

key terms

approximation
expressive writing
modelled writing
poetic writing
praise-question-polish
quick writes
reading-writing connections
reciprocity
responding
transactional writing

questions to guide your learning

By the end of this chapter, you should understand the key terms and be able to answer the following questions:

- What is writing?
- What are some of its uses?
- What are some different forms of writing?
- How do writing abilities emerge and develop?
- What are the connections between reading and writing, and between learning how to read and how to write?
- How can you promote those connections with your students?
- How can you show your students what good writers do?

Looking Back, Looking Ahead

In Chapter 8 and Chapter 9, we described reading as a puzzle to be solved by readers and teachers in a variety of contexts for a variety of purposes. We reminded you of the complexities involved in reading, the individuality of each reader, and the nature of communication in the reading process. We considered both theory and practice in some detail to demonstrate what is currently known about how reading abilities develop and how best to foster that development through the methods and strategies that you use to help our students solve the puzzle and make sense of words, texts, and the world. In Chapter 10, we provided a catalogue of our favourite strategies for classroom practice.

This chapter provides a general overview of theories and research that help to inform you as you try to determine what is truly important so that you can provide excellent instruction in writing. In order to be fully informed about the types of practices you should use in your classroom to promote the development of writing abilities, you must first understand how these abilities emerge and develop. One theoretical assumption in this chapter is that there exists a reciprocal relationship between learning how to write and learning how to read—an assumption with important consequences for instructional decision-making. It means, for example, that writing is not taught in isolation from reading. It also

literacy
notebook
11.1

STOP, THINK, AND WRITE

Your challenge in this chapter is to identify clearly what you believe is most important to know about what writing is, what its functions are, how writing development takes place, and what your goals are in terms of student growth and improvement. You will be asked at the end of the chapter to create a priority list of key classroom approaches and goals.

■ What is writing?

■ What is writing used for?

■ What are some of the factors that determine or influence the development of writing abilities?

■ What is your role in fostering the development of writing?

■ How are reading and writing connected?

Return to these initial thoughts at the end of the chapter, and record any changes in your thinking.

means that expert modelling is a key instructional strategy, just as it is with oral language and reading. This expert modelling includes demonstrating "what good writers do," using rich models from literature and everyday life, explicit modelling of the processes of writing, and arranging high-quality interactions between teacher and students.

This chapter is concerned with understanding the forms and functions of writing and how the abilities and skills to communicate effectively through written language develop. We look at the emergent writing of early readers/writers, their understanding of the functions of writing, and how developing writers gain increasing control over the processes of writing. We consider the vital importance of how you respond to children's writing and how you become an expert role model. A more detailed treatment of the assessment of writing follows in Chapter 12.

What Is Important for Teachers to Know about Writing?

WHAT IS WRITING?

Your beliefs about what writing is and what its purposes are shape your instructional practices. What do young children think writing is? Why do they write? What do they think about the purposes or functions of written language? These are all relevant questions to ask yourself and your students!

Think about a young child's developing concepts about print evident in their early attempts at reading and writing: the concept that the print carries the message, where to start, which way to go, and the concepts of letter, word, sentence, first and last, and so on (see Figure 4.5). Now think of a very young Junior Kindergarten child: what does she think the business of writing is all about?

Just as you can observe children's behaviour to determine which concepts about print they have, you can conduct informal observations or gather information through conversations during a writing conference to determine how they are conceptualizing what writing is and what it is for. You might ask questions such as:

A young child's developing concepts about print are evident in early attempts at writing.

- Is she comfortable with the marker in her hand?

- Does she think there is a difference between writing and drawing?

- Does she understand that writers pick letters deliberately so readers can understand the words?

- Is she a risk taker? Does she attempt new spellings?

- Does she realize that there are different kinds of writing? Does she try any of these genres or forms?

- Does she understand why you have invited her to write?

- Does she realize that writing is meant to be read by others?

(Harwayne, 2001, p. 167)

We might assume that writing involves representing one's "thoughts and ideas" in written (symbolic) form (see Indrisano & Paratore, 2005, p. 2, for example). Surely it is much more than this. Consider that a very young child's first scribbled writing may be telling a personal story to accompany a painting, composing a song about a pet, making a grocery list for a shopping trip, or writing a speeding ticket while playing police officer. Consider children's possible interactions with adults or peers in these instances: they may expect that their writing will be acted upon or that you will participate in their dramatic play. However, in every case, it is expected that you take their written words seriously, as real-world events. As Donald Graves (1983) noted, they are saying "I am," (p. 3) and as Frank Smith (1988) noted, they are saying "I am part of the literacy club."

Writing involves complex social, emotional, and cognitive aspects.

Consider your own attempts as mature writers to capture an elusive emotion or mood by writing a poem. Can this creative process be reduced to "representing our thoughts and ideas" in written form, or is it a much more complex endeavour? Writing a poem often involves revisiting scenes and reliving emotions, searching for words and phrases, playing with their order and placement, reading and re-reading, often aloud, for the rhythms and cadences we capture, often to our own surprise. From the simple transaction involved in writing a grocery list to the emotive forms of the poetic and expressive modes, writing involves complex social, emotional, and cognitive aspects. Those aspects determine the writer's purpose and intended audience, the form and the type of response expected or desired (see Figure 8.7).

The extent to which you keep in mind this complexity of the forms and functions of writing has significant repercussions on how you respond to your student writers as individuals—from their very early attempts to their more sophisticated endeavours.

This emphasis on the importance of response from a real reader—in this case the teacher—underscores the strong interconnections between writing and reading. Reading and writing are now typically taught together. This was not always the case. In the past, many educators believed that students had to learn to read before they could learn to write. Current research clearly shows that reading and writing abilities develop concurrently and reciprocally (Clay, 1975, 1998; Close, Hull, & Langer, 2005). Because learning to read and learning to write are so closely interwoven, our in-depth look into reading and literacy learning theories in Chapter 8 presents many principles that carry over into how children learn to write. Furthermore, the principles outlined in Chapter 4 on the transition from oral language learning to literacy apply to the processes involved in learning how to write. The following is an abbreviated overview of seven of the key principles. This provides the theoretical background to the remainder of the chapter, which will focus on how children emerge and develop as writers within the contexts of reading/writing instruction and learning experiences; on the importance of teacher modelling and student attempts through approximation; and on the crucial role of the teachers' responses to children's writing as interactional participants and expert models.

Writing and Reading: Principles of Literacy Learning Applicable to Learning How to Write and to Read

1. *Writing develops along a continuum.*

Early language use can be viewed as "developing" along a continuum, without necessarily assuming that this occurs in a rigid, stage-by-stage progression. Language is learned *in use*, in social interactions with peers, parents, teachers, family members, and community members.

Writing similarly develops along a continuum, but not necessarily in a predictable sequence. Figure 11.1 traces commonly observed writing behaviours at different phases in development.

2. *Oral language and writing development are related.*

Language structures and concepts acquired in oral language are likely to be transferred into reading and writing in the classroom. Spoken and written language seem to use the same thought processes (Vygotsky, 1979); the more developed children's talking and listening abilities are,

FIGURE 11.1 A Continuum of Writing Development

Opportunities to talk and discuss writing are needed at all stages.

Phase	Developing Writing Characteristics	Concepts about Print	Writing Behaviours and Attitudes	Needs as a Writer
Emergent	• Drawing as writing, scribbled writing	• Has the concept of using signs to convey a message. • Will say that scribbles tell about a picture. • Has some directionality.	• Uses drawing and scribbling to gain control over writing instruments and to imitate other writers.	• Opportunities to write during play • Phonemic awareness activities (songs, chants, rhyming games) • Encouragement • Explicit teaching of concepts about print
Emergent and Early	• Letter-like units, non-phonetic letter strings, copying from environmental print • Use of some letter names ('kt' for 'cat') • Use of some semi-phonetic spelling	• Able to explain a copied message; may not be accurate at first (emergent), but increases gradually in accuracy (early). • Has the concept of words and letters. • Has some sound symbol correspondence.	• Uses sentence patterns (for example, "I like..."). • Rehearses writing out loud and re-reads messages aloud. • Writes mostly for self, not for an audience. • Prefers writing something new rather than revising.	• Phonics and spelling patterns in context • Explicit instruction on concepts about print • To write for a variety of purposes and audiences • Modelled, shared, and interactive writing

FIGURE 11.1 A Continuum of Writing Development (continued)

Phase	Developing Writing Characteristics	Concepts about Print	Writing Behaviours and Attitudes	Needs as a Writer
Early and Transitional	• Noticing "within-word'" patterns such as vowels and silent letters ("cote" for coat) • Semi-phonetic and phonetic spelling • Experiments with punctuation	• Able to record own ideas and read them back accurately. • Has concept of sentences and punctuation.	• Beginning to write for an audience. • More interested in final products. • Willing to spend time revising and editing. • Concern for accuracy may result in apparent decrease in creativity (using only known words).	• Specific instruction on vowel-consonant patterns • How to generate and expand new topics • How to use a variety of strong verbs and adjectives; and become confident with conventions
Transitional and Self-Extending	• Syllable juncture patterns not quite mastered ("shoping" for shopping) • Some phonetic and many conventional spellings • Increased accuracy of punctuation and other conventions of writing	• Able to compose messages and ideas successfully. • Has increasing awareness of purposes of writing and textual forms.	• May copy styles of favourite authors • Increased concern with conventions • Topics tend to be "too big" • Writing may include too many details, run-on dialogue, and may not be structured or sequenced clearly	• Instruction in revising and editing; rules for adding word endings; summarizing; writing dialogue; and structuring a piece using a story map or other graphic organizer • Literary models and teacher modelling

FIGURE 11.1 A Continuum of Writing Development (continued)

Phase	Developing Writing Characteristics	Concepts about Print	Writing Behaviours and Attitudes	Needs as a Writer
Self-Extending and Independent	• "Derivational constancy" ("priviledge") conventional spelling, punctuation, grammar • Inaccuracies may result from risk-taking with unfamiliar vocabulary and usage	• Has increasing control over a variety of forms of writing for a wide range of purposes.	• Begins to: apply revising and editing skills automatically; develop own writing style and voice; write for specific audiences for definite purposes; and use deliberately chosen forms. • Writes increasingly sophisticated stories and informational pieces.	• Guided choice: writing on topics of interest • Instruction on editing and revising and spelling derivations • Instruction on sentence combining and paragraph formation • Opportunities to share writing with peers • Sophisticated models of a range of genres

the better they are able to compose when writing and to comprehend when reading.

The success of early writers depends heavily on their working vocabulary, their implicit understanding of the grammatical structures of language, and their sense of having something to say, that is, their understanding of how writing is "talk put into print."

3. *Emergent writers need to understand concepts about print.*

These are the key concepts about print (Clay, 1993) that emerging readers and writers must understand in order to experience success in learning how to read and write (see Figure 4.5). These include the concept that print carries the message, the concept of directionality and one-to-one matching, and the concepts of a letter, a word, and a sentence.

The same concepts that children need to know when reading—about where to start, which way to go, how each word we say is separated when printed on the page, and so on—are also needed when writing. Knowing the correct technical terms is essential in order to understand the teacher's explicit instruction.

4. *The functions of oral language parallel the functions of writing.*

There are distinct and recognizable "functions" of oral language and "categories of talk" as it is used in the real world (Halliday, 1973; see Figure 4.7).

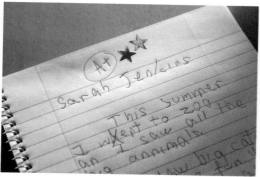

In expressive writing, the writer expresses personal thoughts and feelings.

These functions and categories closely parallel the forms and functions of print, which include concepts about text and the way texts are organized. Concepts about text include awareness of functions of language and print, forms of text, genres, authors, and expository text structures.

Each form, genre, and sometimes author, has its own rules or corresponding concepts that readers must learn how to use in order to comprehend texts of various kinds and writers have to use to construct their own varieties of texts.

The three main modes of writing available to the writer are **expressive writing**, **poetic writing**, and expository or **transactional writing** (see Figure 11.2). As young readers/writers become familiar with these ways of thinking about text, they are able to formulate and create their own texts, and concurrently develop a better understanding of how authors put their ideas together in meaningful ways.

Refining these broad categories further, we can identify more specific forms or genres, which can in turn be organized in various formats using assorted organizational features and visual representations appropriate to the writers' purposes and their intended audiences. See Figure 8.7 as the forms and functions of print are vital for the effective and comprehensive instruction of writing. A fully developed writer (and reader) should have a full command over all forms and functions, from poems and stories to reports and instructions, just as a developed speaker requires command over the many functions of oral language.

5. *Our conceptions of reading and writing as processes are closely connected.*

Reading is a transactional process among reader, text, author, and community of learners.

Writing is a similarly transactional process, highlighting the relationships between writers (the authors) and readers (the audience).

FIGURE 11.2 Three Modes of Writing

Expressive
- reveals the nature of the person
- expresses self; verbalizes consciousness
- includes free flow of ideas and feeling
- often sounds like talk

Form: personal expression
Examples: personal narratives, diary/journal entries, inventories

Poetic
- verbal constructs fashioned in a particular way to make a pattern
- used as an art medium, for example, poems or plays performed

Forms: narrative, poetic
Examples: stories, plays, songs, poems, word play

Transactional
- concerned with getting things done
- involves giving information or instructions
- often attempts to persuade and advise others

Forms: descriptive, argumentative, expository
Examples: information essays, reports, lists, instructions, recipes, letters, notes, messages

---

Reading is a matter of developing strategies and making connections. The development of writing abilities also requires strategic activity, including making of connections. Figure 11.3, which builds on Figure 8.3, shows the parallel between writing and reading strategies.

6. *Reading and writing involve various roles.*

When readers learn how to make sense of text—how to "solve the reading puzzle"—they can be viewed as orchestrating four interconnected, complex roles: word-solvers, concept builders, meaning-makers, and architects (see Figure 8.4). These same roles must be coordinated as young writers try to compose their own text.

1. As word-solvers, writers must "solve" words using a variety of strategies, from letter/sound analysis to drawing on a repertoire of automatically known vocabulary (learned through repeated writing and reading in various contexts).

2. As concept builders, writers use a variety of forms to express ideas, thoughts, and feelings, to convey information, and to record imaginative creations. They use appropriate language conventions and

FIGURE 11.3 Menu of Writing Strategies

Emergent Writers	Early Writers	Transitional Writers	Fluent Writers
• Think about the message or story to be written. • Use writing to accompany, explain, and enhance own pictures and drawings. • Track print. • Use knowledge of patterns. • Use knowledge of visual (graphophonic) cues (beginning and ending letters). • Analyze words from beginning to end, recording letters to match sounds.	• Think about the message or story. • Use writing to express themselves, to create imaginative stories, to record information. • Use spelling patterns. • Monitor and self correct. • Use meaning, structure, and visual (graphophonic) cues together. • Put words together into phrases (fluency). • Re-read own writing for meaning.	• Think about the story: use the think aloud strategy. • Use writing to express themselves, to create imaginative stories, and to record information. • Make a story map to plan a story. • Use a before and after chart. • Retell chapters in writing. • Re-read to clarify meanings. • Choose appropriate genre and format to express ideas, feelings, information.	• Set purposes for writing. • Use writing to express themselves, to create imaginative stories and to record information. • Use text features to organize and to express ideas. • Research, take notes, make data charts. • Write to deepen understanding of stories, factual texts, and poetry. • Create webs and charts (for example, KWL). • Strategy recursively taught at all levels: retell, relate, reflect orally and in writing. • Choose appropriate genre and format to express ideas, feelings, information.

syntax learned through oral language and reading texts. They are developing a metacognitive awareness of author's voice and how to write with a specific audience in mind.

3. As meaning-makers, writers establish purposes for writing and self-monitor and correct their writing with readers in mind.

4. As architects, writers engage in transactions between themselves and their readers, other authors and other texts, and the reading/writing community. They understand writing as a process that involves building and creating through drafting, revising, editing, and sometimes publishing. They write to inform and entertain. They

recognize their use of point of view and its effect on the reader. They engage in critical thinking throughout the entire writing process.

The ultimate orchestration of these four roles occurs when one writes like a reader and reads like a writer. For the author, this entails writing with the reader in mind as one reads and re-reads one's own writing.

7. *The conditions required for learning to read and write are similar to those for learning to talk.*

Two assumptions made by Cambourne (1988) reveal the thinking that encourages effective teachers of literacy to draw on their knowledge of how children learn to speak for powerful clues as to how they might more efficiently and, less agonizingly for many, learn to read and write.

1. "The oral and written forms of language are only superficially different" (p. 28).

   They are different in important ways, but not at the deep levels that affect how we learn them: "The same neural processes are involved, using the same neural machinery" (p. 29). Thus, provided the conditions of learning are the same for learning oral and written language, each should be able to be learned in much the same way.

2. "Learning to talk is a stunning intellectual achievement" (p. 30).

   Once we identify the conditions for oral language learning, we can determine whether they are applicable to the teaching and learning of literacy.

   Note: The key conditions of literacy learning (Cambourne, 1988, 1995) are outlined in Figure 2.7 and Chapter 4 in the section Conditions for Language Learning.

The key conditions for literacy learning, based on how oral language is learned, provide a natural starting point when designing effective writing instruction.

HOW DO THESE PRINCIPLES INFLUENCE HOW WE TEACH WRITING?

While all of the aforementioned principles influence our teaching of writing in important ways, we would like to focus on the following three instructional dimensions of Cambourne's model as fundamental in the teaching of writing:

1. The value of *approximation* of writing behaviours as they occur along the learning continuum

2. The value of *response* in validating and encouraging student writing

3. The power of *modelling* or *demonstration* in the instruction of writing

Here, we recognize the central pedagogical question we articulated in Chapter 8, shifting the emphasis from this question: "How do I teach reading and writing?" to: "How do I teach my students to read and write?" To rephrase further, as you become aware of yourself as a model of good writing practices in your daily writers' workshop, the question becomes, "How do *I* teach my students to write, and to become better writers?"

One of the most powerful approaches to the teaching of writing is to consider your students as apprentices, modelling, guiding, and providing learning experiences for them as they become writers and authors. Do not forget the point made previously that you are also apprenticing them into a complex social practice. The three aspects of Cambourne's model when learning to write through apprenticeship—approximation, response, and modelling—are described in the following sections.

Learning to Write through Apprenticeship

Learning to be literate can be thought of as an intellectual apprenticeship.
—Gordon Wells

In Chapter 4, we thought about how children learn to speak, apparently so naturally and effortlessly, through real interactions with expert users of the language, and we saw how Cambourne made a strong case for using this way of learning as a model for literacy learning. It makes sense to apply this model to the teaching and learning of writing. Viewing your students as apprentices, you can create a picture of students and teachers working together as students learn from your expert demonstrations of how to write in various forms for a variety of purposes. Students can "give it a go" through approximation and experimenting and with your support and encouragement they will extend their learning.

The picture we have in mind is a vibrant writers' workshop—a place where young writers can learn to write by writing. Setting aside classroom time and resources for a writers' workshop has been advocated by many educators and researchers including Donald Graves (1983, 1994), Jerome Harste (1988), Lucy Calkins (1986, 1990 (with Harwayne)), Shelley Harwayne (1987 (with Calkins), 2001), and David Booth (1998, 2001). The details of writers' workshop will be discussed in Chapter 12. For now we would like to say, from our own teaching experience, that this is a way of teaching writing that works. One of the reasons it works is that it is based on sound pedagogical principles: it accommodates how children learn—regardless of learning style or linguistic and cultural backgrounds—and it provides a structure of support and response. The workshop provides opportunities for continued practice and higher-level learning in consistent blocks of time designated for writing. Furthermore, all of this learning takes place within an organized community where each member's contribution is valued. Approximation and response are two features of writers' workshop we shall consider next.

Approximation: Keeping in Mind the Way Young Children Learn

The point of surrounding students with wonderful literature and engaging them in conversations about what makes those pieces work, is for students to internalize the process and begin making connections on their own.
—Shelley Harwayne

Approximation can be described as "having a go." The student makes an attempt or repeated attempts and does not get it quite right at first. Successively more successful attempts occur, where each new effort builds on what has been learned in the previous action, and then modified through self-correction usually in interaction with an expert. The recursive nature of this way of learning is fundamental to all literacy learning. Approximations are one illustration of learning being constructed on what is already known and what is almost known or in one's **zone of proximal development** (Vygotsky, 1978).

In addition to providing demonstrations so that students can compare their performances and adapt them, your role is to foster the attitude that "mistakes are our friends in that they help us adjust and refine our knowledge, understandings, and skills so that next time we do better" (Cambourne, 2000/2001, p. 415).

The goal is that those approximations gradually approach the standard as closely as possible: this is where teachers and students work together toward achievable expectations. Take the case of a child who is progressing from phonetic to conventional spellings. We know this because both kinds of spelling appear in the child's writing. This is probably an appropriate time to discuss spelling approximations as temporary

zone of proximal development A learner's instructional range, which determines the level of support received from the teacher.

spellings (not "invented," a term commonly used, since the approximations are not made in the spirit of "anything goes," but are based on patterns known at this time). It is developmentally appropriate to provide them with standard models, and encourage them to study similarities and differences between their attempts and conventional spellings in order to stimulate them to make the transition.

During approximation, the student "has a go" at writing then modifies it through self-correction, usually with guidance from an expert.

When looking for evidence that children learn how to do many things through a process of approximating expert behaviour, we don't have to look much further than the early writing of young children. Provided they are given the resources and the opportunities, children will imitate what they see others do. They will mark papers and other surfaces with scribbles, "pretend" loops of writing, or mock letters, numbers, and symbols. When they move from drawings and begin to scribble in a linear direction, like sentences, or vertically, like lists, they are writing in gross approximation of adult writing, which they think their teachers and caregivers understand: "This is my grocery list," "This is a thank you card," "This says, 'My dog, Charlie,'" or the dreaded, "Read this. What does it say?" (Clay, 1975).

In the beginning, given the chance, children imitate their adult models, and produce various kinds of approximations of writing for real-world purposes to communicate matters they think are important. In the beginning, children enter willingly into an informal apprenticeship with adults and older children who can write, in order to follow their example and create similar written messages.

It is important to know two things about this arrangement—it helps you to understand how approximation works and you must be aware of how you respond in order to teach effectively.

When we understand how children begin the process of learning to write by approximation of the writing around them, we begin by recognizing how most children progress through phases from scribbles, to letter-like forms, to copying and writing strings of letters, to semi-phonetic (perhaps just the first letter/sound) and phonetic words in sentences with experimental punctuation, and finally to conventional spellings. Awareness of this progression is what is important, not the actual sequence but the realization that this is what children often, and apparently "naturally" do, given the opportunities, resources, and stimulation.

Because this progression takes place along a continuum (although it is highly variable from individual to individual) it makes little sense to expect a young learner who is at the stage of scribbling with strings of letters to move immediately to correct letter formation and conventional spellings. For example, a child in Kindergarten writes the following under a drawing of himself and his family and explains that it says: "This is me and my dog, and my brother, Jake, and my sister, Jessica."

Ds s ME n mi bG n mi BR JAKE n mi str Jss

Understanding approximation and how young children grow in writing capabilities, does it make sense to "correct" this child's writing by writing the dictated words in red pen on the child's composition? On the contrary, you should honour the child's success at expressing his message by responding in a genuine way, orally or in writing, about the message and the drawing, perhaps commenting on his dog (and writing the word in the correct way). Showing an interest in what matters to him validates his writing even further. You can ask the name of his dog, for instance, and perhaps encourage more writing.

Knowing that children will approximate our behaviour as writers, and knowing how they learn and grow gradually based upon their previous learning and what they are ready to learn next, you can provide just the right modelling at the right moment to encourage that new learning. This brings us to the second point about apprenticeship.

How you respond to children's early efforts at writing, that is, the quality of our interactions with them, is the key to whether they will feel encouraged to continue the endeavour, and whether and how new learning will occur. Asking just the right questions can lead them to try new strategies. Debbie Newton, a Nipissing B.Ed. student in 2005/2006, documented the growth of her daughter Hailey's emerging writing from September to February of her Junior Kindergarten year. She reports being impressed

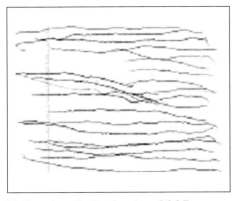

Hailey, Age 3, September 2005

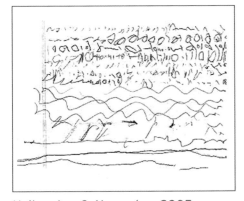

Hailey, Age 3, November, 2005

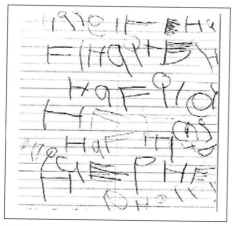

Hailey, Age 4, January 2006   Hailey, Age 4, February 2006

by the rapid growth in Hailey's knowledge of how to use print, and by her awareness of the role she played as Hailey's mother in that progress.

Response: How Can We Respond To Encourage Student Writers?

If you give your students plenty of opportunities to write about
things that matter to them, and you (and the rest of the class)
receive their writing with respect for the ideas they express,
you will have done an enormous amount of good.
—Charles Temple & Jean Gillet

Responding effectively means engaging in quality interactions with your young writers. Classroom size, the wide range of levels of writing ability, and heavy curricular demands mean that, realistically, a busy teacher has only limited amounts of time to spend with each student on an individual basis. These factors strengthen the importance and value of your individual interactions with your students.

Effective teaching of writing requires paying close attention to learners' approximations, repeating demonstrations, and showing clearer, more explicit models as needed when you observe that there are skills and strategies the children do not yet have under control. Thinking of this process in terms of Cambourne's model, this involves "drawing explicit attention to salient features of demonstrations/models that will help learners modify their approximations" (Cambourne, 2000/2001, p. 416).

One practical way to deal with the time constraints that threaten your ability to provide frequent feedback and response to individual stu-

STOP, THINK, AND WRITE

Look carefully at Hailey's writing samples.

■ What does she know about print in each sample?

For example, in sample 1 (September), she knows that print looks different from pictures or drawing, and she may know that it goes from left to right in lines.

In Sample 2 (November), she appears to be becoming aware of letter forms.

■ What does she know about print in samples 3 and 4?

■ What might you want to ask Hailey about her February writing? (She appears to be communicating something special with the circled sections).

■ What would your next step(s) be to encourage Hailey to continue her writing endeavours?

---

guided writing A method of writing instruction in which the teacher teaches small, temporary groups of students the strategies and skills they need at that particular time.

mini-lessons Brief, teacher-directed lessons designed to practise or review a particular strategy or skill, usually within the context of readers' or writers' workshops.

dents is to enable children to receive responses from other students. Responses from other students can be encouraged through specifically designated "peer conference" places and times, dialogue journals or reader response journals. Additionally, you should be constantly alert to small groups of writers with similar needs, and set up small, temporary **guided writing** groups for instruction through **mini-lessons**. The practical details are discussed in Chapter 12.

THE ART OF THE WRITING CONFERENCE

Along with small group instruction, writers' workshop requires a dependable way to track each writer's progress and a manageable way to set up effective one-on-one conferences on a regular basis.

Writing conferences typically include both oral and written responses. To be high-quality interactions, they must provide feedback that is both sensitive and stimulating. Many teachers like to begin a conference with specific praise and one or two interested questions focused on the content and ideas expressed by the writer, and follow this with specific teaching directed at what this writer needs at this moment, and is ready and willing to learn. The praise-question-polish response format shown in Theory into Practice 11.1 shows how to praise an especially good turn of phrase or a strong emotion effectively expressed, how to question a main idea, and how to demonstrate or reinforce a point of writer's craft (a stronger verb here, a comma there). These are three manageable points to cover in a conference that will be useful to the student and that you can quickly record for assessment and tracking.

Theory Into Practice/11.1

PRAISE-QUESTION-POLISH RESPONSE FORMAT

Praise-Question-Polish (P-Q-P) is a simple response format to follow during your writing conferences. While conferring with students, this sequence can also be modelled for students to follow when they are conferring with one another.

Praise: After reading or listening to a student's piece of writing, respond by stating what you thought was remarkable, attention-grabbing, or how the writing made you feel. Be specific with your praise: "Your use of the phrase 'galloped off in pursuit' makes the story really exciting here." Celebrate the particularly successful parts of the writing.

Question: Ask questions about the story, poem, or content itself, remembering to respect the students' ownership of their writing. Ask questions with a view to teaching, but in such a way that the students are encouraged to find their own solutions. If you show an interest in knowing more details about a topic—for the sake of clarity, or to help the writer complete the piece—the author is more likely to take on the task of revision willingly.

Polish: Ideally, ideas for polishing the piece will be the natural result of the conference questions, and will be evident to the student with a minimum of explicit suggestions from you. When making suggestions, ensure that the student is capable of following up on them. If not, model the skill and complete one or two examples with the student. For example, if a student has a dialogue between characters but no quotation marks, ask, "How can we make this easier to read? Let's see how it's done by published authors." Then explicitly show the line breaks and punctuation, pointing out how it helps the reader to know who is talking.

Another possible focus for a writing conference is an assessment conversation where students are invited to discuss areas they have improved upon in their overall writing progress. Kaya assesses her writing progress in the following way at the end of Grade 3:

> *I can write more details, more complete sentences, put more interesting things in my stories, and make people in my writing funny and interesting. I have more characters in my stories too. I can also spell better and use more capitals and punctuation.*

> (Fu & Lamme, 2002, p. 241)

The crucial aspect of effective response to or feedback on student writing is your role of modelling or demonstrating concepts, skills, and the writer's craft, based on the needs you identified during the conference.

STOP, THINK, AND WRITE

Think back to some of your experiences as a writer in an elementary or secondary classroom.

■ Do a five-minute quick write about one unpleasant experience and about a positive experience. How do these experiences inform your teaching?

Peer conferences enable students to receive from other students.

Modelling or Demonstration: Showing Writers How It's Done

1. You can show students excellent literary models during read alouds.

2. You can show students how to write by writing in front of them and using think alouds.

We have seen that young writers display their eagerness to imitate mature writers by approximating their writing behaviours in accordance with their understandings and abilities. Professional writers are similarly attuned to what other writers are creating and publishing, and what is being said about their writing. From the emerging writer to the writer developing in fluency and sophistication, the value of literary models in the form of published material and living models in the form of writing being composed before one's eyes cannot be underestimated. *Students need to be shown what good writers do and how they do it.*

1. *Use literature to demonstrate great writing.*

We can turn to our collection of quality children's literature to demonstrate everything a good writer does. Here are just some of the things you can point out during a read aloud to demonstrate to students that reading can enhance and inform their writing.

- Choosing an engaging topic (*Puffins Climb, Penguins Rhyme,* Bruce McMillan)
- Creating stories with lively characters, well-sequenced plots, and believable settings (*Ramona Quimby, Age 8,* Beverly Cleary)
- Creating mood (*Salt Hands,* Jane Chelsea Aragon)
- Presenting information in a clear and interesting way (Eyewitness series)
- Coming up with a good title (*What's a Penguin Doing in a Place Like This?* Miriam Schlein)

- Composing (and punctuating) good dialogue (*Stella, Queen of the Snow*, Marie-Louise Gay).

- Enhancing writing with illustrations (*O Canada*, Ted Harrison)

- Arranging lines of poetry (*Garbage Delight*, Dennis Lee)

- Creating a circular plot (*Where the Wild Things Are*, Maurice Sendak)

- Using repetition effectively (*Brown Bear, Brown Bear, What Do You See?* Bill Martin, Jr.)

- Keeping it simple (*Grandfather Twilight*, Barbara Berger)

- Expanding ideas (*Birds That Don't Fly*, Bobbie Kalman)

- Choosing strong verbs, descriptive adjectives, and a variety of nouns (*Every Single Night*, Dominique Demers). Here is an excerpt from that book to illustrate the kind of vibrant writing student writers can emulate:

  > *Mighty lions shake their manes, and roar so loud that baobab trees quiver. Then, from every corner of the bush, elephants, zebras, rhinoceroses, giraffes, gazelles and cheetahs race away under the moon. They dash home to their dens, their lairs, their hideaways. They run off to curl up in the arms of the night.*

2. *Write in front of your students to model how you write.*

When students observe teachers writing in front of them, talking about their writing as they go, they learn that even the writing of "experts" often begins tentatively, untidily, and undergoes a process of many decisions about word choice, punctuation, deletions, additions, mistakes, and corrections. Without active demonstration of how writing is accomplished, it remains invisible and mysterious. You can show what a good writer does, and articulate how a writer thinks.

You will recall the importance of think alouds to show our students the invisible, in-the-head strategies and processes we use when reading, particularly at points of difficulty. It is equally vital to model the many problem-solving strategies and the "on-the-run" decision-making that occur as we write. Effective teaching of writing means doing lots of modelling of the processes of writing, with special emphasis on showing the invisible processes that make communication through writing possible.

Beginning with the practice of "quick writing" as described by Donald Graves in Teacher Talk 11.1, you can directly demonstrate this skill for your students on the board, overhead projector, chart paper, or computer screen. As you write, your modelling includes verbalizing your thoughts and decisions about why these ideas are important to you and

Teacher Talk/11.1

DONALD GRAVES TALKS ABOUT THE TEACHER AS WRITER AND THE USE OF QUICK WRITES

Let your mind run, let all things in, but above all write without pausing.

When teachers compose texts of their own—texts they care about—during writing workshop, precious time is saved. Teachers reveal to their students the decisions all writers must make about every aspect of writing and demonstrate the skills that make writing clear and meaningful.

It is unheard of for a math teacher not to show the art of solving problems on the chalkboard. An artist paints with his class, a science teachers illustrates the art of investigation and documentation, and a coach shows how she spreads her fingers to control a basketball. Good teaching means demonstrating the decisions and skills required to participate in the field of study or endeavour being taught. This also applies to writing.

Quick writes are *foundational* to a sound writing program; *they are not the program*. I freely acknowledge that there is no research supporting the case of and the place of quick writes in the writing curriculum. However, research shows that the following instructional techniques, all of which apply to quick writes, encourage better writing. The writer should:

1. Write frequently.
2. Concentrate on main ideas.
3. Re-read what has been written.
4. Organize the writing.
5. Support claims with supporting details.
6. Use a distinct and recognizable voice.

There are many reasons for you and your students to practice writing quickly.

1. **You learn to work from a stimulus.** Writers need to get used to finding a personal response to a general stimulus. Your students' work with quick writes will help then lasso a fundamental idea and develop it.
2. **You learn to get off the mark quickly.** With practice, writers get their ideas moving more quickly. Their first line moves closer to the emotional centre of the piece.
3. **You begin to recognize your natural sense of organization.** Although a quick writer is open to any and all thoughts, rereading the piece almost always reveals a natural structure.
4. **You can identify the emotional center of a piece and provide supporting information.** The most common response to student writing on formal assessments is "lacks supporting details." Quick writes become the laboratory for teaching writing essentials.
5. **You connect conventions to context.** Since quick writes lead authors to topics they care about, they will more likely attend to conventions as they write and refine the text. As you demonstrate writing with students, you will model decision making in terms of say, punctuation.

talking about your thinking as you record those ideas, as you make decisions about conventions, and as you reread to find main ideas, "emotional centres," and organizational patterns. As Graves points out, the quick write is not the entire writing program, but you can demonstrate many principles of good writing by modelling quick writes and giving your students the opportunity to quick write frequently.

In addition to demonstrating good writing through your own quick writes, you can offer models of good writing by established authors, displaying and discussing examples of different kinds of texts, including a wide range of forms and genres. Show students how to be constantly on the lookout for examples from many sources that can be used as models to express their own ideas, information, and feelings through stories, poems, letters, and informational texts. The idea is to constantly model or provide models of how effective writers use various strategies to create meaningful texts for their readers.

CONCEPTS ABOUT TEXTS BEST TAUGHT THROUGH MODELLING

Some concepts can be taught most effectively through modelling. These include genres, formats, purposes of writing (see Figure 8.7) and learning (rather than copying) from other writers.

Additional concepts, which are discussed in Chapter 12, include:

- audience and voice

- importance of conventions in meaning-making (writing like a reader)

- writing as a process (pre-writing, drafting, re-reading, revising, editing, sharing, and sometimes publishing)

- getting started using quick writes, not story starters

- using peer and teacher conferencing to show how to end a story

Students need both literary and living models demonstrating various forms and genres of writing—models that show them how good writers write. Reading and learning how to write are interdependent. Writing cannot take place without reading. How does the argument that reading is a transactional process between reader and text, author, and community of learners, shape your planning when you are teaching writing? The close connections that exist between reading and writing can be referred to as reciprocity. Acknowledging the reciprocity between learning to read and learning to write influences how you teach.

The Reading-Writing Connection: Reciprocity

What is the relationship between learning to read and learning to write? We saw that oral language learning and literacy learning involve the "same neural machinery" (Cambourne, 1988). Reading and writing also involve closely interwoven thought processes (Vygotsky, 1979; Clay, 1991, 1998). The act of composing when writing or creating text not only requires re-reading, but closely parallels the constructive acts that allow readers to make meaning from a written text. The act of writing must be done with readers in mind to ensure that the communication is successful. Writers compose for a specific purpose for a specific audience. In classrooms where writing flourishes, writers talk to one another and collaborate with one another to hone their craft and to enhance the experience of authorship. Just as reading is a transaction among reader, text, author, and the community of readers, writing is a transaction between texts (both written and in progress) and a community of readers and writers.

ADVANTAGES OF LEARNING TO WRITE AS ONE BECOMES A READER

For very young writers, writing seems to complement reading where meaning is at the heart of teaching. In the first year or so of instruction, the ability to read extends beyond the capacity to write; therefore, during this emergent phase, writing activities consisting of composing one's own sentences to tell a story or to convey information appear to be an important complement of the reading program. Being able to compose and write down a sentence "demands that the children pay attention to the details of the print" as they construct words letter by letter and form phrases into sentences.

> *The good reader can work at any of these levels in the hierarchy. The poor reader tends to specialize in sounds and may be ignoring the details by which letters are distinguished. But this is not possible in early writing. All features of the language hierarchy must, inevitably, receive attention as the child builds letters into words, words into phrases and phrases into sentences and stories.*
>
> (Clay, 1975, pp. 2–3)

When reading and writing are taught simultaneously, young children use "common sources of information since there are processing connections that must arise in the learner who is being taught to read texts of many kinds and to write texts of many kinds by the best instruction currently advocated" (Clay, 1998, p. 137).

Clay (1998) lists four key advantages for beginning readers who learn to write as they become readers:

1. *Writing fosters slow analysis.* Writing is the slowest of the six language arts. Speaking and listening can be very fast; reading can speed up or slow down at will; viewing and representing can occur as rapidly as the flick of a switch. Writing is slowed down by the "motor, muscular, or movement nature of the task and by the need to construct every detail of the words, not just in forming letters, but also in juxtaposing one against the other" (p. 137).

2. *Writing highlights letter forms, letter sequences, and letter clusters.* When children learn to hand-print letters into words and into sentences, they are engaged in processes quite different from the processes in using pre-formed letters, word cards, or computer programs. When printing, they must form one letter at a time, paying close attention to the features of letters that distinguish one from another—the shape of the middle, the length and position of the stem, the orientation of similarly shaped letters, and so on. This process "makes the reader/writer analyze print at the letter level and analyze letters at the feature level" (p. 138). Teachers often spend time devising ways or looking for "programs" to help young readers see and remember letters and sounds. When engaged in the authentic task of writing down what they want to say, this detailed analysis is an unavoidable part of the task itself:

   Writing induces pressure to group letters into sequences and clusters because there is an imperative to get the message down before you forget it. Control over a cluster of letters frees attention for other things. Mastery over writing one's own name begins the clustering of letters. (p. 138)

3. *Writing seduces the learner into switching between different sources of knowledge.* Writing a message begins with composing in one's head (or aloud), then writing the first words one letter at a time. As writers build from letters to words, to sentences, paragraphs, and stories or informational pieces, they become implicitly aware of this hierarchy, without the need for a formal analysis. Clay points out that for learners who are concurrently reading and writing, as this process requires, writing will foster competence in reading and vice versa, especially "if the learner becomes aware of the reciprocal nature of these acts" (p. 138).

4. *Cognitive advantages can be predicted.* Since reading and writing are both "performance" skills, being able to connect the kinds of knowing between the two will help the reader/writer monitor and self-correct. Being able to compare how self-correction works in the same way when reading and when writing will bolster their ability to monitor their own performance in both. Because of its slowness and necessary attention to detail, writing is particularly useful in helping learners notice new things about print, and thereby building up a more complex knowledge base for both reading and writing.

(Adapted from Clay, 1998, pp. 137–9)

The argument that reading and writing abilities are learned through the reciprocal nature of their processes is a theoretical one. It can be supported through observations of young learners in programs where reading and writing are taught at the same time (see, for example, Shanahan, 1988, 1996; Langer & Flihan, 2000). But why should this be so? What do reading and writing have in common in terms of the kinds of knowledge involved in each? On one hand, reading seems, at the superficial level, to be more like listening—a receptive process involving absorbing and interpreting or decoding a message. On the other hand, writing seems more like speaking—an expressive process involving the composition and utterance or encoding of a message. Does this imply that different instructional techniques are appropriate to each? Or are there significant commonalities between the two ways of knowing?

What are some of the specific sources of knowledge writers must use that parallel the four roles of the reader? Figure 11.4 builds on Figure 8.4 and compares the sources of knowledge needed by readers to those needed by writers.

It is clear that many similar and some identical strategies are used by both readers and writers as they try to comprehend and compose texts. When we examine the strategies and processes involved in interacting with words and meanings, we see that the superficial differences between reading as "receptive" (decoding) and writing as "expressive" (encoding) are over-ridden by the work the reader and the writer must do to "build" or "construct" something meaningful, whether the black marks are already there on the page, or are in the process of being written down.

What does this mean for young readers and writers? In terms of word knowledge, the reciprocal relationship between writing and reading is evident. When children make the links from reading to writing and back again, this builds their metacognitive awareness of how new words can be used when reading and writing. This awareness strengthens and ex-

FIGURE 11.4 The Four Roles of the Reader/Writer

The Reader/Writer as Word-Solver	The Reader/Writer as Concept Builder
• Draws on a repertoire of known words when reading and writing. • Continually develops a reading and writing vocabulary. • Uses word-solving strategies, such as phonemes and letter clusters, for reading and writing. • Recognizes and uses visual information to read and write. • Demonstrates a continual awareness of own reading and writing strategies and processes.	• Reads and writes for a variety of purposes. • Knows and uses the structures and features of a variety of text forms to aid reading comprehension and text composition. • Uses language conventions (punctuation) and text features to aid in reading and writing. *Uses conventions to aid comprehension of their readers.* • Adjusts reading and writing strategies to match text forms and purposes. • Recognizes and uses the author's voice. • Thinks metacognitively to make meaning. • Demonstrates a continual awareness of own reading and writing strategies and processes.
The Reader/Writer as Meaning-Maker	The Reader/Writer as Architect
• Establishes a purpose for reading and writing. • Recognizes that reading and writing always involve meaning making. • Knows and applies a variety of reading strategies and writes with the reader in mind. • Self-monitors while reading and writing. • Sustains comprehension and composition over extended periods of time. • Responds to texts in a variety of ways including by writing.	• Recognizes reading and writing as transactions between readers, authors, and the reading/writing community. • Builds on and revises ideas, information, and perspectives when reading and writing. • Engages in critical thinking, critical consciousness, and critical literacy/inquiry. • Recognizes points of view, omissions, and multiple perspectives. • Demonstrates a continual awareness of own reading strategies and processes.

Source: Based on Freebody & Luke (1990) and Ontario Ministry of Education (2004).

tends word knowledge. Words become established as known reading and writing vocabulary through the same principles of repetition and flexible use. These vocabulary banks continue to grow and extend through similar sorts of learning strategies (see Figure 8.6).

This strong case for reciprocity between the processes involved in learning to read and to write has major implications for effective instruction in general and individual teaching decisions at the everyday level.

Reading and Writing: Fostering the Connection

HOW DO THE CONNECTIONS BETWEEN READING AND WRITING INFORM OUR INSTRUCTION?

In 1998, Marie Clay published her research on how teachers can introduce a new book to young readers in order to prepare them for successful, independent reading. In that study, she identified the following "teaching moves" that support children's writing:

- Bringing a topic into the conversation
- Maintaining interactive ease
- Prompting constructive activity
- Accepting partially correct responses
- Playing with anticipation
- Asking the child to "learn" something
- Lifting the difficulty level
- Increasing accessibility of the ideas
- Supporting performance
- Asking the child to work with new knowledge
- Accepting child involvement
- Developing attention to…[whatever is needed at the time]
- Praising strategic behaviour
- Revisiting the familiar

(Clay, 1998, p. 155)

Interwoven throughout these teaching moves are the three aspects of writing instruction we discussed earlier—allowing a child to approximate, ensuring a high level of positive responses to the child's work, and setting up new learning through modelling or demonstrating all the other moves.

These teaching moves presuppose a writing program that is based on the constructive principle of learning in interaction with an expert teacher who is interested in the children's writing, and in showing them how to improve as writers. Such a program has no place for previous writing programs where all tasks are assigned on teacher-chosen topics and then corrected by the teacher in red ink. "Accepting child involvement" and "supporting performance" means inviting children to write on topics that matter to them for purposes they understand, including sharing with other writers. It also means supporting their efforts by encouragement and praise and by teaching them new strategies and skills—including self-correcting—so that they can become better writers.

FOUR WAYS TO FOSTER STUDENT AWARENESS OF THE READING-WRITING CONNECTION

1. *Provide explicit instruction on how to write with the reader in mind and read with the writer in mind.*

   • Read aloud excellent children's literature to demonstrate skills or techniques in the craft of writing. For example, read Mem Fox's *Tough Boris* to show the effects on the reader/listener of using just the right adjectives ("Boris was massive. All pirates are massive.").

   • Do modelled writing, using a think aloud to stress the need for proper conventions (spelling, grammar, punctuation, legibility) to ensure writing is readable.

   • Do modelled reading, using a think aloud to ask questions of the author and pose possible answers (Beck & McKeown, 2002).

   • Model how to revise and edit writing by reading it aloud to yourself or to a peer.

2. *Organize an author study.*

   • Have students create a display of books by the same author.

   • Research biographical information from books and websites.

   • Use films, tapes, DVDs, or CDs.

   • Have students discuss the author's work, themes, and writing style.

   • Compare to other authors.

   • Respond through art, for example, murals, book jackets, and posters.

   • Respond through writing. Attempt to imitate the author's style or write a letter or e-mail to the author.

   • Respond through drama using tableaux, role-play, or story drama (Chapter 7).

   • Invite the author to visit or reply to a letter.

   (Based on Booth & Swartz, 2004)

3. *Plan a genre study.*

   • Choose a genre of interest to the class or one appropriate to a theme students are working on.

- Set up a class library of texts of that type and form.
- Experience many examples through read alouds, guided reading, and independent reading.
- With the students, compose a list of characteristics of that genre.
- Compare/contrast with another genre.
- Experiment with this genre and form in their own writing. (Based on Booth & Swartz, 2004.)

4. *Encourage reader response through writing.*

- Read and respond in writing during or after the reading.
- Teach how to write excellent reader responses through oral rehearsal such as retellings followed by discussion of feelings and opinions; explicit teaching through modelling a personal response; providing written feedback in student journals; and guiding student practice through strategies such as shared writing. (In shared writing, the teacher and students compose a written response together; the teacher records it on chart paper or overhead projector for everyone to see and read together. See Chapter 12.)
- Encourage students to record feelings, observations, facts they have learned, opinions, and questions they have about what they have read.

Advantages of reader response:

- When children write in response to what they have read, what they have personally learned and observed from their reading becomes even more evident to them.
- Many formal and informal assessments direct readers to respond in writing in order to show how well they have understood a text.
- Children's reading and writing abilities can be at significantly different levels. Reading ability is usually higher, particularly in the early years. The reliability of writing as an assessment of reading must be questioned. However, by responding in writing to a specific text, developing writers have the opportunity to use a published author's work as a model. They can rely on the text for correct spellings, new vocabulary, how to handle difficult writing skills such as punctuation for dialogue, and how to show the beginning of a new paragraph.
- Reader response is much richer than a comprehension check: it can take many creative forms, both written and artistic. For example,

writing a script for a play based on a story or information text, or creating an illustrated journal or cartoon strip.

- Response activities should lead to deeper insights, more detailed observations, and the ability to discuss controversial ideas, express emotional reactions, and see diverse points of view.
- Response activities motivate.

Figure 11.5 contains a list of options that will both motivate and engage writers in the process of responding through writing.

FIGURE 11.5 Response Options Using Writing			
advertisements	dialogue journals	journal entries	quick writes
articles	diaries	labelled maps	reactions
buddy journals	documentaries	letters	reports
charts	double-entry journals	newspaper reports	story sequels
comic strips	family trees	paragraphs	timelines
creative writing	graphs	plot lines	webs
critiques	interview questions	predictions	writing in role
diagrams	jot notes	questions	

USING WRITING IN READING INSTRUCTION

When you make writing an integral part of reading instruction, you enhance students' awareness of reading-writing connections (see Theory into Practice 11.2). For example, high-frequency words encountered during a read aloud or shared reading can be added to word walls using modelled writing, recorded by students and teacher using interactive writing, and added independently to personal spelling lists. During a guided reading lesson, Junior-level students can display the plot sequence of a novel on a story map, or a double-entry journal (see Chapter 10, Journals), recording quotations in one column, and the reader's reactions or responses in the other.

ADVANTAGES OF WRITING: BEYOND THE CLASSROOM WALLS

The following are just some of the many advantages writing offers to readers as they continue their development as readers, writers, and human beings.

Theory Into Practice/11.2

WRITING ACTIVITIES BEFORE, DURING, AND AFTER READING

Writing activities can enhance reading instruction during any or all of the phases of a reading lesson. Writing before reading can stimulate interest in the text; writing during reading can help students think about their reading and how they are reacting; writing after reading allows revisiting the text and encourages critical thinking.

Before Reading:

Use writing to record various ways of anticipating what will be read; for example, wonder statements, predictions, word or concept webs, or K-W-L charts (see Chapter 10). This stimulates thinking about the topic, special vocabulary, and ideas to be encountered.

Tips:

1. Show just the cover and title when introducing a new book and have students record questions or a quick write of thoughts and feelings.
2. Read aloud the first sentence, and then ask the students to write one sentence that might follow. Record the sentences on the board or chart paper.

During Reading:

Initial readings should be uninterrupted. Model how to stop occasionally during subsequent readings to jot down thoughts and reactions on Post-it notes or in a reading journal. You may provide prompts, such as

- I wonder why...
- This reminds me of...
- I think...
- I'm confused about...
- I don't know this word...
- I like this part because...

Guide students as they jot down their notes; these notes can become the basis of a reading journal entry.

After Reading:

Revisit the text to make connections and inferences, determine important ideas, speculate about the author's purpose and a possible theme, and identify the type of text or genre.

Activities:

- Highlight favourite or key passages.
- Make connections to self, to other texts, to the world, and to related media.
- Summarize key ideas.

Beyond the Reading:

- Re-write from a different point of view, perhaps that of a minor character.
- Compose questions to interview a character.

Theory Into Practice/11.2

WRITING ACTIVITIES BEFORE, DURING, AND AFTER READING (continued)

• Write a diary entry for a character.
• Organize information in the text using a graphic or visual organizer.

At this stage, where the goal is to stimulate higher level critical thinking, avoid simple recall or retellings and activities that are only about decoding the words or noting conventions. Instead, engage students in writing activities that *focus on the meaning, especially reading between and beyond the lines* (see Chapter 8).

Source: Ontario Ministry of Education (2003), sections 10.5-10.7.

Making Reading-Writing Connections:

Harwayne (2001, pp. 147-148) suggests asking the following questions to probe the reader's opinions about the author's writing:

• What do you think of this author's style?
• Are there things this author has done that you would like to do as a writer?
• Are there parts in this book you are envious of, wishing you had written them?
• Are there places where you found yourself rereading because the text was so well written?
• Did you stop to read aloud any lines or sections to your family or friends?

STOP, THINK, AND WRITE

■ What are the disadvantages of constantly requiring students to respond in writing to their reading?

■ How can you ensure there is a balance between reading for pleasure, providing opportunities for creative responses (through the arts, for example), and your need to assess reading comprehension?

literacy
notebook
11.4

• Writing can lead to deepening and broadening of insights regarding everything from a story listened to or read, to a topic learned about through viewing or reading, to a current event or life experience.

• Writing encourages self-expression, the development of an individual voice, and personal power.

• Writing in a community of writers encourages awareness of other voices, of diverse points of view.

• Writing increases awareness of how texts are constructed, allowing growth of the ability to write like a reader, and read like a writer.

STOP, THINK, AND WRITE

At the beginning of this chapter you were told that you would be asked to create a prioritized list of key classroom approaches and goals by revisiting your initial responses to the following questions:

- What is writing?
- What is writing used for?
- What are some of the factors that determine or affect the development of writing abilities?
- What is your role in fostering the development of writing?
- How are reading and writing connected?

Has your thinking changed?

- Writing enhances individuality and self-esteem, especially when it is the ideas and feelings it expresses that we celebrate and respond to, not merely using technical conventions.

These advantages are achievable in a flourishing community of writers made possible through a well-run writers' workshop (see Chapter 12.)

Moving On

In this chapter, we considered some key aspects of effective teaching of writing from the very early years as confident apprentices to the later stages of development as just-as-confident, accomplished, expressive writers. We discussed the all-important connection between reading and writing in terms of reciprocal and interdependent learning processes. We demonstrated the strong similarities between the print concepts and strategies required to acquire reading and writing abilities, and the textual concepts, strategies, and connections required to further develop those capabilities. Based upon the similar principles of how reading is learned and how writing is learned, we made some inferences about what is effective writing instruction.

Assuming that children become literate through learning conditions comparable to those of an apprenticeship, we described the value of creating a classroom context known as writers' workshop. We focused on three salient aspects of the teaching and learning that are essential for the flourishing of young writers: learning to write by approximation, receiving responses to written pieces and compositions through high quality interactions with the teacher, and teaching by modelling expert writing.

In Chapter 12, we will discuss the following:

- establishing, setting up, and maintaining a well-functioning writers' workshop

- addressing the levels of support for writers as part of a balanced and comprehensive program

- teaching the craft of writing in a workshop

- examining how students use the writing process or writing cycle similar to "real" authors, and tracking and assessing progress

> *Every study of young writers I've done for the last twenty years*
> *has underestimated what they can do... Children need to be nudged to try*
> *new things and experiment with new skills...*
>
> *Children who know how they ought to go about learning are easier*
> *to nudge than those who believe the teacher's job is to push them to do*
> *everything. They have a more assertive approach to their future as writers.*
> *They know what they need to learn.*
> —Donald Graves

LIT-FOLIO UPDATE

Your lit-folio should include evidence of your developing awareness of the connection between reading and writing as processes, how they are learned and how they support one another. How does this awareness inform your teaching?

LIT-FOLIO TIP

Use the quick-write strategy to summarize your understanding about learning by approximation, your questions about how to respond during writing conferences, and how you can develop your ability to confidently model good writing for your students.

Resources to Support Your Learning

Professional Resources

Atwell, N. (1998). *In the middle: New understandings about writing, reading, and learning.* Portsmouth, NH: Heinemann.

✦ Booth, D. (2001). *Reading and writing in the middle years.* Markham, ON: Pembroke Publishers.

✦ Booth, D., & Swartz. L. (2004). *Literacy techniques for building successful readers and writers.* Markham, ON: Pembroke Publishers.

Calkins, L. (1986, 1994). *The art of teaching writing.* Portsmouth, NH: Heinemann.

Calkins, L. & Harwayne, S. (1990). *Living between the lines.* Portsmouth, NH: Heinemann.

Clay, M. (1975). *What did I write?* Portsmouth, NH: Heinemann.

Clay, M. (1987). *Writing begins at home: Preparing children for writing before they go to school.* Portsmouth, NH: Heinemann.

Clay, M. (1998). *By different paths to common outcomes.* York, ME: Stenhouse.

Fletcher, R. (1993). *What a writer needs.* Portsmouth, NH: Heinemann

Fletcher, R. (1996). *Breathing in breathing out: Keeping a writer's notebook.* Portsmouth, NH: Heinemann.

Graves, D. (1994). *A fresh look at writing.* Portsmouth, NH: Heinemann.

Harwayne, S. (2001). *Writing through childhood: Rethinking process and product.* Portsmouth, NH: Heinemann.

Indrisano, R., & Paratore, J. (eds.) (2005). *Learning to write and writing to learn: Theory and research in practice.* Newark, DE: International Reading Association.

Rasinski, T., et al (eds). (2000). *Developing reading-writing connections : Strategies from* The Reading Teacher. Newark, DE: International Reading Association.

Routman, R. (2000). *Conversations: Strategies for teaching, learning and evaluating.* Portsmouth, NH: Heinemann.

Routman, R. (2005). *Writing essentials: Raising expectations and results while simplifying teaching.* Portsmouth, NH: Heinemann.

Children's Literature: Our Favourites

Literary Models for Student Writers

✦ *Every single night,* Dominique Demers

✦ *Garbage delight: Another helping,* Dennis Lee

✦ *Jillian Jiggs and the great big snow,* Phoebe Gilman

Painted words: Spoken memories, Aliki

Salt hands, Jane Chelsea Aragon

The tenth good thing about Barney, Judith Viorst

Those summers, Aliki

Tough Boris, Mem Fox

Websites

✦ Ontario Ministry of Education:
   http://www.edu.gov.on.ca/eng/

Read Write Think:
   http://www.readwritethink.org/index.asp

✦ The 2learn.ca Education Society (Alberta):
   http://www.2learn.ca/

The New York Times Learning Network: Grades 3-12:
   http://www.nytimes.com/learning/index.html

The Writing Fix: http://www.writingfix.com/

12

Real Writers Writing

> Our students need what readers and writers the world over need. They need places to go and things to do.
> —Lucy Calkins

key terms

audience

drafting

editing

Elkonin boxes

guided writing

high-frequency words

independent writing

interactive writing

modelled writing

prewriting/ rehearsing

publishing

revising

rimes

shared writing

voice

word pattern

writers' workshop

writing conference

writing cycle

writing rubric

questions to guide your learning

By the end of this chapter, you should understand the key terms and be able to answer the following questions:

- What is the writing process?
- What is writers' workshop?
- How is writers' workshop set up and established?
- How is the craft of writing taught in the workshop context?
- How are conventions such as spelling and grammar taught in writers' workshop?
- How do you assess student writing?

Looking Back, Looking Ahead

In Chapter 11, we considered the critical importance of the reading-writing connection when identifying the general principles of a writing program, and when making decisions about effective writing instruction. We looked at how children acquire and develop writing abilities, and how the general conditions of language and literacy learning apply specifically to writing development.

In this chapter, we take a close look at the methods and strategies you can use to help your students become effective communicators through the written word, to guide and encourage them as they move confidently from approximations to a comprehensive command of a wide range of forms of writing for a variety of purposes. We consider the concrete conditions and practical strategies that make this learning possible. We begin with a discussion of the continuum of support from modelled writing to independent writing. This is followed by a detailed description of teaching the writing process or the writing cycle in a writers' workshop. We then present an overview of our principles for good practice in teaching writing.

Principles of Good Practice in Teaching Writing

There are so many writing skills to teach, and so many strategies to choose from. What will guide your choices as you design your writing program and make daily on-the-run decisions based on what is going on in your classroom? The following principles are suggested as a guide. They are based on the International Reading Association pamphlet, *New Directions in Reading* (2000).

TEN PRINCIPLES OF BEST PRACTICE IN WRITING

1. *Student independence as "real writers" is the ultimate goal.*
   - Guide students to choose their own topics, themes, and purposes for writing.
   - Show students how to monitor their own processes and progress.
2. *Reading and writing connections are emphasized at all times.*
   - Critically examine literature to learn about how and why authors write.

3. *Sufficient time and materials are provided so that students can create their own original written works.*

   • Explicity teach prewriting, drafting, revising, editing, and publishing.

4. *Teacher modelling of all aspects of the writing process is a central feature.*

   • The teacher is an expert demonstrator of writing skills and strategies, working as a real writer alongside students.

5. *Spelling, grammar, and the conventions or mechanics of written language are taught in context.*

   • These are completed at the editing stage of writing, during writers' workshop.

6. *Writing is done for real audiences and work is published for sharing in class and in the wider community.*

7. *The classroom is a community of writers working within the supportive structures of writers' workshop.*

   • Students share and value each other's ideas and writings.

   • Students benefit from peer-to-peer and teacher-student conferencing.

8. *Writing across the curriculum is embedded throughout the school day as a tool for learning.*

   • Students research and write about non-fiction and informational topics as part of the many forms of writing explored during writers' workshop.

9. *Effective evaluation and assessment is frequent and ongoing.*

   • The teacher provides frequent oral feedback and conferencing while circulating during writers' workshop.

10. *How we respond to students' writing is crucial to their success as writers.*

    • All assessment is done in order to improve student writing and encourage risk-taking.

    • Responses must reflect complete respect for the individual writer as a person with a unique history, cultural background, family, and life experiences, and must promote the development of their individual voices.

literacy notebook 12.1

STOP, THINK, AND WRITE

■ What is most important to you at this time in your development as a teacher?

■ With which of the above principles of teaching writing do you feel most confident?

■ Which principles do you feel you need to know more about?

■ Which principles do you think your students would think most important?

Writing Instruction

Recognizing that all students vary in personality, learning style, and reading behaviour, effective literacy teachers understand that there is no single method, theory, or set of learning materials that can successfully teach all children to write. Therefore, teachers must have access to a wide range of writing approaches and methods that will support all students, regardless of grade level, personality, ability, or learning style. In this chapter, we present a range of strategies that will make writing interesting, fun, interactive, and engaging. The strategies reflect a continuum of support from modelled to independent. Figure 12.1 presents our conceptualization of how the degrees of support, introduced in Figure 2.5, support student growth in writing. According to this model, teachers provide a high level of support through modelling, with an ongoing decrease in support through guided and shared writing, followed by opportunities for independent practice. This allows for a **gradual release of responsibility** as students make the transition from being shown how, to trying it on their own.

In Figure 4.6, we discussed emerging characteristics of literacy learners and strategies to support learners in their literacy development. Because this learning occurs along a continuum, and not necessarily in discrete stages, teachers must observe their students carefully, and select strategies and levels of support in response to their individual level of literacy and the literacy contexts of their classrooms. In the same way that strategies are selected responsively and flexibly, so too are the levels of support. Modelled, shared, interactive, guided, and independent writing are equally effective at all grade levels, depending on the purposes, tasks, and contexts that support literacy learning.

After providing a description of the various levels of support as they apply to teaching writing, the rest of this chapter focuses on writers'

gradual release of responsibility The incremental adjustment from a high level of teacher support to a high level of student independence as the teacher gradually hands over responsibility for learning to the student.

FIGURE 12.1 Applying the Continuum of Support to Writing

from	Level of Support	Writing Practices
teacher	**Modelled**	• Teachers write in front of students, thinking aloud to model and demonstrate in-the-head thinking, decision-making, and strategy use. • Teachers compose texts that are beyond what students can write independently—at their difficulty level. Writing should be appropriate to the students' needs and cognitive levels, on a topic of interest to both teacher and students. The teacher is the only one engaged in writing.
support	**Shared**	• Teachers share writing experiences and opportunities with learners, inviting them to join in by offering ideas and composing orally. • Teachers write messages or stories that students can read independently—at their instructional level. Messages should be motivating, engaging, and purposeful, and based on topics of current interest. The writing should be visible to everyone, using chart paper, overhead projector, or computer screen.
to	**Interactive**	• Teachers share writing experiences and opportunities with learners, interacting in a way that permits learners to contribute what they know and can do independently. Students "share the pen," writing independently what they can with the teacher filling in the gaps. • Teachers select texts that students might be able to write independently—at their instructional level. Texts should be motivating, engaging, and serve the current purposes of the classroom, (for example, writing a thank you letter).
student	**Guided**	• Teachers scaffold to bridge the gap, activate prior knowledge, and prepare students to write using new strategies or forms of writing. Students are grouped by similar strengths, needs, and experience to provide intensive strategy instruction. Students write texts at their instructional level on their own, with the teacher supporting their efforts as they try new strategies and problem solving approaches. • Teachers guide students to write new material independently—at their instructional level. All students may be at the same or similar stage in the writing process (for example, first draft).
independence	**Independent**	• Teachers select methods and practices that foster student independence. They make available a wide variety of models for students that are at their instructional level. • Students select their own topics and engage in various stages of the writing process, sometimes joining a peer or teacher conference for feedback and response.

workshop, describing how it can accommodate the continuum of support and literacy strategies for children who are learning how to write and how to become better writers. At times, we revisit concepts and strategies already introduced, not only to underscore their importance in a comprehensive literacy program, but also to link these strategies specifically to writing.

Before we describe each of the levels of support as they apply to writing, we remind you that you do not necessarily need to have regularly scheduled times for each of these instructional levels—they can occur spontaneously as needed. Modelled writing can and should occur frequently during independent writing time, for example, when you have an impromptu conference with a student. On one day, you may decide to write the morning message in front of the students with a think aloud as modelled writing while on another day you may choose to write it with the students interactively. Similarly, a guided reading lesson may end with a brief shared writing activity to summarize and consolidate the learning. All of the levels of support, including those for both reading and writing, can be used for specific instructional purposes in readers' workshop and writers' workshop.

MODELLED WRITING

Chapter 11 provided a strong rationale for the central importance of modelled writing as a key instructional strategy. As indicated above,

literacy notebook 12.2

STOP, THINK, AND WRITE

Thinking about "having enough time for it all."

- How do you envision yourself providing a continuum of support, from modelling writing at the highest level of teacher support, to providing sufficient time and resources to allow students to practise writing independently?

- How might you balance the need to schedule times for modelled, shared, and interactive writing with the whole class, and more spontaneously occurring guided writing sessions with small instructional groups brought together by an identified need (a skill or strategy) they have in common?

- How might you balance whole class demonstrations for new learning, small group instruction, and individual conferences?

modelled writing, where teachers write in front of the students and articulate aloud what they are doing and thinking, can be used during whole class writing lessons or mini-lessons during small group instruction or during an individual conference. Theory into Practice 12.1 is intended as a guide for modelled writing. For maximum benefit, teacher modelling should occur frequently throughout the school day and include a wide range of writing purposes, forms, strategies, and skills.

Theory Into Practice/12.1

GETTING READY FOR MODELLED WRITING

In modelled writing, teachers demonstrate how expert writers get their thoughts, ideas, and feelings into writing. Since this is the highest level of support, the teacher's role is an active one. The students' role is to observe and listen, being attentive to those aspects of writing being demonstrated and explained.

Before

Teachers decide what will be written and why and explicitly explain these decisions as part of the writing process.
- Teachers write in front of students.
- Teachers create text, thinking aloud as they write, describing all decision-making and problem-solving, including self-correcting, re-reading, editing, and revising.
- Teachers write so that all can see the product, on chart paper, the chalkboard, overhead projector, or computer screen.
- Teachers model and explain good strategies and writing skills, providing a model for a variety of styles and forms, producing text that students can read independently.

After

- Teachers re-read own writing, explaining how expert writers must do this continually.
- Teachers summarize the purpose of the model, for example, to show how to do a quick write, or how to combine sentences.
- Teachers post the writing, inviting students to read the written text and use it as a reference when writing.

Teacher Follow-Up

During small group instruction, while circulating around the room during writers' workshop, or during individual conferences, assess the effectiveness of the modelling by observing whether students are using the model and asking them about their learning. What did you notice as I modelled how to write dialogue between two characters? What did you find useful for your own writing? What problems or questions do you still have? What kind of writing or what skill in writing would you like to see me model in the future? What would be helpful?

Topics for Modelling (see also Chapter 11)

The general context of modelled writing is the process of making explicit the reading/writing connection to help students write like readers. Here are some suggested areas for specific focus appropriate to various grade levels.

- JK/SK: Understand the purposes of writing.
- Grade 1: Leave spaces between words.
- Grade 2: Use connecting words to link simple sentences.
- Grade 3: Choose words that are most appropriate—focus on adding descriptive words to create visual images for the reader.
- Grade 4: Use proper forms for paragraphs.
- Grade 5: Produce an advertisement for radio—focus on persuasion.
- Grade 6: Use verb tenses consistently throughout a piece of writing—focus on editing.

You will need a repertoire of scripts to provide think alouds to model specific skills or strategies. Figure 12.2 contains a sample script to model the concept of a word and leaving spaces between words.

SHARED WRITING

In shared writing, teachers and students collaborate to compose a text, with the teacher acting as scribe. The following are the primary benefits of sharing the writing process:

- Students are given the opportunity to compose ideas while being free from concerns about the conventions of writing.
- Concepts about print can be discussed, demonstrated, and developed.
- Writing strategies can be demonstrated and reinforced.

literacy notebook 12.3

STOP, THINK, AND WRITE

Choose another grade level and a curricular expectation for the writing strand from the previous list. Write the script for a think aloud to accompany the modelling of that strategy, skill, or genre of writing.

- Since the teacher does the actual writing, exemplary models are provided.
- Students assist orally by providing ideas, sentences, and high-frequency words, letters, and sounds.

FIGURE 12.2 Sample Think Aloud for Writing

Focus: Grade 1, the concept of a word and leaving spaces between words.

Context: Teacher is writing the morning message, verbalizing thinking while writing, using metalanguage to talk about the what, how, and why.

Teacher: Good morning everyone! Today I am going to write our morning message for you while you watch, so that you can see what I do as I write. I am going to talk out loud as I write, explaining what I am doing and why. I am showing you what I do as I write, and what goes on inside my head as I decide what and how I write. I've noticed that when you write your stories, sometimes it is hard for you, and for me, to read what you have written, because there are no spaces between the words. We don't know where one word ends and the next one starts, and we get all mixed up. I am going to show you what books and good writers do—put spaces between words—so that readers can see each word clearly. It makes it easier for everyone to read. I am going to write:

Good morning! Today we are going to read the book *Willy the Wimp*, by Anthony Browne. We will talk about it and then we will draw and write about the story.

Before I begin writing, I am thinking about who I am writing for—you—and how big the letters should be so that everyone can see and read the message. I begin with an upper case "G" like the one on the alphabet strip (points above on the wall) and I am writing the rest of the word "Good" with lower case letters with a very small amount of space between them, because these *letters* G-o-o-d are all part of the same *word*—the word "Good." Now that I have finished writing the word "Good," I will leave a space, about one finger wide, like this, and then I will start to write the next word, "morning." I write the letters "m-o-r-n-i-n-g" almost touching because they are all *letters* making the *word* "morning." As I write, you can find the word "morning" on our word wall and make sure I get all the letters right. Let's read what I have written: "Good morning." I've written two words with a space between them to make it easier for you to read. Since this is the end of the first part of my message—the first sentence—I have to show it is finished. I could put a period, but I've decided to put an exclamation mark, because I am so happy to see you this morning. Reads "Good morning!"

The teacher continues to write. "Today we are going to read..." verbalizing about the distance between letters in the same word, and the spaces left between the end of one word (the last letter) and the beginning of the next word (the first letter). To reinforce the concept of "word," she directs their attention to each word as she finishes writing it, and invites them to find the word if it is posted in the classroom, including the words in the title of the book, which is sitting on the chalkboard ledge. The teacher continues until the writing is finished and then models re-reading it, once again pointing out the spaces between the words.

The purposes of early and emergent shared writing are to:

- develop and extend awareness of concepts about print (Figure 4.5), functions of print, familiarity with language patterns, and basic written forms such as lists, letters, messages, reminders, poems, stories, and information

- help students make the connection between oral language and print (during shared writing the student is free to compose ideas without having to get them all down before they are forgotten)

- build an understanding and interest in the writing process and its functions

- demonstrate the usefulness of having a repertoire of known words to draw on when writing (a writing vocabulary already known speeds up the process and frees the writer's mind for composing and creating text, rather than becoming bogged down by stopping to analyze sounds and letters for each word)

Theory Into Practice/12.2

STEPS IN SHARED WRITING

Shared writing differs from modelled writing. During shared writing the students do the composing while the teacher does the recording. During modelled writing, the teacher composes and writes while thinking aloud. Note, however, that lots of modelling continues in shared writing!

1. Read something together to warm up and become inspired.
2. Brainstorm topics.
3. Choose a topic/idea from the list (reach a consensus).
4. Students compose one sentence (or one line of poetry) at a time, teacher records, and students may assist by telling known words, letters, and sounds.
5. Read that sentence together and then compose the next sentence.
6. Compose, write, and re-read each sentence as you go.
7. Continue until finished.
8. Revise, edit, re-read together (shared reading).
9. Celebrate the finished piece by having a choral reading, posting in the classroom or school, or by sending a copy home.
10. Continue to revisit the poem, report, story, letter, summaries, or other text form you have created together. Students are always interested in re-reading their own creations on topics they have chosen. Their compositions can be made available during shared and/or independent reading time, or circulated among the students for reading at home. These finished pieces become motivating models for students' own independent writing.

GETTING READY FOR A SHARED WRITING POEM

	Teacher's Role	Learner's Role	Strategies
Before Writing	• Expose students to a variety of poems. • Guide students to identify poetic sounding language, for example, alliteration, sensory imagery, metaphors, and similes.	• Read a variety of poems independently, attending to how they sound, and how they look on the page. • Participate in shared and choral readings of poems. • Respond orally and in writing to poetry.	• Identify "poetic language" and its special features of rhythm, metre, rhyme, metaphor. • Identify the visual appearance of various poems in print. • Connect to previous encounters with poetry.
During Writing	**Brainstorm** • Explore a variety of topics or themes. • Guide students in reaching a consensus when making a choice. **Model and Suggest** • Remind students of key features of a good poem. • Guide phrasing and word choice. • Model how to record a poem.	**Prepare** • Suggest topics and themes of interest and relevance. **Compose** • Suggest lines of poetry one line at a time. • Re-read before composing next line, following the suggested rhythm and style. • Suggest length of lines, line breaks, word order changes, and additions or deletions.	• Connect to topics and themes of importance to the group. • Compare with published poems. • Attend to key features of poetry.
After Writing	**Debrief** • Discuss how the poem sounds, how it looks, and how it expresses emotions and ideas. **Refine** • Allow for feedback from students for suggested revisions. • Make the poem available to everyone for independent reading.	**Re-read, Revisit, Revise, and Celebrate the Poem** • Participate in group evaluation of process and product. • Share reactions to the shared writing process. • Decide together whether and how to publish beyond the classroom (contests).	• Connect • Revise • Revisit • Analyze • Interpret • Respond • Discuss • React

Shared writing at the Junior level can be used to demonstrate and reinforce writing strategies and conventions, writing for various purposes, and writing specific fiction and non-fiction genres. Examples include:

At the pre-writing/rehearsal stage:	At the drafting stage:
• KWL charts	• letters
• concept webs	• persuasive pieces
• time lines	• personal narratives
• story maps	• poems, scripts for plays, or readers' theatre
• report outlines	• advertisements
• formulating working questions for researching a topic	• summaries
• lists of themes and topics	• news reports
	• stories from traditional fables to historical fiction

Shared writing may also be used effectively at the revision and editing stages of the writing process.

INTERACTIVE WRITING

In **interactive writing**, teachers and students compose and create a text together through a process where they "share the pen." When the topic is chosen with a real classroom purpose in mind (for example, to send a thank you note to the custodian for helping to make the set for a play), the learning becomes centred on an authentic opportunity for writing, where the children are contributing to real writing for a real purpose. During the writing, the teacher may model the use of letter-sound matching skills needed to construct an unfamiliar word, or model the use of known words posted on the word wall. For early, transitional, and fluent writers, interactive writing can help increase spelling knowledge as the teacher models using a pattern or cluster such as "ight." The finished piece of writing, which displays both the teacher's and the students' contributions, provides written language resources for future classroom use, talk about writing conventions, problem-solving strategies, and the various purposes of writing.

Interactive writing in the Junior classroom can be used to teach parts of speech, sentence expansion (adding adjectives, adverbs) and the conventions of writing such as punctuation and spelling. The processes of re-

Theory Into Practice/12.4

STEPS FOR INTERACTIVE WRITING

1. **Construct the text.** Children and teacher choose the topic and brainstorm ideas. With the teacher guiding, the children suggest sentences, and the group reaches consensus on each sentence.

2. **Identify the words in the first sentence.** The teacher repeats the first sentence and asks students to identify or "count" the words in the sentence on their fingers as they repeat the sentence, articulating each word slowly and distinctly.

3. **Write the sentence.** Children take turns writing sentences, words, or letters, depending on their knowledge and experience. During the writing, the teacher asks questions or makes comments to focus attention on concepts about written language. Teacher helps children write accurately and legibly.

4. **Read the sentence.** After each word has been written, the sentence is read and re-read until it is finished. The next sentence is then prepared.

5. **Repeat the steps.** Children and teacher repeat steps 2, 3, and 4 for each sentence.

6. **Re-read the completed text.** Children and teacher re-read the completed text; individuals take turns reading sentences.

Possible topics for interactive writing

Lists	Clusters or Webs	Science experiments
Diagrams	Collaborative books	Reports
Classroom news	Stories	Poems
Prediction charts	Story maps	

Letters to another class, the principal, secretary, or an author

vising and editing can be the focus of an interactive writing session, or it can be a specific strategy or skill. The overhead projector is a good tool to use with Junior-level students to keep them engaged. The work can be copied later onto chart paper and posted for reference.

GUIDED WRITING

In **guided writing**, the teacher pulls together small, temporary groups of writers to teach the strategies and skills they need at that time.

- Group work may focus on developing specific writing skills and strategies (for example, forming paragraphs) on using writing as a tool for inquiry, on learning to write in different genres, or on using word processing software to publish writing.

Theory Into Practice/12.5

GETTING READY FOR GUIDED WRITING - PARAGRAPHS

	Teacher's Role	Learner's Role	Strategies
Before Writing	• Scaffolds the concept of a "paragraph" by linking it to newspaper reading they have recently done. • Models a targeted strategy using a think aloud: "I'm going to show you how writers decide where to start a new paragraph."	• Engage in conversation about the strategy. • Raise questions. • Link the writing strategy to readings. • Notice how authors construct paragraphs, and where they begin a new paragraph.	• Connect • Question • Notice
During Writing	• Observes, listens, and interacts, confirming or suggesting strategies to assist with problem-solving. • Prompts include: "I notice you are now talking about where, and not when anymore. Should you start a new paragraph?"	• Independently revise reports. • Use problem-solving strategies to construct paragraphs. • Check organization. • Re-read their writing, guided by the teacher. • Use the 5Ws + H to know when to start a paragraph. • Request help when needed.	• Write with attention to organizing information into paragraphs • Problem-solve • Monitor organization • Apply fix-up strategies (use appropriate proof-reading symbol for "new paragraph")
After Writing	• Invite personal responses and encourage reflective, inferential, and critical-level responses. • Select one or two teaching points and focus on strategies. • Praise for trying new problem-solving strategies. • Encourage students to continue writing on this topic (revising, editing, sharing, or publishing).	• Talk about their writing at the content level and at the organizational level. • Share reports with appropriate audience. • Sometimes engage in extension activities.	• Check, confirm, and revise writing • Connect • Analyze • Interpret • Respond • Re-read • Revise

A JUNIOR GUIDED WRITING MINI-LESSON PLAN

Text: *Terry Fox: A Story of Hope*
Author/Publisher: Maxine Trottier/Scholastic Canada
Genre: Biography
Lesson Objective/Reading Strategy: Organize information recorded on biography maps using the 5Ws + H (Who, What, Where, When, Why, and How) to identify topics for individual paragraphs
Time Frame: This is an introductory lesson on paragraph writing.

1. Instructional Expectations

The following are Grade 4 language curriculum expectations (Ontario Curriculum) that are addressed and modelled in this lesson.

Students:

- Read and write a variety of fiction and non-fiction materials for different purposes.
- Make judgements about what they read on the basis of evidence.
- Begin to develop research skills (formulate questions, locate information, clarify their understanding of information through discussion).
- Use their knowledge of the organization and characteristics of different forms of writing to understand and use content.
- Use various conventions of formal text to reinforce understanding of ideas (charts, illustrations, glossary, diagrams, captions).

2. Pre-assessment

a) Learners:

- Reading level: early Grade 4 (instructional)
- On Day 1, this group of six learners read the text about Terry Fox and were asked to extend what they knew about character maps to biography maps as a note-taking strategy. On Day 2, they continued to read and take notes; they also completed their biography maps.
- This group requires guidance and support to begin to organize their biography maps into full reports with separated paragraphs.

b) Learning Environment:

- Learners are seated at the round table, beside the classroom library.
- The teacher is seated at the back, with a clear view of the entire class.
- The whole class is working on a "famous Canadians" theme and participating in the same literacy centres using texts at their own reading level.

c) Resources:

- Seven copies of *Terry Fox: A Story of Hope*
- Student completed biography maps for note taking
- Newspaper article (overhead)
- Tracking/observation record (teacher)

A JUNIOR GUIDED WRITING MINI-LESSON PLAN (continued)

3. Teaching Content and Strategies

Before Writing

a) Introduce the text

Ask: How will I activate students' prior knowledge? How will I prepare students for the lesson objective? How will I introduce the idea of paragraphs?

b) Activate Prior Knowledge

Review what is already known and has been written about Terry Fox's life. Ask students what they have learned about Terry Fox's life from their reading and writing over the past couple of days. Ask students to summarize, paraphrase, and discuss their biography webs.

c) Establish New Learning

Ask: What is the targeted reading strategy or lesson objective? How will I introduce the strategy? How will I encourage students to practise the strategy during independent writing?

Formulate questions.

Have students develop questions they still have about how to organize their recorded information into paragraphs and suggest that perhaps the answers to these questions are found in how their biography maps answer the 5 Ws + H.

Teacher:

- Meets with small group who have all completed biography maps and are ready to organize their maps into draft reports.
- Uses newspaper articles, which they have previously studied and written, as models of how the 5Ws + H are used to organize the information.
- In the newspaper article, the teacher highlights the "What" or topic sentence, and then the "Who" and "Where" and so on, highlighting each in a different colour and pointing out the change of paragraph for each.
- Directs students to pages in the Terry Fox book, points out how the author used a new paragraph each time something new happened in Terry's life, and notes how each new paragraph is indented with a short space to the right of the margin.
- Summarizes the "trick" for knowing when to make a new paragraph: decide what it's about and if it's something new, like a new "W" start a new paragraph by indenting it.
- Directs students to find information in their biography maps under each of the 5Ws + H and use coloured highlighters to begin to organize their maps to write them as reports with paragraphs.

4. Consolidation

During Writing (consolidation and application): Focus on students' application of strategies

Ask: Do students understand the principle of using the 5Ws+H as a guide for forming new paragraphs?

A JUNIOR GUIDED WRITING MINI-LESSON PLAN (continued)

Ask students to use coloured highlighters to highlight the information on their bio-maps that relate to each of the 5Ws + H.

5. Application

During

Each student identifies the 5W information and begins the first draft of their reports independently. Teacher circulates and assists as required or requested.

After

After the independent reading, the writing is discussed: Were you able to find the 5Ws+H in your bio-maps? Did it help you begin your drafts with some idea of where new paragraphs should be formed?

Beyond this Lesson on Writing

Teachers provide opportunities for follow-up discussion.

Ask: What support will students require as they move on to the revising, editing, and sharing stages of the writing process?

At the revising and publishing stages they may want to:

a) Create a table of contents for *Terry Fox: A Story of Hope*, by labelling phases of his life.

b) Create a glossary that represents Terry Fox's life.

c) Track Terry Fox's life on a map as he travelled across Canada. Be sure to include dates.

d) Use Terry Fox's biography as a model to form their reports into biographies. Students will be encouraged to use visual evidence, with captions.

6. Assessment

Teacher observes and records the strategies used and level of student engagement. Conducts a writing conference with one or two students. The following chart is a suggested format that can be easily transferred into a guided writing "At a Glance" sheet for the whole guided reading group.

Student Name: Aisha
Date: December 20, 2005
Text Used: *Terry Fox: A Story of Hope*
Strategy Focus: Writing Paragraphs
Strategies Used:
Level of Student Engagement:
Writing Sample attached: ❏ Yes ❏ No
Writing Conference conducted: ❏ Yes (attached) ❏ No
Observations:

Source: Lesson Plan Template from Ontario Ministry of Education (2003); Nipissing University (2005).

- Guided writing may also be done individually as the teacher circulates during writers' workshop.

- The teacher plans and teaches mini-lessons on procedures, strategies, and skills with individual or small groups of students with similar strengths and needs; models organization and brainstorming; and guides students through the writing process.

Evaluation and Assessment of Guided Writing

Teachers know when they are using guided reading successfully by watching their students develop self-extending writing, word-solving, and spelling systems that allow them to become flexible and proficient problem solvers and writers. Teachers assess the level of student learning in guided writing through observation before, during, and after writing, and through formal and informal conferencing. The section Assessment in Writers' Workshop presents an overview of the assessment of independent writing samples. Assessment provides significant information for subsequent planning and instruction; it concentrates mainly on the writers' acquisition and application of strategies such as organization, word use, and voice. Once guided writing mini-lessons have been conducted, teachers often challenge students to return to their texts and apply the new strategies. They may be asked to comment on their acquisition and application of strategies during sharing time or workshop checkout.

INDEPENDENT WRITING

Independent writing is typically done in the writers' workshop, with significant scaffolding and support from teacher and peers. During independent writing, students engage in guided practice implementing the writing process, as described below, and supported by the structures of a workshop setting where students write as part of a community of authors who share their writing. We consider first the cycle of writing as a recursive process, and then present the context for its implementation. Figure 12.3 is a detailed diagram of the writing cycle. It is important to note that the shifts between stages occur minute by minute, second by second, throughout the writing process. They are seldom discrete linear steps but overlapping, recursive ones. Writing is a recursive process, as is all literacy learning. As we progress through the stages, we present a brief overview, key characteristics, tips for supporting each stage, and a student example of each stage.

FIGURE 12.3 The Writing Cycle

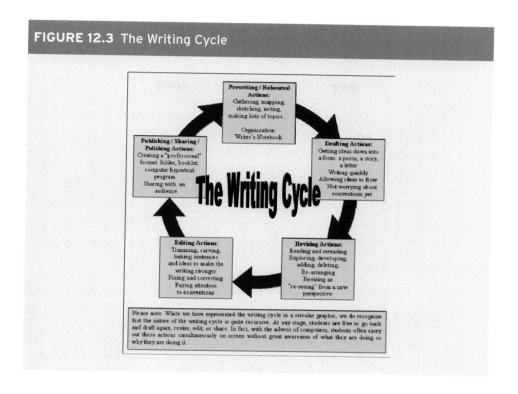

The Writing Process or Cycle

PREWRITING/REHEARSAL

The prewriting or rehearsal phase of writing is a way of life for writers: it involves an almost constant state of awareness, vision, and imagination. It is important that your students realize that real writers see potential stories everywhere at all times. One way to encourage this way of being attentive to the sources of inspiration all around us everyday is a writer's notebook (Calkins & Harwayne, 1990), in which we can record ideas, topic lists, and possibilities to explore in the future. This treasure house of ideas can include quotations from favourite stories, poems from favourite authors, drawings, clippings, cartoons, photos, observations, or the raw beginnings of a poem or story.

This stage of the writing process does not require full topic development. It does include considering a range of possible topics and then choosing one topic or theme as a focus. Once a topic is selected, the writer determines the purpose of the writing and explores appropriate forms. When this aspect of writing is given sufficient attention—when teachers provide time and guidance through talking, reading, and tentative writing activities—it is a highly creative and exciting part of the writing cycle. When time and stimulation are provided at this stage, you do not need to limit young writers to assigned topics or story starters. Sometimes specific topics will be suggested or assigned; however, students need the opportunity to choose topics of personal interest.

Prewriting or rehearsing may involve processes such as reading widely on a topic or examples of a particular genre or style, gathering raw materials, mapping possible lines of development, sketching out patterns or ideas, and thinking about a possible purpose, audience, format, and genre. Activities can include talking, observing, reading, drawing, or brainstorming for ideas.

Generating Topics

Using a writer's notebook is most effective when it is considered a "tool for living and writing" (Calkins & Harwayne, 1991, p. 35). Calkins points out that notebooks can be "just another place for writing, or they can represent a new way of thinking about the writing process" (p. 37). When notebooks are a tool that invites young writers to write about anything and everything without being committed to any draft in particular, this is a shift away from assigned topics. The idea is to accumulate a rich cache of ideas into which the writer can delve and then choose a promising item for further exploration and development. The writer then begins to ask, What do I want to do with this? What form will it take? Who is my audience? The reader response journals in Theory into Practice 8.1 and 8.2 encourage students to collect words, phrases, ideas, images, and connections to texts as they read. These responses are a rehearsal for writing. In the margin is an entry in a writer's notebook by a Grade 3 student, writing in poetic form about her struggle to find a topic.

Topics, Personal Choice, and Voice

If "voice" in writing can be described as the ineffable presence of the author's personality, expressed through a certain style that says "These are my words, and only I could write them," how do you or how can you teach students to write freely so that their individual voices are heard in all their diversity, personality, and individuality?

When students are given the opportunity and freedom to choose their own topics from a rich personal collection of ideas, their writing will be expressed in their own individual voices. That important aspect of quality writing called "voice" is less likely to require explicit teaching when students are able to write about topics and themes that matter to them. Remember that at the elementary level young writers are *children*. While that may seem to limit them in terms of knowledge and experience and the ability to express their ideas and opinions in writing, we must keep in mind that children are more knowledgeable than adults on certain topics and themes.

> *When we put a premium on topics that are considered meaty, deep, or significant to adult eyes and we ask students to probe these issues with sophisticated techniques, we are denying children the opportunity to capture their childhoods through childish eyes. We are also denying them the written texts that will preserve their memories of themselves as children.*
>
> (Harwayne, 2001, p. 10)

When you can't think of what to write.

I can't think of what to write not about a bee and not about a mite. And if I'd think I mite think of what to write

Alex's Grade 3 writer's notebook entry

With this in mind, encourage your students to make lists of writing topics and themes where they, as elementary-school-age children, have something over adults—topics about which they are the experts. Although these topics and themes will vary from Kindergarten to Grade 8 and lists can be generated with your students, the following are some possibilities suggested by Harwayne (2001):

- Pretending: Young children spend time playing and pretending to be animals and characters from stories; their own artwork and early writing reflects this.

- Collecting: Most children collect something, from rocks to hockey cards. Writing about their collections and researching and writing about what others collect are natural extensions of their own activities.

- Rites of passage: Childhood is full of "first times." From the first time they ride a bike to the first time they stay up all night at a sleepover—these crucial events are guaranteed to be of personal importance to children (pp. 23–33).

Choice of topics about which young writers truly have something to say is one way to encourage children to write in ways that display their personal voice. But how can you encourage students to write in a way that communicates who they are as the author of a piece? In Teacher Talk 12.1, Jeff Scott recalls teaching transactional writing to his Grade 2

Teacher Talk/12.1

JEFF SCOTT: FOSTERING STUDENT VOICE IN TRANSACTIONAL WRITING

I feel that too few teachers have opened their doors to the possibilities beyond personal narratives when it comes to teaching writing. How did I promote the use of voice in my students' writing? How did I encourage them to create written reports that reflected more than just the facts? How did I support a more colourful writing style, even though they were writing factual reports?

Before I answer these questions, I would like to begin by defining what I mean by voice and audience awareness. *Voice* refers to the writer's sense of commitment in the writing, which is demonstrated in the choice of information, the style in which the information is presented, and the presence of the writer's personality in the writing. *Audience awareness* refers to the way the writer has written to anticipate the reader's need for information and to maintain the reader's interest. How will this sound to a reader? Will it make sense? Will it be interesting to read?

Students offer personal "wisdom" and "voice" in the classroom, on the playground, or at home, on a constant basis. This voice may be an informed one as a result of personal experiences and knowledge or may be an uninformed opinion. One must recognize the value or importance of this personal idea and support it, whether to clear up a misconception, add to the comment, or merely reply to it. I believe it is our job as teachers to encourage students and teach them how to use their voice, not only in oral discussions but also in print. Often teachers allow students to share orally a personal moment or item in class. Do we allow this to happen in our writing programs?

I have found that students are able to use their voice when researching something that is of interest to them; in the primary grades, animals are always a popular area of research. Students are introduced to frameworks, a tool that is effective for gathering and organizing information effectively on a single page. The use of this tool combines the skills of deciding what information is necessary, how much information is needed and relevant, the use of point-form note-taking, as well as the organization of the final paper, sentence construction, and the composition of each paragraph. The following is an example of a framework.

Heading 1: Penguins	
Criterion 1: Appearance	sharp beaks, smooth belly
Criterion 2: Flight	waddle, can't fly, have solid bones
Criterion 4: Classification	bird family
Criterion 3: Interesting Facts	spiky tongues, Emperor Penguin is the largest, Blue Penguin is the smallest

Students identified and selected the criteria they wished to research (other areas include food, enemies, and habitat). Students read through their material and entered the information in the appropriate cell on the framework. Once they had done this, it became fairly straightforward to organize the writing and students took the information and put it into sentences. Sentences were grouped according to the criteria to ensure paragraphs with similar material. Throughout this process,

Teacher Talk/12.1

JEFF SCOTT: FOSTERING STUDENT VOICE IN TRANSACTIONAL WRITING (continued)

I provided mini-lessons on how to: identify important information in a section of writing; reduce important information to point form; group information according to specific criteria; create interesting sentences using a variety of styles; compose a fluent paragraph; and add their own voice, feelings, and opinions, on the topic. The framework and resulting collected information formed the basis for bringing voice into each student's writing. It has been my experience that as students acquire more information and knowledge on a topic they begin to feel more personally about it and are willing to share their feelings orally. Providing this opportunity to share their feelings with their classmates is an important step in developing voice in their writing.

Another method I have used to encourage the use of voice is modelling. Children were provided with sample articles from magazines such as *Owl, Chickadee, National Geographic Kids, Young Naturalist*, and *Ranger Rick* where the authors used their own voices in combination with researched facts. Portions of these articles were dissected to discover how the authors delivered information while maintaining their voice in their writing. I feel that if we want children to become non-fiction writers, where both facts and personal voice are evident, we need to provide them with a multitude of resources. In addition, we need to ensure that students have the opportunity to share their feelings with others. Providing voice in writing does not come naturally for children; it requires the teacher to provide a variety of examples and a lot of encouragement and opportunities to talk and write. I believe that the addition of voice transforms a piece of descriptive writing into something much more personal and interesting to read. The following piece of writing was produced by a Grade 2 student; it has only been edited by a peer! Although the paragraphs are not well defined, notice the student's use of voice.

Penguins (peer-edited piece by a Grade 2 student)

Penguins are truly famous birds to me and that is why I did this project. Your going to hear about it's description its location and more. Enjoy!

Instead of teeth penguins have sharp beaks. Scientists found out that penguin can see better under water than on land. Penguins are gliding softly threw the water that nobody knew what made them go so softy. It was a smooth belly they were born with. Penguins have spicky tongues like little spikes on knifes. Birds can fly through the air but can penguins? No! because penguins have solid bones and birds need hollow bones to fly in the air so gracefully. Did you know that the emperor penguin is the largest in the entire penguin family? Did you know that the little Blue penguin is the smallest penguin? My brain didn't tell me that the little Blue penguin was the smallest penguin when it was time to do research. Did yours when you found out that penguins were real live animals?

Guess what animal category a penguin fits in? If you guessed birds your right. Lots of people think that penguins are in a different category because they can't fly. Just because they can't fly doesn't mean that they can't be in the bird category. My feelings got hurt when the penguin book that gave me the facts told me that almost every person in South America didn't think that penguins were in the bird category.

Jeff Scott is a science professor in Nipissing University's Education Faculty. He taught Grade 2 when this piece was written.

students and shares some of the strategies he used when his students were developing reports based on their studies of animals.

Deciding on Purpose, Form, and Audience

"Writing is for stories to be read, books to be published, poems to be recited, plays to be acted, songs to be sung, cards to be sent, cartoons to be labelled, instructions to be followed" (Smith, 1983, p. 566). When we consider the many purposes of writing, we are reminded of Halliday's (1973) functions of language, which apply to writing as much as they do to oral language. Figure 12.4 reminds us that we can write for a variety of

FIGURE 12.4 Forms and Functions of Writing

Language Functions or Purposes	Forms of Writing	Audience
Instrumental Language used to get things done	Business letters, memos, reminders	Specific addressee
Regulatory Language used to tell how	Written instructions, directions, posted rules	Students, those we wish to instruct
Heuristic Language used to find things out	Exploratory writing, questioning, research, interviews	Self or an expert
Interactional Language used for social relationships	Friendly letters, greeting cards, e-mail, dialogue journals	Friends, peers
Personal Language of feelings	Letters to the editor, diaries, journals, learning logs	Self, general public
Imaginative Language of the imagination	Poems, stories, scripts, jokes, riddles	Self, teacher, peers, family
Representative Language used to talk about the world	Reports, biographies, summaries, informational texts	Self, teacher, the world

(Compare with Figures 4.7 and Figure 8.7.)

purposes, in forms or formats that correspond to those functions, which Halliday identified for oral language.

Tips for Prewriting and Rehearsal

The following are tips for students for prewriting and rehearsal:

- Keep a writer's notebook (or a reader response journal).
- Read a lot and often and include a wide range of authors, styles, genres, topics, themes, and formats.
- Maintain a list of topics, themes, and writing ideas that you care about.
- Brainstorm orally and in writing; use concept webbing, drawings, charts, diagrams, outlines, and graphic organizers.
- View and discuss films, plays, artwork, and other visual and dramatic media.
- Engage in drama and storytelling.
- Take photographs.
- Make observations.
- Listen to conversations.
- Ask the following questions:
  - What am I really interested in?
  - What do I know about my topic?
  - How could I find out more?
  - Who do I want to write for?
  - How can I make my topic interesting and enjoyable for my audience?
  - Who are my favourite authors? What do I like about their style?

Two student generated samples of prewriting and rehearsal are presented on the following page.

DRAFTING

When drafting a story, William Faulkner advised, "Get it down. Take chances. It may be bad, but it is the only way you can do anything really good." At this stage, the idea is to make light, quick, tentative lines with the awareness that nothing is permanent. The goal is to get the ideas down on paper while they are flowing. This involves putting our ideas into a written context, but not making final decisions about the form the writing may take.

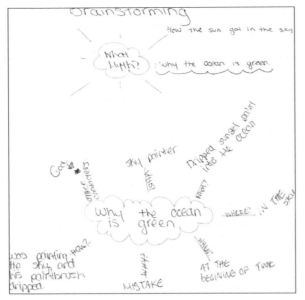
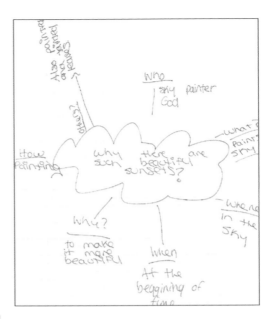

Student Generated Samples of Prewriting/Rehearsal

For student writers, this process of drafting quickly serves the practical purpose of getting ideas down before they are forgotten. How do you explain this free flow of thoughts and feelings from inside the writer to the page? One suggestion is to model it by verbalizing how one lets the ideas tumble out in much the same way we allow it to happen when chatting with family or friends; we don't think about it very much—we just let it happen. On the other hand, there are some guidelines that will help the next stages in the writing process, when you need to be more analytical and critical.

You can model the usefulness of drafting using double spacing on one side of the page, so there is space for changes, rearrangements, and additions. Writers should also get into the habit of reading and rereading their own text as they write, so that ideas can be shaped and connected as they are written. Writers don't necessarily wait until the revising and editing stages to make adjustments.

Tips for Drafting

The following are tips for students for drafting:

• Write quickly and often.

• Let the ideas flow.

• Allow yourself to be surprised by your own writing.

- Keep all copies of drafts and a record of all changes; you may want to go back to your original writing. (If writing by hand, write on one side of the page, on every other line, and draw a single line through deletions so that you can still read them. If using a computer, use the track changes and comment functions.)

- Ask the following questions:

  - What do I really want to say?

  - How long should this be? (Is it too long? Is it too short?)

  - How do I want this to sound?

  - How do I get my feelings about this into the piece?

  - Will this be interesting to anyone besides me?

  - Do I need more information or different ideas?

  - Would this be better expressed through a different form? (If it's a story, maybe it could become a poem or a letter).

  Below are two student generated samples of drafting.

Student Generated Samples of Drafting

REVISING

Drafting becomes revising once the writing has taken on a form appropriate to the writer's purposes. When a writer has what seems to be a more or less complete letter, story, poem, or report, the piece needs to be carefully re-read and looked at from the reader's point of view. This is where the author's sense of style, word order, organization, clarity, and the specifics of the writer's craft are all brought to bear—where, above all, the piece is read with a critical eye to improve the writing itself.

One way to teach the concept of revision is to point out the derivation of the word "re-vision" as a form of "re-seeing," looking again, or seeing our ideas for a second or third time from a different perspective. The processes involved in revising include exploring new and related ideas, developing the ideas already recorded, adding details, and deleting repetitions and sentences or passages that do not serve the writer's intentions and purposes.

Tips for Revising

Teach students that the key actions when revising include re-reading and revisiting the writing several times—aloud if possible—in order to do the following:

- Find what they like in their writing and mark the best words and sentences.

- Find the heart of the piece; underline the part that is at the centre of what you want to say.

- Look at details; for example, find three good verbs, one simple direct sentence, and three nouns that ask for more detail.

(Based on Graves, 2005, pp. 9-14.)

During student conferences, mini-lessons, and modelled writing, teach your students to ask themselves these questions:

- When I read my writing out loud does it flow?

- Is it clear what my goal is throughout the piece of writing? Did I achieve my goal? Did I write what I intended to write?

- Is there a catchy introduction? Does the conclusion leave the reader thinking?

- Does every word count? There should be a reason why a specific noun, verb, adjective, or adverb is used.

- Do the events follow in an order the reader can follow?

- Have I used sentence expansion to add adjectives or adverbs?

- Is my train of thought clear? Are there any parts that don't belong?

- Do I use a variety of verbs throughout the piece? (For example, look at a list of verbs to use in place of "said.")

- Am I using the same words and phrases over and over again? Did I check a thesaurus?

- Do details support *only* the topic sentence of *that* paragraph?

- Is the proper format used throughout?

- Are all sentences complete or are there sentence fragments?

- Is a vivid picture created in the reader's mind?

Conference Sample: Praise, Question, Polish

P: I like the rich imagery that you used throughout your writing and the connections you made to both myths and Bible stories.

Q: I wonder how the skypainter felt when he was finally brought back to God and had to explain how he had been passing his time. What is the strongest part of this piece of writing?

Student Response: I really made an attempt to use words that would evoke imagery. I used the thesaurus to come up with new words and I experimented with how to incorporate them into my writing (for example, splotch, drip, mottle, confusion of colours).

P: On this page, you have used the same word "tremendous" three times. I wonder if you can find synonyms that would make your writing stronger and more interesting.

Days passed, and still no word of the sky painter. God was worried about what had become of his faithful artist.

Finally, one day, God's workers brought back the sky painter, weary and starving. Right away, God prepared a tremendous feast in celebration of his return. During the tremendous feast, God said to the sky painter "Why did you hide from me?" The sky painter bowed his head, and said "Have you looked at the trees recently? I have destroyed their dazzling colors, and now, they appear to be ~~look like~~ a tremendous confusion of colors." As God peeked through the clouds, he noticed the dazzling colors, and thought to himself. "This is the dawning of a new world. I now state

Student Generated
Sample of Revising

EDITING

Editing can occur at any point in the writing process, but it must be addressed specifically before final publication. Editing includes attending to the conventions of writing and making corrections as needed. It also includes looking for possible ways to trim, carve, and change how sentences and ideas are linked. The writer's goal is to correct any errors in conventions to make the text look and sound stronger.

Soon afterwards the sky painter looked below, and to

his astonishment, what he saw was a vast ocean of colour.

In fear of what god would have thought of his work, he

hid under a nearby rock.

The next morning, there was no sunrise, and no sunset.

The sky stayed plain — no beautiful red or pinks, no

brilliant orange or yellows, just simple blacks and whites.

God searched for the sky painter, for he wanted his

beautiful sunsets back once again. He searched high and

low, far and wide, but he could not find him anywhere.

Finally, after days of searching he sent out two of his best

Sample of Editing

Since the ultimate goal for your students is that they have the ability to independently and efficiently edit their own writing, you must be prepared to spend time teaching and re-teaching the use of writing conventions in both reading and writing contexts. It takes time for children to internalize the range of details they should pay attention to when editing and proofreading their work—from spelling and grammar to word choice. While they are learning, we can encourage greater independence by posting reminders to attend to details that typically require attention and correction. For example, the acronym C.O.P.S. reminds students to check their work for Capitals, Overall appearance, Punctuation, and Spelling and grammar. Self-editing checklists, such as the one below, can be included in students' writing folders or notebooks.

Self, Peer, or Teacher Editing Checklist

❏ I have spell checked my work.

❏ I have ensured that my possessives and plurals are correct.

❏ I have checked comma placement.

❏ I had a peer check the conventions and I asked my teacher to do a final editing check as well.

❏ I have compared my final draft to my final copy and made sure that I have made all the changes.

Tips for Editing

The following are some tips for students for editing:

• Read and re-read your work with a critical eye.

• Look for possible errors in spelling, punctuation, and grammar.

• Use dictionaries and writing models to see how the experts spell, punctuate, and put sentences together.

• Have a friend, relative, or teacher proofread your writing after you have edited to the best of your ability.

• Ask the following questions:

  ▪ Is my final draft as error-free as possible?

  ▪ Do I have complete sentences with proper punctuation?

  ▪ Is my handwriting or printing clear?

- If it is a printout, is the font clear and a good size for most readers?
- Is this the best writing I am capable of?

PUBLISHING

Before **publishing** or sharing written pieces, whether with peers or beyond the classroom, they must be polished. It is important to stress that not all pieces make it to the publishing stage. This is where keeping a cumulative folder or portfolio of student work is vital. A crucial aspect of self-evaluation is to go over one's own writing and decide which pieces should be taken to the publishing stage. Although the choice should ultimately be the student's own, this can be discussed during peer and teacher conferences.

Tips for Publishing and Sharing

- Make the decision about what to publish and how to share a piece—a collaborative process, with the final choice being made by the student.
- Ask the following questions:
  - Which work is my best, most interesting, and most powerful piece of writing?
  - What will I have to do to prepare it for sharing?
  - How do I want to publish it or make it public?
  - Do I want to do any the following:
    - Display it on a bulletin board?
    - Enter a writing contest?
    - Contribute to a class anthology?
    - Show it to my family as a booklet, letter, or in another form?
    - Publish it in a magazine or school newspaper?

Writers' Workshop: A Time and a Place for Writing

The content of a writing lesson matters far less than the context of it...
we need to structure the workshop carefully, thinking about time,
schedules, rules, expectations and materials.
—Lucy Calkins

Writers' workshop creates a literacy environment for students to write independently, explore the texts of their lives, and discuss their writing

I have decided to publish my work as a story-book. I will use water colours for my illustrations and a combination of black and white and colour images to support my story.

I intend to share my story with my peers as well as with younger students. I would like to participate in a literacy café or exhibition at either the class level or the school level.

A long time ago, when the world was young, the world looked like a massive coloring book that no one had taken the time to color in. Then, one day, when God got tired of seeing the same two colours, he hired a sky painter. This slender, dwarfish, brittle elderly man had probably never painted anything in his life, never mind a sunset. With whiskers on his chin and wearing an old hat, he walked with a gallon of paint in one hand and a paint brush in the other. God said to him "Go now, and paint me ravishing sunsets, brilliant flowers and textured animals. I want to see colour. Colour is life, stamina, and feelings. Go forth and make me happy."

**A Bird of Many Colours
By Ashley Parr**

Student Generated Samples of Publishing and Sharing

with peers. Students are provided with the time they need to engage fully in the writing process and write, revise, discuss, and share their writing on a variety of levels. During writers' workshop, students acquire and practice writing strategies to construct, extend, and revise meaning as they write a variety of texts for purposes that they choose and control. Large group instruction, mini-lessons, grand conversations, journals, and **writing conferences** with the teacher and other students enable readers to explore, construct, and revise their understandings, make inferences, and respond personally and critically to their writing. In writers' workshop, students have the freedom to construct and write texts that they find personally relevant and meaningful. Teachers make available a range of writing materials for students to explore; they also schedule time for independent writing, discussion, journaling, writing process activities, sharing circles, and grand conversations.

ESSENTIAL ELEMENTS OF WRITERS' WORKSHOPS

Writers' workshops are similar to readers' workshops: the goal of the workshop is independent writing, balanced with literary warm-ups, mini-lessons, self-selected writing, and one-on-one conferencing time. Figure 12.5 is an overview of how activities, time, and space should be organized. Teachers need to spend time in the first term establishing predictable routines and procedures, as well as organizing the time, space, and materials to support independent student writing. In order to ensure that writers' workshops run smoothly, students need:

In writers' workshop, students develop the craft of writing and create and share written work.

- a predictable organizational structure for daily writing

- regular instruction based on ongoing needs

- a well-ordered productive workshop where they can develop the craft of writing, create, and share written work

- information on:

  - how to obtain and return resources such as paper, notebooks, files, reference materials

  - how to manage personal writing folders and portfolios

  - how and where to store finished and unfinished writing

  - how to solve writing problems when the teacher is busy

  - where and when peer and teacher conferences are held (posted daily)

  - setting and meeting deadlines, both teacher and self-imposed

ASSESSMENT IN WRITERS' WORKSHOP

Assessment in writers' workshop can take a variety of formal and informal formats, but each should reflect the individual goals set by the students, the teachers, and curriculum guidelines. Through conferencing, observation, and analysis, writer behaviours can be assessed. Teachers should look for student growth in both holistic behaviours such as organization, voice, fluency, self-monitoring, application of fix-up strategies, risk-taking, engagement, recognition of good writing and what authors do, and more specific strategies such as making use of prior knowledge, predicting, critiquing, establishing criteria for selecting, and purposeful selection of writing genres, and formats.

Since engagement is an essential characteristic of writers' workshop, part of the responsibility for assessment should be shared with the writers,

FIGURE 12.5 Essential Elements of Writers' Workshops

1. **Literary Warm-Up (5 minutes)**
   Literary warm-ups can involve book talks by students or teacher. They might also contain highlights of previous workshops, and quick presentations or responses prepared by students to motivate or interest other students.

2. **Mini-Lesson (5-10 minutes)**
   Mini-lessons are short, teacher-initiated, whole-group instructional sessions for constructing, extending, and revising meaning. Topics for mini-lessons are generally derived from the teacher's assessment and observation of what students need to know today to make them better writers tomorrow. Teachers select strategies that will prepare students to write new texts successfully and independently or support them in their continued development as writers. Many mini-lessons are procedural in nature (responding to issues of "how-to,") but flexibility is an important aspect as well. Teachers may use a combination of modelled, shared, interactive writing, or published works as models to demonstrate the focus of the mini-lesson. There are times when teachers conduct mini-lessons for small groups of learners. Topics for mini-lessons include:

   - organization, sequencing, story grammar, story structure using a story map (beginning, middle, end), how to create a character, how to craft a good ending that is either satisfying for the reader or invites them to think further about a topic
   - voice, imagery, word choice, grammar, sentence fluency
   - conventions, for example, saying words slowly to hear and record all the sounds in a word, capitalization, quotation marks, verb tense
   - presentation, illustration possibilities, word processing, desktop publishing
   - writing cycle stages
   - rules and routines
     1. Use a quiet voice.
     2. Work hard.
     3. Use class resources.
     4. Don't worry about spelling on first drafts.

3. **Self-Selected Writing (remainder of the workshop)**
   During self-selected writing (SSW), students and teacher begin to write quietly, setting and maintaining an atmosphere of focused production. The choices depend on the needs of the students, goals established during mini-lessons, and the writer's purpose. Independent writing topics may be student or teacher generated, but there should always be some choice during the "independent time." Sometimes students will be required to engage in assigned writing. Teachers model a new genre, engage in shared writing, and then assign a writing task. These assignments may occur in conjunction with cross-curricular subject areas, for example, summaries, comparisons, explanations, directions, legends for maps, reports. As students gain control of a variety of genres (in both reading and writing), different forms of writing will appear

FIGURE 12.5 Essential Elements of Writers' Workshops (continued)

in their independent writing. Teachers should spend part of each SSW time writing for their own purposes. During the rest of the period, teachers circulate, support, and conference with writers. During this block of time, students should be engaged in all aspects of the writing process. Students are encouraged to select works from their writing folders and continue to work independently, rehearsing, drafting, revising, editing, polishing, and sharing.

Tips:

- To keep noise and movement at minimal levels, keep a jar of sharpened pencils and a second jar for pencils needing sharpening.
- Organize space to include easy storage and access to the following materials:
  - notebooks or teacher-prepared books
  - writing folders/portfolios (commercial or student made)
  - variety of paper: unlined, lined, different sizes, colours, textures, and shapes for pasting into scrapbooks (Primary)
  - variety of surfaces for writing: blackboards, slates, white boards, magnetic boards, magic slates
  - variety of tools for writing: magic markers, pencils, chalk, paint brushes, crayons
  - resources: alphabet cards, alphabet books, dictionaries, personal spelling dictionaries, word rings (word cards attached to a large key ring), thesauruses, language handbooks
- Post resource charts for easy access to steps in the writing process, word lists, and references charts highlighting common homonyms (for example, to, too, two), theme words, spelling patterns/rules, and commonly misspelled words.

4. **Individual writing conferences should be held with each student as regularly as possible.**
   The teacher usually initiates conferences with students, either based on a schedule or spontaneously based on observed needs. This signals that students may also confer quietly with a peer, obtain resources, or seek help. Teachers observe and record perhaps using a clipboard with class list, or a posted "status of the class" list to identify and track individual and group needs. The student and teacher listen to one another or they read, react, reinforce strategies, ask questions, and evaluate progress toward old goals and set new ones. Teachers should establish rapport, share, listen, comment, encourage, and guide during these conferences. Conferences may include formal assessments, informal writing inventories, or think alouds.

5. **Sharing Time/Celebration/Workshop Checkout or Author's Chair**
   A large-group gathering is usually held at the conclusion of each workshop period. This may be formal or informal. Its purposes should be student-oriented; that is, primarily for feedback and response from an audience of peers to a piece of writing, which may be a completed piece, or a work in progress. The emphasis should be on celebration and offering helpful suggestions for improvement. This is the students' opportunity to share what they are doing in their writing or highlight their favourite passages or topics assigned during mini-lessons.

especially as they evaluate their growth as writers and their progress toward set goals. Teachers share the assessment process with students as they conference and examine reading responses, journals, and a variety of writing samples. Effective evaluation and assessment of writing involves:

- frequent oral feedback as teacher circulates during writers' workshop
- focusing on one or two error-types at a time during student conferences, where teaching correct forms can occur on-the-run
- full evaluation of only a few polished pieces, chosen with the student as representative samples of "best work" kept in a folder or portfolio
- viewing growth over time
- student self-evaluation and self-assessment being taught and encouraged

Ongoing assessment by both students and teacher occurs continuously, often "on-the run" as during the writers' workshop, at all stages of the writing process. A status of the class chart may be posted and used to keep track of which writing stage each student is engaged in, when, and for how long. All assessment is done for the purpose of improving student writing and encouraging risk-taking. Teachers may use anecdotal records and checklists. Students may use self-assessment forms for revision and editing.

Assessment of Independent Writing through Writing Conferences

An effective writing program should include a variety of assessment tools such as surveys, interest inventories, writing logs, checklists, questionnaires, rubrics, and portfolios or cumulative folders.

Published research and our own experience leads us to argue that the most powerful and useful assessment occurs in collaboration with students, during a conference, when authentic feedback can be provided and immediate student needs can be met.

Scheduled Conferences

Conferences are most effective when they are brief and to the point— usually just one teaching point. Conferences may also take place during quiet writing time. Focus on:

- content, organization, imagery
- writer's craft (audience, voice, and word choice)
- revision and editing processes

- design and organization
- publishing formats

Rather than relying solely on finished products to assess writing, anecdotal records and scheduling notes should be kept; they contain important assessment information. Since writing is a process, and it is being taught and learned as fundamentally recursive in nature, the process itself should be assessed, not just the final product. Figure 12.6 contains a detailed list of questions and prompts to support students at various stages of the writing process.

Teaching Students How to Peer Conference

Teach and post the easily remembered, three-step format for questioning: **P**-Praise; **Q**-Question; **P**-Polish. This easily remembered acronym encourages students to first offer specific praise for another student's writing, then ask a question to show interest and request clarification, and then offer a suggestion for polishing the work.

The Art of Assessing Beginning Writers

In the sample, the teacher has interpreted the student's message in red ink below the student's writing—a practice called underwriting. Underwriting difficult-to-read emergent writing can be an appropriate teaching tool. It should be done in collaboration with students as they re-read their written words and the teacher writes to show them the way it would look if "written in a book." It isn't clear that the teacher wrote this as the child dictated because the teacher missed the word "because" (decas). During such a collaborative conversation, the teacher should point out all the things the child did correctly; for example, writing something that matches the picture so well, moving left to right, leaving spaces between some of the words, printing clearly, and writing the letters to match the sounds in the words. Most Kindergarten teachers (junior or senior) would write "WOW!" and then respond to the child's writing in an oral conference. We feel that to write the correct version in an apparent spirit of marking the work, rather than working with the student, may be quite discouraging to a young writer.

We suggest instead that the teacher have an informal conference or collaborative conversation with the child about the picture and its message using the PQP format. The teacher should teach one thing, for ex-

Text (JK sample): I like the cow because it is my favourite.

FIGURE 12.6 Conference Questions that Support and Encourage Independent Writing Development

Note: the following questions can be modified to apply to specific genres or writing formats. They apply whether the writing is a poem, a story, a letter, or a report.

Reasoning
- Why did you choose this subject?
- Do you have enough information? Are you basing this on your own experiences or background knowledge? Tell me about it.
- What is the most important thing you are saying here? (Referring to the whole or to a specific part of the writing.)

Communication, Audience, Voice
- How does this draft sound when you read it out loud?
- Do you feel it is saying what you intend it to say to a reader?
- Who are you writing this for? Who do you picture reading your work?
- Is this the best word here?
- Do we have enough details to be able to visualize your report? Will your reader be able to picture your characters and setting?
- Show me a place where I can tell that you have written this piece.

Organization
- Are you happy with your beginning and ending (introduction and conclusion)?
- Have you tied the introduction to the end? How?
- Does your beginning grab the reader's attention?
- Is the middle well developed?
- Did your organizer help you?

Conventions
- What strategies are you using to revise and edit this piece?
- What do you think needs the most attention when proofreading: spelling, capitalization, or punctuation? Anything else?
- Are you going to publish this piece? How do you intend to present this visually?
- Are there other forms besides a written report that you might use to present this? (For example, multimedia, commercial advertisement, newscast, drama, poem, or letter.)

The above categories are based on Ontario Ministry of Education and Training (1999).

What is your next step?
- Do you want to share this with a peer, a small group, the class, or another classroom?
- What are your plans for your next piece of writing? Which areas do you want to improve?

ample, the word "my" or "like," both of which the student is likely to use again. A high-frequency word can be taught by pointing it out in a story book, having the child construct it using magnetic letters, or practise writing it in sand and on a white board.

The Art of Assessing More Experienced Writers

The following sample is a first draft from a student in Grade 4. The teacher's comments are written in the margin.

Once again we suggest using the PQP format in a conference with this student. Since this is not yet a polished piece presented for publishing, it would not be appropriate to assess the writing formally with a rubric.

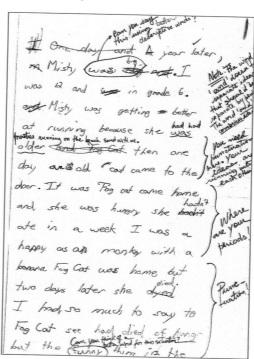

Student Generated
Sample First Draft:
Grade 4

1. Address the content first with some specific praise; for example, "I like the idea of a "fog cat" and your link to a cat named Misty—it makes your story sound interesting and mysterious."

2. Next ask a question to show interest, and to stimulate the student to think more deeply about their own writing, for example, "Where did you get the idea of a fog cat? Were you reading the poem by Carl Sandburg (posted on the wall)? Or did you read a story that made you think about this? Or do you really have a cat like the one in your story?"

3. Finally, teach one thing. All of the comments written by the teacher are valid, but the purpose of assessment should not be to overwhelm the student or discourage him/her. Ask yourself, "What does this student need right now to express these ideas more effectively?" It is also a good practice to ask students for a point they would like to improve.

Writing Assessment Using Rubrics

So far we have discussed classroom assessment of writing in terms of teacher observation, conferencing, anecdotal records, and checklists. When assessing a final published piece of writing, a common practice is to use a writing rubric designed to guide the scoring of the written work according to relevant criteria. Several characteristics of the writing are chosen, and descriptors provided for levels of achievement for each category. A well-designed rubric is tailored to the form of writing being assessed and the grade level. Thus, when assessing letter writing, the rubric would include descriptors under the category conventions such as "uses standard letter format, including date, salutation, body, and closing." The levels assigned for each characteristic or writing trait can be numerical—often ranging from one through four (Ontario), or a verbal scale, ranging from "not yet" to "WOW!" Here are some examples of rubric levels using a verbal, rather than numerical scale:

STOP, THINK, AND WRITE

The following comments are from a B.Ed. student.

The first writing assignments that I remember began in the Junior grades. Although I have never been very creative, I remember a couple of writing assignments that I poured my heart into about subjects that were close to my heart. When I received them back, I remember my disappointment when my marks were mediocre and my beautiful "masterpieces" had many red marks on them from the teacher. I was devastated. How dare they ruin my creation! What do they know anyway! Although I am a great speller and have good grammar, to this day, I have never been a personal writer and I feel that these early episodes may be part of it. My only writing has consisted of the necessities of my work, including proposals and reports.

Think back to a time when your writing was evaluated by a teacher. In particular, think of a time when you had poured your heart and soul into a piece. What was the teacher's response? Was it a positive or negative experience? How can this experience, and the one described above, inform your teaching practice?

Generic Levels

1. Novice—just beginning to use this writing trait or skill; needs assistance.

2. Apprentice—beginning to model the use of this skill using the examples of expert or proficient writers.

3. Proficient—shows independent control over this trait or skill.

Levels used by the rubic-based assessment tool—Six Traits® (which will be discussed further)—include: Not yet, Emerging, Developing, Competent, Experienced, and WOW! The categories targeted for assessment are crucial if the rubric is to be useful in providing students with specific guidance for improving their writing, and in providing teachers with information to plan further instruction. In Ontario, the focus is on the following categories of knowledge and skills: reasoning, communication, organization, and conventions.

While the Ontario rubrics have fairly clear descriptors for achievement levels from one to four and are illustrated with exemplars of student work at each level, we find the categories themselves to be potentially confusing. For example, in the case of a letter, does following the proper letter format apply to *organization*, or to *conventions*? In the introduction to *The Ontario Curriculum: Exemplars: Writing* (1999), letter format is included under Organization (p. 9), while in the rubric itself it is included under *Conventions* (p. 43). This may seem relatively unimportant, until we consider how to guide student improvement based on their scores on a rubric. How can we explain to a student in Grade 3 the differences between *Reasoning* ("uses well-developed ideas that are all connected to the topic") and *Organization* ("the main idea and the supporting ideas of each paragraph are clear and the paragraphs are linked to each other")?

The Six Traits® teaching writing uses the following categories: ideas, organization, voice, word choice, sentence fluency, and conventions. There are many texts and websites about the Six Traits® approach (see resources at the end of this chapter), but the origins of this practical approach seem to be at the grassroots level, among teachers themselves. The development of rubrics designed to describe what each of these traits looks like at different performance levels can be traced to a group of American educators in the 1980s (Spandel, 2005). The strength of the Six Traits® approach is that it is grounded in aspects of writing that are clearly identifiable and can be clearly understood by both teachers and students. When the accompanying rubrics are appropriately designed, the implications for improvement and instruction are apparent to both students and teachers.

In addition to the rubrics provided by the Ontario Ministry of Education (1999), there are many commercially prepared rubrics available online and in print. We suggest that you choose judiciously. Here are some questions to consider as you assess the clarity and usefulness of rubrics:

- Are the categories that are being assessed clearly defined?

- Are they currently a focus in your writing instruction? (Have you taught how to use *voice* in writing or taught what *sentence fluency* sounds like?)

- Is the rubric appropriate for the grade level?

- Can it be adapted for student use in "child-friendly" terminology?

- Is the rubric applicable to the form of writing being assessed?
- Are the levels of achievement applicable to your students' instructional levels?
- Are the descriptors for each level helpful?
- Do you and your students know what a Level 2 means, and how to raise their writing to a Level 3?
- Do you and they know what a piece of writing at the WOW! level looks like?

Rubrics are readily available for different forms of writing, from letters and reports to personal narratives and stories. One form of writing that can be difficult to assess using a rubric is poetry.

literacy notebook 12.5

STOP, THINK, AND WRITE

Using the poem "The Spider Acrobat" and the generic rubric form, create a rubric for writing poetry in Grade 3 and score the poem accordingly.

- How would you encourage this young author to improve her writing?
- Would you use the rubric to show her how to reach the next level? How?
- What are the limitations of using a rubric to assess a poem?

In and out and out and in.
Little spider loves to spin in and out and out and in.
If a fly pases by it shall get stuck in a web so thin.

RUBRIC FOR ASSESSING CHILDREN'S POETRY			
Categories Poet	1. Novice Poet	2. Apprentice Poet	3. Artistic
Ideas: the main message is suited for poetic form			
Word Choice: words chosen make the meaning come alive			
Poetic Devices and Form: rhythm, beat, rhyme, metaphor, imagery, line breaks, visual shaping			
Expression: musical sounding, appealing to the ear; evidence of author's creativity and originality			

Spelling and Word Study

Can spelling be taught adequately in the context of writers' workshop? The approach we are suggesting here is to reinforce the application of spelling skills during real reading and writing activities, including readers' and writers' workshop, where students can apply what they are learning about spelling in their own writing, where spelling is best assessed, rather than only through an isolated test based on a memorized list. This is not to say that spelling should not be formally taught or that well-chosen lists should not be used as part of spelling instruction (Bosman & Van Orden, 1997; Perfitti, 1997; Templeton, 2003).

Because spelling abilities develop through the teaching and learning of increasingly sophisticated problem-solving and pattern-noticing strategies, with the highest levels involving the ability to use words effectively, we feel that classroom activities related to spelling should focus more broadly on *word study*, rather than *just* spelling (which often implies memorization of weekly lists). Word study includes activities to build vocabulary in reading, writing, listening, and speaking, as many high-quality spelling programs do (see Ruth Scott's *Canadian Spelling Program*, for example, listed in the resources at the end of this chapter). We now present specific suggestions and teaching tips for word study—ideas that can be readily integrated into workshop activities.

Among the chief objections regarding the practice of teaching spelling and word knowledge in the context of real writing activities is that it:

> *depends on the teacher's knowledge base to present appropriate words that reflect the appropriate patterns...[and that] even if all teachers had this knowledge base readily available, such* incidental *instruction does not provide students the degree of exposure necessary for abstraction of appropriate spelling patterns.*
>
> (Templeton & Morris, 2000, p. 536)

We are not suggesting that spelling instruction should be left only to *incidental* instruction; on-the-run instruction at teachable moments is powerful, but it does not replace a structured word study program. As for teacher knowledge about how spelling pattern knowledge develops, this is an area for ongoing professional development and continual classroom assessment and careful observation. These goals can be achieved. To begin, here are some suggestions concerning professional knowledge and practice.

1. Be aware of how spelling typically develops, remembering that, as with the learning to read and write, it is a recursive process where writers grow from emergent to independent. Refer to Figure 12.7, with emphasis on spelling and word pattern knowledge.

2. Be able to articulate what spelling is and what word study involves— for you, for your students, for parents.

3. Use modelling, to explain how to problem-solve and pay attention to patterns and meanings. Think of spelling as one component of language learning and a thinking process, in which we use prior knowledge to help predict and confirm what letters to use when writing a word.

4. Be able to articulate the principles and developmental patterns by which children learn to spell and problem-solve words.

The categories in Figure 12.7 are often referred to as stages in spelling development. Note that they occur in and through the contexts where

FIGURE 12.7 A Continuum of Spelling Development

	Developing Spelling Characteristics	Attention to Patterns
Emergent	Drawing as writing, scribble writing	Awareness of repetition in print, for example, a series of repeated lines, dashes or curly-cues (as in Hailey's writing in Chapter 11)
Early	Letter-like units, letter strings, copying from environment	Letter name spelling patterns: "U" for you "KSL" for castle
Transitional	Semi-phonetic and phonetic spelling	Within-word spelling patterns: "enuf" for enough "gote" for goat
Self-Extending	Conventional spelling	Syllable juncture patterns: "hamer" for "hammer" Errors on stressed syllables: "beleaving"
Independent	Fluent writers confidently take risks with spelling unfamiliar words	Derivational constancy patterns: new words keep the meaning of their spelling roots (Canadian from Canada), but make errors such as "rememberince" for "remembrance"

reading and writing are learned. In addition to looking at how spelling progresses from alphabetic and sound knowledge to spelling phonetically or using "temporary" spelling, we can also consider how children gradually use more of their knowledge of word structure, including patterns such as word families (back, pack, Jack), how vowels and silent letters work together (rain, bike), rules such as doubling the final consonant and adding "ing" (running, skipping), and how meanings of words are preserved throughout their derivational forms (port: export, transportation, report, reporter). This knowledge appears to develop along a continuum as well (Templeton & Morris, 2000; Ganske, 2000; Bear, Invernizzi, Templeton, & Johnston, 2004), whereby students attend to more sophisticated pattern layers in English spelling, as indicated in Figure 12.7. See the following samples that illustrate various patterns.

Phonetic: Within-Word Patterns Used
Some words are spelled phonetically, for example "enuf" for "enough" or "uv" for "of." "Frends" in this sample uses knowledge of the "end" pattern.

Text by JK student:
The drawn figures are labelled
"Mrs. B (?)," "me," "Ben," "Lucas," and "Cody."
The text reads "At school, I made lots of friends."

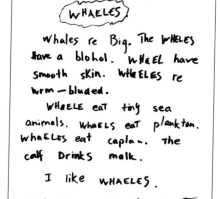

Transitional: Syllable Juncture Patterns
This writer's repertoire includes some phonetically spelled words. Note the spelling of "whaeles" reflecting pronunciation with two syllables instead of one and "bluded" where the pattern of doubling final consonants before added endings is not yet known.

Grade 2 sample:
"Whales. Whales are big. The whales have a blowhole. Whales have smooth skin. Whales are warm-blooded. Whales eat tiny sea animals. Whales eat plankton. Whales eat capelin. The calf drinks milk. I like whales."

The ladder worked wonders. The sky painter painted millions of beautiful sunsets. Some were pink, some were orange. ~~He~~ ~~was~~ He would paint a new sunset once in the evening and paint (sunrises in the morning. One morning, while

Conventional Spelling: Derivational Constancy
This writer has a large working repertoire of known words, including those with regular and irregular spelling. Words with similar meanings share common patterns: paint, painter, painted.

Grade 7 sample

HOW DO CHILDREN LEARN TO SPELL?

Observation indicates that children learn how to spell through cognitive, developmental processes, involving hypothesizing and testing, growing and changing over time in much the same growth pattern as oral language. Just as children drop "goed" from their oral speech, they drop "lic" for "like" from their writing. Learners use what they know to confirm, predict, and relate new information to old. Children learn conventional or standard spelling if they read, write, and receive instruction and encouragement through strategies that are part of a balanced and comprehensive literacy program. Setting aside long periods of time for drilling and testing spelling words results in little permanent learning and minimum transfer to real writing. Spelling is best learned when integrated with reading and writing, and by noticing and using patterns and strategies. With these principles in mind, we have suggested a range of contexts and activities to support spelling development and word study in Figure 12.8, followed by a more detailed account of each.

Teaching Spelling through Large-Group Instruction during Writers' Workshop

- Use minimal cue messages on the board (sentences with words left out—cloze). The teacher composes these first, then later the children write messages for the class.

- Mask a word in enlarged print with Post-it notes. The teacher or child removes the Post-it notes a little at a time, predicting and confirming.

- Make written activities as interactive as possible. Have the children predict the letters that will come next in a word.

- Imitate patterns in reading texts. Substitute a letter in a word to make a new word, a synonym, or a phrase.

FIGURE 12.8 Teaching Spelling or Word Study

Suggested Contexts for Teaching Spelling

- Large group instruction on word study prior to or during writers' workshop (see Teacher Talk 8.1)
- Writing process—usually the editing stage
- Conferencing, especially "side-by-side" editing of student work, where spelling principles, patterns, and strategies can be pointed out and modelled
- Word games and activities (see Chapter 10, Vocabulary Work)
- Word walls (see Chapter 10)
- Technology—teach and encourage exploration of the possibilities and limitations of computer spelling and grammar check programs
- Dictionary and thesaurus skills—teach word origins, especially the meanings of the common roots and affixes (for example, "hydr" as a root comes from the Greek for "water" and "phobia" means fear, hence "hydrophobia" means fear of water; have students look up "hydrant" and "hydroponics")

- Use alphabet books, songs, and chants during large group instruction time. Build on letter names and sound associations and common letter sequences and patterns. Make class alphabet books and charts, personal dictionaries, and other personalized spelling aids.

- Teach spelling through the writing process, during writers' workshop. Concentrate on high-frequency words needed in daily writing. Use mini-lessons and word walls.

- Encourage students to comment on strategies used during workshop conference or sharing time.

Teaching Spelling through the Writing Process

Early Writers

- Using letter sound association knowledge to record new words ("phonetic" or "invented" spelling).
- Write known words quickly.
- Use words posted around the room (word walls, bulletin boards) and in personal dictionaries.

Young writers at the emergent to early stages (Kindergarten to late Grade 1) should not be asked to recopy a piece, but should be helped with changes that need to be made if their writing is going to become a "published" part of the classroom reading repertoire. It takes sensitivity to help standardize a child's spelling without discouraging risk-taking. Balance this with the need to recognize the necessity of "book spelling" in final copies.

Experienced Writers

- Write down ideas as quickly as possible, spelling many known words correctly, but not worrying about risks taken with unknown words or possible errors until the editing stage.

Teaching Spelling through Conferencing One-on-One or with Small Groups

For the child with no letter-sound association:

- Emphasize getting the story in picture form so the meaning won't be lost. Choose a key word and write the initial letter or the whole word, modelling how you associate the sound with that letter. Encourage the child to continue writing the story with their own version of writing.

- Work on letter-sound-association. For example, using an overhead projector and magnetic letters; tracing letters in sand while making associated sounds; practising with alphabet charts and personal booklets with letter-picture-initial sound association (sound and lips/mouth formation should be emphasized); draw attention to initial sounds during shared reading and shared/interactive writing.

- Write a comment or question about the story as read by the child to model writing and provide a reminder of the writer's message.

- Act as scribe.

- Ask the child to underwrite or copy directly beneath the teacher's model.

- If the child has copied randomly from around the room, help the child to read the print. Suggest some small improvisation to make it more their own.

- Provide a colour-coded alphabet desk strip showing the letter-sound relationships.

For children who do not use the letter-sound associations that they already know:

- Encourage them to keep writing and reading. The letter-sound association does not come easily. Some children don't want to slow down and concentrate long enough to use the knowledge they already have. For some children, the "knowledge" isn't completely consolidated or it needs to be "over-learned," that is, taught and applied numerous times.

- Talk about how much easier it is to go back to what we've written if we use a repeated spelling form based on writing down the sounds we hear.

- Have buddies who help children write their stories using a computer. This can be motivating when spelling forms can be retrieved easily.

- Provide a colour-coded alphabet desk strip or stand-up chart.

- Have a written conversation with the child to model and to motivate using a form of spelling that the child can retrieve and use.

For the child with a noticeable and continuing discrepancy between spelling and reading/writing development:

- Teach coping strategies: dictionaries, Word Walls, personal lists, and getting help from buddies.

For the child with difficulties in segmentation (phonemic awareness):

- Prerequisite: Plan lots of poetry, music, clapping, and movement.

- One syllable words: Do the segmentation with the child.

- Multi-syllable words: Say and clap out the syllables; say and write the syllables one at a time.

- Teach Elkonin boxes (sound or letter boxes) for recording sounds as the word is spoken slowly (see Chapter 10)

For the child who is ready to publish a piece:

- Model and encourage synonym substitution. (For example, "Said is Dead," use "exclaimed" or "replied." Refer to student-generated list posted in the writing centre).

- Model proofreading in a whole class conference, using an overhead projector. At first, select or compose an anonymous piece; later the students may volunteer their work.

- Develop a proofreading guide, composed with the class (shared writing), to be posted in the classroom or stored in writing folders.

Teaching Spelling and Vocabulary: Other Methods

Other methods for teaching spelling and vocabulary include word walls and word activities using rhyming, poetry, riddles, and games. Begin with the context in which the words occur; this gives the words their meaning and enhances memory and interest. (See Chapter 10, Vocabulary Work and Word Walls.)

Explicitly Teaching Dictionary Skills

Children should not be told to "look it up" if they have not been taught how to use a dictionary or if they are unlikely to find the word (for example, when "photograph" has been spelled "fotograf"). It is here, in the context of teaching dictionary and thesaurus skills, that you can focus on vocabulary building, particularly for students who are at the meaning or derivational constancy level of understanding how words work.

Assessment of Spelling

The effectiveness of the classroom spelling program is reflected in the students' daily writing. An effective program responds to class and individual needs.

Because spelling knowledge is a developmental process, effective and developmentally appropriate instruction must be based on an assessment of the students' developmental levels. Are they using primarily alphabetic and phonetic knowledge, within-word patterns, or using knowledge of word meanings to spell unfamiliar words? What evidence is there in students' daily writing? To ensure that spelling instruction targets that "just right" level, the level of knowledge about words and word patterns must be carefully assessed. Only then can you provide the level of instruction needed so that students can apply and extend their ability to spell unknown words.

Using Word Lists to Teach Spelling

Words students *need* to know include high-frequency words, which they cannot sound out because they do not follow predictable (alphabetical or phonemic) decoding or phonetic rules. They also need to know words with patterns, which allow new words to be generated, and words needed "instantly" for fluent writing. Words students *want* to know include high-utility words that are often topic or theme related, depending on the student's focus for a piece of writing (for example "mystery," "detective," "clues") and words derived from the students' daily writing including commonly misspelled words and personal words chosen by the student.

The following are some basic teaching tips for using word lists:

• Late Primary: teacher selects five words, student selects a few words

• Junior: list should include no more than 15–20 words, including words misspelled from previous week's dictation

100 WORDS NEEDED INSTANTLY FOR FLUENT WRITING

Words 1-20		21-40		41-60		61-80		81-100	
the	he	at	but	use	up	would	write	first	down
of	was	be	not	an	other	make	go	water	day
and	for	this	what	each	about	like	see	been	did
a	on	have	all	which	out	him	number	call	get
to	are	from	were	she	many	into	no	who	come
in	as	or	when	so	then	time	way	oil	made
is	with	one	your	how	them	has	could	its	may
you	his	had	can	their	these	look	people	now	part
that	they	by	said	if	some	two	my	find	over
it	I	word	there	will	her	more	than	long	new

Prefixes: re, dis, an/an, un, in, im, pro. Suffixes: s/es, ed, ing, ly, er/or, tion/sion, er/est

Booth& Swartz (2004), p. 117.

WORDS STUDENTS WANT TO KNOW: Sample High-Utility Words

K-Grade 1	Grades 1-2	Grades 2-3	Grades 3-4	Grades 5-6
student's name; (friend's names)	of	think	about	between
	can	know	other	brought
I	are	found	first	possible
the	see	together	below	although
a	going	witch	animal	question
am	here	laugh	which	suddenly
is	on	please	castle	beautiful
to	up	different	sentence	already
in	was	because	follow	exercise
like	get	write	picture	mystery
me	this	friend	Canada/	detective
red	play	once	Canadian	poetry
my	home	would	another	problem
mom	for	school	right	solution
dad	got	where	through	answer
and	look	were	often	writing
they	away	when	thought	learned
zoo	funny	people	together	knowledge
said	sleep	boy	friend	remember/
	stop	girl	medieval	remembered/
	day	good	night	remembering/
			knight	remembrance

All grades: family, read, write, school, Thanksgiving, Halloween, Christmas, holiday, and other vocabulary appropriate to school and community cultures.

This list was compiled after consulting: Cunningham (1995), Fountas & Pinnell (1996), and Toronto District School Board (2000).

38 COMMON RIMES: More than 500 words can be made with these patterns		
ack (back, pack) **all** (ball, call) **ain** (rain, plain) **ake** (make, take) **ale** (tale, whale) **all** (ball, fall) **ame** (name, came) **an** (can, than) **ank** (thank, bank) **ap** (cap, map) **ash** (dash, crash) **at** (cat, hat, mat) **ate** (gate, late)	**aw** (saw, draw) **ay** (play, day) **eat** (meat, beat) **ell** (tell, bell) **est** (best, west) **ice** (rice, nice) **ick** (sick, trick) **ide** (ride, slide) **ight** (light, night) **ill** (fill, hill) **in** (pin, win) **ine** (fine, shine) **ing** (sing, wing)	**ink** (think, pink) **ip** (ship, lip) **ir** (sir, girl, fir, first) **ock** (sock, rock) **oke** (joke, smoke) **op** (stop, hop) **or** (or, for) **ore** (more, store) **uck** (duck, truck) **ug** (hug, slug) **ump** (bump, jump) **unk** (junk, dunk)
Source: Saskatchewan Learning. Retrieved May 31, 2006 from www.sasked.gov.sk.ca		

- Spelling lists from a text: words should be grouped in meaningful ways, and modified for individual needs
- Establish the following weekly routine: generate a list, pre-test/self-correct, study, and post-test/self or peer correct immediately. Time should not be wasted on studying words already known; use the time for vocabulary building.

Suggested Components of a Word Study Program

1. Teach and explore word structures (root words, affixes, prefixes, plurals, comparatives, variant endings, syllables, word origins).

2. Have students sort the words according to self-chosen, previously taught categories, for example common endings or rimes, such as "ack," "in," and "oke" or common beginnings or onsets, for example "br," "str," or "th."

3. Have students sort words conceptually (for example by theme) and use the words in writing and speaking activities.

4. Teach strategies for unknown words (demonstrated and practised during shared writing).

   - Say a word slowly and represent each sound heard.
   - Think of analogies and patterns with known words ("cat"—"hat").
   - "Have a go"—write the word three times and see which looks right (magnetic letters are useful).

- Teach mnemonics, spelling patterns, useful rules, and generalizations.

5. Teach study techniques (for example "look, cover, write, check").

6. Post-test—work with a partner, correct immediately.

Teaching Grammar in the Context of Writers' and Readers' Workshops

WHAT IS GRAMMAR?

Grammar is a linguistic science concerned with description. It is a component of language instruction, which refers to the formal, internal patterns of language. When you prompt students to listen to whether something sounds right or makes sense, you are often prompting for syntax.

WHY TEACH GRAMMAR?

Grammar is learned as one learns to talk, read, and write. If it is primarily learned in context, then why should you "teach" it? There are two key reasons. Standard English is the mark of an "educated person," and most educators assume that it should be added to their students' repertoires (not to replace their own dialects, but to add "book language" to their repertoire). Second, and more important, there is a strong connection between using correct grammar and maintaining clarity when communicating.

HOW DO WE TEACH GRAMMAR?

Research shows that formal, isolated teaching of grammar has "negligible" or even "harmful" effects on the improvement of writing (Hillocks & Smith, 1991; Weaver, 1996) and that integrating grammar study with reading and writing produces the best results (Noguchi, 1991; Noyce & Christie, 1983). Grammar is primarily a tool for writers and is best integrated with the revising and editing stages of the writing process.

- The "mini-lesson" is one approach, taught in the context of readers' or writers' workshop, where student needs are best assessed and teaching/learning is best integrated.

- You do not need special worksheets; use excerpts from the books you and the students are reading, or even better, the students' own writing.

- Use a problem-solving approach during the editing stage; this is less threatening than correcting their speech, which is more personal. Students should be encouraged to find and correct their own errors, but teachers must often provide the corrections, saying for example, "We usually write it this way." Use models from books being read in the classroom. Students can accept that book language is a different kind of English.

Mini-Lessons and Activities for Interactive Learning of Grammar

Ideas for Teaching the Parts of Speech

1. *Identify and collect the parts of speech* (or those parts of speech designated for the grade level). Collect the parts of speech from books that the students are reading, listening to during read alouds, or from the students' own writing. Parts of speech such as nouns can be collected from *Chrysanthemum* by Kevin Henkes, adjectives from *Tough Boris* by Mem Fox, and verbs from *I Went to the Zoo* by Rita Golden Gelman.

Activities

- Read aloud *There Were Monkeys in My Kitchen* by Sheree Fitch. Have the children recall and record their favourite verbs from the story and then make up their own silly verbs.

- Create an illustrated class book using the words collected.

- Use grammar concept books as models for illustrated lists and individual dictionaries, small group bulletin board projects, or class books on parts of speech. For example *A Snake is Totally Tail* by Judi Barrett for adverbs or Ruth Heller's books (Scholastic) for nouns, collective nouns, verbs, and adjectives (for example, *A Cache of Jewels and Other Collective Nouns.*)

- Act out adverbs: "Walk the Walk Charades"

  - Students choose a card with an adverb and take turns walking in the manner suggested by the adverb (you may include picture clues).

  - The audience suggests a list of adverbs for each walking style.

  - Record on chart paper or a parts of speech word wall.

2. *Use sentence slotting/completion.*
   Purpose: To teach the parts of speech and the use of a variety of words to enhance and expand writing.

   Context: Shared writing

Parts of speech can be taught using books that the students are reading or from their own writing.

Literature Links: *Officer Buckle and Gloria* by Peggy Rathmann, *A Frog in the Bog* by Karma Wilson

Activities

- With your students, fill in the blanks for specific parts of speech.

  a) The snake slithered _____ the rock.

  (over, around, under, to, behind)

  b) _____ knew more safety tips than anyone else in Napville.

  (Officer Buckle, He, The police officer, The man)

- Sentence Expansion
  Expand "There's a frog on the log" by adding modifiers (use selection of 5Ws + H)

  Sentence: There's a frog on the log.

  What kind? Small, green

  Where? Half-sunk log in the middle of the bog.

The expanded sentence becomes: There's a frog on the log in the middle of the bog. It's a small, green frog on a half-sunk log in the middle of the bog.

Ideas for Teaching Forms of Punctuation and Sentence Type

1. *Use Dialogue*
   Have students work in a group of four and develop a four-sentence conversation, which exemplifies all four sentence types: declarative (statements), interrogative (questions), imperative (requests, commands), exclamatory (exclamations). Have students write scripts using standard punctuation.

2. *Use Literature as Models*
   Have students work in small groups to identify punctuation and sentence types from the books or poems they are reading or from their own writing. Examples of literature include *Where the Wild Things Are* by Maurice Sendak, *The Creature in Classroom* by Jack Prelutsky, and *Who Has Seen the Wind?* by Christina Rossetti. Create a class book using sentences copied from literature that illustrate types of punctuation. Note that punctuation and sentence mini-lessons are often grouped together because punctuation provides a clue to the type of sentence.

Theory Into Practice/12.8

USING DRAMA TO LEARN THE PARTS OF SPEECH

We refer to this activity as Word Plays or Syntax Drama, but our B.Ed. students have affectionately dubbed it "Gramma-Drama." Make words and sentences come to life. The students compose sentences, using big cards with their parts of speech or punctuation printed clearly.

DIP. DIP, AND SWING

The paddle dips effortlessly into the still water.

The – the article that sets the pace

paddle – the noun that takes canoe to town

dips – the verb that provides energy

effortlessly – an easygoing adverb

into – a preposition that tells the paddle where to go

the – the article that tells paddle precisely which water to go into

still – an adjective that calms water

water – a wet noun

period – punctuation that ends the stroke

Once this has been modelled for students (you may use a group you coached prior to the lesson), provide the following instructions:

- The group writes a full sentence that can be used to perform a word play (the sentence should include a variety of parts of speech and a variety of words.)
- Everyone should have a role.
- The group should practise the word play and then present it to the class.

Moving On

In this chapter, we considered some principles and procedures for the effective instruction of writing from the very early years when a student is a confident apprentice to the later stages of development as a confident, accomplished, expressive writer. We continued to emphasize the all-important connections between reading and writing as reciprocal, interdependent learning processes. We investigated strategies and contexts for learning that capitalize on these connections. We also emphasized real-world purposes for writing as a strong motivation for students to write and to extend their growth into powerful writers with control over all parts of the writing process. To set up the learning conditions for "real writers writing," we described writers' workshop and showed how all aspects of writing instruction, guided practice, and independent writing can flourish in a structured, supportive community of writers.

In Chapter 13, we continue our exploration of literacy learning and ask you to extend what you know about "schooled literacy" beyond the classroom and into the community and the wider world. Many of the strategies that students learn as part of their schooled literacy, in terms of examining texts and looking beyond surface level comprehension, are the foundations of critical literacy. We also emphasize the necessity for media literacy—the requirement that students be able to view critically, analyze, evaluate, make sense of, and create a variety of media works (television, radio, film, mass media, computer games, magazines, and popular music). Multimedia literacy implies the ability to deconstruct media messages by applying the same critical-thinking skills used in reading and writing to multiple text genres.

It strikes me that children who have had lots of experiences designing, cutting, pasting, carving, sketching, painting, decorating, pretending, and otherwise messing around creatively take more readily to the process of writing. Children who know how to play seem to approach writing with the required openness it takes to craft quality work.
—Shelley Harwayne

LIT-FOLIO UPDATE

Your lit-folio should have evidence of your developing awareness of the practices that best promote writing as a process and in writers' workshops. The central role of teacher modelling of all stages of the writing process was emphasized in this chapter. Are you confident modelling writing in front of students? Do you find it easy to verbalize your in-the-head thinking through think alouds? Have you begun a collection of think-aloud scripts to model writing skills and strategies?

LIT-FOLIO TIP

Return to Literacy Notebook 12.3 and write a script for one of the grade level expectations listed.

Resources to Support Your Learning

Professional Resources

Atwell, N. (1998). *In the middle: New understandings about writing, reading, and learning.* Portsmouth, NH: Heinemann.

✦ Booth, D. (2001). *Reading and writing in the middle years.* Markham, ON: Pembroke Publishers.

Button, K., Johnson, M.J., & Ferguson, P. (1996). Interactive writing in the primary writing classroom. *The Reading Teacher, 43,* 478–484

Calkins, L. (1986, 1994). *The art of teaching writing.* Portsmouth, NH: Heinemann.

Calkins, L., & Harwayne, S. (1987). *The writing workshop: A world of difference.* Portsmouth, NH: Heinemann.

Fletcher, R. (1996). *Breathing in, breathing out: Keeping a writer's notebook.* Portsmouth, NH: Heinemann.

Graves, D., & Kittle, P. (2005). *Inside writing: How to teach the details of craft.* Portsmouth, NH: Heinemann.

Harwayne, S. (2001). *Writing through childhood: Rethinking process and product.* Portsmouth, NH: Heinemann.

Heffernan, L. (2004). *Critical literacy and Writer's Workshop: Bringing purpose and passion to student writing.* Newark, DE: International Reading Association.

✦ Phenix, J. (2001). *The spelling teacher's handbook.* Markham, ON: Pembroke Publishers.

✦ Phenix, J., & Scott-Dunne, D. (1991). *Spelling instruction that makes sense.* Markham ON: Pembroke Publishers.

✦ Scott, R. (1993). *Spelling: Sharing the secrets.* Toronto, ON: Gage.

✦ Scott, R., & Siamon, S. (1996). *The Canadian spelling program,* Toronto: Gage.

Spandel, V. (2005). *Creating writers through 6-trait writing assessment and instruction.* Boston, MA: Pearson.

Weaver, C. (1996). *Teaching grammar in context.* Portsmouth, NH: Heinemann.

Wheatley, J. (2005). *Strategic spelling : Moving beyond word memorization in the middle grades.* Newark, DE: International Reading Association.

Children's Literature: Our Favourites

Literature with Main Characters Who Are Writers

26 Fairmount Avenue, Tomie dePaola (autobiography)
Amelia's notebook, and *Emma's journal,* Marissa Moss
Anastasia Krupnik, Lois Lowry
Dear Mr. Henshaw, Beverley Cleary
I'm in charge of celebrations, Byrd Baylor
Jenny Archer, author, Ellen Conford
The Jolly Postman, The Jolly Pocket Postman, and *The Jolly Christmas Postman,* Janet and Allan Ahlberg
✦ *Little by little,* Jean Little (autobiography)
My stories by Hildy Calpurnia, Dale Gottlieb
The nature of the beast, Jan Carr
Only Opal: The diary of a young girl, Barbara Cooney
Poor Jenny, bright as a penny, Shirley R. Murphy
Somebody loves you, Mr. Hatch, Eileen Spinelli
Thank you Santa, Margaret Wild
A valentine for Norman Noggs, Valiska Gregory

For Sentence Types and Parts of Speech

Don't let the pigeon drive the bus, Mo Willems
A frog in the bog, Karma Wilson
I went to the zoo, Rita Golden Gelman
Many luscious lollipops: A book about adjectives, Ruth Heller (see other books in the series from Scholastic)
✦ *There were monkeys in my kitchen,* Sheree Fitch
What do you do with a tail like this? Robin Page

For Paragraph Writing

Art for children (series), Ernest Raboff
Communication, David Lowe, and others, Ginn Literacy 2000 series
✦ *Terry Fox: A story of hope,* Maxine Trottier

Websites

✦ Ontario Ministry of Education—The Ontario Curriculum, Exemplars Grades 1-8: Writing (1999): http://www.edu.gov.on.ca/eng/
The Peel Literacy Guild—The Dolch Sight Word List: http://www.peelliteracyguild.com/sight_words.html
Read Write Think: http://www.readwritethink.org/
✦ The 2learn.ca Education Society (Alberta): http://www.2learn.ca/
✦ Early Literacy: A resource for teachers (Saskatchewan): http://www1.sasked.gov.sk.ca/docs/ela/eliteracy/index.html
Everyday Spelling List: www.everydayspelling.com/spellinglist
North West Regional Educational Laboratory (NWREL), Six Traits® of Writing: http://www.nwrel.org/assessment/

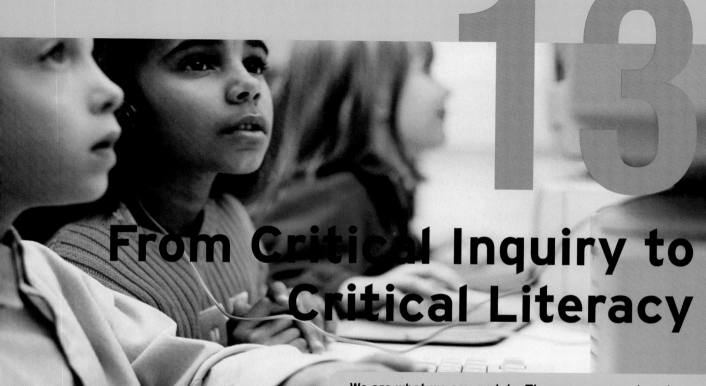

From Critical Inquiry to Critical Literacy

We are what we say and do. The ways we speak and are spoken to help shape us into the people we become. Through speech and other actions, we build ourselves in a world that is building us. We can remake ourselves and society, if we choose, through alternative words and dissident projects. This is where critical literacy begins—words that question a world not yet finished or humane.

—*Ira Shor*

key terms

critical inquiry
critical literacy
multimedia genres
text
touchstone text

questions to guide your learning

By the end of this chapter, you should understand the key terms and be able to answer the following questions:

- How can students develop critical literacy through critical inquiry?
- What are the dominant influences on the development of critical literacy?
- What is your students' role in critical inquiry? Your role?
- How can you select critical inquiries that work for you and your students and that are relevant to their lives?
- What are some of the subtleties in working with different media genres?

Looking Back, Looking Ahead

Chapter 3 presented literacy as our ability to read the W.O.R.L.D. It encompassed words, orality, re-vision, literacies, and discourses. In this chapter, we return to many of these concepts with a focus on deeper level comprehension, re-vision, critical inquiry, and multimedia awareness. This chapter is a natural extension of Chapter 7, which presented a theory of reading instruction, and Chapter 10, which presented a theory of writing instruction, both of which constitute "schooled literacy." In this chapter, we invite you to extend what you know about schooled literacy beyond the classroom into the community and the world. Many of the strategies that your students learn as part of their schooled literacy—examining texts and looking beyond surface level comprehension—form the foundations for critical inquiry. Strategies such as, question-answer relationships, R.A.F.T. writing, and the subtext strategy are pre-requisites and co-requisites for critical inquiry in the classroom.

During the four chapters devoted to print literacy, reading, and writing, we have underscored the importance of multiple ways of knowing and multiple ways of representing knowledge. We continue this theme as we present strategies to support students as they take a step beyond comprehension to an examination of texts from a more critical standpoint. In this chapter, we conceive of text very broadly as including lived experience and oral, visual, print, and multimedia genres.

As you move into critical inquiry, it is essential to recognize your own subjectivities as literate beings. Your views of the world, assumptions about learning, learners, and schooling, and your previous experiences will all shape the types of inquiries you plan for your students. In addition, the views of the world, assumptions about learning and schooling, and the previous experiences of your students will all need to be considered. Each of these factors will determine the level of critical inquiry. As with any other skill, strategy, or way of knowing and representing, practise makes practice. Be patient. Start small with inquiries and actions that are attainable and gradually release responsibility for decision-making to your students.

Conceptualizing Critical Literacy

Critical literacy is described in several ways by literacy educators and researchers. Freire and Macedo (1987) provide a succinct definition where critical literacy "means making oneself present as part of a moral and political project that links the production of meaning to the possibility for human agency, democratic community, and transformative social action" (p.14). Lewison, Seely-Flint, and Van Sluys (2002) offer a conceptualization of critical literacy that is more comprehensive and easily applied in the classroom. Critical literacy involves:

a) Disrupting the Commonplace: seeing the everyday through new lenses where critical literacy is a way to:

 i) problematize all subjects of study and understand existing knowledge as a historical product

 ii) interrogate texts by asking a range of questions, most importantly "How is this text trying to position me?"

 iii) include popular culture and media as regular parts of the curriculum for pleasure and deconstructing how people are positioned and constructed by television, video games, comics, toys, and advertisements

 iv) develop a language of critique and hope

 v) study language to analyze how it shapes identity, constructs cultural discourses, and supports or disrupts the commonplace or the status quo

b) Interrogating Multiple Viewpoints: understanding and experiencing perspectives and viewpoints different from our own as we:

 i) reflect on multiple and contradictory perspectives

 ii) use multiple voices to interrogate texts in an effort to explore whose voices are heard and whose voices are silenced

 iii) pay attention to and seek out the voices of those that have been silenced or marginalized

 iv) examine competing and contradictory narratives

 v) make difference visible and transparent

c) Focusing on Sociopolitical Issues: paying attention to how power relationships and language become part of our classroom teaching where critical literacy requires you to:

 i) look beyond our personal perspective and attempt to understand the sociopolitical systems to which we belong

ii) challenge the unquestioned legitimacy of unequal power relationships by studying the relationship between language and power

iii) use literacy to engage in the politics of everyday life

iv) redefine literacy as a form of cultural citizenship that increases opportunities for participation in society and as an ongoing act of consciousness and resistance

d) Taking Action and Promoting Social Justice: taking informed action against oppression, promoting social justice, and transforming the world through our understandings and perspectives as we

i) engage in reflection and action upon the world in an effort to make it a better place

ii) use language to exercise power and enhance everyday life and to question the practices of privilege and injustice

iii) analyze how language is used to maintain domination and how non-dominant groups can gain access to dominant discourses without devaluing or sacrificing their own language and culture, how diverse forms of language can be used as cultural resources, and how social action can change and transform existing discourses

iv) challenge and redefine cultural borders and encourage students to cross borders as they seek to understand others

Conceptualizing Text

One of your primary roles will be to select texts that provide multiple opportunities for students to explore their thinking and their world from diverse perspectives including historical, cultural, political, gender, and personal. By returning to texts in your classroom on many occasions (as we have suggested in previous chapters), you are giving yourselves and your students time to "ponder, challenge, and rethink" your beliefs (Laman, 2006, p. 212). Teachers and students engaged in critical inquiry seek to understand the problem presented in the text, raise questions, and explore alternative solutions. Like reading, critical inquiry is a transaction between the text consumer, the text creator, the text, and the reading community ("text consumer" refers to readers, listeners, and viewers of text and "text creator" refers to authors, composers, producers, speakers, and performers of text).

Critical inquiry includes four families of practice (Luke & Freebody, 1999): code-breaking, participating with text, using text, and creating space for critical analyses. Literacy teachers understand how to seamlessly integrate these practices into their regular program and continually explore and interrogate the following assumptions about text (Johnson & Freedman, 2005):

- Consumers of text require tools, or what are often referred to as code-breaking practices, that enable them to deconstruct, question, and interrogate texts from a structure, style, or genre perspective.

- Texts, regardless of their source, are not infallible, timeless, universal, or neutral—they represent someone else's ideas and beliefs in the time context of their creation. As we examine underlying ideas, beliefs, and assumptions, we develop our own views of the world and possible re-interpretations as consumers of text.

- Text refers to any language event, whether oral, written, or visual. Conversations, poems, novels, posters, music videos, television programs, performances, video games, and multimedia productions, for example, are all texts. The use of the term text "is an economical way of suggesting the similarity among many of the skills involved in 'reading' a film, interpreting a speech, or responding to an advertisement or a piece of journalism" (Foundation for the Atlantic Canada English Language Arts Curriculum, n.d., p. 11).

- Consumers should not receive texts passively, but should question, interrogate, critique, and challenge the underlying attitudes, values, assumptions, and ideologies. It is within this family of practices that we act on our knowledge that texts are not ideologically natural or neutral, that they represent particular points of view while silencing others.

- Deconstruction of text, construction of meaning, and re-visioning of the world requires collaboration, active discussion, and interaction.

- Construction and production of text is an important component that allows us to apply all that we have learned through deconstruction and positions us effectively for social equity and change.

Learning to question, interrogate, and take a critical stance toward your own text consumption will better position you to share your own sense-making process with your students through discussion, conversation, conferencing, scaffolding (see Chapter 8), explicit strategy instruction (see Chapter 9), and think alouds (see Chapter 6). As you choose texts to fit your program, the needs and interests of your students, and your own personal subjectivities, remember that we advocate careful *selection* of texts, not *censorship* of texts.

> *Schools are about creating equity for individuals as well as groups of people, and are places where favoritism is not appropriate or beneficial. Schools in a democracy are about democracy, tolerance, and an acceptance of multiple voices and multiple perspectives. When we censor texts based on differences of value systems, we close the door to students' learning about others in the world.*
>
> (Johnson & Freedman, 2005, p. 191)

Figure 13.1 presents a list of critical questions that will be useful to you as you consider the texts you read for your own purposes and the texts you select for your students. Dominant themes and categories for inquiry are highlighted. The questions are not intended to be used for every text at every reading in every context. Instead, it is up to you to select carefully those questions that you feel will guide your students' understanding of text and facilitate their critical inquiry.

literacy
notebook
13.1

STOP, THINK, AND WRITE

Using the following questions to guide your response, write about text selection, text use, and critical inquiry in the classrooms you have observed:

- How do teachers talk about text?

- Whose voices are heard? Whose voices are silenced? Does this influence how teachers deconstruct and interpret text?

- How do teachers use text to discover themselves and their functioning in the world?

- Do teachers support student exploration of text in school and beyond?

- Do teachers help students to recognize the relationship between the functions of text and the way texts are structured, their tone, their formality, and their sequence of components?

- Do teachers provide a range of resources? Do these resources reflect any particular perspective on the world?

FIGURE 13.1 Questions for Text Selection, Text Use, and Critical Inquiry

Reader Response

- How do I, as text consumer, respond to and interpret the text? How do I relate to this text?
- Do I make comparisons and connections to events, groups, situations, or phenomena within the text? Why does that happen?
- How do I feel about this text? Why do I like or dislike this book?
- How does my cultural background, attitudes, and values shape my response to this text?
- In what context am I situated as I seek to deconstruct, interpret, and make sense of this text?
- What knowledge do I need to bring to this text in order to understand it?

Purpose of the Text

- What is the text about? How do I know?
- Who would be most likely to read, view, or listen to this text and why?
- Why am I reading, viewing, or listening to this text?

Point of View/Perspective of Reality

- What view of the world does the text present?
- What kinds of social realities does the text portray? How does the text construct these realities?
- How would the text be different if it were told in another time, another place, another culture?
- From what perspective or point of view is the text presented: a) First Person: Story told through the "I" voice; b) Omniscient Third Person: Story told through the narrator who knows and sees everything; c) Limited Third Person: Story told through a narrator with limited knowledge about the other characters and their feelings and motives.
- If I were to view the text from a variety of perspectives, would I hold the same values as the text creator?

Interrogating the Text Creator

- What kind of person, with what interests and values, composed the text?
- What aspects of life does the text creator value? How do I know?
- What view of the world and values does the text creator assume that I hold? How do I know?
- What does the text creator want me to believe about the world? What assumptions are made?
- Did I accept the view of the text creator without thinking and questioning? Why or why not?
- What would the text creator have had to do differently to get me to like or dislike the book?
- In what ways do I agree or disagree with the text creator?

Power and Interest, Gaps and Silences

- Whose views are excluded, whose are privileged? Who benefits from the text? Which positions, voices, and interests are at play? Who has the most power in this text? How do I know?
- Who is allowed to speak? Who is quoted?
- Is the text fair? Does the text represent unequal distributions of power?
- How am I positioned in relation to the text composer?

FIGURE 13.1 Questions for Text Selection, Text Use, and Critical Inquiry (continued)

- How does the text depict age, gender, culture, ethnicity, socioeconomic status, and individual difference?

Text Structure, Features, Characteristics
- What are the fundamental features and architecture of the text? Why has the text been constructed in this way?
- How does the structure of the text direct me to respond in particular ways?
- What genre (narrative, poetry, media, etc.) does the text belong to?
- How does the text creator use language, images, and auditory or visual communication to elicit certain responses from me?
- What language directed my thinking and feelings?

Characters
- How are the characters constructed in the text (children, teenagers, young adults, adults, older adults)?
- How do the male and female characters act differently? Similarly?
- Are my actions similar to the character's actions? Why or why not? How might I have acted differently?
- In what ways are the characters not like people in the real world?
- Why has the text creator represented the characters in a particular way? What would happen if I examined the characters' thoughts and actions from a different point of view or perspective?

Culture
- What does it mean to be an insider or an outsider to a given culture or population?
- Can readers fully engage in pieces of literature when they are outside the culture of the text?
- Are we really insiders of the literature we read that supposedly represents our culture?
- How should I read literature from outside my cultural experience?
- What might I, as an outsider to the culture, miss when reading literature from other cultures?
- What would someone from another cultural group think about this text?

Time, Period, Location
- How do I really know how people acted during another era in history? Have human beings changed, or have the stories told about them changed?
- In what ways do the characters represent how people would have thought and acted during a particular era? How do you feel about them and their ideas?
- How has our society changed since that time? How can our society continue to improve?
- What bearing does historical context have on the way characters are constructed, language is used, and messages are shared?
- Can the text be deconstructed in light of its time or location of creation?
- How does the text creator's time period, location, and culture reflect particular ideas about the world?
- Within which contexts (historical, political, ideological, sociological, psychological, cultural) is this text situated? How might these views be similar or different from the views we have today?
- How does the social context in which a text is encountered influence how readers respond to it?

Source: Adapted from Johnson & Freedman (2005); Department of Education, Tasmania (n.d.).

The Role of the Reader

In Chapter 8, we suggested that one of the roles of the reader was that of architect—one who:

- recognizes reading as a transaction between reader, author, and reading community

- builds on and revises ideas, information, and perspectives in texts

- engages in critical thinking, critical consciousness, and critical literacy/inquiry

- recognizes points of view, omissions, and multiple perspectives

- demonstrates a continuous awareness of own reading strategies and processes

- responds to texts in a variety of ways

We then suggested that the role of the reader as architect was to see beyond the past and present to imagine a different future; this requires readers to understand their world from diverse perspectives and world views that can be acquired through a variety of texts (oral, visual, print, performance) and experiences. In this chapter, we present and discuss specific ways we can engage our students as architects and involve them in the critical roles of planning, creating, designing, implementing, and reflecting. In Chapter 3, we discussed discourses and students' ways of being in the world. We recognized the importance of exploring and extending literacy by linking students' discourses, ways of being in the world, "cultural capital," "ways with words," and "funds of knowledge" to what is needed to participate and engage fully in literacy and to have their voices heard in educational and world contexts (Bourdieu & Passeron, 1977; Heath, 1983; Moll, 1992).

> *All students come to school with cultural and social experiences and particular ways of saying and doing things. These various experiences, or cultural and linguistic resources, connect in multiple ways. What this means is learning environments need to be responsive to the cultural discourses that students have access to and are active in, by looking closely at the things that are important to them or that they feel have importance in their lives.*

(Vasquez, 2001, p. 52)

This approach to language and literacy instruction is responsive to students' interest and needs, and in a sense centres around empowerment, one of our primary goals. Such models engage students in real-life literacy and value students' worlds and their ways of making meaning; such models are empowering for literacy learners and often offset pre-existing power relationships. Empowerment models support students as they explore and acknowledge the importance of literacy in their lives, while also enhancing students' sense of literate self and self efficacy by helping them to recognize and realize their capacity for solving real-world problems (Freire & Macedo, 1987; Powell & Davidson, 2005). "Some argue that the youngest students in elementary schools should not be burdened with issues of the adult world. However, children routinely experience exclusion, bullying, academic tracking, and racial and linguistic prejudice." (Laman, 2006, p. 204)

You need to recognize and accept the complexity of your students' lives and use the classroom as a place to support them in becoming critically literate. Hall (1998) writes, "It is one of the paradoxes of schooling that the kinds of texts most privileged in schools are the ones least likely to be pursued once people leave schooling" (p. 10). One possible solution to this paradox is to use students' popular culture (for example, video games), life experience (for example, donut shops, bullying), multimedia (for example, television, Internet), and performance as starting points for literacy.

The Role of the Teacher

As you teach, you will act as a facilitator, a scaffolder, a model, a participant, and an observer. You will engage students in discussion, observe classroom interactions, and facilitate reflection on issues of diversity and social justice. The role you play in critical inquiry and discussion will be as individualized and unique as both you and your students. Your goal is to lead your students through critical inquiry toward critical literacy.

> *Critical inquiry focuses on larger systems of meaning and connects the personal with the political. Critical inquiry involves the active engagement of learners as they explore issues in the world around them... Critical inquiry weaves critical literacy practices throughout the curriculum and offers children prolonged engagement with issues that are important to them and important to democracy. In such contexts, children read against texts, re-envision the world they live in, and take action within that world. Teachers and children ask questions such as, "Why is it like this?" and "Could this text be written differently?"*
>
> (Laman, 2006, p. 204)

Critical inquiry proceeds along the same continuum of support as the six language arts, engaging each when relevant. Some teachers main-

FIGURE 13.2 Beyond Personal Purposes to World Actions

Intrinsic Motivation and Purpose	World-Oriented Connections, Questions, and Actions
Problem Resolution (Conflict Resolution) Enables readers to see themselves as successfully solving problems or conflicts.	**Problem Resolution** (Conflict Resolution) Enables readers to theoretically solve problems or conflicts that arise in text and then take social action to ensure that these same problems or conflicts are dealt with in their own lives.
Prestige (Self-Esteem) Enables readers to perceive themselves as significant, receiving attention and exerting control in their own lives.	**Privilege** (Power and Control) Enables readers to explore issues of power and control as they arise in text, voices represented in text, and voices that are silent, as a function of race, culture, socioeconomic status, gender.
Aesthetic (Pleasure) Enables readers to appreciate literature that ranges from an appreciation of beauty in nature to enjoyment of family and friends' interaction and harmony.	**Aesthetic** (Culture) Enables the reader to appreciate and experience a range of cultural texts including visual, print, multimedia, and performance.
Escape Enables readers to leave the realities of daily existence, travel to far away places, and do strange, unfamiliar, and exotic things.	**Escape** Enables the reader to understand the privilege or lack thereof of their daily existence in the view of a world that is different from their own.
Intellectual Curiosity (Information) Enables readers to discover new ideas and new worlds.	**Intellectual Ambiguity** (Information) Enables the reader to see the fallibility of texts and underscores the necessity to rate and evaluate a range of media texts in order to understand new ideas and new worlds.
Understanding Self (Self-Concept) Enables readers to understand personal motivations through the motivations of story characters.	**Understanding Others** (Empathy) Enables the reader to understand others, their life situations, the kinds of choices made, stereotyping in the story, and connections to their own lives.
Teacher Expectations (Content Learning, Work) Enables readers to participate in an efferent instructional stance where they are expected to respond to explicit text-based questions and participate in discussions involving pre-determined responses.	**Societal Expectations** Enables readers to participate in what is considered an efferent and critical stance where they are expected to question values underlying texts and text creation, and participate in discussions to understand societal and world-oriented issues.

Source: Adapted from Ruddell (2004, pp. 992-993).

tain a strong presence in classroom discussions, modelling the types of responses, questions, prompts, and comments they would like their students to explore; others see their role as that of a guide where they structure the critical inquiry and then facilitate student access to critical inquiry. Others emphasize student directed and peer led groups where students choose the process of critical inquiry and independently follow it through to completion. Regardless of which level of support you adopt, your participation as a teacher will be necessary to:

- open spaces for all students to share
- ensure that there are no students who are oppressed or marginalized in classroom discussions
- provide encouragement for and validate student contributions
- clarify unfamiliar events or ways of thinking (scaffold)
- support and comfort students who reveal their hardships, pain, and suffering (Möller, 2002)

It is important to recognize that critical inquiry and discussion regarding social justice will not be easy. There will be times when students reveal far greater awareness of issues (for example, discrimination, poverty, individual difference) than you could possibly imagine. Despite the fact that these conversations may be difficult, they are important in your development and that of your students. Without an awareness of these issues, you will not gain the necessary values, skills, and strategies required to re-vision and transform our worlds.

The role of the teacher in initiating and developing critical literacy is multifaceted. It begins with personal understanding and use of critical literacy, modelling reading from a critical stance in everyday teaching and learning experiences, and providing access to a variety of texts that represent critical literacy.

(McLaughlin & DeVoogd, 2004, p. 55)

Before engaging in critical inquiry with your students, it is critical that you first acknowledge your own subjectivities and become critically aware of your own life as a literacy learner and literacy teacher. Chapters 1 and 2 initiated this inquiry; it will continue throughout the remainder of your life as a literacy learner and a literacy teacher.

There are times when we must question our own ideologies, simply because they do conflict with others' in critical ways. For instance, as teachers, we realize that we have ideas about what teaching is, what teachers should be like, and what students should be like. We also have ideas

literacy
notebook
13.2

STOP, THINK, AND WRITE

Engage in 10 minutes of quick writing using the quotation from Johnson & Freedman (2005) as your stimulus.

- What is your immediate and unadulterated reaction to this quote?
- What are your ideas about what teaching is, what teachers should be like, what students should be like, what should happen at home with parents, what their parents should be like, what values should be placed on education?
- How will this affect the way you plan and interact with students and parents?
- How might these ideas and assumptions change from grade to grade?

about the kinds of things that should happen at home with our students, what their parents should do or be like, and what values they should place on education. We live with these assumptions about ourselves and the world. In becoming critically conscious, however, we must begin to situate these ideas in the times we live in, in the ways we were raised and educated, and in the ways that the media and the laws of our societies have decided are right, good, or important.

(Johnson & Freedman, 2005, p. 6)

Critical Inquiries across the Grades

As you engage in critical inquiry, your classroom will resemble a mini-research culture, where you are experimenting with strategies and techniques that will enable you to understand the worlds of your students. As you learn to engage in critical inquiry you will try new things and you will make mistakes. The only mistake that is not acceptable in critical inquiry is not trying. Mistakes are part of learning; they give us a way to grow and a purpose for learning. In the next few pages, we document classroom-based research projects that focus on critical inquiry beginning in Kindergarten. The processes implemented by these teachers were not perfect; what was important, however, was the teachers' willingness to learn with and from their students. These teachers have not used critical inquiry as a subject added on to the curriculum; they have woven critical inquiry into their programs in ways that are responsive to their students' ways of being in the world, funds of knowledge, and ways with words.

As we selected the research studies to present here, we looked for projects that could be easily adapted for other grade levels, as well as those that would inform you about the reciprocal relationship between the lived experience, subjectivity, and inquiry of both you and your students. Because of this relationship, it is difficult to assign a developmental level to projects selected for critical inquiry; it is likely that as you initially embark on the journey of critical inquiry, your confidence and awareness as a teacher of critical inquiry will be the greatest predictor for success. Within each critical inquiry project, you will see the four dimensions of the critical literacy conceptualization offered by Lewison, Seely-Flint, and Van Sluys (2002). In response to the developmental needs, lived experiences, and interests of the classroom community, each teacher attempted to disrupt the commonplace, interrogate multiple viewpoints, focus on socio-political issues, and take action to promote social justice (although not necessarily all at once). These research accounts demonstrate a progression in critical literacy and the types of inquiries that students are capable of making, if given the chance!

KINDERGARTEN: LITERACY EVENTS AT THE DONUT HOUSE

Powell and Davidson (2005) engaged their students in the creation of a classroom donut shop. This research inquiry used the lived experiences of students as a text for inquiry. It enabled students to disrupt what they understood about the everyday workings of a donut shop and adopt alternative perspectives as they explored roles such as construction worker and building inspector. The inquiry began with a field trip to a real donut shop and culminated in the creation of The Donut House at their school. Throughout the project, these Kindergarten students were fully engaged in all aspects of planning, implementing, and running their own donut shop. Most writing was shared, interactive, or guided, with the teacher gradually releasing responsibility as the students gained confidence. As students became familiar with vocabulary, they were able to use words independently to write, to explore sounds, to figure out how words work, and to represent their own ideas. Theory into Practice 13.1 describes the links to literacy throughout the donut shop project.

GRADE 1: OPENING SPACES WITH PICTURE BOOKS

As many teachers do, Huber (Leland, Harste, & Huber, 2005) struggled with text selection and the types of books to read to young students. She recognized this as a need in her own classroom programming and de-

Theory Into Practice/13.1

LITERACY EVENTS AT THE DONUT HOUSE

Before Literacy Event: Field Trip to a Donut Shop
- Mini-lessons on making observation notes (using words and pictures)
- Reading signs and viewing images at the donut shop
- Writing of a list of materials needed to make donuts
- Writing of a thank you note to the donut shop staff
- Writing the field trip summary

During Literacy Event: Donut Shop Construction
- Writing letters: find a construction site, secure a loan, recruit stockholders, pass building inspection
- Procedural writing: instructions on how to make a donut
- Writing a big book documenting process through writing and pictures
- Independent, spontaneous, journal, and guided writing about donut shop project
- Reading of responses to letters, materials list, directions for making donuts, big book

Grand Opening
- Writing invitations to stockholders, parents, builders
- Dramatically and orally practising roles for the grand opening
- Dramatically and orally practising being interviewed by reporters
- Dramatically and orally practising answering phones, greeting customers, selling donuts, making change

After Literacy Event
- Guided reflection with students: What went well? What would they change next time?
- Creating a Donut House dramatic literacy centre
- Ensuring that all texts created during the event are available

cided to question her own assumptions (and those of her students) about what goes on in her classroom, school, and community. Although uncertain, she decided to open spaces for critical inquiry with picture books. What she discovered was that picture books that address world issues enabled her Grade 1 students to make stronger connections than the books with the classic "happily ever after ending" that were normally read without controversy in early primary classrooms (for example, fairy tales). She came to understand that her students took such texts very seriously and were willing to expend greater amounts of energy on their discussion and their work with these texts.

And while she was not surprised that their awareness of social issues showed considerable growth when she started to read books that focused on these topics, she did not expect to find that the children would start treating each other with more compassion and understanding. She was also surprised to find that they put considerably more effort into their written and artistic responses, took on multiple perspectives, and made lots of intertextual connections when the were reacting to these books.

(Leland et al., 2005, p. 258).

Huber re-visioned her read aloud as a way to open spaces for critical inquiry with her students. Questions that guided her inquiry included: What makes books appropriate for critical inquiry with students? What makes these books different than others? Is it possible that her classroom becomes a different place when she shares social issue books with her students? How do these experiences shape the culture of her classroom? Teacher Talk 13.1 contains excerpts from Huber's journal as she engaged her students in critical inquiry.

Engaging your students in these types of inquiries will help them to expand their understanding about the purposes of literacy and connect literacy to their interactions with others. It is not simply the selection of texts that changes and transforms the classroom experience, but the re-vision of instructional practice and the way you talk about text will play a major role in shaping your students' emerging identities as cultural and literate beings (Leland et al., 2005). Engaging students in reading responses that matter (for example, role play, perspective taking, problem-solving, social action, reader response journals, visual arts, comic strips with dia-

Teacher Talk/13.1

KIM HUBER EXPLORES CRITICAL INQUIRY

These children do not all have tidy happy endings in their lives. Using critical texts opens their eyes and my own to world issues. This helps to create understanding and provides connections for kids whose lives do not fit what they think is normal—such as the family of four with both parents and a dog in the backyard.

In my wildest dreams I would never have thought my students would have come so far in just one school year. At the beginning of the year, they simply saw a book as being for their enjoyment, like a Disney experience. They now look critically at texts, looking for clues into the meaning the author intended. They have examined books for hidden assumptions and have looked at how the readers are being positioned through these texts.

Source: Excerpted from Leland et al. (2005, pp. 264, 267).

logue) is essential to adopting a critical stance. Your role as a teacher is not necessarily to tell or question students, but instead, to "nudge" them even when they are reading independently to think and act just outside their comfort zone. Texts do not always need to be followed up with discussion; there are times when the power of words stands on its own.

GRADE 2: WRITTEN CONVERSATIONS AS INQUIRY

Jennings and O'Keefe (2002) describe a project that extends the concept of double entry journals and engages parents and children in collective inquiry about social justice and equity. This inquiry focuses on socio-political and historical issues as well as engaging students in alternative viewpoints. The conversations show parents and children making connections and sharing their views about important issues that might not have emerged otherwise. They had "sincere discussions about how people can make their communities humane and equitable—or not" (Jennings & O'Keefe, 2002, p. 407). In addition, children and parents grappled with complex issues by asking and answering questions, relating and connecting to their own experiences and identities, and extending their understanding of historical and cultural events. Theory into Practice 13.2 outlines the implementation of written conversations between parents and children.

GRADE 3: CONNECTING WRITERS' WORKSHOP AND CRITICAL INQUIRY

On choosing a significant subject:

> *This cannot be stressed bluntly enough. The writer must have something to say... It doesn't matter if a writer begins it cleverly, or ends it neatly, organizes it smoothly, writes dramatically, or writes with voice. The it itself has to have merit.*
> —Ralph Fletcher

This quotation draws our attention to the tensions between student freedom and teaching objectives. On one hand, we want to allow students sufficient choice in their own writing so that their topics matter to them, and on the other hand, we want to nudge or stretch student awareness beyond their present understandings, which may be strongly influenced by media and pop culture. We have all taught children who want to write relentless reproductions of television shows or popular movies, or continue to recycle cartoon or video game characters. How can you push your

Theory Into Practice/13.2

WRITTEN CONVERSATIONS AS CRITICAL INQUIRY

Before Written Conversation

- Practise double entry journals in the classroom—written conversations between teacher and student, or student and student.
- Send a letter or newsletter explaining the purpose of the writing project to parents or caregivers.
- Select literature or other texts carefully that can be used to open conversation and inquiry.
- Introduce the concept of written conversations in the classroom by beginning with a novel familiar to students in your classroom.
- Explore relevant and responsive themes in the classroom.
- Have parent and child read the text; reading can take place along the continuum of support from modelled to independent, or any combination.

During Written Conversation

- Parents and children engage in written conversation about a text (in their language of choice). It is important that parents attempt to write within their child's instructional reading level so that responses can be read independently. You will need to model this in the initial entries created in class. Jennings and O'Keefe (2002) quote the following conversation in response to a one-page article on the roles of Rosa Parks and Martin Luther King Jr. in the civil rights movement:

Elijah: Why can't white and black people drink out of the same water fountains?

Mom: Most of your whites thought of blacks as dirty animals because of our skin colour. So they treated blacks very unequal and cruel because whites also believed that they were better than blacks. How does this make you feel, to know how whites treated blacks?

Elijah: It makes me mad. Why did they kill Martin Luther King, Jr.?

Mom: Before the times of Dr. King Jr. most whites had learned so much hate for blacks that it was impossible to think that we could ever come together to help each others. When Dr. King came as a leader not just for blacks, but of all people, some whites got even more mad. So a few whites decided to kill him to stop his movement for equal rights and justice. Dr. King had words of truth that made whites and blacks want to become helpers of each other. The whites that killed him thought this would scare blacks enough to keep them from wanting equal rights and fair treatment. Do you know the difference between what is wrong and what is right? Would you treat someone wrong because they are not the same colour as you? What if your parents told you to stay away from people who are not the same colour as you? What would you do?

Elijah: Yes, I know the difference between wrong and right. No because they didn't treat me wrong. I will still play with them if I no [know] them (p. 405).

After Written Conversation

- Guided reflection with students: What went well? What would they change next time?
- Support students as they explore ways that they can take what they have learned and apply it to their own lives, empowering them to make their world more equitable.
- Encourage students to bring the issues they have written about and discussed to writers' workshop (see the next section on how we can engage students in developmentally and contextually appropriate critical inquiry and social action through writers' workshop).

students toward topics and themes that not only matter to them, but explore possible related issues of violence, social justice, and fairness?

Heffernan (2004) offers insights into this question through her work with her Grade 3 students during writers' workshop. One powerful suggestion is to read many texts that tackle issues of social justice, and practise "extended conversations" and "talkers' workshops" about issues, which include important things to remember about a book, discussing how the text may link to possible writing topics from the students' own lives, and discussion time to tackle issues currently facing the students, such as racism, sexism, and "playground politics" (Heffernan, 2004, pp. 26-43). By planning time for students to tell their own stories, make their own connections, and examine their own experiences, you are engaging them in actions that can transform not only their lives but the world as well (Johnson & Freedman, 2005).

Nudging your students to move away from retellings of television shows or summaries of texts can be encouraged by emphasizing personal writing during writers' workshop, writing on topics that relate to the students' own lives, on matters that they care about most. What Heffernan suggests is that you use lived experience as a text to examine and interrogate. You must recognize that personal narrative can easily remain superficial and uninteresting to readers outside the familiar circle of family and friends. This is why you should engage students in a discussion of the types of audiences for whom they write.

Students who understand their audiences write in an "authorly" way, interrogating their texts in much the same way that they are encouraged to interrogate another author's text. Understanding the connection between reader, author, text, and context is an important component of becoming a responsive and responsible reader, writer, and world citizen (Johnson & Freedman, 2005).

Heffernan (2004) encourages her students to write around "themes" and not just "topics" in order to move them forward into "social narratives" (pp. 47-51); it is these social narratives that offer the potential to transform and re-vision. Clearly, a healthy amount of reading, talking, and writing, as well as revisiting one's own writing, are required to successfully lead students to explore the more serious issues that underlie their own social experiences of playing on a hockey team or being invited to a sleepover. By examining the texts of their own lived experiences, we are helping them to use writing as a way of understanding, and an impetus for transformation and social action. Theory into Practice 13.3 provides an example that begins with a "real-life" problem and finishes with social action by engaging habits of mind.

ENGAGING "HABITS OF MIND" TO DECONSTRUCT AND RECONSTRUCT LIVED EXPERIENCE

Before Habits of Mind

Negotiate a scenario that is relevant to and presents an issue for your students. For example, many schools have made a shift toward designated play areas before and after school, at recess, and at lunch time. Questions of who uses the equipment, the baseball diamond, the soccer field, and when, become important to students. Encourage students to explore the problem and possible solutions by applying the five habits of mind:

During Habits of Mind

Cause and Effect/Connections

- Why do the teachers designate times for groups of students to use the playground equipment?
- How is the change connected to other changes or issues (for example, incidents of bullying, children getting hurt)?

Point of View/Perspective

- Who wants this change? Why?
- Who would this change affect? How?
- Who doesn't want this change? Why?

Evidence

- What facts are connected to this change?
- How many instances of bullying have been reported?
- How many children were hurt?
- What have teachers and students observed about the situation?

Suppose/Wondering

- What if the play areas were closed for a period of time?
- What would happen if the younger students always had the equipment and the older students always had the areas designated for soccer and baseball?

Debate

- How would the change improve recess or lunch time conditions for students and teachers? Make it worse?
- What are the alternatives? How would each improve or worsen conditions?
- Why is this change necessary?

After: Beyond Habits of Mind to Social Action

Using all of the information that you have collected, design the ideal school yard and the ideal schedule for designated play areas and play times. You might choose to develop a map or a calendar that can be used with younger students. Your plan must include letters to those who would be involved in the changes to your school yard and the implementation of your schedule (parents' committee, principal, teachers, school board, students).

Source: Adapted from Meier (1996) in Johnson & Freedman (2005, p. 4).

Heffernan's (2004) work with her students reminds us that a fair amount of prodding is sometimes required in order to lead students to write stories that "really make people think about big ideas" (p. 50). For example, she describes a student who simply wants to write about the time he got stitches. By really pushing him in her conversation, and through a suggestion from another student, he was encouraged to delve below the surface and explore "the violence that has been happening on the soccer field" (p. 50). Heffernan concludes:

> *As a teacher, I had to face the fact that I did have to* do something *if students were to see themselves as purposeful and powerful writers. I had to take an active role in the types of writing that occurred during writers' workshop. A push for thematic purpose in the workshop is more than an arbitrary restriction of choice—it is a step toward creating a space in which student writers use writing as a tool for exploring and generating social awareness. (p. 51)*

GRADE 4: CONNECTING CRITICAL INQUIRY AND READERS' WORKSHOP

Readers' workshop provides many opportunities for your students to explore and interrogate multiple viewpoints and socio-political issues as well as disrupting the commonplace or what is often taken for granted. Carefully selected texts allow teachers and students to explore issues that otherwise may go unexamined. Literature provides the opportunity to engage your students in "important work" with literature that extends beyond pleasure and enjoyment, and creates spaces for "understanding how language works to construct people, for using language to critique the word and the world, and for changing social practices that advantage some people over others" (Vasquez, 2001, p. 70).

Readers' workshops designed for critical inquiry allow students to linger with literature over an extended period of time, to explore deeper meanings from a variety of perspectives, and to participate actively in meaningful, authentic, and relevant classroom discussion, conversation, and response beyond "I like the book!" (Vasquez, 2001). Books read on many occasions and that foster great discussions often become what Calkins (1994) has referred to as touchstone texts. They are texts that are read on multiple occasions to the point that they become part of the classroom community's collective history (Laman, 2006).

In Theory into Practice 13.4, we present a multi-session readers' workshop approach that capitalizes on the work of Laman (2006) and Vasquez (2001) using *Hooway for Wodney Wat* (Helen Lester).

CRITICAL INQUIRY WITH *TOUCHSTONE TEXTS*

Before Critical Inquiry with Touchstone Texts

Session 1

- Read aloud a powerful text that is relevant to students' lives and will provide a place for them to explore their thinking and their understanding of the world.
- Use a variety of questions that support students as they make connections, ask further questions, and react to the story (see Figure 13.1).
  Why did the author make Wodney a rat and Camilla a capybara, a very large rodent? How does the text depict individual differences? How do the characters' words demonstrate who is stronger and more powerful? Are the pictures consistent with the character's words?
- When discussing and responding to the text, students will likely discuss issues such as:
  Whose voices are heard? Whose voices are silenced? How does language position the characters? Why are things the way they are? How can we change them?
- Ensure that students have the critical reading strategies needed to support inquiry (for example, subtext strategy, character role frameworks).

During Critical Inquiry

Session 2: Roles and Perspectives

- List the four roles of characters (Christensen, 2004 in Laman, 2006) on a chart so students can read it easily during the read aloud.
  Allies help the "targets" in situations where others are unfairly treated.
  Bystanders do not make the situation worse, nor do they make it better.
  Targets are those who are being unfairly treated.
  Perpetrators are those engaged in the unfair treatment of others.
  Allies: *In the hide-and-seek game, all the other rodents become Wodney's allies in the "bullying" although he seems initially unaware of what is happening.*
  Bystanders: *Wodney was initially a bystander, but as he became empowered, supported, and validated by his peers, became a perpetrator.*
  Targets: *Wodney and Camilla are both victims.*
  Perpetrators: *Camilla is a bully and in the game, Wodney becomes a "hero" in the eyes of his peers. The other redents were perpetrators and bullies as well.*
- As the text is read aloud for a second or third time, encourage students to ask questions throughout the reading. Record them on the chart as a record of discussion during the interactive read aloud. Questions raised during an interactive read aloud often reflect students' ways of being in the world and their cultural models; these may include issues related to power, history, friendship, culture. For example,
  Why didn't the teacher do something about Camilla when she was bullying? Why would the teacher let Camilla yell out answers without raising her hand? How did the other rodents feel when they were bullied by Camilla? Did they think about how they treated Wodney? Why didn't the other rodents tell Camilla about Wodney?

CRITICAL INQUIRY WITH *TOUCHSTONE TEXTS* (continued)

- Once students identify the roles played by each character, invite them to rewrite, re-imagine, revise, or comment on the situation:

    I think the other rodents used Wodney. Now he thinks he is a hero but what will happen tomorrow when Camilla is not there anymore? Will they start teasing him and bullying him again? I don't think it was fair for them to run Camilla out of town. It was her first day at a new school. Maybe she was nervous, maybe she didn't want to be teased about how big she was so she used her size to be a bully instead. Everyone knows that bullies don't usually get teased.

Session 3: Literature Circle 1: Small Group Generated Questions

- Students work in small groups and focus on answering the questions raised during the interactive read aloud and during literature circle 1. Each group is given four questions from Session 1 and instructed to record what they really think (Vasquez, 2001). Groups monitor their discussions by putting a star beside the questions that generate lengthy discussion. For example,

    Why do bullies act like this? Why can't they be nice? Why does the teacher look mean when trying to listen to Wodney? It's not Wodney's fault. Why would the other rodents tease him like that? Why did Camilla leave? Didn't she understand it was just a game?

Session 4: Literature Circle 2: Student Response to Guided Prompts

Students work with a partner or in a small group to discuss and respond to the following prompts (these responses may be written down or orally recorded):

- What is important to remember about this book? What surprised you about this book?
- List one or two writing topics from your own life that connect with the story.
- Why do you think people should or should not read this story?
- Write one or two statements about or as someone whose perspective is or is not represented in the story. For example,

    Wodney's perspective is presented well in the story. We know that he is nervous, shy, anxious, scared, and intimidated. We can tell through the pictures and through his lack of talking. If Wodney were to talk a little louder though, he might say, "Don't you know this isn't my fault? Don't you know that I am working hard to fix my 'r's. Don't you know that every time you tease me, you make me feel so very alone?"

Session 5: Grand Conversation (see Chapter 9)

- The whole class engages in a grand conversation about the story, paying particular attention to the questions in Session 3.

After Critical Inquiry

- Students use information from the text and previous steps to collectively select an image or text that best represents their learning from this story. This critical inquiry evidence (photocopy student responses) becomes part of their **audit trail, historical trail,** or **learning wall.**
- Plan with students social justice and action projects related to bullying on the schoolyard (for example, peacemakers, character education, social skills training).

GRADE 5: "HAVING A GO" AT SOCIAL ACTION THROUGH DRAMA AND POETRY

Drama: Constructing "Make-Believe Worlds" to Explore Social Action

Drama is a dynamic tool that opens spaces for learning and critical inquiry. Through process drama that emphasizes problem-solving, students can explore and stretch the limits of their day-to-day perspectives and realities through critical reflection and "have a go" at rehearsed and improvised action.

> *Participants at once inhabit and co-construct a "make-believe world" (O'Neill, 1995) parallel to their own lives. They develop characters and situations that are animated by multiple social positions, and they mediate their own experiences of the world with those of the various roles enacted in the drama.*
>
> (Medina & Campano, 2006, p. 333)

Drama enables students to "try on" new perspectives and ways of being as they come to terms with their own identities. In the non-threatening space of drama, students can disrupt the commonplace and explore multiple perspectives that they may not have previously considered. Stimuli for drama are diverse and include: lived experience where students can "construct and reinterpret multiple aspects of their lives and critically examine forms of marginalization" (Medina & Campano, 2006, p. 333). Texts should provoke dramatic reader response (print, oral, and visual), and scripts specifically designed to explore issues of social justice and equity.

Medina and Campano (2006) cite two dynamic features of drama that are instrumental in teaching and research communities. The first is drama's ability to provide, from a critical inquiry perspective, spaces to explore power relationships and mediate competing and conflicting values that often emerge during role play. In role play, students bring their unique ways of being in the world and their ways with words into their roles. The second feature is drama's potential to evoke students' cultural and social identities as they engage with issues and audiences relevant to their own lived experience. Both features allow your students to step back from their own personal realities, distance themselves, fictionalize their experiences, and then explore alternative perspectives. Theory into Practice 13.5 describes how you can use process drama to engage students in explorations of social justice and equity as they relate to classroom management and what students should think their teachers should know (Medina & Campano, 2006). In this multilingual Grade 5 classroom, the students and teachers collectively created a performance art group *Dancing across Borders*.

EXPLORING SOCIAL ACTION THROUGH DRAMA

Before Drama

- Select or negotiate an issue for critical inquiry.
- Consider how multiple viewpoints can be presented in the drama.
- Ask for volunteers to put together a play that addresses the following questions:
  - When was there a productive classroom atmosphere?
  - Why did some students develop an oppositional stance toward school?
  - When did school require the students to compromise or deny an aspect of who they felt they were?

During Drama (a concrete example reported by Medina & Campano, 2006)

- Students reviewed their writing portfolios for texts and stories that were evidence of intercultural miscommunication, conflict, and social critique.

  Students' writing, including poems and journal entries, addressed issues such as gender, culture, work lives outside school, and punitive aspects of schooling.

- Students wove these texts together as a starting point for a script entitled "What the Teacher Didn't Know." The script became a "living text," "written collaboratively and often altered in the context of practice and performance" (Medina & Campano, 2006, p. 338). For example, the students used a combination of dialogue, freezing, and soliloquies to explore the situation and focus on the perspectives, emotions, and identities of students.

Scene:	Will is asleep
Mr. Sid:	Will! Again, no! I cannot believe it! You are in my classroom, not in your bed. Wake up now and do what I told you.
Will:	This class is boring and you're giving me a headache.
Mr. Sid:	Well, that's your opinion! You can go out now, and find yourself a job in Taco Bell or McDonald's.
	FREEZE
Will:	The teacher didn't know I am on medication and that I felt robotic, lethargic, and withdrawn. Therefore, I fell asleep during class because they make me take the medication in the morning. I told the teacher that I was on medication but he wouldn't listen to what I had to say. I was originally put on medication without my parents' knowledge when I lived in a group home. By medicating children, it makes them depend on medication for their personal problems. I am still struggling with mine. By the way, my mother is working in Taco Bell because she is struggling to feed us, and I don't see nothing wrong with that (p. 338).

After Drama

- Guided reflection on the process with students: Discuss how drama provides a space for students and teachers to take on alternative ways of being and explore diverse perspectives.
- In effect, this group of students engaged teachers in critical inquiry about behaviour. They disrupted interpretations of behaviour as laziness, non-compliance, or disrespect and tried to help teachers explore alternative perspectives in an effort to make the classroom a more responsive, inclusive, and respectful space.

A Poetry of Caring: Evoking Hearts and Heads

The world is ours
A place to help others
Something you don't put on the shelf
Somewhere to express yourself
—Kayleigh, Age 11 (in Pomeroy, 2004)

Damico (2005) explored the transformative potential of poetry to "involve hearts and heads, evoking feelings and provoking thoughts and ideas about complex social issues" (p. 138). Theory into Practice 13.6 describes Damico's implementation of critical inquiry into published and historical poetry. Her focus was less on analysis and more on heartfelt and immediate responses to poetry as she attempted to explore spaces of hope and possibility, restore feeling, and challenge students' prevailing notions of poetry as "flowery" and "sappy."

Pomeroy (2004) took a different approach to poetry. Although reading poetry necessarily precluded its writing, it was not the focus of her inquiry. Instead, she and her students seamlessly wove together issues of homelessness, poetry, and social action. Students began by reading *Fly Away Home* by Eve Bunting, a story about a homeless boy and his father who live in an airport. Students then researched homelessness on the Internet and engaged in many discussions about the issue. Both students and teacher realized that simply understanding the issue was not enough. Enabling and supporting students as they engaged in social action was a natural extension. Pomeroy's students decided to create a poetry anthology, *Making a Difference One Poem at a Time,* that they could sell to raise funds for homeless shelters. This required them to understand a variety of kinds of poetry, including autobiographical poems, cinquains and diamantes, haikus, limericks, and acrostic, lyric, and narrative poems. They identified common elements, such as imagery, emotion, and rhyme, and wrote poems about homelessness.

In addition to writing the book, students also had to coordinate production, marketing, sales, and distribution of profits to charitable organizations. With the guidance of their teacher, they saw the possibility for social action and took steps to transform the world of the homeless. The $218 raised from the sale of their anthology in the first year was donated to a homeless shelter. The transformation and re-visioning continued into the second year as the whole school became involved in the poetry writing project and worked to restore equity and social justice. Pomeroy's story teaches an important lesson: critical inquiry projects do not have to be complex to make a difference, as long as they reflect the thoughts, ideas, and experiences of the students who want to make a difference. By allowing students to decide on social action, they are empowered and come to recognize their ability to shape, transform, and revise the world.

GRADE 6: CRITICAL INQUIRY THROUGH POPULAR CULTURE

Popular culture can be an entrée into students' discourses and world views. When you incorporate popular culture into your programs, you

---

Theory Into Practice/13.6

EVOKING HEARTS AND HEADS THROUGH POETRY

Before Poetry Reading

- Explore students' perceptions of poetry using questions such as:

  Poetry Survey
  1. Poetry is...
  2. When I think about poetry, I think about...
  3. I have written poems about...
  4. Why do people write poems?
  5. Do you have any favourite poems or poems?
  6. What do you think it takes to be a poet?
  7. Are you a poet? How would you know?
  8. Any other ideas or things you want to share or are wondering about?
     (Apol & Harris, 1999 in Damico, 2000, p. 139)

- Discuss the survey with students. Reinforce valid understandings and expose myths and misconceptions about its form and purpose. (For example, most students in Damico's survey equated poetry with the expression of feelings or sharing thoughts; she reinforced this and at the same time dispelled the myth that poetry had to be "flowery" and "sappy").

During Poetry Reading

- Provide a variety of poetry books and anthologies for students to explore; encourage them to select poems that evoke feelings and suggest they explore issues of social justice and equity.
- Invite reader response through the following:
  - Individual and class conversations about poems: For example, who wrote it? When? Why? If it were written today, would it be different? The teacher's role here is that of a critical facilitator, asking key questions and prompting student thinking.
  - Journal writing: For example, prompts such as, What does the poem make you think or feel?

After Poetry Reading

- Invite students to participate in poetry writing about real life issues that affect them (for example, identity, equity issues such as homelessness, individual difference, culture).

recognize the importance of student interest and relevance, and are looking for ways to help them see the "everyday" through a new lens. This multimedia plan (Theory into Practice 13.7) focuses on Roald Dahl's *Charlie and the Chocolate Factory*. Students are encouraged to adopt alternative perspectives and explore the issue of stereotyping as it relates to an author's or director's purpose and point of view. Based on three different media texts, students are asked to explore the impact of genres and their unique characteristics. Students extend their understanding of media stereotypes to stereotyping in their day-to-day lives. Multiple encounters with each text will be necessary in order to provide students with ample time and opportunity to deconstruct, gather evidence, and explore the conventions and structures that influence the way that stereotypes are portrayed.

Multimedia, Perspective, and Education

Multimedia is a powerful tool. It often becomes an instruction manual that creates expectations for groups of people (groups formed by race, class, gender, sexual orientation, disability, ability). In order to understand the inequalities in our society, we need to examine what creates them. It is not fair nor true to say that the media are responsible for producing inequalities in society. The media do, however, perpetuate them. Fairy tales, romance novels, movies, television shows, advertisements, video games, media idols, and live performances typically reinforce stereotypes of groups that are rarely questioned. Through critical inquiry, you can provide your students with the tools to deconstruct and analyze critically problematic

literacy notebook 13.3

STOP, THINK, AND WRITE

Recall your experiences in classrooms both as a student and as a teacher.

- Have you ever participated in a critical inquiry?
- If so, what do you remember about it?
- How was the commonplace disrupted?
- How did you explore alternative perspectives?
- How did this inquiry enable you to explore socio-political issues and power relationships?
- How did you act in a way that promoted social justice?
- How could you adapt this inquiry for use in your own classroom?

A MULTIMEDIA PLAN: *CHARLIE AND THE CHOCOLATE FACTORY*

End of Grade 6 Expectations: Atlantic Canada English Language Arts Curriculum

Students will be able to do the following:

Respond critically to a range of texts, applying their understanding of language, form, and genre.

- Recognize that facts can be presented to suit an author's purpose and point of view.
  - Consider information from alternative perspectives.
- Identify the conventions and structure of a variety of print and media texts and genres.
  - Connect with the purpose of each text or genre.
- Respond critically to texts.
  - Formulate questions as well as understandings.
  - Demonstrate growing awareness that all texts reflect a purpose and a perspective.
  - Identify the point of view in a text and demonstrate awareness of whose voices/positions are and are not being expressed.
  - Discuss the text from the perspective of own realities and experiences.
  - Detect prejudice, stereotyping, and bias.
  - Apply a growing range of strategies to analyze and evaluate a text.

Speak and listen to explore, extend, clarify, and reflect on their thoughts, ideas, feelings, and experiences.

- Defend and support opinions with evidence.
- Listen critically to others' ideas, opinions, and points of view.

Be able to communicate information and ideas effectively and clearly, and to respond personally and critically.

- Contribute and respond constructively in conversations and small group and whole group discussions.

Be able to interact with sensitivity and respect, considering the situation, audience, and purpose.

- Listen attentively and demonstrate awareness of the needs, rights, and feelings of others.
- Detect examples of prejudice, stereotyping, or bias in oral language, recognize their negative effect on individuals and cultures, and attempt to use bias-free language.

Resources

Charlie and the Chocolate Factory, book by Roald Dahl

Willy Wonka and the Chocolate Factory, (1971), film, featuring Gene Wilder, directed by Mel Stuart, writing credit Roald Dahl, 100 min., US

Charlie and the Chocolate Factory, (2005), film, featuring Johnny Depp, directed by Tim Burton, writing credit Roald Dahl, 115 min., US

Pre-assessment

Students have encountered or read the book.

They have learned to crack the code of visual images (see Figure 13.6).

A MULTIMEDIA PLAN: *CHARLIE AND THE CHOCOLATE FACTORY* (continued)

Session 1: Modelled and Shared Deconstruction of the Stereotypes Found in the Printed Text

- Discuss the term "stereotype," drawing on students' lived experience (teachers need to be familiar with media characters).
- Select one character from the story and read selections that create the stereotype. Include description of the character, texts related to the character, words spoken by the character, and the character's actions.

   For example, in Charlie and Chocolate Factory, Dahl (1968, pp. 26-27) describes Augustus Gloop as an enormously fat boy who looks like he has been "blown up with a very powerful pump." The image that Dahl writes about was posted on the front page of the newspaper announcing Augustus's luck in finding a golden ticket. Augustus Gloop was portrayed an enormously fat nine-year old boy whose "flabby folds of fat" bulged out of every part of his body. Dahl likens this fat to a "monstrous ball of dough" with small greedy eyes that peer out at the world.

   To reporter queries of her son's luck, Mrs. Gloop assured reporters that she was sure that her son would find a Golden Ticket because it would be impossible for him not to find one given the number of candy bars he eats in a day. She describes eating as Augustus's hobby all that he is interested in, and something that he requires for nourishment, similar to vitamins. She assures the reporter that in her mind, eating is far better than being a hooligan or shooting off zip guns.

- Engage students in a discussion of how Dahl created the stereotype of Augustus Gloop: What types of language did he use? What did he make explicit? What was implicit? After reading the book, how do they envision this character? What is the character's view of reality? What does Dahl believe about this type of person and how they behave in the world? How do we know?

Guided Deconstruction of the Stereotypes Found in the Printed Text

- Assign other characters from the novel (Willy Wonka, Charlie Bucket, Veruca Salt, Violet Beauregard, Mike Teevee, four grandparents, parent(s), Oompa Loompas).
- Ask students to find text selections that suggest a different stereotype. Give them a response sheet that targets the questions discussed in modelled and shared deconstruction.
- In the large group, students are asked to a) present the stereotype portrayed by Roald Dahl; b) support their presentation with excerpts from the text; c) dramatically present their assigned character making specific reference to words and actions in the text.

Session 2: Guided Deconstruction of the Stereotypes Found in the Film *Willy Wonka and the Chocolate Factory*

- Before Viewing: Ask students what they recall about stereotypes from the previous discussion.
- Critical Viewing: Distribute a response sheet similar to that used in Session 1. Assign a character to each group. As they watch the film, have students collect visual and talk examples.
- Post-Viewing: How does the character in this early film compare to the image they had created as

A MULTIMEDIA PLAN: *CHARLIE AND THE CHOCOLATE FACTORY* (continued)

a result of visualizing the book? How does the language in the film compare to the language in the book? Do the music and dance sequences enhance or detract from the stereotype?

Session 3: Independent Deconstruction of the Stereotypes Found in the Film *Charlie and the Chocolate Factory*

- Before Viewing: Ask students to independently select a new character and then brainstorm four or five questions that they have about their character.
- Critical Viewing: As students watch the film, have them collect visual and talk samples from the film that describe their character.
- Post-Viewing: Discuss how the visual representation and language in the 2005 film compare to the 1971 film. Why do you think the director made these changes? Do they reflect an alternative perspective?

Session 4: Class Discussion

Begin with the following questions and respond to questions, queries, and statements as the discussion proceeds.

Was there any doubt in your mind about the presence of stereotypes?

Why was Roald Dahl so explicit about the stereotypes?

What message was he trying to convey?

What is his perspective or view of reality? What does he value?

What does he want his audience to think, feel, or do?

Session 5: Extending to Writers' Workshop and Social Action

In both the book and the films, we have encountered the stereotypes visualized by Roald Dahl, Mel Stuart, and Tim Burton. Are these stereotypes as explicit in "real" life? Can you recall a time when stereotyping happened in the classroom? In the school yard? In the community? At home? How do stereotypes develop? How can we identify the types of language we use and our own behaviour that perpetuates stereotypes? Are stereotypes fair? What should we do about stereotypes?

Extensions

- The character of Willy Wonka is significantly different in each version. Discuss the differences between Gene Wilder's interpretation of the character and Johnny Depp's. How does this differ from the book? If Roald Dahl could have told Gene Wilder or Johnny Depp how to portray the character, what might he have said? If you were going to play the character of Willy Wonka, how might you do it? How do you think the inner monologue of Willy Wonka differs in each text?
- Explore the point of view from which each version was told. How does this present an alternate view of reality? How does this privilege one character over another?
- Using a two- or three-way Venn diagram, compare the texts.
- If video equipment is available, encourage students to adapt a print text into a film.

representations that the media create and perpetuate. It is important to understand that media is not an exact reflection of reality. Expectations, ideologies, and stereotypes have no meaning outside the context of the media in which they are created and encountered.

Even the youngest children can develop an awareness of the impact of media on their lives and how the media shape and inform their personal narratives. Consider the cycle of television program creation, television viewing, product creation, marketing, and purchasing. Can we identify which came first? And does it really matter? Recall a scenario that many of us have observed—a three-year-old demanding a popular toy as she walks through a mall, turning this way and that, seeing the toys, clothing, even foods that she knows so well because they are part of her everyday life. How can you help your students to grapple with the messages that they implicitly receive and tacitly accept? How can we connect critical inquiry and critical literacy in the home, school, community, and world?

You see the pervasive effect of media in our classroom on a daily basis: in the identities and roles students select, the decisions they make, the games they play, the words they use, and the countless retellings of movies, video games, and jingles. We would like you to consider the necessity to help students see their everyday experiences from different perspectives, exploring and understanding the reciprocal relationship that exists between themselves and the media, and therefore the role that they can have in disrupting the commonplace, re-visioning their narratives, and transforming the inequities of their personal narratives.

As you and your students gain awareness of the more traditional conceptualizations of media (television, film, print: magazines), Thoman (2006) argues that awareness will progress through three overlapping and complementary stages, to which we have added a fourth:

1. Become aware of the amount of time spent with various media, the types of choices made, and the importance of managing one's media "diet."

2. Learn the skills that enable us to become critical viewers and consumers of media—how to analyze, interrogate, and deconstruct texts and how they are created.

3. Develop a deeper probing approach to media that includes questions such as "Who is this message intended for? Who wants to reach this audience and why? From whose perspective is this story told? Whose voices are heard and whose are absent? What strategies does this message use to get my attention and make me feel included?" (Tallim, 2006).

STOP, THINK, AND WRITE

Stage 1: Describe your media "diet."
What is your favourite television show? Radio show? Advertisement? Film? Magazine, newspaper, book? Video game? How much time do you spend as a text consumer?

Stage 2: Choose one text.
What genre of media does this text belong to? What is its underlying structure or architecture? How does this genre distinguish itself from others? What makes this particular text memorable? What is it about this genre that you like best or least? How was this text created?

Stage 3: Interrogate the text.
Who is this message intended for? Who wants to reach this audience, and why? From whose perspective is this text told? Whose voices are heard and whose are absent? What strategies does this message use to get my attention and make me feel included? Refer to Figure 13.1 and select additional questions for inquiry.

Stage 4: Choose a voice that was absent.
How would this text change if this story was told? How could you change this text to ensure that power is distributed equitably and all voices are heard?

literacy
notebook
13.4

4. Participate in social action and re-visioning of the world. Ask questions such as "How might the message change if told from a different perspective? How can I address the inequity present in the text? How can I transform and re-vise the world and make it a better place one small step at a time?"

Figure 13.3 presents a set of guidelines for multimedia exploration in your classroom. Remember that exploration and critical inquiry using multimedia should not be considered an add-on to the curriculum, but instead something that you can naturally integrate on a day-to-day basis.

Understanding Code-Breaking Practices for a Range of Multimedia Genres

You will recall that we adopted a very broad conceptualization of text that encompassed print, visual, oral, performance, and multimedia. Although the process of critical inquiry will remain consistent, there are

FIGURE 13.3 Guidelines for Multimedia Exploration

Focus on Process
- Explore questions that arise as texts are viewed, heard, or read; engage higher-order thinking skills (Bloom's taxonomy) throughout the inquiry process (see Figure 13.1).
- Support students as they identify main ideas, make connections between sources, ask relevant and thought-provoking questions, identify myths, misconceptions, assumptions, stereotypes, ideologies, and erroneous beliefs that are fostered and perpetuated through the media.

Develop a Critical Inquiry Plan in Collaboration with Students
- Brainstorm the types of texts available both in and out of the classroom. Brainstorm topics-related media and text sources.
- Adapt the KWL to include the "where" of information gathering.

Teach Students How to Get the Most from Text
- Teach expository text features and strategies for information gathering (see Chapter 10).
- Encourage students to predict, confirm, and clarify information collected through a variety of texts.
- Discuss information collected from media texts; make comparisons about presentation, credibility, accuracy.

Establish Guidelines for Text Assessment and Evaluation with Students
- Establish specific guidelines to assess and evaluate the effectiveness of a variety of texts (for example, print evaluation, website evaluation, video critique). Encourage students to ask the following questions about the author, format, audience, content, and purpose of a text:
  1. Who created this message?
  2. What creative techniques are used to attract my attention?
  3. How might different people understand this message differently?
  4. What values, lifestyles, and points of view are represented in, or omitted?
  5. Why is this message being sent?

  (Centre for Media Literacy, 2005; Thoman & Jolls, 2004)

Focus on the Basic Language, Grammar, or Code Used in a Variety of Texts
- Ensure that students have the necessary tools to crack the code and follow these codes independently in their own text creation.
- Ask them to sort, analyze, and appreciate the range of techniques used to attract attention, convey emotion, and persuade.

Provide Multiple Opportunities for Students to Discuss and Create Multimedia Texts
- Encourage students to represent their knowledge using a variety of texts (for example, PowerPoint presentations, auditory texts, performance texts, visual texts, HyperStudio, KidPix, video, music).
- Provide students with a range of resources that will support their exploration of multimedia (for example, adding sound effects to a readers' theatre script, adding music to a PowerPoint, supporting oral presentations with visual aids).
- Ensure that there are meaningful and authentic links between assessment and evaluation.

Source: Scheibe (2004); Thoman & Jolls (2004).

unique code-breaking practices that need to be addressed. Your students require a full continuum of support as they develop an understanding of how these "tricks" influence their response as media consumers, the message they gain from the text, stereotypes that are perpetuated, voices that are silenced or marginalized, and the power relationships that emerge (Lundstrom, 2004).

> *Although mediated messages seem to be self-evident, in truth, they use a complex audio/visual "language" that has its own rules (grammar), and that can be used to express multi-layered concepts and ideas about the world. Not everything may be obvious at first; and images go by so fast! If our children are able to navigate their lives through this multimedia culture, they need to be fluent in "reading" and "writing" the language of images and sounds just as we have always taught them to read and write the language of printed communications.*
>
> (Thoman & Jolls, 2004, p. 19)

We have chosen what we believe are the five dominant multimedia genres (besides print and lived experience, which we have discussed at length earlier in the chapter or in other places throughout the text) that will be encountered by students in your classroom. We highlight some of the unique characteristics and features of television, video games, performance, visual texts, and advertisements. This list is by no means exhaustive, but it will enable you to tap into your students' popular culture and media exposure as a site of critical inquiry.

TELEVISION AWARENESS

> *Television and film have become the storytellers of our generation:*
> *these stories tells us about who we are, what we believe,*
> *and what we want to be.*
> —KathleenTyner

How does television create the myths and the stories by which we live? Gerbner (2002) suggests that stories act as attempts to make the invisible visible, revealing the characteristics of human beings that we are familiar with and the actions that we can understand. The stories that are woven into our cultures can be divided into three categories:

1. *Stories about how things work*
   Fiction, drama, and often mythology. The purpose is to develop the underlying message and the significance of how things work in real life. Sometimes these stories are parodies, sometimes comedy… their primary purpose is to "make the inner dynamics of life visible" (Gerbner, 2002).

Critical inquiry of television involves an awareness of television as ritual, institution, entertainment, and as a socialization agent.

2. *Stories about how things are*

   These are factual stories that might include the past or the present. News reports and documentaries are in this category. The underlying purpose is to present life as it was lived or is being lived; its meaning is dependent on the context in which it was created.

3. *Stories of action*

   These are stories of values and choices, which are both prerequisites for action. Lifestyle programs and commercials are in this category, one that challenges us to act—to set a goal, to change something in our lives, to buy a given product. These stories suggest what we "ought to do, ought to buy, ought to vote for, ought to consider" (Gerbner, 2002).

How do you help your students to understand these stories and the impact of television on who they are, what they believe, and what they want to be? You can plan meaningful and authentic activities that support students in their quest to become "media savvy" (Lundstrom, 2004). You can listen to the media discourse as it surfaces in your classroom and respond accordingly. You can begin with the media experience of students and then challenge them to adopt a questioning, interrogative, and critical stance. You can help them understand concepts such as television as ritual, television as institution, television as entertainment, and television as a socialization agent. Figure 13.4 provides specific teaching strategies to address each of these concepts.

VIDEO GAME DISCOURSE

You may be shaking your head and asking what video game literacy could possibly have to do with language, critical literacy, or even media literacy. Let us assure you from the outset that it has everything to do with media literacy, and because it enters the lived experiences of our students and their social narratives, it also becomes a significant force in their language development. Video game characters show up on television, on trading cards so very popular on the school yard, on food packages, and in the books they read. Imagine the possibility of motivating the reluctant writer or reader by making the connection to video games (which often require significant amounts of reading). When we talk about video game literacy, we are not talking about skill and competence with a particular game; what we are looking at is critical

FIGURE 13.4 Spotlight on Television

Television as Ritual

By ritual, we mean the pervasive schedule, pattern, and rhythm of television, which often influences the schedule, pattern, and rhythm of the household. Imagine the bedtime ritual between a 2-year-old and parent as they snuggle and watch *Arthur*. Or imagine the adult who turns down an invitation to a social because "their shows" are on at that time. The ritual aspect of television is a reality; what is important is that students learn how to monitor and manage their media diet.

- Ask students to keep track of how much time they spend watching television each day, using a checklist, graph, or written list. Collate data and calculate frequencies of specific programs, genres of programs, and length of time spent watching television.

Television as Institution

Guidelines, such as those provided by the Canadian Association of Broadcasters, Advertising Standards Canada, and the Alliance for Children and Television, apply to programming and advertising issues. They target issues such as the content and purpose of programming, advertising language, and target audience.

- Ask students to distinguish between the actual program and advertising. Are there similarities? Are there differences? How do their favourite advertisements compare with their favourite programs?
- Ask students to keep track of the number of commercials in a given television program, the percentage of time dedicated to advertising, and where commercials are placed in a program. Ask students to track television commercials over a given period of time, apply the guidelines, and act accordingly (options include writing a letter to the network, writing a letter to Advertising Standards Canada, or the Canadian Radio-Television and Telecommunications Commission, outlining their findings). Television commercials can be analyzed using the following questions (Piazza, 1999, p. 217):
  - How might you characterize the nature and tone of the language? (Childlike, playful, serious, sarcastic?) Why was this tone chosen?
  - Does the commercial lead you to act or not act in a certain way?
  - What is the age of the target audience? Values? Gender? Economic status? How does it appeal to these targets?
  - What effects do the music, pictures, and images have?
  - What techniques does it use to get your attention? (Fast cuts, non-sequential images, surreal images, fast-paced formats, discontinuous images.) Figure 13.6 presents issues related to both lighting and camera shots in advertisements.

Television as Entertainment

There is no doubt that television offers hours of entertainment with a high level of satisfaction for viewers, but at what cost? Without critical viewing skills, viewers are unaware of the impact of ideologies, values, and attitudes implicit in television. Entertainment is rewarding; we all need to relax at the end of a long day, and escape the stresses and pressures of our own lives.

- Ask students to reflect on why they watch television. What types of television programs do they

FIGURE 13.4 Spotlight on Television (continued)

find entertaining? What types make them laugh? What programs allow them to escape from their lives, if only for a little while?

Television as Socialization Agent

This is perhaps one of the most underestimated functions of television. Without realizing it, children are learning how to behave, what to say, what to buy, what to wear, how to look—all by turning on the television.

- Ask students to keep a character journal that applies the subtext strategy. Have them stop every once in a while to climb inside a character's mind and understand what they are thinking, what they might be saying, or how they might react. Ask students to make connections to their own lives. Have they ever been in a similar situation? Have they felt the same way as the character? What did they do? How did they act? What did they say?

- Provide students with a list of questions that they can answer in much the same way that they would questions about print text. Find texts that have multiple representations (print, film, dramatic performance) that will enable students to compare things such as the underlying ideologies and beliefs of the author. Figure 13.3 presents an in-depth multimedia study.

- Students generally stay with television series that perpetuate the same subjectivities in each episode. Ask students to respond to television programs in the same way they would with print texts.

- Encourage parents and caregivers to view and discuss television with their children. Provide response sheets or questions that will support and guide meaningful and focused discussion. A simple framework for discussion is suggested by Davis (2002):

  i) You're smarter than your TV: Reinforce that we can make our own decisions.

  ii) TV's world is not real: Comment on the differences.

  iii) TV teaches us that some people are more important than others: Encourage them to question and talk back to their television... "Give me a break!"

  iv) TV keeps doing the same things over and over again: Help them to understand the formula of sitcoms, cartoons, talk shows, news reports, advertisements. Help them to understand the impact of music, silence, laughter, lighting, camera angle.

  v) Someone is always trying to make money with TV: Talk about advertisements. How do they persuade, convince, and grab attention?

Source: Davis (2002); Gerbner (2002); Piazza (1999).

awareness of the gaming architecture, the visual images, and the implicit assumptions about the world and audiences that need to be interrogated and critiqued.

The work of Gee (2005) is groundbreaking with regard to video games and video game discourse. Using video games as a text source to interrogate will enable learners to explore the underlying beliefs of video game producers and perhaps dispel the myth that video games encourage students to be passive recipients of this particular form of media. The initial question concerns the message that underlies the culture of video games. What is the message of this medium? And how does this medium shape our cultures, our beliefs about the world, and our stories? Figure 13.5 presents a list of key and guiding questions adapted from Center for Media Literacy, which you can use to engage in critical inquiry with video games and its resulting gaming culture. It is important to ensure, especially with video games, that critique is not synonymous with negative judgment, but instead reflects an opportunity for analysis, deconstruction, and discussion. We have provided a full list of questions, but teachers and students alike should feel free to select questions that suit their purposes.

Engaging in critical inquiry of video game discourse is one way of engaging students, particularly boys, who have become distanced from the teaching-learning process. The video game culture is the lived experience of many students, often many who are not fully engaged in the institution of "schooled literacy." Gee (2004) tells us that there is much to learn from the video game discourse about learning (for example, decision-making, scaffolding, power, control, practice, modelling, demonstration). If you can bring some of the learning principles inherent in video games into your classroom, you might naturally engage a greater number of students. The issue of boys and literacy is discussed further in Chapter 14.

VISUAL TEXTS: MORE THAN MEETS THE EYE

> *We live in a world of things seen, a world that is visual, and we expend much of our physical and emotional energy on the act of seeing. Like fish, we "swim" in a sea of images, and these images help shape our perceptions of the world and of ourselves.*
> —John Berger

No matter where we turn, images pervade our lives; some are natural, some artistic, some designed to entertain, some to persuade, some to represent. Pictures are symbolic forms of communication. In fact, pictures and images on the walls of caves were the first texts—stories told from long ago to perpetuate and pass on tradition and heritage. We recall from Chapter 5 that, as children emerge into literacy, one of their initial forms of representation or writing is pictorial. But as with any type of

FIGURE 13.5 Deconstructing the Video Game Culture

Key Question: Who created this video game?
- What kind of video game is it? What are its elements?
- How similar or different is it to other video games you have played?
- Which technologies were used in its creation?
- How would it be different in a different medium (for example, a board game)?
- What choices might have been made differently?
- How many people did it take to create this video game? What are their professions?

Key Question: What creative techniques are used to attract my attention?
- What do you notice about the way the message is constructed? (Colours/shapes? Sound effects? Music? Silence? Dialogue/narration? Props, set, costumes? Movement? Lighting?)
- Where are the cameras? What are the viewpoints?
- How is the story told? What are people doing?
- Are there any visual symbols or metaphors?
- What's is the emotional appeal? Persuasive devices? What makes it seem real?

Key Question: How might others understand this message differently from you?
- Have you ever experienced something like this?
- How close does it comes to what you experienced in real life?
- What did you learn from playing this video game? What did you learn about yourself?
- What did you learn from other people's response and their experience?
- How many other interpretations could there be? How could we find out about them?
- How can you explain the different responses?
- Are other viewpoints just as valid as yours?

Key Question: What lifestyles, values, and points of view are represented in this video game?
- How is the human person characterized? What kinds of behaviours/consequences are depicted?
- What type of person is the reader/watcher/listener invited to identify with?
- What questions come to mind as you watch/read/listen?
- What ideas or values are being "sold" in this video game (for example, aggression)?
- What political or economic ideas are communicated?
- What judgments or statements are made about how we treat other people?
- What is the overall worldview?
- Are any ideas or perspectives omitted? How would you find what's missing?

Key Question: Why is this message being sent?
- Who is in control of the creation and transmission of this message?
- Why are they sending it? How do you know?
- Who is served by, profits or benefits from the message? The public? Private interests? Individuals? Institutions?
- Who wins? Who loses? Who decides?
- What economic decisions may have influenced the construction of the video?

Source: Adapted from Center for Media Literacy, (2003). Teacher's/Leader's Orientation Guide.

media, it is not simply enough to receive the visual information. It is not enough to just *see*. What we need to do is learn "*how* to see and *what* to see…. And what we decide to see is determined by what we know and what we believe and what we want" (Berger, 1989, p. 25).

How do you make sense of visual information? What catches your eye and sustains your attention? Why? How do these images shape your perceptions of the world and of yourselves? Figure 13.6 presents some of the influences of visual images that are often taken for granted. Your students need to be aware of how perspective is shaped by such things as lighting and camera position and angle.

Critical inquiry of video game discourse is one way to engage students.

ADVERTISEMENTS: PRINT AND VISUAL

As with television, one of the first things we need to do as consumers is become aware of our daily exposure to other forms of advertising. Greater awareness of what constitutes advertising and where we encounter it in our daily lives will help us to reduce our advertising consumption as well as resist the persuasive and subversive effects of advertising. Beyond an awareness of the advertising world around us, we need to develop skills and strategies that will enable us to see beyond the visual image to the subtexts and stories beneath the surface. Figure 13.7 suggests questions that will help you to analyze advertisements, describe the stories they tell, and find their hidden messages with your students. As with any other response, responses to advertisements will be shaped by our previous experiences, our own beliefs, assumptions, and ideas about media and the tricks that advertisers use.

PERFORMANCE TEXTS

When you consider the importance of learning "*how* to see and *what* to see" so that your students have greater control over the constant bombardment of visual images they receive through television and advertising, you might do well to turn to performance text as a suitable rehearsal ground for practising what to attend to and what to ignore.

When we experience performance texts, whether in the form of theatre, music, or dance, we enter a *living* world. One of the most fundamental understandings your students can get from the experience of a live stage play or a musical or dance production in a real theatre is how *different* live professional performances are from video, television, or other recorded forms of theatre, music, and dance. Understanding how this difference plays out in real time is crucial to understanding the power of spontaneity—the power of the live interaction on the audience-performer relationship.

> *The more the audience gives to the actors,*
> *the more the actors can give back to the audience.*
> —Claudia Cornett & Katharine Smithrim

By experiencing how an audience's reactions and anticipations can immediately influence the performers on stage, and in turn, the entire dy-

FIGURE 13.6 Cracking the Visual Code

Lighting

Lighting	Effects
Natural light (like fire, sunset, candles)	Creates shadows, quiet moods, time of day (daybreak, dusk)
Artificial light (lamps, streetlights)	Can create romance, routine events
Spotlights	Can focus on a character or object, draw eyes to the centre of what is to be illuminated
Area lighting	Illuminates everything in view, all at once; viewers can focus on whatever they choose
Backlighting	Creates reflections and silhouettes, shadows, fireside glow, halo, faces bathed in sunlight

Camera Talk

Cinematographers and photographers can alter our interpretation by varying camera angles, framing, size of subject, and light filters.

Camera Shot	Effects
Colour, distortions, enlargements, caricatures, angles, and curves	Focus perceptions and shape interpretations
Fast cuts, speed of shift, sequential images	Create illusions of time
Close up, long shot, wide-angle shots, distant shots	Create illusions of space
Angle shots, peripheral visions	Perspective and point of view

Source: Piazza (1999).

namic between performer and audience, your students as audience participants gain first-hand experience with the power of response. In other words, what they decide to see and pay attention to, and how they react, will have an instant effect on the performance itself. How this dynamic

FIGURE 13.7 How to Analyze an Advertisement: Finding Ads' Hidden Messages

There's more to advertising's message than meets the casual eye. An effective ad, like other forms of communication, works best when it strikes a chord with the needs and desires of the consumer— a connection that can be both intuitive and highly calculated.

The following questions can help foster an awareness of this process. Use them for class or group discussions or your own analysis of ads or commercials. You may be surprised by the messages and meanings you uncover.

- What is the general ambience of the advertisement? What mood does it create? How does it do this?
- What is the design? Does it use axial balance or some other form? How are the basic components or elements arranged?
- What is the relationship between pictorial elements and written text? What does this tell us?
- How is space used? Is there a lot of white space or is the ad crowded with graphic and print elements?
- What signs and symbols do you find? What role do they play in the ad's impact?
- If there are figures (men, women, children, animals), what are they like? What can be said about their facial expressions, poses, hair style and colour, age, sex, ethnicity, education, occupation, relationships? What does the background tell you? Where is the action taking place and what significance does this have?
- What action is taking place in the advertisement and what significance does it have? (This might be described as the ad's plot).
- What theme or themes do you find? What is it about? (The plot of an advertisement may involve a man and a woman drinking but the theme might be jealousy, faithlessness, ambitions, passion.)
- What about the language used? Does it only provide information or does it try to generate an emotional response? Or both? What techniques are used by the copywriter: humour, alliteration, definitions of life, comparisons, sexual innuendo, and so on?
- What typefaces and voiceovers are used and what impressions do they convey?
- What is the item being advertised and what role does it play in Canadian culture and society?
- What about aesthetic decisions? If the advertisement is a photograph, what kind is it? What significance do long shots, medium shots, close-up shots have? What about lighting, use of colour, angle of the shot?
- What sociological, political, economic, or cultural attitudes are indirectly reflected in the ad? It may be selling blue jeans but it might also reflect such issues as sexism, alienation, stereotyped thinking, conformism, gender, conflict, loneliness, elitism, and so on.

Source: Excerpted from "How to Analyze an Advertisement" by Arthur Asa Berger in *Media & Values* (37) Fall 1986, published by Center for Media Literacy. Reprinted with permission of Center for Media Literacy (www.medialit.org).

FIGURE 13.8 Discussion Prompts for Post-Performance Experience

- What did you see? What did you feel? Why?
- Do you think other members of the audience reacted and felt the same way? How do you know?
- How did the set affect you?
- How did the lighting affect you? Which colours? How were they used? How did they influence the mood of the audience?
- Was there accompanying music? How did that affect your response? The audience response?
- When did the actors respond to the audience? To what were they reacting? (clapping, laughing, heckling?) How did they respond? Do you think that was planned?
- What was most important about this play?
- What was missing?
- How does it compare to the book or script?
- What do you think of this interpretation?
- What are some other possible interpretations? (For example, how might this line have been said? How might the set, or lighting, or costumes have been different?)

works can be examined during post-performance discussions, which can reveal profound insights. Figure 13.8 includes a list of starting points for discussion. As always, the discussion should reflect the needs, wants, and interests of the students.

Attending a live theatre production is not only an aesthetic experience for students, it allows them to exercise some control and authority over a presentation. Live performances literally cannot be merely passively received. They give your students involved and informed encounters with art. Opportunities for guided discussion will greatly enhance a critical awareness that can be extended to other texts.

Moving On

In this chapter, we looked at using critical inquiries to teach critical literacy. We discussed the complex interaction of text, text producer, and text consumer. We acknowledged the significance of the text consumer's prior knowledge about the way various texts work as well as the influence of their dominant discourse or way of being in the world.

In Chapter 14, we look at some of the issues you face when you bring a wide range of individuals into literacy. We present multiple perspectives from which to look at issues such as students who are considered to be "at risk" and students with "special needs," the many complexities involved in teaching culturally and linguistically diverse learners, as well as some of the issues involved in understanding how gender may play a role in literacy learning. This chapter cannot possibly cover all of the issues; instead its primary purpose is to contribute to your self-inquiry as you become an exemplary teacher for *all* of your students.

> *Beyond the first steps into critical literacy lies an increasingly*
> *fascinating intellectual world. It is a world filled with multiple*
> *perspectives, one in which the subordinated are acknowledged and*
> *valued. It is a world in which we naturally participate in reflection,*
> *action, and transformations; a world in which critical literacy*
> *is not viewed as a classroom activity but rather as a stance used*
> *in all contexts of our lives.*
> —Maureen McLaughlin & Glenn DeVoogd

LIT-FOLIO UPDATE

This chapter has given you a great deal to think about in terms of you own media consumption. Additions to your lit-folio might include an example of your own critical inquiry into television, film, or visual texts using questions chosen from the chapter. You might also choose to develop a multiple-session lesson plan that will engage students in critical inquiries about social issues through literature or media.

LIT-FOLIO TIP

As you engage in critical inquiries with your students, keep a journal that documents your thoughts, questions, ideas, and observations. You can then use these reflections as you plan future inquiries with your students or in your discussions with students.

Resources to Support Your Learning

Professional Resources

Cornett, C.E., & Smithrim, K.L. (2001). *The arts as meaning makers: Integrating literature and the arts throughout the curriculum.* Toronto, ON: Prentice-Hall.

Gee, J.P. (2004). *Situated language and learning: A critique of traditional schooling.* New York: Routledge.

Heffernan, L. (2004). *Critical literacy and writer's workshop: Bring purpose and passion to student writing.* Newark, DE: International Reading Association.

Johnson, H., & Freedman, L. (2005). *Developing critical awareness at the middle level: Using texts as tools for critique and pleasure.* Newark, DE: International Reading Association.

Piazza, C. (1999). *Multiple forms of literacy: Teaching literacy and the arts.* Upper Saddle River, NJ: Prentice-Hall.

Ruddell, R. B. (2004), Researching the influential literacy teacher: Characteristics, beliefs, strategies, and new research directions. In R. B. Ruddell & N. J. Unrau (Eds.). *Theoretical models and processes of reading* (5th ed.), pp. 979-997. Newark, DE: International Reading Association.

Vasquez, V. (2001). *Getting beyond "I like the book": Creating space for critical literacy in K-6 classrooms.* Newark, DE: International Reading Association.

Vasquez, V. (2004). *Negotiating critical literacies with young children.* Newark, DE: International Reading Association.

Language Arts, the journal of the National Council of Teachers of English, is an indispensable resource.

Children's Literature: Our Favourites

Flipped, Wendelin Van Draanen
Fly away home, Eve Bunting
Freedom summer, Deborah Wiles
The lady in the box, Ann McGovern
The magic vase, Fiona French
✦ *The paper bag princess,* Robert Munsch
The quiltmaker's journey, Jeff Brumbeau
So cool, Dennis Lee (a book of poems)
✦ *So far from the sea,* Eve Bunting
The spider and the fly, Tony DiTerlizzi
Stargirl, Jerry Spinelli
Three wise women, Mary Hoffman
Voices in the park, Anthony Browne

Websites

Center for Media Literacy: http://medialit.org
Media Awareness Network
    http://www.media-awareness.ca/

14

Perspectives on Special Issues in Language and Literacy

Let us continue our conversations about difference, power, and literacy in our efforts to serve all the children who walk into our classrooms... Their invitations to stop, think, and locate ourselves should be welcoming to all.

— *Timothy Shannon*

key terms

advocacy

at risk

early intervention

ELD (English literacy development)

ESL (English as a second language) learners

gender gap

Reading Recovery®

with promise

questions to guide your learning

By the end of this chapter, you should understand the key terms and be able to answer these questions:

- What does it mean when a student is perceived as at risk?
- What strategies can I use with students who struggle to read and write for various reasons?
- What are some strategies for helping ESL students develop language and literacy skills?
- How can I meet the needs of my students who are from diverse cultural and linguistic backgrounds?
- How can I use children's literature to address social, cultural, and gender issues?
- How do I address the literacy gender gap?
- How can I advocate for my students?

Looking Back, Looking Ahead

In Chapter 13, we explored the fact that a significant aspect of literacy includes the development of awareness about text creation and production. We looked into various ways in which your students can become critically alert to who creates texts of all kinds, why, and for whom.

In this chapter, we will take a look at a variety of issues and considerations that must be made for the range of differences we find in our classrooms. It returns us to the question of *How do I teach my students to read, write, and become literate?* It returns us to the questions we asked in Chapter 1 when you constructed your own literacy stories. In order to know how to teach the variety of students in our classroom, how to help them to become readers, writers, and literate beings, we have to discover who they are, with full awareness of how our perceptions of them are shaped by our perceptions of ourselves. The sorts of issues we wish to look at from multiple perspectives include some of the challenges of teaching students who are considered to be at risk and students with special needs. We also discuss some of the many complexities involved in teaching a class of culturally and linguistically diverse learners, as well as some of the issues involved in understanding how gender plays a role in literacy learning. Each of these topics is multifaceted; we cannot do them justice in a single chapter. Our goal is to contribute to your self-inquiry, to stimulate questions and discussions, and to explore some of the ways that quality literacy instruction can meet the complex needs of our young students.

Because our school population encompasses children with a diversity of learning styles and levels, it is not enough to simply say, "Yes, I know the strategies and I understand how they work." Knowing and understanding are only one component of teaching. You must be able to analyse, dissect, criticize, apply, and then recreate to be effective and exemplary; you must be able to synthesize a range of ideas and find creative solutions to problems. You must be able to reflect on your experiences and your learning, and make connections to yourselves, your classrooms, and your students. This ongoing process of doing and reflecting leads you closer to becoming exemplary teachers of literacy.

Although in this book, we have explored a wide range of strategies to promote literacy development, we have continued to argue that knowing the strategies alone is not sufficient. Teachers teach children, and both teachers and students constitute an extensive variety of individuals from a multiplicity of backgrounds. In addition to effective teaching strategies, you need to continually explore the personal dimensions of your teaching. You must know who you are and who your students are. The deeper you go into this knowing, the better your teaching will be. You will be better able to determine how to make literacy learning flourish for all of the children in your classrooms.

It is our belief that full engagement of all teachers and learners results in the highest level of thinking, that of creativity—the level where you strive for deeper understanding and greater awareness. Effective teachers are capable of consolidating and making judgements regarding teaching/learning strategies to match all students' needs. This involves implementing a variety of teaching/learning strategies. It requires devising and proposing solutions that are unique to your group of students—your group of unique individuals.

Effective teachers implement a variety of teaching and learning strategies to match students' need.

You are an individual too, however, and everything you decide and do is shaped by your individuality. This is why we emphasize personal knowledge and self-awareness through personal stories. In this chapter, we invite you to revisit and re-vision the personal literacy stories you wrote as you read Chapter 1.

Revisiting Your Personal Literacy Story

Revisiting your personal literacy stories serves several purposes. First of all, it should help you to clarify your conceptualization of what literacy is and is not. Second, it should reveal something about your perceptions of how literacy is learned. This process helps to uncover your assumptions about the ideal conditions necessary to make literacy acquisition and development possible or what constitutes an "ideal" or "normal" learner. Are these ideals and assumptions about what is "normal" myths? Do they reflect the lived experience of real teachers and learners, who come from a variety of ethnic, cultural, social, and economic backgrounds, who have made different life choices, and who teach and learn from multiple perspectives? Re-viewing and re-visioning your stories through a critical lens from a variety of viewpoints should position you to determine more effectively which approaches and practices will best meet your students' individual needs.

Who Am I? Who Are My Students?

To begin an inquiry into your own literacy stories, ask the following questions:

- Does my story illustrate a happy, successful journey into literacy?
- Does my story demonstrate a background of privilege?
- How do I interpret that "privilege"? (Do I assume my background is "normal"?)
- Do I assume privilege involves loving parents, who read lots of bedtime stories, provide plenty of books, conversation, and opportunities to write at home?
- Did I encounter positive experiences in school, and do I attribute those experiences to my background and home support, to good teaching practices, and an encouraging school culture?
- Does my story illustrate a difficult journey toward literacy?
- What were the difficulties?
- Did "traditional" teaching styles fail to match my individual needs? For what reasons? Did I encounter negative experiences with uninspiring teachers, discouraging, non-nurturing school cultures?
- Were my successes and challenges related to my gender? How?
- When I look back on my story, which experiences would I want to change and which experiences would I want to replicate for my students?
- How would I teach a child who is "just like me"?

Compare your story with those of your students:

- How do your students' literacy stories compare with yours?
- How do they compare with one another's?
- How are some students' personal experiences privileged in school settings? How are others not privileged?

By asking yourself these questions, you will be in a better position to make well-informed, critical decisions about what kinds of programs, resources, strategies, and approaches make sense when you think about teaching all the students in all of their diversity. When you think about the gravity of your responsibilities and the complex task of teaching students with infinite individual variations, it becomes dauntingly clear that you must be the real risk-takers with learners who are at risk.

Your stories may reveal that you share many of the characteristics and challenges often associated with learners at risk. Many B.Ed. students have told us that they had been identified as having a learning disability or "had to go to ESL classes." Some were mistakenly labelled learning disabled or faced severe struggles because they came from different linguistic or cultural backgrounds. Some considered themselves "late bloomers" in terms of literacy for a variety of reasons, such as being more interested in sports, science, or the arts. Some still feel culturally uncomfortable. Responsiveness to your own and others' stories remains imperative. Self-inquiry should come first.

This journey of self-inquiry is a continual, lifelong endeavour. We never reach a final destination where we can say, "Now I know myself completely!" and "Now I have a firm philosophical stance!" In spite of our most rigorous attempts at self-interrogation, in spite of every effort to expose assumptions about our students, especially about students from diverse backgrounds, there is always more to learn. When we think we have learned all we need to know, life tends to impose a reality check. This reality is illustrated in the philosophical statement and personal experience story of teacher Carole Richardson in Teacher Talk 14.1.

STOP, THINK, AND WRITE

With your responses to the above questions in mind, consider these questions:

- How is my personal literacy story tied to my identity?
- How does this connect to how I view myself in terms of gender, culture, and social factors?
- How are students' stories and experiences, both in school and out, tied to their personal identities?
- If I don't know enough about my students to answer these questions, how can I find out?
- How does, or might, this knowledge inform my teaching, and truly change my beliefs and practices?
- What assumptions have I been making about what literacy is, and how it is learned?
- What do I consider to be "normal"?
- What are the consequences of my beliefs about literacy learning and teaching for the literacy success of all my students?

Teacher Talk/14.1

CAROLE RICHARDSON TALKS ABOUT CULTURAL EXPECTATIONS AND GENDER

I approach this topic of cultural expectations as related to gender in the schools from two perspectives: My expectations for my students as related to my cultural background and the family expectations for children, reflecting the cultural background of the family.

When I began teaching, I assumed that all my students understood that the right to education is a basic right for everyone; I assumed that all students were valued equally within their homes, I assumed that a good education was as important to every family as it had been to mine. Though individually none of these assumptions seem to have the potential to cause alarm, they did create some communication problems with students who had no reason to share these assumptions.

I learned simple things that raised my level of awareness and forced me to examine more honestly my own assumptions about education. When teaching health, I learned that when discussing female anatomy, it was devastating for some of my students, who had experienced female genital mutilation (sometimes known as female circumcision), to realize that the books and diagrams I was using did not include pictures of female anatomy with which they could personally identify. I learned that though female students of some cultures were not allowed to be present for health classes, the male students could remain. Many of these female students then approached me later to gain the information in a more informal manner so that their male siblings and cousins would not understand more about these issues than they did.

My students taught me not to assume that all families of the same culture had the same expectations for their children. This was similar to my culture—many of my friends' parents had different expectations for them than my parents did for me.

I vividly remember a parent-teacher interview concerning a young girl who was one of my most dedicated and successful students. I had also taught her brother, who had since left the school. He had not experienced the same level of success in my classroom. When her parents arrived, her father wanted only to tell me how well his son was doing. I turned the conversation back to the subject of his daughter's academic ability many times until he finally told me that her education was of no importance and that he was not interested in her progress. Though her mother did not speak throughout the interview, the father admitted that he had only come because his wife had wanted him to. I wondered what my student would hear. She arrived in my classroom the next day, smiling, to tell me that her mother had told her how I had spoken so highly of her and that she wanted to let me know she would continue to work very hard.

I have come to understand, over my years of teaching, that I do not have to agree with the beliefs and understandings of every culture, but, as they are the reality of my students, I must learn about them and respect the influence they have on the lives of my students, in the same way that my culture has so deeply affected me.

As teachers, either experienced or beginning, one of our most important tasks before we enter a classroom is to truly understand who we are, what we believe, what our assumptions are, and how all of this will affect our students, in fact, more than we might ever know. We owe it to ourselves and to our students to know who we are so that we can honour the voices and the differences that our students bring to our classrooms.

Carole Richardson is Assistant Professor of Music, Department of Education, Nipissing University

Who Are the Students At Risk?

Who are the learners in our classrooms who are most at risk of not acquiring and developing full literacy? Typically, we consider those who fall within one or more of the following categories as at risk:

- Emergent or early learners (K–Grade 2) who do not learn to read and write in their first years of schooling, and are therefore in need of early intervention reading instruction

- Learners for whom English is not a first language: ESL (English as a Second Language) or ELL (English Language Learners)

- Learners who are designated ELD (English Literacy Development) whose language development is delayed because they have had "limited access to schooling and have significant gaps in their education," due to a variety of circumstances (Ontario Ministry of Education, 2001, p. 6)

- Learners with "special needs"—from those who are not yet identified to those who are "severely labelled" (Leland, Harste, & Helt, 2000) with learning difficulties or disabilities

- Learners with behavioural and emotional difficulties, including Attention Deficit Disorder (ADD) and Attention Deficit Hyperactivity Disorder ADHD)

- Learners from economically or socially disadvantaged homes

Note: "ELL" is the term used most widely in the United States. We will use "ESL" to refer to students for whom English is not their first language.

According to some studies, students at risk tend to be boys, underachieving gifted learners, or learners from different cultural backgrounds than the prevailing school culture.

Before we discuss the best ways to help students at risk, we need to look at this list, and at the category at risk in the spirit of our self-inquiry. We know we have a wide variety of strategies to choose from, the question is "Which one, when, how, and with whom?" But who are these students? Is there a single program or set of strategies that will work for them all, or for any of the groups labelled in the list? Why do we use the term "at risk" for students who are assigned to one or more of these groups? Why do we demand immediate answers to the question "What to do about them?" Perhaps we should look first for a different perspective on the so-called at-risk category.

AT RISK OR WITH PROMISE?

What does the term "at risk" mean when applied to our students? At risk of what? The answer is not always clear, but in very general terms, it means at risk of failing, or not succeeding in the educational system according to set standards. It has been suggested that the label "at risk" forms the basis of a "deficit view of students who are not from an Anglo middle-class world… this label is used to rationalize their failure if they do encounter difficulty in school" (Flores, Cousin, & Diaz, 1998 in Opitz, 1998, pp. 26–27). What is often ignored are the inequities faced by these students—inequities resulting from factors such as race, class, and linguistic and cultural differences—especially when those differences place them in a minority position in the educational system. The (often hidden) assumption is that *given their background*, these students will have learning problems.

When working with students identified as at risk, strategies should be adjusted as needed.

If the ethnic, linguistic, socio-economic, or cultural backgrounds of some students make it more difficult for them to join the literacy journey in the school setting as it exists, then surely our job is to ensure that the setting is changed to allow them to flourish. It is often assumed, for instance, that these learners don't have the requisite "background knowledge and experiences" on which to build. But what is the background knowledge that they do bring with them? It may not match the content set by the government-approved curriculum. This means that adjustments—sometimes to the *what* but more often to the *how* we teach—will have to be made. We can change our strategies even if we cannot always change the content. Since new learning is constructed upon prior knowledge, we have to investigate, through conversations and interest surveys, our students' ways of being and forms of knowing. Giving all students the opportunity to compose, tell, draw, dance, and write about their own stories and interests is an obvious and powerful place to begin.

Another assumption often made about learners at risk is that their parents cannot, or will not, provide sufficient home support. Numerous studies have shown that there can be many reasons for this appearance of lack of interest. When the school itself initiates the contact, parents often do show they are concerned (Heath, 1983; Moll & Greenberg, 1990; Anderson & Gunderson, 1997). Some of the reasons parents seem reluctant range from their perception that they do not speak English well enough, or perhaps at all, to their uneasiness with an institution—the teachers' jurisdiction. Again, if the home-school relationships appear to be intimidating or unfriendly to children and their families, it is clearly your job to reach out and to make appropriate changes.

When you do invite your students and their families to tell their stories, share their interests, and celebrate their histories and backgrounds, it becomes obvious that these learners are not at risk but rather that they come to school with promise—with the promise of great resources to tell, draw, dance, and display, and to continue to learn with you as you learn from them. An example is *Painted Words, Spoken Memories* by Aliki, which is based on the author's experiences. It depicts an immigrant student who is supported at school and at home as she learns English and who is given the opportunity to tell her family story at school—at first through visual art but later with her new words. We have spoken about changes, adjustments and making settings and strategies more "appropriate." What might this mean for each of the groups mentioned in the with-promise category?

EMERGENT OR EARLY LEARNERS WHO ARE AT RISK: EARLY INTERVENTION

All schools need effective early intervention programs to help those children who are assessed as at risk of not succeeding in learning to read and write in their first years of schooling. This is especially the case in schools where there are significant numbers of children who enter school with few experiences with stories, books, and print. These children may be in need of intensive expert reading instruction to help them reach an average Grade 1 reading level by the end of Grade 1 so that they do not fall further and further behind as they move through the grades. The effectiveness of early intervention as opposed to support provided in later grades (after Grade 2) is confirmed by many research studies (Piluski, 1994; Allington, 2001, 2006).

The children who struggle the most require personalized and intensive one-on-one support by a teacher trained specifically in early reading strategies. One research-based early intervention program that has proven to be successful in accelerating the reading development of struggling Grade 1 students is Reading Recovery®, developed by developmental psychologist Marie Clay in New Zealand (Clay, 1993a). Although considered expensive, success rates are consistently high (Clay, 2001; Shanahan & Barr, 1995; D'Agostino & Murphy, 2004).

Candidates for Reading Recovery® are six years old and in Grade 1. They are identified using scores on assessments of their knowledge of

Children who struggle benefit from personalized one-on-one instruction.

concepts about print, performance on reading and writing tasks such as letter and word identification, writing words, and performance on a dictation task (Clay, 1993b). The lowest achievers then work in daily 30-minute sessions for approximately 16 weeks with a trained Reading Recovery® teacher, typically a Grade 1 teacher in the school. Key features of the program include:

- personalized instruction based on the child's existing reading and writing levels, assessed daily through running records and writing tasks

- instruction supplementary to the child's regular Grade 1 program

- child working faster and more intensely to accelerate progress

- focusing instruction on comprehending messages in print when reading, and constructing messages in writing

- moving the child through increasingly difficult ("levelled") short texts

Reading Recovery® teachers undergo extensive, year-long training and ongoing professional support. They maintain daily assessments and observations of each student; entry and exit assessment data are collected and analyzed by the Reading Recovery® Institute for that country.

A distinguishing feature of Reading Recovery® is that it includes all children who make low scores on the Observation Survey, "regardless of ethnic membership, language achievements, school history, physical handicap, intelligence or learning disability" (Stuart, 1997). It is a program that sees children as with promise whether or not they demonstrate characteristics typically perceived as at risk.

ESL and ELD Learners

There is no one-size-fits-all program or set of strategies that works for all ESL and ELD students. It is worth considering some of the difficulties commonly faced by students who are becoming literate in English and whose first language is not English. Students who are learning to read in a language they are not yet proficient in face the following challenges (Mora, 2006):

- the dissimilarity of sound-symbol relationships between their native language and English

- oral vocabulary constraints

- limitations due to background knowledge

- difficulties with text structure (based on Lenters, 2004, cited in Mora, 2006)

- making rapid gains in speaking and listening, while reading and writing progress may be much slower

These challenges are similar to those faced by many emergent readers and writers, when teachers must keep mind different developmental levels. Most young children's pronunciation and grammar are quite different from "book language." Their oral vocabulary and background knowledge may need considerable development and they are typically more advanced in listening and speaking than in reading and writing. With this in mind, the strategies appropriate for emergent learners are likely to work well for ESL learners. For example, shared reading, where teacher and students read an enlarged text together (see Chapter 8); literacy centres, where students have the opportunity to reinforce literacy skills in a social setting, using hands-on materials (Chapter 8); shared and interactive writing and writers' workshop (Chapters 11 and 12); storytelling, poetry, and drama activities to build vocabulary, knowledge of grammatical structures, and phonemic awareness (Chapter 12); and read alouds and think alouds (Chapter 6) to develop all of the above. It is worth noting that all of these are normally occurring activities in the regular classroom community, where all learners—ESL, ELD, and others—can benefit from the social aspects of language learning.

While many of these instructional strategies may be already in place in the effective literacy classroom, we are not saying that ESL learners do not require differentiated instruction. Recent research indicates that we should question the assumption that the needs of second language learners are not very different from those of other diverse learners, and that exposure to English will result in proficient English speakers (Harper & de Jong, 2004, in Hadaway & Young, 2006, p. 14). Nor can we assume that as students become proficient in social language, which typically takes about two years, they concurrently develop their understanding and use of academic language, which takes five to seven years for children aged 8 to 11, and longer for children aged 4 to 7 (Collier, 1987, in Hadaway & Young, 2006). We also question the assumption that short-term, intense exposure to English creates "school success" for all ESL learners.

Figure 14.1 contains both general and specific ideas that may be helpful in program planning, depending, as always, on the timing, the groups, and the individuals.

FIGURE 14.1 Strategies and Approaches Appropriate for ESL and ELD Students

1. **Cooperative Groupings**
   - Organize in small groups so that all feel a need to participate.
   - Use paraphrasing and active listening games.
   - Use three step interviewing where students interview each other and then share the results.
   - Have all group members facing each other so that they can hear clearly.
   - Ensure group tasks promote interdependence and active participation.

2. **Activities with Partners**
   - Use think-pair-share.
   - Work with peers who are alert to non-verbal signals.

3. **Graphic Organizers for Reading and Writing**
   - Use graphs, webs, timelines, Venn diagrams, story maps.

4. **Visuals**
   - Use pictures, illustration, real objects, and other visuals.
   - Do not rely on abstract pictures and explanations.
   - Bring in objects your students will encounter during lessons and guided reading.
   - Use manipulatives such as magnetic letters, word cards, and pocket charts.

5. **Predictable Text**
   - Use books where sentence patterns repeat and pictures support words.

6. **Read, Read, and Read Again**
   - Schedule shared reading opportunities throughout the day (large and small group).
   - Be aware of idioms, multi-meaning words, homophones, other language peculiarities.
   - Return to books to discuss difficult or tricky language structures.
   - Use the whole-part-whole method (read the whole book, return for individual parts, and then reread the whole book).

7. **Self-Selected Reading and One-on-One Conferencing**
   - Distribute Post-it notes so that ESL learners can mark confusing words and structures.

8. **Pre-Reading Activities**
   - Make text more accessible: provide print in both languages.

9. **Print-Rich Classroom**
   - Display lots of labels, text, environmental print, sentences, questions, word walls, in both languages.
   - Encourage students to build their own dictionary of words (add illustrations when appropriate).

10. **Every-Student Response Activities**
    - Plan open-ended activities with multiple response formats.
    - Use the concepts of multiple intelligences and learning styles to plan for students.

STUDENTS WITH SPECIAL NEEDS

Again, we cannot make generalizations about this group of learners. But they do face many of the same challenges as all learners at risk or with promise because of mismatches between some aspects of school settings and some teaching strategies, and some learners' ways and forms of learning and knowing.

Included in this group are those sometimes referred to as "severely labelled." Along with being tagged with the label "learning disabled" many learners share common experiences of "struggling with the school curriculum, which equate[s] literacy with written language" (Leland et al., 2000, p. 106). This narrow view of literacy disadvantages many children. These students typically do poorly on standardized tests that assume that even reading skills can be measured in terms of what a student can write about what they read. And yet, literacy in the real world is full of "multimodal events" that include art, music, drama, language in many forms, movement, math, and so on. Standard literacy tests such as EQAO and its counterparts in the United States do not measure literacy in these terms (Leland, Harste, & Helt, 2000). Usually they do not even measure computer skills, at which many "learning disabled" learners excel.

Another group of learners with special needs often appears: students with social and emotional differences that, in various ways, prevent them from coping with the general or standard curriculum. How can we hope to teach the students whose family lives are not stable? Who do not have enough food? Or who live in fear of being abused either physically or emotionally? On a smaller scale, we encounter students with attentional needs, those who are hyperactive and those who have such low self-esteem that they cannot possibly hope to engage in a literate world that requires a high level of risk. How can we support these students? How can we value their individual discourses in a way that meets their needs, the needs of the literacy community, and the curriculum? Critical literacy pedagogy and practice are responsive to the unique needs of these learners, especially when it uses the text of lived experience as a source or as a theme for personal writing.

Regardless of special needs or special life circumstances, we do need to support all learners as they develop in each of the language arts: reading, writing, listening, speaking, viewing, and representing. Figure 14.2 presents specific suggestions for supporting students with a wide variety of individual profiles, from intellectually delayed or disabled, to those with emotional or behavioural difficulties, and those who, for whatever reason, are reluctant readers and writers. We continue to stress giving students the

FIGURE 14.2 Extra Support for Those Who Need it Most

General Strategies for Reading and Writing Support
- Modelling and demonstrating: use think alouds to demonstrate how to handle reading a tricky text, and modelled writing to show how text is constructed
- Cooperative groupings, including small group, large group, and partner activities
- Graphic organizers for reading and writing (webs, timelines, Venn diagrams, story maps)
- Visual supports whenever possible
- Picture walks before reading to activate prior knowledge
- Cartoon sequencing as a pre-writing activity
- Real objects: use concrete manipulatives in all subject areas
- Predictable, readable texts, at the readers' level
- Story starters and quick writes (Chapter 11)
- Read alouds and shared reading (reading to and with)
- Modelled and interactive writing (writing for and with)
- Readers' theatre (especially for development of fluency) (see Chapter 5)
- Self-selected reading and writing on areas of personal interest
- Strategies for choosing books at their reading level; for example the "Three-Finger Strategy: read one or two pages of the book, and hold up a finger every time you find a word you can't read. If you are holding up three fingers, the book is probably too hard. Choose another one." Allington (2006) talks about why this well-known strategy is so useful: "I think the key understanding being developed here is one that is important for kids to develop—some books are just too hard...learning that selecting appropriate books is important is a necessary understanding in itself" (p. 67).
- Pre-reading and pre-writing scaffolding: keep students who need it with you when you send the others off to work
- Print rich classroom, with clear and useful postings (word walls, clear, brief instructions)
- "Every student" response activities, for example, holding up YES/NO cards, finger symbols

Schedule 30 Minutes of Open Centre Time Every Day
Set up centres with open-ended materials that children can enjoy and learn from, pursuing their own interests. These may be theme-related, and may include:
- Building materials, Lego, puzzles, board games, computer games
- Manipulatives and games: math, science, etc.
- Clay, Play-Doh, a variety of sculpting materials, chalk, paint, drawing materials
- Magazines, encyclopaedias, reference books, *Guinness Book of World Records*
- Picture books, easy reads
- Letter and word games
- Overhead projector, shadow puppets, etc.

FIGURE 14.2 Extra Support for Those Who Need It Most (continued)

Eventually, if you are determined and persistent, your centers will work almost without you. Leaders will care for materials, and children will know which days they get to choose first. The occasional child who must be removed will, after sulking a few minutes, write the required explanation so that he or she can go to centres the next day.

(Cunningham & Allington, 2006, p. 218, original emphasis).

Form an "After Lunch Bunch"

- 15 minutes during lunch break for easy reading, short writing, storytelling "just for fun"

Find and Train a Tutor for Your Most Needy Child

- This may be your best course of action for the child who is really behind, but has no scheduled one-on-one assistance (may be ESL, or not yet identified.) There are many programs to model here, but all you need are books at easy to instructional levels, a format for a brief writing activity based on the reading, a list of reading and writing prompts for the tutor, and a log sheet for them to fill in together.

- Try the **"Preview-Pause-Prompt-Praise"** strategy. Train your tutors to first **preview** the text (cover, title) and make predictions; **pause** (count to 3) when the reader makes an error to give them a chance to self-correct; **prompt** if needed ("You said *house*; does *house* make sense there?"); **praise** for using a reading strategy, especially to self-correct (Allington, 2006, 97-98).

Partner Older Struggling Readers/Writers with Younger Ones

- The older ones can tutor the younger ones.

Coordinate with Remedial Reading and Resource Room Teachers

opportunities to demonstrate what they know and how they know in multiple ways, including visual art, drama, movement, and hypertext presentations using computer programs such as Hyperstudio and Kidpix.

Again, there is no one-size-fits-all solution. This underscores the need to be close observers when adapting or readjusting instruction to meet assessed needs. Before offering specific teaching instructions, let's consider the general needs of struggling readers, based on research (Allington, 2006):

- They need to read a lot: "sheer volume of reading is a distinguishing feature of high achievement classrooms" (Allington & Johnston, 2000; Pressley et al., 2000; Taylor et al., 2000, all cited in Allington, 2006, p. 45).

- They need books they can read: readers must be matched with texts at appropriate reading levels (see Fountas & Pinnell, 1999, 2001 on the art of "levelling" texts).

- They need to be internally motivated to read: voluntary engaged reading is linked to greater proficiency (Wang & Guthrie, 2004).

- They need to read fluently: "reading fluently requires automatic information processing" (Allington, 2006, p. 92, based on research by Share & Stanovich, 1995). Engaging readers in repeated readings is an effective way of fostering fluency (Kuhn & Stahl, 2003; Samuels, 2002, both cited in Allington, 2006, p. 94).

- They need to develop "thoughtful literacy" (Allington, 2006). They *need to be taught* how to make connections and have opportunities to talk about those connections. On the need for explicit instruction in comprehension strategies, see Almasi, Geras, & Shanahan (2005); Kamil (2004); and Guthrie (2004).

Research-Based Comprehension Strategies for Explicit Instruction

1. Activating prior knowledge: tap into what students already know; make predictions and wonder-statements.

2. Summarizing: select the most important features from informational texts and re-tell just those, leaving out the less important details.

3. Story grammar lessons (story maps): understanding the key elements of a story—characters, plot, setting, problem and resolution.

4. Imagery: internal visual images of aspects of a story (characters, setting, for example).

5. Question generating: teach readers how to generate their own questions about a text (from "things I would like to know" to questioning the author in a critical way; see Chapter 13).

6. Thinking aloud: the internal dialogue good readers use to understand as they read. (based on Allington, 2006, p. 122).

With these general needs in mind, let's now turn to specific instructional practices and strategies especially recommended for students who struggle the most with reading.

Because of the importance of being able to communicate in writing and the reality of standardized tests that place such emphasis on writing, teachers need support strategies for those most in need. Many learners are reluctant to write all the time or at certain times. At these times, they show many of the characteristics of those identified as having learning disabilities. Although it is difficult to describe the "typical" student with writing difficulties, there are characteristics that we can identify. Figure 14.3 includes a list of those traits and behaviours we have encountered with "real" writers. As discussed in Chapters 10 and 11, the causes of writing difficulty should be investigated first with questions such as, "Do you have a list of topics? Is there a topic or theme you really care about right now? What might help you get started here? How can I help you get started? Once you have established that the major issue is not finding the perfect topic or theme, you must turn your attention to strategies and techniques that can support the writer in difficulty. Figure 14.4 provides an in-depth look at the diversity of strategies that teachers need to have at their fingertips regardless of whether a student has special needs or simply falls into the category of reluctant writer.

General Thoughts

- Work on technical skills using games, allow student choice, encourage peer collaboration.

- Teach skills that are useful, relevant, and necessary.

- Teach students a process/a strategy/a way of learning that can be used with different content—once they know how to learn, they are freed up for true learning.

- Provide support as needed throughout the writing process; for example:

  - Promote brainstorming using tape recorders, pictures, outlines, and webs.

  - Model or use author's texts as models for the drafting phase.

  - Conference frequently at revising and editing stages; encourage use of reminders.

  - Use mnemonics such as C.O.P.S. (Capitals, Overall appearance, Punctuation, Sentence structure—see Chapter 11).

  - Provide multiple choices for publishing: posters or other visual arts, board games, computer, or media presentations.

    Source: Tips and suggestions for ESL learners and "Extra Support for Those Who Need it Most" were compiled from our own ideas and from Allington, 2006; Cunningham & Allington (2003, 2006); Kudar & Hasit (2002); Oglan (2003); and Polloway et al. (2003).

Teachers frequently discuss the challenge they face. For example one teacher describes "out of control children who hijack the learning of the other students and drain the energy and sanity of the teacher" (Ms. S., a Grade 1 teacher). We have discussed the difficulties of meeting the learning needs of students with emotional and behavioural problems. But as this teacher points out—and many teachers will agree—"What about the learning of the other students—the ones who are constantly disrupted?" This is a concern that we cannot fully address here. Some of the suggestions in Figure 14.2, including those from Cunningham and

---

FIGURE 14.3 Characteristics of Learners with Writing Differences

In general, learners with writing differences:

- have difficulty starting to write
- focus on accurate spelling (try only a few functional spellings)
- ask how to spell a word before trying it
- use high frequency words (sight words)
- write in the first person
- write on familiar topics
- write about actual events, often the sequences of events in a day
- use limited, unimaginative vocabulary (easily accessible)—sometimes write run-on sentences
- may or may not be able to find a topic
- are reluctant to ask for help from the teacher or peers
- tend to do one draft, have trouble revising, cannot edit independently, do not recognize errors

They may also have difficulty with oral expression or speech and language delays. More specific differences stem from:

- written expression—dysgraphia:
  - difficulty telling or retelling a story
  - difficulty identifying a topic
  - difficulty expressing simple ideas
  - inability to recognize
- spelling difficulty
  - difficulty hearing and saying sounds in words (phonemic awareness)
  - inability to identify a word with a different spelling from a set of three words
- handwriting difficulty—fine motor coordination:
  - immature pencil grasp—difficulty holding a pencil
  - difficulty tracing shapes
  - frequent stops and starts

FIGURE 14.4 Teaching Strategies to Support Learners with Writing Differences

- Provide more structure, guidance, and monitoring.
- Explain expectations for writing and feeling that they are a part of a community of writers (writers' workshop, see Chapter 11).
- Arrange lots of modelling, demonstration, levels of support.
- Set short-term, achievable goals during conferences, use task analysis when necessary.
- Encourage students to select their own topics, topics that are relevant, meaningful, interesting.
- Make sure audience extends beyond the teacher.
- Provide multiple opportunities to work on the same piece of writing.
- Incorporate writing into larger culminating project posters, visual arts, games.
- Select writing projects that have specific purposes and capitalize on students' strengths.
- Make sure resources are always in the same place.
- Encourage 10 minutes of free writing to loosen up and let ideas flow.
- Offer choices.
- Encourage students to read and enjoy formats they want to write in.
- Brainstorm, rehearse, discuss in advance.
- Use concept webs, charts, story maps, organizational frameworks.
- Encourage student feedback and conferencing before, during, and after writing.
- Facilitate writing process, encourage revision and editing.
- Have frequent, regular writing conferences—short, to the point, with open questions about the writing, not just feedback:
  - Why did you choose this topic? What makes you care about it?
  - What do you like about what you have written?
  - What will your next step be?
  - Are there any other characters you could introduce?
  - What kinds of things would they say to each other?
  - Do you have a beginning, middle, and an end?

Quick Tips

- Experiment with page positioning for students (to reduce the movement of the page or book, for example, tape it to the desk).
- Provide individualized word walls, alphabets.
- Use a pencil grip for students with poor fine motor coordination—elastics work well—larger pencils, markers, crayons also have a different feel.
- Provide cues of where to write, for example happy face, arrow, highlighting (for those who have trouble with spatial orientation).

STOP, THINK, AND WRITE

You have a new student, Josh. He is angry. He is angry when you ask him to read, and especially angry when you ask him to write. After your morning literacy block, he typically goes out for recess and ends up in the principal's office for aggressive behaviour. Your colleagues tell you he needs psychological counselling.

■ What do you think he needs?

■ Prompt: have you looked at your language program, and at Josh's literacy assessments to determine whether your routines and strategies are meeting his needs?

■ In other words, are you asking him to do things he cannot do (yet)?

Allington (2006), have been designed for children with behavioural difficulties in mind. Sometimes significant modifications must be made to the program itself, as suggested by teacher Karyn Cooper in Teacher Talk 14.2. But consider first what approach you should take.

Cultural Diversity and Multiple Intelligences

Many, if not most, teachers currently have students from diverse cultural backgrounds in their classes. Many different cultural groups may be represented in a single class—where "different" simply means a culture other than that of the majority of the classroom, school, or wider community. Although teachers may be aware of the difficulties some of their students face and may be extremely sensitive to their power struggles, particularly those in minority situations, they do not necessarily know what to do to address the differences and to capitalize on the rich backgrounds of culturally different students. Becoming "culturally responsive" is a complex process, but you can begin with the following strategies:

1. Build trust: concentrate on the personal dimensions of teacher–student and student–student relationships, rather than primarily on cognitive concerns.

2. Become culturally literate: learn about the students' language, interactional style, learning style, and values. Invite students and their families to share this knowledge.

3. Use effective questioning techniques: research indicates that teachers often address fewer higher-order questions to those students for whom they have low expectations (Allington, 1983, cited in Jackson, 1994).

Teacher Talk/14.2

KARYN COOPER TALKS ABOUT TEACHING STRUGGLING READERS THROUGH THE ARTS

One of the most challenging and rewarding experiences in my teaching career began on the day that I was presented with a class of "disabled" readers. This class of 15 children, aged 8 to 13, was housed in a portable classroom, far away from the main school. They had all been assessed as being two to three years "behind" in Language Arts. It was here that the best learning of my teaching career began, for these children had loud angry voices and I, their teacher, learned very quickly that "survival" (both the children's and my own) meant learning to listen to those voices.

Tensions between my students and me began very early in the morning of the first day. There is little doubt that the students were frustrated with the inane worksheets I assigned that morning, and there was a general sense of boredom with the "cat sat on the mat" type of reading series I had foisted on them. However, the explosion that finally caused me to really sit up and take notice came shortly after my announcement that I was going to administer a required reading test. It was not even noon, when one angry student threw his desk across the room screaming, "I ain't gonna take no reading test! What are you? Stupid? We can't read! That's why we're in this dumb class!"

This truth made clear to me by my frustrated student caused me to summon up the strength to talk to the principal about putting off the testing until a more suitable date. I also managed to convince him to allow me to focus on the arts in my classroom, with the idea that the teaching of strategic skills and evaluation would soon follow and in fact be woven through the curriculum.

After an open and heartfelt discussion with my students about their frustrations in failing at "traditional" reading and writing activities, I talked to them about trying a new curriculum for a while, one that would focus on drama, music, and the arts. With a mixture of moans and groans from the students, I began reading Jack Prelutsky's poem, "Homework, Oh Homework" from *The New Kid on the Block*. That day began an adventure into the drama of shared reading.

"Homework, Oh Homework" is an example of what I would term motivational material because it quickly captured the children's interest and led naturally into a shared reading experience. In shared reading, the teacher and the students read the text aloud together [see Chapters 7 and 8, this book]. Shared reading seemed like a suitable place to begin with my students because most of them had difficulty reading texts independently. Engaging the students in shared reading experiences gave me the opportunity to model the joy of reading, while over time, building reading skills.

Karyn Cooper is Assistant Professor, Department of Curriculum, Teaching, and Learning at OISE/UT.

Source: OISE/UT (2002, pp. 35–36). Reprinted by permission from Orbit Magazine/OISE UT.

4. Provide effective feedback—the same high-level, direct, and specific feedback you would give to any student.

5. Analyze instructional materials—ensure high quality, historically and culturally accurate literature devoid of racist concepts, clichés.

6. Establish positive home–school relations.

7. Build a repertoire of instructional strategies.

Source: Based on Jackson (1994), pp. 57-63.

These strategies are similar to those we have been advocating throughout this book; they are similar to the strategies used by every exemplary teacher of literacy. Nevertheless, it is worthwhile reminding you of the need to reach *every one* of your students, and that different students require different kinds of responses. The final suggestion that you "build a repertoire of instructional strategies" is an enormous part of the art of teaching. Knowing exactly which strategy to use, when, how, and with whom is part of that art.

Among the many approaches you can choose from, it is wise to remember the multiple intelligences, particularly when you are trying to respond effectively to culturally diverse learners. To date, Howard Gardner has formally identified eight intelligences, recognizing that although we all have capacities in all domains, we usually have strengths in only one or two (see Chapter 3 and 7). Schools traditionally teach to the verbal and logical intelligences, and seem to have neglected the visual, musical, interpersonal, intrapersonal, and kinesthetic intelligences (see Gardner, 1993). Individuals who do not exhibit strength in the verbal and logical domains often are less successful in school settings and, as we have pointed out, they frequently make lower scores on standardized literacy tests. Gardner's theory of multiple intelligences offers strong support for providing more opportunities in the arts and in the language domains other than writing, so that students can use those intelligences to bolster the less dominant areas.

Boys and Girls and Literacy

Fuelled by the publication of results from provincial, national, and international standardized tests, the media has been full of reports about the new **gender gap**—boys appear to be falling behind girls. Not only are boys not doing as well as girls in literacy (measured in terms of reading and writing), girls appear to be catching up in science and math, subjects in which boys have traditionally excelled. But we cannot blame only the publication of test scores. Even if we choose to disregard the significance of such assessments because they are based on narrowly conceived ideas about literacy and are biased in favour of certain groups, as well as other well-documented problems with standardized testing in general, there are other indicators that boys may be in trouble. There is a widening gap in dropout rates, and males now form a declining proportion of university enrolments (Froese-Germain, 2004). Certainly, it is the current perception that we should be concerned about boys, especially when it comes to literacy. Is it safe to assume, then, that girls are well provided for? Should you now focus your attention primarily to boys? There are many reasons to question this direction.

First of all, we should not simplify the categories "boys" and "girls" to include all boys and all girls, as if there is no significant diversity within each group. This would add further to the stereotypes of all boys as *this* (boys can't sit still long enough to read a book) and all girls as *that* (all girls like to read).

Second, how closely are we examining what is said by those who use data to support their claims? Do the higher test scores mean that gender equity has been accomplished for girls, so we should now turn our attention to the boys? Research indicates that this is not supported by the real experiences of real girls in real schools, or in the real world: "neither boys nor girls 'rule in school'" (Sadker, 2002, cited in Froese-Germaine, 2004, p. 4). In terms of "achievement, academic enrolment, academic interactions, special programs (including gifted and special education), and athletics … there is evidence that educational progress has been made for each gender [however] many challenges remain for each gender" (p. 4). One significant factor highlighted in this research is that both boys and girls "had more positive things to say about being a boy than being a girl" (Sadker, 2002, p. 240). In addition, while girls may generally seem to enjoy greater school success, this has not translated into major advances in the real world: "the larger equity picture continues to be characterized by an imbalance of social, economic, and political power favouring men" (Bouchard et al., 2003, cited in Froese-Germaine, 2004, p. 5).

Many teachers complain that boys are often reluctant to engage in reading and writing activities. Avoiding generalizations and stereotypes, research does show that boys exhibit different literacy behaviours than girls (Booth, 2002b, p. 22). Boys are two to five times more likely than girls to have a reading disability and they have greater difficulty over-

Boys and girls exhibit different literacy behaviours.

coming it; they are more likely to be placed in remedial classes or be held back a year; and they do not do as well as girls in standardized tests of reading comprehension, writing, spelling, and grammar (Barrs & Pidgeon, 1994, 1998). The learning opportunities and strategies offered in Figure 14.1 may entice, support, and provide success for many students who need that "extra something" from their teachers.

While we agree that researchers need to investigate the relationship between the test scores and classroom marks of boys and girls, we must also look into the complexities of the relationships between school success and other categories, such as cultural and ethnic diversity, disabilities of many kinds, class, and other socio-economic factors. Clearly, if we are going to recommend change based on assessment data such as standardized tests, we must examine these other equity issues as well, and base our responses on individual differences and needs.

> *Socio-economic factors appear to have as much impact on boys' literacy achievements as gender issues... Quality teaching can, of course, overcome the difficulties the children from a lower socio-economic background face when confronting literacy expectations: however, too often schools discriminate (even unconsciously) against some children. The media reports too often describe boys as an underachieving, educationally disadvantaged group, suffering from the support given to girls. Educator Peter Hill suggests we would be better off if we approached the problems by "targeting poorer students, low achievers, picking up disproportionately more boys in the process."*
>
> (Booth, 2002b, p. 12)

We want literacy success for all of our students. Our expectations for literacy success for boys and girls should not necessarily be altered by some suggestions for reform, such as same-sex schools and classrooms, returning to "traditional values," increased testing, using computers, comics, and car magazines to sustain boys' interests, and "injecting a healthy dose of competition into one's instructional approach," which apparently suits boys' learning style (Seeman, 2000, cited in Froese-Germaine, 2004, p. 4). We must remind ourselves that whatever we change for boys will affect girls, and we must question practices that may contribute to gender bias. We must look at the actual research on initiatives such as gender segregation, which is largely inconclusive about the benefits: "The success of single-gender public schooling depends strongly on how carefully it is implemented" (Datnow & Hubbard, 2004). We recognize that there are complex issues at stake here, and that there are no easy answers to the questions raised by these calls for reform. But again, these across-the-board suggestions make assumptions about how all boys learn and about the best ways for all boys to be taught.

Although there are far more cognitive similarities than differences, there is evidence that there are some differences between boys and girls that may affect their literacy learning, especially how they learn. For example, "girls have an additional language-processing centre in the right frontal lobe, which seems to enhance their capacity to process language. Boys demonstrate greater strength and brain activity in the right hemisphere when utilizing their visual-spatial abilities" (Booth, 2002b, p. 15). The fact that boys are more likely than girls to have reading disabilities, and that they are more likely to view themselves as non-readers, are matters that should concern us. As for other literacy behaviours that illustrate differences, such as the fact that poetry is less popular with boys than girls, and that boys appear to be more enthusiastic about reading electronic texts than girls, these preferences could be attributed to the social and cultural environment (both in and out of the classroom), rather than "inherent" differences.

Recognizing that some differences do exist between the ways boys and girls become literate, and between how they view themselves as literate beings, raises the question we have been posing throughout this book:

> *From the wide variety of effective teaching strategies we know and can choose from, which ones are best to use when, how, and with whom?*

Applied to endeavours to bring both boys and girls into full literacy, we can ask specifically:

> *What are the most effective ways, using which resources, at what key times, and setting up what kinds of learning tasks and activities for engaging both boys and girls in literacy learning?*

The approach we wish to emphasize and to encourage is to continue to develop literacy programs that balance and integrate the language arts: reading, writing, listening, speaking, viewing, and representing, and to implement a wide range of strategies that engage, support, and set up success for all kinds of learners. Clearly, this goes well beyond designing classrooms for boys using more computers, comics, and car magazines—strategies that may work quite well for some boys and for some girls, too. For both boys and girls, classroom and school libraries need to stock an inviting assortment of fiction and non-fiction materials, in a variety of formats from picture books and novels to magazines, comics, graphic novels, and e-texts, plenty of opportunities for choice, and sufficient time to read them.

We must also remind ourselves, as we observe the boys and girls in our classrooms, that they may explore and display their literacy in different ways—ways that reflect our ever-changing conceptualizations of what it means to be literate. When we observe girls and boys with open minds, we recognize that there are multiple ways of knowing and that as the world changes, the demands for different forms of literacy change. To maintain this open minded stance, Hilary Minns (1991) suggests that we need to:

• recognize the differences between some girls and some boys

• recognize the similarities between some girls and some boys

• identify the diversity within groups of girls and boys

• highlight multiple forms of literacy and literate practice

• celebrate multiple figurations of masculinity and femininity

(Cited in Booth, 2002b, p. 15)

To sum up the very complex issues regarding boys and girls and literacy, we need to remind ourselves that boys and girls themselves need to discover how their community, media, and pop culture, their school's culture, and their classroom subculture all affect their view of what it means to be a boy or a girl, and how this in turn affects how they view themselves as readers, writers, and literate beings. We must continue our self-inquiry into how we contribute to our students' identity formation, and how this affects their literacy success, which will in turn affect their success living and working—males and females together—in a pluralistic democratic society. Consider the following questions, keeping that ongoing self-inquiry in mind.

WHAT DO WE DO ABOUT BOYS WHO ARE STRUGGLING?

The foregoing discussion may imply that this question may be misguided. Many of the suggestions in Figure 14.1 will be useful at different times with different boys. Many boys do fall within groups who are non-readers or writers, or who struggle for a variety of reasons, such as being ESL learners, or having ADD or other exceptionalities. To take into account some of the general characteristics often observed in boys who are reluctant or who struggle on the journey to becoming literate, the following comments may be helpful.

When we perceive a boy to be reluctant or to have little interest in reading, we should take a good look at what they *are* reading. David Booth reports research where several mothers who were concerned about their sons' lack of interest in reading were interviewed. The researcher found that the boys were reading as much as before, but they were reading materials such as newspapers, baseball cards, magazines and manuals—materials that apparently did not fall within the mothers' concepts of literacy (Booth 2002b, p. 42).

Boys need to see themselves as readers and writers.

Boys need to see themselves as readers and writers. This statement is true for all literacy learners, of course. But as we have seen, some boys face particular difficulties here—some may be brain-based; others are probably social and cultural in origin as illustrated in the statement, "My father only reads the newspaper." Acknowledging that there are many different kinds of struggling readers and writers, we need to find out what they can do, and proceed from there. One general strategy that works well for many boys (and girls) is to model or demonstrate different forms or aspects of reading and writing. Boys will often say, "Show me!" We need to keep in mind how necessary this highest level of support is in literacy learning (see Cambourne, 1988, 2000/01).

David Booth also identifies the following as particularly important for boys:

- Uninterrupted silent reading times
- Opportunities to listen to you read aloud and tell stories
- Guided reading times for attending closely to the meanings and the functions of different genres of texts
- Occasions for talking to others about what they have read
- Constantly hearing about new books and other print resources
- Opportunities to act upon what they have read
- Feeling that they *own* the reading; to feel that reading matters to them

(Booth, 2002b, pp. 42-43)

These suggestions reflect the sort of quality literacy teaching we have explored throughout this book. Without this thoughtful and responsive teaching, many students—probably many of them boys—will not succeed.

STOP, THINK, AND WRITE

In his book, *Even Hockey Players Read*, David Booth takes us through a colourful, balanced, and thoughtful array of stories, analyses, and suggestions about how to guide boys into literacy. He lists the following questions to further our endeavours into self-inquiry:

■ Do schools (and parents) unconsciously discriminate against many boys in their attempts at becoming literate?

■ What resources do we select for boys and girls to read?

■ How do we ourselves react to boys' and girls' literacy behaviours?

■ Do we reinforce socially constructed frames of being a boy or a girl, or do we help youngsters to expand or to redefine them?

■ How do we handle male peer groups who pressure others in the class to respond in "stereotypical male" fashion to ideas that are shared?

■ Do we encourage different ways of participating in print-focused contexts, modelling and demonstrating alternative possibilities for literacy behaviours?

■ Do we make explicit the stereotypes that the media (and society) throw up about what men and women are expected to read?

■ Do we open up response discussions so that boys and girls can note the different ways of becoming a reader and a writer?

■ Can we help boys extend who they are, and alter their life's directions through their reading of others' lives, accepting the challenges that books offer to their own becomings?

■ Why do so many boys and girls construct their images of being a reader and a writer in very different ways?

■ What roles does gender play in this definition of a literacy self? Are girls, too, confirming their gender identities by conforming to the norms of their peer groups in choosing to read certain books and to write about particular issues? From the observations and research of several teachers, parents, and researchers, reading (and to a degree, writing) appears to reflect and affirm gender identity.

■ If reading "reflects and confirms" gender, can we use that influence on behaviours in boys and girls to see gender issues through a critical lens?

■ Are we as teachers and parents powerless over peer group pressures? Why is it that some classrooms are able to extend the literacy behaviours and constructs of so many boys and girls? Why are these effective changes happening in some schools, regardless of their socio-economic contexts?

Source: Excerpted from Booth, D. (2002b). *Even Hockey Players Read: Boys, Literacy and Learning*. Markham, ON: Pembroke Publishers, pp. 111–112. Reprinted by permission.

Using Children's Literature to Address Social and Cultural Issues

In Chapter 6, we discussed the power of stories and quality literature in children's lives and literacy development. We identified several general features that characterize the best in children's literature, including the following:

1. Appeal: stories that are delightful, entertaining, and enlightening for children

2. Good story: a drama unfolding through a clear, clean plot structure

3. Vivid language: language that makes the story come alive

4. Richness: stories offering many layers and possibilities for multiple interpretations; many types of characters, in a wide variety of social, historical, cultural, and moral settings

5. True to life: stories that address "truths" about life, regardless of possible controversy

6. Not too moralistic: good stories have the potential to morally transform the reader, and many stories offer "lessons" through their themes; however, this should not be an obvious explicit purpose

7. Integrity: all of the story elements must come together to create a pleasing whole

A review of these qualities reminds us that many children's stories meeting these criteria are candidates for our classroom programs and libraries, whether we are directly or indirectly addressing issues such as multicultural and linguistic diversity, problems such as racism, or social issues such as gender relationships or bullying. Our goal ideally is to include a wide and rich variety of authors and genres, to ensure that as many ethnic and cultural groups and family groupings as possible are represented. Many books meet these criteria. We do not want to shy away from strong stories that are true to life, since students come from a wide variety of backgrounds, experiences, and family settings. We want each student, in particular those experiencing personal hardships, to be able to find themselves and their situations reflected in literature. We want all children to experience the wonder of identification with a character who "thinks and feels just like I do." We need to assemble an array of powerful stories to stimulate thought and discussion, arouse emotions, and provide new perspectives on difficult and pervasive issues such as stereotyping, violence, and social injustices.

With these high standards in mind, we need to go beyond quickly choosing a picture book because it has the word "bully" in the title to address a recess problem. We want to go beyond reading books about "chopsticks and dragons" to introduce Asian cultures to students from non-Asian backgrounds (Pang et al. 1994, in Opitz, 1998). Surely we must go much further than just reading Tomi dePaola's *The Legend of the Indian Paintbrush* and having a little discussion, to understand First Nations' cultures. If we are serious about bringing our students into true appreciation and understanding of culturally diverse groups and their values and beliefs, and finding real insights into social problems such as bullying and violence, we must go much deeper than what can transpire in a typical story time or a single read aloud.

Although good literature can certainly make a difference, complex issues such as racism and bullying must be closely woven into the curriculum, throughout the school day. Rasinki and Padak (1990, in Opitz 1998) use a four-level model to show how the degree of sophistication with which we approach the use of literature for multicultural learning can increase.

1. The contributions approach uses literature to highlight the lives and contributions of persons from different cultures and abilities, for example, *I Am Rosa Parks* by Rosa Parks (American Civil Rights movement) and *What's the Matter with Albert?* by Frieda Wishinksy (the story of Albert Einstein), which describes Einstein's early troubles succeeding in regular school settings.

2. The additive approach takes literature that is readily recognizable as multicultural, with content themes and characters from different cultures, and includes them in the literature curriculum; for example, adding multicultural folktales to the read aloud time and the classroom library.

3. The transformation approach encourages students to view problems, themes, and issues from the perspective of different cultural groups; for example, seeing the Canadian experience during World War II through the eyes of a Japanese Canadian in an internment camp through *Naomi's Road*, by Joy Kogawa, or the experiences of Jewish children, through *Hana's Suitcase*, by Karen Levine.

4. The decision-making and social action approach challenges students to study problems within their own school, or look at how certain groups are treated in their local newspaper.

Source: Adapted from Rasinki & Padak, 1990, in Opitz, 1998, pp.199–200.

Books such as *The Hundred Dresses* by Eleanor Estes, first published in 1944, confront the reader with the issues of bigotry and how teasing can escalate to bullying. It is the story of an immigrant family, the Petronskis, who leave their town because of bullying. We are drawn into the point of view of the bystander, who does nothing about the teasing and realizes at the end of the story that there is nothing she can do about its severe consequences for the victim, Wanda Petronski. This is the sort of story that can lead to transformation and re-vision, by taking on different points of view, and to social action, for there can be few children who have not occupied some point on the bully–victim–bystander triangle.

How do we lead our students to this level of enlightenment? One approach that encourages making higher level connections and comparisons is to engage in an in-depth study of story types or themes found across cultures, such as Cinderella and trickster tales (Young & Ferguson, 1995). Such studies promote critical examination of themes such as stereotypes and humour, with its key role in cultural understandings.

Another powerful tool is role-play, both through dramatic re-enactments and writing in role (Swartz, 2004). It encourages and makes possible the adoption of new perspectives and viewpoints. As Kathleen Gallagher (2002) puts it:

> I have long found that doing drama with kids in classrooms can be an especially effective community-building activity. It is not because drama is all "fun and games" (although it can be) nor is it because drama is all about agreement and consensus. In fact, in my experience, drama is an effective community-building activity in classrooms precisely because it engages—in enabling ways—questions of diversity and the multitude of perspectives and knowledge contained in most classrooms. (p. 27)

We should take part in these role-plays with our students. We have stressed in this book that it is important that we not ask our students to do anything that we ourselves are not willing to do. Regular participation in activities such as drama and storytelling plays a key role in our transformation and re-vision, both personally and professionally. Role-play in particular emphasizes the fact that part of one of our roles is often that of a "shape-shifter," whereby we take on a different persona at different times in various situations with individual students according to their varying needs. In order to become as responsive as possible to the virtually infinite diversity in terms of personalities, backgrounds, learning styles, and needs, we must respond to on a daily basis; we must have an ever-growing repertoire of strategies ready to use in a wide array of real-life scenarios.

In encouraging fearful children to enter the pool, sometimes we teachers have to get wet to remember the feel of the water, the sense of being at one with the medium. And that is my metaphor for being within the teaching in any discipline, why I need to add my voice, once in a while, to the choir.

(Booth, 2002b, p. 56)

Other ways to nudge our students toward higher (or deeper) levels of awareness about social issues through literature were discussed in Chapter 13. In Figure 13.1, we suggested questions to consider as you select literary and information texts. They are also applicable to 'text' in the broader sense that encompasses multimedia, visual, performance, and lived experience texts. Even more importantly, students can be taught to ask these questions and use these prompts when they are choosing and critiquing texts. We can begin with questions such as "Why do I like or dislike this book?" and "What is real in this text?" with children in Kindergarten, prodding them to go deeper into their reasons by considering the author's writing style, the colours of the illustration, and even physical factors such as the size ("It's big enough for the whole class to read together") or the presentation of the text ("It comes with a tape"). In Grade 3, students can be taught how to respond to the text: "How does this make me feel?" and to analyze why the text had that effect on them: "How does the author use images and visual communication to elicit certain responses from readers?"

By Grades 6 to 8, readers and viewers are ready to engage in a full-fledged print (novel) and media (film) comparison, such as that described for *Charlie and the Chocolate Factory* (Theory into Practice 13.7), which focuses explicitly on stereotypes. In this mini-unit, students have opportunities to pose and discuss questions about cultural and gender-based stereotypes. The experience of reading and discussing the novel and viewing and discussing the two versions of the film has the potential to significantly deepen students' appreciation for adopting different points of view or alternative perspectives on reality and ask "If I were to view the text from a variety of perspectives, would I hold the same values as the text creator?" Lively discussions and response activities can revolve around the following profound moral questions: *How would I feel if I had been portrayed as that stereotypical character (in the book or film)? Why did Roald Dahl choose to create these characters? Was he right or wrong? What are my beliefs and values? How do I feel when they are misrepresented or challenged?*

But is it enough to lead and guide our students into these heights of awareness? What does this show them about how to act on these new understandings? Of what practical use is their newfound critical appreciation of the role of the author or film director? What are they supposed to do with their indignation over cultural or gender-based stereotyping? What are *we* supposed to do? We'll discuss the question of teacher advocacy in the next section of this chapter. Before we do, we make one major suggestion. There is a powerful method for guiding our students toward taking active, rather than passive roles as listeners, speakers, readers, writers, viewers, and representers. That is to provide opportunities to create their own literary and media works. Encourage and give students the resources to create their own versions of novels, plays, or advertisements, or encourage them to map out a story board for a film version, act it out, film it, and show it.

Advocacy and Political Involvement

As citizens who refuse to mind their own business, teachers must not act as if their business is only in the classroom, and must realize that what happens outside the classroom can profoundly affect their work for better or worse. Most obviously, refusing to mind your own business means taking political action… teachers with purpose and passion must protest damaging government action, not because they are in despair, but precisely because they are hopeful and actively determined to make things better for their students.

(Hargreaves & Fullan, 1998, pp. 99–100)

There are times when teachers are called on to advocate either personally or politically—which often overlap—for a student or group of students, at the school, local, provincial, or federal level. Your responsibility is to ensure that you do what is best for your students. This means at times promoting and defending policies, programs, and actions that allow you to implement best practices in your classroom. If there are impediments to being effective teachers of literacy, ensure that you voice your concerns to your communities and governments.

Teachers advocate for their students every day, in many ways, without thinking that these actions are necessarily "political" in nature. But when Karyn Cooper (Teacher Talk 14.2) lobbied her principal to allow curricular changes to better serve her students' needs by going beyond the government-mandated curriculum, her actions were political. When a teacher calls a parent–school meeting with psychologists, social workers, and medical personnel to discuss a student's individual program, that teacher is advocating at the school and community level for that student. When teachers organize a storytelling festival to celebrate the stories of the culturally and linguistically diverse families in their school, they are taking social action on everyone's behalf. When principals organize school meetings to discuss ways of addressing inequities in literacy success because of income and social status, they are educational advocates.

If you determine that a student's or group of students' best interests are at stake, and action "outside the classroom" is needed, we suggest that you prepare carefully by first of all, knowing yourself, your students, and your own stand on the issue, as well as the issue itself, as thoroughly as possible. You must be clear, articulate, and persuasive. You must know when to present your case, how and to whom, so that it will be most effective.

If the issue you wish to take a stand on is standardized testing, for example, you must be able to explain your conceptualizations of literacy (and numeracy) and to cite research that shows how these assessment tools fail to measure key modes of literacy. Your target will most likely be the provincial ministry of education. Will you write letters to your local newspaper, member of the legislature, the minister of education, or the premier? Will you organize other teachers and members of the community to do the same? How effective will you be making presentations at the local or provincial levels? Have you considered launching a public relations campaign using your local newspaper? Educational advocacy is hard work, and so is

literacy notebook 14.4

STOP, THINK, AND WRITE

■ What is your response to the following statement?

There are strong pressures today to dehumanize, to depersonalize, to industrialize our schools. In the name of cost effectiveness, of efficiency, of system, of accountability, of minimal competency, of a return to basics, schools are becoming turned into sterile, hostile institutions at war with the young people they are intended to serve.

(Goodman, in Opitz, 1998, p. 234)

Ken Goodman goes on to create a "declaration of professional conscience" for teachers. Two of the 10 pledges he makes are:

1. We will make the welfare of our students our most basic criterion for professional work with parents and policymakers to formulate programs that are in the best interests of our pupils.

2. We will do all we can to make school a warm, friendly, supportive place in which all pupils are welcome. Our classrooms will be theirs. (pp. 234-5)

What points would you add as important to your "professional conscience"?

teaching. Some teachers prefer to fight the system "from within" by refusing to "teach to the test" for example. Our point is that the more you know about any topic, the stronger your position will be from which to act.

Moving On

In this chapter, we looked at some of the issues you face when you are challenged with the task of bringing a wide range of individuals into literacy. We returned to your personal literacy stories in our search for insights into how best to teach all students to become readers, writers, and literate beings. We sought multiple perspectives as we looked at issues such as students who are considered to be at risk and students with special needs; the many complexities involved in teaching culturally and linguistically diverse learners; and some of the issues involved in understanding how gender plays a role in literacy learning. We hope this chapter has contributed to your journey of self-inquiry, and your exploration of some of the many creative ways that quality literacy instruction can be implemented.

In Chapter 15, we offer an assortment of teachers' tried and tested suggestions and survival tips for preparing for and getting through your first September—that first crucial month of the school year.

I simply want to communicate the idea that there is always more to be found, horizons to be breached, limits to be broken through, always untapped possibility.
—Maxine Greene

LIT-FOLIO UPDATE

Consider what you might include in your portfolio as evidence that you personally have shown growth in your self-awareness of how your literacy identity influences your teaching of literacy—to boys, to girls, to non-English speakers, or to students of a different ethnicity than yours. What have you learned about how to meet the needs of this diversity of learners? What do you know about what counts as *normal* in classrooms in your community?

LIT-FOLIO TIP:

Comment on your confidence level about teaching in schools in economically disadvantaged neighbourhoods. What can you do to develop greater assurance in teaching students from all kinds of backgrounds? Return to your personal literacy story. What insights do your own experiences offer?

Resources to Support Your Learning

Professional Resources

Allington, R. (2001, 2006). *What really matters for struggling readers.* Boston, MA: Pearson.

Beers, K. (2003). *When kids can't read: What teachers can do: A guide for teachers 6-12.* Portsmouth, NH: Heinemann.

✤ Booth, D. (2002). *Even hockey players read: Boys, literacy and learning.* Markham, ON: Pembroke.

Cunningham, P. & Allington, R. (2003, 2006). *Classrooms that work: They can all read and write.* Boston, MA: Pearson.

✤ Hargreaves, A. & Fullan, M. (1998). *What's worth fighting for out there?* Toronto: Ontario Public School Teachers' Federation.

Ontario Ministry of Education, 2001, *English as a second language and English literacy development: A resource guide.*

Opitz, M. (Ed.) (1998). *Literacy instruction for culturally and linguistically diverse students.* Newark, DE: International Reading Association.

Children's Literature: Our Favourites

Crow Boy, Taro Yashima

The dragon prince, Lawrence Yep

The girl who spun gold (West Indian version of Rumplestiltskin), Virginia Hamilton

✤ *Magic shop books*, Bruce Colville

Molly Bannaky, Alice McGill

Moses goes to school (deafness), Isaac Millman

Night visitors, Ed Young

Paul Goble gallery: Three Native American stories, Paul Goble

Stargone John (emotional disabilities), Ellen Kindt McKenzie

The time warp trio, Jon Scieszka

Cultural and Social Issues Junior Level Books

The bone talker (aging, communication, lasting values), Shelley Leedahl

The day of Ahmed's secret, Florence Parry Heide, Judith Heide Gilliland

Catherine, called Birdy (girls and women, historical roles), Karen Cushman

Charlie and the chocolate factory (stereotyping, poverty), Roald Dahl

✤ *The elders are watching* (cultural values), David Bouchard

Fly away home (poverty, homelessness), Eve Bunting

The girl who loved the wind (diversity), Jane Yolen

✤ *The hockey sweater* (cultural values), Roch Carrier

The hundred dresses (bullying, discrimination), Eleanor Estes

Knots on a counting rope (blindness, courage, First Nations' values), Bill Martin, Jr.

Monster Mama (differences, bullying, problem-solving, beauty/ugliness), Liz Rosenberg

Painted words/spoken memories, Aliki (immigration, learning a new language)

Rose Blanche (war, Holocaust), Roberto Innocenti

The seeing stick, (blindness), Jane Yolen

The table where rich people sit (poverty, family values), Byrd Baylor

The wall (war), Eve Bunting

Traditional Literature Representing Various Cultures

Aesop's fables, Jerry Pinkney

Arabian nights, Brian Alderson

✤ *Canadian fairy tales*, Eva Martin, Laszlo Gal

✤ *Out of the everywhere: New tales for Canada*, Jan Andrews, Simon Ng (eds.)

The wonder child and other Jewish fairy tales, Howard Swartz

World folktales, Atelia Clarkson (ed.)

Websites

✤ Ontario Ministry of Education. See *English as a Second Language and English Literacy Development: A Resource Guide* (2001): http://www.edu.gov.on.ca

✤ Saskatchewan Learning ESL links: http://www.sasked.gov.sk.ca

✤ TESL Canada (Teaching English as a Second Language in Canada): http://www.tesl.ca/

✤ Canadian Council of Teachers of English Language Arts: http://www.cctela.ca

Linda's Learning Links: Ideas for Literacy Centres: http://www.lindaslearninglinks.com

Intercultural E-Mail Classroom Connections: http://www.stolaf.edu/network/iecc/

Multimedia Connections

Compare the movie to the book.

Shrek the movie

Shrek! the novel by William Steig

15

Putting Literacy into Practice

Getting Ready for September

The courage to teach is the courage to keep one's heart open in those very moments when the heart is asked to hold more than it is able so that teacher and students and subject can be woven into the fabric of community that learning, and living, require.
—*Parker J. Palmer*

key terms

assessment and record keeping

balanced and comprehensive language and literacy programs

classroom community

classroom set-up

collaboration (students, parents, teachers, administration)

first day/week considerations

language across the curriculum

routines and expectations

school culture

student engagement

questions to guide your learning

By the end of this chapter, you should understand the key terms and be able to answer the following questions:

- How do teachers prepare for the start of school?
- How do teachers create community from the first day?
- How do teachers manage the classroom in a way that promotes risk-taking and success?
- How do teachers prepare for students they don't yet know?
- How do teachers plan for the language learning for a wide range of students?
- How do teachers assess learners in terms of reading and writing?

Looking Back, Looking Ahead

In this chapter, we discuss the critical questions of teachers getting ready for September. How do I organize my classroom? How do I prepare for students I don't yet know? How do I arrange for the learning of a wide spectrum of individuals? How do I become acquainted (quickly!) with the expectations for this grade level (or levels if it is a split grade)? How do I determine what level they are at in reading and writing? How do I pull everything I've learned together and plan an effective and engaging program?

While this chapter is not intended to be a "how-to," it is intended to provide support to teachers who just aren't sure where to begin. The thoughts and ideas in this chapter will not be entirely new; you have encountered them in previous readings, in seminar discussions and activities, and through practicum experiences. What is new are the suggestions and insights offered by experienced and practising teachers in the field.

Suggested Reading Guide

We suggest you begin with the following sections:

- Heli Vail's "Supporting the First-Year Literacy Teacher: An Administrative Perspective"
- Rosalind Zimbalatti's "Preparing for Learners Who Have Special Needs"

When you know the grade level you will be teaching, read the relevant section. Then read the advice from teachers of grade levels before and after your grade, to get an idea of where your students have come from, and where they are going.

If you are about to teach Grade 1, for example, be sure to read Susan Sitter's "Preparing for the Transition from Kindergarten to Grade 1" because your student have enormous adjustments to make!

Where *does* one start? One of the reasons preparing adequately for September seems such a daunting task is that every teacher recognizes the absolute necessity of getting the best start possible. Once September is over and the school year begins in earnest, it is impossible to erase September and start over again. There is so much to do!

Experienced teachers know that the best approach is to begin with what you are able to control. When we read the contributions from teachers telling us about how they typically prepare for the beginning of the year, we see that, for some, this means focusing on the physical set-up of the classroom; for others, it means establishing routines in the first few days. For teachers new to a school, it means spending time getting to know the school—teaching and administrative colleagues, custodians, and neighbours in the school community. For others, it means studying the student records of the children they will be teaching. For many, it means carefully mapping out long-term planning to ensure curricular expectations will be met. For others, it means reviewing best practice strategies such as guided reading, and figuring out the best ways to manage time, resources, and assessment records. There is a great deal to orchestrate; beginning with the "big picture" and those things that we have control over is important for maintaining the energy required for the day-to-day work of teaching.

The voices you hear in this chapter are those of teachers who have mastered the art of teaching: they have managed the day-to-day business of teaching well, and have also taught with courage, recognizing that responsive and best practice instruction requires the courage to teach what is needed, when it is needed, in a way that makes the most sense and keeps learners at the heart of instruction.

Putting it All Together

There is no magic formula and no one-size-fits-all program; instead, you need to build into your balanced and comprehensive programs what we referred to in Chapter 2 as ranges of instruction, a continuum of support, and diverse models of instruction. Balanced and comprehensive programs naturally value the diversity of learners as they incorporate the six language arts, multiple intelligences, and multi-literacies, and extend beyond comprehension into critical literacy.

Where to Begin: The Big Picture

Before the first day of school is one of the few times busy teachers get the opportunity to think and reflect on the "big picture," and on what really matters to them in their teaching. This is the time when you can think about and discuss with your colleagues school and program goals, principles, priorities, and creating conditions for learning. In this chapter, we present literacy stories of teachers, ranging from fairly recent graduates to those with many years of experience. We asked

STOP, THINK, AND WRITE

As you proceed through the remainder of the chapter, jot down anything you definitely want to remember. You can do this holistically or you can select a specific grade (likely your preferred grade). Keep the following questions and prompts in mind:

Teaching: Quality of Instruction

■ What curriculum expectations stand out?

■ How do these teachers make the curriculum relevant to students?

■ How do these teachers incorporate a W.O.R.L.D. (**W**ord, **O**rality, **R**e-Vision, **L**iteracies, **D**iscourses) view into their teaching?

Excitement: Personal Characteristics

■ How do these teachers demonstrate care, commitment, and passion for their students?

Attitude: Attitude toward Subject

■ How do they share their enthusiasm for literacy and learning with learners?

Caring: Understanding of Learner Potential

■ What do they believe about learners?

■ What levels of support are built into their September set-up that demonstrate an understanding of learner potential and learner development (the need for multiple entry/exit points that allow for success)?

Helping: Life Adjustment

■ How do they demonstrate an acceptance of student discourses and their "ways of being" in the world?

■ How do they demonstrate awareness and attentiveness to learning differences, academic problems, and personal difficulties?

them, "If given the opportunity to talk to beginning teachers, what would you say?" These are their stories, suggestions, and insights. They offer their advice to help smooth your transition from theory to classroom practice—a process you have already begun. The topics and themes we will discuss are woven throughout these teachers' stories and do not proceed in any particular order; there is no sequence to follow in planning and focusing on each of these categories. On many levels, we agree with Sue Sitter, a Kindergarten teacher and one of the contributors, when she says that she is "always getting ready for

September." In preparation for reading their stories and ideas, we take a brief look at each of the key themes teachers consider as they prepare for the start of a new school year.

CREATING COMMUNITY

Before you even meet your students, you know that they will represent diverse backgrounds, interests, and abilities. This diversity may relate to culture, language, religion, learning styles, and interest preferences, and intellectual, social, and emotional differences. While celebrating diversity, you also need to create a community of learners who can work together side-by-side, respecting and enhancing their own learning and that of their classmates. Achieving community is the result of conscious effort. The stories teachers tell indicate some of the ways a true working community can be created through well-run readers' and writers' workshops, a variety of problem-solving discussion forums, such as literature circles and literary conversations, and richly diverse literature to promote awareness, tolerance, and compassion.

Creating community is one of the most important aspects of the start of a new school year.

In the first days and weeks of the new term, most teachers focus on creating the conditions that allow a **classroom community** to flourish: As one teacher put it, the first days are about "bonding and routines; routines and bonding." With this in mind, many teachers focus their planning for the first few days and weeks on activities for building relationships and establishing working rules and routines in a positive way.

KNOWING YOUR SCHOOL'S CULTURE, INCLUDING DIVERSITY, TRADITIONS, NEIGHBOURHOOD

Doing your homework ahead of time, perhaps during the summer, can contribute greatly to your knowledge of your **school's culture**. You can get a feel for the school by asking about the sorts of events and traditions held in the school and nearby, by talking to neighbours, custodians, and colleagues. Reviewing newsletters from the previous year, finding the school handbook or mission statement, even wandering down the halls and looking at bulletin boards contributes valuable information. Gathering this information will require your full engagement as a literacy learner—this is the time to listen, talk, read, write, view, and represent. Your school's culture will become part of you and you will become part of it.

PLANNING THE VERY FIRST DAY

The first day of the school year is crucial for both teacher and students and there are many **first day/week considerations**. Just as you need to get to know them, your students need to know who you are. You want your students to feel welcome and at ease with you as their new teacher. You want this to be balanced by the expectation that everyone in the class will be learning to their potential, and that while this can be fun at times, it always involves an engaged effort from everyone. First day activities that promote "getting to know you" and that offer a glimpse into the coming year with its promises and expectations are included in many of the teachers' stories. One of the stories provides a snapshot of how a first day might unfold.

ESTABLISHING ROUTINES AND EXPECTATIONS

Every experienced teacher emphasizes the fact that the establishment of **routines and expectations** in the first days and weeks of school is absolutely vital to the success of the program and, our particular concern, to the success of each individual literacy learner. Many teachers highlight the role that good organization plays in establishing useful routines that allow learners to focus on learning.

GATHERING AND ORGANIZING RESOURCES; ORGANIZATIONAL PRINCIPLES; AND CLASSROOM SET-UP

As a first-year teacher, you may be overly worried about organizing and setting up. There is lots of support here—from administration (see Heli Vail's suggestions) and from colleagues. Collect resources from a variety of sources: gather new and used materials from garage sales and retiring teachers, keep an eye on used book stores and dollar stores, and capitalize on book clubs that offer monthly "free picks." For school orders or if you are asked to choose your own materials using a designated budget, consult experienced teachers, become familiar with the catalogues, go back to your notes from previous classroom experiences, envision your program, and then order away!

Organize books and resources simply and conveniently: if they are children's resources, store them where the children can reach them and easily put them back in an orderly fashion. Be creative and use a system of labelling that students can read easily (pictures and words for younger students). Teaching students how to retrieve and store materials is a simple routine that is easily managed and that builds the independence necessary for future learning.

For your classroom set-up, begin with the type of program you plan to put in practice. If you are implementing workstations or literacy centres, you will need to plan for movement flow, adequate workspace, storage of materials, and student record keeping. You will also need to envision routines and expectations for centres and workstations, and how you will gradually release responsibility for independence to students. These topics are discussed at several grade levels in the teacher contributions later in the chapter.

STUDENT ENGAGEMENT

Planning ahead for this is implicitly embedded in your program planning. If you are planning for student involvement in activities that are enticing for their age level and interests, with a wide variety of possibilities and some degree of personal choice, student engagement usually just happens. When it doesn't, it's time to re-evaluate your program and ask whether the tasks and strategies you have planned are meaningful and relevant to your students, reflective of their needs and interests, and appropriate in terms of difficulty. If you want your students to be engaged in their learning, you must give them a reason to be engaged and this is where program planning, literature selection, interest inventories, and so on become indispensable.

If students are to be engaged in their learning, they must have a reason to be engaged.

COLLEAGUES AND COLLABORATION

The value of collaboration among colleagues, for everyone involved, but particularly for teachers in their first years of teaching, cannot be over-emphasized. Many boards have mentoring programs in place for new teachers—some are one-on-one mentors whereas others gather first year teachers on a monthly basis for induction and orientation. Beyond these formal initiatives, get to know the other teachers in your school community. Many believe in the importance of collaboration. The numbers of teachers who generously offered their time and expertise to participate in this chapter is testimony to the collegial and collaborative nature of teaching.

ASSESSMENT AND RECORD KEEPING

Depending on your grade level and program needs, you will need to think about how you will assess your students in reading, writing, listening, speaking, viewing, and representing. We have made many suggestions throughout the book, but you will need to design the assessment and record keeping system that works best for you. You will need student folders for ongoing work, portfolio folders for "best work," as well as checklists and tracking charts. Remember that assessment drives instruction and that your assessment must focus on both process and product. Use a variety of tools, from formal tests to informal anecdotal notes. Before the first day, you can set up your "system." Sue Sitter's account provides some practical advice.

A BALANCED AND COMPREHENSIVE LANGUAGE PROGRAM INCLUDING LANGUAGE ACROSS THE CURRICULUM

You are probably thinking, "How can I manage it all?" Balanced and comprehensive literacy and the continuum of support, assessment, language across the curriculum, a collection of quality literature, managing guided reading groups and writers' workshop—the list seems endless. The next section, Stories from the Classroom, offers practical teaching tips on these very components of the language program. The teachers range from Kindergarten to Intermediate level, and include a resource teacher and a former administrator.

The teachers' stories reflect the transfer of theory into practice, where balanced and comprehensive language and literacy programs become a reality. Our concluding summary takes a look at the recursive interaction of student need, teacher reflection, and classroom practice; it summarizes the most important aspects of a balanced and comprehensive language program: what it should include and why, and what it looks like in the classroom.

COMMUNICATION WITH FAMILY/PARENTS/CAREGIVERS

Communication with family, parents, and caregivers must be conceptualized and planned prior to September. How will you introduce yourself? How will you ensure that family, parents, and caregivers understand your rules, routines, and expectations? When are appropriate times to collaborate and ask questions? All of these questions must be considered; the more information you can share, the easier your job will be. Newsletters and agendas go a long way in fostering interactive communication and general questions. Establishing home contact early and often is one of the most important things you can do to ensure your students' success. And don't forget, just because you have it all worked out doesn't mean that you'll avoid the parent who shows up in your classroom because there is something they have to tell you. Be ready for them and have a plan in mind. Let them know that you are willing to meet with them, but that your first commitment is to your students. Have a task or activity available for the parent while they wait, invite them to sit in on a lesson, or suggest they wait at the office until you can have someone take over your class for a few minutes. The bottom line is to be prepared in a way that is respectful and acknowledges their need to talk to you.

Stories from the Classroom

As you read the stories from experienced teachers, you will see that we have alerted you to the five dominant themes of each one. This will provide you with a quick reference as well as an orientation for reading.

SUPPORTING THE FIRST-YEAR LITERACY TEACHER: AN ADMINISTRATIVE PERSPECTIVE

☑ Knowing Your School's Culture

☑ Gathering and Organizing Resources

☑ Colleagues and Collaboration

☑ A Balanced and Comprehensive Languages Program

☑ Communications with Family/Parents/Caregivers

Heli Vail, a former principal with many years of experience at the elementary and intermediate levels, offers sage advice for new teachers about the kind of support they should expect and can rely on from the school administration. How does a good administrator (principal) support a first year teacher of literacy?

Introductory Meeting with Your Principal

Your principal will want to meet with you very shortly after you have been offered the teaching position to discuss the established policies and procedures of the school. Part of that discussion will also centre on the school's action plans for literacy program development and implementation.

The principal will give you a list of the support personnel in the school and the board who can provide assistance and support during the course of the year. To help facilitate that contact, the principal may have also invited the school's lead literacy teacher, resource teacher, and/or team/division leader to attend part of this meeting. Or, the principal will arrange for you to contact these resource people to set up a meeting. In addition, the principal will also tell you when the groups meet to discuss strategies that support the development of literacy. Your principal may suggest one of them as a mentor.

The principal will tell you about in-school resources for literacy use and the availability of additional literacy materials from the board's resource centre. An inventory of information technology hardware and software that can be used will be provided. The principal will also tell you how to access petty cash.

The principal will discuss the school's improvement plans for literacy and give you a copy of the standardized data on school literacy results as well as individual results of students who will be in your class. The principal also needs to advise you where the student records or files are located and the procedure for examining them. You will also be given the names of your students' previous teachers so that you can contact them for additional information; they may have anecdotal notes, writing portfolios, and so on, that show students' progress in literacy.

The principal should discuss the school's expectations around long- and short-term planning in your literacy program and encourage integration of other subject areas into this plan. This will include how much time should be devoted to literacy during a day. Your principal will encourage you to incorporate guest speakers and field trips into your plans for an effective literacy program. You will need to know how to fund and organize school trips.

Communication with parents about literacy is extremely important and your principal should let you know what the expectations are around this. For example, is there a curriculum evening at the beginning of the year when you will be expected to talk about aspects of your program including literacy? Should you send home an outline of your themes, units, long- and short-range plans on a regular basis? Is there a school newsletter that you can contribute to or are you expected to write a class newsletter where you talk about your program?

Future Meetings with Your Principal

Your principal should schedule regular meetings with you throughout the year to discuss issues and concerns. The principal should also be an occasional visitor in your class, either having been invited to read to the students or to have students share accomplishments in their literacy development.

PREPARING FOR LEARNERS WHO HAVE SPECIAL NEEDS

☑ Knowing Your School's Culture

☑ Knowing Your Students

☑ Gathering and Organizing Resources

☑ Colleagues and Collaboration

☑ Assessment and Record Keeping

How do you prepare for those students who are identified as learners with special needs, for those who are receiving extra support, and those who perhaps should receive extra support? Rosalind Zimbalatti, resource teacher and Reading Recovery® teacher, uses this checklist with the teachers in her school.

- The resource teacher will probably have an up-to-date list of the students in the school who have received resource intervention or support from outside agencies and board support services.

- Look in the student files for reports on students who have had Occupational Therapy (OT), Physiotherapy (PT), and/or Speech and Language Pathology (SLP). Each report will contain valuable recommendations, often ideas that can benefit all students (pencil grip, specific computer programs, and strengthening and balancing exercises for gym class).

- Take time to read new OT, PT, and SLP reports when they come in. The up-to-date information will be useful when you write report cards, as student strengths and weaknesses will probably be highlighted.

- Observe, record, and then notify the resource teacher of any specific concerns you may have. The resource teacher may give suggestions for addressing the concern, put in a referral for outside assistance, or call a school resource committee meeting to discuss the student. A school resource committee is usually made up of the resource staff, the principal, and the teacher. The aim of the committee is to solve dilemmas using a collaborative approach, before an issue becomes a big problem.

- If resource intervention takes place in the classroom as part of the program, make sure there is a good workspace for the resource teacher and a small group. A table, with folding stools stored underneath, is one option.

- If students leave the class for resource intervention, plan and practise a procedure so that this coming and going does not disrupt the whole class. Develop a quiet sign-in/sign-out system for outside professionals who come to collect a student for weekly therapy.

- Be sure to read the accommodations section of a student's Individual Educational Plan. It is the teacher's responsibility to provide the accommodations or discuss any necessary changes with the resource teacher.

REAL-WORLD KINDERGARTEN: JUNIOR/SENIOR KINDERGARTEN

☑ Classroom Set-up

☑ Resources

☑ Assessment

☑ Communication with Family/Parents/Caregivers

Patrick Duncan teaches Junior/Senior Kindergarten. He graduated from Nipissing University in 2002.

I have found that the best recipe for managing Kindergarten in the real world is preparedness along with a healthy dose of flexibility and a pinch of humour thrown in for good measure. Consider the following as a few words of advice to help you deal with the real world of teaching in a unique Kindergarten environment.

Coming into a new school year prepared is of the utmost importance when entering into Kindergarten or any other year for that matter. Being prepared allows you to be able to handle all those little things that come up day in and day out.

Getting ready for September in Kindergarten also means getting ready for meeting, teaching, and working with the new students. Most school boards still have some sort of JK intake interview system where the students, along with their parents, come to meet the teacher and see the classroom. This is a fantastic opportunity to establish a baseline for each child and to really start to form a strong home-school connection. You should plan for a fairly comprehensive, yet quick, assessment of the student's current skills. The areas to focus on are the child's fine and gross motor skills, articulation, the ability to follow verbal instructions, and a general idea of each student's numeracy and literacy skill level along with social maturity. Use this information to talk to parents about any concerns you may have. Make referrals at this time to the necessary professionals to address concerns about occupational, physical, or speech language therapy. Having the parents there helps you to stress how important it is to get a good start in school and enables them to fill out the necessary referral information and consent forms right away.

Also, set the parents at ease by giving them copies of a sample day plan and a short summary of your teaching philosophy. Have a sign up sheet for volunteers, ask for and answer their questions, and have them provide contact information as well as an emergency contact person.

Classroom Setup

The classroom setup is an integral part of having a well-run and fun Kindergarten classroom. An important rule of thumb when looking at how to set up the classroom and centres is to work smarter not harder. Centres should be set up with literally every material the students will need to accomplish tasks; this allows the teacher to change the activities at that centre with little or no work. Having a fully stocked craft cupboard allows the teacher the flexibility of changing the structured task at that centre easily, as well as allowing the students the creative freedom to enhance the assigned task or create their own original piece of work.

When setting up your classroom centres, pay particular attention to traffic flow and, more importantly, sight lines. Remember that an important part of your job is to teach proper social interactions through observing play/learning situation so you must have unobstructed views of all of your centres. I have learned that it is crucial to have totally unobstructed sight lines to your gross motor centres, specifically if you have building blocks, and centres which require a great deal of sharing. If accidents are going to happen or disputes occur, they are more likely to occur in these centres and it is hard to fill out the accident report or tell the parents how their child was hurt if you could not see what happened. As well, try as best as you can to physically separate your potentially loud centres from your "quiet" centres. Creating a classroom setup which allows for "quiet" centres where you can con-

ference and assess student progress without too much distraction is definitely beneficial to your ability to carry out the assessments and to maintain your own mental well being.

Resources

Most school boards have central resource centres that can be accessed through the Internet; however, if you visit the resource centre and get to know the staff, they will be one of your greatest resources. The staff will help you to match the resources in their centre with the curriculum you are planning to teach and to coordinate the arrival of these resources. If they do not have a specific resource, they will direct you to another resource or sometimes consider purchasing it. Having this done over the summer certainly helps when it comes to dealing with the real world of teaching during the school year. Another absolutely necessary resource for teaching Kindergarten, which I consider the Kindergarten bible, is the *Kindergarten Teacher's Resource Book* by Miriam Trehearne.

Language Program Planning

As the pendulum swings from phonics-based programming to whole language, throughout your career in teaching, remember one key phrase – Balanced Literacy Program. I try to not get too caught up in the debate of which one is better as I believe each child learns differently and therefore, should be exposed to both philosophies of teaching language. Learning letter sounds is as integral to learning to read as exposure to and learning sight words from a word wall. Also, don't forget the importance of singing in the Kindergarten classroom. Singing with children is strongly correlated to further success in reading. If you are not a good singer, don't worry, Kindergarten children are very forgiving.

It is really important to establish early where each student is with letter recognition, letter sounds, sight words, and phonemic awareness so that you can keep them moving forward and challenged.

Ongoing and frequent assessment makes report card writing easier and allows for early identification of children at risk of later reading difficulties.

In the Kindergarten program, language permeates all that you do. Language is part of the graph you are labelling, the data you are collecting for your mathematics curriculum, the parts of the plant you are labelling in science, and the letter you are writing to thank the community members for allowing you to come and visit.

Parent Contact

Parental involvement in your students' learning is imperative. Initiate parent contact early, usually at the intake interview, and keep contact often. Establish a shared writing activity every day where the students write about their day. Quickly type this up or write it out, photocopy it, and send it home. Parents will love it because it helps them find out what their child did at school that day and it also helps with the child's oral communication skills. Send home a weekly newsletter informing parents of the week's events and where you will need parental assistance. Don't be afraid to ask for help. I have as many parent volunteers in my classroom as I can get and, trust me, I can keep them all busy! Have parental home helpers who can assist you from home by cutting things out, writing things up for you, creating your web page and updating it, or creating manipulatives that you can use at your fine motor table. Some parents want to be totally involved in their child's education, so let them. They are not coming into your classroom to judge you; they are coming to help you, so make them feel welcome.

Make up some quick and easy-to-complete teacher notes for home, photocopy them and have them readily available for when you need them. When you catch a student doing something noteworthy, grab a teacher note, check off the appropriate box, place a sticker on it, sign it, and have the student put it in their note-home bag. This way, good news goes home twice as often as the not so good news and it makes it more palatable for parents as they notice how often you notice their child's good side. More importantly, train anyone in your room on how to quickly fill out one of these forms as they can greatly assist you in catching the good things as well as dealing with those little problems that frequently occur.

Assessment and Record Keeping

Personally, I try to do as much of my assessment and record keeping using technology. I have the expectations and rubric I am working on at each centre pasted on the back of the centre logo. I assess the students on an ongoing basis by using a digital voice recorder. I record the expectation, the child's name I am assessing, the level of the rubric they have achieved, and any further information to support that assessment of their work. I can also record the conversation that I have with the student that I am assessing to review later if I have concerns about their ability to accomplish the expectation. This is a great tool when trying to get support for students who are struggling. The special education teacher and the principal can hear the conversations that I have with the students during assessment period or during times when they are exhibiting a behaviour problem. The digital voice recorder has separate files that I can create which makes downloading to my laptop easier. During an evaluation period, I can refer back to these recordings (which can also be formatted into print with voice recognition software), to have a firm understanding of each student's achievement level.

Conclusion

Remember that no matter what happens, you are teaching students—not a curriculum. There is no one special formula for successfully teaching Kindergarten. However, you have to love what you do. Take care of your physical well being as every known virus will come through your classroom and most importantly, love the kids!

PREPARING FOR THE TRANSITION FROM KINDERGARTEN TO GRADE 1

☑ Creating Community

☑ Planning the Very First Day

☑ Gathering and Organizing Resources; Organizational Principles; Classroom Setup

☑ Student Engagement

☑ Assessment and Record Keeping

Susan Sitter uses the metaphor of the teacher as an artist in the midst of a work in progress. She continually works with her students to guide them toward becoming self-regulating, self-extending learners of literacy and life. Susan is a Senior Kindergarten teacher. Her previous assignments have included teaching a split Kindergarten–Grade 1. She reports that she survives by listening to *Cat Stevens' Greatest Hits* during learning centre time.

Always Getting Ready for September

In my teaching I am always "getting ready for September." As I consider the journey children undertake as they proceed from Kindergarten to Grade 1, I want to make sure they are prepared to meet the challenges and enjoy the adventure. As I get ready for *this* September, I am looking ahead to their *next* September.

Organizing for Assessment and Record Keeping

To start, I follow a simple routine that requires minimum effort with maximum gain: I set up my assessment binders for the year. I purchase six different coloured, two-inch binders with pockets on the inside covers. The binders are labelled: Anecdotals/Communication, Running Records, Observation Survey, Guided Reading, Writing Assessment (includes a pink copy for each child of Miriam Trehearne's Writing Continuum from *Kindergarten Teacher's Resource Book*), and Mathematics. I prefer the "D" rings because they're easier to use. I include a class set of dividers for each binder and invest the time to write the name of each child on front and back of the tabs (alphabetical order by first name). The hour or so the process takes pays off throughout the year, as I accumulate assessment pieces and samples and file them in chronological order for each child. Once my binders are set up, I focus my effort on organizing the classroom.

A Guiding Metaphor

At some point, the thought occurred to me that "I am an artist and the classroom is my canvas." In September, my vision is to begin with a plain canvas and to get a feel for my palette of children before beginning to create our masterpiece of learning during this school year. The room is inviting, engaging, and welcoming. The children become co-artists in learning and creating. While I imagine the themes or titles for our bulletin boards in September it is their artwork and writing that adorns them. Decorations such as posters are left for the highest reaches where I have no intention of climbing more than once during any given year! I indulge in purchasing paper borders but keep things simple so as not to detract from the real focus: the children's work. I cover bulletin boards with fabric so that I don't have to repeat the time-consuming process of covering them each year. I invest in two colour tones that complement one another and are a deep enough tone to show off the children's work (Elizabeth MacLeod's inspiration). I have one classroom bulletin board and hallway boards covered in black to highlight visual art (Patti Muir's inspiration). September planning for language, art, and math focuses on creating bulletin boards that showcase the children's early writing, art, and math. The highest bulletin boards have artwork that features each child's name; these stay up for the whole year (to build community and because of the height!). In June I have the children redo the same art activity to emphasize their growth in writing their own names.

Classroom Set-up

The blackboard space is carefully staked out for the competing "real estate demands." I must leave space for a name chart (developed over the first days or weeks); an alphabet link chart (for letter recognition and phonemic awareness); possibly a behaviour management chart (for example, "Quiet Owls in Room 118" to promote and reward quiet—not silent!—work). I leave room for a "colour ladder" of colour word cards. I want plenty of space for developing a word wall together. I start with lower case letters of the alphabet and add words only as they are introduced through shared reading and interactive writing. For much of the year, I avoid having more than one word per letter (to avoid confusions) but as words are mastered I move them to a "Words We Know" list. This keeps the word wall up-to-date and relevant. It also emphasizes that the purpose is to *learn* the words! The word wall needs to be placed so that the children can see it from the places where they need to refer to it (from the carpet during shared reading and interactive lessons; from their tables during guided and independent writing). Finally I need to establish sites on the blackboard space, wall, bulletin boards, and chart stands for displaying anchor charts, pieces of shared reading text, and class interactive writing for current and future reference (for example, during instruction; for "reading around the room"). A blank "Blue Book" is kept throughout the year for adding word lists, copies of anchor charts, and shared reading pieces. This becomes a "mini-Room 118" for easy reference from anywhere in the room or at home. My hope is that by June the Blue Book is embedded in their brain so that they head to Grade 1 with a solid foundation in reading and writing.

Perhaps the most effective piece of equipment for early literacy is the white board easel for mounting big books, posters, and chart paper for shared reading lessons; for using in interactive writing lessons; and for manipulating magnetic letters during letter and word work. Even the "real estate" of the easel needs to be carefully planned so that its multipurpose value is not lost in a storm of overlapping materials! I keep the magnetic letters wrapped around in alphabetical order from bottom left up and across the top and down the right side (Rosalind Zimbalatti's inspiration).

Throughout the process of preparing the class-room for the first days and weeks I make a concerted effort to de-clutter. If the classroom is new to me my intent is to have it as streamlined as possible before I begin. My ongoing goal (and struggle!) is to maintain this standard throughout my own practice. I have opted to allow no personal items. All materials such as pencils, crayons, markers, scissors and glue are communal. We share everything and take responsibility for returning materials to their proper place. Work that isn't collected for display, portfolio, or assessment purposes is sent home daily.

Gathering Resources

As I ready this streamlined, well organized, inviting classroom to display children's work and creations, and to mount our jointly prepared anchor charts (for example, routines, family word list, fire safety), word wall, and name cards, I need to collect resources for reading, writing, and oral language to support the evolving and wide-ranging needs of early readers and writers. Within a given month, I strive to strike a balance among a variety of text forms and purposes. My starting point is usually selecting the shared reading piece. Each month, I select a piece of poetry or a song, a simple yet effective pattern book, a nursery rhyme and a children's book with text large enough for a shared piece. I tie much of my interactive writing and independent writing to the shared reading. Early on we write many class books together interactively (whole group, small group, and one-to-one as needed). We also write weekly "Weekend News" in our writing books (spiral bound scrap books) to emphasize the composition and writing of brief messages to complement the repetitive nature of the pattern writing.

Teaching Real-World Writing and Reading

Most importantly for writing, I model from Day 1, during learning centres or workstations or "play time," how writing is embedded in our daily living. At the house centre, I take a phone message from the Cat in the Hat because I have no time to talk to him just then. For months the children write messages, first in squiggles and waves, then with a single name copied from the word cards, and eventually full fledged written messages as more words and approximations become part of their writing repertoire. Samples of independent writing from learning centres are snatched and photocopied, dated, analyzed for writing stage/progress/next steps, and filed in the writing assessment binder. To become a portfolio piece, the author needs only to assess what they have learned from it. My interaction and modelling of writing during learning centre time helps drive the momentum and love of writing within our community. The children take it from there and spread their own writing spirit as they discover their own purposes (writing songs, checking appointments at the dental clinic, making posters for the puppet show, writing news stories about Saturday's hockey game, making blueprints for the block structures, recording distances for paper airplane launches, noting the many "mysteries" in Room 118 such as Matthew's missing shoes). A separate bulletin board is devoted to the children's independent writing during centre time (or that they've brought from home). This is a dramatic testimony to the energy, passion, and transitions they experience as writers. Once the children are hooked on writing (all the while reading their own text and listening to others as they read theirs), the children are ready to reap the rewards of reading. With simple class books such as *Look at me! By Room 118*, children can read or at least recite a simple pattern book in very short order. Each page features the children's own (interactive) writing of a pattern sentence such as "Look at Emily," with a photo of Emily on her first day of school (or at SK Orientation the week before).

The focus early on is for students to establish concepts about books and print, to solidify (or learn) letter identification, to develop fluency and expression, and of course to love reading, writing, and lots of oral language. Early reading behaviours (one-to-one matching, directionality, locating known and unknown words) are modelled and encouraged. Early on, attention is also drawn to self-monitoring (for example, matching one-to-one or attention to meaning, structure and visual details of print). All of these skills and behaviours are built upon in subsequent weeks and months, but the foundation is laid from the outset.

The key to all reading and writing is to develop a strong and eventually fluent repertoire of "known words" in reading and writing. These words are gleaned from shared reading pieces and also from the children's independent writing. Some of my favourite texts for gathering these high frequency words include *Chrysanthemum* by Kevin Henkes, for an introduction to celebrating their own names and our name card pocket chart; *The Maple Leaf* (Porcupine Collection) and *Colours* (Nelson) for our colour ladder; *Today is Monday*, by Eric Carle for days of the week; and *The Photo Book*, by Beverly Randell for family words. "Essential" words are mounted on the word wall or on a special word list (name cards; family words, colour words, days of the week). During transition times students can be asked to "read the walls"; during lessons I refer to these supports for both reading and writing; during learning centres they may choose to "read around the room" (Fountas & Pinnell, 1996). They may choose to copy words for various purposes; or they may simply enjoy writing letters and words on their own small easel or writing board.

Books and texts are carefully selected to teach the use of comprehension strategies, especially with making connections to their own lives and experiences. For read alouds, series such as Paulette Bourgeois' *Franklin* promote a strong sense of community while helping children realize others share similar problems.

Establishing Community

On Day 1 in September, I come armed with my repertoire of teaching skills and I have established the classroom so that the children and I will create supports together for ready reference during the year. From the earliest moments I have two goals: to connect with the children and to create a learning community. The children learn from each other—for better or worse. Early on I invest teaching time in helping the children who learn *best* to get reading underway. The better they can, read the better their neighbours will read, and I will have easily and efficiently maximized the teaching ratio in the class. (For the over-eager "teachers" I may even teach some helpful prompts such as "Have a go" or "Do your best" so that they don't overpower the others). Children who may not learn to read as easily may have well-established interests (in reading or in life); these children are also exemplary models for our main purpose—to love learning and literacy.

From the first day, one of my main goals in reading is for the children to take care of the reading resources. I start with a limited number of books. I set clear boundaries and attempt to keep sorting manageable by having "little books" and "library books" available in two locations so they learn to put books away where they found them. As the children demonstrate as a group that they are caring for the materials and returning them properly, I add to the classroom collection and practise managing a growing collection of beautiful books and reading materials.

Now my teaching is made more powerful by the classroom environment (established with the children as new charts, routines, and texts are introduced) and by having the children serve as models to each other of reading behaviours, strategies, and preferences. I have a set of systems to help maintain an organized and smoothly managed community. I have gathered a variety of resources to help establish us as a literate community that embraces the joys of learning and literacy. And I am committed to connecting with my students so that I can continue to learn about them and from them as I teach.

> As a teacher I am always "getting ready for September." The spiral continues each year as I adapt and learn from my best laid plans. "I am an artist and the classroom is my canvas." If the masterpiece turns out to be more of a Picasso when I had envisioned an Alex Colville then I can thank my palette of children for introducing me to a new style.

GRADE 2 IN A FRENCH IMMERSION SCHOOL

- ☑ Creating Community
- ☑ Establishing Routines and Expectations
- ☑ Gathering and Organizing Resources
- ☑ Classroom Set-up
- ☑ Student Engagement

Cilla Dunn is presently the Coordinator for French as a Second Language in a Catholic district school board. The first years of her career were spent as a core French teacher and an early French immersion teacher in the Primary division.

Let Your Own Passion Shine!

I start the year with questions that I need to reflect on and answer, both now and throughout the year:

- Who am I, the teacher? Who are you, the students?
- How will I provide a learning environment that is inviting, positive, supportive?
- What is non-negotiable in our room?
- What will be my approaches to assessment?
- How will I balance the curriculum demands and the realities of my learners?

A Guiding Metaphor

I consider the fact that my students and I will be living together in this classroom for a whole school year. If I am going to create a learning community, there must be relationship. I want my students to know me and I want to know them really well. I want my students to sparkle and shine. I want us all to have fun!

I choose a guiding metaphor to establish my vision for how the relationships will occur. Kathy Gould Lundy talks about this in her book *What Do I Do about the Kid Who...?* (2004). Her metaphor is a door—you can imagine the possibilities. The metaphor for my vision is "light." I want us to see each other and what is around us. Light as a flood of illumination, a flash of insight, light in excited eyes, or the light you want to turn on. This metaphor permeates everything we do—both from the perspective of the student learners and from my own as teacher and learner. It will be about seeing ourselves in our best light: igniting interest, fanning the flame of curiosity, uncovering hidden talents, celebrating shining moments. What guiding metaphor will you choose?

The Learners

My Grade 2 French Immersion students will come to me with varying skills and styles of learning. I like to find out about their multiple intelligences, their preferred ways of working, their interests and so on, so I prepare surveys for them to respond to and devise various observation sheets as ongoing records of their behaviours, actions, preferences, strengths, needs, responses to tasks—these are the signposts that point me toward the next step to take to match instruction to learners. I would do this whether they were second language learners or not. I do also want to have a good idea of their French language achievement so far, especially because I feel this is the gateway year—if they are struggling now, chances are it will be tricky to accelerate them, but after this year, almost impossible without very intensive support. What texts do they enjoy reading? How much writing have they done? Have they acquired the basic oral vocabulary and structures of French in Kindergarten and Grade 1? I will check the assessment records

from last year and chat with previous teachers—eventually—but I want to get to know the students myself first. A simple oral activity with the whole class, where students complete the sentence "*Je m'appelle* ____ *et j'aime* ____" ("My name is ____ and I like ____") gives me a first glimpse of personality, interest, and vocabulary bank.

Room for Independence and Interdependence

I really enjoy setting up the physical environment (hands-on learner!) as early as possible. I want to make sure that we have spaces for everything we need to use or do. What will the room look like? Well, I joke about being able to tell a lot about a teacher's instructional style by the furniture arrangement, but it does tell a tale. I want to facilitate the social and collaborative processes of learning, so desks or tables will be set up to allow for small group interaction. I like to have a place we can gather as a whole group, too. There may be some students who will want to work alone at times, so planning for flexible groupings is important. I like to have "central storage" for most items, rather than having students cram and crush items in their desks. I have storage areas designed for student access: a box file for each student to store personal folders, crates of hanging file folders labelled (print and visual) for all kinds of paper and pre-printed graphic organizers (self-serve style), bins labelled for other manipulatives and materials, workstation containers, and finished-work bins. We will work together to change anything along the way if it improves our environment.

The students soon discover that they have the power to act independently—the set up is intended to support independence. Group leaders (rotating daily) are responsible for many routine tasks, such as distribution and collection of resources and work. Everything is labelled to reinforce vocabulary, nouns are always written with *un/une/des, le/la/les*. Words are posted in sentences whenever possible to reinforce structures. The bulletin boards and walls are almost bare at the start because we will need the space for student work and our reference (anchor) charts, word wall items, and other works in process. I will browse through the school book storage to find out what resources are available to suit a range of reading levels and interests, probably anywhere from a low Level 3 at the start to maybe even Level 16 for some by the end of the year. My choices will be a mix of informative and narrative texts. I will look for resources in the school library and staff room. Other books will be ones I have bought or borrowed for read alouds and student browsing. I have gathered many visuals (pictures, photos, clip art, old calendars) over time so that I have conversation starters to foster oral language and prompt writing in social studies and science. (A great book on teaching non-fiction writing K–3 with an approach that works for immersion is *Is That a Fact?* by Tony Stead (2002). I have decided that I don't need a teacher desk. I have a conference table instead. I have my own area (shelf or cupboard) where I keep manuals and resources. I make sure that curriculum documents are available.

Rules and Routines

Once the students and I have decided what our rules should be, they can be posted. We discuss what someone would see us doing if they came into the room, what it would sound like, and how we want to feel. This covers a lot of the basics such as noise levels, productive activities, and attitudinal aspects. *Dans notre salle de classe...on écoute attentivement, on parle doucement, on lit, on écrit, on n'interrompt pas, on dit "s'il te plaît" et "merci."* Icons or pictures help convey the rules. Students can sign the rules poster, as if it were a contract.

Routines for entry and transitions—any beginning, ending or change—are necessary. I use songs or music for transitions; reliable cues for predictable movement. If you have no musical talent and can't sing catchy rhymes with the students to signal cleanup or getting ready, recorded music works just fine as long as it is recognized and responded to.

Routines for workstations are about purpose. If students know what they are supposed to be doing, most potential problems are solved. Keep it simple and avoid focusing on "stuff." A basic bingo grid can have many incarnations! The materials I have on hand, such as magnetic letters and construction paper, will be adapted to different purposes. I should be able to teach the *process* involved in a literacy workstation quite simply. Once taught, the actual materials or content can vary and the students still understand what to do, especially when task cards and the task management board are supported by visuals (icons or photos of students at work).

Instructional Approaches, Assessment, Curriculum, and Realities

I have two big ideas to ponder here:

1. You've heard it so many times: gradual release of responsibility. However, what I think we miss when this becomes a buzzword are the ideas of gradual release of support, gradual handing over of responsibility when ready, gradual assumption of independence on the part of the student. There needs to be a sensible flow from teacher modelling to independent student activity in the same focus area. "I do it, we do it, you do it." There is a lot of information available on scaffolding and instructional approaches, so no excuses.
2. What is necessary for some is usually good for all. This ties in nicely with Universal Design for Learning and differentiated instruction (see *Education for All*, Expert Panel Report, Ontario Ministry of Education, 2005).

The first point emphasizes creating a balance between the curriculum (sometimes seemingly mismatched to the particular students in the class) and the realities faced by the students. We provide explicit teaching and opportunities to practise before expecting students to know or do something. Thinking of learning as a continuum allows us to work from where the student is and light the way to the next step.

Knowing the students really well is essential to making the second point work in their favour. How do they learn best? Look through the eyes of the students. Plan with a goal in mind. Then, for both learning and assessment, design multi-modal response possibilities so all can succeed. Determine all the ways that Grade 2 students can demonstrate understanding, including dramatic, musical, visual, and kinesthetic responses. This is particularly significant in second language teaching, where linguistic responses are limited. Determine who needs more time, more space, or more support. Let students know that what is important is their spirit, fire, smile, desire—however they manifest themselves. And, just as importantly, let your own passion shine!

TIPS FOR STARTING YOUR YEAR IN A PRIMARY GRADE

☑ Colleagues and Collaboration

☑ Gathering and Organizing Resources

☑ Knowing Your School Culture

☑ First-day Activities

☑ Communication with Family/Parents/Caregivers

We continue our discussion of how to prepare for primary grade teaching with a contribution from Kristen Ferguson, who has taught a range of primary grades over the past five years. She offers a list of tips covering "things she wishes she had known or had thought of in her first year of teaching."

Administrative Details

Ask the principal about required long-range plans early. They vary from board to board and can be detailed. Give yourself lots of time during the summer to work on them. Make time to talk to your principal before school starts to find out what the school norms are. What is the protocol for behaviour on yard duty? How do you do bus duty? Do you have a classroom budget and petty cash? How are supplies ordered? What is the procedure for a hot dog or pizza day? Do letters sent home by the teacher need to be read first by the principal? Where are the student records kept? Are there any children with severe medical problems or allergies? Will there be an assembly the first week of school? Make a list of all the questions you have for your principal. The principal will probably be impressed by your initiative and organization.

Elicit Parent Support

I like to send home a questionnaire for parents to complete (See Theory into Practice 15.1). I usually attach it to the class newsletter that goes home the first day of school. At the beginning of the questionnaire, I tell parents that I want to get to know their child better through their eyes. I ask them questions such as: What makes your child happy? What upsets your child? What does your child like/dislike about school? How often does your child read at home? I find this truly gives an excellent insight into a child's personality and life at home. It also tells the parent(s) that you care about the child and that you want their input.

First-Week Activities

A great way to start literacy activities with JK/SK/Grade 1 is to do lots of fun activities with the students' names. Have them on cards and spell them out, clap the letters, cheer the letters, sing the letters, sound them out, print them, paint them, sort them, add them to the word wall. It's a great way to learn the children's names and for them to learn their classmates' names.

While there is much emphasis on routines and

establishing a classroom community the first week in the primary grades, I like to delve into the curriculum, too. I spend a few days on review from the previous grade, but the students like learning and I like to get going! Pick some of the more manageable expectations and get started! Don't be afraid to do this. My first couple of years I was nervous about starting to teach the curriculum, it seemed so daunting. I found that I wasted a few valuable weeks by doing too much review that wasn't all that useful (I found this out as I ran out of time near report card deadline!).

Time Savers

Invest in a paper sorter. I bought a relatively inexpensive cardboard one from an office supply store. Give students a cubby with their name on it and it's a quick and easy way to distribute newsletters, completed worksheets to go home, etc. Students love picking up their "mail" at the end of

the day. It's also much quicker than handing back work to students at their desks. It's also a great way to ensure that students have taken home everything that they're supposed to and that things are not left in their desks.

It is important to find all of your resources and programs weeks before school starts. You need to find out which programs your school has, if any are mandated by the board, principal, etc. Resources are often spread throughout a school rather than located in one central place. It's important to remember that if the school bought the resources, equipment, texts, etc., that they don't belong to an individual teacher; they belong to the school. Even though they're stored in a specific teacher's room, they're for any teacher to use.

(Note: This is where collegial collaboration comes in—even if some teachers need a friendly reminder!)

Getting Ready for Standardized Testing

As you prepare for standardized testing (at the end of grades or divisions), it is important to understand that, as an individual teacher, you are only one member of the assessment team. Students, parents, caregivers, teachers, schools, and communities are all involved in the ongoing assessment and instruction of students. Ongoing literacy assessment (whether standardized or school-based) is essential for student learning and success. Standardized testing usually targets the areas of literacy and numeracy. In Ontario, for example, the Education Quality and Accountability Office (E.Q.A.O.) conducts provincial assessments at the end of Grade 3 and Grade 6, and at the end of the first semester in Grade 10, as well as the Ontario Secondary School Literacy Test.

Students will encounter standardized testing, often for the first time, at the end of the primary division (often Grade 3). Remember that this test is not a test of your effectiveness, but is intended to assess the students' acquisition of knowledge, skills, and strategies by the end of the primary division or selected grade. Effective school teams recognize the benefit of working together to ensure the success of their students and their literacy programs. There are several things you can do as part of a team that is committed to ensuring that every child can read and write.

- Collaborate with other teachers in your division or grade. Share the strengths and needs of your students and program. Develop common assessment and instructional practices that will support the continuum of student learning (for example, agree on a standardized printing program or a common language block that will support student mobility for guided reading groups).

- Participate in a school-wide plan for managing and keeping track of literacy assessment information. For example, agree that you will conduct running record assessments at the beginning of each term and that each student's results will be recorded in their lit-folio and passed from one grade to the next. Or keep writing samples from beginning, middle, and end of year and engage students in a review of their writing skills and strategies.

In order to learn to negotiate the format of the test or avoid its tricks and traps, it's important to use materials that closely resemble the test your children actually take (Santman, 2002, p. 209).

- Make use of practice tests. Teach students how to work with true–false, multiple choice, short answer, and problem-solving questions. Make these formats part of your day-to-day literacy program.

- Ensure that your students have extensive practice with the following reading, writing, and language for learning across the curriculum strategies and skills:

  - Listening to oral instructions
  - Following written instructions
    - Developing stamina and persistence as readers
    - Reading unfamiliar texts and applying problem-solving strategies
    - Working on their own without help
    - Completing tasks on a specific timeline
    - Using time wisely
    - Reading and understanding information
    - Writing paragraphs
    - Solving problems with several steps
    - Using language across the curriculum (for example, in math)

Students who are taught to use the framework of Retell, Relate, Reflect (Bowness & Hirsch, 2004; Swartz & Bone, 1995) score higher on written components of standardized tests, especially in the areas of problem-solving, communication, and reasoning.
Retell: Explain in your own words how…
Relate: Explain why… give examples from the text (or problem).
Reflect: Explain your thinking.

- Creating and reading charts, tables, and graphs

- Explaining their thinking

- Read through the guidebooks for standardized testing and make sure that you fully understand the process of test administration, accommodations, and exemptions.

- Don't be afraid to ask others for help. On your first time round in standardized testing, there should be plenty of support at both the school and board levels.

- Ensure that your day-to-day classroom assessment and instruction structures support effective classroom management principles, responsive and best practice instruction, and balanced and comprehensive literacy.

> - *Remain true to excellence in teaching.*
> - *Be true to sound theory and practice.*
> - *Provide students with the tools to be successful.*
> - *Help students to understand the criteria required for successful responses*
> *(Buckner, 2002; Wolf & Wolf, 2002).*

Stories from the Classroom: Junior Grades

Let's begin our consideration of how to get ready for the start of the school year with Junior level students, by looking at Terry Campbell's snapshot of a Day 1 with her Grade 4 students.

PICTURE IT! TERRY'S FIRST DAY SNAPSHOT— GRADE 4

- ☑ Creating Community
- ☑ Creating a Culture of Risk-Taking and Success
- ☑ Planning the Very First Day
- ☑ Classroom Set-up
- ☑ Student Engagement

When I taught at the elementary level, Grade 4 was my favourite because I liked the age group—9 years old, on average. One of my most important goals was to build a working community of collaborative learners. I valued creating an atmosphere of safe risk-taking and to accomplish that we all had to trust each another. The process of trusting one another and working together had to begin the first day. Forging positive relationships between me and the students, and among the students, and establishing the routines that underscore respect for one another all help to create community qualities that resonate throughout the year.

This first day was at a school in North Bay—a beautiful, early 1900s brick school with its original hardwood floors gleaming in the foyer as you entered. The students all met in the gymnasium for the principal's opening remarks, the singing of "O Canada," the introduction of the teachers, and then a roll call for each grade. Twenty-four Grade 4 children lined up behind me and I led them to the classroom I had organized so carefully in August. It was the first time I had decided to use tables instead of desks, with community bins and covered tins for supplies. Each child had a cubby for personal possessions, a box file for independent reading (two or three fiction, and at least two non-fiction materials). I had central file stands for work folders such as writing portfolios and reading logs. The bulletin boards were labelled "Art Work," "Music," "News," and "Work Committees." My desk was in the back corner, and a conference table was strategically placed near the door, with "Status of the Class" charts for Writers' Workshop, and a "Conference Sign-up" for reading. As the children entered they found their name tags on large manila envelopes, ready for them to decorate. With four very large tables, I could place six children at each table. Perfect!

To help the students get to know me, I began with a story. I told them about one of my favourite places on earth—the lower Niagara Glen beside the rushing river. I then asked them to talk to the person across from them about their own favourite place to be. We later shared these stories, orally first, and then by writing and drawing about them when I gave each of them their "Writer's Notebook," and explained what it was for (see Chapter 12). By Friday this illustrated writing had become our first bulletin board display.

We went to the carpeted area to read together the poem, "Whatif," by Shel Silverstein, printed in large letters on chart paper. This poem became a theme—Grade 4 children worry a lot, especially at the beginning of the school year. We added our own "whatifs" to Silverstein's list, using interactive writing. (*Whatif I have no friends, Whatif I get in trouble the very first recess, Whatif I hate my lunch*...they had no problem coming up with ideas). We were in the middle of adding our whatif's, when

the principal came to the door with a small 9-year-old boy. He was sobbing. He had been moved from the Grade 3–4 to my class. He didn't like changes. I'd like to say I didn't think about my perfect seating arrangements, but well, I'm not perfect. We fit him in and he stopped crying.

Later in the afternoon, I read the class Byrd Baylor's *Everybody Needs a Rock*, which lists the 10 rules for finding a perfect rock. We then went outside to find our own perfect rocks. My only rule (about the rocks) was that it had to fit easily in your hand. I'm afraid that my rules for going out were copious: lining up down the right hand side of the stairs, going outside in an orderly way (this is not the same as recess!), walking in pairs on the sidewalk, moving to the right for neighbours (especially the elderly ones), and so on. I explained that they had to be able to walk as a group in a safe, orderly way, because I had lots of exciting places to go with them this year—the public library, the arts centre, the Y, skating rinks—all within walking distance. We returned in one piece, labelled our rocks, displayed them in the Science Station, and investigated rocks and minerals later in the month. We finished our day with the traditional Irish song "Tell My Ma" (the Rankin Family version), and posted it on the Music Board.

Before they left for home, we reviewed the day and I handed out the newsletters about the exciting year ahead of us. That first day everyone went home (down the right hand side of the stairs!) smiling (some still singing). This is my favourite memory of an almost perfect first day.

Well begun is half done.

BEST PRACTICE TIPS—GRADE 5

☑ Creating a Culture of Risk-Taking and Success

☑ Establishing Routines and Expectations

☑ Classroom Set-up

☑ Assessment and Record Keeping

☑ A Balanced and Comprehensive Language Program

Anna-Marie Aquino has extensive experience at the Junior level. She currently teaches Junior/Intermediate Language Arts and Literacy in the Bachelor of Education program at Nipissing University.

Setting the Stage

It is important that you spend the first weeks of school creating the proper climate and atmosphere you wish to establish for the remainder of the year. The physical arrangement of the classroom is one that you will spend considerable time organizing, but will depend on the structure of the room, number of students, special needs, and the resources available to you.

I strongly suggest creating boxes of reading materials that meet a variety of needs. Traditional novels are often the first resource teachers acquire, but they represent only a small portion of possible materials. Magazines, especially sports and science publications, are often a good way to reach reluctant readers. Newspapers, game guide books, non-fiction texts, and comics are other excellent resources that meet a variety of interests and reading abilities. These book boxes can be used at the beginning of the year to get all students reading and can continue to be used throughout the school year.

A classroom library is also necessary and again should reflect the diversity of learners in terms of ability and interest. A variety of fiction and non-fiction materials including picture books, novels, and reference materials should provide the basis of the library. It is also important to note that diversity of culture should also be represented in the texts found in the classroom. Students should be able to see themselves reflected in the texts they are reading. Some research on your part may be necessary as these materials should be authentic in that they should be written by someone who has the authority to write from the perspective, culture, and ethnicity that they are writing about.

Best Practice Tip #1: Develop a "Today in Grade 5" Rubric

Purpose

To create a positive climate in the classroom, extend responsibility to students, develop student accountability, and develop rapport with parents.

Procedure

On the first day of school, enlist your students to collectively decide on five actions that they need to do in order to have a good day. Suggestions might include being respectful to one another, listening and responding using a positive tone and words, keeping hands and feet to oneself, completing homework assignments, and so on. These actions are criteria that form the basis of the rubric. Each of the criteria now needs a descriptor to meet each level of a 4-point rubric. For example, Level 1: rarely, never, or with assistance. Level 2: sometimes or with limited assistance. Level 3: most, usually, or almost always. Level 4: consistently, always, or thoroughly. When put on a grid, these criteria with levelled descriptors make a rubric.

Process

Make a copy of the rubric for each student and paste it in their agenda. A student agenda may take the form of a commercially prepared book or a scribbler where students record events, homework, and notes on a daily basis. The agenda should be signed daily by the teacher before students go home and then by parents before it is returned to school the next day. Each day, students record in their agendas the level they achieved for each of the criteria.

Advantages

For the teacher: You will be able to see if student opinion of classroom behaviour matches your own. If not, make sure you record your own assessment in the agenda for parents to see. In addition, parents now have a record of behaviour for each day, which can be used as the basis for further communication.

For students: Students are required to reflect on the day and take responsibility for their actions. For the parent: Parents have the opportunity to see how the day went for their child and are able to initiate a discussion about any areas of concern. It also serves as a basis for communication between school and home.

Baseline Assessments

It is critical that you take a baseline assessment of each student's reading ability early in the year. This information helps you with grouping and planning. It is difficult to plan a program if you do not know the strengths and weaknesses of each student in your class.

The baseline assessment consists of three things. First, you should conduct a reading survey with your students to determine reading behaviours. This might include asking students about the books they have read in the last couple of months and what they are currently reading; favourite books and authors; strategies used when encountering difficulties with text; and opinions of themselves as readers. Second, a running record that indicates the oral reading behaviour of each student, including phrasing and fluency, needs to be conducted. Finally, an assessment of student comprehension must be completed. This is the most important component and tells whether the student understood the material, is able to retell and recall details,

was able to make connections, and so on. A caution: a student may score very high on the running record, but low on the comprehension component. In fact, my experience has been that this is often the case. Therefore, it is not enough to conduct only the running record. The comprehension test is critical to understanding your students as readers and retrieving the data you need to identify weaknesses and identify the strategies you will need to teach.

Balanced Literacy

A good Language Arts program is one that has a balance of reading, writing, oral and visual communication, and word study opportunities, as well as the development of critical literacy skills.

Reading: A read aloud should be conducted daily and may take the form of picture books, non-fiction texts, articles, Internet sites and so on. Shared reading, guided reading, and independent reading should be used at various times throughout the week depending on your timetable. Remember that all reading components can be used in other subject areas.

Writing: A solid writing program includes modelled writing, interactive writing, guided writing, and independent writing. These too can be used in other subject areas. Students should be familiar with the writing process and the traits of writing.

Critical Literacy: Students need explicit instruction in being critical of the texts they are exposed to. At this age they are bombarded with information and persuasive advertising. They need to be able to distinguish fact from fiction, what is real, what is manipulative, and so on. Opportunities to interrogate the texts they encounter, especially on the Web, should be built into everyday learning experiences.

Oral and visual communication and word study need to be built into your program and can be addressed across the curriculum.

Best Practice Tip #2: Explicit Instruction

It is important that you begin teaching new concepts with plenty of teacher support and gradually release that support until your students can work independently. This means that, in most cases, you will have to explicitly teach new concepts by providing a model of how a strategy works and how it is to be implemented. Thinking aloud while you model a new strategy is effective and provides students with a model that demonstrates both *how* the strategy is used and *why* the strategy is used.

Meeting the Needs of All Learners

Many educators today are keenly aware of the need to address the diversity that our youngsters bring to the classroom. This diversity is manifest in many ways, including multiple cultures, ethnicity, religious beliefs, life experiences, familial relationships, socio-economic status, and so on. Students have multiple ways of knowing and reading the world around them. To address and embrace this variety, teachers must ensure that the literature and texts (print, visual, technology) represent diversity. Are all students represented in these materials?

Assessment

Equally important is the fact that if you are willing to acknowledge that children have multiple ways of knowing, then it follows naturally that children have and require multiple means of expression. By this I mean that traditional paper and pencil tasks for expressing understanding taps into only one of the many intelligences and, as a result, may be inhibiting and restricting for others. Ways to meet the variety of needs in your classroom may include, for example, using the arts, such as visual representation, drama, and dance, which can and should be used a means for allowing students to demonstrate what they know and have learned.

Conclusion

As a teacher new to Grade 5, you bring with you notions, assumptions, and understandings of what it means to be a teacher of Language Arts. These ideas come from your own lived experiences as an elementary, secondary, and university student, as a pre-service teacher, student teacher, practice teacher, and a number of other possible influences. I encourage you to embrace these understandings and use them to guide your teaching. More importantly though, I encourage and challenge you to interrogate your taken-for-granted assumptions about teaching; reflecting daily on what is and what is not working in the classroom and what your role is when there are conflicts. I challenge you to do this not only in Language Arts, but in all facets of what you do as an educator.

THE MOLDING OF AN ATTITUDE: PRE-REQUISITES FOR CLASSROOM COMMUNITIES—GRADE 6

☑ Creating Community

☑ Creating a Culture of Risk-Taking and Success

☑ Establishing Routines and Expectations

☑ Language across the Curriculum

☑ Student Engagement

Ab Falconi is currently a principal in the Simcoe District Catholic School Board. As a classroom teacher, he spent many years teaching all types of learners. His formal placements included every combination of Grade 5, Grade 6, and Grade 7.

Grade 6, in my opinion, has got to be one of the most rewarding and interesting grades to teach. With high expectations, solid routines, and a proper approach, you, as the teacher, can facilitate classes where Grade 6 students can become primary students again and enjoy Dr. Seuss books and can participate in a mature conversation about national politics. With this in mind, I will attempt to provide you with a glimpse into what allowed me to be successful with Grade 6 students.

Expectations

It is very important that the students understand that you are the teacher and that although you can be friendly, you have the final say within the classroom. It is essential that as you prepare for the school year, you establish goals and expectations. It is equally important that you develop these goals and expectations with the students in the first couple of days.

On the first morning of school, I would intentionally not have the "rules" discussion. The students are programmed to expect this and yes, they all know the answers that you want to hear. Instead, it is important to have meaningful activities set up for the students so that you can, through your plans and techniques, guide them toward success. Remember that during this initial period the students are trying to figure you out as their teacher at the same time that you are trying to figure them out as students. There is usually a "honeymoon period," which you can take advantage of if you plan for it.

As I followed my plan for that morning, I would point out the behaviours that I valued. I would not do this in the sense that I would say "I like the way that Sally is listening" to the whole class (as they would expect in a primary class), but rather I would discreetly tell Sally individually that I appreciated her attention (or whatever the expectation might be). I would say this quietly to her but just loud enough that a few students around her would hear me. This sent the signal to some of the students that I valued that behaviour. This allowed me to later call upon Sally or someone around her for a suggestion during the conversation about expectations and have a very good idea of what the reply might be.

During this discussion on expectations, I would write all the ideas on the blackboard in order to be able to draw connections between students' ideas and to come up with a maximum of three rules or expectations. I would try to get the students to come up with something such as "Respect others" as most behaviour that you will want to reinforce will fall under this expectation. The other expectations that I would try to get them to develop were "Keep your hands, feet, and objects to yourself." The students would always add in a few others like "No name calling" and "Put your hand up before answering questions." When the students know that you have high expectations and that you will consistently enforce them, they will strive to meet them.

Routines

To be successful in any grade you need to develop solid routines, but I found this to be crucial in Grade 6. When the students knew what to expect and the structures that I insisted on, they were more successful in their studies and I believe achieved better academic results. For example, I believe that when students can follow simple routines such as lining up and coming into the classroom in a straight, quiet line then they are more likely to follow a more complex routine such as listening quietly to a peer as they provide their interpretation of a piece of writing.

For my routines to be successful, I needed to plan to practice them over and over again. It is important that practising routines does not become monotonous or boring for the students. To be successful in the routines, they needed to know that I valued them and expected each student to follow them.

Establishing Community and Language across the Curriculum

As you develop the expectations and routines in the first few days of school, it is imperative that you establish a community of caring within your classroom. Grade 6 students need to know that they are all part of a classroom community and that you expect them to take care of each other.

An activity that I enjoyed using to develop expectations, routines, and community was to apply the Novel-in-a-Day strategy (see Chapter 10) to a short novel such as *Abel's Island* by William Steig. This strategy requires that students work together, take risks, discuss group successes, and build a positive classroom environment where conversations about the text were grounded in respect and sensitivity to each other's feelings. This process helped the students to see themselves as a part of a community and to value everyone's place within it.

As we discussed the chapter presentations (each chapter was acted out by a group), we would discuss what was effective about the presentation and how the next group could improve upon it. We talked about how the characters felt and how their feelings would apply to a community. We would discuss how each student in our class was an important part of our community and how each one had something to contribute.

So What?

All of this sounds great in theory. So what? My point in all of this is that without high expectations, solid routines, and a good sense of community within your Grade 6 classroom, you will not be as successful in moving your students along the literacy continuum or in any other necessary learning. In order to earn trust and foster risk taking, you will need to:

- Ensure that all students achieve success by celebrating their strengths.
- Teach that we will have individual needs and that we need to work together in order to overcome those needs.
- Ensure that all children feel safe and free to take risks in front of their peers. They need to know that no one will laugh at their efforts.
- Create an atmosphere of mutual respect within the classroom (teacher to student, student to teacher, and student to student).

BEYOND ELEMENTARY

☑ Creating Community

☑ Creating a Culture of Risk-Taking and Success

☑ Establishing Routines and Expectations

☑ Assessment and Record Keeping

☑ Communication with Family/Parents/Caregivers

Intermediate Perspectives: Things a New Teacher Should Know, but May Not Be Told in Teacher's College!

We would like to qualify this by saying that it is not that these things are neglected in teacher's college, but that many of these practices are often incidental and best learned in practice.

Andrew Boivin is another fairly recent education graduate, who offers these tips for intermediate grades.

- I send an information letter home the first week of school to open the lines of communication immediately between parents and the school. In the information letter, I introduce myself, explain my expectations for the students, the use of agendas, and so on.

- On the first day of school, I start the class photo album. I like to take pictures of the students on the first day of school then continue to take photos throughout the year of the students and their projects, of the students doing special assignments, classroom celebrations, etc. I keep the album in the classroom for students to look at. I also take photos the last few weeks of school in the same location as the first day of school. It's interesting to document special events throughout the school year as well as see their physical growth! The photos can also be digitized for a slide show for their Grade 8 graduation.

- I have a folder for each student where I keep signed tests, copies of projects and assignments, and other important information. The information is then easily accessible for parent–teacher interviews and report cards.

- An effective management tool for the intermediate grades involves the class seating plan. I ask students to confidentially submit to me the names of the people they would like to sit near as well as the area of the class they prefer (front of the class, etc.). To keep the privilege of sitting near friends, they must control their behaviour. I then create the seating plans keeping their request in mind, but I am ready to redo the seating plan if management becomes an issue. It also rewards those students who can do their work while they sit near their friends. It also lets me know which students are friends and which ones do not work well together.

- As with all grades, it is important to reinforce positive work habits in the intermediate grades. I give students a ticket (from big rolls of admission tickets) for having their agendas signed by their parents daily, completing work early, and exceeding expectations for classwork, etc. Then every two weeks, I draw tickets for small prizes. This encourages and motivates students not only to complete their work, but to complete it accurately and with care.

Initiating and Maintaining Communication with Parents, Caregivers, and Families

Implicit and explicit throughout the field notes is the need to communicate and collaborate with parents, caregivers, and families. They know their children best and, with some encouragement from you, will willingly share their awareness with you. The tips that we offer here are the same ones that were offered to us when we were beginning teachers trying to bridge the gap between home and school. Establishing home contact early and often is one of the most important things you can do to ensure your students' success. The following are the best bits of advice that we received as new teachers.

- Phone every home, and be sure to say something positive you have noticed about that student. The first call home should never be about a problem such as misbehaviour or an academic concern. Balance the negative calls home with positive calls and always start with something positive. Also consider sending a note home to parents (see Theory into Practice 15.1).

- Send a newsletter home telling parents what they can expect from you. Give them the critical information that will support you (for example, your classroom rules and routines, how to contact you) and invite their involvement from the outset. Many teachers send home weekly newsletters that provide a snapshot of the students' week. What content did they learn? What songs, stories, or poems were learned? What special events were planned? What should they know about for next week? And don't forget to make sure that there is something the child has done in the newsletter—added a border, copied their spelling words, or practised their numbers (this heightens the likelihood that the newsletter will be read!). See Theory into Practice 15.2 for a sample weekly newsletter sent to parents and caregivers of senior Kindergarten students.

- Invite parents to send in a "Note from Home." Figure 15.1 contains excerpts from a parent's note. Remember, parents love their children and know them best! Most parents welcome the opportunity to share a little personal information about their child whether it be in response to a specific question or "tell me about your child in one million words or less." Parents recognize through this contact that you are interested in their child and want to learn more about them.

- Maintain communication books for all children (this might be a homework book or commercial agenda); choose five students each day and write a quick note home to tell parents something you have learned about their child that week.

- Determine where you will store notes and reminders from parents or caregivers (find out the school policy about keeping and storing notes).

- Consider how you will accommodate a parent who wants to talk to you when you are in the middle of teaching (one teacher suggests inviting them in, tell them when you will be able to talk to them, and give them a "helping" task to do while they wait).

Theory Into Practice/15.1

A NOTE TO PARENTS

Welcome to Grade 2! This is going to be an exciting year for us as we journey into the world of reading and writing. In order to make our classroom a special place and deepen our understanding of your child's literate life outside of school, we are asking that you share some of your memories, traditions, experiences, or even pieces of literature. Your child will be invited to share these memories, traditions, experiences, and literature in class as we explore our similarities as literate beings. Throughout the year, we will be asking you to share our literacy journey—your child needs to hear your stories and your memories; needs to see you reading and writing for real purposes—this will help them understand why reading and writing are important.

- Describe any special times, spaces, and places that you have for sharing a story in your home (These may be stories read or stories told). Who does your child like to read with or to? Where do they like to read? When do they like to read? When you read with your child, what are some of the things that they do or some of the things they ask you to do? (For example, Does your child join in or ask to have the story read over and over again?)
- What was your child's favourite book? What is your favourite memory of reading this book with your child?
- What was your favourite book as a child? Have you shared that book with your child and your memories of being read to?
- Please tell me about your child's early attempts at reading and writing.
- What were your child's first words? First sentence? What is your favourite memory of something that your child said? Can you recall a story that your child loved to retell?
- Does your child like to pretend and play make-believe? Does your child tell stories to stuffed animals or to friends?
- Are there any other stories or special memories you would like to share to help us gain a better understanding of your child's language practices?

Thanks for sharing!

Sincerely,

Theory Into Practice/15.2

SENIOR KINDERGARTEN WEEKLY NEWSLETTER

The following newsletter highlights the best of the week, the skills practice, the strategies learned, and the songs and rhymes sung. It also contains a thought for the week—just for parents!

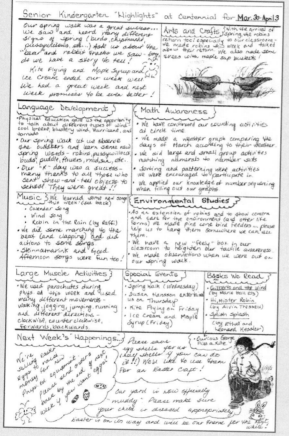

FIGURE 15.1 Excerpts from a Parent's Note

Madison is excited about school and ready to embark on the wonderful world of learning. She loves to talk, read, write, and play.

Madison started to talk at a very young age. Her first words were "mama" and "dada." She has always been very articulate; it seems that she went from words to sentences overnight. Her vocabulary is extensive and she sometimes says things that you would not expect to hear from a three-year-old. She has been heard to tell her brother not to do something because it is dangerous or to tell her dad that she is confused. Her sense of humour is highly developed and she loves to tease anyone who will laugh and have fun with her.

Our special time for reading is primarily before bed—we usually snuggle up on a blue wingback chair in our living room or in my daughter's bed. Madison likes to read with just about anyone who is willing but particularly with her mom and dad. She likes to read all the time. When we read, Madison looks at the pictures and talks about what the story is about. Sometimes she will ask to have the same stories read over and over again; it is always a relief when someone comes to visit and they can take a turn reading the same book I've read hundreds of times (or so it seems!).

Madison's favourite book is *If You Take a Mouse to School* by Laura Numeroff. My favourite memory of reading with Madison is at the age of two when she sat and told me the story word for word. We had read the book to her so often that she had memorized it and could recite it word for word. Imagine our surprise when she offered to read to us!

Madison loves to pretend and make believe. She especially enjoys being a princess or a fairy as you can see in the picture I've attached. I quite frequently hear her talking to her dolls and stuffed animals and taking care of her "babies." She loves to read her doggies and babies stories once she goes to bed at night and most nights, I go in and re-shelve the books that she has read on her way to sleep. I know she will have as much fun with books, pretend, and make-believe at school as she has had at home. Thank you for the opportunity to tell you about my daughter.

Catch 'em Being Great! Michelann's Plan for Managing the Classroom

Following is a list of my favourite "tried and true" strategies to manage a classroom and create a culture of risk-taking and success. Regardless of which grade your find yourself teaching you'll need a range of proactive strategies. You will note that I have made reference to strategies that were either explicitly discussed throughout this book or were implicit in many of the strategies and approaches we have presented.

- To begin, one of the most important lessons we can teach our students stems from the phrase, "What is fair is not always equal!" This is a tough concept for students, but can be easily accomplished with a few pointed statements: Would it be fair for a student not to have glasses if they were needed? What if someone needed a hearing aid? Students are capable of understanding the concept that our classroom is a fair classroom, it is a place where we all get what we need to succeed, and sometimes that is not equal!

What is fair is not always equal!

The continuum of support that we have described provides multiple entry points and fosters a culture of success—all students get what they need to be successful because it is naturally built into our language program.

- Select teaching/learning strategies that support student independence and responsibility. By focusing on personal bests, creating manageable chunks of information, incorporating explicit instruction, using areas of learner strength, planning learning opportunities that are relevant, meaningful, realistic, and appropriate to individual student needs, providing opportunities for guided and independent practice, supporting at key times, believing in students, and never giving them more than we think they can handle, we are celebrating individual difference and demonstrating our belief that *all* learners can be successful.

Never give students more than you think they can handle!

Open-ended activities, tapping into multiple intelligences, multi-literacies, and learning styles demonstrate our belief in the potential of learners.

- To foster a culture of risk-taking, your students need to understand that "mistakes are our friends." "I can't" should be put to rest and they should instead look forward to "having a go." Providing students with alternative phrasings such as "This looks tricky but…" gives them a positive statement rather than a negative one. A favourite activity that students find great fun is the creation of both "I can't" statements and "I can't" poems. Once these have been drafted, students collect them and then put them away until the end of the year. On the last day of school, they can return to their box and see what they accomplished that they thought they couldn't.

Accentuate the positive!

The power of positive thinking is critical in language and literacy. Students who think they can't, likely won't feel comfortable to take a risk.

- Make sure that you reward the behaviour and not the student: Avoid phrases such as "Good boy, good girl"; use "I like how you solved that word. That is impressive." Phrases such as these provide an explicit response to what the students did well; and it is likely they will try it again. Provide appropriate praise and positive reinforcement, but don't overdo it! Ensure that your students feel believed in, trusted, listened to, cared for, and important in both life and literacy!

Catch 'em doing great things!

Strategy instruction, mini-lessons that are responsive to learner needs, and just-in-time instruction target both behaviours that require support and those we want to reinforce.

- Expectations for behaviour and consequences must be made explicit. You can do this by brainstorming codes of conduct or classroom contracts; developing levels of behaviour, privilege, or intervention systems; posting explicit examples of effective and ineffective behaviour; posting strategies for students to manage their own behaviour; or engaging them in goal setting and behaviour plans. Ensure that the expectations for behaviour and learning are respectful of your students' unique strengths and needs and that the consequences for behaviour are respectful of individual students, teachers, and the classroom community. When you plan your expectations, ask yourself who is in control of the behaviour—you or the student?

Do make your expectations explicit!

Helping students to understand who they are as literacy learners and to recognize their own ways of being in the world, explicitly talking about strategies, and helping students to share their own strategies is making expectations for literacy behaviour explicit; behaviour management is therefore a natural extension.

- For students who struggle with behaviour below the "average," provide legitimate and limited choices that create win-win situations for both you and the student. "You can do Task A or Task B—either one is fine with me, or you can choose your order." Students who have some choice in their program and some negotiation are more likely to be engaged as they feel a sense of ownership, power, and control of their learning. Make sure that students understand the cyclical nature of choice, decision, behaviour, and consequence.

Provide legitimate and limited choices! Create win-win situations!

Be positive! Be fair! Be consistent! Be respectful! Be a guide!

Providing multiple intelligence response options, building in time for discussion, ensuring adequate rehearsal for writing, and planning guided and mini-lesson approaches all provide opportunities for students to make choices.

One Final Summary

The stories presented in this chapter show significant reflection and thought on the part of the writers. Each teacher considered the optimal conditions for language learning (Cambourne, 2000, 2001) in conjunction with the needs of their learners, the requirements of the curriculum, and their school culture. We began this book with a description of our goals for you as literacy learners. We conclude with a list of theoretical principles that should underpin your goals for your own learners.

Literacy learners need to:

- participate in a language and literacy program that meets their diverse individual needs

- understand the purposes of literacy so they can fully appreciate and enjoy literacy in their lives

- be actively involved in their own literacy learning

- read, listen to, and view high quality children's literature to develop story sense, appreciate diverse cultures and ways of life, and learn how to adopt multiple perspectives

- hear written language (stories and informational texts) so they can learn its structures and take in new information and ideas

- learn the conventions of print and how books work so they can use this knowledge as readers and writers

- develop a wide range of strategies to enhance comprehension and the enjoyment of reading and writing

- play with language: to enjoy and manipulate the sounds of language, to attend to the relations between sounds and letter and word patterns, and to use this knowledge as a tool in developing oral language, and developing as readers and writers

- explore words and learn how words work so they can use this information effectively and efficiently in reading and writing

- have many experiences working with written symbols so they can learn how to look at letters and use this information to read and write

- be assessed both in "standard" ways and in ways that reflect "multiple ways of knowing"

Theory into Practice 15.3 presents a detailed summary of a balanced and comprehensive program that is grounded in what students need, what literacy teachers should think about, and how you can begin on Day 1 with meaningful and authentic learning opportunities. We have referred you to previous concepts, strategies, theories, and models discussed throughout the book. These are the connections that we see. Because you come to this task with your own perspective and your own experiences, your connections may be different. Feel free to revise to fit who you are as a literacy learner and a literacy teacher.

Theory Into Practice/15.3

THE RECURSIVE SPIRAL OF NEED, REFLECTION, AND PRACTICE

Theory Students need:	Reflection Literacy teachers should think about how to:	Classroom Practice Create meaningful and authentic opportunities for students to engage in:
A language and literacy program that meets their diverse individual needs (Chapters 1 & 2)	• Conceptualize "literacy" and what it means to become a fully literate being	• Multiple ways of displaying literacy learning using the six language arts and optimal conditions for literacy learning
To understand the purposes of literacy so they can fully appreciate and enjoy literacy in their lives (Chapters 1–3)	• Help literacy learners understand the importance and power of words and why learning to read and write matters in the real world	• Discussions about books and films; guest presenters who read and write for real-life purposes and talk about literacy in their lives • Literacy practices for real-life purposes, for example, letter writing, current events
To be actively involved in their own literacy learning (All chapters)	• Scaffold new learning from students' experiences/interests • Build in student choice and responsibility • Ensure that students have sufficient choice, time, resources, and opportunities for sharing and self-assessment	• Classroom activities that celebrate individual differences and connect literacy to their personal experiences • Making appropriate and limited choices about the work they undertake as literacy learners (for example, purpose, audience)
To read, listen to, and view high-quality children's literature to develop story sense, appreciate diverse cultures and ways of life, and learn how to assume multiple perspectives (Chapter 6)	• Important it is for developing readers and writers to understand entire forms and structures rather than just "bits"	• Read alouds and exposure to continuous text everyday with think alouds that focus on analysis of story structure, critical thinking, critical literacy
To hear written language (stories and information texts) so they can learn its structures and take in new information and ideas (Chapter 4)	• Help learners become familiar with grammar and syntax not always heard in everyday speech	• Lessons about unusual language structures (for example, games that use phrases such as "Once upon a time") • Read alouds each day
To learn the conventions of print and how books work so they can use this knowledge as readers and writers (Chapters 4, 8, 9)	• Build in awareness of the key concepts about print throughout the school day using a variety of contexts and strategies appropriate for emergent readers/writers	• Explicit instruction about conventions of print (for example, concepts about print, visual features and print lay-outs, glossaries, and indexes)

THE RECURSIVE SPIRAL OF NEED, REFLECTION, AND PRACTICE (continued)

Theory **Students need:**	Reflection **Literacy teachers should think about how to:**	Classroom Practice **Create meaningful and authentic opportunities for students to engage in:**
To develop a wide range of strategies to enhance comprehension and the enjoyment of reading and writing (Chapters 5–12)	• Foster this development through scaffolding, fluency, and flexibility	• Opportunities for repeated readings of familiar texts, choral reading, drama, U.S.S.R., readers' and writers' workshops
Opportunities to play with language: to enjoy and manipulate the sounds of language, to attend to the relations between sounds and letter and word patterns, and to use this knowledge as a tool in developing oral language, and developing as readers and writers (Chapters 4 & 5)	• Engage literacy learners in meaningful and authentic opportunities to hear and say sounds in natural conversations • Develop phonemic and phono-logical awareness through oral activities and games	• Opportunities to repeat and expand phrases and sentences in everyday classroom conversation, so they can hear them over and over, and become confident in their ability to hear and say sounds (phonemic awareness)
To explore words and learn how words work so they can use this information effectively and efficiently in reading and writing (Chapters 8 & 9)	• Help literacy learners make connections from personal knowledge to build a wide network of understandings • Create and implement a powerful word study program	• Word work, word walls, word games, vocabulary building, word study
To have many experiences working with written symbols so they can learn how to look at letters and use this information to read and write (Chapters 8–12)	• Help literacy learners notice and recognize that letters are the building blocks for words, sentences, and stories	• Opportunities to differentiate between shapes, pictorial objects, and letters • Proper letter formation in Primary manuscript printing and Junior cursive writing
To be assessed both in "standard" ways and in ways that reflect "multiple ways of knowing" (Chapters 7–14)	• Ensure that assessment reflects the fact that literacy can be demonstrated in many ways	• Continual "literacy" assessment during daily language blocks and across the curriculum

Source: Adapted and revised from Pinnell & Fountas (1998, p. 3).

Moving On

As you journey forward, remember that it is the journey itself, not the destination, that is worth striving for. The process that you have undergone to this point is one that will likely continue for years to come as you engage in literacy acts, practices, and rituals as a student, a teacher, and a member of a literacy community. Our best advice is to keep your mind and your heart open to the reciprocal nature of teaching and learning, and strive to learn something new each and every day.

The connections made by good teachers are held not in their methods but in their hearts—meaning heart in the ancient sense, as the place where intellect and emotion and spirit and will converge in the human self.
—Parker J. Palmer

LIT-FOLIO UPDATE

We expect that by this point in your reading and in your development as a teacher, you have collected a variety of evidence that demonstrates your knowledge, skill, and values as both a literacy learner and a literacy teacher. You may still be in the process stages, but you are well situated to begin to select evidence that best represents your teaching self and your awareness of your self as a literacy learner.

It is now time to polish and get ready to share the very best of you. As you decide on the final format for your presentation lit-folio, envision that your philosophy reflects what you believe about literacy. Ensure that your lit-folio introduction, reflection, and table of contents reflects what you know about literacy teaching, and that the evidence you include reflects what you can effectively do in practice.

Resources to Support Your Learning

Booth, D. (ed.). (1996). *Literacy techniques for building successful readers and writers.* Markham, ON: Pembroke Publishers.

Clay, M. (2000). *Running records for classroom teachers.* Portsmouth, NH: Heinemann.

Fountas, I., & Pinnell, G.S. (2001). *Guiding readers and writers: Grades 3-6.* Portsmouth, NH: Heinemann.

Lundy, K. G. (2004). *What do I do about the kid who…?*
50 ways to turn teaching into learning. Markham, ON: Pembroke Publishers.

Schwartz, S., & Pollishuke, M. (2005). *Creating the dynamic classroom.* Toronto, ON: Pearson Education.

Stead, T. (2002). *Is that a fact? Teaching nonfiction writing K-3.* Portland, ME: Stenhouse Publishers.

Trehearne, M. (2000). *Kindergarten teacher's resource book.* Scarborough, ON: Nelson Thomson Learning.

Trehearne, M. (2004). *Grade 1-2 teacher's resource book.* Scarborough, ON: Nelson Thomson Learning.

Glossary

Aesthetic stance When a reader is primarily concerned with becoming actively involved in a text, for example, when a reader lives vicariously through the characters. One of two poles on a continuum; the other is efferent stance (Rosenblatt, 1978).

Approximation When a student makes an attempt at a task and does not get it quite right, but makes more successful attempts; each new effort builds on what has been learned in previous attempts and is then modified through self-correction usually in interaction with an expert.

At risk A term applied by teachers and other professionals to describe students who must strive or struggle to develop full literacy, for example, ESL students and students with emotional and behavioural difficulties.

Attention Determines the amount and type of information that the student can extract from a text. Student may focus on individual letters and words, text structures, and other types of information.

Audience The person(s) for whom the student is writing. The piece must anticipate the readers' need for information and maintain their interest.

Audit trails, **historical trails**, and **learning walls** Ways track of touchstone texts encountered and lessons learned throughout the year. Students participate in the selection of evidence that best represents their inquiry.

Automaticity Performing a task with little attention necessary; the reader engages a range of strategies without explicit attention to the underlying processes. It is closely tied to fluency. Both require fast processing and flexible use of strategies.

Balanced literacy A literacy program that includes:

• reading, writing, speaking, listening, viewing, and representing

• shifts in responsibility from teacher to student in modelling, sharing, guiding, and independent classroom work

• skills and strategy instruction and integration of learning in authentic contexts of reading and writing across subject areas

Bloom's taxonomy (cognitive domain) A hierarchical classification of educational objectives, progressing from knowledge and memory to comprehension, application, analysis, synthesis, and evaluation (Bloom et al., 1956).

Browsing boxes Colour coded storage boxes to organize books by reading level; each colour representing a reading level.

Cambourne's model of literacy learning: A set of conditions for literacy learning based on features of the learning environment that make oral language learning possible.

Choral reading/speaking Reading or recitation of a poem or short passage by the entire class, in unison, or in parts.

Cloze passages A test to determine a student's reading level. Words (usually every fifth word) are deleted from a 250- to 300-word prose passage and the reader is required to fill in the blanks. The test measures a student's ability to use context to construct meaning.

Comprehension strategies Instructional techniques that help readers find meaning in texts. For example, by confirming or rejecting inferences, predictions, or conclusions based on textual information, and confirming understanding by re-reading.

Concepts about print The key concepts relating to how language is represented in print that an emerging reader must understand in order to learn to read and write. For example, directionality, and the concepts of a letter, a word, and a sentence.

Conditions of literacy learning Characteristics of the classroom environment arranged by the teacher to optimize language learning.

Constructivist learning theory Students actively create knowledge of the world around them by connecting what they already know or have previously experienced with what they are learning.

Critical inquiry Questioning texts and identifying the multi-level transactions between the reader (consumer of text), the author (creator of text), the text, and the reading community.

Critical literacy An awareness of issues beyond literal interpretations of texts, including analysis of what is present and what is missing, and evaluation of social justice, fairness, and equity.

Cueing systems The four systems (semantic, grapho-phonemic, syntactic, and pragmatic) that are part of every language. Used by teachers to support students' different methods of developing literacy.

Discourse Communication through language, which is largely influenced by our ways of being in the world.

Early literacy The stage of development (approximately Grades 1 to 2) in which the reader begins to rely less on pictures; becomes more aware of and pays attention to print; knows high-frequency words; has some fluency; and composes written messages using words copied from the environment—some known words, some phonetically spelled.

Efferent stance When a reader is primarily concerned with acquiring information from text. One of two poles on a continuum; the other is aesthetic stance (Rosenblatt, 1978).

Elkonin boxes A way to help students understand phonemes and sound/symbol correspondence. Each phoneme (single sound) in the word is printed in a separate box. For examples: f/r/ie/n/d

ELD (English Language Development) ELD students have delayed language development because they have had "limited access to schooling and have significant gaps in their education," due to a variety of circumstances (Ontario Ministry of Education, 2001).

Emergent literacy The stage of development in young children (approximately pre-school to early Grade 1) in which an awareness of and interest in writing and books develops. Children tell stories using "book language" and write down approximations of words and messages as they begin to link their own oral language to print.

Engagement Reading, writing, speaking, and listening characterized by intrinsic motivation and total involvement and enjoyment in those activities for their own sake.

ESL (English as a Second Language) learners Students for whom English is a second language and who have little or no fluency in English.

Expository genre Text written to inform readers, provide new information, or clarify details on a topic that is somewhat unfamiliar.

Expressive genre Text written to describe the writer's personal thoughts and feelings, often in the first person.

Fix-up strategies Alternate reading comprehension monitoring strategies used when the purpose for reading is not being met or when the text is not making sense to the reader; for example, correcting a word by checking the picture.

Fluency Fast processing in which the student recognizes words and spelling patterns quickly and automatically and so is able to focus on the meaning. Student uses context and structure to make predictions and checks ensure what is read makes sense, sounds right, and matches the print. Fluency requires a bank of known words that can be accessed automatically.

Found poetry Quotes, phrases, and words from a variety of genres, texts, and formats are manipulated and combined to create a poem.

Functions of language Halliday identified seven purposes of language: instrumental, regulatory, heuristic, interactional, personal, imaginative, and representative (Halliday, 1973, 1975, 1993).

Genres Categories of literature having distinct forms and functions.

Good talk Conversations and dialogues characterized by honesty, fairness, and caring collaboration.

Gradual release of responsibility The incremental adjustment from a high level of teacher support to a high level of student independence as the teacher gradually hands over responsibility for learning to the student.

Grand conversation An aesthetic discussion of literature to make meaning and interpret stories through conversation with co-readers.

Grapheme The smallest part of a word that represents a phoneme (a single sound). For example, p/l/ay.

Graphic organizers Visual aids used to organize textual information. For example, story maps, KWL, and before-and-after charts.

Grapho-phonemic cues The visual cues that help readers decode the words using their knowledge of letter-sound relationships, word patterns, word families, and sight words.

Guided reading A small-group approach to reading instruction based on the principles of Reading Recovery® designed by Marie Clay (1993). The teacher supports students as they develop the skills and strategies that will help them to become independent and flexible readers.

Guided writing A method of writing instruction in which the teacher teaches small, temporary groups of students the strategies and skills they need at that particular time.

High-frequency words The 100, 200, and 300 most common words in the English language.

Hybridity A characteristic of meaning-making that requires the producer and consumer of text to creatively merge, connect, and activate prior knowledge related to texts, culture, and personal experience.

Independent literacy Readers are able to read on their own for informational, recreational, and aesthetic purposes.

Independent writing Students engage in guided practice and are supported by the structures of a writers' workshop, where they write as part of a community of authors sharing their writing.

Instructional level One of three levels determined by the percentage of errors the student makes when reading a text sample: 90% to 95% accuracy – text matches student's reading level and is at student's instructional level; 95% or more – text is too easy; 90% or less – text is too difficult.

Interactive writing Teachers and students compose and create a text together by sharing the composing and recording processes.

Intertextuality A characteristic of meaning-making that refers to the complex relationships that emerge or are created between text

and other modes of meanings, real or imaginary, print, media, or otherwise (New London Group, 2000). When readers make these "text-to-text" connections they enhance their meaning-making processes.

KWL What do I **K**now? What do I **W**ant to know? What did I **L**earn? By answering these questions (usually in a chart) students activate prior knowledge and become engaged with text.

Language experience approach A method of early literacy instruction in which the student dictates what he/she wants to say, the teacher writes this down, and the student then reads the text. This approach combines speaking, listening, reading, and writing in such a way that they reinforce each other.

Literacy The ability to read, write, speak, listen, view, represent, and think critically about ideas by understanding and using language in diverse ways.

Literacy centres Permanent or temporary work stations equipped with task cards for independent practice of a previously introduced reading or writing strategy.

Literature circles Groups that are formed to discuss student-selected books. Each student adopts a role in the group according to specific guidelines and keeps written records, including a self-assessment checklist (Harvey, 2002).

Literary conversations Discussions held by the entire class community about major ideas such as themes, genres, and textual connections.

Literacy-enriched play centre A play area equipped with familiar reading and writing materials (Owocki, 2001).

Literacy story The construction of a narrative that outlines an individual's literacy and learning development.

Literacy works-in-process Items in a process lit-folio that represent the process one has undergone as a literacy learner and as a developing literacy teacher.

Lit-folio See Presentation lit-folio and Process lit-folio.

Matthew effect Describes the relationship between active engagement in reading and reader development. By actively engaging in reading, effective readers develop the characteristics that make them skilled, life-long readers (Stanovich, 1986).

Metacognition The process of thinking about one's own thought processes and so being able to be responsible for one's own learning.

Metalinguistic awareness Recognizing the phonological, syntactic, and semantic tasks involved in the acquisition of language.

Meta-talk A form of metacognition whereby students talk about their own talk processes and articulate how they learn through talking.

Mini-lessons Brief, teacher-directed lessons designed to practise or review a particular strategy or skill, usually within the context of readers' or writers' workshops.

Modelled reading A method of support in which the teacher reads texts aloud that are at the difficulty level of the students. Often the teacher will also think aloud while reading to demonstrate the components of the reading process.

Modelled writing A method of support in which the teacher models and thinks aloud about the writing process while composing a text.

Multiple intelligences Howard Gardner's (1987, 1999) psychological and educational theory asserting eight forms of knowing, learning, and performing: linguistic, logical-mathematical, musical, bodily-kinesthetic, spatial, interpersonal, intrapersonal, and naturalist.

Multiliteracies The diversity of learners, classrooms, schools, and contexts, and recognitions that there is no one conceptualization of literacy, no one right way, or best time or place to teach literacy. (New London Group, 2001).

Multimodal An integration of the five literacies—linguistic, audio, visual, spatial, gestural—in meaningful, authentic, and real-life activities.

Multiple ways of knowing Alternate or non-traditional methods and paths for learning and for showing what one has learned. For example, demonstrating new knowledge by dramatizing or drawing.

Orality Verbal language used in communication through the activities of listening and speaking. Literacy integrates listening, speaking, reading, writing, viewing, and representing.

Orthography Correct or conventional spelling of words. Initially this involves an understanding of phonics, but as students become more competent word-solvers, it will also require an understanding of how words work (root words, prefixes, suffixes, etc.).

Poetic writing Primarily fictional writing used as an art medium, for example, stories, plays, songs, poems, word play.

Phoneme The smallest unit of sound in a word. For example, a single or several letters (ph/o/t/o/g/r/a/ph).

Phonemic awareness The ability to identify and use the smallest units of sound in a word.

Phonological awareness Students study phonemes, as well as parts of language such as words, syllables, and rhymes to understand the sound systems.

Phonological cueing system The sound patterns in language and how they combine.

Phonics A method of instruction in which the student learns the relationships between the components of written language (graphemes) and the individual sounds of spoken language (phonemes).

Pragmatics A system of understanding how discourse must be adapted to fit specific contexts. It is applied when using language for specific purposes for designated audiences.

Presentation lit-folio The product and final representation of who one is as a literacy learner and a literacy teacher.

Process lit-folio A collection of items that represent the process one has undergone as a literacy learner and a developing literacy teacher.

Quick writes A writing strategy that allows ideas to flow and voice to develop. Writers focus on content without concern for conventions of spelling or grammar. They write brief, free responses to a specific prompt.

Read alouds Part of the first level in the continuum of support from modelled to independent reading. The teacher reads aloud to the class to show enjoyment of literature, to model intonation, expression, pronunciation, and comprehension strategies for both story and content texts.

Reader response An activity or strategy focusing on the reader's personal response (in written, oral, or visual form) to a reading experience, including feelings, thoughts, images, and memories (Rosenblatt, 1978). Although the focus is on the reader, the teacher provides instruction to stimulate revisiting and refining initial responses.

Readers' theatre A group of readers prepares and performs a script, usually with one or two narrators and several characters. Students use their voices to convey the meaning of the tale. The exercise helps to develop collaborative group work skills, literary appreciation, confidence in oral language ability, reading fluency, and increased vocabulary through repetition.

Real discussion A classroom dialogue on a student-selected question or problem that relates to an event that the whole class or a small group of students has participated in. Members of the group contribute equally.

Reciprocity The principle of interdependence between the processes involved in learning to read and learning to write.

Recursive learning A learning strategy that focuses on repeating or returning to previous learning in order to build new learning.

Representing Communicating meanings in nonverbal forms, such as visual art, diagrams, charts, multimedia performances, and drama.

Retell, relate, reflect A response format used to develop different levels of comprehension. Students retell a story or informational passage in their own words, relate what they have read to their own experiences, and *reflect* on meanings and possibilities (Schwartz & Bone, 1995).

Re-vision Critically viewing the past and present and imagining a different future. It implies reconstructing education, using informed theory to guide new pedagogical practices, and fundamentally restructuring educational institutions (Kellner, 2004).

Rime The part of a syllable that contains the vowel and all that follows it (for example, *at* in *cat*; *oy* in toy *or ew* in new). Rimes are smaller than syllables but larger than phonemes.

Role-playing Taking on the part of a character or representing a point of view, such as that of an 'expert.'

Rubric A scale used to score performance, according to a set of criteria or descriptors for each level of achievement (usually 3–4 levels) from least to most proficient.

Running records A systematic method of recording and analyzing a student's ability to read accurately for meaning, developed by Marie Clay.

Scaffolding A metaphor for the temporary support and guidance provided for students as they acquire skills and understandings. It stays in place until their skills and knowledge become self-supporting.

Schema (*pl.* **schemata**) Organizing principle, such as a rule, script, or concept based on a learner's prior knowledge.

Self-extending literacy The stage of development (approximately Grade 3 and up) where the student uses sources of information flexibly, solves problems independently, reads a wide range of texts, reads for meaning, reads longer more complex texts in a variety of genres, and uses conventional spelling.

Semantic cueing system The meanings of individual words and how words can be combined to make meaning in a given context. To develop semantic awareness, students need many opportunities to develop vocabulary and learn the features of language, such as poetic and story sense, through listening, speaking, reading, and writing activities.

Shared reading An expert reader and developing reader read together. This allows the developing reader to integrate story sense and extend control over language.

Shared writing Teachers and students collaborate to compose a text. The teacher acts as scribe.

Socio-cultural learning theory Students construct understandings and interpretations primarily through interaction with others. Learning is a social process that reflects the community and culture in which the students learn and live (Gee, 1990; Heath, 1983; Vygotsky, 1978, 1986).

Sound blending The combination of two or three sounds to form a word. For example, /c//a//t/ to form 'cat.'

Sound isolation Isolating individual sounds in words (being able to identify sounds at the beginning, middle, or end of a word, for example, /t/ is the end sound of cat).

Sound matching Matching words to corresponding sounds. For example, cat is the word that starts with the sound /c/.

Sound segmentation Separating the sounds of a word into its beginning, middle, and end sounds. For example, brown can be broken down into three sounds /br/ /ow/ /n/. Elkonin boxes may be used to teach sound segmentation.

Sound substitution Isolating one sound and substituting a different sound to make a new word. For example, changing 'cat' to 'hat.'

Strategic supports Scaffolding new learning by activating prior knowledge and talking to students about the purposes and functions of literacy.

Story drama Students dramatize or enact a story in a variety of ways after they have read or listened to the story and discussed it.

Story map Graphically plotting the structure (such as beginning, middle and end) and elements of a story (such as setting, characters, events, and theme).

Story sense Understanding the structure and elements of narratives.

Storytelling The art of orally recounting events in narrative form, such as real-life anecdotes or fictional tales.

Student portfolio An organized, systematic collection of student work, usually used for self-assessment and teacher evaluation of progress over time in reading and writing.

Subtext strategy A natural extension of think alouds but focuses directly on the thoughts, feelings, and emotions of characters. This strategy enables students to make personal connections to text, develop inferring skills, empathize with characters, and understand multiple perspectives.

Suffix A syllable added to the end of a word to form a derivative. For example, ic in historic means of *history*.

Syntactic cueing system The grammar or structure of a language. It determines word order, tense, and inflection.

Tableau Frozen action shot or picture created by a group of students performing in statue-like form. The tableau represents the fundamental nature of a significant moment in the action of a story.

Temporary spelling Words spelled using letter-sound and word pattern knowledge to approximate conventional spellings; sometimes called "invented" or "phonetic" spelling.

Think alouds A method of instruction that demystifies the comprehension process by making in-the-head thinking while reading, explicit and visible to students so that they have a framework for thinking and a common language for talking about books.

Thinkmarks Bookmarks inserted by readers to mark passages requiring problem-solving strategies. The reader's thinking is recorded on the bookmark.

Touchstone texts (Calkins, 1994) Texts that are read on multiple occasions for multiple purposes over time. They are texts that are returned to over and over again, and become part of the classroom community's collective history (Laman, 2005).

Transactional writing A descriptive, argumentative, or expository mode of writing, for example, information essays, reports, lists, instructions, recipes, and letters.

Transitional literacy The stage of development (approximately Grades 2 to 3) when the student uses multiple sources of information and cues when reading; possesses a large core of frequently used words; notices, but does not need pictures; reads fluently; has the ability to read longer, more complex texts; uses some invented, phonetic spelling in writing.

Voice A writer's unique style, expressed through diction, tone, syntax, and awareness of audience.

Word plays Using drama to learn the parts of speech. Students make words and sentences come to life by acting out sentences and displaying cards with words and their parts of speech.

W.O.R.L.D. view A comprehensive and balanced view of literacy drawing on literacy research about **W**ords, **O**rality, **R**e-vision, **L**iteracies, and **D**iscourses

Writers' workshop Collaborative group in which students write independently, explore the texts of their lives, and discuss their writing with peers.

Writing conference Student and teacher read and discuss the student's writing and react, reinforce strategies, ask questions, and evaluate progress toward previous goals and set new ones.

Writing process/cycle The recursive stages of writing: prewriting/rehearsal, drafting, revising, editing, and publishing/sharing/polishing.

Zone of proximal development A learner's instructional range, connecting what is already known or was previously experienced with what is being learned. This determines the level of support received from the teacher (Vygotsky, 1978).

References

A

Aaron, P. G., Joshi, M., & Williams, K.A. (1999). Not all reading disabilities are alike. *Journal of Learning Disabilities, 32*(2), 120-138.

Adams, M.J. (1990). *Beginning to read: Thinking and learning about print.* Cambridge, MA: MIT Press.

Adams, M.J. (1998). The three-cueing system. In F. Lehr & J. Osborn (Eds.), *Literacy for all: issues in teaching and learning* (pp. 73-99). New York: Guilford Press.

Alexander, P.A., & Fox, E. (2004). A historical perspective on reading research and practice. In R. Ruddell & N. Unrau (Eds.), *Theoretical models and processes of reading* (5th ed., pp. 33-68). Newark, DE: International Reading Association.

Allington, R. (2001, 2006). *What really matters for struggling readers.* Boston, MA: Pearson.

Almasi, J.F. (1995). The nature of fourth graders' sociocognitive conflicts in peer-led and teacher led discussions of literature. *Reading Research Quarterly, 30,* 314-351.

Almasi, J.F., & Gambrell, L.B. (1997). Conflict during classroom discussions can be a good thing. In J. Paratore & R. McCormack (Eds.), *Peer talk in the classroom: Learning from research* (130-155). Newark, DE: International Reading Association.

Almasi, J., Garas, K., & Shanahan, L. (in press). Qualitative research and the report of the National Reading Panel: No methodology left behind. *Elementary School Journal.*

Almasi, J., O'Flahavan, J., & Arya, P. (2001). A comparative analysis of student and teacher development in more and less proficient discussions of literature. *Reading Research Quarterly, 36*(2), 96-120.

Alvermann, D.E. (1996), Peer-led discussions: Whose interests are served? *Journal of Adolescent and Adult Literacy, 39*(4), 282-289.

Alvermann, D.E., & Eakle, A.J. (2003). Comprehension instruction: Adolescents and their multiple literacies. In A.P. Sweet & C.E. Snow (Eds.) *Rethinking reading comprehension* (pp. 12-29). New York: Guilford Press.

Alvermann, D.E., O'Brien, D.G., & Dillon, D.R. (1990). What teachers do when they say they're having discussions of content area reading assignments: A qualitative analysis. *Reading Research Quarterly, 25*(4), 296-322.

Anderson, J. & Gunderson, L. (1997) Literacy learning from a multicultural perspective. *The Reading Teacher,* 50, 514-516.

Anderson, R.C. (1994). Role of the reader's schema in comprehension, learning, and memory. In R. Ruddell, M.R. Ruddell, & H. Singer (Eds.), *Theoretical models and processes of reading* (4th ed., pp. 469-495). Newark, DE: International Reading Association.

Anderson-Inman, L., & Horney, M. (1998). Transforming text for at-risk readers. In D. Reinking, M. McKenna, L. Labbo, & R. Kieffer. (Eds.), *Handbook of literacy and technology: Transformations in a post-typographic world* (pp. 15-44). Mahwah, NJ: Lawrence Erlbaum.

Anthony, H.M., & Raphael, T.E. (1989). Using questioning strategies to promote students' active comprehension of content area material. In D. Lapp, J. Flood, & N. Farnan (Eds.), *Content area reading and learning: Instructional strategies.* Englewood Cliffs, NJ: Prentice Hall.

Applegate, A.J., & Applegate, M.D. (2004). The Peter effect: Reading habits and attitudes of preservice teachers. *The Reading Teacher,* 57(6), 554-563.

Armstrong, T. (1994). Multiple intelligences: Seven ways to approach curriculum. *Educational Leadership,* 52(3), 26-28.

Atwell, N. (1987). *In the middle: Writing, reading, and learning with adolescents.* Portsmouth, NH: Boynton/Cook.

Atwell, N. (1998). *In the middle: New understandings about writing, reading, and learning.* Portsmouth, NH: Heinemann.

B

Bakhtin, M.M. (1986). Response to a question from the *Novy Mir* Editorial Staff. In *Speech genres and other essays,* (pp. 1-9). Trans. V. W. McGee. E. C. Emerson & M. Holquist. Austin, TX: University of Texas Press, 1986.

Banaszewski, T.(1999). Poetic Surfing: How I used a focused Internet search to keep students on the crest of a wave. *Learning & Leading with Technology,* 26(4), 20-21.

Barnes, D. (1993). Supporting exploratory talk for learning. In K. Pierce & C. Gilles (Ed.), *Cycles of meaning: exploring the potential of talk in learning communities.* (pp. 17-34). Portsmouth, NH: Heinemann.

Barrs, M., & Pidgeon, S. (Eds.). (1998) *Boys and reading.* London: Centre for Language in Primary Education.

Barton, B. (1992) *Stories to tell.* Markham, ON: Pembroke Publishers.

Barton B., & Booth, D. (1990) *Stories in the classroom.* Markham, ON: Pembroke Publishers.

Bear, D. R., Invernizzi, M., Templeton, S., & Johnston, F. (2004). *Words their way: Word study for phonics, vocabulary and spelling instruction.* Upper Saddle River, NJ: Pearson/Merrill Prentice Hall.

Beck, I., & McKeown, M. (2002). Questioning the author: Making sense of social studies. *Educational Leadership, 60* (3), 44-47.

Beck, I., McKeown, M., Hamilton, R., & Kucan, L. (1997) *Questioning the author: An approach for enhancing student engagement with text.* Newark, DE: International Reading Association.

Beers, K. (2003). *When kids can't read: What teachers can do.* Portsmouth, NH: Heinemann.

Bellanca, J., Chapman, C., & Swartz, E. (1997). *Multiple assessments for multiple intelligences* (3rd ed.). Arlington, Heights, IL: Allyn & Bacon Skylight.

Berger, A. A. (1989). *Seeing is believing: An introduction to visual communication.* Mountain View, CA: Mayfield.

Bettelheim, B. (1976). *The uses of enchantment.* New York: Alfred Knopf.

Birdseye, T. (1993). *Just call me stupid.* New York: Holiday House.

Block, C.C., & Israel, S.E. (2004). The abc's of performing highly effective think-alouds. *The Reading Teacher, (58)* 2, 154-167.

Block, C.C., & Mangieri, J.N. (2005). *Powerful vocabulary for reading success, grades 3–6.* New York: Scholastic.

Bloom B. S. (1956). *Taxonomy of educational objectives, Handbook I: The cognitive domain.* New York: David McKay.

Bogdan, D. (1992). *Re-educating the imagination: Toward a poetics, politics, and pedagogy of literary engagement.* Portsmouth, NH: Heinemann.

Bogdan, D., Cunningham, E.J., & Davis, H.E. (2000). Reintegrating sensibility: Situated knowledges and embodied readers. *New Literary History, 31,* 477-507.

Bogdan, D., & Straw, S. (Eds.). (1993). *Constructive reading: teaching: Beyond communication.* Portsmouth NH: Boynton/Cook.

Bomer, R. (2006). Reading with the mind's ear: Listening to text as a mental action, *Journal of Adolescent and Adult Literacy,* 49(6), 524-538.

Boomer, G. (1993). How to make a teacher. *English Education,* 25(1), 3-18.

Booth, D. (1993). *Doctor Knickerbocker and other rhymes: a Canadian collection selected by David Booth.* Toronto, ON: Kids Can Press.

Booth, D. (1994). *Story drama: Reading, writing, and role-playing across the curriculum.* Markham, ON: Pembroke Publishers.

Booth, D. (1996). *Literacy techniques for building successful readers and writers.* Markham, ON: Pembroke Publishers.

Booth, D. (1998). *Guiding the reading process: Techniques and strategies for successful instruction in K-8 classrooms.* Markham, ON: Pembroke Publishers.

Booth, D. (2001). *Reading and writing in the middle years.* Markham, ON: Pembroke Publishers.

Booth, D. (2002a). *Story drama.* Markham, ON: Pembroke Publishers.

Booth, D. (2002b). *Even hockey players read: Boys, literacy and learning.* Markham, ON: Pembroke Publishers.

Booth, D. (2002c). The deep end of the pool. *Orbit Magazine,* 32(3), 56

Booth D. (2005) *Story drama: Creating stories through role playing, improvising, and reading aloud.* (2nd ed.). Markham, ON: Pembroke.

Booth, D., & Barton, B., (2000) *Story works: How teachers can use shared stories in the new curriculum,* Markham ON: Pembroke Publishers.

Booth, D. & Lundy, C. J. (1985). *Improvisation: Learning through drama.* Toronto, ON: Harcourt Brace Jovanovich.

Booth, D., & Moore, B. (2003). *Poems please! Sharing poetry with children.* Markham, ON: Pembroke Publishers.

Booth, D., & Swartz, L. (2004). *Literacy techniques for building successful readers and writers* (2nd ed.). Markham, ON: Pembroke Publishers.

Bosman, A. M. T., & Van Orden, G. C. (1997). Why spelling is more difficult than reading. C. A. Perfetti, L. Rieben, &M. Fayol (Eds.), *Learning to spell* (pp. 173–194). Mahwah, NJ: Erlbaum.

Bourdieu, P., & Passeron, J. C. (1977). *Reproduction in education, society, and culture.* London: Sage.

Bowness, R., & Hirsch, D. (2004). Beyond the test: Practical strategies for student success. Workshop presented at Checkmark 2004, Nipissing University, North Bay, Ontario.

Braunger, J., & Lewis, J. (2006). *Building a knowledge base in reading,* (2nd ed.). Urbana, IL: National Council of Teachers of English.

Bressler, D., & Siegel, M. (2000). Portfolios as literacy conversations among parents, teachers, and children: Collaboration, negotiation, and conflict. In M.A. Gallago & S. Hollingsworth (Eds.), *What counts as literacy: Challenging the school standard* (pp. 153-172). New York: Teachers College Press.

Britton, J. (1970). *Language and learning.* Markham, ON: Penguin.

Bruner, J. (1983). *Child's talk: Learning to use language,* New York: Norton.

Bruner, J. (1986). *Actual minds, possible worlds.* Cambridge, MA: Harvard University Press.

Bryant, P.E., & Bradley, L. (1985). *Children's reading problems.* Oxford, UK: Basil Blackwell Ltd.

Buckner, A. (2002). Teaching in a world focused on testing. *Language Arts,* 79(3), 212-215.

C

Cadiero-Kaplan, K. (2002). Literacy ideologies: Critically engaging the language arts curriculum. *Language Arts,* 79(5), 372-381.

Calkins, L. (1986, 1994). *The art of teaching writing.* Portsmouth, NH: Heinemann.

Calkins, L. (2001). *The art of teaching reading.* New York: Longman (Addison-Wesley).

Calkins, L. & Harwayne, S. (1990). *Living between the lines.* Portsmouth, NH: Heinemann.

Cambourne, B. (1988). *The whole story: Natural learning and the acquisition of literacy in the classroom.* Gosford, AU: Ashton Scholastic.

Cambourne, B. (1995). Toward an educationally relevant theory of literacy learning: Twenty years of inquiry. *The Reading Teacher,* 49(3), 182-190.

Cambourne, B. (2000/2001). Conditions for literacy learning: Turning learning theory into classroom instruction: A minicase study. *The Reading Teacher,* 54(4), 414-417.

Cambourne, B. (2002). The conditions of learning: Is learning natural? *The Reading Teacher,* 55(8), 758-762.

Camp, D. (2000). It takes two: Teaching with twin texts of fact and fiction. *The Reading Teacher,* 53(5), 400-408.

Campbell, D.M, Cignetti, P.B., Melenyzer, B.J, Nettles, D.H., & Wyman, R.M. (2001). *How to develop a professional portfolio: A manual for teachers* (2nd ed.). Boston, MA: Allyn & Bacon.

Campbell, L., Campbell, B., & Dickinson, D. (2004). *Teaching and learning through multiple intelligences* (3rd ed.). Boston, MA: Pearson Education.

Campbell, T. (2005). Good talk about great literature: Addressing the problem of subjectivity in moral education. Unpublished Ph.D. dissertation, University of Toronto.

Canadian Education Association. (2004). *Policy brief: The promise and problem of literacy for Canada: An agenda for action.* Toronto, ON: Canadian Education Association.

Carbo, M. (1987). Deprogramming reading failure: Giving unequal learners an equal chance. *Phi Delta Kappan,* Spring, 197-202.

Cazden, C.B. (1988). *Classroom discourse: The language of teaching and learning.* Portsmouth, NH: Heinemann.

Cazden, C.B. (1992).*Whole language plus.* New York: Teacher's College Press.

Center for Media Literacy. (2002/2003). How to analyze an advertisement: Finding ads' hidden messages, Retrieved February 21, 2006, from http://www.medialit.org/reading_room/article 227.html.

Center for Media Literacy (2003). Teacher's/Leader's Orientation Guide. Santa Monica, CA: Center for Media Literacy.

Center on English Learning and Achievement. (2001). Participating in classroom dialogue helps struggling readers. Retrieved April, 2005 from http://cela.albany.edu/newslet/spring01/struggling.htm.

Chall, J. (1989) *Learning to Read: The Great Debate 20 Years Later - A Response to 'Debunking the Great Phonics Myth'.* Phi Delta Kappan, 70 (7), 521-538.

Chall, J. (2000). *The academic achievement challenge: What really works in the classroom?* New York, NY: Guilford Press.

Chomsky, N. (1975). Reflections on language. New York: Random House.

Clandinin, D.J. (1990). Learning to live new stories of practice: Restorying teacher education. *Phenomenology and Pedagogy,* 9, 70-79.

Clandinin, D.J. (1991). Narrative and story in teacher education. In T. Russell & H. Munby, (Eds.), *Teachers and teaching: From classroom to reflection* (pp. 124-137). London, UK: Falmer Press.

Clark, B. (1997). *Growing up gifted.* Upper Saddle River, NJ: Prentice Hall.

Clark, K.F., & Graves, M.F. (2004). Scaffolding students' comprehension of texts. *The Reading Teacher,* 58(6), 570-580.

Clarke, L.W. (2005). "A stereotype is something you listen to music on": Navigating a critical curriculum. *Language* Arts, 83(2), 147-157.

Clay, M. (1975). *What did I write?* Portsmouth, NH: Heinemann.

Clay, M. (1979). *Reading: The patterning of complex behaviour.* London, UK: Heinemann.

Clay, M. (1985). *The early detection of reading difficulties,* (3rd ed.) Auckland, NZ: Heinemann.

Clay, M. (1993a). *Reading Recovery: A guidebook for teachers in training.* Portsmouth, NH: Heinemann.

Clay, M. (1993b) *An observation survey of early literacy achievement.* Portsmouth, NH: Heinemann.

Clay, M. (1994). Foreword. In R. Ruddell, M.R. Ruddell, & H. Singer (Eds.), *Theoretical models and processes of reading* (4th ed., pp. ix-xiii). Newark, DE: International Reading Association.

Clay, M. (1998). *By different paths to common outcomes.* York, ME: Stenhouse.

Clay, M. (2000a), *Concepts about print: What have children learned about the way we print language?* Portsmouth, NH: Heinemann.

Clay, M. (2000b). *Running records for classroom teachers.* Portsmouth, NH: Heinemann.

Clay, M. (2001). *Change over time in children's literacy development.* Portsmouth, NH: Heinemann.

Clay, M. (2004). Talking, reading, and writing. *Journal of Reading Recovery,* 3(2), 1-15.

Close, E., Hull, M., & Langer, J. A. (2005). Writing and reading relationships in literacy learning: Theory and research in practice. In R. Indrisano & J. R. Paratore (Eds.), *Learning to write, writing to learn* (pp.176-193). Newark, DE: International Reading Association.

Clyde, J.A. (2003). Stepping inside the story world: The subtext strategy: A tool for connecting and comprehending. *The Reading Teacher,* 57(2), 150-160.

Collins Block, C. (2001). *Teaching the language arts: Expanding thinking through student-centered instruction* (2nd ed.). Boston, MA: Allyn & Bacon.

Collins Block, C. (2003). *Literacy difficulties: Diagnosis and instruction for reading specialists and classroom teachers,* (2nd ed.) Boston, MA: Allyn & Bacon.

Collins, J., & Blot, R.K. (2003). *Literacy and literacies: Texts, power, and identity.* Cambridge, UK: Cambridge University Press.

Cooper, K. (2002) Teaching struggling readers through the arts. *Orbit,* 32(3), 35-36.

Cornett, C.E., & Smithrim, K.L. (2001). *The arts as meaning makers:*

Integrating literature and the arts throughout the curriculum. (Canadian ed.) Toronto, ON: Prentice-Hall.

Culbertson, H. (2000/2001). *Top ten ways to listen to lectures.* Bethany, OK: South Nazarene University. Retrieved April 19, 2006 from, http://home.snu.edu/~HCULBERT/listen.htm.

Cunningham, P.M. (1995). *Phonics they use.* New York: Harper Collins.

Cunningham, P. M., & Allington, R. (2003, 2006). *Classrooms that work: they can all read and write.* Boston, MA: Pearson.

D

Damico, J.S. (2005). Evoking hearts and heads: Exploring issues of social justice through poetry. *Language Arts,* 83(2), 137-146.

D'Agostino, J.V., & Murphy, J. (2004). A meta-analysis of reading recovery in United States schools. *Educational Evaluation and Policy Analysis,* 26, 23-38.

Daniels, H. (2002). *Literature circles: Voice and choice in book clubs and reading groups.* York, ME: Stenhouse.

Datnow, A., & Hubbard, L. (2004). Single-sex public schooling: Lessons from California's experiment. *Orbit,* 34(1), 9.

Davis, J. (2002). Five important ideas to teach your kids about TV. *Center for Media Literacy,* Retrieved February 21, 2006 from http://www.medialit.org/reading_room/article 52.html.

Day, J.P., Spiegel, D.L., McLellan, J., & Brown, V.B. (2002). *Moving forward with literature circles.* New York: Scholastic.

De Castell, S., Luke, A., & MacLennan, D. (1986). On defining literacy. In S. de Castell, A. Luke, & K. Egan (Eds.). *Literacy, schooling, and society: A reader* (pp. 3-14). London, UK: Cambridge University Press.

Delpit, L. (1990). Language diversity and learning. In S. Hynds and D. Rubin (Eds.), *Perspectives on talk and learning* (pp. 247-266). Urbana, IL: National Council of Teachers of English.

Diller, D. (2005). *Practice with purpose: literacy work stations for Grades 3-6.* Markham, ON: Pembroke Publishers.

Department of Education, Tasmania (Retrieved February 8, 2006, from http://www.education.tas.gov.au/english/critlit.htm).

Dressel, J.H. (1990). The effects of listening to and discussing different qualities of children's literature on the narrative writing of fifth graders. *Research in the Teaching of English,* 24(4), 397-414.

Duncan, B. (2006). Quoted in Approaches to Media Education, Media Awareness Network, Retrieved February 5, 2006, from http://www.media-awareness.ca/english/teachers/media_literacy/media_ed_approaches.cfm.

Durkin, D. (2004). *Teaching them to read,* (6th ed.) Boston, MA: Pearson Education.

Dymock, S. (1993). Reading but not understanding. *Journal of Reading,* 37, 86-89.

Dyson, A. H. (1999). Transforming transfer: Unruly children, contrary texts, and the persistence of the educational order. *Review of Research in Education,* 24, 473-489.

E

Eeds, M., Wells, D. (1989). Grand Conversations: An exploration of meaning construction in literature study groups. *Research in the Teaching of English,* 23, 4-29.

Egan, K. (1988). *Primary understanding: Education in early childhood.* New York: Routledge.

Egan, K. (2001). *Working Paper No. 5: Cognitive tools and the acquisition of literacy.* Montreal, PQ: Centre for Literacy of Quebec. Retrieved March 3, 2005, from: http://www.nald.ca/litcent.htm.

Eisner, E. (1978). *Reading, the arts, and the creation of meaning.* Reston,VA: National Art Education Association.

Eisner, E. (2002). *The arts and the creation of mind.* New Haven, CT: Yale University Press.

Ellis, C., & Bochner, A. (2000). Autoethnography, personal narrative, reflexivity: Researcher as subject. In N. Denzin & Y. Lincoln (Eds.), *The handbook of qualitative research* (2nd ed.) (pp. 733-768). Newbury Park, CA: Sage.

Evans, K. (1997). Exploring the complexities of peer-led literature discussions: The influence of gender. In J.R. Paratore & R.L.McCormack (Eds.), *Peer talk in the classroom: Learning from research,* (pp. 156-175). Newark, DE: International Reading Association.

F

Feldman, C.F. (1991). Oral metalanguage. In D.R. Torrance & N. Olson, (Eds.), *Literacy and orality* (pp. 47-65). Cambridge, UK: Cambridge University Press.

Fletcher, R, (1993). *What a writer needs.* Portsmouth: Heinemann.

Fletcher, R. (1996) *Breathing in breathing out: Keeping a writer's notebook.* Portsmouth, NH: Heinemann.

Ford, M. P., & Opitz , M. F. (2002). Using centers to engage children during guided reading time: Intensifying learning experiences away from the teacher. *The Reading Teacher,* 55(8), 710-717.

Foucault, M. (1988). *Politics, philosophy, culture: Interviews and other writings 1977-1984* In L. D. Kritzman, (Ed.)., & A. Sheridan et al. (Trans.). New York: Routledge.

Fountas, I.C., & Pinnell, G.S.. (1996). *Guided reading: Good first teaching for all children.* Portsmouth, NH: Heinemann.

Fountas, I.C., & Pinnell, G.S. (1998). *Word matters.* Portsmouth, NH: Heinemann.

Fountas, I.C., & Pinnell, G.S. (1999). Matching books to readers: Using leveled books in guided reading K-3. Portsmouth, NH: Heinemann.

Fountas, I., & Pinnell, G.S. (2001). *Guiding readers and writers: Grades 3-6.* Portsmouth, NH: Heinemann.

Freebody, P., & A. Luke (1990). Literacies programs: Debates and demands in cultural context. *Prospect,* 5(7), 7-16.

Freedman, A. (1993). Show and tell? The role of explicit teaching in the learning of new genres. *Research in the teaching of English* 27 (3): 222–251.

Freedman, L. (1997). Teacher talk: The role of the teacher in literature discussion groups. In K.M. Pierce & C.J. Gilles (Eds.), *Cycles of Meaning: Exploring the potential of talk in learning communities.* Portsmouth, NH: Heinemann.

Freire, P., & Macedo, D. (1987). *Literacy: Reading the word and the world.* Boston, MA: Bergin and Garvey.

Froese-Germain, B. (2004). Are schools really short changing boys? Reality check on the new gender gap. *Orbit,* 34(1), 3-6.

Frye, N. (1963). *The Educated Imagination.* Toronto, ON: CBC Publications.

Frye, N. (1988). Criticism as education. The Leland B. Jacobs Lecture. In *On education.* Markham, ON: Fitzhenry & Whiteside.

Fu, D., & Lamme, L. (2002) Assessment through conversation, *Language Arts,* 79(3). 241-250.

Fulford, R. (1999). *The triumph of narrative: Storytelling in the age of mass culture.* Toronto, ON: House of Anansi Press.

G

Galda, L., & Cullinan, B. (2003) Literature for literacy: What research says about the benefits of using trade books in the classroom. In M. Kamil, P.D. Pearson, & R. Barr (Eds.), *Handbook of reading research: Volume 3.* Newark, DE: International Reading Association.

Galeano, E. (1988). In defense of the word. In R. Simenonson & S. Walker (Eds.) *Multi-cultural literacy* (pp. 113-125). Saint Paul, MN: Graywolf Press.

Gallagher, K. (2000). *Drama education in the lives of girls: Imagining possibilities.* Toronto, ON: University of Toronto Press.

Gallagher, K. (2002). Drama builds content and relationships: Learning through the arts can significantly enhance learning experiences. *Orbit,* 32(3), 27-30. Gardner, H. (1987). *Frames of mind.* New York: Basic Books.

Gambrell, L.B. (1996). Creating classroom cultures that foster reading motivation. *The Reading Teacher, 50* (1), 14-25.

Gambrell, L.B., Morrow, L.M., & Pennington, C. (2000). Early childhood and elementary literature-based instruction: Current perspectives and special issues. *Reading Online.* Retrieved March 16, 2006, from http://readingonline.org/articles/art_index.asp?HREF=handbook/gambrell/index.html.

Ganske, K. (2000). *Word journeys: Assessment-guided phonics, spelling, and vocabulary instruction.* New York: The Guilford Press.

Gardner, H. (1991). *The unschooled mind: How children think and how schools should teach.* New York,: Basic Books.

Gardner, H. (1993). Multiple intelligences: The theory in practice. New York: Basic Books.

Gardner, H. (1995). Reflections on multiple intelligences: Myths and messages. *Phi Delta Kappan, 77*(3), 200-208.

Gardner, H. (1999a) *Intelligence reframed: Multiple intelligences for the 21st century.* New York: Basic Books.

Gardner, H. (1999b). *The disciplined mind: Beyond facts and standardized tests: The K-12 education that every child deserves.* New York: Simon and Schuster.

Gardner, H., & Boix-Mansilla, V. (1994). Teaching for understanding within and across the disciplines. *Educational Leadership, 51*(5), 14-18.

Garey, S. (2002). Brands R us: How advertising works. *Center for Media Literacy,* Retrieved February 21, 2006, from http://www.medialit.org/reading_room/article50.html.

Gee, J.P. (1990). *Social linguistics and literacy: Ideology in discourses.* Basingstoke, UK: Falmer Press.

Gee, J.P. (2001). Reading as situated language: A sociocognitive perspective. *Journal of Adolescent and Adult Literacy, 44*(8), 714-725.

Gee, J.P. (2004). *Situated language and learning: A critique of traditional schooling.* New York: Routledge.

Gee, J.P. (2005). The classroom of popular culture: What video games can teach us about making students want to learn. *Harvard Education Letter,* Retrieved February 22, 2006, from http://www.edletter.org/current/gee.shtml.

Gerbner, G. (2002). Society's storyteller: How TV creates the myths by which we live. *Center for Media Literacy,* Retrieved February 21, 2006, from http://www.medialit.org/reading_room/article 439.html.

Gitlin, A. (1995). Teacher education: What is good teaching and how do we teach people to be good teachers? In J. L. Kincheloe & S. Steinberg (Eds.), *Thirteen questions: Reframing education's conversation.* (2nd ed., pp. 111-120). New York: Peter Lang.

Goatley, V.J., & Raphael, T.E. (1992). Non-traditional learners' written and dialogic response to literature. In J. Zutell & S. McCormick (Eds.), *The fortieth yearbook of the National Reading Conference* (pp. 313-322). Chicago, IL: National Reading Conference.

Goodman, K.S. (1968). The psycholinguistic nature of the reading process. In K.S. Goodman, *The psycholinguistic nature of the reading process,* (pp. 13-26). Detroit, MI: Wayne State University Press.

Goodman, K.S. (1987). Acquiring literacy is natural: Who skilled Cock Robin? *Theory into Practice, 26,* 368-373.

Goodman, K.S., & Goodman, Y. (1983). Reading and writing relationships: Pragmatic functions. *Language Arts, 60*(5), 590-99.

Goodman, K.S., & Goodman, Y. (1988). *The whole language evaluation book.* Portsmouth, NH: Heinemann.

Goody, J., & Watt, I. (1968). The consequences of literacy. In J. Goody (Ed.), *Literacy in traditional societies* (pp. 27-68). London, UK: Cambridge University Press.

Goswami, U., & Bryant, P. (1990). *Phonological skills and learning to read.* East Sussex, UK: Lawrence Erlbaum Associates Ltd.

Gough, P.B. (1985). One second of reading: Postscript. In R.B. Ruddell & N. J. Unrau (Eds.), *Theoretical models and processes of reading* (5th ed., pp. 1180-1181). Newark, DE: International Reading Association.

Graesser, A.C., McNamara, D.S., Louwerse, M.M. (2003). What do readers need to learn in order to process coherence relations in narrative and expository text? In A.P. Sweet, & C.E. Snow (Eds.) *Rethinking reading comprehension* (pp. 82-98). New York: Guilford Press.

Graff, H. (1981). *Literacy and social development in the west.* Cambridge, UK: Cambridge University Press.

Graff, H. (1987). *The labyrinth of literacy: Reflections on literacy past and present.* London, UK: Falmer Press.

Graves, D. (1983). *Writing: Teachers and children at work.* Exeter, NH: Heinemann.

Graves, D. (1990). *Discover your own literacy.* Toronto, ON: Irwin Publishing.

Graves, D. (1994). *A fresh look at writing.* Portsmouth, NH: Heinemann

Graves, D., & Kittle, P. (2005). *Inside writing.* Portsmouth, NH: Heinemann.

Graves, D., & Sunstein, B. (1992). *Portfolio portraits.* Portsmouth, NH: Heinemann.

Greene, M. (2000 [1995]). *Releasing the imagination: Essays on education, the arts, and social change.* San Francisco, CA: Jossey-Bass.

Guthrie, J.T. (2001, March). Contexts for engagement and motivation in reading. *Reading Online, 4*(8). Retrieved December 29, 2005, from http://www.readingonline.org/articles/art_index.asp?HREF=/articles/handbook/guthrie/index.html.

Guthrie, J.T. (2004). Teaching for literacy engagement. *Journal of Literacy Research, 36*(1), 1-28.

Guthrie, J.T., & Wigfield, A. (2000). Engagement and motivation in reading. In M.L. Kamil, P.B. Mosenthal, P.D. Pearson, & R. Barr (Eds.), *Handbook of reading research: Volume III* (pp. 403-422). New York: Erlbaum.

H

Hadaway, N.L. & Young, T.A. (2006). Changing classrooms: transforming instruction. In T.A. Young, & N.L. Hadaway (Eds.), *Supporting the Literacy Development of English Learners: Increasing Success in All Classrooms.* Newark, DE: International Reading Association.

Hall, N. (1998). Real literacy in a school setting: Five-year-olds take on the world. *The Reading Teacher, 52,* 8-17.

Halliday, M.A.K. (1969) Relevant models of language, *Educational Review, 22* (1), 26-37.

Halliday, M.A.K. (1975a). *Explorations in the functions of language.* New York: Methuen.

Halliday, M.A.K. (1975b) *Learning how to mean.* New York: Elsevier.

Halliday, M.A.K. (1993). Towards a language-based theory of learning. *Linguistics and Education, 5*(2), 93-116.

Hansen, J. (1992). Literacy portfolios: Helping students know themselves. *Educational Leadership,* May, 66-68.

Hargreaves, A., & Fullan, M. (1998). *What's worth fighting for out there?* Toronto, ON: Ontario Public School Teachers' Federation.

Harste, J.C. (1994). The sign systems. In R. Ruddell & H. Singer (Eds.) *Theoretical models and processes of reading* (4th ed.)(pp. 1220-1242). Newark, DE: International Reading Association.

Harste, J.C., Leland, C., Schmidt, K. Vasquez, V., & Oceipka, A. (2004). Practice makes practice, or does it? The relationship between theory and practice in teacher education. *Reading Online:* January/February 2004. Retrieved from www.readingonline.org; January 20, 2006, 2:17 pm.

Harste, J. C., Short, K.G., Burke, C.L. (1988). *Creating classrooms for authors: The reading writing connection.* Portsmouth, NH: Heinemann.

Harwayne, S. (2001). *Writing through childhood: Rethinking process and product.* Portsmouth, NH: Heinemann.

Harwayne, S., & Calkins, L. (1987). *The writing workshop: A world of difference.* Portsmouth, NH: Heinemann.

Havelock, E. (1991). The oral-literate equation: A formula for the modern mind. In D. R. Torrance & N. Olson (Eds.). *Literacy and orality* (pp. 11-27). Cambridge, UK: Cambridge University Press.

Harvey, S., & Goudvis, A. (2000) *Strategies that work: Teaching comprehension to enhance understanding.* Markham, ON: Pembroke Publishers.

Heath, S.B. (1983). *Ways with words: Language, life, and work in communities and classrooms.* New York,: Cambridge University Press.

Heath, S.B. (2004). Learning language and strategic thinking through the arts. *Reading Research Quarterly, 39*(3), 338-342.

Heathcote, D. (1984). *Dorothy Heathcote: Collected Writings,* London, UK: Hutchison.

Heffernan, L. (2004). *Critical literacy and writers' workshop: Bring purpose and passion to student writing.* Newark, DE: International Reading Association.

Heilbrun, C. (1988). *Writing a woman's life.* New York: Norton.

Hillocks, G., Jr., & Smith, M. W. (1991). Grammar and usage. In J. Flood, J. M. Jensen, D. Lapp, & J. R. Squire (Eds.), Handbook of research on teaching the English language arts (pp. 591-603). New York: Macmillan.

Hirsch, E.D. Jr. (2003). Reading comprehension requires knowledge of words and the world: Specific insights into the fourth-grade slump and the nation's stagnant comprehension scores. *American Educator,* Spring, 10-29.

Holdaway, D. (1979). *The foundations of literacy.* Gosford, NSW: Ashton Scholastic.

Hornsby, D. (2000), *A closer look at guided reading.* Victoria, AU: Eleanor Curtain Publishers.

Huck, C., Hepler, S., Hickman, J., and Kiefer, B.Z. (2004). *Children's literature in the elementary school.* (8th ed.) Dubuque, IA: McGraw-Hill.

I

Illich, I. (1973). *Tools for conviviality.* New York: Harper & Row.

Indrisano, R., & Paratore, J. (Eds.) (2005). *Learning to write and writing to learn: Theory and research in practice.* Newark, DE: International Reading Association.

International Reading Association. (2000). Excellent reading teachers: A position statement. *The Reading Teacher,* 54(2), 235-239.

J

Jackson, F. (1994). Seven strategies to support a culturally responsive pedagogy. In M. Opitz (Ed.) (1998). *Literacy instruction for culturally and linguistically diverse students.* Newark, DE: International Reading Association pp. 57-63.

Jennings, L.B., & O'Keefe, T. (2002). Parents and children inquiring together: Written conversations about social justice. *Language* Arts, 79(5), 404-414.

Johnson, H., & Freedman, L. (2005). *Developing critical awareness at the middle level: Using texts as tools for critique and pleasure.* Newark, DE: International Reading Association.

Juel, C. (1991). Beginning reading. In R. Barr, M.L. Kamil, P.B. Mosenthal, & P. D. Pearson (Eds.), Handbook of reading research (Vol. 2, pp. 759-788). New York: Longman.

Juel, C., Griffith, P.L., & Gough, P.B. (1986). Acquisition of literacy: A longitudinal study of children in first and second grade. *Journal of Educational Psychology, 78,* 243-255.

Just, M.A., & Carpenter, P.A. (1980). A theory of reading: From eye fixations to comprehension. In R.B. Ruddell & N. J. Unrau (Eds.), *Theoretical models and processes of reading* (5th ed., pp. 1182-1218). Newark, DE: International Reading Association.

K

Kamil, M.L. (2004). Vocabulary and comprehension instruction. In P. McCardle & V. Chhabra (Eds.), *The voice of evidence in reading research,* (pp. 213-234). Portsmouth, NH: Heinemann.

Keene, E.O., & Zimmerman, S. (1997). *Mosaic of thought: Teaching comprehension in a readers' workshop.* Portsmouth, NH: Heinemann.

Kellner, K. (2004). Technological transformation, multiple literacies, and the re-visioning of education. *E-Learning,* 1(1), 9-37.

Ketch, A. (2005). Conversation: The comprehension connection. *The Reading Teacher,* 59(12), 8-13.

Kintsch, W. (2004). The construction-integration model of text comprehension and its implications for instruction. In R.B. Ruddell & N. J. Unrau (Eds.) *Theoretical models and processes of reading* (5th ed.) (pp. 1270-1328). Newark, DE: International Reading Association.

Kogawa, J. (1990). Where there's a wall. *More than words can say: Personal perspectives on literacy.* Toronto: McClelland & Stewart.

Kudar, S., & Hasit, C. (2002). *Enhancing literacy for all students.* Boston, MA: Pearson.

L

Laman, T.T. (2006). Changing our minds/Changing the world: The power of a question. *Language Arts,* 83(3), 203-214.

Langer, J.A. & Flihan, S. (2000). Writing and reading relationships: Constructive tasks. In R. Indrisano & J. Squire (Eds.), *Perspectives in writing: Research, theory and practice* (pp. 112–129). Newark, DE: International Reading Association.

Lankshear, C.K., & Knobel, M. (1998). New times! Old ways? In F. Christie & R. Misson (Eds.), *Literacy and schooling* (pp. 155-177). New York: Routledge.

Lankshear, C., & Lawler, M. (1987). *Literacy, schooling, and revolution.* London, UK: Falmer Press.

Lazar, A. M. (2004). *Learning to be literacy teachers in urban schools: Stories of growth and change.* Newark, DE: International Reading Association.

Leland, C., Harste, J., & Helt, C. (2000). Multiple ways of knowing: Lessons from a blue guitar In M.A. Gallago & S. Hollingsworth (Eds.), *What counts as literacy: Challenging the school standard* (pp. 106-117). New York: Teachers College Press.

Leland, C., Harste, J., & Huber, K.R. (2005). Out of the box: Critical literacy in a first-grade classroom. *Language* Arts, 82(4), 257-268.

Lemke, J.L. (1998). Metamedia literacy: Transforming meanings and media. In D. Reinking, M.C. McKenna, L. Labbo, & R.D. Kieffer (Eds.), *Handbook of literacy and technology: Transformations in a post-typographic world* (pp. 283-302.). Mahwah, NJ: Lawrence Erlbaum.

Lewison, M., Flint, A.S., & Van Sluys, K. (2002). Taking on critical literacy: The journey of newcomers and novices. *Language* Arts, 79(5), 382-392.

Livingston, N., & Kurkjian, C. (2005). Circles and celebrations: Learning about other cultures through literature. *The Reading Teacher,* 58(7), 696–703.

Lonsdale, M., & McCurry, D. (2004). *Literacy in the new millennium.* Adelaide, AU: Department of Education, Science, and Training, Commonwealth of Australia. (Retrieved, February 25, 2005, from http://www.ncver.edu.au).

Luke, A., & Freebody, P. (1999). Further notes on the four resources model. *Reading Online.* Retrieved January 20, 2005, from http://readingonline.org/past/past_index.asp?HREF=../resarch/lukefreebody.html

Lundstrom, M. (2004). Media-savvy kids. *Instructor,* 114(4), 16-21.

Lundy, K.G. (2004) *What do I do about the kid who…?: 50 ways to turn teaching into learning.* Markham, ON: Pembroke Publishers.

Luongo Orlando, K. (2001). *A project approach to language learning.* Markham, ON: Pembroke Publishers.

M

Manning, M., & Manning, G. (1994). Managing literacy portfolios. *Teaching Pre-K-8,* 24(7), 84-86.

Many, J.E., & Wiseman, D.L. (1992). The effect of teaching approach on third grade students' response to literature. *Journal of Reading Behavior,* 24, 265-287.

McGee, L.M. (1992). Exploring the literature-based reading revolution (Focus on research). *Language Arts, 69,* 529-537.

McKeown, M.G., Beck, I.L., & Worthy, M.J. (1993). Grappling with text ideas: Questioning the author. *The Reading Teacher.* 46, 560-566. McLaughlin, M., & Allen, M.B. (2002). *Guided comprehension: A teaching model for Grades 3-8.* Newark, DE: International Reading Association.

McLaughlin, M., & DeVoogd, G. (2004). Critical literacy as comprehension: Expanding reader response. *Journal of Adolescent and Adult Literacy,* 48(1), 52-62.

McLaughlin, M., & Vogt, M. (1996). *Portfolios in teacher education.* Newark, DE: International Reading Association.

McMahon, S.I., Raphael, T.E., with Goatley, V.J. & Pardo, L.S. (Eds.). (1997). *The book club connection: Literacy learning and classroom talk.* New York: Teachers College Press.

McTighe, J. (1992) Graphic organizers: Collaborative links to better thinking. In N. Davidson & T. Worsham, (Eds.), *Enhancing thinking through cooperative learning.* (pp. 182-197) New York: Teachers College Press.

Medina, C.L., & Campano, G. (2006). Performing identities through drama and teatro practices in multilingual classrooms. *Language Arts,* 83(4), 332-341.

Meyer, R.J. (1996). *Stories from the heart: Teachers and students researching their literacy lives.* Mahwah, NJ: Lawrence Erlbaum.

Miller, J. (1990). *Seductions: Studies in reading and culture.* Boston, MA: Harvard University Press.

Mitchell, J.P., Abernathy, T.V., & Gowans, L.P. (1998). Making sense of literacy portfolios: A four-step plan. *Journal of Adolescent and Adult Literacy,* 41(5), 384-387.

Moffett, J. (1968). *Teaching the universe of discourse.* Boston, MA: Houghton Mifflin.

Moll, L.C., Amanti, C., Neff, D., & Gonzalez, N. (1992). Funds of knowledge for teaching: Using a qualitative approach to connect homes and classrooms. *Theory Into Practice,* 31(2), 132-141.

Moll, L.C., & Greenberg, J.B. (1990). Creating zones of possibilities: Combining social contexts for instruction. In L.C. Moll (Ed.), *Vygotsky and Education: Instructional implications and applications of sociohistorical psychology.* (319-348), New York: Cambridge University Press.

Möller, K.J. (2002). Providing support for dialogue in literature discussions about social justice. *Language Arts,* 79(6), 467-477.

Mora, J. (2006). Differentiating instruction for English learners: The four-by-four model. In T. Young, & N. Hadaway (Eds.) *Supporting the literacy development of English learners: Increasing success in all classrooms.* (pp. 35-38). Newark, DE: International Reading Association.

Morrow, L.M. (1988). Young children's responses to one-to-one story readings in school settings. *Reading Research Quarterly,* 23. 89-107.

Morrow, L.M. (2000). *Beginning literacy: Research-based principles and practices,* Sadlier Oxford.

Morrow, L.M., & Smith, J.K. (Eds.). (1990). *Assessment for instruction in early literacy.* Englewood Cliffs, NJ: Prentice Hall.

Morrow, L.M., & Weinstein, C.S. (1986). Encouraging vocabulary reading: The impact of a literature program on children's use of library centers. *Reading Research Quarterly,* 21, 330–346.

N

Nagy, W.E., & Scott, J.A. (2000). Vocabulary processes. In M.L. Kamil, P.B. Mosenthal, P.D. Pearson, & R. Barr (Eds.), *Handbook of reading research,* (Volume 3) (pp. 269-284). Mahwah, NJ: Lawrence Erlbaum Associates, Inc.

National Council of Teachers of English. Elementary Section Steering Committee. (1996). Exploring language arts standards within a cycle of learning. *Language Arts.* 73, 10-13.

National Institute of Child Health and Human Development (2000) *Report of the National Reading Panel. Teaching children to read: An evidence-based assessment of the scientific research literature on reading and its implications for reading instruction.* (NIH Publication No. 00-4769). Washington: Government Printing Office.

New London Group. (1996). A pedagogy of multiliteracies: Designing social futures. *Harvard Educational Review,* 66(1), 60-92.

New London Group 2000. A pedagogy of Multiliteracies designing social futures. In B. Cope & M. Kalantzis (Eds.), Multiliteracies: Literacy learning and the design of social futures. London: Routledge, 9–37.

Newman, J.M. (1991). *Interwoven conversations: Learning and teaching through critical reflection.* Toronto, ON: OISE Press.

Nichols, R.G. (2005). *Successful listening.* International Listening Association: Retrieved June 18, 2005, from http://www.listen.org.

Noguchi, R. (1991). *Grammar and the teaching of writing: Limits and possibilities.* Urbana,IL: National Council of Teachers of English.

Norton, D., & Norton, S. (2003). *Through the eyes of a child: An introduction to children's literature.* Upper Saddle River, NJ: Pearson.

Noyce, R., & Christie, J. (1983). Effects of an integrated approach to grammar instruction on third graders' reading and writing. *Elementary School Journal,* 84, 63-69.

O

Oglan, G. (2003). *Write, right, rite!* Boston, MA: Pearson.

Ogle, D.H. (1986). K-W-L: A teaching model that develops active reading of expository text. *The Reading Teacher,* 39, 564-570.

Ohlhausen, M.M., & Jepsen, M. (1992). Lessons from Goldilocks: "Somebody's been choosing my books but I can make my own choices now!" *New Advocate,* 5, 31-46.

Olson, D.R., & Torrance, N. (2001). Conceptualizing literacy as a personal skill and as a social practice. In D.R. Olson, & N. Torrance (Eds.), *The making of literate societies* (pp. 3-18). Oxford, UK: Blackwell.

Ong, W.J. (1982). *Orality and literacy: The technologizing of the word.* London, UK: Methuen.

Ontario Ministry of Education (1991). *Assessing language arts.* Toronto, ON: Queen's Printer for Ontario.

Ontario Ministry of Education (1999). *The Ontario curriculum exemplars: Writing.* Toronto, ON: Queen's Printer for Ontario.

Ontario Ministry of Education (2001). *English as a second language and English literacy development: A resource guide.* Toronto, ON: Queen's Printer for Ontario.

Ontario Ministry of Education (2003). *A guide to early reading instruction: Kindergarten to Grade 3.* Toronto, ON: Queen's Printer.

Ontario Ministry of Education (2003). *Early reading strategy: The report of the expert panel on early reading in Ontario.* Toronto, ON: Queen's Printer for Ontario.

Ontario Ministry of Education. (2004). *Literacy for learning: The report of the expert panel on literacy in Grades 4 to 6 in Ontario.* Toronto, ON: Queen's Printer for Ontario.

Opitz, M., Ford, J., & Zbaracki, J. (2005): Are you listening? Listening comprehension as the missing link to reading comprehension. Presentation at the 50th International Reading Association Conference, San Antonio, TX.

Owocki, G. (2001). *Make way for literacy! Teaching the way young children learn.* Portsmouth, NH: Heinemann.

P

Palincsar, A.M. (1987). Reciprocal teaching: Can student discussions boost comprehension? *Instructor,* Jan., 56-60.

Palincsar, A.M. (2003). Collaborative approaches to comprehension instruction In A.P. Sweet, & C.E. Snow (Eds.) *Rethinking reading comprehension* (pp. 99-114). New York: Guilford Press.

Palincsar, A. S., & Brown, A. (1984). Reciprocal teaching of comprehension-fostering and comprehension monitoring activities. *Cognition and Instruction,* 1(2), 117-175.

Palmer, P.J. (1998). *The courage to teach: Exploring the inner landscape of a teacher's life.* San Francisco, CA: Jossey-Bass.

Parr, M., & Campbell, T. (in press). 'Poets-in-practice' practice poetry: More than just a little 'poet-itude'! *The Reading Teacher.*

Paterson, K. (1989). The spying heart: more thoughts on reading and writing books for children. New York: Lodestar.

Pattanayak, D. P. (1991). Literacy: An instrument of oppression. In D. R. Olson & N. Torrance (Eds.), *Literacy and orality,* (pp. 105-108). New York: Cambridge University Press.

Pearson, P.D., & Stephens, D. (1994a). Comprehension of text structures. In R. Ruddell, M.R. Ruddell, & H. Singer (Eds.), *Theoretical models and processes of reading* (4th ed., pp. 448-468). Newark, DE: International Reading Association.

Pearson, P.D., & Stephens, D. (1994b). Learning about literacy: A 30-year journey. In R.B. Ruddell, M.R. Ruddell, & H. Singer (Eds.), *Theoretical models and processes of reading,* (4th ed., pp.22-42). Newark, DE: International Reading Association).

Pérez, B. (2004). Creating a classroom community for literacy. In B. Pérez (Ed.), *Sociocultural contexts of language and literacy* (pp. 309-338). Mahwah, NJ: Lawrence Erlbaum.

Perfetti, C. A. (1997). The psycholinguistics of spelling and reading. In C. A. Perfetti, L. Rieben, & M Fayol (Eds.), *Learning to spell* (pp.21-38). Hillsdale, NJ: Erlbaum.

Peterson, R. & Eeds, M. (1990). *Grand conversations: Literature groups in action.* Richmond Hill, ON: Scholastic.

Phenix, J. (2001). *The spelling teacher's handbook*. Markham, ON: Pembroke Publishers.

Phenix, J., & Scott-Dunne, D. (1991). *Spelling instruction that makes sense*. Markham ON: Pembroke Publishers.

Piaget, J. (1959). *The psychology of intelligence*. Totowa, NJ: Littlefield, Adams.

Piazza, C.L. (1999). *Multiple forms of literacy: Teaching literacy and the arts*. Upper Saddle River, NJ: Prentice-Hall.

Piluski, J.J. (1994). Preventing reading failure: A review of five effective programmes. *The Reading Teacher*, 48, 31-9.

Pinnell, G.S., & Fountas, I.C. (1998). *Word matters: Teaching phonics and spelling in the reading/writing classroom*. Portsmouth, NH: Heinemann.

Polloway, E.D., Patton, J.R., & Serna, L. (2005). *Strategies for teaching learners with special needs* (8 ed.). Boston, MA: Pearson.

Powell, R., & Davidson, N. (2005). The donut house: Real world literacy in an urban kindergarten classroom. *Language Arts*, 82(5), 248-256.

R

Raphael, T.E. (1984). Teaching learners about sources of information for answering comprehension questions. *Journal of Reading*, 27, 303-311.

Raphael, T.E. (1986). Teaching question-answer relationships. *The Reading Teacher*, 39, 516-520.

Raphael, T.E, Pardo, L.S., & Highfield, K. (2002). *Book Club: A literature based curriculum*. Lawrence, MA: Small Planet Communication.

Rasinski, T., Padak, N.D. Church, B.W., Fawcett, G. Hendershot, J., Henry, J.M., Moss, B.G., Peck, J.K., Pryor, E., & Roskos, A. (Eds.). (2000) *Developing reading-writing connections: Strategies from* The Reading Teacher. Newark, DE: International Reading Association.

Richards, J. C., & McKenna, M. C. (2003). *Integrating multiple literacies in K-8 classrooms: Cases, commentaries, and practical applications*. Mahwah, NJ: Lawrence Erlbaum.

Robbie, S., Ruggierello, T., & Warren, B. (2001). *Using drama to bring language to life: Ideas, games, and activities for teachers of languages and language arts*. North York, ON: Captus Press.

Robinson, F.P. (1961). *Effective study* (rev. ed.). New York: Harper & Row.

Robinson, R.D. (2002). *Classics in literacy education: Historical perspectives for today's teachers*. Newark, DE: International Reading Association.

Rog, L.J. (2001) *Early literacy instruction in Kindergarten*. Newark, DE: International Reading Association.

Rosenblatt, L.M. (1978). *The reader, the text, the poem: The transactional theory of the literary work*. CarbondaleIL: Southern Illinois University Press.

Rosenblatt, L. M. (1985). Language, Literature, and Values. In S. N. Tchudi (Ed.), *Language, Schooling, and Society* (pp. 16). Upper Montclair, NJ: Boynton/Cook.

Rosenblatt, L.M. (1994). The transactional theory of reading and writing. In R.B. l & N. J. Unrau (Eds.), *Theoretical models and processes of reading* (4th ed., pp. 1363-1398). Newark, DE: International Reading Association.

Roser, N., & Martinez, M. (Ed.) *Book talk and beyond: Children and teachers respond to literature*. Newark, DE: International Reading Association.

Routman, R. (1988). *Transitions: From literature to literacy*. Portsmouth, NH: Heinemann.

Routman, R. (1991). *Invitations: Changing as teachers and learners K-12*. Portsmouth, NH: Heinemann.

Routman, R. (2000). *Conversations: Strategies for teaching, learning and evaluating*. Portsmouth, NH: Heinemann.

Routman, R. (2005). *Writing essentials: Raising expectations and results while simplifying teaching*. Portsmouth, NH: Heinemann.

Rubin, D. (1990). Introduction: Ways of talking about talking and learning. In S. Hynds and D. L. Rubin (Eds.), *Perspectives on talk and learning*, (pp. 1-17). Urbana, IL.: National Council of Teachers of English.

Ruddell, R.B. (2004). Researching the influential literacy teacher: Characteristics, beliefs, strategies, and new research directions. In R.B. Ruddell & N.J. Unrau (Eds.), *Theoretical models and processes of reading* (5th ed., pp. 979-997). Newark, DE: International Reading Association.

Ruddell, R.B. (2006). *Teaching children to read and write: Becoming an effective teacher* (4th ed.). Boston, MA: Allyn & Bacon.

Ruddell, R.B., & Ruddell, M.R. (1994). Language acquisition and literacy process. In R.B. Ruddell, M.R. Ruddell, & H. Singer (Eds.), *Theoretical models and processes of reading* (4th ed., pp. 448-468). Newark, DE: International Reading Association.

Ruddell, R.B., & Unrau, N.J. (2004). The role of responsive teaching in focusing reader intention and developing reader motivation. In R.B. Ruddell & N.J. Unrau (Eds.), *Theoretical models and processes of reading* (5th ed., pp. 954-978). Newark, DE: International Reading Association.

Rumelhart, D.E. (1994). Toward an interactive model of reading. In R.B. Ruddell & N. J. Unrau (Eds.), *Theoretical models and processes of reading* (4th ed., pp. 1149-1179). Newark, DE: International Reading Association.

S

Sadoski, M., & Paivio, A. (2004). A dual coding theoretical model of reading. In R.B. Ruddell & N. J. Unrau (Eds.), *Theoretical models and processes of reading* (5th ed., pp. 1329-1362). Newark, DE: International Reading Association.

Samuels, S.J. (1994a). Toward a theory of automatic information processing in reading, revisited. In R.B. Ruddell & N. J. Unrau (Eds.), *Theoretical models and processes of reading* (4th ed., pp. 1127-1148). Newark, DE: International Reading Association.

Samuels, S.J. (1994b). Word recognition. In R. Ruddell, M.R. Ruddell, & H. Singer (Eds.), *Theoretical models and processes of reading* (4th ed., pp. 359-380). Newark, DE: International Reading Association.

Santa, C. (1988). *Content reading including study systems*. Dubuque, IA: Kendall/Hunt.

Santman, D. (2002). Teaching to the test? Test preparation in the reading workshop. *Language Arts*, 79(3), 203-211.

Saskatchewan Education. (1997). *English Language Arts 10: A Curriculum Guide for the Secondary Level*. Regina, SK: Saskatchewan Education.

Scheibe, C.L. (2004). A deeper sense of literacy: Curriculum-driven approaches to media literacy in the K-12 classroom. *American Behavioural Scientist*, 48(1), 60-68.

Schuster, E. (2003) *Breaking the rules: Liberating writers through innovative grammar instruction*. Portsmouth, NH: Heinemann

Schwartz, S., & Bone, M. (1995). *Retelling, relating, reflecting: Beyond the 3R's*. Toronto, ON: Irwin Publishing.

Scott, R. (1993). *Spelling: Sharing the secrets*. Toronto, ON: Gage.

Senn, J.A. (1992). *325 creative prompts for personal journals*. New York: Scholastic.

Shanahan, T. (1988). The reading-writing relationship: Seven instructional principles. *The Reading Teacher*, 41, 636-647.

Shanahan, T. (1996). Reading-writing relationships, thematic units, inquiry learning. In pursuit of effective literacy instruction. *The Reading Teacher*, 51(1), 12-19.

Shanahan, T., & Barr, R. (1995). Reading Recovery: An independent evaluation of the effects of an early instructional intervention for at-risk learners. *Reading Research Quarterly* 30, 4: 958-996.

Shor, I. (1999). What is critical literacy? *Journal for Pedagogy, Pluralism, & Practice*, 4(1), Retrieved September 4, 2005, from http://www.lesley.edu/journals/jppp/4/index.html.

Sipe, L. (1999). Children's response to literature: Author, text, reader, context. *Theory into Practice*, 38(3), 120-129.

Slavin, R. E. (2003). *Educational psychology: Theory and practice* (7th ed.). Boston, MA: Allyn & Bacon.

Smith, F. (1978, 1979). Reading without nonsense. New York: Teachers College Press.

Smith, F. (1983). Reading like a writer. *Language Arts*, 60(5), 558-67.

Smith, F. (1988). *Joining the literacy club*. Portsmouth, NH: Heinemann.

Smith, F. (1990, 2004). *Understanding reading*. Mahwah, NJ: Lawrence Erlbaum.

Smith, M. K. (2002) Howard Gardner and multiple intelligences. Retrieved March 21, 2005, from *The Encyclopedia of Informal Education* at http://www.infed.org/thinkers/gardner.htm.

Snow, C.E., Burns, S.M., & Griffin, P. (Eds.). (1998). *Preventing reading difficulties in young children*. Washington, DC: National Academy Press.

Snow, C.E., & Sweet, A.P. (2003). Reading for comprehension. In A.P. Sweet, & C.E. Snow (Eds.) *Rethinking reading comprehension* (pp. 1-11). New York: The Guilford Press.

Spache, D.G. (1976). *Diagnosing and correcting reading disabilities*. Boston, MA: Allyn & Bacon.

Spandel, V. (2005). *Creating writers through 6-trait writing assessment and instruction*. Boston, MA: Pearson.

Spender, D. (1982). *Invisible women: The schooling scandal*, London, UK: Writers and Readers Publishing Cooperative.

Stanovich, K.E. (1986). Matthew effects in reading: Some consequences of individual differences in the acquisition of literacy. *Reading Research Quarterly*, 21(4), 360-407.

Stanovich, K.E. (2000). *Progress in understanding reading: Scientific foundations and new frontiers*. New York: Guilford Press.

Stanovich, K.E., Siegel, L.S., & Gottardo, A. (1997). Converging evidence for phonological and surface subtypes of reading disability. *Journal of Educational Psychology*, 89(1), 114-127.

Stead, T. (2002) *Is that a fact? Teaching nonfiction writing K-3*. Portland, MN: Stenhouse.

Straw, S.B. & Bogdan, D. (Eds.). (1993). *Constructive reading: Teaching beyond communication*. Portsmouth, NH: Boynton/Cook.

Street, B. (2003). What's "new" in new literacy studies? Critical approaches to literacy in theory and practice. *Current Issues in Comparative Education*, 5(2), 1-14.

Stuart, D. (1997). Reading Recovery: What's in a name? *FWTAO/FAEO Newsletter*, May/June, 1997, 38-41.

Sudbury District Catholic School Board. (2004). Welcome to Kindergarten: A solid foundation for your child's future. Sudbury, ON: Sudbury District Catholic School Board.

Sullivan, M. (1995). *Making portfolio assessment easy: Reproducible forms and checklists and strategies for using them*. Richmond Hill, ON: Scholastic.

Swartz, L. (2002). *The New Dramathemes* Markham, ON: Pembroke Publishers.

T

Taberski, S. (1998). Give shared reading the attention it deserves. *Instructor-Primary*, 107(7), 32-34.

Taberski, S. (2000). *On solid ground: Strategies for teaching reading K-3*. Portsmouth, NH: Heinemann.

Taberski, S. (2001). Fact and fiction. *Instructor*, 110(6), 24-27.

Tallim, J. (2006). What is media literacy? Media Awareness Network, Retrieved February 5, 2006, from http://www.media-awareness.ca/english/teachers/media_literacy/what_is_media_literacy.cfm.

Temple, C., Martinez, M., Yokota, J., & Naylor, A. (2002). *Children's books in children's hands: An introduction to their literature*. Boston: Allyn & Bacon.

Temple, C. & J. Gillet, J. (1996). *Language and literacy: A lively approach*. New York: HarperCollins.

Temple, C. (1993). "What if Beauty had been ugly?" Reading against the grain of gender bias in children's books. *Language Arts, 70*(2), 89-93.

Templeton, S. (2003). Spelling. In Flood, J., Lapp, D., Squire, J. R., & Jensen, J. M. (Eds.), *Handbook of research on teaching the English language arts* (2nd ed., pp. 738-751). Mahwah, NY: Lawrence Erlbaum Associates.

Templeton, S., & Morris, D. (1999). Questions teachers ask about spelling. *Reading Research Quarterly*, 34, 102-112.

Templeton, S., & Morris, D. (2000). Spelling. In M. Kamil, P. Mosenthal, P.D. Pearson, & R. Barr (Eds.), *Handbook of Reading Research*: Volume 3 (pp. 525-543). Mahwah, NJ: Lawrence Erlbaum Associates.

Thoman, E. (2006). The 3 stages of media literacy. Media Awareness Network, Retrieved February 5, 2006, from http://www.media-awareness.ca/english/teachers /media_literacy/what_is_media_ literacy.cfm.

Thoman, E., & Jolls, T. (2004). Media literacy: A national priority for a changing world. *American Behavioural Scientist*, 48(1), 18-29.

Tierney, R.J., & Readence, J.E. (2005). *Reading strategies and practices: A compendium*. Boston, MA: Allyn & Bacon.

Tompkins, G. E. (2002). *Language arts: Content and teaching strategies* (4th ed.). Upper Saddle River, NJ: Merrill Prentice Hall.

Tompkins, G.E. (2003*). Literacy for the 21st century*, (3rd ed.) Upper Saddle River, NJ: Merrill Prentice-Hall.

Tompkins, G.E. (2004). *50 literacy strategies*, (2nd ed.) New York: Merrill Prentice-Hall.

Tompkins, G.E., Pollard, M.J., Bright, R.M., & Winsor, P.J.T. (1999). *Language arts: Content and teaching strategies*, (Canadian ed.). Scarborough, ON: Prentice-Hall.

Toronto District School Board. (2000). *Teaching children to read and write: A literacy guide for teachers*. Toronto, ON: Toronto District School Board.

Tough, J. (1976) *Listening to children talking: A guide to the appraisal of children's language use*. Portsmouth, NH: Heinemann.

Tough, J. (1977) *Development of meaning*. Portsmouth, NH: Heinemann.

Townsend, J., & Pace, B. (2005). The many faces of Gertrude: Opening and closing possibilities in classroom talk. *Journal of Adolescent & Adult Literacy*, 48(7), 594-605.

Trehearne, M. (2000) *The kindergarten teacher's resource book*. Scarborough, ON: Nelson.Treiman, R. (2001). Reading, In M. Aronoff & J. Rees-Miller (Eds.), *Blackwell handbook of linguistics* (pp. 664-672). Oxford, UK: Blackwell.

Tyner, K. (2006). The storytellers of our generation, Media Awareness Network, Retrieved February 5, 2006, from http://www.media-awareness.ca/english/teachers/media_literacy/why_teach_media_liter.cfm.

U

UNESCO. (2003). *Literacy: A UNESCO perspective*. Paris, France: UNESCO.

V

Vacca, J.L., Vacca, R.T., Gove, M.K., Burkey, L., Lenhart, L.A., & McKeon, C. (2003). *Reading and learning to read* (5th ed.). Boston, MA: Pearson Education.

Vacca, R.T., Vacca, J.L., & Begoray, D.L. (2005). *Content area reading: Literacy and learning across the curriculum* (Canadian ed.). Toronto, ON: Pearson Education.

van Manen, M. (1997). *Researching lived experience: Human science for an action sensitive pedagogy* (2nd ed.). London, Canada: Althouse Press.

van Manen, M. (2002). *The tone of teaching*. London, ON: Althouse Press.

Vasquez, V. M. (2001). *Getting beyond "I like the book": Creating space for critical literacy in K-6 classrooms*. Newark, DE: International Reading Association.

Vasquez, V. M. (2004). *Negotiating critical literacies with young children*. Newark, DE: International Reading Association.

Vygotsky, L. (1978, 1979). *Mind in society*. Cambridge, MA: Harvard University Press.

Vygotsky, L. (1986). *Thought and language*. Cambridge, MA: MIT Press.

W

Wagstaff, J.M. (1999). *Teaching reading and writing with word walls*. New York: Scholastic.

Wang, J.H., & Guthrie, J.T. (2004). Modeling the effects of intrinsic motivation, extrinsic motivation, amount of reading, and past reading achievement on text comprehension of U.S. and Chinese students. *Reading Research Quarterly*, 39, 162-186.

Weaver, C. (1994). *Reading process and practice: From socio-psycholinguistics to whole language*. Portsmouth, NH: Heinemann.

Weaver, C. (1996). Teaching grammar in context. Portsmouth, NH: Heinemann.

Weaver, C. (1998). Introduction: A perspective. In C. Weaver (Ed.), *Reconsidering a balanced approach to reading*, (pp. xv-xxvi). Urbana, IL: National Council of Teachers of English.

Weber, E. (2005). *MI strategies in the classroom and beyond*. Boston, MA: Pearson.

Wells, G. (1986). *The meaning makers: Children learning language and using language to learn*. Portsmouth, NH: Heinemann Educational.

Wheatley, J. (2005). *Strategic spelling : Moving beyond word memorization in the middle grades*. Newark, DE: International Reading Association.

Whitehead, M.(1999) Supporting language and literacy development in the early Years. Buckingham, UK: Open University Press.

Whitmore, K.F. (1997). Inventing conversations in second language classrooms: What students say and how they say it. In Paratore, J.R. & McCormack, R.L. (Eds.) *Peer Discourse in the Classroom: Learning from Research* (pp. 102-128). Newark, DE: International Reading Association.

Wiencek, J., & O'Flahavan, J.E. (1994). From teacher-led to peer discussions about literature: Suggestions for making the shirt. *Language Arts*, 71, 488-498.

Wiggins, G., & McTighe, J. (1998). *Understanding by design*. Alexandria, VA: Association for Supervision and Curriculum Development.

Wilhelm, J.D. (2001). *Improving comprehension with think-aloud strategies*, New York: Scholastic.

Wilhelm, J.D., & Smith, M.W. (2002). *"Reading don't fix no Chevys": Literacy in the lives of young men*. Portsmouth, NH: Heinemann.

Wilkens, D.K. (1996). *Multiple intelligence activities: Grades K-4*. Huntington Beach, CA: Teacher Created Materials.

Wilkinson, L. (1999). An introduction to the explicit teaching of reading. In J. Hancock (Ed.). *The explicit teaching of reading* (pp. 1-12). Newark, DE: International Reading Association.

Wilson, D.E., & Ritchie, J.S. (1994). Resistance, revision, and representation: Narrative in teacher education, *English Education*, 26(3), 177-1 88.

Wirt, B. Bryan, D., & Wesley, K. (2005). *Discovering what works for struggling readers: Journeys of exploration with primary-grade students*. Newark, DE: International Reading Association.

Wolf, S.A., & Wolf, K.P. (2002). Teaching *true* and *to* the test. *Language Arts*, 79(3), 230-239.

Worthy, J. (2005). *Readers Theater for building fluency*. Toronto ON: Scholastic.

Worthy, J., & Prater, K. (2002). "I thought about it all night": Readers' Theatre for reading fluency and motivation. *The Reading Teacher*, 56(3), 294-7.

Wray, D., & Medwell, J. (1999). Effective teachers of literacy: Knowledge, beliefs, and practices. *International Electronic Journal for Leadership in Learning*, 3(9).

Y

Yolen, J. (1981). *Touch magic: Fantasy, faerie, and folklore in the literature of childhood*. New York: Philomel Books.

Yopp, H.K. (1992). Developing phonemic awareness in young children. *The Reading Teacher*, 45, 696-703.

Yopp, H.K., & Yopp, R.H. (2000). Supporting phonemic awareness development in the classroom. *The Reading Teacher*, 54, 130-143.

Yopp, H. K., & Yopp, R.H. (2001, 2006). *Literature-based reading activities*. Boston, MA: Pearson.

Young, T.A., & Ferguson, P.M. (1995). From Anansi to Zomo: Trickster tales in the classroom. *The Reading Teacher*, 48, 490–503.

Young, T., & Hadaway, N. Eds. (2006). *Supporting the literacy development of English learners: Increasing success in all classrooms*. Newark, DE: International Reading Association.

Z

Zimmerman, S., & Hutchins, C. (2001). *Seven keys to comprehension: How to help your kids read and get it!* New York: Three Rivers Press.

Photo Credits

All images copyright © PhotoDisc/Getty Images except where noted below.

Chapter 1, pp. 6, 12; Chapter 2, p. 58; Chapter 3, p. 67; Chapter 4, p. 98; Chapter 5, pp. 130, 136; Chapter 9, p. 288; Chapter 11, opener, p. 376; Chapter 14, p. 522: Corbis Digital Stock.

Chapter 4, p. 94: Courtesy of Amanda Brownlee.

Chapter 5, p. 142: Iconica/Peter Cade

Chapter 6, opener, p. 159; Chapter 8, p. 256; Chapter 9, p. 285; Chapter 13, p. 507: Purestock.

Chapter 6, pp. 161, 174; Chapter 15, opener: Ryan McVay/PhotoDisc/ Getty Images

Chapter 7, p. 194: Dynamic Graphics, Inc.

Chapter 9, p. 276, illustrations and text from Stella, Queen of the Snow copyright © by Marie-Louise Gay. Reprinted by permission of Groundwood Books Ltd.

Chapter 13, p. 502: Photograph by S. Jamasji.

Chapter 14, pp. 515, 536: Image 100 Ltd.

Index